DIARY
OF
COTTON MATHER

The TOWN of
BOSTON
IN
New England
by
Capt John Bonner

1722

Ætatis Suæ 80

Fox Hill.

Roxbury Flatts

AMERICAN CLASSICS

DIARY

OF

COTTON MATHER

VOLUME II
1709-1724

FREDERICK UNGAR PUBLISHING CO.
NEW YORK

Second Printing

Printed in the United States of America

Library of Congress Card Catalog Number 57-8651

CONTENTS

LETTERS. PAGE

ILLUSTRATION

DIARY
OF
COTTON MATHER

Diary of Cotton Mather

1709

THE XLVIITH YEAR

He that has God on his side, does all things, with Ease. A saying of one of the *Greek Poets*.

Castitas periclitatur in Delicijs, Humilitas in Divitijs Pietas in Negotijs, Veritas in Multiloquio, Charitas in hoc mundo. *Bern.*

Somnium narrare, vigilantis est, et vitia sua confiteri, sanitatis indicium est. *Sen.*[1]

12 *d*. 12 *m*. [*February*.] 1708. *Satureday*. Tis amazing, tis amazing, that such a feeble, and such a fruitless, and such a sinful Thing as I am, should be still continued in the World! I am gott thro' that Year, which for many Years I imagined would at the furthest be the Year of my Death.

However, O my Soul, do not fall asleep now; be not secure for the Year that is coming on.

This Day I sett apart for the Exercises of a *Thanksgiving*, unto the Lord. I employ'd it in Exercises proper for such a Day; which having often occurr'd in the mean Story of my Life, there is no Need of now repeating the Mention of them.

The more special Endeavour of this Day was to give Thanks unto the Lord, and acknowledge the Triumphs of sovereign Grace in it; for His using me in what Services to the evangelical Interests, I have had Opportunity to pursue, in my Life hitherto; and this notwithstanding my being

[1] *Epist. Mor.* Lib. VI. Ep. i. 153.

[1]

so foolish and shallow a Creature, as not He only, but His People also know me to be, and so filthy a Creature as tis known to Him that I am.

The Affairs wherein I may be concerned for the next Year, I now also did committ unto the L[or]d.

About this Time, a small Accident befel me which look'd like a very particular Answer of Prayer.

Tho' I am furnished with a very great Library yett seeing a Library of a late Minister in the Town to be sold, and a certain Collection of Books there, which had it may be above six hundred single Sermons in them; I could not forbear wishing myself made able to compass such a Treasure. I could not forbear mentioning my Wishes in my Prayers before the Lord; that in case it might be a Service to His Interests, or to me in serving His Interests, He would enable me in His good Providence, to purchase the Treasure now before me. But I left the Matter before Him, with the profoundest Resignation willing to be without every Thing that He should not order for me. Behold, a Gentleman, who a year ago treated me very ill; but I cheerfully forgave him! carried me home to dine with him; and upon an accidental Mention of the Library aforesaid, he, to my Surprize, compelled me to accept of him a Summ of Money, which enabled me to come at what I had been desirous of.

15 *d*. 12 *m*. *Tuesday*.   This Day, the Reforming Societies mett all together, and kept it as a Day of Prayer.

To bewayl our Unfruitfulness; and obtain Pardon thro' the Blood of Jesus, with Grace and Strength, to bring forth more Fruit.

It was a good Day. The Lord helped me to carry on the Exercises of the Afternoon. I preached near two Hours; a Sermon about *Good Works*.

4 *d*. 1 *m*. [*March*.] *Friday*.   I sett apart this Day, for the Duties wherewith a Day of Prayer and Fasting is to be carried on.

There was nothing very remarkable, either in the Occasions, or in the Exercises of the Day.

But there is one Thing, which I desire to take Notice of. My Life has been strangely filled with *Temptations*. But I have been lately Tempted with a *new Assault* from Hell, violently made upon me. I am assaulted with Sollicitations to look upon the whole *Christian Religion*, as — (I dare not mention, what!) Wherefore, I now cried unto the Lord, for the Quenching of these *fiery Darts;* and for my Præservation from the least Approach towards that *Blasphemy* which would be the *unpardonable Sin*. And I earnestly professed before the Lord, my *Resolutions*, that I will adore His Glorious *Christ*, as the Son of God, and employ my *Life* in diligent, exquisite, rapturous Endeavours, to serve Him unto the uttermost. As for the *dark Things* that occurr, in His *Providence;* and the *unaccountable Proceedings* of that glorious One, in His Government of His Church, and His Permission of *ill Things* to be *suffered*, yea, and which is worse, to be *done*, by His own most faithful Servants; and His Permission of *Evil Spirits*, to do astonishing Things for a considerable While, in the Countenancing and Encouraging of Christianity. I did resolve humbly to rely upon his unsearchable *Wisdome;* and make it part of my *Homage* unto Him, to beleeve Him wise and just and good, and confess myself *unable to judge* of His Dispensations, but *refer* all unto a Time, when He shall please to entertain His People in another World, with a *Discovery* of what He has done and meant, in His former Dealings with the World. For, what He does, tho' *I know not now, I shall know hereafter*.

I found a wonderful Peace, in being thus resolved. I found this Faith, to be my best *Wisdome*. The Damp which there began to grow upon my Piety and Usefulness, vanished. The Flame revived; and I went on with Joy in my usual Methods of a flaming Zeal, to do good abundantly.

About this Time, thro' the Largeness of my Family, and the Negligence of those that should have been concerned for me, and perhaps from some other Causes, I fell into some Wants and Straits. I had not Cloathes fitt to be worn; I was *cloathed with Rags;* (which, O Lord, I acknowledge, that such a *Sluggard* as I am, deserve to be!) And one or two of my Children are no better accommodated. This Poverty thus pinching and humbling of me, had some very grievous Temptations in it. But the Lord presently helped me, not only to bear my Poverty with Patience, but even to rejoice in it; sweetly to rejoice in these Considerations.

First. Oh! my Conformity to my Glorious Lord JESUS CHRIST, it is, how agreeable! how desirable! Poverty was one special and signal Article of His Condition in the World. And particularly, He was robb'd of His Garments. Why, why then should I complain of the Want of Garments! Any thing that makes my Condition resemble His, tis acceptable to me!

Secondly. Tho' I am cloth'd with Rags, yett I am Owner of the most splendid and glorious Robe in the World. My Saviour has invested me with the matchless Robe of His Righteousness; wherein I stand before the Holy God. O Priviledge, enough to swallow up all Uneasiness at the meannest Habit, that ever any Person was abased withal!

Thirdly. Tho' I can gett no better Clothes than Rags for myself, yett the Lord honours me, by making me the happy Instrument of cloathing other people. The Poor have numberless Releefs, out of my Purse, and by my Means from others, and the Naked are cloathed.

Such Considerations brought me, not only to Submission but even to Cheerfulness, under my Humiliations. I resolved, I would bear my Trials, with the Frames of true, vital, joyful, Christianity; and wait on the Lord with a

Beleef of the sixth Chapter of *Matthew*, and be any Thing that God will have me to be.

The Work of Repentance in me, and a Resolution to be Rich in good Works, was quickened on this Occasion.

24 *d.* 1 *m. Thursday.* A public Fast; in which I enjoy'd merciful Assistences of God.

1 *d.* 2 *m.* [*April.*] *Friday.* I sett apart this Day, for Prayer with Fasting, in Secret; on such Occasions as use to employ me this way.

Nothing very remarkable occurred in either of these Dayes.

The Evening before the latter of them, I could not but observe, that if I had not had a very earthly Heart, I might lead an heavenly Life.

I counted, from the Beginning of the Evening, to the Time of my going to Rest, (the Occasions for the Sick, and for Marriages, &c. were so many,) I had been called to pray no less than ten Times; to make no less than ten several Prayers.

This Month has rolled away, with little remarkable in it. Special Services, attempted or purposed, are hinted in my Book of daily Memorials.

After my Lecture, on 21 *d.* 2 *m.* I was taken ill; and by Illness confined, from the Services of the Lord's-Day. But in the next Week, I recovered.[1]

29 *d.* 2 *m. Friday.* I enjoy'd more of Heaven, than at some Times, in the Prayers of this Day; which Day I sett apart, as usually. My Faith in the glorious Jesus, as both my Saerifice and Advocate, was lively. And I was assured, that my great Saviour would own me, as one of His people.

4 *d.* 3 *m.* [*May.*] *Wednesday.* This Day, the Lord employ'd me in a special Service for Himself, and for His People, and beyond my Expectation. I was to carry on

---

[1] April 26. "Visited Cotton Mather, who has been indisposed." Sewall, *Diary*, II. 253.

the Exercises of a Day of Prayer at *Malden*.[1] In the Morning when I arrived there, the principal People gave me to understand, that the Church (both the male and female Part of it,) had been together, and proposed this Day, solemnly to renew their *Covenant* with God, and one another; and to confess their Sins, particularly their late, long sinful Contentions, and forgive one another, and ask Forgiveness of God and of one another; and bring themselves most explicitly under other Engagements for further Instances of *Piety*, which the Declensions of the Time invited them to take more particular Notice of. They desired me to furnish them, with an Instrument expressive of these holy Purposes; which I did that Morning. It was also their Desire that I would manage the Action, which was to be done this Day, with all possible Solemnity. Having at Noon, between the Meetings, further prepared the Church, for what was anon to be done; anon, in the Close of the Afternoon, I went thro' the solemn Action; in which, and in the several Speeches, which I made upon the several Parts of it, I enjoy'd most precious Assistences from the Lord. There was a most gracious and powerful Presence of God, in the Assembly; and this Day, will be a Day much remembred among the People, who were concerned in it, or Spectators of what was transacted on it.

Oh! sovereign Grace! How wonderfully doest thou continue, to employ the Chief of Sinners!

11 *d.* 3 *m. Wednesday.* My dear Son *Samuel*, was last Friday, taken very sick, of a Feavour, which proves very grievous and mortal, to our Children. The Sickness of the Child growes upon him so far, that the Physicians, begin to conclude he will dye, to despair of his Life.

Beholding the *Angel of Death* with a drawn Sword thus

---

[1] In 1708 David Parsons was called to the church at Malden, but does not appear to have come before April, 1709, or been ordained till summer. Corey, *History of Malden*, 470. See p. 9, *infra*. Mather's text is given on p. 30, *infra*.

over my Family, I sett apart this Day (tho' myself also much Indisposed,) for Prayer with Fasting before the Lord.

I bewayled the Sins, by which the Life of my Children, and of this desireable Child, has been forfeited. I besought the Pardon of them, thro' the Blood of the Lamb of God; and I pleaded that Blood, as a *Family-Sacrifice*. I resigned the Child unto the Lord; submitted unto whatever Disposal, the infinite Sovereignty and Faithfulness of God, should make of the Child. I was first and most of all concerned, that the Soul of the Child might be bound up in the Bundle of Life, and that I and mine, might reap spiritual Benefits and improve in Piety, from what befalls the Child. I declared, that I did not ask, that the Child might live, and be a Rebel and a Traitor to God; no, I had rather have him dy in his Infancy, than live in cursed and lothsome Wickedness. And then, I presented my Petition for the Life of the Child. This Petition, with the Child himself, I putt into the Hands of the glorious Advocate, whom I by Faith saw in the Heavens concerned for me; when this Faith came into Exercise, I found my Mind strangely quieted about the Child, and about the Issue of the Danger now upon him.

That my Prayers might be the more effectual, I was willing to have Alms accompany them.

Both my Prayers and my Alms, I putt into the Hands of my Advocate, that He sprinkling of them with His Blood, they may be my acceptable Præparations for the Mercies of the Lord.

So, I sent unto the Press, an Essay to advance Knowledge and Goodness among *Children*, and resolved that I would have a considerable Share in the Expence of the Impression. And thus also, from the Evil that befalls, and afflicts my Child, there will arise much good, unto many other Children.

On this Day, the Child gave some Hopes of Revival.

But the Day following his Feavour growes to an Extremity. Wherefore on

13 d. 3 m. Friday.   I kept another Day, of Prayer with Fasting, in my Study, for the Life of my Son, and for the Compassion of Heaven to all my Family.

I had also some other Errands unto Heaven.   One was, that I might obtain the Presence of the Lord with me, in the Services of the next Week.

Another was, that I might be sheltered from the Malice of our Governour, and Council, and Clergy, who suspect me, to have an hand, in a Book newly come over, which does expose and chastise their criminal Mismanagements.

A great Expedition that is now forming, from Great Britain, and all these Colonies, against our French Neighbours, was another Matter which I had to spread before the Lord.[1]   And the sick Families in my next Vicinity, do likewise bespeak my Supplications for them, as well as my own.

Among other Considerations with me this Day, one was, that my Saviour has *Healing in His Wings*.   Now, His *good Angels* are His *Wings*.   I relied on Him then, to send one of His good Angels, to do good, and bring some Help and Health, to my dying Child.

On this Day, the Child began to revive.

The Essay, which I published on this Occasion, has in it, several Instruments of Piety, besides the *Abridgment* of the *Assemblies Catechism*.   Especially, *The Desires of the Repenting Beleever* on the Ten Commandments.   It is entituled, THE SUMM OF THE MATTER.

16 d. 3 m. Monday.   My Wife watch'd last Night, (as she had done every other Night) with the languishing Child.

In the Morning between six and seven a clock, she suddenly fell into her Travail, and quickly, (in a few Minutes

---

[1] April 30. as Sewall records, the "Queens Letter is read in Council about the Canada Expedition, and Col. Vetch's Instructions, to which exact Obedience is commanded."

and before that more than one or two of the Neighbours
could run in unto her, and before that she could reach her
own Chamber, and safely) she was delivered of a SON.[1]
There was a great Complication of Mercies, in all the Circumstances of this Matter. And now, the Gracious Lord,
instead of taking one Son from me, has given another to
me; whom I also humbly dedicate and consecrate unto
Him.

It is a time of Exercise in my Family. An epidemical
Feavour is raging in my Neighbourhood. Several of my
Children, are threatned with the Beginnings of it; as well
as one of them is but slowly, and at a languishing Rate,
recovering from it. But thro' the Compassion of my
heavenly Father, all goes over.

And this Week, the Lord employes me, and strengthens
me, to do several public Services.

On the Wednesday, I preached a Sermon, at the Ordination of a Pastor, in *Malden*.[2]   On the Thursday, I preached
the Lecture, to a great Assembly in *Boston*. The Service
of the Sick, is also very heavy. But the Lord mercifully
carries me through all.

22 *d.* 3 *m. Lord's-Day*.   After those Thoughts and Acts
of Piety, which were proper for such an holy Occasion, I
did this Day baptise my Son, and I call'd his Name
NATHANAEL; as much for the Signification of the Name, as
because I had a valuable Brother and Uncle of the Name.

In the ensuing Week,[3] the Lord made use of me, at the
Convention of the Ministers, both on *Wednesday* and on
Thursday; to speak many Things, (especially in Prayer with
them, on both of those Dayes) which may have a Tendency
to serve the Interests of His Kingdome.

The Ministers, devoting the Time they were together

[1] Nathanael.

[2] David Parsons. See p. 6*n*, *supra*.

[3] Election was on May 25, the sermon being preached by Grindall Rawson, of
Mendon. His text was Jer. XIII. 16.

on *Thursday*, unto Prayer; and I foreseeing, that I should meet with much Interruption on the Day following; I did not sett apart *Friday*, as I use to do.

In the Month of *June*, there did not occur much, that I had either Cause, or Time, to insert in these Memorials.[1]

[1] "20 *d*. 4 *m*. [*June*.] *Monday*.   Divers votes passed at a Church Meeting.

"Whereas there are several Members of this Church, who on various pretences, do not attend on the Ordinances of the Lord, here dispensed; and their disorderly walking herein is offensive to the Church;

"It is desired, that the Elders of the Church speak or send unto them, to make them sensible of their Error and their Duty, and oblige them to take an orderly Dismission, where it is fitt they should have it, unto some other Church, walking in the Order of the Gospel.   And the Elders of the Church are desired, in the Name of the Church, to sign a Dismission for them.

"And where any do refuse, one way or another, to do their duty, it is desired, that report may be made unto the Church, in order to further Proceeding.

"Whereas a Woman belonging to this Church, whose name is *Miller*, has been seduced unto something of *Quakerism*, but the Church is informed, that her Circumstances have peculiar Temptations in them: It is desired, that the Elders of the Church, and so many of the Brethren, as may in their Charity be moved unto it, use as many Methods as they can for her Recovery.   And that, if in six Months' time, she be not brought out of her Entanglement, a Report be made unto the Church, that so our Duty towards her, may be further considered.

"One whose Name is *William Perry*, having long since pretended that another Brother, whose name is *Benjamin Gypson*, had defamed him; but the Difference was made up between them: nevertheless, after the Reconciliation, *Perry* took a fancy that an Apprehension expressed by some people of his being sometimes crazy-headed, had its original in something spoken by *Gypson*, or somebody before that Reconciliation, he withdrew from the Communion of the Church, and from so much as joining with the public Worship on the Lord's-Dayes in the Assembly. Continuing in this Course, he was more than once or twice privately dealt withal; but he treated all with much Inconsistency and Obstinacy.   He now appeared before the Church, and was charged as guilty of,

"A most palpable Breach of Covenant with the Church of God;

"An implacable Spirit of Malice towards a Brother that has done him no Wrong;

"A slandering and belying the Officers of the Church and others, as not having done him Justice.

"His Behaviour before the Church was such, as gave much Dissatisfaction, and obliged as many as then expressed themselves, to declare that they look'd on him as distracted.

"It was desired, that the Elders of the Church, with the Deacons, and any others whom they may see Cause to consult on this Occasion, enquire further into the State of the said *William Perry;* and make Report unto the Church, that they may proceed accordingly.   In the mean time, the Church declared him to be suspended from the Communion.

I procured the Reprinting of several Composures, for the præserving and promoting of Piety, both in our Army and our Navy now going against Canada. My, *Souldier told what he shall do;* and my, *Golden Curb.*[1] These I disperse to as good Purpose as I can; and I study other Methods, to pursue the same Designs of Piety.

My public Prayers and Sermons are adapted unto the present great Occasion. And I enjoy a precious Presence of the Lord with me in them.

It pleased the Holy One, to take away to a better World, my dear Friend, Mr *Jonathan Pierpont*, the painful, faithful, useful and humble Minister of *Reading*. I was enlivened somewhat by his Death to pursue my Services, with yett more of Industry.[2]

His Flock had a Day of Prayer, after his Death; (on Jun. 22.) Then I served them; all the Exercises of the Afternoon were performed by me; wherein I enjoy'd a very great Assistance of the Lord, and in a very great Assembly. The spirit of the Holy One came upon the

"Whereas the arrears of a Legacy piously bequeathed by Mr. *Samuel Scarlett* unto this Church have not been paid for very many years, it is desired and directed, that Messieurs *Foster, Howard, Clark, Winthrop, Hutchinson, Ruck, Martyn*, be joined with the Deacons, to inspect the State of that Affayr, and advise what is to be done, that it may be brought into some certain reasonable Issue. And that in case, a Composition be judged advisable, the Church be further informed of the Matter, before anything be concluded on." *Cotton Mather's MS. Records of the Second Church*, II.

[1] *Ye Soldier told what he shall do*, was first issued in 1707. The title of the issue of 1709 had *taught* in place of *told*.

The Golden Curb; or, Sober Checks given to Rash Passions, formed part of Mather's Batteries upon the Kingdom of the Devil, printed in London, in 1695. In this new issue the title read *A Golden Curb, for the Mouth, which with an Headstrong Folly, rushes into the Sins of Profane Swearing and Cursing*. Boston, John Allen, 1709, p. 12. It has no separate title-page.

The manner in which Mather exerted his efforts to secure the publication of his sermons is well illustrated in his letter to John Winthrop, December 16, 1707 printed in 4 *Proceedings* VIII. 406, and to Dr. Penhallow, p. 169, *infra*.

[2] He was the fourth minister of Reading, son of Robert and Sarah (Lynde) Pierpont of Roxbury. Some extracts from an early journal are given in Eaton, *History of Reading*, 104 *n.* Sewall says his death "was a very great Loss!"

Chief of Sinners, and there was a memorable Solemnity in the Congregation.

I think, I may also say, I exercised some Faith in the *ascended Jesus* for them.

Inasmuch as I kept one Fast this Week already, (at *Reading*) I did not keep another, on the *Friday* following, as else in Course, I should have done.

I nevertheless enjoy'd a precious Communion with the Lord, at His holy Table.

I conversed with each of the three Persons in the Eternal Godhead. I addressed the three Prayers, unto the three glorious Persons. But still in the Beginning of each Prayer, acknowledged that Person to be the God, who is the Father, and the Son, and the Holy Spirit; that so, I might not erroneously separate them, when I distinguish'd them. I wondered at this Grace, that when those three glorious Persons were from all Eternity conversing with one another, they would now bring such vile Creatures, as we are, into an heavenly Conversation with them. I celebrated the particular Things done by each Person, for His People. I glorified each Person, with such Praises, and such Desires, as were adapted unto our Consideration of the Deity subsisting in it. I was carried into the Suburbs and Earnests of Heaven, by this evangelical Action. Herein also, as in a thousand and a thousand other Things, the Lord is my Teacher.[1] Oh! lett me love Him, who is thus ripening of me, for the heavenly World!

The Month of *July*, brings with it, as little as the former.

Only, on 22 *d.* 5 *m.* [*July.*] *Friday.*

I sett apart the Day, for Prayer with Fasting before the Lord, and had some sweet Conversation with Heaven in the Day.

The Lord is again favoring me, with precious and mul-

[1] Two lines struck out in this place.

tiplied Opportunities, to bring forth Fruit, and serve Him,
in the Way of the Press.

I shall have Opportunity, quickly to take Notice of
several Essayes, which the Glorious Lord, allowes the Chief
of Sinners, to make, for the Service of His Kingdome.

One thing that I now do is this.

I am extremely concerned, that they who lay hold on
the Covenant in our Churches, especially in my own, may
be saved from the Snares of a wretched Formality, in what
they do, and be made very sensible of the great Obligations
which are laid upon them, to lead a life of serious Religion.
I therefore preached a Sermon upon *Sins against the everlasting Covenant;* and then, I fitted it for the Press, and
printed it.[1] It is entituled, THE BONDS OF THE COVENANT.
My Design is, to lodge it in the Hands of all that have
offered themselves unto the Covenant in my own Church,
or that shall do so. And also to send it into most of the
Towns in the Countrey, with some Intimations, to have it
lent, on that Occasion.

Moreover, having preached [2] a Sermon about, *Communing with our own Hearts*, there were devout Hearers, who
desired that they might be furnished with Copies of it; and
offered the Expence of the Impression. So I fitted this for
the Press also; and entituled it, WORK WITHIN DOORS.[3]

20 d. 6 m. [*August.*] *Friday.* This Day I sett apart, as
usually before the Celebration of the Eucharist; for Prayer
with Fasting, in my Study.

But Nothing very remarkable occurr'd, relating to it.
I enjoy'd something of Heaven. It left some heavenly
Impressions upon me.

I am so full of Employments; and in such an happy
way of continually every day, doing a Variety of Services,

---

[1] This seems to refer to the sermon preached on July 17. See p. 31, *infra.*
[2] Preached June 19. See p. 30, *infra.*
[3] Printed by T. Green, 1709.

which yett I do not ask to have remembred, that I have not
the Liesure which else I might have to replenish these
Memorials. Tis possible, I may, if I live to the End of the
Year, make some Recapitulation.

One going from hence for *England*, about this Time,
I did committ into his Hands, an Essay to be there pub-
lished; under the Title of, A MAN OF REASON. The
Design of it, is to show, that Men ought to hearken to
Reason, and therefore to the Maxims of *Religion*.

But there was another Peece of Work, in which my Heart
was at this Time, very much engaged. I have of late,
begun a Method, of lodging *Books*, which may be Instruments of Piety, in all the Vessels of any Burden, that may
sail out of these Colonies. But now, that I may be more
accommodated, with Instruments for my purpose, I fitted
for the Press a Discourse, designed first of all, to awaken the
unregenerate Sailour, out of his dangerous Condition, *sleeping on the Top of a Mast in the midst of the Sea;* and then
to provide and direct a various Employment for him. I
fitted the Work, with Admonitions of Piety, fetched out of
the various *Objects* and *Actions* aboard; and with Devotions
accommodated unto the various *Occasions* of the *Mariner;*
and with Proposals for the keeping of *good Orders* in the
Vessels. I convey'd it unto the Press, with a Resolution
that by the Hands of the *Naval Officers*, in our several Ports,
there should be lodged convenient Numbers of these Books,
in every Vessel that clears and sails from them. Who can
tell, what may be done? Whether some of the Elect of God
may not be found out upon the Waters! It is entituled,
THE MARINERS COMPANION AND COUNSELLOUR.[1]

Moreover, I considered, that the glorious Mystery of
the *Trinity*, tho it be one of the first Articles in our holy
Religion, yett is not enough liv'd upon. Tis a *Mystery of
Godliness;* and a practical Improvement of it, in and for

[1] *The Sailours Companion*, etc.   Printed by B. Green, for Samuel Gerrish.

the Life of Christianity, I thought, would much tend unto the Advancement of *Godliness*. I thought, it would be a Service unto Religion, and unto many Christians, if I answered the Desires of some, who asked me to publish a Discourse, wherein I practically improved and applyed the Doctrine of the *Trinity*, and plainly brought it into the Life of Christianity. Accordingly, I fitted for the Press, and gave to the Printer, such a Discourse; entituled; A CHRISTIAN CONVERSING WITH THE GREAT MYSTERY OF CHRISTIANITY.[1]

2 *d*. 7 *m*. [*September*.] *Friday*. The other Ministers of the Neighbourhood, are this Day feasting with our wicked Governour;[2] I have, by my provoking Plainness and Freedom, in telling this *Ahab* of his wickedness, procured myself to be left out of his Invitations. I rejoiced in my Liberty from the Temptations, with which they were encumbred, while they were *eating of his Dainties* and durst not *reprove* him. And, considering the Power and Malice of my Enemies, I thought it proper for me, to be this day *Fasting*, in Secret, before the Lord.

Accordingly, I sett apart this Day, for *Prayer* with *Fasting*. And the special Intention of the Day was, to obtain my Deliverance and Protection, from the Enemies, which *hate me with a cruel Hatred*, and sometimes *breath out Cruelties*. I mentioned their Names unto the Glorious Lord, who has promised me to be my *Shield*. I pray'd for Mercies to be bestow'd upon them, and yett I pray'd, that my precious Opportunities to be serviceable, may not ly at their Mercy. I entreated this Favour, with my whole Heart, that I may make a good Use of their Enmity, and that I may rather do the more Good because of it. I sang agreeable *Psalms*, and left my Cause with the Lord, resolving to conform unto that Word; Prov. 20. 22. *Say not thou, I*

---

[1] Printed by T. Green.
[2] Joseph Dudley.

*will recompense Evil; but wait on the Lord, and He shall save
thee.*

14 *d*. 7 *m*. *Thursday*.   It was now a General *Fast*, thro'
the Province.[1]   I enjoy'd a precious Presence of the Lord,
with me in the Services of the Day.

But in Conformity to what I have once and again press'd
upon others, I did, among other Services of this day, sett
myself to consider,

*What further have I to do, in that Work of Reformation,
either upon myself, or among others, which the heavy Judgments of God upon our People, have so long been calling for?*

The principal Articles and Purposes, which I could now
pitch upon, were these.

I. In myself:

I observe, the peculiar Spirit, and Error of the Time, to be
Indifferency in Religion.   I would therefore be more zelous,
more active, than ever, more sollicitous about my own Salvation, and that Sin may be discouraged in the World.

I would be exceeding watchful against all *Impurity*, and
the least Glance of my Mind that way, shall but provoke
me to holy Contemplations and Resignations.

I would be afraid of too easily and suddenly taking up
evil Reports; which is a very common Miscarriage among us.

I would endeavour a more prudent and early Dispatch
of my Studies for the *Lord's-Day;* that I may better enjoy
the *Saturs-day Evening* and employ it in some religious
Exercises, with such as are under my Charge.

II. In my *Family:*

Besides the numberless Wayes, which I am using to carry
on a good Education there, I would use if I can, more of a
continual Dropping, of the Maxims of Piety on those under
my Charge; and this particularly in the way of *occasional
Reflection,* to make the Maxims more easily and more dura-
bly remembred with them.

[1] Error for 15th.   See p. 32, *infra*.

And I renew my Purpose of praying successively with each of my Folks *alone*, after I have engaged their Consent and Purpose, to be the Lord's.

III. In my public Circumstances:

I would, besides my careful Visits, in my Flock, to inculcate those Lessons of Godliness, which I may see their special Circumstances recommending unto them, express in certain Prayers and Sermons, a great Concern, in a way of Pitty, for several Sorts of ensnared ones among my People, who do not pitty themselves. It may be, God will sanctify this Way of treating them, and awaken them to pitty themselves.

I would also bear, and procure to be born due *Testimonies*, against all prevailing Iniquities in the Land.

And I would compose and publish many *Essayes*, accommodated unto the Interests of Christianity in the Land; such as may find out all Sorts of People, in the several Wayes, wherein they may be sett athinking on such Things, as may be for the Glory of God.

23 *d.* 7 *m. Friday.* This Day, I undertook a Journey to the Town of *Bridgewater*. My Design was to comfort and honour, a pious, aged, afflicted Servant of God, Mr. *James Keith*, the Minister of the Place.[1] And to answer the Desire of the people in that Place, who flatter me with Hopes that by preaching there, I may do some sensible Service to the Interests of languishing Religion.

I made many Prayers over the Journey; and humbled myself before the Lord, that so the fond Expectations of the People might produce no Inconvenience; and I resigned the whole Affair before me, to the Conduct of the Lord, whose are all my Wayes. Inasmuch as the Journey was for the Service of the Blessed Jesus, the second *Adam*, I hoped, that no Curse would attend it.

---

[1] He was the first minister of Bridgewater, a Scotchman, educated at Aberdeen, and came to New England in 1662. He was ordained in 1664, and died July 23, 1719.

The Lord smiled upon my Journey, in all the Circumstances of it wonderfully. I travelled in a *Calash*. I had above thirty Miles to go. Much of the Road, was very bad, rough, dangerous Way. Yett I gott to the Journey's End, safe, and long before Night.

I preach'd both Parts of the Lord's Day, and with great Assistences from above.

On Monday, my Journey homewards, was yett more comfortable. It was dispatch'd in a little Time, and admirably accommodated.

6 *d*. 8 *m*. [*October*.] *Thursday*. The Lord is multiplying the Testimonies of His Favour to me. He showes me many Tokens for good, at the Sight whereof my Adversaries are ashamed. The wicked see what is done for me; they see it and are grieved; they gnash their Teeth, and melt away.

On the Occasion of some Judgments which God has dispensed on some Sinners (especially, Drunkards) in my Neighbourhood, I thought, that I would watchfully endeavour an holy Improvement of them. I preached a sermon at the Lecture, on that Subject, how Sinners are punished in their very Sins themselves.[1] But after I had greatly humbled myself before the Lord, and my Spirit had been reduced into præparatory Frames of Contrition and Repentance, I enjoy'd a mighty Presence of the Lord with me. There was a vast Assembly of People; perhaps of some Hundreds more than the great House could hold. The Spirit of the Lord came upon me, and quickened me, and strengthened me, and enabled me to discharge the Service I had now before me. And I hope, the Minds of the people had uncommon Impressions made upon them.

14 *d*. 8 *m*. *Friday*. This Day, I sett apart for Prayer with Fasting, (and Alms) in secret before the Lord.

---

[1] "Mr. C. Mather preaches from Prov. 14. 14. Backslider in heart shall be filled with his own Ways. Mentioned the indulgence of Adonijak; the prophet Micajah; not the prophet, but the King was hurt by his Estrangement." Sewall, *Diary*, II. 266. See p. 32, *infra*.

It was a Day, in which I received some inexpressible Satisfactions from Heaven, that my Sins are all pardoned.

I also felt the sanctifying Work of the Holy Spirit upon me; which furnishes me with a Witness in myself, to the Truths of Christianity.

In this way, I kept waiting for what Advice may be coming to me from *England;* and for my Defence against my Enemies; and for a Blessing on my Family and my Ministry.

The Glorious Lord, goes on, in a marvellous Manner, to employ me in glorifying of Him, and to testify His Acceptance of me, in my bearing Testimonies for Him.

I preached a Sermon at the Lecture,[1] in the Audience of the General Assembly, on the *Street* or *Market-place* of the City of God, being *Pure Gold;* and I bore due Testimonies against the Corruptions of the *Market-place.* I fill'd the Sermon with Testimonies for God and Right, and against the Sins of Dishonesty, and the Snares of Intemperance; and added my Hopes for a City of God, yett to be seen in *America.* I thought it might serve the Interests of Piety and Equity, to spread these Testimonies, into every Part of the Countrey. Providence favoured my Intentions; and the Discourse was published; under the Title of, THEOPO-LIS AMERICANA. *An Essay, on the Golden Street of the Holy City; publishing a Testimony against the Corruptions of the Market-place; with some good Hopes of Better Things to be yett seen in the American World.*[2] After the Publication, there was care taken to disperse the Book, into every Town of all these Colonies; and into some other Parts of *America.*

11 *d.* 9 *m.* [*November.*] *Friday.* I sett apart this Day, for Prayers (in Secret,) with Alms, before the Lord.

As the Intentions of the Day, had nothing in them

---

[1] November 3. See p. 32, *infra.*

[2] It was published by B. Green, in 1710. Sewall notes on November 25: "*Theopolis Americana* is finished, the last half-sheet printed off. I stitched me up a Book, and sent the Revd. author one to compleat his."

Remarkable, to distinguish them, from the other Dayes, which I have kept of later Time, so neither had the Employments or Enjoyments of the Day. But in this way, I kept waiting for the Mercies of the Lord, unto me, and mine, and unto all His People.

24 *d.* 9 *m. Thursday.* A Week ago, my little Son *Nathanael*, was taken very sick of a Feavour, with a grievous Oppression, (as it seem'd on his Breast and Stomach,) but after some time, he seemed somewhat releeved and revived; the Physicians concluded, he would live. I had a strange and sinful Stupidity on my mind. I did not pray for his Life, with such Agony, as I have used for my spared Children. I did not sett apart a Day of Prayer for his Life, as I could, and should have done. In the Night, and as the Dawn of this Day approached, the Child began to have the evident Symptoms of Death upon it. I rose, and with several successive Prayers, resign'd it unto the Lord.

This Day, was a public Thanksgiving for the Mercies of Heaven to the Province in the Year, that is past. I laid aside the Subject I intended; and in the Morning I composed a Sermon on, 1. Sam. 1. 7. *She wept, and she did not eat,* i.e. of the Thank-offering: prosecuting that Observation, that a sense of Affliction was oftentimes an Hinderance to the work of Thanksgiving; but that it ought not to be so. My Son died about Noon. My Sermon in the Afternoon proved very acceptable, and seasonable, and serviceable.

The Lord helped me on this Occasion to glorify Him with Resignation, and with many studies how to make the Death in my Family, profitable unto myself, and unto my Family.

I attended the Funeral on the Day following; and there were many merciful Circumstances accompanying of it.

Wanting a Book, to be lodg'd and left, with such as are in sorrowful Circumstances of Affliction; inasmuch as all the Impressions of my former Essayes that way, are disposed of; I gave to the Bookseller, a Lecture, which is fitted up into an agreeable Book, for such Persons; and I design immediately to purchase forty-shillings worth of them, (and afterwards, if I live, many more,) to be dispersed among the Afflicted. It is entituled, THE CURE OF SORROW.[1]

About this time, a nameless and unknown Gentleman, sent me his Desire, (with what was needful to defray the Charge of it,) that a paragraph in my *Theopolis Americana*, relating to the Abuse and Excess of *Rum*, should be printed by itself, and sent into every Part of the Countrey. I ordered, that there should be annexed unto it, certain *Proposals*, relating unto that Matter, to be considered by religious and ingenious Men, in every Part of the Land. The paper is entituled, PROPOSALS OF SOME CONSEQUENCE; *humbly offered to the publick, from a private Hand.*

9 *d.* 10 *m.* [*December.*] *Friday.* I sett apart this Day, for *Prayers* (and *Alms*) as I use to do. One special Intention of the Day, was that I might obtain Mercy for my Family, and spiritual and eternal Advantage unto all the Souls in it, from the Death which has lately been sent into it; and a prospering Direction, and Assistence of Heaven, for the good Education of my surviving Children.

Thus I went on for the Rest of this Month, after my poor Manner, endeavouring to serve Christ and to do good. Nothing very observable occurred in the Actions, or Accidents of the Month; except perhaps, what may be hinted, in the daily Memorials of my *Purposes*.

Indeed, I added one thing unto the Devotions of my Family. For, whereas we catechise, and read, and sing, and pray, usually in the Beginning of the Evening; I now add this; that we sing a short Psalm, or Hymn, together, the last thing we do, before our going to Bed.[2]

[1] Printed by B. Green in 1709.

[2] "*Susanna Fling,* having fallen into scandal, by an unlawful conversation with the man, whom five months after she married, she this day offered those public and open expressions of Repentance, which were accepted." *Cotton Mather's MS. Records of the Second Church,* II.

6 *d.* 11 *m.* [*January.*] *Friday.* I sett apart this Day for *Prayers* (with Fasting) and abundant *Alms;* on such Occasions as use to bring me thus before the Lord. I was ill; and in Hazard of a Feavour, from a Cold contracted by my Visits to the Sick, in very bad Weather. But I sang the Beginning of the *forty first* Psalm. And my Malady vanished beyond Expectation.

I enjoy'd a mighty Presence of the Lord with me, in one Action after this. Having intimated in a Sermon about the *Sins of Youth,* my Purpose the next Lord's-day [1] to deal faithfully with the Neighbours, about the Sins and Snares of our young People, and as one who knowes the *Terror of the Lord;* a vast Assembly came together from all Quarters of the Town. The Spirit of the Glorious Lord came upon me, with His precious and powerful Influences. I preached a long Sermon, and it was heard with much Attention, with much Affection. And tho' I expected much Malice and Mocking from some of the Hearers, I was happily disappointed of my Expectation. The Things delivered, had a great Impression on the Hearers, and good Effects of Religion and Reformation followed. [2]

3 *d.* 12 *m.* [*February.*] *Friday.* I sett apart this Day also, for Prayers (with Fasting) and abundant *Alms.* Particularly, (as usually) to prepare for Interviews with

---

[1] January 22. See p. 33, *infra.*

[2] "At a Church-Meeting held 10 *d.* 11 *m.* 1709, *Tuesday,* this vote was passed, *Nemine contradicente.*

"The Church, considering the Encumbrance of a course of Law, to recover their just Right in Mr. *Scarlett's* pious Legacy to them, and being willing to sett an Exemple of all Christian and possible Moderation and Compassion to an Orphan, do consent that the Committee, already employ'd about this Affayr, namely Messieurs *Foster, Howard, Clark, Winthrop, Hutchinson, Ruck, Martyn,* with the three Deacons, shall be entrusted and empowered by the Church, to proceed and finish that matter, and make all the legal Provision that shall be necessary; so that the Church may have clear of all Encumbrance, at least the summ of one hundred and fifty pounds in money, or province Bills.

"At this Meeting, *Eliza Renmore* offered her pœnitent Acknowledgement of her Offence in striking a Neighbour. Which the Church accepted." *Cotton Mather's MS. Records of the Second Church,* II.

Heaven, on the Lord's-Day (and the Lord's Supper,) approaching.

Which I enjoy'd unto some Satisfaction.

That this year might prove with me, a pretty *bearing* Year, I concluded it, with two Publications more by the way of the Press.

The Designs of them, will be sufficiently apprehended from the Titles of them.

The one is entitled; THE HEAVENLY CONVERSATION. *An Essay upon the Methods of Conversing with a Glorious CHRIST in every Step of our Life. With Directions upon that CASE, How may the Consideration of CHRIST, be brought into all the Life of a Christian.*[1]

The other is entitled; DUST AND ASHES. *An Essay upon, Repentance to the Last; Advising a watchful Christian upon that CASE; How to keep alive the Daily Exercise of REPENT-ANCE, to the End of his Life!* [2]

My Intention was to lodge these Treatises in the Hands of many of the Ministers, throughout the Countrey.

I represented, the Methods of *Piety* proposed in these Essayes, as being the true *American Pietism.* I considered that the People who are shortly to be the *Stone cutt out of the Mountain*, will be a People of these Principles and Practices. And I was willing, to contribute unto the Shaping of that People; and furnish them with Instruments of Piety, that may be of Use among them. I shall also endeavour to send these things unto Dr. *Franckius*, in *Saxony*.

What remains is, to make some Recapitulation, of my Proceedings, on the *Devices of Good* which I form and write in the Morning of each Day in the Week, on the Quæstion for the Day. I shall not here transcribe all the particular *Devices* and *Purposes*, thus produced; but only touch on a few, that may give some Intimation how my Year has rolled along.

---

[1] These works were issued without author's name.
[2] Published by B. Green in 1710.

I. The Quæstion every *Lord's-day* Morning, was, *what Service to be done for my Saviour, in the* FLOCK *whereof I am the Pastor.*

Here I purposed, that I would endeavour much Service in my *occasional Visits.* Learning (from the Bills putt up, or otherwise,) who has received any *special Mercy,* I would visit them, and agree with them on some *special Return* of Glory to God. Learning who are in any *singular Affliction,* I would visit them, and propose unto them some singular Fruits of *Repentance* and *Obedience.* The *Handmaids of the Lord* that are near their *Travail,* I would visit, and make their Circumstances an awakening Occasion to settle the Peace of their Souls.

That I would use more than ordinary Endeavour to rescue the *Children of the Covenant,* from the woful Formality, with which many of them lay hold on the *Covenant.*

That I would in the most pathetical and emphatical Wayes imaginable, warn the *young* people, against the Snares of Death, whereby many are endangered.

That I would labour mightily to begett a *Temper of Benignity* in the Neighbourhood; and among other Methods for it, preach as winningly as I can, on the Duties of *good Neighbourhood.*

That I would sett up a *Charity-School,* and make it a precious Opportunity of Good unto many Children. Particularly, visit it often, and instruct the Children and give pecuniary Rewards unto them, when they have learn't the good Things, which I sett 'em to learn.

That I will animate an Addition to the *Religious Societies* in the Neighbourhood.

That I would write a Letter unto the principal Person in each of the *Religious Societies* (or at least mention the Matter to them,) expressing my Desire, that the Societies would suggest unto me, what *Subjects* they most want or wish, to hear publickly preached on; and preach accordingly. &c. &c. &c.

II. Every MUNDAY Morning, *what to be done in* MY FAMILY?

Here, among many other things, I purposed,

That I would order the Children to read over the *Mother's Catechism*, written by Mr. *Baxter*, in the most profitable Manner.[1]

That to increase in my Family, their Attention to, and understanding of, the Scriptures, each Person shall have a Bible in their hands, and read the *Verse*, as I am going to make my Observations upon it.

That the Children shall have their Apartments well-fitted up, in which they may read, and write, and pray.

That I would oblige each of the Children, to retire, and ponder on that Quæstion, *what should I wish to have done if I were now adying!* And report unto me their Answer to the Quæstion; of which I may take unspeakable Advantage, to inculcate Piety upon them.

That I would cause those of the Children who can write, ever now and then, to draw up a *Prayer* in writing, and shew it unto me.

By which Means, I may see, how far they *consider the State of their own Souls:* and it may bring them to consider it. I would particularly putt them upon drawing up of *Prayers*, against such Miscarriages of Temptations, as they may be most of all in a Danger of.

That I would spend the *Saturs-day* Evenings in the most exquisite Wayes of instilling Piety into my Family, by successively taking each Person alone into my Study, and there Talking and Praying with them. And alwayes make that Evening an Opportunity of Praying with my Wife, before the Communion of the *Lord's-Table*, and preparatory to it.

That I would labour to discharge unto my Son-in-Law,

[1] First published in 1701. No American issue seems to have been published before 1729.

the Duty of a Father, in a most exemplary manner; see that he be tenderly used, and well-provided for. Assist his Education; and instil the Lessons of Piety into him, with all possible Assiduity. &c. &c. &c.

III. On TUESDAY Morning, I came to consider two *Quæstions* alternately.

On the First week, I thought; *what Service to be done for Christ, and my* RELATIVES ABROAD?

Here, I contrived several things to be done, that I may assist some *aged Relatives* in their Præparation for the heavenly World.

And, I contrived to find out my most *distant Relatives* and reach them with Books of Piety, and such Things as may be useful to them.

And some of my Sisters, having their Husbands abroad; I constantly, at least once a week, visited their Families, and pray'd with them. &c. &c. &c.

But then, every other Week, instead of my *Relatives*, I considered my *Enemies.* I singled out my *personal Enemies*, as many of them, as I can know of, and considered, *what good may I do unto them?*

I am in the Way of it, and I have made good Progress in the Way; that I shall not know that I have one Adversary in the World, but what I have explicitly charged my Soul, to take heed of all personal Revenge of him; yea, I have actually done some good Office for him.

I will not here mention the *Persons*, or the *Purposes;* because tis better they should be forgotten.

IV. Every WEDNESDAY Morning, my Quæstion was, *what Service to be done for Christ, and the Interest of His Kingdome, in the Countrey, or among other People?*

Here, I scattered *Books of Piety*, about the Countrey; yea, in all the Towns of these Colonies. Books, upon such Intentions of Religion, as appeared most necessary and seasonable to be prosecuted.

I did the like for all the *Vessels*, of Burden, that sail out of these Colonies.

I published, near as many *Books*, as there have been *Months* in the Year.

I send Numbers of Books, to serve the Designs of Religion, in the other Plantations.   Yea, in *England*, in *Scotland*, in *Ireland*, in *Saxony*.

And many Services were done for particular Churches here and there; for which there were frequent Occasions administred.

V. Every THURSDAY Morning; *what Service in and for the* SOCIETIES?

Here, many Things were done, to stop the Torrent of Wickedness.

Proposals for general Advantage, were hence made unto the General Assembly.

More *Charity-Schools* were erected; and the Methods of supporting them agreed upon.

A new *Society for·the Suppression of Disorders*, was formed.

I proposed a Method, that every Person in the *Reforming Societies*, might be obliged in their Turn, to mention some thing, that be a Proposal of Consequence to the main Intention.

I visited the other *Religious Societies;* and where some of them were languishing I preached, on Eccl. 4. 9.   *Two are better than one;* the Benefit of *Associations* for *religious Purposes.*

VI. Every FRIDAY Morning, *what particular Objects of Compassion have I to do good unto?*

Here, I fill'd my *List*, successively, with *afflicted* People. And, I did what I could for them.

Unto the same List, I added, *particular Persons*, who in regard of their Souls ensnared by the Destroyer, called for my *particular Labours* to address them, and rescue them.

VII. My last Quæstion, and that for the SATUREDAY Morning, has been;

What remains to be done for the Kingdome of God in MY OWN HEART AND LIFE? I thought,

That I am favoured with surprising and uncommon Opportunities, to publish many *Books of Piety.* There is nothing of so much Concernment for me, as to take effectual Care, that my *own Books,* do not at last prove my own Condemnation, by my failing in those *Points of Piety,* which I commend unto others. Wherefore, (with Prayers to be delivered from so great a Confusion) I would, on the *Lord's Day Evenings* read over my own *Books of Piety,* and work them over again upon my Heart; that my Soul may be exquisitely conformed unto them.

That whatever *bodily Infirmities* I labour (or can call to Mind, that I have laboured) under, I would make them the Occasions and Incentives of some *Dispositions* and *Purifications* in my Soul, which they may agreeably mind me of; and I would sett myself to consider *what.*

That I would, at my Meals, think more frequently and thoroughly on the *super-essential Bread,* the *Food that endures to everlasting Life.*

That I would invent agreeable *Motto's,* and have every Room, in my House furnished with them; as Admonitions of Piety and good Management, for myself and others.

That I would sett myself more distinctly to consider, first, what were the more special *Sins,* and *Crimes* of my Youth; And thereupon, what more *special Service* I should now do for the Kingdome of God, in the directest Contrariety and Contradiction to my former Sins.

Then, to consider, what *Reproaches* I have mett withal; and thereupon, what *Services* I should be awakened thereby to do for the Kingdome of God.

Yea, that when I hear of any Abuse offered me, I would instead of giving way to any Passion, presently sett myself to think, *what good to be gott by it? What use to be made of it?*

That I would sometimes insist on that Enquiry, *what do I that no Hypocrite ever did?*

And many more such things. *Sic volvitur Annus.*

THE COURSE OF MY PUBLIC MINISTRY.

13 *d.* 12 *m.* [*February.*] 1708. I preached, in the Forenoon, (being suddenly putt upon it, and with scarce an Hour's Warning by my Father's Illness,) on 2. Thess. 3. 5. *An Heart directed into the Love of God.* In the Afternoon (in my Course of handling select Passages, in the first Epistle of *John:*) on 1. Joh. 4. 8. How *God is Love.*

20 *d.* 12 *m.* I preached, on Prov. 21. 25. *The Desire of the Slothful.* (Some having Desired a sermon on the Subject.)

24 *d.* 12 *m. Thursday.* I preached the Lecture, on Isa. 6. 5. The Methods of carrying on a *Life of Repentance,* as long as we live.

27 *d.* 12 *m.* I preached on 1. Joh. 4. 18. How *Love* brings us into a *fearless* Condition.

6 *d.* 1 *m.* [*March.*] 1709. I preached on, 1. Joh. 4. 9. The *Love* of God in *sending His* only *Son* into the World that we may *live.* (And I administred the Eucharist.)

13 *d.* 1 *m.* I preached, on 1. Joh. 5. 3. The *Commandments* of God *not grievous* to the Children of God.

20 *d.* 1 *m.* I preached on Prov. 23. 34. The unregenerate *Sleeping* in a dangerous Condition, and not sensible of it.

24 *d.* 1 *m. Thursday.* A General Fast. I preached on Lam. 3. 25. The *Goodness* of God, unto them that *seek* Him, and *wait* for Him.

27 *d.* 1 *m.* I preached on, 1. Joh. 5. 4. *Overcoming* the *World.*

3 *d.* 2 *m.* [*April.*] I preached on 2. Cor. 13. 5. The *Advantages* and *Inferences* to be made, from our *knowing ourselves.*

10 *d.* 2 *m.* I preached, on, 1. Joh. 5. 14. A Beleever praying *according to the Will of God,* and finding the Answer of his Prayers. (When my Sermon was near three quarters finished, a Fire breaking forth in the Town, broke up the Assembly. When the Assembly returned, after the Fire was conquered, I went on, and preached another Sermon, an extemporaneous Essay, from Job. 20. 26. on that Case, what shall we do, that we may escape the Judgments of God, by *Fire* consuming our *Habitations?* Much Notice was taken of this latter Sermon.)

17 *d. 2 m.* I preached on 1. Joh. 5. 14. and went on, where I left off the last Lord's-day; and added a Discourse on five remarkable *Cases*, about our making Prayer, and God's Hearing it.

21 *d. 2 m. Thursday.* I preached the Lecture, on Job. 13. 6. That Men ought to *hearken to Reason.* Applying it unto certain Maxims of Piety.

1 *d. 3 m. [May.]* I preached on, 1. Joh. 5. 6. Our Saviour coming under the Advantages, both of *Water* and of *Blood.* (And I administred the Eucharist.)

4 *d. 3 m. Wednesday.* I preached, on a Day of Prayer at *Malden,* on 1. Joh. 5. 14. And assisted the Flock, in Renewing their Covenant.

8 *d. 3 m.* I preached, on Job. 5. 24. That Case, how a good Man should so *visit his Habitation,* as *not to Sin.*

15 *d. 3 m.* I preached, on, Jer. 30. 15. *Sin,* the Cause of Affliction. (A Time of much *Affliction,* especially by Sickness, in the Neighbourhood.)

18 *d. 3 m. Wednesday.* I preached, at the Ordination of a Pastor, in the Church at *Malden;* on Psal. 147. 2. The *Lord Building up Jerusalem.*

19 *d. 3 m. Thursday.* I preached the Lecture, on Hos. 6. 1. The *Repentance* necessary for a *wounded People.* And applied it unto the great Expedition, which is now forming, for *Canada.*

22 *d. 3 m.* I preached, on Ezek. 16. 21. *My Children.* The Lord owning the Children of His People, as His *own Children.* (And I baptised my Son, *Nathanael.*)

29 *d. 3 m.* I preached on, 1. Joh. 5. 19. The *whole World lying in Wickedness.*

5 *d. 4 m. [June.]* I preached, on Rev. 2. 19. Our Lord's *knowing,* who *serves* Him, and what *Service* they do for Him. (On the Death of my dear Friend, Mr. *Pierpont,* the Pastor of *Reading.*)

12 *d. 4 m.* I preached, on 1. Joh. 5. 21. The Idols that endanger us; the Spiritual *Idolatry,* from which we are to keep ourselves.

16 *d. 4 m. Thursday.* I preached the Lecture, on, Heb. 1. 13. Our Saviour *making His Enemies His Footstool.* With relation to the great Expedition against the Idolaters of *Canada.*

19 *d. 4 m.* I preached on, Psal. 4. 4. The great Exercise of *Communing with our own Hearts.*

22 *d. 4 m. Wednesday.* I preached at *Reading,* on Rev. 2. 19. where a Fast was kept, for the Death of their Minister and about the Calling of another.

26 *d.* 4 *m.* I preached, on 1. Joh. 5. 7. The Testimony given by the *three Persons* in God, unto the Character, and Religion of our Saviour. (And I administred the Eucharist.)

3 *d.* 5 *m.* [*July.*] I preached, A. M. to the South-Church, on Job. 5. 24. P. M. to the North Church, on Prov. 23. 7. The Character of Men, fetch'd from the *Thoughts*, which their *Hearts* are fill'd withal.

10 *d.* 5 *m.* I preached on Prov. 1. 32. The *Prosperity* of ungodly People, thro' their own Foolishness *destructive* to them.

14 *d.* 5 *m. Thursday.* I preached the Lecture on Jer. 4. 18. Sin the procuring Cause of Affliction; applying it, to our public Circumstances.

17 *d.* 5 *m.* I preached on, Isa. 24. 5. Violations of the *everlasting Covenant.* Proposing solemn Admonitions, to the many among us, who with too much Formality and Forgetfulness, enter into the *Covenant.*

24 *d.* 5 *m.* I preached, on Rev. 7. 16. The Time, when the People of God, shall not complain of any *distressing* Heat upon them. (It now being a very hott, faint, sultry Time.)

31 *d.* 5 *m.* I preached on, Psal. 25. 1. The main Business of every distressed one, with the Lord; and the main of his Business, to *lift up* a distressed *Soul* to the Lord. (Intending if God will, a Course of Sermons on the Psalm, in this Time of many Distresses.)

7 *d.* 6 *m.* [*August.*] I preached on, Jer. 13. 23. The Danger and Mischief, of *evil Customes.* I concluded with Warnings to our *Ethiopians.*

11 *d.* 6 *m. Thursday.* I preached the Lecture on, 1. Sam. 1. 15. 18. *Pouring out the Soul to the Lord*, the Cure of *Sadness.*

14 *d.* 6 *m.* I preached on, Psal. 25. 2. Acknowledging the Lord as *our God*, and then *Trusting* in Him.

21 *d.* 6 *m.* I preached on, 1. Joh. 5. 8. The *three Witnesses on Earth*, to the Truth of Christianity, (And I administred the Eucharist.)

28 *d.* 6 *m.* I preached on, Psal. 25. 2. Our being *ashamed* of Sin; but being delivered from the *Shame* of *disappointed Hopes.*

4 *d.* 7 *m.* [*September.*] I preached on Prov. 4. 27. The avoiding of *Extremes* and *Errors on both hands.*

8 *d.* 7 *m. Thursday.* I preached the Lecture, on Prov. 1. 24, 28. Sins *retaliated* in their Punishments; and the Lord's punishing our Deafness to His Calls, by His being as deaf to our Cries. (Præparatory to a General Fast, the next Week.)

11 *d*. 7 *m*. I preached, A. M. at the Old Church, on Luk. 24. 32. The *warning* Efficacy, which the Words of Christ may and should have on the Hearts of Men. And P. M. at the North Church, on Psal. 119. 176. The Description of a *returning Sinner*.

15 *d*. 7 *m*. *Thursday*. A General Fast. I preached on, Psal. 25. 2. The Calamity of being under the *Triumphs* of our *Enemies;* and the Way to be delivered from the Calamity, by getting into good Terms with Heaven.

18 *d*. 7 *m*. I preached on, Prov. 23. 17. That *Sinners* are to be (not envied, but) *pittied*. Several objects of Pitty among them specified.

25 *d*. 7 *m*. I preached at *Bridgwater*, A. M. on Luk. 24. 32. And, P. M. on Jer. 8. 6.

2 *d*. 8 *m*. [*October*.] I preached on Job. 14. 10. The State of Man, (*where is he?*) after he has *given up the Ghost*. Several Deaths having happened the last Week in my Neighbourhood.

6 *d*. 8 *m*. *Thursday*. I preached the Lecture, on Prov. 14. 14. Sinners (*filled with their own Wayes,*) having in their very *Sins* themselves, the *Punishment of* their Sins. (Occasion'd by strange Things befalling some Sinners among us.)

9 *d*. 8 *m*. I preached, on Luk. 24. 32. The *warning* Efficacy in the Words of our Saviour.

16 *d*. 8 *m*. I preached, 1. Joh. 5. 10. The *Witness within;* the Testimony to the Truth of Christianity, which we have in a work of Grace, within us. (And I administred the Eucharist.)

23 *d*. 8 *m*. I preached on, Psal. 25. 3. *Prayer* for *others* as well as ourselves; and a concern that *others* may not be discouraged in Piety by any thing in us; and the Enemies of good Men, *without a Cause;* and Sinners *asham'd*, because they are causelessly so. And who are *Waiters on God*.

30 *d*. 8 *m*. I preached on Act. 10. 44. The *Holy Spirit* falling on the Hearers of the Word, while they are *Hearing* of it.

3 *d*. 9 *m*. [*November*.] *Thursday*. I preached the Lecture, on Rev. 21. 21. The *Street* of the City, *pure Gold;* against Corruptions in the *Market-Place*. (The General Assembly then sitting.)

6 *d*. 9 *m*. I preached on Psal. 25. 4. The *Wayes* of God; the Wayes that we shall not be ashamed of; and a Desire to be *taught* those Wayes.

13 *d*. 9 *m*. I preached on Gen. 20. 11. The Dangers of *Places*, in which there is not the *Fear of God*.

20 *d*. 9 *m*. I preached on Psal. 25. 5. *Reiterated* Prayers, and

Knowledge in order to *Practice;* and the Necessity of being *led* by God; and the Christian Religion being the *Truth* of God, and *pleading* in *praying;* and Salvation turning on our keeping the Wayes of God; and waiting on Him, *all the Day.*

24 *d.* 9 *m. Thursday.* A public Thanksgiving for the Mercies of the Year. I preached on, 1. Sam. 1. 7. *She wept and did not eat.* That a Sense of Affliction is often an Hindrance to the Work of Thanksgiving; but should not be so. (My Son *Nathanael,* dying about Noon, made the Discourse in the afternoon, seasonable and observeable.)

27 *d.* 9 *m.* I preached, on Ps. 25. 5. How God is the *God of our Salvation.*

1 *d.* 10 *m.* [*December.*] *Thursday.* I preached the Lecture, on Jer. 18. 2. The Sovereignty of God; how tis to be acknowledged; particularly in the Condition of our Families.

4 *d.* 10 *m.* I preached, on Jam. 1. 27. The Offices of good *Neighbourhood;* labouring to inspire a Temper of Benignity into the Neighbourhood. The Time of the Year makes it a special Opportunity.

11 *d.* 10 *m.* I preached on Cant. 2. 16. The glorious Priviledge, of an Interest in the only Saviour. (And I administred the Eucharist.)

18 *d.* 10 *m.* I preached, on Tit. 2. 14. Our Saviour's *giving Himself.*

25 *d.* 10 *m.* I preached on Psal. 25. 6. The experienced, and everlasting Mercies and Bounties of God; how to be improved for our Encouragement.

29 *d.* 10 *m. Thursday.* I preached the Lecture, on Luk. 10. 29. The Duties of *good Neighbourhood.*

1 *d.* 11 *m.* [*January.*] I preached, on Luk. 13. 8. *One Year more* of Divine Patience, by Intercession obtained for the Unfruitful. Taking advantage from the Time, (*New-Years Day,*) to inculcate Instructions of Piety, which it is proper to begin the year withal.

8 *d.* 11 *m.* I preached on Tit. 2. 14. Our Saviour's *Redeeming us from all Iniquity.*

15 *d.* 11 *m.* I preached on Psal. 25. 7. The *Sins of Youth,* what to do, that they may be not *remembred,* but pardoned.

22 *d.* 11 *m.* I preached a second time, on Ps. 25. 7. The Lord gloriously helped me, to bear my Testimonies against the *Sins of Youth,* which threaten the young People in my Neighbourhood. A vast Assembly of young People, from all Parts of the Town, came

together on this Occasion; and my Testimonies found a great Acceptance, and beyond my Expectation.

26 *d.* 11 *m. Thursday.* I preached the Lecture, on Gal. 2. 20. *Living by the Faith of the Son of God;* and the excellent Methods to fill a Life with Acknowledgments of a Glorious CHRIST, and have Thoughts of Him in all Manner of Conversation.

29 *d.* 11 *m.* I preached on, Psal. 25. 8. The *Goodness* and *Faithfulness* of God; particularly appearing, in showing Sinners the *Way* to Blessedness: and what is the *Way*,

5 *d.* 12 *m.* [*February.*] I preached on Tit. 2. 14. The *redeemed*, becoming a *purified*, and *peculiar* People. And I administred the Eucharist.

To SAMUEL PENHALLOW.   M.H.S.

BOSTON, 16 *d.* 10 *m.* [December.], 1709.

Sir, — You have alwayes allow'd me, all possible Freedom with you; and I have alwayes practis'd it.

I continue to do so. And I Entreat that by your obliging Hand, there may be convey'd the Little Books, of the *Golden Street*, unto those, unto whom I have directed them.

The Books of *Sober Considerations* I Entreat you, to disperse where you think, there may be most occasion for them.

The other paper of PROPOSALS, I am desired by a Nameless Gentleman (I could never Learn, who; tho' when I saw the Second Leaf, I could Easily call to Mind, who was the Author of what fell into the Hands of the unknown Gentleman;) to scatter; and I Leave this Parcel of them, unto your Discretion, for the Dispersion of them.

I pray the glorious Redeemer to multiply His Blessings, on your person and Family. I am, Syr, Ever and heartily your Servt.

Co. MATHER.

To SAMUEL PENHALLOW.   M.H.S.

BOSTON, 4 *d.* 2 *m.* [*April.*], 1709[10].

SIR, — If I prove Troublesome, tis your most obliging Invitation, that has made me so.

We suppose the Fleet not yett sailed.

I humbly entreat you, Sir, to make this Packet, (unto my Brother,) find Mr *Emerson;* unto whose care I committ it, as being partly indeed for his Service; that is, to recomend him unto what my Brother may do for him.

If you meet not with Mr *Emerson* I pray, lett Mr *Stoddard* have it; who has already a Cargo of my providing.

We have no manner of Newes; that is to say, public.

Ever now and then, we discover *New Roxburisms* but those whether committed here, or at *Piscataqua,* (when you take People in their way,) must not as yett be talk'd of.

I don't understand, that the publication of Mr *Stoddard's* pretended Answer goes forward.[1]

I pray your Acceptance of an *Opening Temple,*[2] and wish you a part in it. I am, Syr, Your hearty Servt,

Co. Mather.[3]

To Samuel Penhallow. M.H.S.

Boston. 22 d. 3 m. [*May.*], 1710.

My Honoured Friend, — After a thousand Obligations which you have heretofore laid upon me, you have by your late kind Presents, entred pretty far into another Chiliad. Should I write you as many Letters of Thanks, as I have obligations, I should make you but an ill Requital, and but oppress and injure you with a Load of Acknowledgments. In one word, I thank you, I love you, I wish I could serve you.

I proceed unto the next Part of my Duty; which is to inform you, That the Arrival of our *Ingenuous, Generous, and prosperous Friend, Capt. Wentworth,* surprizes us with a large Cargo of Intelligence. I will offer you nothing, that you may expect from our public Newes Letter.

But, we may every day expect the *Dragon,* as a Forerunner, of Six Men of War, with a thousand Marines, of whom etc. Col. *Nicolson* is General, to pursue an Expedition, *first* against *Port-royal.*[4] The

---

[1] Solomon Stoddard's *An Appeal to the Learned,* a reply to Increase Mather, and printed this year.

[2] *The Temple Opening,* printed in 1709.

[3] "9 d. 2 m. [*April.*] 1710. This Day a Confession of *William Perry,* expressing a Repentance of his Error and Evil, in withdrawing from the Communion of the Church, was offered unto the Church, and accepted." *Cotton Mather's MS. Records of the Second Church,* II.

[4] Palfrey, *History of New England,* IV. 277.

Arrival of our Mast-fleet, and the Maqua's, may perhaps, a little retard, and alter, some of the Motions and Measures, but the thing will go on; and you will foresee that it is like to be a Summer of extreme Distress unto us.

The Parlaiment, were willing to exert a Trial of skill, on the High-flyers in the Nation; and impeached one *Sacheverel* before the House of Lords, for some fiery Sermons, which he published. He had a long Trial of ten Dayes; And the Friends of his Cause in the House of Lords, were so many, that a very easy Sentence was passed upon him; of three years suspension from the preaching Part of his priestly Function. Immediately an High-Church Mob was raised, by some Incendiaries; who did horrid Things, and pull'd down six Presbyterian Meeting-houses, (*Burgesses, Bradburies,* etc.) and were proceeding to pull down the Bishop of *Salisburies* House, and endless Outrages; But the City Trained Bands suppressed the formidable Tumult. Almost all Men of Thought, expect a Civil War; at least, as soon as Opportunity shall be given for it, by a Peace with *France;* which now is diverted, until some further Decisive Action.[1]

What remains is, to comfort you, concerning a Good Friend of ours, in whose Welfare we have both reckoned our selves Concerned. Mr *Emerson* is returned. And I cannot learn any other, but that he has behaved himself honourably, and come off with a very good Reputation. Several eminent Persons write unto me concerning him; and all of them, very respectfully. He is, you know, of a vivid, and active Genius; and of an hearty Inclination to Do Good. So far as I can understand, he has done it; and has endeavoured all good Offices to the Publick as he has had opportunity. I beleeve, his Friends, (as well as his Talents,) to be such, that, if his own Flock do not give him a very agreeable Reception, he may soon, much mend his Condition and Serviceableness, on the other side of the Atlantic. It will be some Difficulty for him, to reach *Piscataqua,* till he hath spent a little Time here, in doing and settling some Affairs, of Consequence to others as well as himself, here; for there are many who rely upon him, for his Guidance, and Advice, and Management in their Affairs. If he don't hurry home, his Conduct must not be censured.

I will add no more at this Time. I commend you to the Pro-

---

[1] The story is briefly told in the *Dictionary of National Biography*, L. 81.

tection and Comunion of our only Saviour. And I am, Syr, Your very obliged Servt.

Co. MATHER.[1]

To SAMUEL PENHALLOW.   M.H.S.

BOSTON 1 d. 11 m. [January.], 1710–11.

MY HONOURED FRIEND, — It is not in flourishing and flattering Words, but in very speaking Matter of Fact, that I continually declare, my Esteem for your Person and Conduct, and my entire Satisfaction in your good Affection to me.

Tis from hence, that I ever presume upon such Points of a Friendship and Freedom with you, as I do not with any Person in your Province, nor with many in the whole world.

I readily subscribe this Testimony, that I find you a Constant, Faithful, and useful Friend.

And I now address you with a Request which I would make to none but such a Friend.

On the astonishing Exemple of outrageous wickedness among *the Sailors and Strangers lately broke into your Neighbourhood*, and the Quick and Strange Destruction brought by the Judgments of God upon some of them, I Entertained a great Auditory, with a Lecture on the Last Thursday.

The publication of the Sermon is desired; and I am willing to grant the Desire.

But it ought to be accompanied with an Expressive and Punctual Relation of the horrid Matter, and such an one, as being well attested, may be Relied upon. The Least material Mistake, may be a great Inconvenience.

Now, no Man more able than you, to furnish me. Write me then, this week, a Letter that shall give me the Story with all the Circumstances, which you think proper to have Exposed unto the world. Yea, and such a Letter, as may (except you forbid me,) be joined with my Sermon. For truly, Syr, I am not ashamed of appearing very publickly in your Company, if you are not afraid of appearing in mine. And thus much for that Affayr.[2]

---

[1] "4 d. 4 m. [June.], 1710. David Norton, having been overtaken with a scandalous Degree of Drunkenness, the Church this day accepted his pœnitent and ingenuous Confession." *Cotton Mather's MS. Records of the Second Church*, II.

[2] This must refer to *Compassions called for*, but there is no letter from Penhallow in it.

My dear, and youngest Sister, *Jerusha Oliver*, is now lying dead (in Childbed of her first Child,) and to-morrow to be interr'd. She was an Exemple of shining Piety from her Infancy and has left admirable Memorials of it, with her Pen, whereof she was a considerable Mistress. I mention this; because your Good Affection, makes the Concerns of our Family your own.[1]

God continue to you, your excellent and amiable Consort; and give you much Comfort in all your Children. May the Knowledge and Image and Service of a glorious Christ, exceedingly Beautify them all. I am, Syr, Your very obliged Servt,

Co. MATHER.

Tis to be feared, Capt Hobby can continue but a little while.

[1] Mather printed a tract about the Christian experiences of Mrs. Oliver, entitled *Memorials of Early Piety*, 1711.

1711

THE XLIXTH YEAR OF MY LIFE

12 *d.* 12 *m.* [*February.*] 1710. *Munday.* Should the Chief
of Sinners live to the End of this Year, I shall have seen a
Jubilee of Years. It becomes me to begin the Year, with
a Sort of *Jubilation;* and to spend this Day in Songs of
Praise unto the *God of my Life.*

I began the Day, with Cries to Heaven, for Help to go thro' the
heavenly Work of praising the glorious One.

I laboured all the Day long to multiply on all Occurrences and
Occasions, the heavenward Ejaculations of a praising Soul.

I attended my usual Exercises in the Religion of the Morning.

I then deeply humbled myself before the Lord, for the Sins of
my past Life; and particularly, the more notable Sins of the last
Year; most of all, my criminal Idleness and Barrenness; that I have
done so little Good, in Comparison of what I might have done. I
confessed myself worthy of all the Afflictions which I have suffered
all this while; yea, of all the Afflictions, Distresses and punishments,
which I can see any Sinners any where languishing under. I own'd
the shining Displayes of sovereign and marvellous Grace in all the
Favours that Heaven bestowes upon me.

I sang agreeable *Psalms* now and then in the Day.

I proceeded unto Meditations and Acknowledgments of the
Mercies which my past Life has been brightened withal. Especially,
in that having obtained Help from God I continue to this Day. And
I am free from grievous and painful and horrible Diseases. And my
Family is in comfortable Circumstances. And I have been fetch'd
a foolish and filthy Creature from forlorn Wretchedness, and made
a Preacher of the everlasting Gospel, and accommodated with an
Utterance and a Library beyond most in the World. I have had
precious Opportunities to preach the glorious Gospel; in very great
Assemblies; my Auditory is alwayes one of the greatest that is
ordinarily seen among the People of God. My Writings also, have

been published, and accepted, (near two hundred several Times,) and serviceable to the best Interests. And tho' I have had cruel Enemies I have been strangely preserved from their Power and Malice; and victorious over it.

I then considered the more particular Blessings which crowned the last Year unto me. The Smiles I have had on my Family; and the Helps in my Ministry; the Triumphs of my continued Serviceableness over the Attempts of my Adversaries to hurt it. And the Strength added unto my Serviceableness, by the Civility I received from the University of *Glasgow.*[1]

I adored the Grace of God in these Things; and considered the Intercession of my Saviour as procuring of them for a Sinner, who is worthy of nothing but sore Plagues and of long Continuance.

Afterwards, considering how I am endebted unto my admirable *Jesus,* for all the Favours of Heaven, I perused with Deliberation, and suitable Meditations and Resolutions, my Proposals for living by the Faith of the Son of God. And then I did on my Knees before the Lord, express my Dispositions, to make my daily Flights unto my *Jesus,* as my Sacrifice and my Advocate; and rely upon His Providence to supply me, and protect me and comfort me; and sett His Exemple alwayes before me, and make my Conformity to Him, even in Sufferings and Abasements, my sweet Satisfaction; and be acted from a Principle of Obedience to Him in all Things; and be filled with continual Thoughts of Him. That I might arrive yett more perfectly to these Things, I resigned myself up to His holy Spirit, and requested Him to take Possession of me.

Anon, that I might glorify the great God, in each of His three Persons, I pondered the distinct Acknowledgments thereof, in my Treatise of, *A Christian Conversing with the Greatest of Mysteries.* And then I did in my Prayers distinctly make those Acknowledgments.

Besides these Things, I call'd to Mind, who had been special Instruments used by God, in doing of me Kindnesses, in the year now expired. I blessed God for them, and pray'd for a Blessing of God upon them. And then I gave Thanks for the Ministry of the holy Angels, and the good Offices which had been done for me, by those Ministers doing the Pleasure of the Lord.

Finally. I made this an Opportunity to bring my Petitions unto the God of my Praise: in some special and important Articles. More especially, that some, eminent and opulent Persons may be raised

[1] The degree of Doctor of Divinity, conferred in 1710.

up; to forward the Publication of my *Biblia Americana*. And, that my Serviceableness may not be overwhelmed by the Floods of the ungodly whereof I am afraid; but some Token for Good be shown unto me, which may cause them that hate me to be ashamed.

And, that the Lord may be glorified in the Conversion of that poor Jew, for whom I was concerned now sixteen or seventeen Years ago; and towards whom the Dispensations of Heaven have been singular and wonderful.

I concluded with Prayers, that the Year upon which I am now entring may be filled with the Blessings of Goodness; that I may be comfortably carried along to the End of the Year. But, that if my Death come upon me this Year, it may prove happy, and easy, and joyful.

Arriving to the Question, *What shall I render to the Lord?* I considered, that I should be answering this Question, every Day of my life; the Morning of every Day would bring an explicit Answer to it. And whereas I have heretofore noted every Day my Contrivances to do good, in other papers, and then transferred the Principal of them unto the End of these Memorials at the End of the Year, I would for the future, save that Labour, and note them, in the Midst of these Papers, and in the Order that I think upon them. There is no need of my repeting here, the Questions assigned for each Day of the Week. My Answer to each of them, will be a GOOD DEVISED, for which a G. D. will be the Distinction in these Memorials.

2.[1] G. D. Unto the Sacrifices of the Lord's-Day Evening in my Family, I would often add this; take a Book of Piety, and make each of the capable Children read some short pungent Passage in the hearing of all that are present, and then apply it, firstly to the Readers, and also to all the Hearers; that they may be taught the way of Life, with a most awakened Attention unto it.

3. G. D. I have a little Nephew, for whom I have not hitherto done all that I have to do, towards his Conversion and Salvation. His Name is J. C.[2] my wife's

---

[1] In carrying this plan of a daily entry into effect, Mather uses the day of the week, and thus begins to number again with every seven. To assist the reader in fixing the exact day, the Sunday's entries are fully dated by month and day of the month.   [2] Clark.

Brother's Son. I will send for him; and bestow on him the little Book of the *Religion of the Morning;* with the Life of little *Von Extor*,[1] and suitable Admonitions and Encouragements.

4. G. D. By a Vessel now going for *Carolina*, and thence for *Scotland*, I would send some Instruments of Piety, especially my *Bonifacius* and my *Religion of the Morning*, and my Sister's *Memorials of Early Piety*, unto those Hands thro' whom they may, if God please, do good unto many others.

5. G. D. One of our *Societies for the Suppression of Disorders*, have thro' I know not what Feebleness, disbanded. I would, by the means of an active Person or two, try to revive it.

G. D. When any good Thing is agreed and resolved in a Society, where I happen to be present, I would alwayes take special Care that there be some or other alwayes appointed for to execute the Resolutions. Many good Things miscarry, because there are not particular Hands, to whom there is assign'd the Execution of them.

6. G. D. An aged and pious Man, fallen into great Penury, (Κοναντ).[2] I will procure needful Garments for him.

A Godly young Man, a Ship-carpenter, having been long languishing in a Consumption, (Ιγγερϛολλ)[3] I will stir up some good Men of his profession; to releeve his Necessities. There is a poor Woman, (Ταλκερ)[4] to be taken care of.

7. G. D. When I visit a sick Person, I would use to fetch an Admonition, relating to the moral Distempers in my own Heart and Life, analogous to something that I may see in the Circumstances of the Sickness, upon the Person, whom I go unto. I would think; *What Thing*

[1] Christlieb Leberecht von Extor, son of the physician to the King of Prussia. See Mather, *Man eating the Food of Angels*, 1710.

[2] Conant.   [3] Ingersoll.   [4] Walker.

*amiss in my own Soul and Walk, should I be led now to depre-
cate?* I would make this Deprecation, an Article of my
Prayers to God. And why not an Article of my Prayers
with the visited Person; and of my Discourses also, my
Addresses to the Person? The Diseases that Sin has brought
on our Spirits, worse than any on our Bodies; and the Releef
we may find in our admirable Saviour.

17–18 *d.* 12 *m.* I kept something of a Vigil, to obtain
with Prayers and Psalms, in, and after the middle of the
Night, certain special Favours of the Lord. Most especially, that my Serviceableness may be rescued from the
Mischiefs my Adversaries intend unto it, and that my
glorious Lord would appear with some comfortable Testimonies for me. I pleaded, that I durst not make any
Essayes for my own Defence, much less for my own Revenge,
lest I should in any measure take my Cause out of His
Hands, where I desired entirely to leave it.

1. [*February* 18.] G. D. I would renew my ancient
Care of the Flock in this one Point. I will have the Catalogue of the Communicants in our Church, Yea, and of
all that have entred into the Covenant; lying before me.
And I will take my proper Times, to spread the Names of
them all successively before the Lord; and ask for them
the Blessings of Goodness, and such Blessings as may
appear to me most suitable for them. This will give me
an Opportunity for much Exercise of Goodness; and lead
me also to find out the Condition of the Flock.

G. D. Being to baptize two Negro's;[1] I would make
it an occasion to glorify the great Saviour of all men, in
several Instances; especially in such Admonitions to that
black Part of the Flock, as may be needful for them.

2. G. D. It will be a great Service and Honour unto
my little Daughters to have them very good Mistresses of

---

[1] James and Ruth are the names given in the *MS. Records of the Second Church*,
but no further information is given.

their Pens. I will prosecute and cultivate this Point of
their Education, with all possible Encouragement.

3. G. D. There is a Merchant in this Town, who has
been wickedly, absurdly, sordidly abusive to me. It lies
in my Power many Wayes to hurt him. I will totally ab-
stain from doing the least Hurt unto him. I will earnestly
pray unto God, for all Sorts of Blessings upon him; and
particularly, that the Danger of his Breaking, and coming
to nothing, may be prevented. And I will sett myself to
invent wayes to do him good Offices.

No sooner had I written these Words, but there was a
pretty Occurence in the Family, which carried with it a
fine Picture and Emblem and Incentive of the Disposition,
which I am endeavouring. My little Son *Sammy*, did not
carry it so kindly to his little Sister *Lizzy*, as I would have
had him. I chid him for his Crossness, and gave her a Peece
of *Pomecitron*, but would give none to him, to punish him
for his being so cross to her. I had no sooner turn'd my
back, but the good-condition'd Creature fell into Tears,
at this Punishment of her little Brother, and gave to him
a Part of what I had bestowed upon her.

4. G. D. It would be a great Service to the Kingdome
of God, if the *Funerals*, that are so frequent among us,
were made greater Instances and Incentives of *Religion*.
A Discourse on that CASE, *What should be the Behaviour
of a Christian at a Funeral?* may be of good Use among
us. At the Lecture, I may, if God please endeavour it.[1]

5. G. D. I propose to send for a principal Person or
two, belonging to each of the *religious Societies of young
Men*, and consult with them together, about the State
of the Societies, and what may be done for the Growth of
them, and for the best carrying on their Exercises.

6. G. D. There is an aged Gentleman, who has very

[1] Two years later he printed an essay upon *A Christian Funeral*, and the
conduct of a Christian at a funeral.

little to subsist him, (Ραυλινς).[1] I will study [to] make his Life comfortable to him, and have him at my Table every Week, and as often as he pleases.

7. G. D. The mysterious Nature and Working of *Pride*, and *Self*, in my depraved Soul, must be my most exquisite Study; and I must be restless until I find the Dispositions thereof mortified in me by a superiour and Cœlestial Principle; and I must proceed, not only to a constant Rebuke of my Sin in all the Motions of it, but also to do those Actions wherein it shall be evident unto me, that *Grace* has had the Upperhand of *Sin*. How else can I be meet for the *Inheritence of the Saints in Light?*

1. [*February* 25.] G. D. What if I should preach a Sermon, about the *Errands* upon which the Faithful should come unto the *Table* of the Lord, and *Methods* of bringing them? Our People need greatly to be instructed and quickened in this matter; and if they wisely did their Duty herein, it would greatly promote Piety among us! What if I should afterwards publish the Sermon, and scatter it into the Families of the Neighbourhood, and throughout the Countrey?

2. G. D. My Consort is now near her Time, I will order my Prayers for her and with her, and my Discourse and Carriage to her, after such a Manner, as may best suit her present Circumstances.

3. G. D. To an aged Gentlewoman, related unto my Wife, (Mrs. Ταρδ)[2] I will immediately write a Letter, that may assist her Preparation for the heavenly World; and send some agreeable Books unto her.

4. G. D. There are some Gentlemen, who are willing upon Funerals in their Families, to devote some of the Money, they save out of the needless Expences on such Occasions, unto the Service of our three Charity-Scholes, and the Education of poor Children. I would move, that

---

[1] Rawlins.   [2] Ward.

the three Gentlemen who are the Stewards for the Supporters of the said Scholes, may unite in calling on the Gentlemen proper to be address'd for their Bounty on such Occasions; and receive then the Direction of the several associated Supporters, concerning the Disposal thereof.

5. G. D. There is a bereaved Church in our Neighbourhood, running into Divisions and Confusions, by delaying to invite a worthy Minister among them. What if I should prevail with the neighbouring Ministers, to join with me, in writing a monitory Letter unto them, to prevent the Devices of Satan, which are operating on them?

6. G. D. A poor young Woman, the wife of a sober young Man, gone to sea for the Releef of his Poverty, (Μορσε)[1] is in the Straw, very Indigent. I will send in Releefs unto her.

2 *d.* 1 *m.* [*March.*] 1711. *Friday.* This Day I sett apart, for Prayers with Alms, and Fasting before the Lord; that I might obtain His Favours on my Family and my Ministry; and Abundance of Grace; with the Pardon of all my Miscarriages.

I mett with many Hindrances (by Company coming in upon me) in the Duties of the Day; which made me fear that I had not sett about the Duties with a due Preparation and Application; for which this may be a Chastisement upon me; and I humbled myself accordingly.

7. G. D. When any Thing begins to raise any Ebullition of *Anger* in me, I would endeavour to allay it, by one or both of these Considerations. First, What provocations have I given to the Great God, like those, but infinitely greater than those, which I receive of them that are about me? And, What was the Meekness and Wisdom of my blessed Jesus, when He was provoked by the Contradiction of Sinners?

[1] Morse.

1. [*March* 4.] G. D. Should not I do well, to take the Number of those who have died in our church; and make it a lively Argument and Incentive to quicken Piety in the Survivers?

4 *d.* 1 *m. Lords-day.* My great Errand unto the Lord at His Table, was, to renew my Hold of the everlasting Covenant. Methoughts, I now saw more clearly than ever, that the Covenant of Grace, is but the Covenant of Redemption between God the Father and our Saviour applied unto Us. And that my Saviour is He, who has engaged for me unto His eternal Father, that I shall beleeve and repent, and be holy in all Manner of Conversation, and be found in the sincere Discharge of the Duty which the Covenant has prescribed as the Way unto Salvation: and that what I have to do, is by His Assistence to consent, that the blessed Jesus be my Saviour, and that I be united unto Him as unto the Head of all His People, and that He shall by the efficacious Grace of His holy Spirit, bring me to my Duty, and help me in it, and make me prayerful, and watchful, and fruitful, and zealous of good Works; and anon raise me from the Dead. And I consented accordingly. And then sealed it.

2. G. D. It is high Time for me, to draw up for my Daughter *Katharin*, the main Questions relating to the Experiences of Conversion and of Piety, and oblige her with her Pen to answer them: and so bring her forward into the Covenant of God, and the Communion of His holy Table.

3. G. D. I can't call to mind any one Person in the World, who has injured me, and Abused me, but I have requited them Good. All I can think of this Morning is, to continue in this Disposition, with the Help of the divine Grace, and continually lay hold on all Occasions, as they may occur, to overcome Evil with Good.

4. G. D. A remarkable Relation of a Distress under-

gone and a Deliverance received by some sea-faring People, is putt into my Hands. I will endeavour the Publication of it in such a Manner, as may not only glorify the Power, and Wisdome, and Goodness of God; but also do good, especially among that sort of People.[1]

5. G. D. I would procure a strict Enquiry, about the late way of Admission into the particular Church-State, practised among our Christian Indians; lest it should (which I hear) degenerate into a very lax Proceedure.

I would also obtain it, that the Oppressions of some English upon those Indians, (which I hear a fresh complained of) may be exactly enquired into.

6. G. D. There is a poor Scotch young Woman, who is near her lying in, and is destitute of all Necessaries and Conveniencies. I will send her some Releef, and move my Wife (who is near her own lying in) to do so too; and stir up the Neighbours to join in releeving of her. There are some others in the like Circumstances, for whom I would be in the like Manner concerned.

7. G. D. I am afraid, lest while I am conversing with my Neighbours, (tho' it be always with the Intentions of doing some Good unto them) I may, ere I am aware, be betray'd into some Degree of Slothfulness, which may be a Prejudice unto my greater Usefulness. Wherefore, when I am abroad among my Neighbours, I would often putt that Question to myself, *Would it not be more pleasing unto my glorious Lord, that I should be in my Study at this Time?* If I find myself in a Temper and Vigour to be carrying on greater Services in my Study, I would break off the most agreeable Conversation, and fly thither, with a Zeal of redeeming the Time, upon me.

1. [*March* 11.] G. D. Tho' I often encourage Liberality in Almsgiving, yett upon further Consideration I find, that I have not spoken enough. I propose therefore to

[1] See p. 71, *infra.*

Discourse yett more distinctly and more cogently upon it; and press my Flock with a new Vigour, to be liberal in their Expences upon pious Uses.

2. G. D. My Son *Increase* is now of Age enough, to know the Meaning of *Consideration*. I would now more than ever, oblige him to attend upon me, at such Times of the Day, as can be best spared for it. And I would never lett him spend many Minutes with me, without entring upon a Point of Conversation, that may instruct him, and enrich him, so that he may be the wiser and the better for it.

3. G. D. Think, what Subjects, my aged Father may do most good by studying and insisting on: and whatever Subjects I find him at work upon, look out for him, as many good Writers thereon, as I can, to entertain him with a grateful Variety in his Meditations.

4. G. D. The People of the *Scotch Nation* in this Town, form a Society, which have a Quarterly Meeting. That Society have a Bank, for the Releef of their Poor. Since the University of *Glasgow*, have taken such Notice of me, as they have lately done, I have some Claim to an Admission into their Society. This Admission may give me a precious Opportunity to do good unto them, and by them unto many others. I will take the matter into consideration, and proceed and project (if Heaven allow of it,) what Good may be done by this new Opportunity.

5. G. D. I am concerned for the Welfare of the great *Grammar School* of the Town. I would unite Counsils with a learned, pious, honourable Visitor of the School, to introduce diverse good Intentions into it. This among the rest; that *Castalio*, and *Posselius*, be brought into the School; [1]

[1] Sebastian Castalio [Chateillon] (1515?-1563), writer of *Sacred Dialogues for the Instruction of Youth*, and Johann Posselius (1528-1591). No work of either writer had been republished in America at this time; and this may have been one of the reasons for Mather's preference. A school book would have a certain market, and, of course, a preface would be required, recommending the work to

and that the Lads for their Latin Exercises, turn into Latin such Things as may befriend the Interests of Christianity, in their Hearts and Lives; — particularly, the Quæstions and Answers, in our *Supplies from the Tower of David.*

6. G. D.   A Man who has been commander of a Vessel, (Κολλαρ)[1] is fallen into a distracting Trouble of Mind; another Neighbour, who is altogether distracted (Κισε)[2] has a Family thereby in great Affliction.   I will consider these Objects of Compassion, and I will study and contrive as well as I can, to make their Condition comfortable.

7. G. D.   I am now so sick, that I have not Presence of Mind and Vigor of Thought, enough to project a good Answer, unto the Question, which I would this Morning think upon.   My Sickness will help to make me yett more sick of this World.   It must also quicken my Dispatch of what must be done before I go out of the world.

17 *d.* 1 *m.*   Prostrate in the Dust before the Lord, I declared with Tears, (among other Things,) my sweet Satisfaction, with all those afflicting and abasing Circumstances, which might produce in my Condition at any time, a Conformity to what was in the Condition of my once abased Saviour.   But then my Soul was filled with Joy, in an Expectation, that my glorified Saviour, will one Day bring me to partake with Him, in the Glories of the heavenly world.

1. [*March* 18.]   G. D.   I hear of some young Men in my Flock, who abandon themselves to the ruinous Courses of Gaming; and who especially betake themselves thereto, for the Quieting of their Minds, when they meet with any Thing in the public Sermons that proves troublesome to their Consciences.   Oh! lett me with all possible Fervency, and Compassion, dispense to them the Warnings of God.

---

the student and enlarging upon the opportunities thus given. I am unable to learn that either writer was introduced by Mather in his lifetime.

[1] Collar.   [2] Keyes?

2. G. D.   To accomplish my little Daughters for House-keeping, I would have them, at least once a week, to prepare some new Thing, either for Diet, or Medicine; which I may show them described, in some such Treatise as the *Family Dictionary*. And when it is prepared, I will also make some Remarks of Piety, in a way of occasional Reflection upon it.

3. G. D.   My Mother is now entred the seventieth Year of her Age. What shall I do, that I may assist her Preparation for her Appearance before the Lord? I will discourse with her; as prudently and as takingly as I can, on that illustrious Point; and I will putt into her Hands to read, what may be most agreeable and serviceable for her.

4. G. D.   A lively Discourse about the Benefit and Importance of *Education*, should be given to the Countrey. The Countrey is perishing for want of it; they are sinking apace into Barbarism and all Wickedness. It should be considered of.

5. G. D.   Shall not I do well, to write a Letter unto one or two of the principal Ministers in *Connecticut*-Colony; concerning the fearful Circumstances, into which the Love of *Rum*, has brought several, even of their principal Ministers, and by Consequence very many of the miserable People? And awaken them, to dispense their laweful Admonitions? The Consequences of the affected Bottel, in that Colony, as well as in ours, are beyond all Imagination.

6. G. D.   A poor Woman in my Neighbourhood (ʻΟλλανδ)[1] labouring under Distraction; her Family must needs labour under Necessities. I will procure for them some Releef. The Deacon of the Church of *Wenam*, is also worse than Distracted; and the Pastor and the Church, are embroiled by him, in Abundance of Trouble.[2] This

[1] Holland.
[2] Rev. Joseph Gerrish (1650–1720) was the pastor at Wenham.

furnishes me with Occasions for me to do many charitable
Offices, which I shall watch to do, for them all.

7. G. D. Many, many Things I have to do; many
Things of the greatest Consequence. I shall either leave
them undone, or do them not well, or miss the Time of
doing them, if I do not with much Resignation unto it,
obtain the heavenly Conduct. I would therefore now more
than ever, putt this Article most explicitly and expressively,
into my morning-Prayers; *Oh! Lett me be led unto those
Works which it would be well for me to do this Day, and be
help'd in the doing of them!*

24 *d*. 1 *m. Satureday*. I have been of late, much afflicted
and enfeebled with Sickness in my Stomach; a palled, and
a pained Stomach. I would be awakened from hence, to
bewayl my Want of a Stomach for the Service of God,
and for Meditations on my Saviour. I have not had a due
Appetite for the best Objects and Actions; nor have I
duely relished them. I would bewayl my not being sick of
Sin, as I ought to have been; and my being more sick
of laborious Perseverance in some duties, than I should
have been. The Offences of my Stomach in the Intemperance of the Table, are also to be bewayled. A Pardon
of these Miscarriages, thro' the Blood of the great Sacrifice,
and the Grace to carry better, are to be more pursued by
me, than a Deliverance from my bodily Malady, and in
the first Place obtained.

In the Evening, I attended the Devotions of a *Vigil*.
Therein I sought unto the Lord, for the Pardon of all my
Iniquities. I beleeved, and received His pardoning Mercy,
and I relied on the Merit of my glorious Advocate, thro'
whom it comes unto me. I then told my strong Redeemer,
that the Floods of the Ungodly made me afraid. I fear'd
lest the Power and Malice of my Enemies might ruine my
Serviceableness. I cast myself Entirely into the Protection of my strong Redeemer, and I besought Him to show

me a Token for Good, that they who hate me, may see and be ashamed. Particularly, I pray'd, that a remarkable Remorse, and Horror of Conscience, may be sent into one of them, from the Spirit of the Lord; from whence there might arise a Testimony for me.

1. [*March* 25.] G. D. Some of the Neighbourhood, not having Seats to their Minds in our Assembly, run to a Congregation, which is held in the Meetinghouse of the Anabaptists.[1] Hereby, they never see the Baptism of the Lord administred, nor hear the pathetical and affectionate Prayers made on that Occasion; They miss an Ordinance, in which a gracious Presence of the Lord, is to be looked for. I should in the most proper and prudent Wayes I can contrive, make these unadvised People sensible of the Wrong they do their own Souls, in wandring where they do.

2. G. D. I find, it will be necessary or convenient for me, almost every Night, to take an Account of my Children, what they have been doing in the Day, and how they have spent their Time; and make it an Occasion of continual Admonitions of Piety unto them.

Especially for *Cresy.*

3. G. D. I have a Nephew, becoming a prentice to a Goldsmith, (Βαρθολομεε Γρεεν)[2] and now I would (with agreeable Advice accompanying of it) putt into his Hands, my Book of, *A Good Master well-served*,[3] as a continual Monitor unto him, of his Duty.

4. G. D. To take some Scores of my Treatise on, *The Trinity* and on, *Christianity demonstrated*,[4] (and make agreeable Dedications) and send them unto the Universities in *Scotland;* particularly to that of *Glasgow,* may be a sensible

[1] The First Baptist Church in Boston was constituted May 28, 1665, and Rev. Ellis Callender was in charge at this time. It did not enjoy a building of its own until some years after.

[2] Bartholomew Green, son of Maria Mather and Bartholomew Green.

[3] Printed in 1696. [4] Printed in 1710.

Service to the Interests of Religion there; and so I shall, if the Lord please, endeavour it.

5. G. D. My Purpose, is, to draw up a List of the many *Societies* whereto I belong, and have Distinctions by which I may denominate them; and then with my weekly Deliberations upon *Good Devised* for them, distinctly consider them in their Order, and what shall be done in them, or for them.

I drew up the List this Morning, and found them above twenty.

6. G. D. There is an hopeful Candidate of the Ministry, (Αβερεε) [1] who is destitute of Books. I will begin his Library by bestowing some valuable Books upon him, out of my own. There is also a Man and his Wife in my Neighbourhood, (Ροβερ) [2] who have long languished under Sickness and now conflict with distressing Poverty. I will myself releeve them, and procure for them Releef in the Charity of others.

7. G. D. My Garden, I would make it a Place of such Devotions, and I would employ all the Trees, and Herbs in it, and all the Circumstances of it, in such a devotionary Way, to produce Acknowledgments of the great God and of His Christ, in my Mind, that it shall be unto me a Sort of an earthly Paradise, and putt (as far as may be attained here) unto such an Use, as the new Earth will be by the Saints in the World to come.

31 *d.* 1 *m. Satureday.* I have lett this Week pass, without keeping a Day of Prayer with Fasting, in my Study: because I kept such a Day on the last *Wednesday*, with a great Company of Christians, who mett at the House lately forsaken by the Death of the two most eminent Persons in my Neighbourhood. [3] Where their Children desired me to preach on Psal. XXVII. 10. the Care which the Lord graciously takes of *Orphans*. But then, in the Night following

---

[1] Avery?   [2] Rober?   [3] John and Abigail Foster.

this Day, I applied myself, unto the Devotions of a *Vigil;*
in which I kept crying and singing unto the Lord, until
after Midnight; and spred before the Lord, the same Cases
that I brought unto Him in such Devotions, a week ago;
but with growing and greater Comforts. I felt the Operations of the Spirit of Grace and of Supplications upon me,
in these Exercises; and some Assurances of my Acceptance
with the Lord.

In this *Vigil*, I entirely devoted myself unto the Service of the
blessed JESUS; I resolved upon spending the rest of my little Time,
in the most assiduous Endeavours, to render and procure all possible
Homage unto my lovely JESUS; I purposed, that I would myself
live continually in the Thoughts of the Son of God, and contrive all
the Methods that I can to bring my precious JESUS, to be more
considered, and acknowledged and magnified in the World. I own'd
my Unworthiness to be employ'd in such honourable Service, but I
ask'd for a Display of sovereign Grace in the matter. I resign'd
myself up unto the Spirit of God, and of my glorious JESUS, to
be kept from Errors, and to be led and help'd on, to such Things
as might be for the Glory of my Saviour. So I cast myself, with a
triumphant Faith, on His Providence and Protection!

There was another Thing, which in this *Vigil*, I besought of the
Lord. I besought Him, that His holy Spirit might go mightily to
work in the Assembly, which I serve with my weekly Ministrations;
that He would not withdraw from this Assembly, but make a marvellous Descent upon us, and do wondrously among us, especially upon
our young People, that a Christ may be formed in them. Yea, that
He would in His Providence order Things to fall out, which may
administer unto me, notable Occasions to apply the Maxims of Piety,
with an uncommon Pungency unto the Souls of the People in the
Neighbourhood.

[This Petition had before the year Expired, many and marvellous
Answers given to it.][1]

1. [*April* 1.] G. D. It would be well for me, often
to do, what I have lately done; When the People of my
Flock are all asleep in their Beds, I will have my *Vigils*,
in which I will cry mightily unto the Lord, that the Spirit

---

[1] This paragraph is written in the margin.

of Grace may make a gracious Descent upon our Congregation, and do wonderful Things upon the Souls of our Children there.

1 *d.* 2 *m.* [*April.*] *Lord's-day.* At the Lord's Table, my first Errand was, to consider my blessed Jesus, as purchasing for me a part in the heavenly World, the Pardon of my Sin, that would shutt me out of it, and the Grace to qualify me for an Admission into it; and accordingly I made my Application unto Him.

My second Errand was, to obtain those two Blessings of Purity in Heart and Life, and Activity in the Service of God. I bewayled my Distempers, which ly in the want of these Things. I beheld my lovely Jesus, as purchasing by His Blood, the Pardon of my Sins wherein the Cure of my Distempers must begin; and then, the Grace, to abhor all Sin, to dread and shun every sinful Pollution; the Grace also, that would render me lively in the Works of God, quicken me in all Obedience, dispose me to redeem my Time at the best rate imaginable. And since I found myself in a Disposition to employ the Blood of my Saviour unto *such* Purposes, it was powerfully born in upon my mind, that I had a Right unto it. I applied myself hereunto accordingly. But then I thought, Meditations on the Sorrowes which my Saviour suffered for my Pollutions, and on the astonishing Vigour wherewith He went thro' the work His Father call'd Him to, would be sanctified Means to obtain the Grace I was now pursuing after, I did now also employ some Time in those Meditations.

A fortnight ago, I was taken so sick, that I could not study; for which Cause I was compelled to preach a Sermon, which lay by me, already prepared, on Gal. iv. 19. *Little Children, of whom I travail in Birth again, till Christ be formed in you.* I could not then finish what I intended; so there was reserved for me an agreeable Opportunity; this Day to address the Children of [the] Flock, upon the

great Intention, of having a *Christ* formed in them; and
to do it with a *travailing* Agony.   I had a secret Imagination above a Fortnight ago, that while I should be in this
Travail, I should receive the Blessings of another *Travail*,
in my own Family.   It fell out so; my Consort was detained at home, in the sensible Approaches of her Travail,
this Afternoon; and with all the agreeable Circumstances
that such a Matter could admitt of, and most encouraging
Answers to our Prayers, just after seven a Clock, she was
delivered of a Daughter; an Infant of a very promising
Aspect.

2. G. D.   And so I have a new Article provided, for
the weekly Quæstion of Munday Morning, to go upon.
The *Good Devised* for my newborn Daughter, is first of all,
to give her up unto the Lord, with all Solemnity of holy
Dedication.   Then, to take a sweet Satisfaction in the
Thought of having the Kingdome of My Great Saviour
enlarged, by the Addition of this Child unto it.   And one
thing more; to putt upon her the Name of her deceased
Aunt JERUSHA; whose Name is by her published *Memorials of Early Piety*, rendred precious among the People
of God.

3. G. D.   My Elder Sister,[1] being a Widow, I will sett
myself to take all possible Care of her; and I will also
comfort her with my Visits and my Prayers, as often as
I find myself capable.

4. G. D.   Which of the Tribes of *Israel*, have I left
yett unserved?   The *Orphans*.   They are numerous and
afflicted.   I know not how soon, I may be of the Number,
or by leaving my own Children, may increase the Number.
I have an Opportunity to publish a Book for *Orphans*.   I
will ask the Help of Heaven to Compose the Book, in as
agreeable and profitable a Manner, as may be.

5. G. D.   Why may not I order the Printer who pub-

---

[1] Maria (Mather) Green.

lishes my Discourse about and unto *Orphans*, that he would print and bind a particular Hundred, or two thereof, to be lodged in every Town of these Colonies, with a, *Given to be lent in mourning Families*, upon them?

6. G. D. In my Book for *Orphans*, I will move the *Orphans* who are brought into the Possession of good Estates, to make this one special and speedy Consideration with them; *What shall I do for poor Orphans?* And contrive some signal Expence and Action for the Releef of such.

7. G. D. I propose, as soon as I can, to acknowledge and glorify the great God, in a solemn *Thanksgiving*, for the sensible Displayes and Favours of His interposing Providence unto the World of Mankind in general; in diverse remarkable Instances, and especially some, on the Score of which the glorious One, has hardly ever yett received any distinct Praises from among the Children of Men. How comfortably may I carry on the Part of an holy Priesthood, in such an Action!

About this Time, it was desired, that I should committ unto the Press, a Discourse, of Counsels and Comforts for *Orphans*. I look'd on it, as a further and precious Opportunity, to proceed in my fulfilling of my Ministry. So I fitted the Discourse for Publication: under the Title of, ORPHANOTROPHIUM, *Or, The Orphan well-provided for. An Essay, on the Care taken in the Divine Providence, for Children, when their Parents forsake them; With Proper Advice to both Parents and Children, that the Care of Heaven may be the more conspicuously and comfortably obtained for them.*[1]

1. [*April* 8.] G. D. Many in my Flock, are lately advised of new and great Losses at Sea; they lose Relatives and other Interests. It will be a seasonable and a serviceable Thing for me, now to strike in, and suit their Condition in the public Prayers and Sermons, with such

---

[1] It was the sermon preached March 28, 1711, a day of prayer kept by the children of John and Abigail Foster. Printed by B. Green, 1711.

Hints as may have a Tendency to their getting a great
Deal of Good, by the Losses they meet withal.

8 *d.* 2 *m. Lords-Day.* Having first in Secret, with all
Solemnity, dedicated my Little Daughter (with the rest
of my Children) unto the Lord, I openly and publickly
renew'd the Dedication, at her Baptism. I then declared,
what we did, when we had our children Baptised; admiring
the Free-Grace of God, in taking our Children into His
Covenant, and so laying Hold on the Covenant for them,
and resolving with His Help, to do our Part, that they may
know and serve the only Saviour, and have a Part in Him.

I called the Child's Name, JERUSHA; to admonish her,
if she lives, that she should walk in the Steps of Piety,
which were taken by my deceased Sister of that Name,
the Memorials of whose Piety are published and preserved
among the People of God.[1]

2. G. D. I am considering what I am to do for the
Welfare of my Children. I am shortly to leave them
Orphans in an evil World. The grand Provision that I
am to make for my *Orphans*, is in the following *Deed of
Betrustment*, which prostrate in the Dust, I spread before
the Lord, and beseech Him to look upon it.

O my great and good Saviour, and thou Son of God, in my glorious JESUS: and the Lord in whom the Fatherless find Mercy.

The principal Satisfaction and Consolation, with which I receive
the Children, which the Lord graciously gives unto me, at their
Birth into the World, is, the Prospect of more Subjects for my
Saviour, and the Propagation and Continuation of His Kingdome in
the World. For this Purpose, tis my own strong and full Purpose, to
do my Part, that my Children may know their Saviour, and serve
Him with a perfect Heart and a willing Mind; and I will earnestly
cry unto Him, to produce a Work of His Grace in their Souls, and to
take them under the perpetual Conduct of the Spirit of Grace, that
they may do so.

Now I firmly beleeve, that the World is under the Government
of my admirable Saviour; He sitts at the Right Hand of God, and

[1] See p. 57, *supra.*

the affairs of the divine Providence are under His Administration. He does particularly employ the Ministry of His mighty Angels, in governing the Children of Men; and yett more particularly make them the Guardians of His little Ones; most of all, when in His Providence He makes them fatherless Children. O Orphans well-provided for!

Wherefore, O my Saviour, I committ my Children unto thy saviourly and fatherly Hands. I pray to thee, that thy gracious Providence *may*, I trust in thee, that it *will*, be concerned for them. Oh! Lett nothing be wanting to them, that shall be good for them! Oh! cause them to fear thee, to love thee, to walk in thy Wayes, and make use of them to do good in their Generation: Oh! Be thou their Friend, and raise them up such Friends as may be necessary for them, and in a convenient Manner supply all their Necessities. Give thy *Angels* the Charge of them; and when their Father and their Mother forsake them, then do thou take them up.

This is the Supplication, this the Resignation, this the Dependence of,

COTTON MATHER.

3. G. D. I have a Kinsman, who is Minister of *Saybrook*, and who has also an Opportunity to do good unto the Colledge there.[1] I will send unto him our *Bonifacius*,[2] and some other Things, that may prove Instruments of good unto him, and through him unto others.

4. G. D. It is complain'd unto me, that in the Places, where Churches are gathered, under the unhappy Government of N. *York*, the Pelagian Doctrines are so obtruded on the People by their Neighbours of the Ch[urch] of E[ngland] profession, that it is become a dangerous Crime to bear a due Testimony to the Doctrines of Grace. I would therefore procure some little Essayes for the Defence of the labouring Truths, to be printed here, and sent thither, that they may be scattered among the people, for their Preservation from the Error of the Wicked.

11/12 *d.* 2 *m. Wednesday/Thursday.* Tho' I am enter-

---

[1] Rev. Azariah Mather (1685-1737), son of Rev. Samuel Mather and Hannah, daughter of Robert Treat. He served as a tutor in the college at Saybrook.

[2] Printed in 1710.

ing upon the Duties of a general *Fast*, yett I was desirous
to be employ'd this Night in the Duties and Actions of a
Vigil.

In this Interview with Heaven, having first received the pardoning Mercy of God, and the Blood of my Saviour as purchasing and
procuring the Passage thereof unto me; I proceeded then to entreat
for a Favour of the Lord, whereof I confessed my greatest Unworthiness. I beheld my admirable JESUS, as the promised Messiah of
God, and Redeemer of Men; I beheld Him as taken into a personal
Union with the second Person in the eternal Godhead; I beheld
Him, as having once offered Himself a sacrifice to divine Justice, and
now enthroned at the right Hand of God, and governing the World,
unto the more visible Judgment whereof He will one Day make His
Appearance; and having all the mighty Angels of the Heavens under
His illustrious Authority. I entertained His Religion, as the Truth
of God, and a Revelation forever to be relied upon; All faithful
Sayings and worthy of all Acceptation. I bewayl'd it, that so few
among sinful and woful Mankind are yett acquainted with Him;
that in baptised Nations, and in our own wicked one, there are so
many who deny Him, and deride Him; that among the Professors
of His Name, He is no more known, and lov'd, and priz'd, and
honoured with a zelous Obedience. The Favour which I now begg'd
with Tears, lying prostrate in the Dust before the Lord, was, that He
who with Triumphs of sovereign Grace in it, had already employ'd
such a foolish and filthy Creature, as I am, in Services for the Kingdome of my Saviour; would now employ me to do some signal
Services for His Glory. I desired, that I might myself, be first continually and exceedingly affected with the Excellencies of my Saviour,
and live by the Faith of the Son of God, and have my Life perpetually
filled with Acknowledgments of Him. I then desired, that I might
bear such Testimonies for my glorious Lord, as might bring many
others to acknowledge Him. I declared, that I made Choice of this
as the Top of my Happiness, and my Ambition; and that whatever
Abasements he would have me to undergo in conformity to my
humbled Jesus, I would embrace them with all possible Submission,
and have my Spirit reconciled unto them. I renounced all other
Ends, and Aims, in Comparison of this; To be used as a Servant and
a Witness of my Incomparable *Jesus*, and be employ'd in testifying to
His Glories. Nothing would satisfy me so much as this: Nothing but
this would Satisfy me; This would yeeld me a full Satisfaction.

I entreated, that in my Ministry, under the Conduct of the Holy Spirit, who Glorifies my lovely JESUS, I may be led unto the Preaching and the Writing of those Things, which may exhibit His Glories, at a Rate that had never yett been done in the World. I hoped, the Glories of my dearest JESUS, would ere long be more considered in the world, than they have ever been heretofore, and I wished, that I might be concerned in the Exhibition of them. I went on with my Petition, that some remarkable Thing might fall out, which might furnish me with some special and precious Opportunities, to bear some very victorious Testimonies to the Existence, the Advancement, the Deity of my amiable JESUS. I consented unto the Lord, that if any breaking Dispensations of His holy Providence, must befall me, and praises to my glorious JESUS would arise from them, I would most heartily submitt unto them; this Effect of them should change the very Nature of them to me, and make me take a Sort of a Pleasure in them. Hereupon my Mind was irradiated with a sweet Assurance, that, no, I should not be so dealt withal. But I should be accommodated with some Opportunities; which I was not yett aware of, to bear the Testimonies, to which I had so strong an Inclination. I cried unto the Lord, that I might yett see one, and a very Rich one, in the Conversion of that poor Jew, for whose Conversion and Salvation we have been for six or seven Years more than ten, waiting on Him. And for this Purpose I now again did committ that Soul into the Hands of my Saviour, and His Holy Spirit, with a strong Faith of thy being, O Lord, able to enlighten him, and sanctify him, and conquer all his Obstinacy. To these Things I added my repeted Request, That some, at least one, of the most notorious and malignant Enemies to my Serviceableness, might be Smitten with such an Horror of Conscience, for his Wickedness, as may prove to me a Token for Good, which they that hate me may see and be ashamed.

12 *d. 2 m. Thursday.* A general Fast; in the Duties whereof I enjoy'd the special Assistences of the Lord. But I made it a Day of Alms, as well as of Prayers.

5. G. D. And in my Sermon I earnestly called upon the Members of the Church, to be more concerned for the Welfare of the particular Church to which they belong, and to take it into their frequent and serious Consideration.

6. G. D. I hear of a Family, wherein Parents and

Children are at grievous Variance; [Υιλλις and χιλδρεν].[1]
I would endeavour to bring the Family into a better
Condition.

7. G. D. It was proposed and advised unto me, to
wear my *Signet-Ring*, as a Token and Assertion of the
Doctorate in Divinity, whereto a foreign and famous University has admitted me; and to do it, not from any Vanity
of Ornament, but out of Obedience to the Fifth Commandment, which directs us to assert the Honour of any Dignity,
wherein the Providence of God may station us.

If I do it, I will make even so mean an Action as this, an Engine
of Religion, with me.

First. This Ring shall be a continual Admonition unto me, to
do nothing below the Character, whereof that is the Memorial;
nothing disagreeable to the Gravity, the Discretion, the superiour
Behaviour, which a *Doctorate* ought alwayes to be attended withal.

Secondly. Yea, it shall effectually admonish me, that in my Discourse there pass nothing out of my Lips, that shall be vain, or
mean, or not according to the Lawes of Wisdome and Goodness and
Usefulness.

Thirdly. The Sight of the Gold, shall frequently excite in me
Wishes and Prayers of this Importance.

Oh! *may I have the Grace, the Gain whereof is better than Gold!*

Oh! *may I be a Son of Zion comparable to fine Gold!* [2]

And, on the *Signet;*

Oh! *May I be preserved from so provoking the holy Lord, that if
I were the Signet on His right Hand, He would pluck me thence!*

Fourthly; One Original to the Ceremony of a *Ring* for *Doctors
of Divinity*, was to intimate, that they should be ready to sett their
Seal to the Advice which may be received from them. I would
improve this, as a Caution unto me. My Advice is very often asked,
and on many Occasions. I would be very considerate, very deliberate, seriously look up to Heaven on such Occasions, and speak nothing,
but what I should be willing to seal it, and stand to it.

Fifthly. The Emblem on the *Signett*, is a *Tree*, with, Psal. I. 3.
written under it; and about it, GLASCUA RIGAVIT. May the
Cast of my Eye upon it, continually provoke my Cry unto my

---

[1] Willis and children.   [2] Four lines are here struck out.

Saviour; *O make me a very fruitful Tree, and help me to bring forth seasonable Fruit continually!*

1. [*April* 15.] G. D. A noted Child in the Neighbourhood, about fourteen Years of Age, is newly come to a sudden and awful End; crush'd to Death, by a Cart falling on him. I would on this Occasion preach a Sermon, wherein Children shall be particularly and importunately called upon, to prepare for the Day, wherein the Small as well as the Great, shall stand before God.[1]

2. G. D. And I will make that sad Accident, an Occasion of more than ordinarily importunate Admonitions unto my own Children, especially unto my Son *Increase*, to become serious, and prayerful and afraid of Sin, and concern'd to gett a part in their only Saviour.

3. G. D. I must be much of a Father, to the fatherless Child of my Sister, βιλες.[2] One thing I particularly now propose; that I will give him the little Book of, *Good Lessons for Children;* and give him a Peece of Money, for every one of the Lessons, that he learns without Book.

4. G. D. I would send a Letter to *Taunton*, by the writing whereof, the Minister of the Place informs me, a service may be done for the evangelical Interests.[3] I would also propose and promote an hopeful Gentleman, to the vacant Presidency of the Colledge at *Connecticut*.[4]

5. G. D. Because I would reprint in a single Sheet, a System of the *Doctrines of Grace*, first, in the Words of the *Articles of the Church of England;* and secondly, in the Armour offered by our *Supplies from the Tower of David;* that it may be dispersed in Places, where the Pelagian Errors are most likely to be mischievous; I would ask a

[1] See p. 82, *infra*. The name of the child, Richard Hobby, is not given in the tract, but that of his grandmother is, Mrs. Elizabeth Winsley.

[2] Mather Byles (1707–1788), who followed in the paths of his uncle in methods, and for forty-three years served the Hollis Street Church.

[3] Rev. Samuel Danforth (1666–1727).

[4] The affairs of the college were now in the hands of Rev. James Pierpont.

little Help from our general Society, towards the expence of my undertaking.[1]

6. G. D. There are two Widowes in my Neighbour-hood, for whom I will alwayes be doing such Things as may make their Hearts to sing. [Μαιες and Γοοδαλε].[2] Espe-cially, I will be sure to have them at my Table once a Week; and oftner, if they please to be there.

7. G. D. A sad and a dark and a dismal Time is come upon the World. How shall I provide for my own Safety at such a Time? I promise a *Vigil* to be quickly attended by me; and therein to state more distinctly my Thoughts on this important Matter.

1. [*April 22.*] G. D. I am given to understand, that among the Communicants of the Church under my Charge, there are several wicked People. Some that frequently drink to Excess. And some that have enticed, if not se-duced, others to Adulteries. On this Occasion, first, I would exceedingly humble myself before the Lord, on the Account of my own manifold Sinfulness. Then I would mightily plead the great Sacrifice for the Congregation, that the Wrath of God may not break out against the Flock. Next I would find the most convenient Wayes I can, to warn the Sinners in Zion, and make a just Fear to seize the Hypocrites thereof. Lastly. When I do on the forgoing Lord's-day mention in the Congregation, the Lord's-supper to be administred the next Lord's-Day, I would lett fall a brief, but pungent and awful Intimation of the præparation that should be endeavoured.

2. G. D. *My Deed of Betrustment*, which I made and spred before the Lord for my *Orphans*, I will cause all my Children, that are of Age capable of writing, to tran-scribe Copies of it; and I will have Copies provided for such of them, as are yett in their Infancy; That they may

---

[1] *Old Pathes restored*, 81, *infra.*
[2] Mays? and Goodale.

often look upon it, when they shall be made *Orphans*, and make use of it, in Distresses that may come upon them.

3. G. D. I would write unto my Kinsman at *Saybrook*, and by his Help, find out the Children of my late Kinsman *Richard Mather*,[1] and send unto them such Books of Piety, as may be useful to them.

4. G. D. That I may do good in *Scotland*, and particularly to the University of *Glasgow*, to which I am now related, I propose, to take a Number of my little Books about the *Trinity*, and the *Witness within*, and bind them together, and prefix a Dedication unto the Faculty of the University, and present them unto the Students there.

5. G. D. Tis desired by some, that the Meeting of the Ministers on the *Thursday* after Lecture, may be revived; I would therefore endeavour it; and if it be brought about, I would make it an Opportunity of doing what good I can, and of setting forward such Things as may serve the Kingdome of God.

6. G. D. It is a thing propounded by Austin, in his Book *De Doctrina Christiana;* That if a man have something to bestow upon the Poor; and there are several objects that may seem so æqually to challenge his Charity, that he knowes not well, how to distinguish them, he may do well to employ a *Lott* for the Decision and the Direction of it; *Nihil Justius faceres, quam ut sorte eligeres cui dandum esset.* This is often my own Case. Especially on my Dayes of Prayer; (Such an one as this Day.) I sett apart Portions of Alms, to be dispensed unto the Poor. I am at a Loss, what Objects to single out from among them; there being many who may seem unto me, to stand æqual in their Claims. Why may I not write their Names on Papers, and looking up to Heaven, to dispose the Lott,

---

[1] Richard Mather (1653–1688), of Lyme, Connecticut, who left four children. His wife was Catherine Wise.

then draw, and give accordingly? Doubtless the good Angels of Heaven, would operate on this Occasion.

[I afterwards here enter in the margin, this Observation: I have received a strange Direction from Heaven in taking this way sometimes for the dispensing of my charities. The Declarations of the releeved Objects. How seasonably the Releefe came to them, and how they had been looking up to God for His compassions, having a little surprised me!][1]

27 *d. 2 m. Friday.* I sett apart this Day, for Prayers, and Alms, with Fasting before the Lord; On this Day, I received the pardoning Mercy of God, in the Blood of my Saviour, with some Assurance of its being applied unto me.

And I implored mercy for myself, and on the Concerns of my Ministry, and my Family (resigning my *Orphans*, when they shall be such, unto the faithful and wondrous Care of my great Saviour;) and the Concerns of my Ministry; and my Flock; (in which there are so many wicked Actions done, that I find it necessary to fly unto the great Sacrifice for the Congregation, that the Sinners in *Zion* may not procure the Wrath of Heaven, to break forth against the Flock:) and our Land, and the whole Church, in this evil Day of the pouring out of the seven last Plagues upon the World.

7. G. D. The more shall I befriend the Interests of Piety in my own Heart and Life, the more I become furnished with agreeable Thoughts, of a pious Tendency, and Prayers to be annexed unto the Actions that are of a daily Occurrence with me; among the rest, I do this day particularly propose, that what I have often done heretofore, I will now more exactly, and constantly do, on the *Washing of my Hands.* I would on that Occasion alwayes lift up my Soul unto the Lord, with a Wish of this Importance; *Lord, give me the clean Hands, and the pure Heart, of them*

---

[1] This paragraph is written in the margin.

that are to stand in the Holy Place of the Lord! Or, *Lord,
Deliver me and recover me, from all sinful Pollutions!*

1. [*April* 29.] G. D. I greatly incline, to sett up a
monthly Catechising of Children, at my own House; inasmuch as I have now visited all the Families of my numerous
Flock, and also given my Visits unto the Schools, upon
such an Intention. This Exercise if managed wisely, and
in a Way most likely to take for the Winning of Souls, may
prove an Introduction to Abundance of Good; Yea, I
may insensibly draw me on, to more public Actions, and
Lectures, that may be for the Good of many. I will humbly
look up to the Lord, for His Direction and Assistence.

29 *d.* 2 *m. Lords-Day.* My special Errand (tho' I had
many) unto the Table of the Lord, was, to consider that
my admirable Saviour had undertaken and promised, to
make me a man of an excellent Spirit, and had purchased
the vast Blessing for me. So I consented unto it, that He
should accomplish what He had engaged, and purchased;
and that it should appear in three glorious Instances; great
Purity, great *Patience*, and great *Fruitfulness:* For I was
very sensible, that I was grievously Defective in all of these.

2. G. D. It may be much for the Interest of my little
Son *Samuel*, if I send him to learn to read, with the Wife,
of him that is Master of the *Grammar-School*, and then the
Master of the School may take all Opportunities to forward
him in further Learning.

3. G. D. What if I should be so communicative, as to
lodge my *Paterna* a while in the hands of my Brother-in-
Law, Mr. *Walter;* but with a due Care to preserve Modesty
and Concealment? It may sensibly assist him to discharge
his Ministry, and improve in experimental Christianity!

4. G. D. For my more effectual Proceeding upon my
midweek Point-of-Consideration, I purpose to have lying
before me, a more distinct List of the several Places
abroad which are the Field wherein I am to labour for the

Kingdome of God, and bring them all under a successive Consideration.

5. G. D. Thinking, what shall be done, relating to the evangelical Affayr, wherein I am concerned as one of the Indian Commissioners, I resolve, not only to promote Prayer for the Success of the Gospel among the Indians, every Time we hold a Meeting, but also more than ever to make it an Article of Prayer in the public Assemblies of Zion, my Omission of it has been blameable.

6. G. D. A Family in my Neighbourhood, are in great Affliction, by a Daughter violently sett upon a Match, to which the Parents are as violently indisposed. They all cast themselves into my Hands to help them; and I will gladly give what Help I can unto them.

7. G. D. There are with me, in common with all the Children of Men, the usual Evacuations of Nature, to be daily attended. I would not only improve the Time which these call for, to form some Thoughts of Piety, wherein I may differ from the Brutes, (which in the Actions themselves I do very little) and this I have usually already done; but I would now more particularly study that the Thoughts I form on these Occasions, may be of some *abasing Tendency*. The Actions themselves carry Humiliations in them; and a Christian ought alwayes to think humbly of himself, and be full of self-abasing and self-abhorring Reflections. By loathing of himself continually, and Being very sensible of what are his own loathsome Circumstances, a Christian does what is very pleasing to Heaven. My Life (above any Man's) ought to be filled with such Things: and now I contrive certain Spotts of Time, in which I shall be by Nature itself invited unto them.

1. [*May 6.*] G. D. There is among the Communicants of our church, a Number of exceeding wicked People, and yett such as cannot easily be reached by our Discipline. My Flesh trembles for Fear of God, and I am afraid lest

His Judgments break forth againt the Flock. I will with all possible Agony plead the great Sacrifice for the Congregation; and plead in such a Manner at the Lord's-Table, as may affect the Minds of the whole Church, but especially touch the Consciences of the guilty Sinners in *Zion*. But I must not ly still. I will study the best Wayes I can, to recover the Wicked out of their Miscarriages, or to remove the accursed Things.

2. G. D. Questions of this Importance putt unto the children every Night; when we are parting from one another with the concluding Devotions; *Child, have you sought the Face of God, and read His word, this Day? How have you spent your Time to Day? What Good have you done today?* These might produce happy Effects upon the Children.

3. G. D. I find a new Kinsman, (Mr. ʽΕμιγγναι)[1] a Minister of the Gospel in *Dublin*. I would entertain a serviceable Correspondence with him, and send him such Letters and Packets as may do Services for the Kingdome of God in those Parts of the World.

4. G. D. The Colledge at *Connecticut*, languishes for Want of a President. I have a Gentleman in my Eye, who, I hope, would prove a Blessing to them. And by my Letters to the Government there, I endeavour to recomend him unto such a Station.

5. G. D. In Conversation with the Representatives of the Town, lett me project and putt them upon projecting, what Services may be done for the Public, in the General Assembly.

6. G. D. Among other Objects of Charity, for whose Releef I am daily contriving, I would particularly be thoughtful on one at *Wenham;* a Woman under great Necessities, (with her sickly Husband) related unto a wealthy Gentlewoman, who lately died in this Place, and left her Wealth unto Children that are willing to do for the Poor.

[1] Hemmingway.

7. G. D. Sometimes I have kind Presents made unto me. I must therein see the Kindness of God. But I would thereby alwayes be drawn to more particular Acknowledgments and Resolutions; and such as may be most agreeably awakened by the Quality of the Presents. I would think, *What good Thing should that Man wish, and what good Thing should he do, whom God obliges, by bestowing such Things upon him?* And I would alwayes add a Reflection on the Humiliation of my dear JESUS, who wanted such Things, and mett with barbarous Ingratitude from an evil World.

I was willing to make a good Use of much Evil occurring in the World, and especially of the strange Punishments inflicted by God on many Sinners in the World, and most especially of the Things befalling the Sea-farring Tribe; and to warn this Tribe of men in a singular Manner; as also to stir up all Men in their several Capacities to bear due Testimonies against prevailing and outrageous Wickedness. Upon such Intentions, about this Time, I published a Book under this Title; COMPASSIONS CALLED FOR. *An Essay, of profitable Reflections on miserable Spectacles. To which is added, A faithful Relation of some late but strange occurrences, that call for an awful and useful Consideration. Especially, the surprising Distresses and Deliverances of a company Lately Shipwreck'd, on a desolate Rock, on the Coast of N. E.*[1]

12/13 *d.* 3 *m.* [*May.*] *Satureday/Lords-Day.* This Night I visited Heaven, in a comfortable *Vigil.*

Herein I beleeved and received the pardoning Mercy of God, and the Blood of my Saviour purchasing my Pardon. I proceeded then to mention certain Desires before the Lord. I pleaded that Word of my admirable Saviour; *If yee abide in me, and my Words abide in you, yee shall*

---

[1] Printed by B. Green for Eleazer Phillips, 1711. The vessel was the Nottingham Galley, wrecked on Boone Island. The narrative of the shipwreck, obtained from Captain John Dean, a survivor, is appended.

ask what yee will, and it shall be done unto you. I considered the Articles of my *Abiding* in my dear JESUS, and having his Words *abiding* in me, and my Heart closed with them. Then I declared, that *His Will* should be *my Will;* I would have no Will of my own; I entirely left unto Him, as my Advocate, the Prosecution of what *He will*, on my behalf. Yett I proceeded then to mention some Things that I should be glad of. Particularly, my Defence from the *Floods of the Ungodly* that make me *afraid*. I mention'd several other Desires; and especially this; that the Holy Spirit may fall on my poor Flock, and may do wondrously!

The most agreeable Psalms in the world, are strangely brought unto me in these my *Vigils*, at my first Opening of the Psalter. The LXXI Psalm this Night, so occurring, afforded me *Songs in the Night*.

1. [*May* 13.] G. D. This would I do for my Flock. I would in extraordinary Prayers, and particularly in *Vigils*, cry to the Lord for a powerful and wonderful Effusion of His Holy Spirit, on my poor People, especially on the young People; that He would breath upon them, with a mighty Operation in His Ordinances, and not withdraw from His Institutions. When they are all asleep, thus would I be watching and praying and weeping to Heaven for them.

2. G. D. When any one of my Children is touched with any Illness, I would make that an Occasion for Admonitions unto all the rest; that they should be thankful to God for their Health, and serve him in the Time of their Health; And that they should be sensible of their being obnoxious to the early Stroke of Death, and pray for Life, but prepare for Death. Who can tell, how far the Lord may sanctify such Admonitions!

3. G. D. There is one become a Preacher in this Town, who has been a false, base, mischievous Tale-bearer and Slanderer. And tho' he has ow'd his Improvement and

Subsistence very much to me, yett he has ingratefully made me an Object of his Calumnies and Injuries. I will endeavour still to treat him with Goodness, and the Wrongs I have suffered from him, shall but suppress and restrain the Character which else I should give of him unto the Neighbourhood.

4. G. D. By writing some agreeable Things to some considerable Men in *Holland*, particularly in the Universities there, and by sending some Treatises thither, many good Ends may be accomplished, and Services done for the Kingdome of God.

Yea, I would send my *Orphano-trophium* and some other such Things, with a present of Gold, as far as the lower *Saxony*, for the use of the University, and the Orphan-house there.

5. G. D. In the *General Society for Reformation*, I would move, that a Master of good Pen, would still Note, what is on each *Point of Consideration* proposed and purposed; and that it be still read over at the next Meeting, and enquired how far tis proceeded in.

6. G. D. Here are some Families, in Pain and Fear (and with extream Reason,) that their Friends abroad are miscarried. I would visit them and comfort them, with pure Religion and undefiled.

7. G. D. Every Present that is made unto me, or mine, I would look upon it, as coming from the Hand of God; immediately pay some Acknowledgment unto Him; and consider, *To what special Duty or Service of Religion, should I be by this awakened?*

1. [*May 20.*] G. D. So many Losses abroad at Sea, are multiplied unto my Neighbours, that I must use a fresh Contrivance and Endeavour, to suit their Case in my public Ministry, and make them Gainers by what has befallen them.

2. G. D. My little Son *Samuel*, has lain all the last

week, dangerously sick of a Feavour. I made the Sickness of the Child, an Occasion of Supplications, Humiliations, Resignations. Thro' the Favour of God, the Child is now upon a Recovery.

I would with all possible Artifice now insinuate into the young Child, the Admonitions of Piety, and make him know, what the glorious Lord, that makes him well, does expect from him.

3. G. D. It is not only a Time of Affliction, but also like to be a Time of much Temptation, with a foolish and faulty Kinsman of Mine, who has lately buried his Wife: (Ναθαναελ Κονει.)[1] I would therefore apply myself to him with suitable Admonitions; and more than ever watch over him, to do him good.

4. G. D. Having some epistolar Conversation with Mr. *De Foe*, I would in my Letters unto him, excite him to apply himself unto the work of collecting and publishing an History of the Persecutions which the Dissenters have undergone from the Ch[urch] of E[ngland]. And give him some Directions about the Work. It may be a Work of manifold Usefulness.

5. G. D. The Ministers of the Province in their anniversary Meeting at the Time for the Election of our Counsellors, ought to have a Quæstion gott ready for them to discourse upon. The Quæstion which I would prepare and propose for them, is this:

What may we perceive arising in any Part of the Countrey, which may injure or threaten the Interests of Piety; and what may we propose, for the preventing of such Evils, and the preserving of our best Interests?

6. G. D. When I send unto *Dr. Franckius* in the Lower *Saxony*, I would enclose a Present of Gold, for his *Orphanhouse*, which may be to the Value of four or five Pounds in that Countrey.

---

[1] Nathaniel Coney?

25 *d.* 3 *m. Friday.* This Day I sett apart for Prayers, and Psalms, and Alms, with Fasting, before the Lord; that I might renew my Confession of my Corruptions, and Miscarriages, and obtain a Pardon thro' the Blood of the great Sacrifice, and obtain Grace with a fresh Consent unto the Influences of my Saviour in the Covenant of Grace, to glorify God with a more heavenly Piety, and walk more exactly in the Fear of God. And, that I might entreat the Favour of Heaven on my Ministry, and Family, and on His People, the great Concerns whereof, in this day of doubtful Expectation, I laid before Him.

7. G. D. I would anatomically and particularly consider, every Part of my Body, and with as explicit an Ingenuity as may be, consider the several Actions, and Uses thereof; and then go on to consider, on what Methods I may serve my glorious Lord with them, and in what Regards the Service done by them, is to be a Service for the Lord. These Considerations must be accompanied with Consecrations, and Satisfactions, entreating the Lord, that He would accept my Body, as being employ'd for Him, in these Applications, and preserve me from ever perverting my Body, unto any Employments forbidden by Him. As I would sett apart some Times for an effectual Management of this holy Exercise, thus I would occasionally be awakened unto something of it, when I suffer any Pain or Disorder in any Parts of my Body. Herein I would propose, not only to have my Body more notably, made a Temple of God, but also to præpare for a blessed Resurrection of this Body from the Dead by the Saviour of the Body.

1. [*May* 27.] G. D. Many Strangers come among us; I would in my Ministry, as well as my Exemple, mightily press it on my Neighbourhood, that they would not only maintain the Practice of religious Duties, but also treat the Strangers with such unspotted *Honesty*, and such obliging *Courtesy*, as may recommend our holy Religion unto

them, and give them Cause to bless God for bringing them into such a Place as this.

27 *d.* 3 *m. Lords-Day.* My Errands unto the Table of the Lord were these.

First: (And at the Administration of the First Element) I considered, the Blessedness of the heavenly World, as purchased and obtained for me by my admirable Saviour. Then I received Him as the Purchaser, and Promiser, and Bestower of that admirable Blessedness. Whereupon I assured myself of my Interest in it; and I proceeded then, to take up the Resolutions of a patient, fruitful, heavenly Life; and the Dispositions of Love to my Saviour, who had been the Author of eternal Salvation to me.

Secondly: (And at the Administration of the second Element;) I considered certain spiritual Sins in my Soul, the Desires of the Mind, as well as of the Flesh, which unfitted me for the heavenly Blessedness. I beheld the Blood of my Saviour, as purchasing for me a Deliverance from these Corruptions; and upon this blessed and holy Intention I received it. Hereupon I cried unto the Lord, that I might be delivered, first, from all pride; secondly; from all tendencies to envy at the Prosperity of other Men; thirdly; from all Earthly-mindedness, or Inclination to seek Satisfaction in the Things of this World. While I spent my Thoughts and Cries on each of these Corruptions, I meditated on the contrary Dispositions of my Saviour, which were expressed, when He came to shed His Blood for my Salvation from such Things as these. In this way I hoped for the Cure of them.

2. G. D. I am full, full of Distress, concerning my little Son *Increase;* lest some vicious and wicked Lads do corrupt him and ensnare him. I will not only forewarn him of their Company, but with all possible Watchfulness also find out what Company he keeps: and see that it be the wisest I can find for him. And I will cry mightily to God for the Child. *O my God, my God; give to my Son* Increase, *a changed Heart; a perfect Heart and a gracious!*

3. G. D. I have a Kinswoman at *Glocester,* who is very poor and low, and aged. (Συμονδς.)[1] I will send

---

[1] Elizabeth, widow of Harlakenden Symonds.

her, with an agreeable Book of Piety, some Releef of her Necessities.

4. G. D. In the Assembly of the Ministers from all parts of the Province, I design to propose many Things of great Consequence for the public Welfare.

But then, I would also pursue a Proposal, that a Committee of proper Persons, be appointed upon each Article, to consider it, and cultivate it, and bring it forward with a desireable Efficacy.

5. G. D. What Things may be proposed among the Ministers, may be some of them also, very agreeably proposed in the Societies for Suppressing of Disorders. And these may do their Parts about many of those Things.

6. G. D. There are two godly Widowes in poor and low circumstances, living together in my Neighbourhood, (Περκιυς and βαναυ)[1] whom I will take into my more peculiar Care, to visit them, and releeve them, and see that they want nothing that may be good for them.

7. G. D. There is nothing of more Consequence to my Safety and Welfare, than a constant Strain, of the most self abasing Humility. Wherefore, I would constantly chase all vain Thoughts, and vainglorious Ones out of my Mind, with the greatest Abhorrence of them. And if at any Time I begin to look upon any of my Circumstances which may carry in them any Temptation to Pride, I will presently ballance them with some other of my Circumstances (and alas, I have enough of these!) that have sufficient Humiliations in them.

1. [*June* 3.] G. D. The Church whereof I am the Servant, is distinguished by God, with some singular Circumstances of Honour and Figure. It shall be improved by me, and I will endeavour that they may also improve it, as an Awakening unto us, to be a people of singular Piety and Sanctity, and Fruitfulness, and an Exemple to all the People of God in the Land.

[1] Perkins and Vaughan.

2. G. D. The Consideration of bringing my eldest Daughter into the married State, now she is arrived unto such Maturity, and has enjoyed so polite an Education, is a Thing, that will now engage my more than ordinary Supplications to the Lord.

3. G. D. There is in my Neighbourhood an ingenious Gentlewoman, my Sister-in-Law, (Mrs. Σαρα Κλαρκ,)[1] with whom I have a frequent Conversation. The Lord has given me, I think, a great and undeserved Esteem with her. I would at all Times render my Conversation useful to her; never take a Dish of *Tea* with her, without pursuing some holy Intention. And I would particularly excite and assist, at this Time, her Preparations for Approaches to the Table of the Lord.

4. G. D. I would do my part in presenting to our General Assembly, a *Memorial*, proposing three Things of common Concernment and Benefit. First, That the Grants of new Præcincts, might be limited unto such Numbers of Inhabitants, as may be Capable of supporting the evangelical Ministry; and inclined and resolved to do it, comfortably. Secondly, that the prudent Projection formerly offered, and in some Towns already practised, may be now enforced upon all; To cast the Tax for the Salary of the Ministry, into one Bundle of [   ] with what is made for the other Town-charges. Thirdly. That the care of our paganizing Plantations, may be revived.

5. G. D. Among the Commissioners of the Indian-affayrs, there are diverse good Things to be quickly sett on foot. I also stir up such of the Representatives, as I am acquainted withal, to forward on the General Assembly many good Things, for the Welfare of the Province. Especially the three Things proposed in the former Paragraph.

6. G. D. There are some old Professors of Religion in my Neighbourhood, that are fallen into the way of drink-

[1] Sarah Clark.

ing to Excess. Their Intoxications begin to be observed;
there is Danger lest they hasten upon themselves Rebukes
and Censures from the Church of God; and their Souls
are in the mean time horribly wounded. I would consult
with some Discreet and pious Neighbours, the best way to
admonish them, so as to recover them.

7. G. D. Tho' my Life be filled (after my poor Manner) with continual Services, yett I have now litt upon a
noble Way, very much to increase the Number of them.
When I behold any Services to the Kingdome of the glorious
One, done by any one whomsoever, I will rejoice in them,
and I will give Thanks to Him for them, and I will be
pleas'd with, and glad of, the Use He makes of other Men.
As a Complacency, will involve men in a Fellowship with
the Sins of other men; their unfruitful Works of Darkness;
thus a Complacency will interest men in the Services done
by other *Men;* in the Consolations thereof; perhaps in
the Recompences.

1. [*June* 10.] G. D. Worldly-mindedness, the *Præcip-
uum crimen humani Generis;* there is nothing my Flock
is more in danger of. I must preach upon it, yett more
searchingly, more livelily; and show them the Snares of
Death, which they are in danger of.

2. G. D. My dear *Katy* being fallen into an ill State
of Health, I must not only apply myself to the best Methods
for the Recovery of the Health she has lost, but also
improve the Occasion, for her Quickening to the greatest
Points of Christianity.

And for all my Family, at my Parting with them, when
I go to my Rest, (and sing my Song of the Night with
them,) I would not only still enquire, how they have spent
their Time in the Day; but also contrive to utter some
Sentence, which I may leave with them, as worthy to be
remembred and applied, in the Conduct of their Lives.

3. G. D. As I would bestow a new Suit of Cloathes

on a little Nephew, who is an *Orphan;* so I have a Neece, in whose Conduct, there are some Vanities and Fooleries, whereof she needs to be admonished; and I would endeavour for her the most engaging and effectual Admonitions.

4. G. D. From the Disposition of Things in the *Ottoman Empire,* I have a confirmed Hope, that things may have a Tendency towards a great Revolution. I have much at heart the Condition of the poor *Greek* Churches, and the Millions of Christians languishing under the Oppressions of that Empire. I would not only cry much to God for their Deliverance, but also excite and bespeak Prayers in all the Churches throughout this Countrey for them.

5. G. D. Tis a Time of more than ordinary Resort of Strangers to this Town. It requires a more than ordinary Study, to preserve the Morals of our people, from Corruption at such a Time. I would move, both among the Ministers, and in the Societies, what may be done.

6. G. D. There is a woman in my Neighbourhood, full of Afflictions and of Difficulties, in regard of her Husband, entangled with another Woman, with whom he has debauched himself in another Countrey. I will do what I can to support her, and advise her; but I would particularly write unto her Husband, such Things as may have a Tendency to bring him home, and unto Repentance.

7. G. D. Whenever I encounter with any Thing that is not as I would have it, (any *crooked Thing,*) I would look on it as a Call from Heaven, to entertain a Thought of this Importance; *My Will is cross'd; but what particular Instance of my Contradiction and Disobedience to the Will of God, should this Affliction lead me to consider of?* Both Repentance and Patience may be produced by this Consideration.

1. [*June* 17.] G. D. God renews His Calls unto me, to do some special Service for Him, in catechising the Children of the Flock. I would hasten into the Service;

but I would contrive a sweet Variety of obliging and engaging Circumstances to attend it; which call for some further Consideration. My God, I look up unto thee for thy Conduct!

2. G. D. I must not only know that my Children maintain the Religion of the Closet, but also know what they pray for there. I would therefore not only oblige them to write the Desires of their Prayers in general, but also assign them the several Subjects on which they are to employ their Prayers, and successively have them to write down their Petitions on each of those Articles.[1]

One to whom I am a little related, has a great Interest in him that is now the greatest Man in *Britain*. I will write unto him earnestly to improve his Interest in that great Man, and putt him on doing of great and good Things for Mankind.

About this Time, that I might serve the Cause of God and of Truth, both at home and abroad, I took the *Testimony to the Doctrines of Grace*, formerly published, and a Chapter in the *Supplies from the Tower of David* relating thereto, and contrived them into a single Sheet, (adding an advantageous Circumstance, of a Quotation from Dr. *Edwards*, and a Dedication to him.) and I printed it, especially to be dispersed in the Southern Colonies, where the Christians cry for Help against the *Pelagian* Encroachments. It is entituled, THE OLD PATHES RESTORED. *A brief Demonstration, that the* Doctrines of Grace, *hitherto preserved in the Churches of the* Non-conformists, *are not only asserted in the Sacred Scriptures, but also in the* Articles *and* Homilies *of the* Church of England; *And that the General Departure from those Doctrines, especially in those who have subscribed them, is a most unaccountable Apostasy.*[2]

4. G. D. There seems one Thing much wanting, to

---

[1] Six lines were here struck out in the MS.

[2] Printed by T. Green, 1711. A London edition appeared in 1713.

the Devotions of Christianity, among the Professors of
it; that is, the *Gospel* of the *Rainbow*. That Meteor is
a Spectacle and a Sacrament, which the Holy Lord has
afforded and appointed, for the Encouragement of our
Faith, in many glorious Articles. And the Minds of Men
may be awakened from it unto excellent Points of Piety.
I will take the Subject under my Consideration, and
endeavour with the Help of Heaven, to cultivate it, and
prosecute it, for general Edification.[1]

5. G. D. My Treatise of *Manly Christianity*, which I
have just now received from *London*, (where it was lately
printed,) I would procure to be read in many of the private
Meetings; as containing Things which are of great Importance to be inculcated on our Christians.

And my *Old Pathes*, I would endeavour to gett into
the Hands of the Students at the Colledge, that so the
Doctrines of Grace may be preserved there.

About this Time I have another Treatise, in the Press.
The Discourse, I delivered on the Occasion of the Child,
who was crush'd to Death, two Months ago, has been desired
of me. I have accordingly fitted it for the Press; in Hopes
to do Good among all Sorts, but especially our younger
People. It is entituled, PERSWASIONS FROM THE TERROR
OF THE LORD. *A Sermon concerning the Day of Judgment;
preached on a Solemn Occasion.*[2]

6. G. D. There is a poor Widow in my Neighbourhood,
whom I would invite and oblige, to be at least one Day
in a Week at my Table; besides what I have every Lord's-
Day.

22 *d.* 4 *m. Friday.* This Day I sett apart for Prayers
and Alms with Fasting before the Lord. My Occasions for
such Duties grow upon me, in the critical Time, come upon
the Countrey, by a vast Undertaking to subdue the Col-

---

[1] Sewall also has an entry on the rainbow, June 30. *Diary*, II. 318.
[2] Printed by T. Green, 1711. See p. 64, *supra*.

onies of our Northern Enemies;[1] and in the sickly State
of my eldest Daughter.

It proved unto me a Day of no great Enjoyments.

7. G. D. The Disposition with which I enquire after
Newes, needs a little more of Regulation, and of Sublima-
tion. I desire, that when I make that enquiry; *What
occurs remarkable?* it may be with a Disposition and a
Resolution to form, if it may be, some *Lesson of Piety* upon
the Answer; and putt this Lesson, into a Wish presently
and silently sent up to Heaven. And if it be proper, to
mention unto the Company, that Reflection which I would
have to be made upon it.

23/24 *d.* 4 *m.* I attended something of a Vigil this
Night before the Lord. The main Thing, I begg'd, prostrate in the Dust, was, that I may first know the Glory of
my dear JESUS, and then be alwayes acknowledging His
Glory; and then be the happy Instrument of bringing many
others into the Acknowledgments thereof. Hereupon, I
was assured, that I loved Him, and I grew into a joyful
Assurance, that He loves me, who am yett the Chief of
Sinners, and will do wondrous Things for me. Next, I
cried unto Him, for shelter against my Enemies. I cried
unto Him also, for wonderful Effusions of His Grace, on
my Flock, and on my own poor Children. Lastly, I begg'd
of Him for Illumination and Satisfaction, in the true Evi-
dencing of the late strange Extasies and Prophecies, which
first South *France*, and then both Parts of Great *Britain*,
have been alarumed withal, and entertained with so much
Derision: That I may comply with the Will of God in
such Things; but be preserved from Delusions.

1. [*June* 24.] G. D. I would proceed, not only in considering the several Callings of the People in my Flock, but
also, the different Ages, Estates, and Sexes, and suit them,
with my public Discourses.

[1] See Sewall, *Diary,* II. 316.

24 *d.* 4 *m. Lords-Day.*   My Errands to the Table of the Lord, were, first, to seal my Consent unto the Covenant made between the great God, and my dear Saviour for me. And, secondly, to beg for that grand Blessedness engaged in the Covenant, that I should have the Grace to do the Will of God in every good work; for, I look on all my Duties to be indeed but so many Blessings.

2. G. D.   I have some Thoughts, of putting my Daughter *Katharin*, on writing brief Essayes of Piety, on such agreeable Subjects, as I may from Time to Time assign unto her. Who can tell, of what use these Essayes may prove, to the Interests [of] Religion?

3. G. D.   I must not give over, but renew my Applications to a kind Kinsman, (Mr. Κονει) until I have prevailed with him, not only to give up himself unto the Lord, but also unto the People of God, and come to the Fellowship of His holy Table.

4. G. D.   Having received a Collection of good and great Things doing of later years in *Germany*, (excellent Advances of the Kingdome of God,) I think it may not only glorify God, in the Praises of His People, but also animate the like Things among ourselves, to publish it unto the Countrey.

5. G. D.   I have an intimate Friend, who is arrived and admitted unto a great Intimacy, with the greatest Minister of State in the Nation.[1] I would earnestly write unto him, to improve this Advantage, for the doing of the most extensive Services that are possible unto such good Interests as he may think upon.

6. G. F.   There is a poor, pious, praying Woman, (Αλλεν)[2] a Widow, that lives by a continual Supply sent in from a Charity, which Heaven directs, in answer to her Supplications. I will take a particular Care, that she be well and oft supplied.

[1] Sir Robert Walpole is probably here intended, as also on p. 81, *supra.*
[2] Allen.

7. G. D. I would alwayes have about me some little Matters, (as Pennies, or Fruits, or Paints,) proper to be bestow'd on little Children. And in the bestowing of them, I would alwayes endeavour to commend some Lesson of Piety, to be remembred, with them: and the more likely to be remembred, for the Token that accompanies them.

1. [*July* 1.] G. D. Tis a Time, in which there is a vast Access of Strangers to the Town.[1] It is probable, that they may, some of them, look into our Congregations. I would cry mightily to God, that His Word may take hold on some of their Hearts, and that it may be found, He has brought some of His Elect hither, on purpose to be in the way of their effectual Calling 'here.

2. G. D. My little *Lizzy*, — more care must be taken, about the *Catechizing*, at the School she goes to, and her own particular Share in it; And every Thursday, and Saturday in the Afternoon, she must now learn by Heart, some Lesson of Piety.

3. G. D. A Kinswoman of mine, is married in the west of *England*, unto a Clergyman; if her Friends here advise me to it, I will send unto her some little Books, and what may discharge my Duty to her, in regard of her greatest Interests.[2]

4. G. D. Being furnished with a considerable Number of Bibles, to disperse among the Poor, in the most edifying manner that may be, I would particularly consider my careless, wretched sea-faring Tribe; and lodge in many of our Vessels, a Bible for the use of the Ship's Company, with a Promise from the Captain, that there shall be a suitable Use made of it. (If this be judg'd necessary.)

5. G. D. There is one good Interest, which I have never yett served, and yett I am capable of doing some

---

[1] The English transports with the troops for Canada were in the harbor.

[2] He is, as usual, silent as to the commencement exercises in Cambridge on this day. They were of more than usual importance, because of the presence of the British officers.

small Service for it. The Improvement of Knowledge in the Works of Nature, is a Thing whereby God, and His Christ is glorified. I may· make a valuable Collection of many Curiosities, which this Countrey has afforded; and present it unto the Royal Society. May the glorious Lord assist me, in this Performance.

6. G. D. I will try whether I cannot with the most exquisite Methods of Insinuation, engage in the Thoughts of Piety, some of the Gentlemen, belonging to the Army, lately arrived from Gr. *Britain* here.

7. G. D. When the good God blesses me at any time, with a real, cordial, useful Friend, I would make an holy and a various Improvement of so rare a Blessing, more particularly,

First, I would return my Thanks to the glorious God, who has the Hearts of all men at His Disposal, and behold the Friendship of my Neighbour, as one effect of that Reconciliation with Him, which has been obtained for me, by my admirable Saviour.

Secondly. I would return to my Neighbour all the Acts of his Friendship, and even disdain to be outdone, but overcome him in kind Offices; and I would remember his Name, and whatever I may see to be his Case, in my Supplications before the Lord.

Thirdly. I would employ the Interest which the Friendship of my Neighbour gives me in him, as an Opportunity, to study and enquire, what good I may stir him up unto the doing of; that so the People and Kingdome of God, may fare the better, for my Acquaintance with such a Person.

1. [*July* 8.] G. D. I entertain Thoughts of renewing a Course of *pastoral Visits*, to my Flock. I would earnestly cry to the glorious Lord for His Direction and Assistence, in so important and laborious an Undertaking. I would then, with great Exactness and Watchfulness, consider what are those Enquiries which I should make in every Family; besides the various Points of Discourse, which I may occasionally insist upon.

2. G. D. The Continuance of my Life seems a Thing

of great Consequence to the Welfare of my Family. I must therefore not only make my own fervent Prayers for it, unto the God of my Life, but also oblige the Children to pray for it continually, and sett before them, the Importance of their making this an Article of their daily Supplications.

3. G. D. I have a Kinsman at *Newhaven,* who was once my Scholar, now a Physician and a Justice of Peace, (Ταραμ Μαθερ)[1] to whom I will send such Things, as may have a particular Tendency, to rescue him from his Temptations, and quicken him in his Services.

4. G. D. My Essay of, *The old Pathes Restored,* I would not only convey to our Colledge, but also to that of *Connecticut;* yea, and unto all the Ministers far and near, as I have Opportunity; that so the Doctrines of Grace, may be every where, exhibited and established; and the Kingdome of Truth advanced.

5. G. D. It may not be amiss for me, to press all the Ministers of the Town, that they would contrive into their public sermons, agreeable and awakening Passages, by which the Souls of the many Strangers who at this time especially, drop into our Congregations, may be mett withal.[2]

6. G. D. A worthy Minister (Υιλλιαμς)[3] a Chaplain to our Forces now going against *Canada,* needs the Kindnesses of some good People, to furnish him, with Convenencies for his Voyage; I would promote his Accommodation.

I would also procure him to be furnished with Books of Piety to be dispersed among our Souldiers.

7. G. D. From my private Papers, I incline to make an Extract of such things as peculiarly belong to the Christian *Asceticks;* my Life having been filled with Projections

---

[1] Warham Mather, probably son of Rev. Warham Mather and Elizabeth Davenport, and grandson of Eleazar.

[2] He preached his sermon on the Rainbow this day; "many chaplains at meeting," says Sewall, *Diary,* II. 319.

[3] Williams.

and Contrivances for Methods to carry on the Conversation
of refined Christianity. This Composure, if I make no
further use of it, yett by having my own Eyes often upon
it, I may keep alive the Notion and Practice of the Things
wherein I have been taught of God; whereas now, thro' a
vast Variety of Employments and because my Proposals
ly scattered here and there among thousands of other
Things in my Memorials, I many times forgett the Directions of Piety, which I have resolved upon.

1. [*July* 15.] G. D. I would not only consider every
Class of People in my Flock, by preaching on Subjects that
may be most suitable for their Conditions, but also I would
suit their Conections in my Supplications. Nor would
I only present public Petitions for them, but also more
secretly cry to God, on the behalf of each of these Classes;
for such Mercies to them, as they may have most occasion
for; and for such a Direction likewise of my own Studies,
as may be most for their Advantage.

2. G. D. I would shortly keep a Day of Thanksgiving
to God, in private; chiefly with relation to His Favours
whereof my Family partakes in various and wondrous
Instances. I would spend a great Part of the Day, in the
agreeable Exercises of Religion with my Family. And I
would lay hold on the precious Opportunities, which I may
therein have to bring every Soul in my Family, home unto
my Saviour.

3. G. D. My Brother at *Witney*,[1] is præparing for the
Public, an Abridgment of our *Church-History*. I would
make this an Occasion of putting him upon several Things,
that may prove Services to the Kingdome of God.

4. G. D. That sottish Bigotry is growing; that all the
pastoral Acts done by those who have not episcopal Ordination are Invalid. It seems necessary, that the Churches
be fortified against it. I would consult and agree with

[1] Samuel.

some of the Ministers of the Neighbourhood, about the best
Methods of encountering the follies of unreasonable Bigots.

5. G. D. I would make a Motion unto each of the
religious Societies in our Neighbourhood, that they would
sett themselves very much to pray for Effusions of the
divine Grace on the rising Generation, and a mighty Success of the Gospel among us; and sett apart special Times
on this holy Intention.

6. G. D. The Apostasy of that famous French Con-
fessor, Mr. *Elias Neau*[1] at *N. York*, is to me one of the
most grievous and shocking Things that I have mett withal.
I desire to do something towards his Recovery, or at least,
a Testimony proper for this Occasion.

20 *d.* 5 *m.* [*July.*] *Friday.* I sett apart this Day for
Prayers, with Alms, on the usual Occasions; and because
a great Force is now going from hence against the *Canadian*
Enemy.

My Soul arrived unto some sweet Assurances, that my
Sin is pardoned, and that in Token of it, I shall have a
pure Heart given to me, and be filled with the Grace of
God.

But by reason of Illness upon me, I could not so ply
my Supplications as I would have done. I made it up in
Benignities.

7. G. D. There is a beautiful Creature of God, whereon
He has enstamp'd a sacramental Character. He has made
the *Rainbowe*, a Sacrament of His Covenant that He will
preserve His Church in the World. And His faithful Servants may apply this Covenant, unto their own particular
Circumstances, in regard of any Mischiefs which may
threaten to overwhelm them. I would endeavour more
affectionately, more comfortably, more explicitly than ever,
to apply the *Rainbowe* unto the Use for which the glorious
One has appointed it, when I see the Cloud in the Day of

---

[1] See Vol. I, p. 300. He became a communicant of the Church of England.

Rain brightened with it, and have proper Meditations raised in my Mind.

About this time, considering what an Use the glorious Lord has assigned unto the *Rainbowe*, but how much the Use of it is neglected among His People, and what a Service it might be unto Religion, to teach our People the *Use of the Bowe*, and recover this *Engine of Piety* into that Improvement, for which the Maker of it intended it; especially now the Time is coming on, for an Angel to descend with a *Rainbowe* about His Head, and the great Covenant of God for His Church in the World is hastening to an Accomplishment; I prepared for the Public a Treatise under this Title, THOUGHTS FOR THE DAY OF RAIN. *In two Essayes.* I. *The* Gospel *of the* Rainbowe. *In the Meditations of Piety, on the Appearance of the Bright Clouds, with the Bowe of God upon them.* II. *The* Saviour *with His* Rainbowe. *And the Covenant which God will Remember to His people, in the most cloudy Times that are passing over them.*[1]

1. [*July* 22.] G. D. The Representation of the particular Cases occurring among the People, is not, methinks, made so fully, so pungently, so usefully, in the public Prayers, as it might be. I would apply my Thoughts this way, with more Endeavours to accommodate the Edificacon of the Neighbourhood.

22 *d.* 5 *m. Lord's-day.* My Errands to the Table of the Lord, were especially these two.

I. I considered, That my Lord Jesus Christ is the Object of His Father's infinite Love. That He is in Himself altogether lovely. That in what He has done, and what He will do, for me, He has obliged me to love Him with all my Heart and Soul and Strength. I considered, That the Grace of Love to my dear Saviour, is that wherein I am still very defective. But yett it is purchased for me by the Death of my Saviour, wherefore I consider the Sacrifice of my Saviour, as procuring for me, the Pardon of the Defects in my

[1] Printed by B. Green, 1712.

Love to Him. And such a precious Gift, as an Heart full of Love to him. With this Disposition I took the Bread of the Eucharist. I proceeded then to form these Resolutions, of the Things werein I would express my Love to my Saviour. That I would often, often think of Him, and with unspeakable Delight. That I would watch all Occasions to make an advantageous Mention of His Glories. That I would in my Sermon and in my Writings, use extraordinary Methods to declare His Glories. And that I will Rejoice in all Conformity to Him; yea, when it shall be in the most abasing Circumstances.

II. I considered, that Fruitfulness is a most illustrious and comprehensive Blessing of the new Covenant. But that it is a Thing wherein I am extremely Wanting. My Barrenness! My Barrenness! Tis a killing Thought unto me. I considered, That in the Blood of my Saviour, I have the Pardon of my criminal Unfruitfulness. And I have also the Purchase of Grace to glorify my heavenly Father, by bringing forth much Fruit. I received the Cup with these Dispositions. And with Hopes, that the Spirit of God, who makes His People fruitful, would now more than ever enter into me. I proceeded then, to contrive and resolve the Methods of being very fruitful.

2. G. D. I would carefully observe the Tempers of each of my Children. And, first, I would warn them against the peculiar Indiscretions and Temptations, whereto they may be exposed in their Tempers. Then I would see, whether I can't suit their Tempers with Motives that may encourage and animate their Piety.

3. G. D. My Nephew (Ινκρεασε Ταλτερ)[1] is now disposing to fitt himself for Service in the Study of Physick; I would more than ever be thoughtful for him, and direct and supply his Studies, and do all I can to render him serviceable.

4. G. D. I procure a Sum of Money, to be laid out in Books of Piety; which I propose to lodge in each of our Transport-ships, for the Good of the Sailors, as well as more to be putt into the Hands of our Souldiers, now bound for *Canada*.

[1] Increase, son of Nehemiah and Sarah (Mather) Walter.

5. G. D. There are some hopeful young Merchants, of whom I am thinking, whether it were not a possible and profitable Thing, to associate them in a Conversation, that may turn on Points of Service to themselves and others.

26 d. 5 m. Thursday. This Day, I attended the Prayers and Alms and other Duties of a Fast,[1] which was kept throughout the Province, relating to our great Enterprize against *Canada*.

I enjoy'd a gracious Presence of the Lord with me in the Works of the Day.

6. G. D. There is a minister at *Endfield*, who conflicts with distressing Poverty.[2] And with my Letters unto him, to direct and hearten him, I would also send him such Releefs as I am able.

7. G. D. When I read, or see, any new Book, wherein the Truth, and Church, and Cause of God, has any notable Service done for it, I would offer up my solemn Thanks unto the glorious Head of the Church, for His thus expressing His Care of it, and His Dispensing such Gifts unto the Children of Men.

1. [*July* 29.] G. D. There are very many Widowes in our Neighbourhood. I incline to preach a Sermon on purpose to them, and for them. Yea, and then also to publish it, and so to disperse it among them.

2. G. D. Would it not be for my Son's Advantage, if I should procure him the Company of three or four more serious Lads, to join with him, in spending the Lord's-day Evening together, and reading over by Turns, those Things which I shall recommend unto them, and forming such Resolutions of Piety, as they shall acquaint me withal?

3. G. D. I have a poor Kinswoman, a Daughter of my cosen-german, (Ευνικε Τιλλιαμς)[3] who has been six or seven

---

[1] It was a public fast, ordered by proclamation.

[2] Rev. Nathaniel Collins. His pay appears to have been twenty pounds a year.

[3] Eunice Williams. See Sewall, *Diary*, II. 374.

years a Captive, in the hands of the French Popish Indians. I am afraid, I have not considered the miserable Condition of that Child, with such a frequency and fervency of Supplication, as I should have done; tho' I have not forgotten it.[1]

But I would now with a more importunate Supplication than ever, continually carry that Child unto the strong Redeemer.

4. G. D. Upon further Thoughts, I grow into an Opinion that my writing a Book of, *Christian Asceticks*, may prove a great Service to the Interests of Piety in the World. I will make my Cries to Heaven, for Direction and Assistence in it, and go about it, as soon as may be.

5. G. D. I would write such things unto *Annapolis*, as may be of use to our poor People there; and procure some good People to join with me, in sending thither, Bibles, and other Books of Piety.

6. G. D. There is a poor Man, a prisoner for Debt, for whom I would do all possible good Offices; but particularly, visit him and supply him with Books of Piety; and counsel how to spend his Time well, and make a good Use of his bad Circumstances. (Περκινς).[2]

7. G. D. I think, it will be highly expedient for me, at least once a Month, to look back upon my *Good Devised*, and in the Perusal of the registred Articles, consider what has been forgotten or neglected; and so quicken the Execution of my Proposals.

The Lord's-day Evening, may be a good Season, for these Reflections.

1. [*August 5.*] G. D. I entertain Thoughts of going thro' my large Flock again, with pastoral Visits. And I will therefore cry mightily to the Lord, for His Direction

---

[1] Eunice Mather (1664–1704), daughter of Rev. Eleazar, and thus cousin of Cotton, married Rev. John Williams of Deerfield. Her daughter Eunice (1696–1786?), the captive, married an Indian.

[2] Perkins. Probably John Perkins, the physician.

and Assistence, in so great an Undertaking. I would preface it with a Day of Supplications.

2. G. D. I will cause my four Children (who can use their pen,) to retire, and write each of them an Answer to that Question: *What will be the best Manner and Method of my spending my Time in the World; and how shall I best answer the End of my coming into the World?* When they give me this, I will as far as I can oblige them to conform unto it.

3. G. D. I have a sick Parent, unto whom I owe Abundance of Duty, that I may render his Condition comfortable to him. I will ply it, with all possible Assiduity.

4. G. D. From the Fright on the Minds of the People, apprehending a French Invasion, I would now take Occasion to carry the People unto the Thoughts of the blessed Jesus as our great Preserver, and unto those Methods of Piety which may have a Tendency to our Preservation.

5. G. D. I would lodge in the Hands of the old Gentleman, who is the Master of the French School, a number of my *Vrai Patron des saines Paroles;* to be studied by the Scholars; that they may at once learn the Language, and improve in Knowledge and Goodness.[1]

6. G. D. An Officer of the Army is tak'n sick, and left here; I will visit him, instruct him, do all I can to engage him in the wayes of our holy Religion; and on his begun Recovery, I will perswade him to take up suitable Resolutions; and putt Books of Piety into his Hands.

10 *d.* 6 *m.* [*August.*] *Friday.* This Day, our Town, and the adjacent Countrey have had, the most real Alarm that ever we had.[2] The Symptoms of an approaching Enemy appeared in very awakening Circumstances. But in the Issue it proved only a Fleet of our Friends.

[1] The congregation of French Protestants held their services in the Free School House in Boston. Rev. Pierre Daillé was at this time the minister, and possibly the master of the French school.

[2] Also mentioned in Sewall, *Diary,* II. 321.

7. G. D. Hereupon, I sett myself to think, In what Points my Walk with God should be quickened, by the continual Preservation of this Town, from the Invasion of a formidable Adversary?

I gave to my glorious JESUS, the Glory of being our Preserver. I acknowledged the Sacrifice He has offered for the Congregation, as the Ransome found for us. I resolved, that I would continue to do so. I considered, that since I enjoy the Comforts of a quiet Habitation, delivered from Enemies, I ought to serve the Lord in more Holiness and Righteousness, and make the Religion of my Family yett more full of lively Exercises, and study to have His Worship carried on with a more heavenly Assiduity; and engage every Person in my Family, to think, what they owe unto the Lord on this Occasion. I resolved on these Things, and on doing my Endeavour, that the People of the Town may all come into the like Resolutions.

1. [*August* 12.] G. D. A Delinquent must appear before the Church with his Repentance. I would make it an Occasion to proclame unto every one the Necessity of Repentance, before the Gates of Heaven can be sett open to us; and quicken every one to examine what Evils they may find in themselves which call them to the Exercise of Repentance. I would also make it an Occasion of good unto the Man himself.[1]

2. G. D. I am now providing *Patrons* for my Children, when they shall be *Orphans*. For my Daughter *Lizzy*, I particularly have my Thoughts on a religious and ingenious Woman in our Neighbourhood; which has no Children of her own. I will visit her, and I will do what I can to engage her, that she will deal with that Child as her own.

3. G. D. I have a Kinsman, who is a preacher to the

---

[1] "John Brewster, having given Scandal by assisting a Souldier in deserting from the Camp, his Repentance and Confession was this day [12th] publickly offered unto the Church and accepted."— *Cotton Mather's MS. Records of the Second Church*, II.

Indians. I would endeavour not only to offer him Directions, but also procure him Encouragements, for the Service wherein he is engaged.

4. G. D. The Time drawes near, for the *Connecticot* Ministers to meet at their Commencement in *Say-brook;* I will sett myself to think what matters of profitable Entertainment and Consideration I may lay before them, and seasonably send such Things thither for them.

5. G. D. Move among the Ministers, for the Encouragement of some agreeable Preacher, to be sent unto the English Garrison at *Annapolis*.

6. G. D. There is a Family in my Neighbourhood, which are People of no Religion, but a Composition of Quaker and High-Church and a little Atheistical. These are in great Affliction; by long Sickness, which brings on impoverishing Circumstances. I will make their Affliction an Opportunity to visit them, and releeve them, and instruct them, and do all the Good that is possible for them, and stir up the Neighbours to do so too. (Κρυνσιλ).[1]

17 *d. 6 m.*[2] 7. G. D. I would never putt on the Civilities (of a Glove, or a Ring, or a Scarf,) given me at a Funeral, but endeavour to do it, with a Supplication of this Importance; *Lord, prepare me for my own Mortality.* And, *Lord, Lett me at my Death be found worthy of a Remembrance among the Living!* And inasmuch as I have a distinguishing Share, above the most of them who ordinarily attend a Funeral, in such Civilities, I would look at it, as an Obligation on me to press after the Instances of Godliness and Usefulness, that may render me more excellent than my Neighbour; and particularly, in an holy Behaviour at a Funeral; exemplary in the Religion of the Funeral.

17 *d. 6 m. Friday.* This Day I sett apart for Prayers and Alms, with Fasting before the Lord, (Tho' I had spent part of a Day, praying and preaching, in the Com-

---

[1] Crowninshield?   [2] A confusion in date, as the 17th fell on a Friday.

pany of some Godly Christians, with a dying Gentleman in my Neighbourhood, the beginning of this week.)

My Addresses to Heaven, had some singular Occasions; besides those of the Public, and of my Houshold.

Especially, for the Direction and Assistence of Heaven to me, in cultivating the Subjects of my Ministry.

For a mighty Help of Heaven to me in Renewing my pastoral Visits.

For a merciful Smile of Heaven on the Circumstances of a little Journey, I have some Thoughts of undertaking.

And for some good Newes from beyond-Sea, relating to the Acceptance and Encouragement of my Labours to serve the Kingdome of God.

1. [*August* 19.] G. D. Among the Exercises of my Ministry among my People, I am afraid, whether I am so edifying as I should be, in the celebrating of the *Marriages*, for which I am applied unto. I would therefore more exactly consider, what are the most suitable Confessions and Petitions to be made in the Prayers on that Occasion. And what Maxims of Piety, I may with Brevity, but Pungency, lett fall on the People with whom I am concerned.

19 *d.* 6 *m. Lords-Day.* My Errands to the Table of the Lord this Day were, to mourn over what there is in me Displeasing to God; And Plead the well-pleasing Sacrifice of my Saviour for the Pardon of it. And, profess my Abhorrence of every Thing displeasing to God. And, obtain for the Sake, and by the Spirit of my sacrificed Saviour, a work of His upon me, and the Growth of it, that shall dispose me, and strengthen me, to the Things well-pleasing in the Sight of God; And make an Enumeration of those Things.

2. G. D. It would be for my Wife's Advantage, and also sett a good Exemple unto others, if she would be prevailed withal, to write the Sermons after the Preacher in the Public.

3. G. D. I have a little Kinsman, (an Orphan) at *Hampton*, for whom I would endeavour to do all possible Good offices on all Occasions; but now I would particularly send him the Sermon lately, published, which was preached on the sudden and awful Death of a Child. (Θομας Κοςτον).[1]

4. G. D. There is a considerable Church in my Neighbourhood, which is falling to Peeces, by Temptations gaining upon them, and on very trivial Occasions. I would use all possible Endeavours to prevent and conquer the Devices of Satan, which are now in their Operation among that poor People. It may be, some Letters of mine, may be blessed for that Intention.

22 d. 6 m. A Lord-Chancellor of *England*, who was also Archbishop of *York*,[2] said in his Latter time, "That in his time he had pass'd thro' more Posts of Office and Honour than most Men in the World; but if he were sure that any one Soul had been by his Means converted unto God and Christ and Holiness, it would give him unspeakably more Satisfaction, than all the Dignities which had ever been conferr'd upon him." How happy, how happy, am I! that have so often this astonishing Satisfaction! I had not been many Months a Preacher, before I found among the Declarations of those who joined unto my Father's Church, no less than thirty Seals of my Ministry![3] How many have been by my Addresses to them, either with Tongue or Pen brought home to God, I shall never know in this World. I will now only take some thankful Notice of it, that some excellent Souls, who within these few Dayes have taken their Leave of this World, have spoken strange Things to me on their Death-beds, of what the glorious Lord has by my Ministry done for them. And on this Day, one with Rapture triumphing over the Sting and Fear of Death, cried out unto me. *Oh! Dear Syr, you are*

---

[1] Thomas Coston.
[2] Probably Thomas Wolsey (1475?–1530).   [3] See vol 1. 68.

*the Man! You are the Man, that have brought me home unto
God! It is by your Means, that the Lord has brought me
home to Himself. I must love you dearly; I shall do so, to
my last Breath. God has a wondrous Glory for you.*

Q. Must not a Messenger of Satan buffet me after
this?

5. G. D. Tho' in my Conversation with other Men,
I am continually putting them upon doing of the Good,
which I see they may be capable of doing, and thousands of
Things projected by me in this way find no Place in my
poor Memorials: yett inasmuch as the Day now recurrs
in which my Morning-Thoughts are to consider that Question, what Good may I excite any other Person to do?
I do here enter my Purpose, that when any of my Neighbours have been bless'd with a good Voyage, or an Arrival
of their Interests from Sea, I would make it more than
ever (tho' it has heretofore been my Practice to make it)
an Opportunity of more urgently and cogently persuading
them to apply some of their Gains to pious Uses. And I
would be alwayes able to mention a Variety of pious Uses,
out of which they may make their Choice of what Good
they may chuse to do.

6. G. D. I am in Distress for a Minister in my Neighbourhood, embroiled with a froward people; I will endeavour by the best Methods, to make him and them also,
prudent, patient, and easy.

24 *d.* 6 *m.* This Day I was *buffeted* with a libellous
Letter from a Merchant in this Town, fill'd with Scurrilities
that I suppose were hardly ever æqualled in the World.
The Divel stared in every Line of it. A Legion together
could scarce have out-done it. It is a little odd; tho' the
Libeller, were one of the last, whom I find mention'd among
the Enemies for whom I projected Kindnesses, yett one
Article of his Foam is, that I am a Stranger to the Practice
of a forgiving Spirit which I preach unto others.

I spred the Letter of this *Rabshakeh*[1] before the Lord.
I ask'd the Pardon of his Sin, and the Mercy of God unto
him. I ask'd also the Pardon of my own Sin, that might
provoke the Lord to sett such a Dog upon me. But above
all, I ask'd the Grace of Heaven, for a wise, patient, fruitful
Conduct, under such Outrages from the Wickedest of Men;
and that God would requite me Good for the Cursing of a
Shimei![2]

It may be, some remarkable Good is coming to me.

7. G. D. It is a Law with me, that when Abuses are
offered me, I be awakened unto some agreeable Improvement in Piety upon them. I see especially two Things,
I am now called unto. First, to be yett more consummate
in the Exercise of a forgiving Spirit, when I have been
Injured. Secondly, To be more watchful and fruitful in
my Visits unto my Neighbours. And yett, when I look
back on my Conduct, I find it scarce possible for so feeble a
Creature as I am, to do much otherwise than I have done.
But, be sure, I may do better, and I will endeavour it.

25/26. I kept something of a *Vigil*, in which I putt
over my Cause into the Hands of a righteous Lord; and
I exercised a strong Faith in my glorious Jesus, for His
Defence; and for the Rescue of my Serviceableness from
the Malice of One very wick'd Man, and from all the Floods
of the Ungodly; and that some remarkable Good may follow the Cursing which I have mett withal. But, above all,
I begg'd the Grace, to carry it as I ought to do.

1. [*August* 26.] G. D. In some of my *Vigils*, I have
proposed it unto Heaven, that such Things may happen
in my Neighbourhood, as may prove exceeding Serviceable
unto the Kingdome of God, and furnish me with Occasions
to awaken the Minds of the People unto a most serious
Consideration of their greatest Interests. There have happened several such Things, whereof I have taken a watch-

[1] 2 Kings, XVIII, XIX.   [2] 2 Samuel, XVI.

ful and a lively Hold in my Ministry. And now there is another. The dying Woman, whom I have mention'd, three pages ago, did yesterday speak after this manner to me.

Syr, I was once under the Power of a foolish and wicked Perswasion, that it was in my own power to Repent at my Pleasure. With this Præsumption, I went on in my Sins. I only begg'd of God Almighty that He would not send a sudden Death upon me. I then thought, there was no Fear of such a Repentance as would make sure of everlasting Life. But God has horribly convinced me of my Error. Oh! it has cost me the dreadful Anguish of six, or seven sad Months to come at that, which I thought I could have done when I pleased. Syr, I desire you, that you would from me warn the Neighbours, and all the World, against this dangerous Opinion, whereby so many Souls are destroy'd forever.

I purpose with the Direction and Assistence of the Lord, to do what has been thus proposed unto me, in as pathetical a manner as may be.

2. G. D. There is a particular Projection to be pursued, relating to the Welfare of my *Katy*, in which I desire the Conduct of Heaven, and would seasonably advise with such as may be properly spoken to.

3. G. D. My Kinsmans widow at *Hampton*, hears of the Death of her only Brother. I must write unto her the Consolations of God, and as far as I can, do the Part of a Brother unto her.

4. G. D. The next Month, a Convention of Ministers in the Southern Colonies of *North-America*, meets at *Philadelphia*. As I have Occasion to write unto them, on the behalf of a Church on Long-Island, which sollicit me to do it; So I will take the Occasion, to animate them unto the contriving of Things that may be of extensive Consequence to the Kingdome of God, and Services for me to do as well as themselves; and particularly also to keep a Day of Prayer together.

5. G. D. It is this Day a general Fast thro' the Province. It would be a proper, and may be an useful thing, for me in my Sermon this Day, solemnly to call upon all the religious Societies in the Neighbourhood, that they would when they are together, take this Quæstion into their serious Consideration; *What shall we do, to promote Religion and Piety in our Neighbourhood?*

30 *d.* 6 *m. Thursday.* This Day was a general Fast, thro' the Province, on the behalf of our Forces gone to *Canada.*

The Lord graciously assisted me in the Services of the Day.

In my secret Supplications this Day my Soul was Comforted with a strange and strong Perswasion, that my glorious Jesus, will wonderfully appear, in surprising Dispensations of His Providence, to hearten and reward my Serviceableness, and confound my malicious Adversaries. But for our *Canadian* Enterprise, oh! I fear, I fear, *an horrible Tempest.*

6. G. D. There is a poor Woman, languishing in much Poverty, and by long Sickness brought into a very helpless Condition; I must not only myself releeve her, but also unite my Counsels with others, about the best way of having her well-provided for. (Poθa).[1] There is a poor Widow also whom I would assist and advise in some temporal Circumstances. (Poιaλ).[2]

7. G. D. It must be, (and it has been) my way, when I find myself barren of *Good Devices,* and my Enquiries after them in my Thoughts not presently and easily answered, *then* to form a more deliberate Act of Resignation, wherein I confess my Inability to so much as Think a good Thought, and I beseech the glorious God, who is my Father, and my Saviour, and my Leader, and who formes the Spirit of man within him, to take possession of my Mind, and lead me

---

[1] The name is obscure, but may be Rotha.   [2] Royal.

to such Inventions for the Doing of Good, as may be pleasing unto Him, and for the Service of His Kingdome and Interest.   In the way of this unexceptionable *Quietism*, I still find Thoughts of a surprising Tendency to Good, strangely darted into my mind; Thoughts of too superiour a Character for me to pretend that they are my own.

This Morning, on my *Satureday Quæstion*, finding right Thoughts not arising so quickly in my dull and dark Mind, as I would have had them, I took this Course.   And my Thoughts immediately were such as these.   When I hear or see, any Person using any singular Industry or Contrivance, to serve his own Interest, or to hurt other Men's, I will sett myself to think on some Interest of my admirable Saviour, or Benefit unto Mankind; and such an one, as the Circumstances of that Man's Pursuit may most naturally lead me to think on; and I will then propose, how my Industry and Contrivance in pursuing of that Good, may not fall short of his; but be altogether, as exquisite, as vigorous, and as indefatigable.

1/2 *d.* 7 *m.* [*September.*] *Satureday./Lords-day.*   I applied Myself unto the Devotions of a *Vigil*.

I begg'd for such Tidings from beyond-sea, as might Encourage my poor Essayes to do Good.   I begg'd for a mighty work of awakening and converting Grace on the People, especially the young People, of the Flock whereof I am the Servant.   I begg'd also for a Deliverance from the Malice of those horrid Men, who are the venemous Enemies of my Serviceableness; unto whose malicious Abuses, I make no Answer, but leave them in the Hands of my glorious Redeemer; He will graciously appear for me, and confound them wonderfully!

When my prostrate Supplications were over, I went into my Bed, and kept awake for some while there singing, (for I retired into a Chamber where I lodged alone) unto the Lord.   It was a little Surprising to me, that the first Place, at which my Psalter opened, was, Ps. CXLIX. 5.

The Gracious Holy Ones, Lett them
most gloriously rejoice.
Lett them upon their Beds also
Lift up their singing Voice.

The next Place that opened, was, Psal. XXXVIII. 14.

As one that heareth not was I,
And in whose Mouth Reproofs none were.
For I, O Lord, on thee rely.
O Lord my God, Thou wilt me hear. etc. etc.

These, and many more such Passages, I sang unto the Lord.

1. [*September* 2.] G. D. Some sad young Wretches on their Death-beds lately, had earnestly desired me, to warn other young People, against such Courses as have ruined them. This gives me a fresh Occasion for the dispensing of new, and solemn, and lively Warnings in my public Ministry. As also to speak more privately unto certain particular Persons in the Flock, such Things as they need to be advised of.

2. G. D. When any of my Children have any Illness upon them, I would make it an Occasion to putt them in mind of the Evil in Sin, and especially of such Sin, as their Illness may most naturally mind them of; I would show them the analogous Distempers of their Souls, and instruct them how to look up unto their great Saviour for the Cure of those Distempers.

3. G. D. I have a Kinswoman (Εννικε Τιλλιαμς)[1] which has been diverse Years a Captive in the Hands of the Indians. As I have often pray'd for her Deliverance, I would now grow in the Importunity of my frequent Supplications for her; every Day constantly remember her and mention her. And I would make her condition an Argument in Discourses with my own children, for Thankfulness and Piety.

[1] Eunice Williams.

4. G. D. Things are not in a very good Condition at *Salem*. I have some Thoughts taking shortly a Journey thither, in hopes of doing Abundance of Good there. I will humbly commend this Matter, in all the Circumstances of it, unto the gracious Conduct of the Lord.

5. G. D. My glorious Lord has in His gracious Providence ordered it, that very eminent Persons beyond-sea, take notice of me, and such as I myself never have written unto, send me their Letters and their Presents, which I have this Week received. The Cursing of a *Shimei* was but to prepare me for such Things; and weighs nothing in the Ballence against them. I had a secret Faith, I should find it so. Among these, I must in the first Place reckon the admirable Sir *Richard Blackmore*.[1]

Now I will sett myself to improve these new Correspondencies, for the Honour, and in the Service of my dearest Saviour; and I will sett myself to think, what Service to His Kingdome I may animate each of these eminent Persons to the doing of.

6. G. D. There are poor Gentlewomen, who have long been confined by Illness; but yett are able to read, or hear others read unto them. I will visit them, and comfort them, and supply them with Books of Piety, that may be a profitable Entertainment for them.

7. G. D. It is a Time, when many in the Neighbourhood, are sick and weak, and some sleep, of an uneasy Malady; The Flux with Vomiting. As my Time is pretty much spent among the sick and weak, so I have myself been this week, much weakened with the Distemper. God calls me to look inward; and be very thankful for His merciful Sparing of me; and to consider the analogous Maladies in my own Soul, which I am to deprecate. First, I must be careful that my Soul do not cast up any glorious

---

[1] A physician and voluminous writer in prose and verse. See *Dictionary of National Biography*, v. 129.

Truths of God; nor nauseate any Interests and Practices of Piety. Secondly, I must be careful, that my Bowels be alwayes kept in a due Frame; even those of Compassion to all the miserable in the World.

8/9 *d.* 7 *m. Satureday./Lords-day.* I employ'd myself in the Exercises of a *Vigil* before the Lord. Herein I cried unto Him for a Defence against the Malice of the wicked Men, that are Enemies unto me, and unto my Serviceableness; and for a mighty Success to my Ministry, and Presence of His with me in the Services of the Day ensuing. But that which called me more particularly into the Dust before the Lord, was this. My learned Friend *Whiston* (from whom I have this week received an Account of his Proceedings,) is likely to raise a prodigious Dust in the world, by reviving the *Arian* Opinions. He revives them with more than ordinary Advantages, and I am likely to have my own Mind shock'd with more than ordinary Temptations on this Occasion. Wherefore, I cry most ardently unto the glorious Lord, that He would graciously enlighten me; cause me to take up right Thoughts of my dear Jesus, and of His Holy Spirit; lead me into all Truth, and keep me from Error, and show me my Duty, and never leave me to hurt any Interest of His Kingdome in the World.[1] And,

1. [*September* 9.] G. D. Great Prayer and Study, that I may not mislead my Flock in any Thing, must be one Article of my *Good Devised* for them. And an Endeavour to establish them in the true Doctrine of the Trinity.

2. G. D. I will write down certain Questions of the last Importance to his great Interests, and oblige *Cresy* to write as distinct Answers as he can unto the Quæstions, and show me his Answers.

[1] It could not have soothed Mather's pride to hear the President of Harvard College, at Commencement in 1712, take publicly the Whistonian notion of the Flood. Sewall, *Diary*, II. 355. See also a curious letter of the deist Thomas Chubb written in 1745, on the Whiston theory. *Proceedings*, XLIII. 648.

Q. 1. *What was the Errand which God sent you into the world upon?*

Q. 2. *What can you see in your present Condition to be bewayled?*

Q. 3. *What is your Plea with God, for the Pardon of your Sin?*

Q. 4. *What is it that you desire your great Saviour to do for you?*

Q. 5. *What Exercises of Piety do you resolve to make your daily Practice?*

Q. 6. *How do you desire and resolve, with the Help of Heaven, to spend your Time?*

3. G. D. There dwells in this Town, a Daughter to my late Kinsman of *Hampton*. I will discourse with her about her greatest Interests, and bestow some agreeable Book of Piety upon her.

4. G. D. To explain and maintain the glorious Doctrine of the *Trinity*, is now like to be as great a Service to the Church of God, as can be called for since the learned *Whiston*, does with so surprising Circumstances of Assurance, revive the Cause of *Arianism*. That Person particularly applying himself to *me* on this Occasion, it will be my Duty to do something on the Behalf of the Truth which is now endangered I would therefore now bend my Studies that way; and lift up humble and fervent Cries to the glorious Lord, for His Direction.

5. G. D. The religious Societies are languishing. I would in my public Discourses, earnestly call upon the Christians in the Neighbourhood, to revive them, and increase them; and among the Exercises at them; to sett apart Evenings for Prayers that the Spirit of converting Grace may be poured out upon the Neighbourhood.

6. G. D. Here is a poor Stranger and Scotchman cast into my Neighbourhood, who is languishing with an Hectic, and in Circumstances both of Soul and Body which call for great Compassion. I will endeavour to do all I can for him, and stir up the Neighbours also to bestow all needfull Succours upon him. (αρεσκιν)[1]

[1] Areskin.

14 *d.* 7 *m. Friday.* I sett apart this Day, for Prayers and Alms; with Fasting before the Lord; that I might obtain the Pardon of my manifold Offences to Heaven, and the Blessings of God, òn my Ministry, and on my Family, and on His People.

This Day was brightened, with sweet Communications from Heaven to my Mind. I am this Day assured, that my Sins, which are many are forgiven me; and that the glorious Lord has wondrous Blessings in store for me.

7. G. D. Our Saviour has left *His Peace*, as a Legacy to His Disciples, and, *glorious Things are spoken of thee, O Thou Peace of God!* I am afraid whether I so fully understand the Meaning of that *Peace*, as I ought to do; and much more, whether I live in the Enjoyment of it. I will therefore now apply my Prayers and my Studies, this Way more than ever in my Life before. Oh! that I may prosper therein and arrive to that Peace, in which I have hitherto been so defective!

1. [*September* 16.] G. D. The Bills putt up in our Congregation, will not only direct my Visits, but also afford a Direction to my Dispersion of Books of Piety in the Neighbourhood. Especially in three Cases:

First, when Persons are bound to Sea;

Secondly, when Persons are fallen into some great Affliction.

Thirdly, when Persons have been blessed with a Recovery from Sickness.

In these Cases, I would endeavour to give or send suitable Books unto the Persons concerned in them.

16 *d.* 7 *m. Lords-Day.* I went unto the Holy One at His Table this Day, on two important Errands.

First, I considered the Sacrifice of my Saviour, as making Atonement for all my Sins, which are Works of Darkness, and so Redeeming and Rescuing of me, from the Darkness which my Sins have brought upon me. I considered that Sacrifice as purchasing for me a Deliverance from eternal Darkness; but then also purchasing my Deliverance from the Darkness of Ignorance in the Things of God. I applied this in a singular Manner to the glorious Mystery of the Trinity: that I may not be in the Dark, or left unto any fatal Errors about that Mystery; that I may entertain right and bright Thoughts concerning it; that I may be able to serve the Church of God in that grand Concern, when it shall be Labouring.

Secondly. I considered, that astonishing Benefit, of the Peace, which my Saviour has made His Legacy to His people. I considered the Death and Blood of my Saviour as purchasing of it, I pleaded it with God; and laid Hold on the Peace of an offered Reconciliation with Him. I thereupon, look'd up unto the Lord, that I may be brought into an Acquaintance with the whole Mystery of Practical Christianity, which belongs to the Peace of God, ruling in the Hearts of His children; yea, an experimental Acquaintance with it. And indeed, the Lord now gave me a clear Idea of it; what were the Disturbances which are allay'd and suppress'd and conquer'd in it, and how it conquers them, and on what Principles; and what Satisfactions it fills the mind withal. I may hereafter enlarge upon it.

2. G. D. Yesterday preaching on the Improvement we should make of the Confusion come upon us, by the Defeat, which an horrible Tempest has occasion'd unto our *Canadian* Enterprise,[1] I described the Conduct of the prudent and pious on such an Occasion; especially in point of an awakened Repentance; which Advice I desire myself most particularly to conform unto.

But then, I would on this Occasion, mightily sett before my Children, the Evil that pursueth Sinners, and warn them to avoid it. I would also do more than ever to gett my Children under the shadow of the Wings of their Saviour; since tis likely to be a very calamitous Day among ourselves, and in the World.

3. G. D. I have a Nephew in the Town, who lives with a Ship-builder. I will consider his Temptations, and call for him, and talk with him, and bestow Books of Piety on him. (Ἰω᾽ν Φιλιπς.)[2]

---

[1] See Sewall, *Diary*, II. 322.   [2] John Phillips.

4. G. D. I have a Thought coming into my mind, that by bespeaking and procuring the Praises of the glorious God, acknowledging of Him, and bringing others to acknowledge Him, I answer the End of my Being. There are certain Points, wherein the great God has infinitely obliged Mankind, and yett they take little Notice of His Goodness. I am desirous, as soon as I can find Time, to consider certain common Favours, wherein Mankind enjoy most comprehensive Benefits, but are not suitably affected with the divine Goodness in them. And I would bespeak the Praises of devout Minds unto God, on these Occasions. Such are, the Use of *Spectacles*, the *Mariner's Compass;* Printing; *Shorthand;* the Instruments whereby *Time* is measured.

5. G. D. Propose in the *Society for Suppression of Disorders*, whether it may not be worth the while, to publish and scatter thro' the Countrey, a very brief Essay, about the Nature of an *Oath*, with some serious and suitable Directions about the Duty of *Swearing;* because, the *Fear of an Oath*, is too much laid aside, and forgotten among us; our Courts have too much inconsiderate *Swearing* in them.

6. G. D. There is a poor, helpless Woman, in our Neighbourhood, of whom, among the rest, I will take a very particular Care, when the Winter comes on. (λαξ.)[1]

7. G. D. Happening to lodge in a Place, where some Vermine assaulted me, I thought, the Assault of those Vermine should be improved by me, as a call to Repentance and Piety; not only in the way of considering myself, as among the Enemies of God, contemptibly punished by these his little Armies; but also, in the way of occasional Reflection, considering the ill Qualities and Actions of those Vermine, and what I have Analogous to them in my own Heart and Life, and bewayling of those things before the Lord.

[1] Lax.

22/23 *d. 7 m. Satureday night.* I sett apart a Portion of this Night for the Exercises of a Sacred *Vigil.*

First, one Prayer from the Cheef of Sinners prostrate in the Dust, epresented unto the Lord, my Faith of One God, in three Subsistences, and of the Second of these, assuming and advancing the Man Jesus into an ineffable Union with Himself. But then, I cried unto Him, that I might be led into right Thoughts about the glorious object of my Love, and Hope, and Joy, and of all my Life; and not be left unto any Errors about that glorious Mystery; and that I may be made an happy Instrument of communicating Light unto His People Concerning it. I declared, my only Design, and Desire, to be, that I may pay due Acknowledgments unto Him; and bring others in a right Manner to acknowledge Him. I thought I would then go Sing, Psal. xxv. 14. and Lo, it was the very first Place, at which my Psalter opened! Then, in another Prayer, I cried unto the Lord, for Defence and Shelter against the Enemies of my Serviceableness. Having obtained the Pardon of my Sins, with a joyful Assurance of my pardon, I found my Heart melted easily to forgive and forgett all the Injuries of my Enemies. Yett I could not but ask of the Lord, that the Floods of the Ungodly may not be able to hurt my Serviceableness; but that He would grant me some further Tokens for Good, that may confound their Malice wonderfully. Oh! For some good News from the other side of the *Atlantic!* Rising to sing some agreeable Psalms, my Psalmbook, again surprizingly opened, at the Conclusion of Psal. LVI. and the Beginning of Psal. LVII.

I also besought of the Lord, several other Favours. The Conversion of my Children; especially of my son *Increase;* and a mighty Effusion of the Spirit of Grace on my Flock. And a right Understanding of the strange Dispensations of Heaven at this Day in the World; Especially in the late Inspirations of so many Extaticks beyond Sea; which appear to me, a Matter to be entertained and considered with a very great Attention.

And a Smile of Heaven, on my intended Journey to *Salem.*

1. [*September* 23.] G. D. I am strangely accommodated, with a Number of *Bibles*, to be distributed among the poor Children of my Flock. I will use all the Discretion, and all the Diligence I can, in making the Distribution. And I will make it a sweet Occasion to bring People into a

Resolution, to Read the Word of God, with Supplications over it.

2. G. D. It is Time for me to fix my three elder Daughters, in the opificial and beneficial Mysteries, wherein they should be well-instructed; that they may do good unto others; and if they should be reduced into Necessities, unto themselves also.

For *Katy*, I determine, Knowledge in Physic, and the Preparation, and the Dispensation of noble Medicines.

For *Nibby*, and *Nancy*, I will consult their Inclinations.

3. G. D. I have a young Kinsman, who has entred on the evangelical Ministry, and has taken the charge of a little Flock in *Connecticot*-Colony. I would not only discourse to him such Things as may be of Use to him, in his Discharge of his Ministry, but also out of my Library bestow some useful Books upon him; such as P. *Martyr's Common Places*, etc. and by which his young Studies may be assisted. (ελεαζαρ Τιλλιαμς).[1]

4. G. D. I am, with all possible Resignation to the Disposals of the glorious Lord, intending a Journey to *Salem* this Week. My Intention is, to endeavour an Healing of all Tendency to Discord there, and to do all the other Good that I can possibly devise. Wherefore, acknowledging that the Way of Man is not in himself, I humbly cast myself on the Conduct of my admirable Saviour.

5. G. D. The worthy Minister of *Fairfield*,[2] meets with much Ingratitude and Discouragement from his people. Tho' they be a very numerous People, yett they afflict him with grievous Meannesses of Subsistence.

The Deputy-Governour of that Colony,[3] is a member of his Church. I have an Inclination to write as cogently and as pungently as I can unto that Gentleman, and mind him of his Duty; and press him to stir up the People unto

---

[1] Eleazar Williams, of Mansfield, Connecticut..

[2] Rev. Joseph Webb (1666–1732).   [3] Nathan Gold (1723).

their Duty; it being in his Power doubtless to do much that way, if he do what he ought to do.

28 *d*. 7 *m*. 6. G. D. I am this Day undertaking, with the Leave and Help of my glorious Lord, a Journey to *Salem*. There are many Poor in *Salem*. I would endeavour there to sett forward Things for the Releef of the Poor. And I will particularly carry a Number of Bibles to be bestow'd upon them.

7. G. D. Putting on my Cloathes in the Morning, I considered, that I might find in the Habits and Actions of Christianity, something that might be very Analogous to the several Parts of my Apparrel; and that I might here-upon be furnished with such Thoughts, and Wishes, and Prayers, as that having them, while I am Dressing myself, often formed in my Mind, I may have my Soul at length cloathed with glorious Garments. I must reserve this Design to be prosecuted and exhibited in a Collection of Thoughts, elsewhere to be laid together.

1. [*September* 30.] G. D. Tho' I am continually doing such a Thing in my Practice, yett I would hereafter more explicitly and with plainer Intimations of my Desire, in my Conversation with the more polite Part of my people, make it fashionable to have this Point brought into Con-sideration, when they are in a Conversation: *What Good is to be done before we part?*

2. G. D. The Children, whom I have travelling with me, in my Chariot, on the Road, I would fill my Time, with many profitable and agreeable Instructions to them.

3. G. D. And here at *Salem*, I forward the setting up of a charity Schole.

2 *d*. 8 *m*. [*October*.] *Tuesday*. Returning from *Salem*, where I have seen marvellous Blessings and Favours of Heaven, I find about 7 h. in the Evening, at my coming home, the poor Town of *Boston* in Flames; A Fire broke forth in the Heart of the Town, which Consumes the famous

Old-Meeting house, and the Statehouse, and whole Streets of other Buildings, not stopping till near 2 h. in the Morning.[1]

4. G. D. This lamentable Occasion, brings me into a new Field of *good Devices;* and a large one. Wherefore I sett myself this Day, to go among the afflicted, and see what is to be done for the Welfare of the distressed Inhabitants; and apply myself with all possible Assiduities to be useful unto them. The Contrivances are not capable of Enumeration. I will only mention this; that I would endeavour with the Help of Heaven, on the Lecture to morrow, to dispense the Admonitions of Piety, that shall be most agreeable unto the present Occasion.

5. G. D. Behold also a fresh Occasion to excite the general Society, for the suppression of Disorders, to do some singular Thing, in Prosecution of their main Intention. Lett that be the Question of this Evening; *What singular Thing shall we now do, under our present Awakenings?*

4 *d.* 8 *m. Thursday.* The Glorious Lord this Day renewes to me astonishing Testimonies of His Favour for me. A very vast Assembly of people came together, at the Place assigned for the Lecture. I was greatly assisted of the Lord, in praying with them, and yett more in preaching to them. I had an Opportunity to entertain the People of this, and the Neighbour Towns, with such Things, as were seasonable to the solemn Occasion, which the late awful Dispensations of the divine Providence had laid before us. The Hand of the Lord was mightily with me; and the People were after an unusual Manner affected with what was delivered; a strange Impression was made upon them. These Triumphs of Serviceableness, are marvellous

---

[1] He prefixed to the sermon preached two days after the fire, an account of the visitation, which was reprinted in I. *Mass. Hist. Collections*, v. 52. One of the shops destroyed was that of N. Boone the printer, but six other printers suffered in the same way. A volume of Mather's was "pluckt out of the burning" and afterwards printed, with a title *Meditations on the Glory of the Heavenly World.* See Sewall, *Diary*, II. 323.

Answers of Prayer, Tokens for Good, and Confusions to my foolish Adversaries.

I am this Day also surprised with some other Favours of the Lord, graciously hearing my Supplications.

One of them is this. Letters from *London*, this Day received, give me to understand, that the Libels which an abominable Crue, sent over from hence thither the last Winter, to be published for my Defammation there, were suppressed and destroyed and burnt, by the Influences of one, from whom I had as little Reason to expect such a Thing, as from almost any Man in the World. God raised up our new Lieutenant Governour[1] to be a mighty Friend unto me there.

6. G. D. Poverty appears in very many new Objects of Charity, made such, by the late Conflagration. I now, first encourage the charitable Gentlemen, who are looking out for them. And, then; I am dispensing among them so many Kindnesses, that it is unto no Purpose, for me to mention particular Instances.

7. G. D. There is a particular Improvement in Piety, to which I am to be awakened, by the Circumstances of the late Calamity, brought upon this Town of my Nativity.

1. [*October* 7.] G. D. The sad Condition of the Old Church in the Loss of their Temple, by the late Fire, administers unto me an Occasion of warning my own Church, to take heed of offending Heaven by such Things, as may procure to us, the same Calamity.

2. G. D. Good God, quicken me to a greater Vigour, and Fervour, and Frequency, in inculcating these great Points upon my Children; even with daily Admonitions.

First: That and how the Acknowledgments of God are to fill their Lives; this to be made the chief End of their Lives; and what Encouragements they have to live unto God.

[1] William Tailer.

Secondly. The Methods of Conversing with their admirable Saviour.

Thirdly. The Worth of Time, and the noblest Way of spending it.

Fourthly. The Excellencies and Expedients of Usefulness as far as they can extend their Influences.

Fifthly. A Spirit reconciled unto low, mean, humbling Circumstances in an evil World.

3. G. D. My Wife has a Cosin-german, who is a Gentlewoman, capable not only of Improvements in refined Piety, but also of doing much Good with her Estate in the World. The feeble State of her Health, will add unto my Opportunities in my Conversation with her, to pursue both of those Intentions; and I would accordingly endeavour it. (Mrs. Κλαρκ)[1]

4. G. D. It may serve the Interests of Piety, and be serviceable and agreeable to many good Purposes, if I give to the Public by the way of the Press, the Sermon which I preached the last Thursday.

Wherefore I do transcribe it for the Press, and give it the Title of, ADVICE FROM TABERAH. *A Sermon preached after the Terrible FIRE, which (attended with some very lamentable and memorable Circumstances) on Oct. 2. 3, 1711), laid a considerable Part of* Boston *in Ashes.*[2]

5. G. D. There is a single Gentlewoman in this Town, who is Mistress of a pretty good Estate; I would endeavour to have some effectual Advice convey'd unto her, that she may both living and dying devote a considerable Interest unto pious Uses.

11 *d.* 8 *m. Thursday.* This Day was devoted unto Supplications with Fasting, thro' the Province. I bore my Part, and had the Help of Heaven, in the Work of the Day.

[1] Mrs. Sarah Clark. See p. 78, *supra.*

[2] Printed by B. Green. Taberah was the name of a place in the wilderness of Paran, given from the fact of a burning among the people by the "fire of the Lord" which there occurred. Num. XI. 3.

Our Congregation also did theirs. And they made a Collection for the Releef of the poor Sufferers by the Fire, amounting to near two hundred Pounds.

6. G. D. There are poor Men, wounded in the late Fire, by the Blowing up of Houses. I would visit them, and use my best Endeavours, that they may come as Gold out of the Fire. I would also take some Care that they and their Families be releeved from the Money which the public Charity has provided for them.

7. G. D. The glorious Lord having remarkably preserved me and my Serviceableness (my darling,) from the Power of the Dog, I propose quickly to keep a *Day of Thanksgiving* in Secret on that Occasion; and then I shall more particularly excogitate further Methods of Improvement in all Holiness of Conversation.

1. (14 *d*. 8 *m*.) G. D. This Day, being the Day for the Administration of the Eucharist, I earnestly call upon the Church, whereof I am the Servant, especially for four Things. First; that none of them secretly indulge themselves in any Way of Wickedness. Secondly; that many watchful, fruitful, exemplary Christians may be found among them. Thirdly; that they be not unmindful of the Holy Covenant, whereof they ly under the Strongest Obligations. Fourthly; that they approach and observe the Supper of the Lord, with all possible Solemnity. I warn them, that I am afraid the glorious Lord, is coming out against the Church, and going, perhaps quickly to give a terrible Shake unto it.

14 *d*. 8 *m*. *Lords-Day*. This Day at the Lord's-Table, my Errands were, to acknowledge the Mysteries of Redemption, and venture my Soul upon the evangelical Revelation of them. And to lay hold on the Benefits proposed in them; especially the Cure of the Maladies yett remaining in my Spirit; most of all, my Disposition to envy the Favours of God unto other Men. But then, I laboured mightily to

obtain it of the Lord, that His Displeasure against the Church may be turned away; and that abundance of Holy watchful, fruitful Christians, may therefore be found among us.

2. G. D.   Tis a Consideration that should find some room in my Mind. I am continually crying to God, for His Favour to my Children; that they may be pious, useful, happy Children. But I ought to bewayl some inexpressible Circumstances of Meanness, relating to their Original, their Production and Conception. I ought to obtain a Pardon thro' the Blood of that Holy Thing, which was Born of the Virgin. That so no Vileness of that Nature may have any Influence, to render them abominable to Heaven, and cast them out of its favourable Protection.

3. G. D.   The Husband of my late Sister *Jerusha*, what shall I do for him?[1] Such Discourses as may befriend and advance the Interests of Piety in him, whereof he is an hearty Lover; the presenting of him with agreeable Books of Piety; and the perswading of him, to unite with a Number of serious young Men of a suitable Quality, in a conversation of a religious Importance; these are the Things, which I do at present think of.

4. G. D.   My *Advice from Taberah*, will be published this week; I would use my Endeavours, that all or most of the Persons, who have been Sufferers in the late Fire, may have the Book presented unto them. It may be very seasonable to lodge these Admonitions with them, while the Sense of their Calamity is yett fresh upon them.

5. G. D.   Methinks, it would be a practicable, and a profitable Thing, for me, once a Quarter, to have either the principal Persons belonging unto our several religious Societies together, or, separately to discourse with them, about the Interests of the Societies; what may be further done, that Piety may flourish in them, and by their Means, in the Neighbourhood.

[1] Peter Oliver.

6. G. D. Here is in my Neighbourhood, a Family, where the poor old Man, has for more than threescore Years followed the Sea, and is to this Day in his Sins; the Woman, is sick, and in Distresses. I must endeavour to releeve their Wants; and to do what I can for the Souls of both of them.

7. G. D. In order to the Comfort of my own Mind, and that I may the better walk in the Light, I form an Examination of myself, relating to the grand End of my Life, and all my Actions; and relating to the three Idols, to which all ungodly men devote themselves.

The End at which I would aim in all, is, that the great GOD, and His CHRIST, may be acknowledged, gratified and glorified. My supreme Satisfaction lies in serving this End. When I find, that I reach unto this, here I stop. I ask to go no further. I am satisfied; I am fill'd with Joy unspeakable and full of Glory.

I abhor and I renounce, all that gives any obstruction to me, in prosecution of this glorious End.

More particularly,

I renounce the FLESH.

I make no further Allowance to, and Provision for, the *Flesh*, than God allows me.

I durst not please the *Flesh*, with anything that is displeasing to God.

I rebuke, I restrain, I deny the *Flesh* in its irregular Inclinations.

I don't place my *chief Good*, in having my *Flesh* accommodated.

I renounce the WORLD.

I do no wicked Thing to gain the *World;* would not sin for the *Gain of the whole World.*

I am content with such a Condition in the *World* as God will order for me; it appears well-ordered.

I dream not of Happiness in the great Things of this *World;* I see nothing here will make me happy.

The *sinful Customes* of this *World* do not carry me down the Stream thereof.

I renounce the DIVEL.

I do not hearken to my grand Adversary.

I am afraid of his *Devices.*

My Life is a continual *Warfare* against his *Temptations.*

1. [*October* 21.] G. D. The grievous Losses that are suffered by our Neighbours in their Interests, both at Sea, and on shore, give me fresh Opportunities, which I would employ with all possible Contrivance and Fervency to putt them upon such an Improvement in Piety, as these Dispensations call for. Oh! how earnestly will I now bespeak an Abatement of their Love and Zeal for this World, and their Concern to secure a Portion in a better World!

2. G. D. My Evening-Sacrifice in my Family when the Evening arrives, must have some Accessions made unto it. I am considering, what?

3. G. D. I am thinking, that I will sett myself to consider, which of my Relatives, have not yett very visible and credible Marks of serious Piety upon them; and I would in various Methods address them, and address Heaven for them, with unspeakable Importunity, that victorious Grace may visit them.

I take Notice of it with Wonder. We have religious People, whose nearest Relatives are poor, vain, carnal Creatures, utterly destitute of the Symptomes of Regeneration. And yett they seem very easy and thoughtless about them. While they are in this World well provided for, and carry it well towards them, they seem to take no further Thought about them. I would therefore not only myself be concerned for unregenerate Relatives, but also in my Ministry awaken all religious People to be more so, than many of them seem to be.

4. It will be a Service unto the common Cause of our holy Religion, to obtain from the southern Colonies, an Account, how the Missionaries of the Society for Propagation of Religion, invade and molest the Churches which are well instructed in Christianity, but leave neglected the Plantations that are paganizing.

5. G. D. I have now obtained, that by a prudent and faithful Visitation of the Indians, we are furnished with a

very punctual Account of the State of Christianity among them. We have a distinct and exact Account of their Circumstances; and we have something on which we may proceed unto numberless Actions for the Kingdome of our Saviour, and the Welfare of that miserable People. I propose, that the Commissioners of the Indian-affayrs, may now have their very frequent Meetings, and I suppose that we shall at every one of them, be led into such Projections and Purposes as will be of a lasting Advantage.

Those which I am now upon, are, to render Thanks unto some that have been useful unto our Affairs. To augment the Salaries of some that have been meritorious in the Service. To procure some Strength unto the Indian-Justices. And, to commission a worthy Englishman to be a Ruler unto them at *Little Compton.*

6. G. D. Diverse in my Neighbourhood, have uncomfortable Tidings, concerning the Death of desireable Relatives abroad; I would immediately visit them, and comfort them, and putt into their Hands those Books of Piety, which may help to carry them thro' their Afflictions.

7. G. D. A morning Cough, a little tussient Expectoration, at my first Waking and Rising in a Morning, has these many Years attended me. It is doubtless become useful to me; and the Stopping of it would be an hazardous Inconvenience. But now, it ought to raise a Disposition of Piety in me. I would have my Cough always accompanied with a Thought of this Importance; *Oh! that I may always cast up, and throw off, whatever may be inimical to the Health of my Soul! Every Lust, which like this Flegm, should be parted with; Lord, help me to part with it; yea, to take Pains that I may do so!*

1. [*October* 28.] G. D. I find it a marvellous Consolation, and Satisfaction unto the Neighbours, and a sensible Advantage unto the Exercise of Piety in them; for me in the Conclusion of my public Prayers, earnestly to entreat

of the glorious Lord, that He would graciously and suitably look down on the unmentionable, conceled, and reserved Cases in the Neighbourhood; the Bitterness known only to the Hearts that feel them. I would go on; and in this Action study to be yett more pathetical.

2. G. D. One of my Servants going to marry away, I must make it an Article of special Supplications before the Lord, that He would send a good Servant into my Family. I would therefore bewayle the Sins of my Behaviour towards my Servants; and bewayl my own being so poor a Servant of the Lord; and plead the Sacrifice of my Saviour, who appear'd in the form of a Servant, for my pardon, and for the desired Blessings.

3. G. D. I have a Brother-in-Law, that meets with new, and sad and sore Losses. I am afraid, I am afraid, the Spirit of this World is too much yett upon him; the Business of this World still too much hurries and ensnares him; a new Business adds to his Entanglements. I wish, I could see his Conversion to God accomplished. I would now take this Occasion, with all possible Insinuations, to prosecute the Intentions of Piety upon him.

4. G. D. It may be a Service to my Countrey, and an Imitation of our glorious Advocate in the Heavens, for me to vindicate this poor, envied, abused People of God, from the Reproaches of its malignant Adversaries. I purpose in the Audience of the General Assembly to make a Recapitulation and Acknowledgment of the *good Things* as yett found in the Countrey. If they see cause to order the Publication of it, it will give some satisfaction to the People of God abroad in the World. If they do not, however, I shall hereby be enabled with the more of Insinuation and Efficacy, to bear my faithful Testimonyes, which I propose to do, against the *ill Things* that are also found among us.[1]

[1] He preached this day the Lecture, but the Governor remained away because Mather was the preacher.

5. G. D. *The Society for the Suppression of Disorders;* must be extraordinarily call'd upon, to do something extraordinary upon their great Intention. Several Things are to be proposed unto them. Especially two orders, which are of late not observed. The one, that at least one good Proposal, be written down every Meeting, to be afterwards again examined, whether it have been prosecuted. The other that he, at whose [House] we meet in the Turn, shall be particularly obliged to offer one Proposal unto Consideration.

6. G. D. I am advised of some young Men in my Neighbourhood, who are undoing their Souls by running away from God, into great Apostasies and Impieties. I must earnestly call upon as many of them as I can, and endeavour to recover them.

7. G. D. I am very sensible, that *Envy* is a very considerable part of the *Satanic Image* in the Soul; and the working of it, very displeasing to the good *Spirit* of God. The *Charity that envies not*, is a very vital and lovely Stroke in the *Image* of my sweet Saviour, after which I ought to aspire exceedingly. And how far it may engage the good Providence of the Holy One, to look favourably upon me, tis with Him. I am desirous to have one Stroke more at this Matter, by more distinctly forming these Resolutions, with an Eye unto my dear Saviour, to form in me the Dispositions proper for them, and to help me in the Executing of them.

First: The first and least Ebullition of an *envious Thought* at the Prosperity of another Man, I would rebuke it and suppress it immediately, with all possible Indignation; and in a Way of the most expressive Contradiction to it, lift up my Heart unto God, with my *Thanks* to Him for the Good He has done to that Man, and my *Prayers* and *Hopes* for the Continuance of it.

Secondly; Upon all *occasional Views* of the Blessings and Comforts enjoy'd by other Men, I would shape a Thought of Satisfaction in the *Sovereignty*, and the *Wisdome*, and the *Goodness* of the Glorious

God, which is exercised in it; and make that Article of their Prosperity, a particular Article of my Praises unto the Lord on their behalf; with my Wishes, that they may improve it for His Glory.

Thirdly: When I am sitting with my Friends in their Houses, and walking the Streets where I may see some of their most visible Possessions, I would employ the Ejaculations of my Mind, unto the blessed God, in as real, and sincere Acknowledgments of His granting this Prosperity unto them, and with as true a Pleasure of Soul at the Prospect, as if it were *all my own*. Yea, and I would obtain a Liesure, to walk about the Place; and go round about the Neighbourhood, and tell the Smiles of God upon it, and mark well their Enjoyments, and consider their Consolations, and upon each of them gett my Soul raised into those Dispositions of Joy, which I ought to have, when I see the *Goodness* of the blessed God shining forth in so obliging a Manner; with Supplications for my Neighbours, that they may bring forth much of that Fruit, by which He may be glorified.

1. [*November* 4.] G. D. Entertaining a Purpose, if the glorious Lord, will give me Life and Strength, to visit again all the Families of the Flock, I would furnish myself with an agreeable Book, to be left in them all. I would therefore compose, and preach, and print a little Book, that shall contain the principal Things which a Pastor has to desire from and for his People. I would form the Composure, with all suitable Contrivance and Adaptation, and look up to Heaven about it; and when tis in my Hands, I would putt it into theirs.

2. G. D. My Little Daughter *Nancy*, is under an ill State of Health. I must not only look up to God and use all due Means for the Health of the Child, but also make her Illness an Occasion for most earnest Inculcations of Piety unto her.

3. G. D. The Minister of *Water-town Farms* is my Kinsman, and one desirous to do good in the World.[1] The best Service I can do for him, is to procure him Opportunities of being serviceable. I would particularly procure him some Opportunities to be useful, in the Inspection of the

[1] Rev. William Williams.

Indians at *Natick;* where the Interests of Christianity are extremely languishing.

4. G. D. God has blessed my Applications unto *Woburn,* for the bruising of Satan, who had begun to raise grievous Contentions there.[1] It was thought, that it would be a confirming and Finishing stroke on that Good work, if I would give a Lecture unto that People. I assign a Time for it; purposing to preach as charming Things as I can unto them, on Rom. 15. 14. *I am perswaded you are full of Goodness.*

7 d. 9 m. [*November.*] *Wednesday.* This Day I accomplish my Purpose for *Woburn,* and had many Smiles of Heaven on my Journey; some that were surprising ones.

5. G. D. Tis moved that the Ministers in this Place may join in an Address to the Queen, that may be of Consequence to these Colonies. I would consider the Motion; and if it may do any good, I would prosecute it.

6. G. D. There is a Woman arrived in my Neighbourhood, who was once in better Circumstances, but is now reduced unto the lowest Poverty; and but meanly provided for the Circumstances of the approaching Winter. I will dispense Releefs unto her. (Δαβιε).[2]

9 d. 9 m. Friday. I sett apart this Day for Prayers and Alms, with Fasting before the Lord, that I might procure such Blessings as I want for myself, my Family, my Ministry, my Friends, and the People of God. And especially, that I may from *Scotland,* and from *England,* receive such Things, as may further encourage me in the Service of the Lord.

The Work of the Day left a desireable, and a purifying Impression on my Mind.

7. G. D. Tis a practice that I am not unus'd unto; but I find, it will be for the Interest of God, and the Advance-

---

[1] On the "disorderly seating of many persons in the house of God." Sewall, *History of Woburn,* 186.   [2] Davie.

ment of His Kingdome, in my Heart and Life; that I should most explicitly and pathetically renew my Resolutions for the Practising of it; that whenever I perceive an ill Thought arising in my Mind, I will forever extinguish it, and contradict it, with forming a good Thought, that shall be directly contrary unto it. More particularly; upon a *proud* Thought, I will immediately form a Thought that shall carry the greatest Self-abasement, and Self-abhorrence in it. Upon an *impure* Thought, I will immediately form a Thought, that shall carry in it, a Resignation of myself unto the Spirit of Holiness, and an Invocation of Him to take possession of me. Upon an *envious* Thought, I will immediately form a Thought that shall carry in it, some ardent Wish for the Prosperity of the Person whom I had in my View. Upon a *revengeful* Thought, I will immediately form a Thought that shall carry in it some sincere Desires for Blessings on the Person that has injured me. Finally, upon a Thought of *Discouragement*, from the Labour of being serviceable, or from the Malice, and the Number, and the Power of them that are Enemies to my Serviceableness, I will immediately form a Thought, that shall carry in it, a cheerful Dependence on the Assistence, and Protection of the glorious Lord, and an unfainting Resolution to be always abounding in the Work of the Lord. My best Way will be to putt these Thoughts usually into the Form of *Ejaculations*, and so send them up to Heaven.

1. [*November* 11.] G. D. There has been this last Week, a remarkable Instance of the divine Judgments on an infamous Harlott. There are more of her Tribe, and of their bewitched Followers, in the Neighbourhood. I would make a public Improvement of this Instance; to warn them against the Pathes of the Destroyer.

11 *d.* 9 *m. Lord's-Day.* The special Errands on which I went this day unto the Table of the Lord, were these.

First, I considered, that as Bread strengthens the Children of Men, so my Spirit was to look for Strength to be comunicated from a Christ, becoming my Food, in the ordinance now before me. I considered such a spiritual Strength as purchased for me, by the Death of my dear Jesus, and conveyed from Him to those who rely upon Him for the Conveyance of it. I declared my Faith of this; and in Token thereof received the Bread of the Eucharist. Then I considered, and confessed my own Feebleness in many Instances. And I look'd up to my glorious Lord, for Strength; to be more fixed with my Thoughts on the proper Objects and Matters in the Worship of God; to be more able in Reasoning and Arguing for the Cause of God; and in Discerning some dark Things about His Kingdome. To be more vigorous and courageous in doing my Duty. To repel Temptations with more of Resolution. To overcome the Lusts of the Flesh, with a Strength within. To bear Afflictions from God, and Injuries from Men. And be strong in every Grace of Christ Jesus; especially, strong in Faith giving Glory to God.

Secondly. Being very sensible, what need I have to grow in Humility, I entred into a Contemplation of the Humiliation whereto my humble Jesus, did submitt, when He appeared among us. I herein beheld the Price, for the Grace of Humility to be given unto His People. I declared my Desire of this Grace. And receiving the Cup, I proceed thereon to implore my glorious Lord, that I may have the Grace; to think so meanly of myself, as a Sinner of such Vileness ought to do. To justify God in all my abasing Circumstances, and entertain them with a due Judging and Loathing of myself. To entertain the common Lott of mankind in various Frailties, with a suitable Submission to them. To be afraid of seeking to aggrandize myself in this World. To encounter Indignities with much Patience, and Silence; and be only driven thereby to be more affected with my own evil Deservings. And be one of the poor in Spirit, and of the lowly whom the most High will have Respect unto.

2. G. D. If any little Occasion for my Anger, do occur by any Neglect, or by something amiss, in my Family, I would with all possible Decency govern my Passion. My Anger shall not break out, into any froward, peevish, indecent Expressions. I will only lett them see, that I don't like what I take notice of. But this is not all. I would

on such an Occasion, immediately divert, and break off, —
But what shall I say? — and proceed unto the sorrowful
Mention of some greater Miscarriage, in our Conduct about
our Souls, which what now offends me, may lead me to
reflect upon.

3. G. D. I have a Nephew now a Student at *Cambridge.* I would use various Means, both to preserve him
from Temptations and prepare him for Services. I would
send for him, talk with him, and bestow agreeable Books
of Piety upon him. (θομας Ταλτερ.)[1]

I thought it might be a service for this poor Countrey
abroad in the World; especially among our European
Brethren that enquire after us; if my late Sermon wherein
I vindicated the Countrey might be published at *London.*
My Concession for such a Publication, has the more
of something like Vertue in it, inasmuch as the General
Assembly shew'd themselves covetous and ungrateful and
unworthy enough, in their taking no public Notice of a
Service, which they would Man by Man, every one confess
to be a meritorious one. Wherefore I sent the Sermon to
our Agent in *London,* with an agreeable Dedication thereof
unto him; that it may be there printed, if he please, and
sent into all Parts, where it may be serviceable. As I
thought a sweet Satisfaction in the Neglects of a people
here, to acknowledge the good that is done for them, is
an Imitation of my dear Saviour; so it would be to be an
Advocate for them in a far Countrey. I entituled it; THE
BALANCES OF EQUITY. *A brief Essay on the Just Allowances, to be made, both for* Good *Things, and for* Evil, *wherever
they are to be mett withal. And some Justice particularly
done, to a countrey, that has been sometimes Misrepresented
in the world.*

4. G. D. With the Service newly mention'd which will
be productive of many more, if God smile upon it, I am

[1] Thomas Walter.

now furnishing our Agent at *London*, with such things as may be serviceable to our distressed Countrey.

14 *d.* 9 *m. Wednesday.* This Day, I endeavour to execute of my purpose of keeping a Day of THANKSGIVING, in Secret before the Lord; Especially, to render my Thanks unto Heaven, from my Remarkable præservations from the Malice and Envy of the Men, that are disaffected unto me, and unto my Serviceableness.

After the præparatory Duties of the Morning; and after the Praises offered up to God, for personal and domestic Blessings, in my Family-Sacrifices, and with Endeavours to have my Mind filled with parenthetical and occasional, and ejaculatory Hallelujahs dispatch'd unto Heaven, upon all Occurrences that presented themselves, I spent much of the Forenoon, in such Acknowledgments of the glorious Lord, as I intended in the Devoting of this Day unto Him.

In particular, prostrate in the Dust before the Lord, I humbly confessed my Sins, which had provoked Him, to raise me up Adversaries, who were many, and hate me with a cruel Hatred; and I begged the Pardon of them, thro' the Blood of the great Sacrifice. But then I did with Admiration and Astonishment, celebrate the good Hand of God; which had restrained these Adversaries, and prevented from time to time the Publication of their Libels; and continued and multiplied my Opportunities to do good; and employed me in the Greatest Congregations; and made use of my Pen to write many Books for the Advancement of His Kingdome; Yea, and had strangely encouraged and fortified my Serviceableness, by such Marks of Respect from other Parts of the World, as no Person in *America* has ever yett received before me. And I praised the Lord for this, as a Favour not inferiour to the rest; that He had made my Adversaries useful unto me, for the increasing of my Circumspection, in my Walk, and my Conversation with Heaven; and He had also helped me to forgive my Adversaries, and to treat them with the meek Spirit of Christianity. In these Things, I magnified the sovereign Grace of God unto the Chief of Sinners. I adored His Power, His Wisdome, His Mercy, and His Faithfulness, and His Readiness to hear the Prayers of them that seek Him, and serve Him. I glorified God as the Father, who had used a fatherly Compassion in His Dealings with me; God the Son, who had brought me into an Adoption by the Father; God the Spirit, who had made me one of His Temples, and kept me from

Hurt by the Stones thrown at me.   But I more particularly addressed with my Praises, God the Son, as Incarnate in my blessed JESUS. I glorified Him, as the Head of the Church, and as having the divine Providence in the Government of the World under His more immediate Management.   I glorified Him, as having purchased my Deliverance from Reproaches, by His own suffering Reproaches, and matchless Indignities and Contumelies, when He made Himself a Sacrifice on my behalf.   I glorified Him as having the Divels in a Chain, and as having chained up the wicked Men who are under the Energy of the Divels.   I glorified Him, as having the good Angels under His Command, and as having sent His Angels to do good Offices for me.   I gave myself up to Him; and resolved with His Help, to go on in serving Him unto the uttermost; serving Him with all possible Activity all my Dayes; trusting Him to shelter me from the Rage of wicked Men, to which my Activity for Him and His Interest may render me obnoxious.

I sang agreeable Psalms.

In the Afternoon again prostrate in the Dust before the Lord, I begg'd of Him, to show me how I might glorify Him, in more significant Wayes than meer verbal Acknowledgments.   Particularly to direct me, and assist me, in my Design to preach over the Body of Divinity, with considerations of the Interest which the glory of my admirable Saviour has in every Part of it.   And because, I thought these two were very expressive Wayes of glorifying Him; first, I forgave my Adversaries, and heartily pray'd that they might have the Blessings of Goodness heaped upon them.   I declared, how much I should rejoice to see them turned unto God, and prosperous in the good Wayes of Piety.   I entreated, like a Child of *Jacob*, that these wicked *Edomites* might have their Hearts turned and changed. Secondly, I putt my Trust in my great Saviour to rescue me from the Mischiefs which these Adversaries may do unto me; to defend me from their implacable Fury; to make me, and keep me, a green Olive-tree in the House of my God.   I left my Cause in His Hands; I utterly forbore all Revenge upon them.   I did it purely out of Obedience to Him.   I relied upon Him to fulfil His Word unto me, in pleading my Cause against them.

After this, in some other Exercises I proceeded unto some Acknowledgments of the glorious God, in mentioning His Favours to me; which I reduced unto two Heads; those which related unto my *Ministry*, and those which related unto my *Family*.   Adding such as my Friends and the Public were Partakers of.

O my dear Saviour, wilt thou not encourage me in my Essayes to offer praise and glorify thee! Ah, my Lord, I will hope continually, and I will yett praise thee more and more.

5. G. D. I have now litt upon a good Projection to revive the languishing, and near expired Society, for Suppression of Disorders, in our part of the Town; which I would immediately putt in Execution.

6. G. D. There be two or three poor Creatures, under the Watch of our Church, who are fallen into Scandal. I must first of all, do all that I can to Recover them, and bring them unto Repentance, by private Applications to them. I must then proceed with the Discipline of the Church, that others may hear and fear.

7. G. D. I am now getting on my *Winter-Garments*. I would endeavour to do it, with agreeable Dispositions of Piety.

First, I would heartily bless the glorious God for supplying me with suitable and sufficient Garments. I would bewayl my Sin in my first Parents, that sinned away the Garments of Glory with which we were at first accommodated, and brought a wretched Nakedness upon us. I would confess my Obligations to my dear JESUS, who by submitting to the sufferings of being disrobed, purchased the Comforts of my Garments for me.

Secondly. I would putt on the Lord Jesus Christ, by a new Consent of my Soul, to be found in His Righteousness; and by fresh Contemplations and Resolutions, of such a Conformity to Him, that they who see me, may see much of Him.

Thirdly. I would come into a further Degree of Solicitude, that I may be clothed with the Spirit; and possessed by the Holy One, evidently resting on me, in the Inclinations of Holiness and Usefulness.

Fourthly. I would be sollicitous, to provide Clothing for the Poor that want it, and convey some Garments unto those who in the Cold may want a Covering.

1. [*November* 18.] G. D. Having dispatched a Course of Sermons on the Parable of the *Prodigal*, I would humbly look up to my glorious Lord, for His Direction, about

another Subject, which I may spend some Time upon, if He please to allow me any longer Time among His People.

2. G. D. There are Books of Piety, which I would look out for my wife, and commend unto her the Perusal of them.

And I would particularly advise her, that in the Religion of the Closet, which I know she maintains, it may [be] her practice, not only to preface her Prayers with Reading somewhat, either in the sacred Scriptures, or in such Books as these, but also to fetch from thence, and form, still some new Matter of Supplication.

3. G. D. I have an aged Father-in-Law at *Charlestown*, concerning whom I have a Suspicion arising in my Mind, that he may be very speedily and suddenly call'd out of this world. I would visit him as soon as I can, and in my Visit address him with such Discourse as may have a mighty Tendency and Cogency, to quicken his Præparation, for the heavenly World, and putt his Mind into the Posture wherein his Change is to be waited for.[1]

4. G. D. The Town of *Jamaica*, on *Long-Island*, is a sort of a Frontier for the Interests of the Non-Conformists and of true Piety in these Colonies. The Settlement of a worthy Minister there, would be a real Service to Religion. I have already laboured pretty far in it, and brought it near to an Accomplishment. But some further Strokes are necessary, which I [am] now endeavouring to give, that it may be perfectly accomplished.[2]

5. G. D. It will be of little Importance for me to enter into my Memorials, the Things projected and proposed from time to time, when I have my Interviews with the Commissioners for the Propagation of the Gospel among the *Indians*. However I will at this time insert here two

---

[1] John Phillips, who is intended, lived until 1726.

[2] George McNish, who came to this country in 1705, with Rev. Francis Makemie, became minister at Jamaica some time in 1711. Macdonald, *Sketch of the History of the Presbyterian Church in Jamaica*, 49.

or three Proposals, which I no sooner make than they are putt in Execution. One is, to send a couple of Missionaries unto the *Mohegin* Indians, and their Neighbours, in the Colony of *Connecticot*, which unto the Shame of us all, continue still in Paganism. Another is, to hasten the Ordination of a fitt Person unto the Church of Indians, whereof *Japhet* is the Pastor.[1] I also procured Presents to be made unto certain Indians, who are uncommon Examples of Temperance, and Abstemiousness, and Sobriety. An Hatt for each of them; which may be an Encouragement unto others to follow the Pattern these have given them.

6. G. D. There is a Family of a Justice in this Town, wherein the Man and his Wife, live in horrible Variance; a strife which threatens confusion and every Evil work. They will both of them hearken to me sooner perhaps than to any Person in the world. I will do what I can to sweeten their Spirits towards each other, and perswade them to such a Behaviour as may be for their Comfort and Honour. (Λυνδς.)[2]

7. G. D. Many, many, and marvellous, are the Obligations which my dear Saviour has laid upon me, to love Him, and serve Him. Among the astonishing Favours with which He has obliged me, I find my Heart very deeply affected, with this, that He has given me His *Laws*, which are all holy and just and good; He has taught me how to live unto God; He has prescribed me Rules how to escape the Pollutions and Confusions of this World; He has instructed me in the Methods of Piety; He has directed me, and commanded me to do those Things, by which my Mind immediately becomes rectified, enriched, and ennobled beyond all Expression. And He has advised me, how to spend my Time, in such a Manner, as is most worthy of a reasonable Creature.

[1] An Indian minister, who had labored for some years in the Narragansett country. Mather, *Bonifacius*, 199. See p. 190, *infra*.

[2] Lyndes.

It may not be amiss for me to cultivate this Disposition in me.

1. [*November* 25.]   G. D.   I have distinguished my large Flock, into many Tribes.   There are many Sorts of People whereof it is composed.   The Condition of the Souls in each, ought to be pertinently, and pathetically considered with me.   I would not only suit it in my Sermons, but also in the public Prayers, wherefore, when I am going forth to Minister before the Lord, I would often sett myself to think, what part of my Flock shall I now single out, and employ one considerable Part of the public Prayers on the Condition of it?   By this Method, that Part of the Flock may be singularly awakened unto the Consideration of their own Condition.   They may be instructed how to pray for themselves.   They may be quickened themselves to ask for the Blessings which we desire on their behalf! Yea, who can tell, how far the Holy Spirit of God may fall upon them?

2.   G. D.   There has been a surprising Display of Providence, and Answer of Prayer, in the neat Garments, wherewith my *Cresy* is clothed and armed for the Winter.   I will have the Child apprised of it, and made sensible what an efficacious Thing tis to trust in the Lord, and do good; and I would improve it as a most[1] Encouragement unto him, to apply himself unto the Service of his only Saviour.

3.   G. D.   I have another Kinsman at the Colledge, to whom I purpose to dispense Books, with such Admonitions of Piety, as may be useful to him.   (Στεφαν Τιλλιαμς.)[2]

I would particularly press upon my Kinsmen there, the Reading of two Lives in our Church-History; The Youngest *Shepards*, and my Brother's.

4.   G. D.   The Minister of *Newhaven*, having preached a Sermon in our Assembly, about the *False Hopes*, wherewith many deceive themselves, and some of our Hearers

---

[1] A word omitted.　　　　[2] Stephen Williams.

being willing to publish the Sermon, I encourage that
Matter; and more than so; because I take the Subject to
be of great Consequence for the Interests of Piety, and the
Souls of Men.   I will write a Præfatory Discourse upon it.[1]

5. G. D.   My *Religious Fisherman,* is now published.[2]
I will now have my Agents in several parts of the Countrey,
to lodge the Book where it is intended; and I will also
address diverse Merchants who carry on much of the Trade
of the Fishery, that when they have made good Voyages,
they will apply a few Pieces of Eight, unto the further dispersing of this Book among those for whom it is designed.

29 *d.* 9 *m.* 1711. *Thursday.*   The Mixtures of Mercy remembred in the Midst of Wrath, to this poor People in the
year Past, have obliged us unto a public *Thanksgiving;*
which was this Day attended.   The Lord favoured me with
precious Assistences, both in the private and the public
Duties of the Day.   Especially in this thing; I sett myself
to consider, that an Improvement in the *Love of God,* is
the Use, that I should make of all His favourable Dealings
with me and others.   And, I hope, I found the Flame of
that Holy *Love* enkindled in my Soul, with all the Dispositions of it.   My Heart also expanded in one Article of
praising the Lord in the Congregation; this was, when
with a Soul purified from Envy, I gave Thanks unto the
blessed God, for His Blessings granted unto other men.
I was glad of their Prosperity, and gave Thanks to a good,
and a wise God for it, as for my own.

6. G. D.   I have a Neighbour, my next Neighbour,
who is a very froward, frappish, peevish Creature; and
who in his ungoverned Passion committs many Offences;
He is an Aged Professor of Religion.   I must therefore, as
lovingly, as winningly, as prudently and faithfully as I can,
take him into my Hands, and labour to recover him out of

---

[1] Printed by T. Green, 1712.   Rev. James Pierpont was the minister.
[2] *The Fisher-mans Calling,* appearing in 1712 without a printer's name.

a Distemper, which renders him so uneasy unto himself, and unto all about him.

7. G. D. As it is a great Point of Religion with me to keep out of Debt, so when I pay any Thing that I owe, be the Summ larger or smaller, I would have this Thought still raised in my Mind; *O my dear Saviour, Thou hast paid my Debt unto the Justice of Heaven. Oh! help me to love thee, and praise thee, and serve thee for thy Goodness.*

1. [*December* 2.] G. D. I have newly written a brief *Manual for Self-Examination.* I incline to publish it, and furnish myself, with what Numbers of Copies I can, to be lodg'd in the Hands of all our Comunicants. It may prove a considerable Service to the Interests of Piety among them.

2. G. D. I would putt each of my Children (capable to do it) on Pondering and Answering, that Question; *What Course do I take, and must I take, that I may have the Fatherly Providence of the Great God, and my Saviour, concerned for me? that I may not be abandoned of God unto the Miseries that some Orphans are left unto?* Yea, lett them write their Answer to it.

3. G. D. There is a Family related unto me, in which Family I am treated with exceeding Affection and Civility. I have done something, but never done enough, in the Service of that Family, and for the Welfare of it. I would visit them, and entreat them to think for me, and show me what I shall do for them. I will myself also think; and in all their Exercises and Difficulties, I would study all possible Wayes to comfort them.

4. G. D. The Time is drawing on, for the Sailing of our Mast-fleet into *Europe.* I have many and great Correspondencies to cultivate, with my Letters hither; which I am quickly beginning to write. I will impose it, as a Law on myself, that still, when I am going to write any of these Letters, I will sett myself to think, *what Service may I do for the Kingdome of my admirable Saviour in what I*

now address to my Friend?   And, what Service is there that
I may putt my Friend upon?   I shall not have Time to
record the Services which I shall thus think upon; and it
may be, t'wil be of no Importance to do it.   It is enough,
that they will all be known unto the glorious Lord.

5. G. D.   There is a small Society of younger Persons,
who are Communicants in our Church, and hold a Meeting
in the Friday Evening præparatory to the Communion.   I
will send some very agreeable and profitable Things unto
them, to be read at their Meeting.

6. G. D.   I hear of a very poor, but a very pious,
Woman, at the South End of the Town; to whom I would
therefore not only dispense my own Charities, but also
procure those of other Peoples.

7 d. 10 m. [December.] Friday.   I am this week pretty
much confined, and very much afflicted, with grievous Pains
on the right Side of my Head and in my Jawes.   I improve
these Pains as Admonitions unto me, to humble myself
before the Lord, for the Barrenness of my Head, which has
had no more good Thoughts in it, and so few Designs to
do Good.   And adore the Love of my dear Saviour, who
has delivered me from everlasting Pains.   My Miseries the
last Night were almost insupportable; But I found so
much Releef by an epispastick, that I was able to sett
apart this Day for Prayer with Fasting in my Study, as I
use to do.   However I went thro' the Duties after a feeble
Manner.   And what I fell short in the Prayers, I made
up in Dispensations of Instruments of Piety, which I sent
this Day, with short Letters, to many Quarters.   I much
cried unto the Lord this Day, that I may have such Tidings
coming over the Water to me; as may encourage me in
my poor Endeavours to serve Him.

7. G. D.   I thought, it might contribute unto the
Intentions of Piety, not only in my own Soul, but also in
my Family, if I should have a short Hymn, relating to the

Lord's-day, to be sung (besides the many others which I so employ,) with my Family, every *Lord's-day* Morning. That which I prepare for this purpose, is this.

The Sons of God shouting for Joy at the Arrival of the *Lord's-day*.

My Saviour's risen from the Dead,
    And lives enthron'd Above.
The Price of my Salvation's paid;
    My Life is in His Love.
With holy Sabbaths and Peace
    Hath me victorious Blest.
Lord, bring thou me Holiness,
    To Victory and Rest.

9 *d.* 10 *m. Lord's-Day.* The Prevailing of my Pains upon me, has this Day chased me from the Services and Enjoyments of the Sanctuary; and particularly those of the Holy Table, at which I should have ministred before the Lord. I desire to improve this Humiliation, as a great Incentive to Repentance for my many Miscarriages, by which I have rendred myself unworthy of the Blessings in the Sanctuary. Especially my Unthankfulness for such Mercies, and my Unfruitfulness under them, and my unsuitable Attendence on them; as also the many Impurities of my Life, which make me deserve to be shut out, from the Sanctuary, as one too unclean to be admitted there. On these Accounts, my Flight unto the great Sacrifice, is quickened this Day.

1. [*December* 9.] G. D. But I would endeavour that my Flock, as well as myself, may reap some Good out of my Affliction. I would make up what I have left of an Opportunity to serve them this day, by arriving more serviceable to them, when I come abroad again. My next Sermon may very seasonably and serviceably be on the Communion which the great God maintains with His People, in His Institutions; the Calamity of a Banishment

from that Communion; the Importunity wherewith such a Communion is to be desired; and the Voice of God communing with each sort of People from the Mercy-seat in the Sanctuary.

2. G. D. I must keep a strict Eye on my Servant *Onesimus;* especially with regard unto his Company. But I must particularly endeavour to bring him unto Repentance, for some Actions of a thievish Aspect. Herein I must endeavour that there be no old Theft of his unrepented of, and left without Restitution.

But then, upon every observable Miscarriage of any Person in my Family, I must make my Flight unto the Blood of my Saviour, as a Family-Sacrifice; that so the Wrath of God may be turned away from my Family.

3. There is an horrid and very wicked Blade, a Finished Rake, who a year ago, (and ever since) has treated me with all the Malignities and Indignities, that Hell could inspire him withal, and now in a long Journey made it his business to load me with his lying Calumnies, wherever he has come. I have begg'd of my glorious Lord, that He would pitty and pardon this poor Man, and give him a new Heart, but graciously stop him in his Career of Wickedness. I have entirely left him in the Hand of the Glorious One. Last night, I understand, that God has broken the Arm of the wicked Wretch; by a Fall he has received in his Journey. I thought it now a Time to pray for him, (which I did before I slept,) that God will be merciful to him, and sanctify to him his Affliction, and bring him to Repentance. And I now renew my purpose to do so; and mightily to keep under the Awe of that Word, *Rejoice not when thine Enemy falleth.*

This Day I had a surprising Experiment. I have been for some while Afflicted with grievous Pains in my Head, that seem to have a gouty Aspect upon them. A neighbour-Minister last Night asked me, whether the Dragon

might not be (by the wise Permission of Heaven) taking
some Revenge upon me, for some notable Mischief, which
my Head may have lately done unto His Kingdome? The
Consideration of a Peece of Work, which I am now upon,
harmonizes well enough, with such a pleasant Fancy. But
I am now passing from the evil Angels to the good ones.
All Methods and Medicines for my Cure, fail me. I have
used Unguents, and Plaisters, and Cataplasms, and Epis-
paspicks, and Sinapisms, and Catharticks, and what not!
But all to no purpose. My Physicians are of no value.
My Pains this Morning are more violent than they use to
be. I ly down like a Stag in a Nett, with a very despairing
Discouragement. However, I thought, I would make one
Experiment more. But before I made it, I fell down before
the Lord. I acknowledged the Power of my Enthroned
Saviour, over the World, and over Diseases; and His
Empire over the mighty Angels. I bewailed before His
holy Majesty, my Foolishness and Filthiness, and my
Unworthiness of His Favours. I begg'd the Removal of
my Malady, that I might go on with His desired Service;
and that the Pains which He suffered might be the Price
of my Deliverance. I pleaded with Him, that His good
Angels were able, at His Order, to do marvellous Kindnesses for the Children of men, in releeving of their Weak-
nesses, and those kind and sweet Spirits took Delight in
helping us, especially if they might look on us as their
Fellow-Servants. I besought Him to send one of His
Angels, to touch my Head with His healing Hand; which
I knew would immediately releeve me. Behold, I had no
Occasion for any further Application. My Pains imme-
diately went off. And as yett (I write the Day following,)
I have no Return of them. This Occurrence has a very
sanctifying Effect upon my Mind. It causes me to resolve,
"Oh lett me now be more Industrious than ever; in the
Service of my Glorious Lord! Oh! lett me be more solli-

citious to avoid every Thing that may be offensive to the Angels of the holy Lord."

4. G. D. My Book of, *The true way to shake off a Viper* is published in *London*, and this week arrived here. I would sett myself, in the Dispersion thereof, to consider how it may be most serviceable unto the great Interests of Religion.

5. G. D. I would write unto Sir *Richard Blackmore*, my Desires, that His incomparable Pen may make its furthest Efforts, in paying an Homage to our admirable JESUS; in celebrating His Beauties, before which those of the whole Creation languish and vanish; in uttering the awakened Songs of His Love to the Children of Men; in describing the illustrious Exemple of all Goodness, which He has given us; in asserting His Government over the Works of God; and Painting out the Grandeurs wherein He shall come to raise the Dead and judge the World, and the Delights of the new Heavens and the new Earth, which shall succeed the Resurrection.

6. G. D. I hear of a very poor Woman in my Neighbourhood, perishing in three woful Circumstances; Wickedness, Poverty, and a Consumption. I would sett myself to do all that I am able for her. (πεppιε.) [1]

After two or three Dayes of unaccountable Repose, I suffered some Return of my Pain; upon which I made my Renewed Supplications unto the Lord, as before. And I putt on an Epispastic, which suddenly and mightily releeved me.

7. G. D. It has long been my Custome, when I write a Letter, tho' it be but a short one, to think, *What honourable Mention can I make of my dear Saviour here? What Occasion can I make to insinuate Something of His Glory?* But I would more than ever carry on my Consideration, to this further Point: *What Service may I do for the King-*

[1] Perry.

dome of my dear Saviour, on this Opportunity? What Good may I putt my Friend upon the doing of?

And now, taking my Correspondencies into Considera-tion, I would add these three Resolutions more. First when I am sealing a Letter and sending it away, I would with an Act of *Resignation* putt it over into the Hand of the *divine Providence*, for the Safety and Success of it. Secondly, when I am going to open any Letter that arrives with a Direction to me, I would lift up my Heart unto God, that He would *præpare me* for whatever Matter grievous or joyful, I am therein to encounter withal. Thirdly, in my last Prayer in my Study, before I go to my Rest, I would call to Mind, from whom I have received any Letter this Day, and make a particular Mention of that Person, unto the Lord, with Supplications for suitable Mercies to him.

1. [*December* 16.]   G. D.   There are two Persons of some Fashion and Interest, whom I may with a little of my Advice bring into our Communion. It may be a Ser-vice, not unto them alone, but also unto the whole Flock and therefore I would endeavour it.

2.   G. D.   By the gracious Providence of God, it is come to pass, that the religious, ingenious, and sweet-spirited *Isaac Watts*, hath sent me the new Edition of his *Hymns;* wherein the Interest of Piety are most admirably suited. I receive them as a Recruit and a Supply sent in from Heaven for the Devotions of my Family. There I will sing them, and endeavour to bring my Family in Love with them. I would also procure our Booksellers to send for a Number of them; and perswade my well-disposed Neighbours to furnish themselves with them; and in this way promote Piety among them.

3.   G. D.   Great Service may be done for the Church of God, and some for my Brother himself, by giving my Excitations and Assistences to my Brother *Samuel*, for the

Work he is upon; the abridging and publishing our Church-History. I am now, for that Purpose writing to him.

4. G. D. In my Letters to *Britain*, I would call upon the *Non Conformists*, to institute an Enquiry into the Reproaches and Calumnies, with which their Enemies do load them, and the Prejudices against them, with which their Enemies Endeavour to leaven the Minds of them who do not know them; and consider hereupon, what is the Voice of God unto them in all these things; what Lessons they have to learn from the Abuses of their Adversaries; what should be their Studies that they may effectually confute the Ignorance of them that speak Evil of them; Wherein they may have given any Shadow of Occasion unto disaffected Men to be so; or, what other Miscarriages in them the Holy God may design to chastise in the Abuses of unreasonable Men; and, in fine, what Improvement in the Things that are excellent, they should make under the Discipline of the disadvantageous Character, which foolish and factious Men endeavour to putt upon them; and, thus to gain Wisdome from their Enemies.

5. G. D. Would it not be a thing of good Consequence, if I should write unto some of the Ministers employ'd in the evangelical Service among the *Indians*, that they would procure as soon as may be, a Consultation with the Rest of their Brethren; about the Mischiefs which most threaten the Christian Indians, and the Methods of preventing those Mischiefs; and be more in earnest than ever to advance the Kingdome of God and of His Christ among them; and with a true evangelical Spirit give Demonstration, that the little Pension received by them, is the least Thing they aim at?

6. G. D. I have now gott by me, a pretty large Summ of Money, to be dispersed among the poor. I will first cry to the glorious Lord for His Direction. I will then look out for Objects of Piety, both at home and abroad. And

I will annex Books of Piety, to accompany the Parcels in the Dispensing of them.

7. G. D. There is a Thought which I have often had in my mind; but I would now lay upon my Mind, a Charge to have it yett oftner there; that the Light of *Reason*, is the Work of God; the Law of *Reason* is the Law of God; the Voice of *Reason* is the Voice of God; We never have to do with *Reason*, but at the same time we have to do with God; Our submission to the Rules of *Reason* is an Obedience to God. How much will this Expedient contribute unto a Life of Obedience to God? Lett me as often as I have evident *Reason* sett before me, think upon it; *the great God now speaks unto me!* And lett me from this Principle yeeld a present Compliance with it; always *hearken to Reason*, from this Consideration.

1. [*December* 23.] G. D. There are some religious Societies belonging to the Flock, to whom I would earnestly recommend it, that in the Close of every Meeting they would effectually discourse on certain Points of Consideration, which may render them great Blessings to the Neighbourhood, and promote the Good and Growth of the Flock in very many Instances.

2. G. D. There is an Ingenuity, which I may use, to insinuate the Maxims and Lessons of Piety, into the Minds of my younger Children. I would observe what Games and Sports they are upon, when the Hours of Recreation recur unto them. And I would by way of occasional Reflection, as plainly as tis possible, mind them of those pious Instructions, which the Circumstances of their play may lead them to think upon. Hereby their Minds will insensibly improve, and be drawn on to higher Matters; and perhaps the Maxims and Lessons thus convey'd unto them, will be of use to them, and abide by 'em all their Dayes.

3. G. D. I have a Sister, a Widow, in some Wants

and Straits. I will dispense Releefs unto her particularly in regard of her Habit. (βιλες.)[1]

4. G. D. It may prove many Wayes a Service to the Interests of Piety, if I compose a short Essay, on the most agreeable Points, and in the most agreeable Terms that I can, about the Methods of Piety, wherein we may propose to meet with our blessed Saviour at His Temple in the *Winter;* and first utter this Discourse unto the People of the Town, in a Lecture on a *Winter-day*, and then publish it by the Way of the Press, if I meet with Encouragement.

5. G. D. There is a great Concern which the Ministers of this Town have now before them. A Party in the old Church are in a distempered and a discontented Frame and are for separating themselves into a new Church by themselves. There is hazard of a greater Fire, than what raged the Second of *October*. The Ministers of this Place have great Occasion hereupon, to consult what is to be done, and use exquisite Wisdome, and Meekness, and a very nice Conduct. I would on this occasion give my best Assistences, and ask for those from above.

I would make this an Article of my Advice to the N. C. Ministers in *London;* that whereas the Societies pretending the Propagation of Religion, do disperse numberless Books, which obtrude a very defective Christianity on the Nation, the N. C.'s would write little Books, on the same Arguments, with more of the true Spirit of the Gospel in them; and erect Funds for the Publishing and the Dispersing of them. And send Numbers of them over to our southern colonies; with little Books of the same import with the *Letter of the Aged N. C.* to arm the People there, against Seducers.

6. G. D. There is an aged, (I hope, a pious) Woman in my Neighbourhood; reduced unto very low Circumstances. I will take some Care that her Condition may

---

[1] Byles.

be made more easy and comfortable to her. She is the
Daughter of one, who was once a noted Servant of the
churches. [πρνη the Daughter of Συμs.][1]

There is also a poor pious, praying widow, who has
two Sons, under the unhappy Character of Deserters from
Annapolis; in her Distress for them, she applies herself
to me. I will endeavour to make her Heart sing for Joy,
and do all I can to accomplish their Deliverance from their
unhappy Circumstances.[2]

7. G. D. It is most certain, I am a man full of Ignorance, and full of Corruption, and my Life has been, yea,
still is full of Miscarriages. That I may have the due
Temper of Humility alwayes preserved in me, I would impose it as a Law upon myself; that whenever I have darted
into my Mind, the least Thought of any exalting Circumstances with which the sovereign God has favoured me,
or whenever any of my Friends do happen to flatter me
with the mention of any Thing that they apprehend considerable in me, I will immediately make my Flight unto
some of my abasing Circumstances, for which I have cause
to abhor myself before God and Man; and especially single
out such Abasements as do carry most of Opposition to
my proposed Advancements, and may be employ'd as a
dead Weight against them. Thus would I ly exceedingly
low, and in the Dust before the Lord continually.

1. [*December* 30.] G. D. I hear of a Number of young
People of both Sexes, belonging, many of them, to my Flock,
who have had on the Christmas-night, this last Week, a
Frolick, a revelling Feast, and Ball, which discovers their
Corruption, and has a Tendency to corrupt them yett more,
and provoke the Holy One to give them up unto eternal
Hardness of Heart. I must acquitt myself as prudently
and as faithfully as ever I can, in the Discharge of my

---

[1] Prue, daughter of Syms.
[2] This paragraph is written in the margin.

Duty to them, on this Occasion, and endeavour to bring them unto Repentance, and prevent such Follies for the Time to come.[1]

2. G. D. It must be a particular Article of my Conference with my Children, and I will with much Artifice manage it; how exceeding acceptable to me, their Conduct is, in that they steer clear of such Company as may give any Taint unto them, and they keep an unspotted Character; how honourable it is also to themselves, and likely in the issue to prove more than a little Serviceable.

3. G. D. I have a Kinswoman, who dishonours God, and wounds her own Good Name, and brings a Blemish on her Friends, by her inconsiderate Behaviour. I must use the kindest and wisest Method I can, to save her out of her Follies.

About this Time, I gave to the Public in the Form of a Treatise by itself, what I had prepared for a Preface unto a Sermon published by the Minister of *Newhaven;* a little composure entituled, A SOUL WELL-ANCHORED. *A Little Manual for Self-Examination; To assist a Christian, in Examining his Hopes of a Future Blessedness.*[2] I thought it a Subject of the greatest Consequence. And I laid out a Quantity of Silver, in purchasing a Number of them, to disperse where they might be serviceable.

4. G. D. I must endeavour to save the Town of *Newbury* in this Countrey, from some Devices of Satan, which manage a little and wretched Party, that pretend for the

---

[1] On this last day of the year the ministers of Boston assembled at the house of Major [John] Walley, to pray for his recovery from some disorder that affected his foot. Sewall, *Diary*, II. 330, with unconscious humor describes it as an exercise in prophecy on the part of two of the ministers. "Mr. Wadsworth insisted pretty much, that several in the room might dy before Major Walley; all of them might. Dr. C. Mather very near the conclusion of his Prayer, said, Probably some remarkable person in the room might dye before Major Walley. Major Walley was easy all the time of the exercise, had not one Twinging pain." All the same he died eleven days later.

[2] Printed by B. Green, 1712. Rev. Mr. Pierpont was the minister.

Church of *England* there.[1] A true Account sent home, will be of some consequence.

This Week I also publish, what I prepared the Last. It is Entituled, WINTER-PIETY. *A very brief Essay, on the Methods of Piety, wherein a serious Christian may propose to meet with his blessed Saviour, at the Temple, in the Winter.*[2]

5. G. D. I write unto the N[on] C[onformist] Ministers, that their having been putt upon raising Money for the Support of Missions, for which they have Reason to express the greatest Aversion, may excite them to erect Funds on the other Hand, for the Encouragement of more evangelical and agreeable Missions; and in the mean time, with kind Presents, or at least Letters, encourage their excellent Brethren who are conflicting with extreme Difficulties, in our *southern* Colonies.

6. G. D. I have Thoughts of sending a little Quantity of Silver, with some agreeable Books of Piety, to be dispensed as from an unknown Hand, unto certain Widows in *Salem;* that are poor, but pious and praying Handmaids of the Lord.

4 *d.* 11 *m.* [*January.*] 1711[-12.] *Friday.* I sett apart this Day for Prayers and Alms, with Fasting before the Lord. The Occasions were such as are usual with me. As also, to ask for a Blessing on the Letters and Packetts I am now sending to *Britain.*

I did this day comfortably receive and apply the pardoning Mercy of God, with the Blood of my dear Saviour. And importunately cried unto Him, for Abundance of Grace; in regard of the abundant Occasions, which I have, and am like to have, to exercise it.

---

[1] "Some of the inhabitants living in the vicinity of Sawyer's hill, by the advice and with the assistance of Mr. John Bridger, of Portsmouth, N. H., erected in 1711 'Queen Anne's Chapel.' On Sundays and holy days they held service there 'according to the rubrics and ritual of the established Church of England' until the close of the year 1766." Currier, *History of Newbury*, 228.

[2] Printed by B. Green, 1712.

7. G. D. Whenever I am sensible of any good and great Instrument, raised up to serve the Church and Cause of my dear Saviour; particularly, in the Reading of any Books written by such; I would make it an Article of my rapturous Thanksgiving to the glorious Lord. I would fly to Him, with my Thanks and Praise on the Occasion. I would have this to be very particularly considered by me, among my many Invitations into Communion with God.

1. [*January* 6.] G. D. Having some special Occasion for it, I would in the publick Exhortations, with most pathetical Importunity commend unto the Flock, the Duties and the Tempers of a good *Neighbourhood;* and then also, of *heroic Piety*, which, alas, may be called, *uncommon Piety*, in the several Conditions which God has assign'd unto them.

6 *d.* 11 *m. Lord's-day.* I visited the Table of the Lord, (and administred the Eucharist,) in a very cold Season. I went upon the usual and proper Errands. But I very particularly look'd up to Heaven for Grace to bestow a very excellent Education on my Children.

2. G. D. There is hardly any Thing, that would more contribute unto a Religion and excellent Education for my Children, than to revive my Cares to have them fill their blank Books, with agreeable and valuable Things. I would therefore first of all, settle an Hour with them, have a stated Hour, that shall be for this Purpose constantly kept unto. I would then furnish them, with Materials, both devotionary and scientifical, that may fill the Chambers of their Souls, with precious and pleasant Riches.

Moreover, at the Time of my Short-supper, I would endeavour to hold a Conference with my Children, that shall be as instructive, and impressive, as it can be made, by a Father, in my Circumstances, who am quickly to be taken from them. I have done something this way; but I would improve to a greater Exactness in it.

3. G. D. My honest Brother-in-Law, who was made a

Widower, a year ago, shall have my best Advice and Assistence, in his Return to the married State; and I will endeavour every Way I can devise, to be useful unto him.

4. G. D. I incline to write a little Treatise, about *the Peace*, which is the Legacy of our Saviour unto His People.

5. G. D. I am sensible of some Disorders in the Place, which I would animate the Societies, to rebuke with their Admonitions.

I am again writing to the University of *Halle* in the Lower *Saxony*, sending a present of Gold for the *Orphanhouse* there. I would move their Translating some English Books of Piety, into their own Language.

6. G. D. It is a Time of more than ordinary Severity for the Cold. The last Night, I joined with several other good Men, in sending a Portion to seven of the poor; for whom I have my Soul grieved at this Time. I am also assisting the Distribution of a Legacy of an hundred Pounds left them about ten months ago. My Catalogue of the Poor, which has more than four score in it, is that which directs the Distribution.

7. G. D. At a Time, of severe Cold, I and mine are surrounded with so many Conveniencies and Consolations, that I would have my Heart raised up to the highest Flights of Thankfulness, not only in my Retirements, but also in the Sacrifices of my Family. Yea, I entertain Thoughts, of Keeping a Day of Thanksgiving with my Family.

1. [*January* 13.] G. D. There are some Objects of Rebuke and Censure, in the Church. I must with all Faithfulness dispense what belongs unto them. I hope, God will sanctify what is to be done, both unto them, and unto many others.

2. G. D. I find it requires exquisite Study, and a Mind intensely sett upon doing of Good, and mindful of Death; but I would prosecute this Matter with yett a more lively Application; rarely to lett one of my Children

to come anear me, and never to sitt any Time with them, without some explicit Contrivance and Endeavour, to lett fall some Sentence or other, that shall carry an useful Instruction with it.

But my Son *Increase*, now being of Age for it, I would often call him into my Study, especially on the Lord's-day Evenings, and make him sitt with me and hear from me such Documents of Piety, and of Discretion, as I shall endeavour to suit him, and to shape him withal.

3. G. D. I would repeat my Endeavours to prepare my aged Father-in-law for his approaching Change; and allow to his wife also a Share in my Endeavours that way; by putting some extremely suitable Books for that purpose into theirs which are now in my Hands.

4. G. D. The high-flying Church of *England*, are Endeavouring to poison and seduce and divide the Dutch Christians which are under the Government of *New York*. I have thoughts of writing and sending to the University at *Utrecht*, several Things that may be of great Consequence to the general Interests of Religion.   But among other Things, I would remonstrate this Matter to them; that so they may admonish and caution their People in those Colonies.

16 *d.* 11 *m. Wednesday*.   This Day I was, with some Christians at *Roxbury*, keeping a solemn Thanksgiving with and for a Family, that has received special Favours of God, for which we made our Supplications, two Years ago.

5. G. D. Into my Catalogue of *excellent Things*, I propose to insert some Directions relating to our *religious Societies*, that may have a Tendency to render them all, yett more serviceable to the Intentions of Religion.

Moreover, having Occasion to dispense a Releef of Cloathing this Week, unto a poor Mohegin Indian, and his wife, sojourning at *Braintree*, I would at the same time send unto the Ministers there, to take the poor Pagans into their Hands, and bestow the best Instruction in Christianity upon them, and make our Kindness; an occasion of recommending the christian Religion unto them.

6. G. D. My List of the Poor to be cared for, has about Ninety in it; and it is a time wherein a particular care is to be exercised about most or all of them. Wherefore to distinguish One, in the Thoughts of my *Friday*-morning, seems too confining an Action. Yett there is one poor old Man, to be a little Distinguished. ($\Sigma\nu\alpha\sigma\iota\epsilon$)[1] And another poor old woman, to be particularly this Day look'd after. ($\Upsilon\alpha\rho\kappa\epsilon\varsigma\epsilon\rho$)[2]

7. G. D. It is now a very extreme Winter; and we are now in the Extremity of it.

As I have already from the Circumstances of the Winter, been awakened unto many Strokes of Winter-Piety; particularly, to consider and acknowledge, the Sufferings of my dear Saviour, as purchasing for me, the Comforts that succour me in, and shelter me from, the Difficulties of the Winter; so I would now go on to form certain *Supplicationes Hyemales* or, Winter-Desires and Prayers, which from the several Accidents of the Winter, I would be quickened both to insist upon myself, and also to draw my Friends with me to take notice of.

On, The Distance of the *Sun* from us.
Oh! Lett not my Soul, nor the World, languish in a miserable Distance from our Saviour.

The *Snow*. *Lord, Thro' the Blood of my Saviour applied unto me, render my Guilty and stained Soul, whiter than the Snow.*

The *Frost*. *Lord, Lett not my Capacities, and Activities for thy Service, ly under any Congelation.*

The *Ice*. *Lord, save me from the Fate and Fall of them whom thou hast sett in slippery Places. Glory be to Him, who is able to keep me from Falling.*

The *Vermine* suppress'd. *Lord, Lett the Lusts in my Soul, which are worse than, the worst, and most noxious of all Creatures, be destroy'd, without ever being revived any more.*

[1] Swasie.   [2] Worcester?

The *Fruitless Face* of the Earth. *Lord, Tho' my Life be too much without good Fruits, yett thou canst bring me to be Fruitful in good Works. And tho' the Face of the world at this Day be horribly barren and wretched, yett I will hope in thee, to give it a better Face, and bring on a better Time.*

My *Garments. Lord, I am not afraid of the Winter, because of my double Cloathing. But, oh! putt upon me the Righteousness of my Saviour; lett me be also cloathed with thy Spirit; under such Influences of the Spirit, that none other shall be seen upon me! O glorious, O durable Cloathing!*

My *Fuel. Lord, Enable me to warm all that are about me, with holy Dispositions, and speak those gracious Words to them, which may cause their Hearts to burn within them. And, oh! save me and mine from the eternal Burnings; from the Fiery Indignation, which is to, devour thine Adversaries.*

1. [*January* 20.] G. D. It might be attended with a Train of excellent Consequences, to preserve and promote the Interests of Religion in this Neighbourhood, if such a Projection as this might be accomplished. We have many *religious Societies* in this Neighbourhood. What if I, furnishing myself, with a List of all the Names belonging to each of them, should appoint an Evening once in two or three Months; and single out one or two Members from each Society, and direct them to meet me at the Time and Place assigned; and then learn from them the State of each Society; and concert with them, and propose to them, such Things, as may have a Tendency to serve the Cause of Christ and Piety in the Neighbourhood. I would see what I can do, to accomplish this comprehensive Design for Good.

2. G. D. It may be many Wayes for the Advantage of my Daughters, to have them well-instructed in *Shorthand*. I would therefore apply myself unto this part of their Education; and make the Stated Hour in the Day for this, an opportunity to employ their Pens in all those Things, that may fill the Chambers of their Souls with precious and pleasant Riches.

3. G. D. I have several Cosin-germans and their off-

spring, living at *Salisbury*. I would this week send agreeable Books of Piety, to each of them.

4. G. D. There has been this Winter, an horrible Mortality raging in the Colony of *Connecticot*.[1] The Mortality has very much fallen, on their more useful People, and their more hearty People. I incline to preach a Sermon on that Occasion; and then to print it; and so to send a good Number of the Copies, into the afflicted Colony. By this I propose, not only that my Neighbours here, may make a due Improvement of the divine Dispensations towards our Brethren; but also that the Survivors in the smitten Colony may be Entertained with suitable Admonitions, at a time, when God makes their Heart soft; and the Almighty sends Troubles on them, that may awaken them to hearken unto the Maxims of Religion.

5. G. D. What if I should move among the Ministers that, in case the Sickness continue among our Brethren, we should in this Town publickly keep a solemn Day of Prayer for them? This would not only express our Charity to our Brethren, but also bespeak our own Preservation.

6. G. D. A poor Man, and now an old one, that has been fifteen Years under the Censure of the Church, is now so far coming out of his Impœnitency, that he is applying himself unto us, to be Restored. I would with great Love and Joy cherish his Dispositions, and assist him in this Action; and also do my best, that it may not be a Peece of Hypocrisy (Κολεμαν.)[2]

---

[1] The disease, then believed to be a species of putrid pleurisy, broke out in Waterbury, and raged for eleven months. It was so general that nurses could scarcely be found to tend the sick.

[2] "3 *d.* 12 *m.* Mr. *William Coleman*, appearing this day before the Church, with an expressive Acknowledgment of the miscarriages for which he had been censured, and with some Testimony of a reformed Conversation, the Church did by order vote, restore him to their Fellowship, and also allow him to transfer his Relation, when he shall desire it, unto that Flock in this Town, with which, for a Reason well known unto us all, he may chuse to give his most usual Attendance." *Cotton Mather's MS. Records of the Second Church*, II.

7. G. D. My Mind, with all the Dispositions, and all the Operations of it, is continually under the Eye of the omnipresent God. Not only my Wayes, and my Words, but also all the Thoughts and Frames of my mind, come under the Observation of the glorious One. He takes Notice of all that passes in my Mind, and is intimately acquainted with it all. This is a Consideration, that often visits my Mind, and chases away from it such Things as ought not to be lodged in it. But then I also consider, that it is unto the glorious One, a graceful Thing, to see His Image on my Mind; and my Spirit employ'd as a Temple for Him, in the Inclinations and Contemplations of a godly Mind. I propose, to improve exceedingly in my most frequent and cogent Employing of this Reflection; *Is my mind now tending that way, and doing that Work, that is most pleasing to the glorious God?* And walk under the Power of it.

O my dear Saviour, Help me, help me, to a great Improvement in this Piety!

1. [*January* 27.] G. D. It may administer many and solemn Occasions, to disperse very serviceable Admonitions unto the Flock, if I take the Parable of the *Tares*, and handle it in a Course of Sermons upon it. This I propose to do, and pray the Direction and Assistence of Heaven, in the doing of it.

2. G. D. It may prove of excellent Consequence to my Son *Increase*, if he may turn into Latin, after the rate of one Quæstion per day, my *Supplies from the Tower of David*. It may also supply me, with an Engine, which after my bestowing further Limations on it, and Additions to it, may do inexpressible Good in other Countreys.

How marvellously does the glorious Lord glorify me, in that which is the First-born of my Desires, and multiply my Opportunities to do Good!

My late Sermon on the mortality of *Connecticot*, as it

was heard by a great Assembly, and mett with a great Acceptance, and had its good Operation here; so, it is like to have a further Operation; tis like to do Good in all the Towns of the afflicted Colony. A Copy of it is desired; it is committed unto the Press; it is intended to be sent into every Part of the Colony; and it goes furnished with Lessons and Engines of Piety, accommodated unto the Condition of the poor People there, and such, as tis hop'd, under the Impressions of their Calamity, they will very much take nonce of. It is entituled, SEASONABLE THOUGHTS UPON MORTALITY. *A Sermon occasioned by the raging of a Mortal Sickness in the Colony of Connecticut, and the many Deaths of our Brethren there.*

That which renders this Favour and Honour the more agreeable, is, that a certain finished Rake has lately been abusing and belying of me, in several Towns of that Colony.

3. G. D. Tis now a Time, for me particularly to pray for the Lives of my useful Kinsmen at *Connecticut;* and also, to putt them upon particular Essayes to do good, when I send my seasonable Thoughts unto them.

4. G. D. My little Book of *Seasonable Thoughts on Mortality*, now in the Press; is calculated for Service to the Interests of Piety, not only at *Connecticot*, but in any Place that has been suffering under a raging Mortality. *Carolina* is now such a place, as well as our *Connecticut*. I would therefore sett apart a Number of the Books to be sent thither, by the first Opportunity.

5. G. D. I am calling upon all the *religious Societies*, once again, to putt on the Character of *reforming Societies*, and consider when they are together, *what Good they may do in the Neighbourhood?*

6. G. D. I am inclinable, as soon as I can, to furnish myself, with Books of Piety, that shall be very much adapted unto the Condition, and Edification of the *Poor*, and to make a Present thereof, to each of the Poor, which amount

unto above ninety, in my Catalogue. In the mean time, to keep doing that way, according to my Ability and Occasion.

1 *d*. 12 *m*. [*February*.] *Friday*. The many Sermons I have preached, both more publickly and more privately this Week, and the Colds, I have taken in the damp Evenings, have much indisposed me. Nevertheless, I sett apart this Day for *Prayers*, and *Alms*, with *Fasting*, before the Lord.

One of the Exercises which distinguished this Day, was this. I took the Catalogue of the Books which I have been the Father of. The Number in the Catalogue is, two hundred and five. On each of the Titles I made a Pause. And I obliged every one of them, to suggest unto me some remarkable Article of Humiliation; which I thereupon with an abased Soul mentioned before the Lord.

Another was this; I considered my blessed JESUS, as having first made Expiation for my Sins on the Cross; but now placed on the Throne of God, and with the Fulness of the Godhead bodily dwelling in Him. He has Power to dispense a Pardon, with all the Blessings of Goodness, unto those that belong unto Him. I considered, that the infinite and eternal God, has directed me to make my immediate Applications unto my exalted Redeemer. I considered, that my exalted Redeemer, is full of Love, Goodness, and Kindness to them, who thus repair unto the Shadow of His Wings. Wherefore, I now addressed Him, declaring at the same Time, that I did not exclude any one of the Subsistences in the almighty Godhead, from the Adoration which I now paid unto Him. I addressed Him, full of a lively Faith in Him, and full of Dispositions and Resolutions to serve Him with all my Heart, and Soul, and Strength. I addressed Him, with Petitions, that my Sins may be all forgiven me; that I may have Abundance of Grace given to me; that I may be employ'd in great Works for Him, and carried thro' my Ministry and my Pilgrimage, and sheltered from the Attempts of wicked Men, to hurt my opportunities to do good in the World. Many particular Petitions I carried unto Him; under the Advantage of the clear *Idea*, of addressing Him in this Way; and my Spirit was taken up into the Heavens, in these Addresses; and I received strange Assurances, of the Blessings which are to be bestow'd upon me.

7. G. D. Of my dear JESUS, I read, Heb. v. 8. *He*

learned Audience [1] *from the things that He suffered.* In the Supplications which He made under His bitter Sufferings, He had Audience of His Father. His Father heard Him, and sav'd Him from Death, with a Resurrection unto Life. God has now exalted Him; and He has the Wisdome of God united unto Him, and forever dwelling in Him; and our Supplications are by the Order of God more immediately to be made unto Him, in our Distresses. By what His Father did for Him, He has learnt now to give Audience unto us, in our Supplications. And indeed, in this Compassion of His unto us, there is an Obedience of His unto His Father. I would now entertain a more lively Sense of this Thought, than ever I have had. In the Distresses, that come upon me, I will fly to my lovely Saviour. In the Things that I fear, I will pour out my Supplications to Him, still expressly declaring that I exclude not the other two Persons of the Godhead. I will consider Him, as not only being the Wisdome of the Almighty, but also the Advanced Man on the Throne of God, who has learn'd from His own Condition under Sufferings in the Dayes of His Flesh, to give Audience unto the Supplications of His afflicted Servants. I will yet more particularly call to Mind the Sufferings undergone by Him. And with Importunity, order my Cause before Him, and fill my Mouth with Arguments. Who can tell, what a Train of blessed Consequences, Piety in this way exercised, may be attended withal.

1. [*February* 3.] G. D. I would with more solemn and thundring Admonitions than ever, advise those who are under the Discipline of the Church, to be afraid of bringing upon themselves the Censures, which will be dispensed at length unto them that shall be convicted of being the Workers of Iniquity. There are some, for whom there is peculiar Occasion, that I should shake the Rod over them.

---

[1] Should be "Obedience."

And this Day will give me an agreeable Opportunity for
it, in the Repentance and Reception of One that has been
long a Censured Offendor.[1]

3 *d.* 12 *m.* *Lord's-Day.*   At the Table of the Lord, I considered my great Saviour, as having first purchased for me
the best of Blessings by the Sacrifice of Himself; and being
then ascended unto the Throne at the right Hand of God,
where being united unto the second Subsistence in the Godhead, He knowes our Wants, hears our Prayers, dispenses
from thence to us all the Blessings of Goodness.

Wherefore I applied myself then unto Him upon two
Intentions; beleeving Him infinitely ready therein to do
me good.

First.   I look'd up unto Him, that my Sins may be all
pardoned; and that my Pardon might extend not only
unto a Release from all Punishment in the future State;
but also unto a Deliverance from all spiritual Plagues in
this Life; and particularly, from that of being rejected from
serving of Him, and from being employ'd in great Services
for Him; and from that of being denied such Influences
of His Grace [as] may render His Image very Conspicuous
upon me; for which Influences I now sought unto Him.

Secondly.   I look'd up unto Him, that He would bestow
upon me those Communications of His holy Spirit, which
may mightily furnish me for the Discharge of the evangelical Ministry; and that His holy Spirit may after a very
powerful Manner breathe in my Speeches, and in my Writings, and very particularly in my Sermons, and cause them
to come with a mighty Efficacy on the Souls of them with
whom I may be concerned, and make their Hearts to burn
within them.

2. G. D.   In my Discourses with my children, I will
mightily propound and commend it unto them, that they
do excellent Things, and that tho' others may do vertuously,

---

[1] See p. 154, *supra.*

they may excell even their most vertuous Neighbours. I would therefore earnestly putt them upon consideration of that Point, *What do you more than others?* And they shall join with me in considering what more *particular Excellencies*, they shall be studious of.

3. G. D. On the Occasion of the late Mortality at *Connecticot*, I would write such Things unto my Kinsman at *Say-brook*, as may assist and excite his good Improvement of the divine Dispensations; and employ his Hand also, in dispersing Books of Piety, thro' the Colony.

4. G. D. The Peace of the Church at *Sherborn*, is likely to be prejudiced, by a poor Man, whose misguided Conscience leads him to make a Disturbance there.[1] He applies himself to me; and so I have the more sensible opportunity, to do service for that Church, by diverting the Man from the wrong Way that he is in. The Church at *Groton* is also in miserable Circumstances.[2] My Endeavours to releeve them are called for.

5. G. D. In the Society for the Suppression of Disorders, I will propose, that there be prepared a List of the wicked Houses in the Town, the Disorders whereof call for animadversion upon them; and then proceed unto the assigning of particular Methods and Agents, for the putting of a Check upon them.

6. G. D. That Woman, who was my Mother's Maid, at the Time when I was born, and in my most early Infancy, is a pious, but now an aged, Woman: and she conflicts with Poverty. I will therefore Endeavour to dispense what Releefs I can unto her. [Mrs. Γαλε.][3]

7. G. D. It is of the greatest Consequence imaginable

---

[1] Rev. Daniel Gookin had been the minister for more than a quarter of a century, and being in 1711, a "crazie and infirm man and well stricken in years," Rev. Daniel Baker was called.

[2] The case of Rev. Dudley Bradstreet, which involved the church of Groton in its difficulties, is told in the paper contributed by Dr. Samuel A. Green to 2 *Proceedings*, XIII. 298.   [3] Mrs. Gale.

to me, that I should have upon me the evident Characters of such as the infinite and eternal Father has given unto my Saviour. (Joh. XVII. 24.) How joyfully may I live, and with what Joy may I dy, with the Assurance that such Characters would give unto me!

Now to putt this most important Matter out of Doubt, I would first, come unto the blessed JESUS, and often, often give myself unto Him. Then I would sett myself to consider, for what it is, that the blessed JESUS, has His People given by His Father to Him; and I would fall in with all those Intentions, unto the uttermost of my Capacity. I would much engage and affect myself in the Study of my Saviours incomparable Glory. I would give Him the Glory of all the Good that is to be done for me. I would receive all the Blessings of Goodness, as passing thro' His Hands unto me. I would embrace His Laws as the Perpetual Rules of my Conduct. I would apply myself with a most active, exquisite, and contriving Zeal, to serve His Kingdome in the World, and bring as many as ever I can, to join with me in admiring and adoring of Him.

1. [*February* 10.] G. D. Having resolved, if the Lord permitt, that I will now proceed unto a new Method of catechising the Children of the Flock; I would first open the Exercise at my own House, once a Month; and cry unto the glorious Lord, that He would graciously direct me, assist me, and succeed me in the doing of it; and then contrive the best Methods I can, to carry it on. But I beleeve, this will be but an Introduction to a more public Action; which may issue in a Lecture to the Church, preparatory to the Communion.

2. G. D. Now my Son *Increase* is arrived unto the Exercise of making *Themes*, at the School, I would make this become an Engine of Piety for him; and I would procure such Subjects to be assign'd unto him, as may most assist the Study of Goodness and Vertue in him.

Thus I am come to the End of another Year, overwhelmed with Confusion, when I look back on the Sin and Sloth constantly attending me in it.

It is true, I have been help'd by Heaven this Year,

To lett not one Day pass me, without contriving and recording, some Invention to do good. And these which have pass'd thro' my Pen, are but a few of the Projections, which I have had; but not had either Heart or Time to write them down.

To lett not one Day pass me, without actually expressing something of my Revenues and Possessions on pious Uses.

To write some Illustrations for the most part every Day; doubtless the Number which I have this Year added unto the *Biblia Americana*, has been many more than a thousand.

To preach many Sermons unto the private Societies, besides those in the Course of my public Ministry,

To publish near as many Books, as there have been Months in the year, (to bring forth Fruit every Month,) besides, to prepare others that are not published.

To make many hundreds of Visits; but never one, without some explicit Essayes or Desires to do good in it.

To manage some scores of Correspondencies; and some ultramarine ones, that required an exquisite and an expensive Cultivation; but to propose the Service of my glorious Lord in every one of them all.

To discharge numberless Exercises, referring both to the Lord's House, and to my own that it may be the Lord's.

To read over many scores of Books, and gather into my *Quotidiana* from them, etc., etc., etc.

But after all, O my dear Saviour, I stand in infinite Need of thy Sacrifice.

I have been a most unprofitable servant.

God be merciful to me a Sinner!

The Course of my Public Ministry.

1710.

18 *d.* 12 *m.* [*February.*] 1710[–11.] I preached on Eccl. 1. 4. The Notice we are to take of one Generation *passing* off, and another Generation *coming on*, while the Earth *abideth* forever; and the Improvement we should make of it. (A Sermon occasioned by the Death of Mr *John Foster.*)

22 *d.* 12 *m. Thursday.* I preached the Lecture, on Eccl. 7. 2. and handled that Case; *What should be the Behaviour of a Christian at a Funeral?*

25 *d.* 12 *m.* I preached, on Luk. 15. 16. That a *mean Food* is the best that ungodly People have to feed upon. That people who live in *Wealth*, may before they dy, come to *Want*. That among *bad* People, there is little Care of *poor* People. And, that the Case of People may be such that *no Friend* will or can do any thing for them.

4 *d.* 1 *m.* [*March.*] 1711. I preached, on Heb. 13. 20. The *Covenant* of God, and of *Grace;* and in what regards it is *everlasting.* (And I administred the Eucharist.)

11 *d.* 1 *m.* I preached, on 2. Cor. 12. 4. *Paradise*, the Receptacle for the departed Spirits of the Faithful; the Communion we should maintain with them; by what Means, and in what Acts, that Communion is to be carried on. (A Sermon occasion'd by the Death of Mrs. *Foster.*)

18 *d.* 1 *m.* I preached on Gal. 4. 19. The Nature of the Blessedness, *A Christ formed in the Soul;* and the Notice we are to take of it; the travailing Agony, wherewith we should be concerned, that our Friends may be Partakers of it.

22 *d.* 1 *m. Thursday.* I preached the Lecture, on Job. 14. 10. Man *giving up the Ghost;* and then, *where* he is; the State after Death.

25 *d.* 1 *m.* I preached, A. M. at the South Church; on Dan. 4. 34. *Religion* the best Use and Proof of *Understanding.* P. M. at the North Church; On Luk. 15. 17. The Sinner a *Madman*, and *Repentance*, the Cure of his *Madness.*

1 *d.* 2 *m.* [*April.*] I preached on Gal. 4. 19. And with a *travailing Agony* prosecuted the Formation of a Christ; in the Souls of the Children of the Flock.

8 *d.* 2 *m.* I preached on Luk. 15. 17. Some serving God with

a *mercenary* Spirit; None *Losers* by serving God; People having *enough* and *to spare*, yett no true Children of God; How the ungodly could hardly continue what they are, if they would *consider* what there [they are]; and what *good* God often does to men by *afflicting* of them.

12 *d*. 2 *m*. *Thursday*. A general Fast. I preached on Rev. 1. 11. The *Care* which Christ in Heaven, has of His Churches on Earth.

15 *d*. 2 *m*. I preached on Rev. 20. 12. The *Small* as well as the *Great*, standing before God, in the *Day of Judgment*. Concluding with solemn Admonitions to the Children in the Congregation; on Occasion of a Child of some Note in the Neighbourhood, killed with a sudden and awful Stroke, two Dayes ago.

19 *d*. 2 *m*. *Thursday*. I preached the Lecture, on Ezr. 8. 15. *Ezra's* Account how he spent his Time in his Journey: that Men should so spend their Time, that they may give a good Account, how they have spent it.

22 *d*. 2 *m*. I preached on Luk. 15. 18. A serious *Resolution* of Repentance and Religion, a proper, needful, hopeful Introduction to it.

29 *d*. 2 *m*. I preach'd on Heb. 13. 20. The *Blood of the everlasting Covenant*, and I finished what I began two months ago. (And I administred the Eucharist.)

6 *d*. 3 *m*. [*May*.] I preached, on Luk. 15. 18. The Confession of Sin, which must accompany Repentance, considering, *against whom*, and *before whom*, we have sinned.

13 *d*. 3 *m*. I preached on Prov. 13. 19. And handled that Case, What shall we do that the *Desires* of our Souls may be accomplished, and that the Accomplishment thereof may be sweet unto our Souls.

17 *d*. 3 *m*. *Thursday*. I preached the Lecture, on Neh. 5. 9. The Manner and Method of, *Walking in the Fear of God*.

20 *d*. 3 *m*. I preached, on Luk. 15. 19. The Worth of Mercies known by the Want of them. Our *Unworthiness* of the divine Faith; what a great Thing tis to be a *Child of God;* what an Honour to do the *least Service for* the Lord.

27 *d*. 3 *m*. I preached on, Exod. 9. 26. Other people, and even wicked People, faring the better, for living among the People of God.

3 *d*. 4 *m*. [*June*.] I preached on, Luk. 15. 20. Good *Resolutions* follow'd with good *Executions*. *Repentance* having in it, both a *Rising* from Sin, and a *Coming* to God. And, that we ought to repent *immediately*.

10 *d*. 4 *m*. I preached on, 2. Tim. 4. 10. The *Love of this present*

world; what it is, and how it makes Men *forsake* the Service of God; and what Resolutions we ought all to take up, relating thereto.

14 *d.* 4 *m. Thursday.* I preached the Lecture, on Eccl. 1. 15. The *crooked* Things, and our unavoidable Exercises of Patience, which cannot be cured; a right Behaviour under them.

17 *d.* 4 *m.* I preached, on Luk. 15. 20. The Infinite *Readiness* of the merciful God to show mercy unto repenting Sinners; to be *reconciled* unto them, and to give them comfortable *Signs* of Reconciliation.

24 *d.* 4 *m.* I preached, on Heb. 13. 21. The Great and glorious Blessing, of a Work of *Sanctification,* wherewith God pleases to præpare and dispose the Minds of His People to do *His will in every good Work.* (And I administred the Eucharist.)

1 *d.* 5 *m.* [*July.*] I preached, on Luk. 15. 21. A pardon to be *asked* for, else not hoped for. We are not only to *say well,* but also to *do well. Humility* the Disposition and Concernment of Repentance. Sin to be *repented* after tis *pardoned;* And Repentance with best *Advantage* after *Assurance* of a Pardon; with Observations on the *Omission* of one Clause in the Speech of the Prodigal.

8 *d.* 5 *m.* I preached on Eccl. 2. 14. On what regards, the *Eyes* of a wise Man, are *in his Head.*

12 *d.* 5 *m. Thursday.* I preached the Lecture, on Rev. 10. 1. The *Rainbowe* about the Head of our Saviour. His Remembrance of His *Covenant,* in the most *cloudy* Times that pass over His People.

15 *d.* 5 *m.* I preached on Tit. 1. 16. How Men do in *their Works, deny God.* I thought the Subject suitable, in regard of the many Strangers and Souldiers who drop into our Assembly.

22 *d.* 5 *m.* I preached on, Luk. 15. 22. Sin *forgotten,* when *forgiven.* The *Servants* of God made the Instruments of conveying the Blessings of God. God's doing *more* for His people than they ask Him to do. Not only the *Necessities,* but also the *Conveniencies* of the Children of God provided for; a *repenting* Soul *well array'd* from the Wardrobe of God; the Meaning of the *Robe,* and *Ring,* and *Shoe.*

26 *d.* 5 *m. Thursday.* A general Fast. I preached on Luk. 18. 8. The *Elect, Children* of God, having their *Enemies,* and *Sufferings,* that seem *long* unto them; but *crying to God,* on which He *certainly* and *speedily* delivers them, and executes *vengeance* on their Enemies.

29 *d.* 5 *m.* I preached on Luk. 15. 23. The *Feast,* and the *Joy,* on the Repentance of a Sinner.

5 *d.* 6 *m.* [*August.*] I preached on, Prov. 14. 10. The *Heart knowing* its own *Bitterness;* and after some Discourses on the Bitterness of Sin, and of Repentance for it, I discoursed on the *secret*

Sorrowes of the Neighbours; what should be their Conduct under them.

9 *d*. 6 *m. Thursday*. I preached the Lecture, on Matth. 2. 23. The blessed Jesus of *Nazareth*, our *Nazarene*, or our Preserver. And I took Occasion of the Fears now in the Town, expecting a destructive Invasion from the French, to inculcate those Things, by which we may engage the Care of our glorious JESUS, for our Preservation.

12 *d*. 6 *m*. I preached, on Luk. 15. 24. A Sinner, a Dead, and a lost Creature, till Conversion to God changes him, enlivens him, recovers him.

19 *d*. 6 *m*. I preached on Heb. 13. 21. (my eighth and last Sermon,) God working in His chosen People, the Things well-pleasing in His Sight, thro' Jesus Christ. (And I administred the Eucharist.)

26 *d*. 6 *m*. I preached on Luk. 15. 24. The Wondrous Matter of *Joy*, in the Conversion of a Sinner.

30 *d*. 6 *m. Thursday*. A general Fast. I preached on Isa. 45. 19. The Offspring of *Jacob*, seeking the glorious God, not in vain.

2 *d*. 7 *m*. [*September*.] I preached a second time, on Luk. 15. 24. The *Joy* on the Conversion of a Sinner.

6 *d*. 7 *m. Thursday*. I preached the Lecture, on 1. Joh. 4. 18. The *Love* which does cast out *Fear;* and how?

9 *d*. 7 *m*. I preached a third Time, on Luke. 15. 24. The *Joy* on the Conversion of a Sinner; and made the most pathetical and importunate Conclusion, I could, with passages [*illegible*] death beds in the Neighbourhood.

16 *d*. 7 *m*. I preached on Josh. 7. 8. The Confusion which attends the Defeat of an important Enterprise; and what we should say in such a Confusion. (This was, that I might take an Advantage to inculcate the Maxims of Piety, from the universal Distress, into which our People are cast yesterday, by the Tidings of the Defeat of our *Canadian* Enterprise.)

23 *d*. 7 *m*. I preached on Luk. 15. 25. 26, 27, 28. *Elder-brothers* to beware lest they miss of being found among the Children of God. *Elder sons* not to be *idle* ones: that we must *enquire* before we *censure*. Ungodly People ignorant of the Meaning of what is done in practical Godliness. Fidelity requisite in a *Report*. *Envy* the Character of wicked People. God *entreating* Sinners, not to refuse Happiness.

30 *d*. 7 *m*. I preached both parts of the Day at *Salem*. A. M. on Gal. 1. 18. *After three Years I went up to Jerusalem*. That we ought so to spend our Time, that we may give a good Account of it.

P. M. on Eccl. 1. 15. How to manage *crooked Things;* whereof that Place has at this Time a sufficient Number.

4 *d.* 8 *m.* [*October.*] *Thursday.* I preached the Lecture, to a very great Auditory, at the South-meetinghouse, and had a very great Opportunity (from Jer. 5. 3.) to bear Testimonies for the Lord, and call the People of the Place, to a due Improvement of the Desolations newly made by Fire, on the Heart of the Town.

7 *d.* 8 *m.* I preached on Job. 3. 25. Living in daily Expectation of, and Preparation for, troublesome *Changes.*

11 *d.* 8 *m. Thursday.* A Fast thro' the Province. I preached on, 2. King 10. 32. The Hand of God cutting People short in their Enjoyments; a right Behaviour under such Dispensations.

14 *d.* 8 *m.* I preached, on Rev. 2. 16. The dreadful Condition of the Church, against whom our Saviour shall come, in the Quality of an Enemy. (And I administred the Eucharist.)

18 *d.* 8 *m. Thursday.* I preached the Lecture (he that should have preached it, being hindred by lameness,) on Ps. 13. 4. The *Triumphs* of a prevailing Enemy to be dreaded and deprecated. Directing a right Use of the Defeat we have lately suffered. (The General Assembly now come together.)

21 *d.* 8 *m.* I preached on Prov. 23. 5. *Riches,* what they *are not,* and what they *are,* how certain and sudden their *Flight* from us; and what Eyes we ought therefore to look upon them withal. (Because of repeated Losses befalling the Neighbourhood.)

28 *d.* 8 *m.* I preached on, Luk. 15, 29, 30. An *Hypocrite* having an high Opinion of his own Righteousness; and having fair Colours for foul Actions; and being ready to rise up and cry down the Follies of others, when they can't see their own Failings; and being ready to complain of the Dealings of God.

1 *d.* 9 *m.* [*November.*] *Thursday.* I preach'd the Lecture on 1. Chron. 19. 3. *Good Things* found in some that are to blame for *ill Things.* And I transferr'd the Discourse into the State of the Countrey; taking the Part of an *Advocate,* as well as a *Reprover.* Because we suffer much by the Calumnies of our Enemies. And the General Assembly was now sitting.

4 *d.* 9 *m.* I preached, on Luk. 15. 31. 32. My twenty-ninth Sermon (as I take it,) concluding my Discourses on the Parable of the Prodigal; with several Observations; but chiefly *that;* How a converted sinner is *enlivened* and *recovered.*

7 *d.* 9 *m. Wednesday.* I preached the Lecture at *Woburn,* on Rom. 15. 14. Being *Full of Goodness.*

11 *d.* 9 *m.* I preached on Isa. 63. 17. *Sinful Hardness* of Heart, a *fearful Judgment* of God. I also improved a remarkable Vengeance of God, upon an Harlot in the Neighbourhood, for a Warning unto others who may wallow in Adulteries.

18 *d.* 9 *m.* I preached, on, Job. 4. 21. *Dying without Wisdome;* who do so, and what Course we are to take that we may not do so.

25 *d.* 9 *m.* I preached, on 2. Thess. 2. 16. The *good Hope thro'* *Grace,* which the People of God have to comfort them.

29 *d.* 9 *m. Thursday.* A general Thanksgiving. I preached on Psal. 31. 23. The *Love* of a good God, as the use to be made of all the good Things, with which He favours us.

2 *d.* 10 *m.* [*December.*] I preached, on, Job. 30. 24. The Cry usually made by the Children of Men, when God by Death brings His Destruction upon them.

16 *d.* 10 *m.* I preached on Exod. 25. 22. The great God maintaining a Communion with His People thro' the Mediation of our glorious Jesus, in the Wayes and Means of His own Appointment. (This I designed, as an Improvement of my own Calamity, in being banished the last Lord's-Day from the Communion.)

23 *d.* 10 *m.* A very cold Day. I preached on 2. Cor. 11. 27. *In Cold.* How the Service of God, is to be carried on, in the *Cold.*

27 *d.* 10 *m. Thursday.* I preached the Lecture, on Joh. 10. 22, 23. What we shall do, that we may meet with our *Saviour* at His *Temple,* in the *Winter.* A very winterish Time.

30 *d.* 10 *m.* I preached on Phil. 1. 10. The *excellent Things* which a true Pastor will desire to see His People, approving of, and abounding in.

6 *d.* 11 *m.* [*January.*] I preached on Phil. 1. 10. and carried on, what I began the last Lord's-Day. (And I administred the Eucharist.)

13 *d.* 11 *m.* I preached on, Phil. 1. 10. and further carried on what I had begun upon the Subject.

20 *d.* 11 *m.* I finished my Catalogue of, *excellent Things.*

27 *d.* 11 *m.* I preached, on Joh. 7. 27. That the knowledge of holy Truths is *Good;* and how and why we should know them for our *Good.* An Introduction to a Course of Sermons, intended (if God will) on the Parable of the *Tares.*

3 *d.* 12 *m.* [*February.*] I preached on Matth. 13. 24. The Church on Earth, being the *Kingdome of Heaven* upon Earth. And began my Course of Sermons on the Parable of the Tares.

10 *d.* 12 *m.* I preached on Matth. 13. 24. The Church, a *Field;* Christ the Owner of it; good Men the good Seed, by Him sown in it.

BENJAMIN COLMAN TO COTTON MATHER. M.H.S.

REV. SIR, — I return you all your late kind Communications, with many thanks for the pleasure and profit I have had from 'em. Mr. Watts is a great Master in Poetry, and a burning Light and Ornament of the Age; nor like the sun of less Use his Heat, from which nothing is hid. Yet how finely does he lay aside his Ornamental dress in his Reformation Sermon and only shows his fire. I'm highly pleas'd in his undertaking the Psalms, and the length that he's already got. His Touches upon the Canticles are I think the Glory of these which I return. Great are my Expectations from his next. You will forgive me that I emulate, and have dar'd to attempt to imitate, his Muse in the Inclosed; its flame, brevity and Metre. Be candid, and think not that I name 'em with the least of His. Yet have I succeeded better, I confess, than I expected. But you shal correct me. What Watt's has taught us of Charity will secure me from your Censure. I'm glad to find your heart so enlarg'd on that subject, and essay. Yet will you not be perfect in it, without as much a Care not to provoke Wrath, as power afterward to despise, or triumph over, it. I am, Sir, in perfect Charity, (asking your prayers, and waiting for your further Communications,) Your obliged and Affec. Servt.

BENJ. COLMAN.

BOSTON. Dec. 25, 1711.

TO SAMUEL PENHALLOW. M.H.S.

BOSTON, 11 d. 11 m. [January.] 1711–12.

MY HONOURED FRIEND, — You give me Leave, to be continually employing your kind Hand, for the noble Purposes of Services to the Kingdome of God. I præsume still on your Kindness and Goodness, which I have alwayes found to be such, that when that which another Person would count a Trouble, is imposed on you, you count it but a Pleasure. My *Fishermen*,[1] I suppose, are by this time in your hand; and will shortly pass from thence to such as are most concerned in them. I now pray your Acceptance of another small Thing; that what, I think, entertained your Ear when you were here, may now entertain your Eye.

My Book of, PASTORAL DESIRES,[2] which is to sett before my Neighbours, the *Excellent Things* we desire for them, now waits for

---

[1] *The Fisher-man's Calling.*   [2] Printed by B. Green, 1712.

some Help to be given unto it. I was thinking, about a Line or two
of yours unto Mr. *Archer*,[1] to this Effect; 'That C.M. having delivered in the public, as he knowes, a Discourse of *excellent Things*,
and having signified, as he also knowes, his Intention to publish the
Discourse, and lodge it in all the Families of the Neighbourhood, for
the Assistence of their Piety; it would be a noble thing in him, and
a Demonstration of his own Piety, to enable the said C. M. to prosecute his good Intention, by a generous Tender of three or four pounds
unto him, to help him in the Charge of the Impression. And it would
be an excellent offering both unto Heaven, and unto the Church,
whereto he has the Happiness to be now related.'

But I know not, whether I am not guilty of a great Impertinency
in this Proposal. I pray you to consider it with the Candor that
alwayes accompanies you; and by no means do any thing, but what
you shall upon Deliberation judge, will best square with the nicest
Rules of Discretion.

At this time I add no more; but commend you to the Constant
keeping and Conduct of the glorious Lord; and subscribe, Syr, Your
very obliged Friend and Servt

Co. MATHER.

To SAMUEL PENHALLOW.   M.H.S.

BOSTON, 28 *d.* 11 *m.* [January.] 1711-12.

HONOURED SIR, — Tis a very cold Time, tis true; But you take a
Course, to make me even—sweat under the Heap of Obligations that
you lay upon me.

Your Friendship I have alwayes found, cordial, generous, useful,
and very obliging. But it bids fair to grow into what the Writers
call, *heroic Friendship*. I shall be in perpetual Assiduities, to do my
part in it; I am not altogether insensible of what belongs to *Reciproca-
tions* in these Cases; and shall assiduously endeavour it in this. Old
Austin writing, *De Amicitia*, has a Saying; *Quid sit vera Amicitia,
non eum novit, qui vult aliam esse mercedem, quam ipsam.* Yours I
have alwayes esteemed so.

But, behold, you have thrown in upon me, *aliam quam ipsam*.
For which I render you my Thanks; with my Prayers to Heaven,
that as we have been united in serving glorious One here below, we
may at last, be so in praising Him above.

I have not yett had Opportunity to see our Friend Master *Archer*,

[1] Thomas Archer was admitted into the Second Church, January 6, 1711-12.

on whom you have done the Part of such a *cunning Archer*. But, I make no doubt, I shall suddenly feel the Operation of your Letter to him.

I wish all Blessings unto you, and unto One of the best of Consorts, and unto your Hopeful Offspring and am, Sir, Your obliged Servt.

Co. MATHER.

My Letter to Mr *Reinoles*, has in it, the Effect of your kind care at *Newberry*.

To SAMUEL PENHALLOW.[1]   M.H.S.

[April 17, 1712.]

The Negotiation of PEACE, is going on; and all Things conspire to give us a strong Expectation, that it will speedily be accomplished. The Conferences at *Utrecht* are carried on, with a greater Spirit of Accommodation on both Sides, than has appeared in some former Conferences on such occasions. The French King makes an *Explanation of his offers for a general Peace;* wherein he acknowledges the Q[ueen] of Great Britain, and the Succession according to the present Settlement. He demolishes *Dunkirk*, for an Equivalent that will not be much disputed about. He gives up St. *Christophere*, *Hudsons* Bay, and *Acady*, to Great Britain; and *Newfoundland*, only reserving the Fort at *Placentia*. He consents to a Treaty of Commerce on the most agreeable Terms. He allowes the Dutch, the Barrier they desire in the Netherlands. He brings the *Spanish Indies*, into the Condition wherein it was before the Death of King *Charles* II. He obliges his Grandson to renounce the Kingdoms of *Naples* and *Sardinia*, and the Dutchy of *Milan*. He consents to have things in *Portugal* and *Germany*, as they were before the War, and Contents the Duke of *Savoy*. And finally, comes into all the just Measures, the Allies can propose to hinder the Crowns of *France* and *Spain*, from ever being united on the same Head. On the whole, the public Writers are pleased to express themselves in these Terms, *That here is much more promised unto the English than was even demanded in those famous and numerous Articles, fallaciously term'd praeliminaries, which were signed by the* Duke *of* Marlborough, *and the Lord* Townshend, *at this Place in the Year* 1709. And, indeed, as we have nothing left now to fight *for;* so we have as little to fight *with*. The Difficulty which the Exchequer finds to pay what it owes, causes a general Discontent. Our Debts amount unto more than fifty Millions. A

---

[1] A good example of a "newsletter" of the day.

great Part of the Revenues of the Crown are Mortgaged. We have brought upon our grand Children such encumbrances as their posterity will hardly see themselves discharged of. We may add, the Queen and the present Ministry, seem resolved upon a Peace, if it can be in any tolerable Manner accomplished.

The Duke of *Marlborough* is thrown down, with all the Indignity imaginable. He is not only stript of all his Offices and Employments, and has his three Daughters dismiss'd the Bed-Chamber, but also he is charged by the House of Commons, (a Majority of an 100, in a very full House,) with *illegal and unwarrantable Practices;* and with wronging the Nation of Vast Summs of Money; above threescore thousand Pounds, in the one Article of Bread, and Bread-Wagons; near two hundred thousand pounds, taken as a Deduction of two and half per *cent*, from our Allowances to the foreign Troops. His Secretary, Mr. *Walpool* [1] was expell'd the House, and sent to the Tower. And it is apprehended, His Grace will not be long after him.

The Act against occasional Conformity runs to such an Heighth, that if a Man be present at any one Meeting of the Dissenters for the Exercise of Religion, he is *ipso facto*, deprived of all Places and Offices of any Trust or Profit whatsoever.

Not only the Dissenters, but all that part of the Nation, who have been distinguished by the title of, *the Moderate Party*, are treated on all Occasions, as an, *undone Faction* (the Term expressly given to them,) and insulted with all manner of Provocations. The Conduct of the Whiggish Lords (in whose House, the Bill was passed first, and went, *Nemine Contradicente*,) in this Matter was very wonderful. The Earl of *Nottingham* hired their Concurrence to the Bill, by a Bargain to bring over unto them, so many Lords of the High Church, as would break all the Measures now taking, and save the Nation. So they sacrificed the best Friends they had; and, if my Lord fail in his Part of the Bargain, lett them gett their Act repealed again how they can.

The Ferments in the Nation are boiled up to such an astonishing and prodigious Heighth, as fills all People with Consternation. Every one seems apprehensive of the most mischievous and tremendous Consequences. The Bishop of *Salisbury*,[2] lately preaching at the *Temple*, on, *Can these dry bones Live?* assured his Auditory, that no Good Times could be Look'd for; nothing but a Miracle could pro-

---

[1] Robert Walpole.

[2] Gilbert Burnet (1643-1715), whose *History of his own Time* is one of the standard sources of history.

duce them; all good Men must hasten what they can, to gett furnished with the Spirit of Martyrdome. Another famous Doctor,
preached on; *He shall cause Craft to prosper in his hand, and by
Peace he shall destroy many.*

The King of *Prussia*, is doing what he can, to promote Conferences among the Protestant Princes, that they may unite in Points,
to demand upon the Peace in favour of the Protestant Religion and
Interest.

There are great Probabilities of a new Rupture, between the
Czar and the *Ottoman* Empire. The King of *Sweden*, delayes his
homeward Motions from *Bender*, till the War, or Peace, be effectually
declared. He has managed himself in a wondrous Manner, and had
a mighty Influence on the Affairs of the World; and his Return home
will have Consequences wherein all *Europe* will be greatly concerned.

The Whiggish Lords and those that came into their Measures,
had made so strong a Party in their House, that they were proceeding
to Impeach the Earl of *Oxford*. But the Q [ueen] by a Creation of
twelve new Lords delivered him.

The *Canadien*-fleet upon their Arrival, fill'd the Court and Nation
with Clamours against *New England*. The Countrey was charg'd
with Treachery, and Stubborness, and accused as having designedly
ruined the Expedition. Mr. *Dummer* did the Countrey the Justice
and Honour of publishing an elegant and sufficient Vindication even
before the Arrival of Col. *Nicholson*, who carried with him a great
Addition of Materials whereupon the clamour was very much abated;
and Col. *Nicholson*, thank'd for his Activity and Fidelity. My Lord
Privy-seal, our Plenipotentiary at *Utrecht*,[1] gave particular Thanks to
Mr *Dummer*, for that Vindication,[2] and assured him, he would at the
Congress prosecute the Claim, which he had therein so well made out
unto *Canada*.

From Glasgow, they write (Feb. 12) "The Parliament is going
on with such a Toleration for the Episcopal men in *Scotland*, (who are
generally *Jacobites*,) and in such Terms, as to carry a manifest Breach
of the *Union*, according to the Sentiments of our best Lawyers and
others. We are like to have a speedy Peace with *France*. The
Commons have voted a great many Resolves, about the Mismanagements of the late Ministry, and about the Deficiences of the Allies
abroad as to Men, and Ships, and Money. Hence People say, the
former Alliance is near an End, and a new one with *France* is at hand.

[1] John Robinson, Bishop of Bristol (1650–1723).
[2] *A Letter to a Friend in the Country, on the late Expedition to Canada*, 1712.

The new Ministers are Impatient for it.   Men of Revolution-Prin-
ciples in this Island are little regarded;   while those of the French
Mode are like to carry the Day.

To Samuel Penhallow.   m.h.s.

Boston 28 *d*. 5 *m*. [July.] 1712.

Sir, — Tis my Duty to unite my Praises with yours, in an Oblation unto the glorious Lord, who carried you with part of your Family,
safe home to your Family; at a time when an Enemy might so easily
have intercepted you, and just after did captivate some of our Friends
even between this and *Marshfield*.   But I will add my Advice, that
you don't run any more such Ventures.   *Boston* is alwayes a *Placentia*
to me, while you are in it; but I can't consent, that you take *Placentia* in the Way to *Boston*, or from it.

We have nothing very remarkable since you left us.   Our domestic Intelligence is not worth relating, our Foreign (besides what you
have in *Johannes* Antiquities,) is, what our Agent [1] writes, about the
Middle of May; that there is great Expectation of a Peace, which
will make N[ew] E[ngland] as well as Gr[eat] Britain, easy and happy
But that all Things are carried on with such a Secrecy, as to be understood by none but those that are next the Candle.   And Major *Handy*
writes, that a Friend of his, (whom yee ken very well) is to come over
shortly, Governor of N[ew] E[ngland] and of *Annapolis*.

I am, as when you Left me; and alwayes, Syr, Your sincere
Friend and Servt.

Co. Mather.

My next Lecture prov'd, as you foretold.   A very vast Assembly
was, and with no small Assistence from Heaven, then spoken to.
The Sermon you have here enclosed.

To Samuel Penhallow.   m.h.s.

Boston, 1 *d*. 7 *m*. [September.] 1712.

Sir, — We are kept under so rigid a Famine of Intelligence from
the other side of the Atlantic, that it has kept me from writing to
you, as not having any Thing worthy to be written of.   And the
Speculations upon this Embargo of our Intelligence, are very various
and uncertain.

[1] Jeremiah Dummer.
[2] "June 12.   Dr. C. Mather preaches from [Psalm] 110, ult."   Sewall, *Diary*
II. 350.

But I call to mind, that you desired my Opinion upon a Case of Scandal in a Church, not prosecuted. It is this; Lett the Proofs of the Scandal be gathered, and lett the Brethren furnish the Pastor with them. (Tho' indeed, it his Duty, to look and send after them.)

Lett the Brethren, then demand of the Pastor, to go thro' with the instituted and necessary Discipline.

If the Pastor deny to do it, lett them inform him, that they will apply themselves with just Remonstrances to the Neighbour-churches, and procure their Admonitions to him.

Certainly, he will not run the Hazard of such a Proceeding.

May the Glorious Lord, multiply His Blessings on you, and on your whole Family and Interest, both at home and abroad. I am, Syr, Your sincere Servt.

Co. Mather.

To Samuel Penhallow.   m.h.s.

Boston, 19 *d.* 7 *m.* [September.] 1712.

Sir, — Tho' you have already one of them, yett I now send you eight more, of a good Book, Entituled, *A Letter of some Aged N.C.'s* [1] My Request is, that you would (with the Assistence of good Mr *Kaies,*) disperse them, where they may best answer the End of them, in your Province. If it be possible, I would have them generally spread, and read, and lent and operative among all your People; especially on the Bank and the Great Island; and that all your Ministers particularly have the perusal of them. The best Thing I can do is to refer all to your Discretion; which I do most heartily.

It afflicts me to hear of the Loss you have sustained in your fishing Interest. But God has taught you Patience, and Submission and Fruitfulness, under such Dispensations. And you have no Fear of being well-Provided for.

The Protection which our glorious Lord, has of late given to our Frontiers, notwithstanding some Desolations there, is an observable matter, and calls for our Thankfulness.

I hope, you will find a Time, to perfect the Collection of Occurrences you once gave me some Expectation of.

I will at this Time, with my usual Freedome, request one more Favour from you. *I have been told, That some years ago, the People digging a Well, in a Town of your Province: (I think, Dover:) did at an Unaccountable Depth under ground, encounter with Trees, that were*

---

[1] This letter, dated August 24, 1701, was printed in a fourth edition, Increase Mather, editor, in 1712.

surprising to them. If you could obtain a more full Account, where the Well; what the Depth; what the Trees; which way they lay; how far from the Sea: I should be able to answer some Obligations that ly upon me, from the other side of the Water; and should with your leave, do myself the Honour, of using your Name in the Communication.

At this time I add no more; but commend your Person, Consort, Children at home and abroad, unto the Blessing and Keeping of the glorious One. I am, Syr, Your obliged and faithful Servt,

Co. MATHER.

TO SAMUEL PENHALLOW.   M.H.S.

BOSTON, 22 *d.* 7 *m.* [September.] 1712.

SIR, — When my last was dated, I had not received the sad Advice, of the Inroads and Assaults, which the Enemy is making on your Neighbourhood. I exceedingly sympathize with you in the Desolations and the Difficulties, that renew so many Troubles upon you. May the glorious Lord be your Protector; and help us all to hear His Voice in these calamitous Dispensations.

You hear of a Peace as good as concluded at home; The Queen, Ministry, Parliament, sett upon it.[1] You hear, that the Allies are very angry; treat us wth much Contempt; carry on their Conquests, and without us, have taken *Quesnoy.* You hear, that tho' the learned among us, and no doubt in *Britain* too, cry up the Terms of the Peace, as the most honourable and sufficient that ever were in the World, yet Multitudes of people, think, we are all betray'd; and the Ferments rise to an astonishing Elevation.

We still have, Psal. XCIII. 4. to friend; and there we must leave all.

The *Caribbee* Islands, it may be feared, they are every one of them lost. The Tidings of what is done there, will have little Tendency to abate the Ferments at home. I am, Syr, Your hearty Servt,

Co. MATHER.

TO SAMUEL PENHALLOW.   M.H.S.

BOSTON, 26 *d.* 11 *m.* [January.] 1712–13.

SIR, — My Friend, Mr *Timothy Thornton* (than whom I have not in my whole Neighbour, one more sincere and friendly,) gives me the

[1] The Queen's proclamation (dated August 18) for a cessation of hostilities reached Boston, October 24.

agreeable Opportunity, of Conveying to you, a Packett, wherein I renew after my poor Manner, my Testimonies of the Sense which I always retain of the many Obligations you have laid upon me.

Whatever Civilities you shew to this Friend of mine, will be placed unto my Account, and add unto the Number of my Obligations.

To him I refer you, for all matters of Intelligence, after which you may be inquisitive; tho' indeed, I scarce know any that are worth enquiring after.

In this Packett, you find a Book written by your Friend, Mr. *Reinoles;* [1] whereof I make a present unto your Lady; as apprehending it more valuable than any thing of my own composing.

May the glorious Lord multiply His Blessings, on your Person, and Family. I rejoice in His late Favours to Captain *Penhallow.*[2] I am, Syr, Your Sincere Friend and Servt,

Co. Mather.

I hope, the Packett I sent you (for *Bradshaw*) cost you nothing For I paid the Post, unto his Satisfaction; and he promised me to make no demand upon you.

[1] Probably Thomas Reynolds, *Practical Religion.* See p. 171, *supra.*
[2] John Penhallow, the younger, who married Ann, daughter of Jacob Wendell.

1713

THE LIst YEAR.

This Year, there have been preached LXXII public Sermons, besides private ones.

Not one Day has pass'd without, some Contrivance to do Good, invented and registred; besides Multitudes of such, not entred in these poor Memorials.

Not one Day has passed, without being able to say at Night, something of my small Revenues dealt out unto pious Uses.

Never any Time spent with any Company without some Endeavour of a fruitful Conversation in it.

A considerable Accession to our *Biblia Americana*, many more Illustrations than Dayes in the Year.

Seventeen Books præpared for publication, and most of them actually published.

Dayes of Prayer, no more than xx. Vigils, very few.

But, oh! the Sins, the Sins, which this Year has been fill'd withal! Oh! the Slothfulness that has attended me, in the Duties of both my Callings! Oh! the Miscarriages that have accompanied all the little Services that I have endeavoured.

My God, I fly to the Blood of my Saviour, for the Pardon of all.

12 *d.* 12 *m.* [*February.*] 1712 [-13.] *Thursday.* I have now seen a Jubilee! The Goodness and Mercy and Patience of the glorious GOD, I cannot but exceedingly acknowledge and glorify.

It being this Day, the Time of our public Lecture, and so there being some Necessity of my going abroad, I suffered thereby some

Interruption, to certain Exercises, to which this Day would otherwise have been entirely devoted.

However, in the former Part of the Day, I bewayled before the
Lord, the Sins of my Life past, and particularly of the Year past,
and received the Pardon of them, thro' Faith in the Blood of my
only Saviour.

And I perused, a Discourse of my own, on the Story of Life;
(from Psal. xc. 9.) delivered publickly on one of my Birth-dayes.

In the latter Part of the Day, I gave Thanks to the Lord, for
the Blessings of my former Life, and particularly of the year now
expired.

I perused the Memorials of the Year, and made my prayerful
and adapted Reflection thereupon.

I marked with my Pencil, such Projections, as I had not prosecuted unto so much Effect, as I would still endeavour to do.

And I praised the God of all Grace, for the Services in which He
had employ'd me, and for which He had enabled me.

Finally, I besought of the glorious One, to spare me this Year
also, and to præpare me for all the Changes which may be this Year
to come upon me, and to grant that this Year may prove more Fruitful, than any I have yett seen, ever since I came into the World.

5. G. D. There is a considerable Motion on foot,
about erecting an Hospital in this Town, for the Education
of poor Children. My Directions and Assistences, which
are called for, on this Occasion, must be afforded in the
best manner I can give them.[2]

6. G. D. There are some hopeful Candidates for the
Ministry, who may be made the more useful to the Church
of God by having such Additions to their Libraries as their
poor Circumstances well scarce allow them, to make. I
would from some Libraries now to be sold, where I may
meet with some good Penn'orths, make agreeable presents
unto them.

7. G. D. I would endeavour this day, particularly to
examine each of the more notable Afflictions, with which

---

[1] The abrupt beginning shows that certain pages of the Diary have been lost.

[2] Could the "circular letter" of Mather, mentioned in Sewall, *Diary*, II. 371,
have been on this motion?

I have been chastened, and impartially to examine what good Effect my Chastisements have had upon me.

1. [*February* 15.]   G. D.   I purpose, as soon as I can, to sett apart a Day, for Supplications before the glorious Lord, it may be, more than one, to obtain Mercies for my Flock, and those Influences of Heaven that may over-rule their Humours and Follies; and a gracious Direction from above to me, in my whole Conduct, and the Discharge of my Ministry.

2. G. D.   There is a Projection relating to my *Katy's* being well-disposed of, which I would consider, and if it be convenient, prosecute.

3. G. D.   There being an hopeful Opportunity for one of my Sisters to be disposed of, I would act in that Matter with all suitable Application.[1]

4. G. D.   That important affayr of setting up a *Christian Hospital*, for the good Education of poor children in this Town, is coming into its Operation; and many services are expected of me on that Occasion, which I would endeavour to perform.

Among the rest, the preaching of a Lecture, to encourage works of Charity.

5. G. D.   Among the Instructors of the Indians, I would promote a short Essay, to be written and printed in the Indian Tongue, to excite and assist the Worship of God in their Families.

6. G. D.   There is a young Gentleman at *Portsmouth* (a Son-in-Law, to a Friend of mine there,) who is under dying Languishments. I have been told, that some godly and worthy People there, look upon him, as being smitten with Judgments of Heaven, particularly for the Expressions of Malignity, whereof he has made me the Object. I would be far from taking any Notice of his malignant Abuses to

---

[1] This may refer to his sister Maria, who married, in 1713, for her second husband Richard Fifield. She was the widow of Captain Bartholomew Green.

me ; but I would now pitty him, and pray for him, and send to him ; and present him with certain Treatises, which may have a Tendency to prepare him for his Dissolution.

7. G. D. God calls me, at this time, to a more than ordinary Exercise of Piety, and of Patience. A very great Number of the Flock, whereof I have been all along hitherto, a trembling servant, imagine our large Meeting-house to be overstock'd with people ; and that they mightily want larger Accomodations for themselves and their Families. They are therefore violently sett upon building a new Meeting-house ; in which Affayr my Concern is the greater, because it proves a Grief of Mind unto my Aged Parent, and I must keep a watchful Eye upon his Conduct on this Occasion.[1] I must treat these People, very lovingly, candidly, courteously and prudently. I must continually cry to the Glorious Lord, that He would guide all my Steps. I must humble myself before Him, for all my Miscarriages in my Ministry and my whole Behaviour. I must be full of Humility and have my Spirit reconciled unto little Circumstances. I must keep a mighty Guard on my Words, and all my Wayes, and on the very Frames of my Heart, as lying all open to the View of God. I must maintain a strong Faith in my dear Saviour ; for a good Issue of this thorny Affair, and for the Continuance of my Opportunities to do Good and for the support of me and mine. My God, I look up unto thee !

1. [*February* 22.] G. D. That critical, important, threatening Affair of our People swarming into a new Meeting house, is now pushing on. It will be a great Service unto the Church, and unto Religion, if I do all that is possible, to keep up the Spirit of Love, and prevent Contention, and preserve a Temper of Kindness, Courtesy, and Charity, in the Management of the Matter. My God, make me Prudent and Patient.

[1] On Mather's omission to notice a new Church, see Sewall, *Diary*, II. 348.

I would speedily sett apart some whole Dayes on this occasion.

I would also forward the Repairing of our Meeting-house into a Condition, that may render it more accommodable.

2. G. D.   I would study as ingenious Wayes as I can to make Remarks of Piety, on our domestic Occurrences; and put in agreeable Clauses into the evening Prayers of the Family, relating to them; and when we are going to those Prayers, employ my Thoughts accordingly.   One Instance to illustrate this Intention I have now to mention. My pretty little Daughter is a weaning.[1]   Meditations on the Characters of a weaned Child in true Christianity, are proper now to entertain my other Children, and the rest of my Domesticks.

3. G. D.   It will be mightily for the Honour of my aged Parent, that he should in a most courteous, candid, condescending Manner, treat the nice Affair of our People swarming into a new Meeting-house.   I will do the best I can, to sollicit such a Conduct in him, and study his Comfort, in the whole Affayr.

4. G. D.   It may serve many glorious Interests of my Great Saviour, if I prepare and publish, a Discourse on the various Injuries, which are done unto my Saviour. For this Purpose, I would fitt up for the Press, a Discourse on the unsuspected Wrongs often done to the Son of God among the Children of Men.   And add unto it, a summary Conviction of Judaism, and of Arianism.

5. G. D.   The next thing, I am doing for the Service of the Christianized Indians, is to give the finishing Stroke, unto the Affair of their Cohabitation at *Natic;* to which I am now giving my best Assistences.[2]

6. G. D.   There is a very poor Child, who has a more than ordinary Disposition and Capacity for Learning, and

---

[1] Jerusha, who died in the following November.
[2] Bacon, *History of Natick,* 21.

has also made a surprising Progress in it; not without a prospect of serious Piety also in him. I would exert my own charity, and sollicit that of others, to procure for him, a learned Education.

7. G. D. The Lord having very graciously instructed me, in the Mystery of three Persons in one God, and the Godhead of my Saviour, and the Government of the World administred by the Son of God incarnate in my enthroned Jesus, I would be exceedingly thankful to Him, for His thus highly favouring of me; I would also endeavour very much to strengthen my Idea of the Mystery, by an assiduous contemplation of it; and I would study more than ever to live upon it, and walk in the Light, having a Mind enlightened with a clear View of Him who is the object of my Love, and my Prayers, and my Praises, and who offers Himself to be my God.

28 d. 12 m. Satureday. This Day I sett apart, for prayer with Fasting, in secret before the Lord. And I enjoy'd much precious Communion with Heaven in the Day.

One peculiar Occasion of my Supplications before the Lord, was, the Motion and Ferment of a new Meeting-house, which our people seem resolved upon swarming into. I am jealous, lest it be a meer Design of Satan, to ruine the North Church; and furnish ill-humoured Men, with an Engine to break to peeces this flourishing and envied Society. However, lest the Thing be of God, and that I may prevent the Devices of Satan, to sow Discord, I treat the whole Matter, with all the candid, and courteous, and compliant, Condescensions imaginable. I now employ my Cries to Heaven, for Wisdome from Above, and all the Patience, which this critical Occasion may call for. I judge and loathe myself before the Lord, for all my Miscarriages, by which I may have provoked Him, to take away a Considerable part of my Flock from me; All my Vanity, my Slothfulness, my Unfruitfulness, and my Unthankfulness.

I repaired unto the great Sacrifice, for the Pardon of my own Miscarriages and of all that has been amiss in the Flock also. I left this whole Matter unto the Divine Management, and relied upon the Influences of the Glorious Head of the Church, for a good Issue of it. I made a Sacrifice of the Flock, and of all my Opportunities to do Good in the World, unto the Great God; with a most consenting Resignation, and became willing to be a Preacher unto a very small Auditory, and to be reduced unto very diminutive Circumstances, and to encounter any Humiliations and Annihilations, that He shall please to order for me.[1]

(I.)[2] Here may be a proper Place, to insert, that from some of the Southern Colonies infested with Antinomian Troublers; I am earnestly cried unto, that I would help them with some Armour against their Errors; and with a Testimony against a Foolish pamphlett spred among the People to disseminate them; and the Concurrence of the other Ministers in this place unto the Testimony. Accordinly, with some Look to Heaven, and Help from thence, I prepared, all that has been desired. And my Treatise is now in the Press, under this Title; ADVERSUS LIBERTINOS, *or, Evangelical Obedience described and demanded. In an Essay, to Establish the Holy Law of the Glorious GOD, upon the principles of Justification by the Faith of the Gospel.*[3]

1. [*March* 1.] G. D. I hope, the Lenity, the Charity, the Humility, and the Good Spirit, and conduct, with which I endeavour to treat the Flock, in their Critical Affair of a

---

[1] Six lines struck out follow.

[2] He begins to number thus the paragraphs in which a new publication is mentioned.

[3] Printed by B. Green, for Samuel Gerrish, 1713. The "foolish pamphlet" bore the title of *A Spiritual Lawyer*, which the Boston clergy declared to be "full of dark, unsafe and unsound Passages." Jedidiah Andrews expressed the wish that an answer might be prepared to Antinomianism, and Mather, as was not unusual with him, secured the countenance of his "most Honour'd (and now Aged) Parent, and my Reverend Brethren, the rest of the Ministers in this Town." A characteristic letter of Andrews will be found in *Proceedings*, XLIII. 646.

New Church, will be blessed of God, as an useful Exemple unto them, and be for the prevention of the Satanic Devices which would operate among them, and be an occasion of Abundance of Good.

1 d. 1 m. [*March.*] *Lords-Day.* At the Lord's-Table this Day, I was brought near unto the Lord. Had I Time, yett I should want Words, to express the Irradiations wherewith I was favoured of the Lord.

At the Administration of the former Element, I considered the Son of God, assuming the Man Jesus, in whom there was offered up unto God, a most valuable Sacrifice; and how far the divine Person of our Immanuel was concerned in the Sacrifice. I was astonished, at the Invitation given unto me, to come and plead that Sacrifice, for my Atonement. I then did receive it, and admire it, and rely upon it. And I considered the six Sorts of Sacrifices, in the former Dispensation, and fetch'd Glories from each of them, which I beheld, and embrac'd and ador'd in my sacrificed Saviour.

At the Administration of the latter, I considered what a Cup of Suffering, my Jesus was willing to drink, that he might procure me the Cup of Salvation. And, then I sett myself, thankfully to offer myself and my all, in a Flame of Love, unto God, who had provided for me such a wonderful Sacrifice as that of my Saviour. I relied on the Blood of my Saviour, to purchase this Grace for me, that I may be willing to be nothing, and lose myself, and every Thing; and my own Will in God; and be willing to undergo all Sorts of Annihilations, which I more particularly specified, and be satisfied in what ever the wise, and just, and good Will of my heavenly Father shall order for me. I then called to mind with inexpressible Consolation, that this will of my heavenly Father, was gone over into my Saviour; it was the Will of my Saviour too; who is by the divine Constitution, the Governour of the World My whole Condition, will be ordered, by my dear, kind, enthroned JESUS!

2. G. D. In my Discourses with my Consort, I would often insist on three Points, wherein the Wives of Ministers have rendred themselves famous, and had their Names precious among Survivers.

The first: Much Constancy and Fervency of Devotion

with study to improve in the Knowledge of the great Saviour, and in Communion with God.

The Second: Much Ingenuity with Assiduity, in the Instructing of their Families and Instilling of Piety into their Domesticks, and well-ordering the Manners of those under their Charge.

The Third; much Compassion, and Helpfulness and Benignity, with Charity in all sorts of Expressions, towards the Miserable in the Neighbourhood.

3. G. D. I have litt upon a Book, fill'd with excellent Passages, the dying Words and Frames of some Holy Souls, full of Resignation to the Will of God, and rejoicing in the Hope of His Glory. I would convey this Honey, to my aged Parent, and present the Book to him, that I may sweeten to him, and assist him in, his finishing Work; which, tho' he be in perfect Health; and of bright Faculties, he seems hastning to, by Longing for.

4. G. D. I have now prepared for the Public, a Discourse on the *unsuspected Wrongs* which are commonly done to our glorious and only Saviour; part whereof was preached on a remarkable Occasion, almost nineteen Years ago. I have now incorporated thereinto, a couple of long Paragraphs, The one, the Sum of what is to be said, for the Conviction of the *Jewish* Infidelity. But the other, a clear Elucidation of the Doctrine of the Trinity; and the Godhead and Kingdome of our JESUS; and a Confutation of the *Arian* Heresy. I propose; in both of these, to some considerable Service to the Interests of Religion. And the latter of them, I propose as an Antidote against the wretched Poison, wherewith *Whiston* is endeavouring to corrupt the Church of God; and particularly to defend the Students in our Colledge from the Corruption.[1]

---

[1] It is impossible to identify the writing of Whiston against which Mather felt such opposition, but none of Whiston's works were printed in America during Mather's life.

5. G. D. There is a sett of wretched, idle, gaming Fellowes in this Town, whose Families are starving in great miseries, while they are following vain Persons. I would move in the Societies, that some effectual Provision may be endeavoured, for the Chastising and Restraining of such wretched Fellowes.

6. G. D. There is a Family in my Neighbourhood, conflicting with much Poverty and Misery, and long Illness and sickness. I must make it an object of my peculiar Charity. (αλκιν.)[1]

7. G. D. My pretty little Daughter *Jerusha*, on whom we have been so fond, as to make me fear whether we should not lose her, now lies very sick of a Fever. I would endeavour exceedingly to glorify God, by making a Sacrifice of the lovely Child; and be awakened unto a fresh Repentance of all the Miscarriages, for which I may fear a Chastisement is now threatned unto me.

1. [*March* 8.] G. D. This Week we give the Church a Meeting, that we may discourse on the critical Affayr of a New Church, as well as repairing our own old Meetinghouse. If the Lord enable me to treat the Church with Prudence and Patience, and a good Conduct on this occasion, He will be glorified, and the Church will be edified. I shall study it exceedingly; and, in order to it, send up ardent Cries unto Heaven, that I may be directed and assisted, and that the whole Affair may have an happy Issue given unto it.

2. G. D. I would make the sickness of my youngest Child, an occasion of Warning unto all the Children in the Family, to gett into a Condition of Safety for Death, and Eternity. And I would be awakened unto further Considerations, what more ought to be done for the Honour and Service of God, in the Sacrifice of my Family.

3. G. D. There are several Women, and aged Ones,

---

[1] Alkin.

among my Relatives, to whom I would present my late
Book, which inculcates the good works of a vertuous
Woman.[1]

10 *d.* 1 *m. Tuesday.*   Because our Church is to-morrow,
to hold a Meeting about those two Points; the repairing
and rendring more Commodious, our Meeting-house; and
then that critical Point, of a great Number swarming
into a new Meeting-house.   And I am afraid, how far the
Deevices of Satan may operate, on these Occasions; I sett
apart this Day, for prayers with Fasting, before the Lord;
that I might obtain the necessary and seasonable Favours
of the Lord.   I bewayled before the Holy One, the Sins
by which I have exposed myself to His Displeasure, and
particularly forfeited my Opportunities of preaching His
Gospel to so vast an Auditory.   And I was assured, that
my Sins are pardoned.   I entreated, that the Sins of the
Flock might also be forgiven; for which I pleaded the great
Sacrifice.   I cried unto Heaven, that I might be furnished
with Abundance of Prudence and Patience, for the critical
Occasion that is before me; and that my aged Parent also
may not be left unto any Word or Frame unsuitable.

I besought the Influences of the Holy Spirit, that the
Evil Spirit may be chained up, and that the Minds of the
Brethren may be kept in the Temper that is most of all
to be desired.   I offered up as a Sacrifice unto God, my
Congregation, and all my Opportunities to do Good; and
became willing to undergo any Condition, that the Divine
Will, should appoint for me.   I besought a comfortable
Issue of the whole Matter now before us, and left it with
the Lord, and cast the whole Burden of the Care thereof
upon Him.

I also carried my sick little Daughter to the Lord.

4. G. D.   I am giving a Peece of Land, unto a People
between *Wenham* and *Ipswyche*, to build a new Meeting-

---

[1] His *Tabitha Rediviva.*

house upon; and I would lay hold on the Occasion, and improve the Interest which I may hereby have in the Hearts of the People there, to lay the People under Obligations, to do some special Services for the Gospel, which I may think upon.[1]

10. [11.] *d.* 1. *m.* *Wednesday.* This Day, I received a gracious Answer to the Prayers of yesterday. We had a great Church-Meeting, of above one hundred Brethren, The Lord enabled me so to discourse on the two great Occasions we mett upon, and so to manage the Brethren, that the whole was carried thro' without one contentious Word: All done, without Murmurings, without Disputings.[2]

---

[1] This probably was the church at Hamilton. On May 22, 1712, the town of Ipswich consented to a church in " the Hamlet, so called," and on October 14, 1713, by an act of the General Court a district precinct was established. In the course of that year a church building was erected, and in the following year Samuel Wigglesworth (1689–1768) was chosen pastor. Cutler, *A Century Discourse delivered in Hamilton,* 1814. The donation of land by Mather receives no mention.

[2] "At a meeting of the Church, Wednesday, 11 *d.* 1 *m.* 1713, these two votes had a general concurrence with them.

"*Voted.* That the Honoured Committee, which has been chosen by this church, to consider and regulate the temporal Affaires thereof, be desired and empowered to proceed according to their Discretion and Ability, as in all needfull Reparation of the Meeting-house so particularly in Arching and Ceiling of it, and bringing the Galleries of the second Range, into such a condition as may be most commodious for the Congregation in general, and for those that shall be seated in them.

"*Voted.* Whereas fourteen of the Brethren in this North Church, have in an Instrument signed by them, addressed the church for their Allowance of their proceeding in an orderly way, which they have in the said Instrument expressed their Intention for, to the Building of a New Meeting-house, and forming themselves into a Church-state, when things are come to a due Maturity for it. The Church does grant the Request of the said Brethren; advising therewithal, that for the Circumstances of their Proceedings, and also for the Choice of their Minister, they endeavour to follow the best Advice, and what may be most for satisfaction.

"A vote passed at a former Church-meeting, vizt. 11 *d.* 1 *m.* 1713. The church desires and betrust *John Clark,* Esq., Mr. *Adam Winthrop,* Mr. *Thomas Hutchinson,* Mr. *Edward Hutchinson,* Mr. *John Ruck,* Mr. *Robert Howard,* Mr. *John Frizzel,* to act as a committee on the behalf of the Church, in directing such affaires thereof, as may concern the Repairing and Ordering of the Meeting-house, the advising of the Deacons about occasional Expences, with a due regard unto

My sick little Daughter now also begins to recover.

5. G. D. Some Godly Indians, having uttered very edifying Passages in their last Hours; Master *Japhet* in particular;[1] I would propose a convenient Collection of them, to be anon employ'd for many valuable Purposes.

6. G. D. A worthy Minister, who was of the same class with me in the Colledge, is fallen under some great Infirmities in his Health; I would as soon as I can, write and send unto this my Brother, such things, as may be most comfortable unto him, under his Affliction.

7. G. D. I ought to be exceedingly Thankful, and grow in my Thankfulness to the glorious Lord, in that I have had my Mind preserved from hypocondriac Maladies, which considering my Studies and Sorrowes, tis a Wonder, they have not utterly overwhelmed me. The View I have of some other men, unhinged and ruined that Way, very much awakens my Gratitude unto God my Saviour.

(II.) Near nineteen years ago, I preached a Lecture on the Wrongs done to our Saviour, by persons who little Imagine or Consider what they do. A Spirit who with a wondrous Lustre, made his Descent into my Study, declaring himself to be a good Angel of God, and expressing his Desire to have Act. IX. 5. preach'd upon, was the occasion of my preaching it. I then sent a Copy of it, unto *London*, to be published there; but it miscarried; and no Noise was made of the Occasion. A good Man in my Neighbourhood, lately asked me for the Notes of that Sermon, that he might repeat it unto a religious Meeting of the Neighbours. Hereupon, it came into my Mind, that I would augment and

the main Ends of the Church's Treasury; and inspecting their Accounts thereof, and the securing such Rents and Legacies as may belong unto it; and other such lesser Matters as may be judged needless for the whole Church to assemble upon. All which Trouble is imposed on the forementioned Gentlemen, but for the Space of one Year ensuing; at the Expiration of which Term the Church propose to renew the Choice of their Committee, as they may judge convenient." *Cotton Mather's MS. Records of the Second Church*, II.

[1] Of Martha's Vineyard. He left a widow, Sarah. See p. 133, *supra*.

enrich the Composure, with two considerable Paragraphs; The one, a Conviction of the *Jewish* Infidelity, with the Summ of those Demonstrations, wherewith Christianity triumphs over Judaism; the other, a confutation of the *Arian* Hæresies, which are horribly revived at this Day, and the Mystery of the Trinity in God, and the Godhead and Kingdome of our Saviour, opened for the Satisfaction of the Faithful. Having done this I proposed the Publication of the Composure; and all the Difficulties of it, are immediately and surprisingly conquered! I cannot but suspect that there will be some uncommon Effect of this Publication. I give it unto the Bookseller, under this Title; THINGS TO BE MORE THOUGHT UPON. *A brief Treatise on the Injuries offered unto the glorious and only Saviour of the World; In many Instances wherein the Guilty are seldome Aware of their being so Injurious to the Eternal Son of God. With a more particular Conviction of the Jewish and Arian Infidelity.*[1]

1. [*March* 15.] G. D. Having with much Patience and Candor, carried our swarming Brethren on to the Allowance of their Proceedings, which the Church has granted them, I would now wholly give myself up to the Methods of Supplication, and Resignation, and committ the Matter to the Lord, and watch against all the Devices of Satan, which may operate unto the Disturbance of the Neighbourhood on this Occasion.

2. G. D. It is of absolute Necessity, that my Family be reformed of their late Hours, in going to Bed; the Reformation will be attended with many happy Consequences.

3. G. D. The dark Dispensation of Providence, which detains my poor Kinswoman, in her Indian Captivity, calls upon me, to address her nearest Relatives, with the best Consolations I can study for them; as also to inculcate on my own Children, Admonitions of Piety and Thankfulness.

[1] Printed by Thomas Fleet for Daniel Henchman, 1713.

4. G. D.   I purpose to make a Present; not only unto our own Colledge, but also unto the University of *Glasgow* of my Treatise, wherein Evangelical Truth has a Triumph over the Arian Hæresies. Having a mighty desire, to fortify the Students there, against those revived Hæresies.

18. *d.* 1. *m. Wednesday.*   Because, it is a very critical Time with my Flock, and there need more than ordinary Methods to defeat and prevent the Devices of Satan, in the Affair of a new Church, and I need much Prudence and Patience and Resignation on such an Occasion, I sett apart this Day, for Prayers and Alms and Psalms, and employ'd it in such Petitions and such Exercises, as I have done two other Dayes, in the two former Weeks. And I left with the Lord, the Matter of our new Church; entreating that if it be of Him, it may be peaceably and lovingly carried on; but if it be not as yett a good Motion, He would please in His marvellous Providence to over-rule it. I also carried unto the Lord, my Opportunities to Glorify Him; entreating that they may be continued and multiplied,

Having thus *besought the Lord thrice*, on this Occasion. I silently wait for the Issue of it.

5. G. D.   I would earnestly prosecute the Affair of having the Indian Lands lett out on such Leases, as may bring in Revenues for the Support of the evangelical Interests among the Indians.

6. G. D.   A young woman has been two or three and twenty Years a Captive, in the Hands of the French. Having been transported from *Canada* to *France*, there she finds herself, at Liberty, with an Inclination to return unto N. E. My Assistence, particularly, to bear the Expences of her getting home is asked for, and I would now do the best I can. I offer, unto a Gentleman, who will give a Letter of Credit, unto our Agent for that Purpose, that he may supply the young Gentlewoman with Money for this occasion, that I will enter into an Obligation to see it all reimbursed.

7. G. D. I take notice of admirable Piety, shining among the Professors of the modern Pietism (tho they are not without their Errors:) [1] and I look on the Strains of Piety conspicuous in them, as notable Dawns of the Kingdome of God among the Children of Men. I would endeavour as in Reading their Books, I find the Passages of a raised and noble Piety occurring, to pant and strive after a lively Impression thereof, on my own Mind. And in this Way I would seek a particular præparation for Services which I may do, in the coming on of the Kingdome of God.

1. [*March* 22.] G. D. As I would readily fly with my best Releefs and Councils to every Person of my Flock, in any special Affliction, which I may know to be upon them, so when I see any of them, under the Arrest of Death going from me, I would with much Solemnity and Affection resign them as part of my Charge unto the great and good Shepherd of Souls. But this is not all. When any of my Flock are taken away by Death, I would seriously examine myself, *how have I discharged my Duty to that person?* And fly to the Blood of the great Sacrifice, for the Pardon of my Deficiencies.

2. G. D. Præfatory to the evening Sacrifices in my Family, I would have two of the younger Children alternately to read a Paragraph, in a poetical History of the Bible, until the Book be gone through. And I would make still some agreeable Remarks upon it, for their Instruction.

---

[1] Beginning with Jakob Boehme, Johann Arndt, and others in the middle of the XVII century, the Pietist movement was carried on in Germany by Philip Jacob Spener, Paul Gerhardt, and August Hermann Francke, of Halle, the last of whom was a correspondent of Mather. They inculcated an earnest study of the Bible, a practice of Christianity, a share in the spiritual government of the Church for the laity, and a more devotional training in the Universities. It was a short-lived movement, but it was, says Rudolf Sohm, " the last great surge of the waves of the ecclesiastical movement begun by the Reformation; it was the completion and the final form of the Protestantism created by the Reformation. Then came a time when another intellectual power took possession of the minds of men."

3. G. D.   Still my aged Parent must be the Object of my Cares.   To make him easy, under his Resentments of the Proceedings about our new Church; and to procure him Releefs against bodily Distempers that somewhat incommode him; and to gett his Mind raised unto the Points of Resignation to God and Satisfaction in His Will, which become us in the Suburbs of the heavenly World.

4. G. D.   I have in View, a special Service for the Kingdome and People of God at *Newbury;* and so in all our Churches, which I must endeavour this Day to prosecute in the General Assembly.

5. G. D.   I would make certain Presents of Books, not only among the Students in *Harvard-Colledge,* but also in the University of *Glasgow;* Books peculiarly adapted unto them, and unto the Interests of Piety among them.

6. G. D.   There are some young Gentlemen, (the Sons of Ministers,) who are out of Employment, and in destitute Circumstances.   I must look out very sollicitously, to find Employment for them.

7. G. D.   God calls me, in an extraordinary Manner, to be armed for the Trials, which I may undergo in a Church, breaking all to peeces, thro' the Impertinencies of a proud Crue, that must have Pues for their despicable Families; a Church so forsaken of God, that there are no Men appearing in it, who consult or desire the Prosperity of it; a Church that seems to be ripe for something little short of a miserable Dissolution.   O my God, and my Saviour; Help me to look up unto thee, for sufficient Measures of Grace, to encounter these uneasy Circumstances!

28. *d.* 1. *m. Satureday.*   This Day I also sett apart for Prayer with Fasting before the Lord; and I humbled myself before Him in a sense of all my Sins, particularly those which may have provoked Him to bring me into very humbling Circumstances, relating to the Church, whereof I have been the Servant.   Having obtained the Pardon of

my sinful Miscarriages, thro' and from the Mediation of my
Saviour, I therewithal cried unto Heaven for Grace, and
Help to behave myself wisely on this Occasion which I
have before me. I did also committ the whole Affair of
our boisterous, ambitious, ill-bred Company, in the Hands
of the glorious Lord, the Head of the Church; casting
upon Him the whole Care of a good Issue to it. I did
likewise present my Supplications on the Behalf of my aged
Parent, who is greatly wounded in his Mind by what is
now adoing; that he may be supported, comforted, made
easy under it.

On this Day, I called my Son *Increase* to me, and having
discoursed unto him, about his interiour State, I then pray'd
with him; and with Tears besought of the Lord, that the
Spirit of Grace and of Supplications may fall upon him.[1]

1. [*March* 29.] G. D. The poor Church, whereof I
have been hitherto the unprofitable Servant, seems to have
near unto it, a dreadful Convulsion, and something of a
Dissolution. Satan seems to have obtained a Commission
to sift the Church, and shake it wonderfully, and bring it
into very diminutive Circumstances. I would now keep
a very watchful Guard on all my own Steps and Words,
that I may not contribute in the least unto the Satanic
Devices. And I would employ many Dayes of Prayer with
Fasting before the Lord, that the Satanic Energies may be
restrained, and conquered, and over-ruled. I would also
make a Sacrifice of the Flock, and of all my Opportunities
to do Good, and of whatever my glorious Lord may call
me to putt into my Resignation.

29. *d.* 1. *m. Lords-Day.* At the Lord's-Table, I celebrated the Love of God unto His peculiar People; and
endeavoured those Dispositions and Exercises which might
be Demonstrations of my Share in His peculiar Love.

But a singular Errand on which I went thither, was,

---

[1] Five lines are here struck out.

that I might obtain the Grace, to glorify God, by a wise, patient, humble Conduct, and an incomparable Resignation, under the miserable Desolations, which are threatned unto the poor Church, whereof I have been the unprofitable Servant.

2. G. D. A more early Rising in the Morning for every one in my Family, would be of unspeakable Advantage unto us all; and particularly befriend the Interests of Piety among us; I would give the Exemple, and oblige the rest unto it.

3. G. D. Still my aged Parent, hastening to the better World, lies much upon my Heart; and I am extremely sollicitous, that his Life prolonged unto us, may be made easy and cheerful, and that he may be kept from every Step or Word that may cause any Confusion in the Flock; and that when the Time of his Death arrives, it may be attended with all the good Circumstances, that he may wish for. My Prayers for such Things must be incessant and importunate.

4. G. D. Tis hardly possible for me to do a greater Service than to publish unto the World, the Maxims, which are to unite the People that the glorious God will form for Himself, and that will quickly be the Stone growing into a great Mountain, which the whole Earth shall be filled withal. There is a mighty Tendency to Reformation, which has been long working in the Minds of Multitudes and Millions of People, both among the Romanists and Protestants. The Efforts made by this Inclination in the Souls of Men, have hitherto, thro' the Temptations of the Day, been generally encumbered with Errors, and Follies, and with naughty Superfluities. But when the pure Maxims of Truth, and of real, vital, spiritual Religion, and manly Christianity, are sett before the People of God, who can tell, what may be done in some new, and the next Essayes, to bring on the Kingdome of God? The proposing of an

agreeable Name for that People, who shall combine upon these Maxims, may be of some use also for the main Intention; and that which I have thought upon it, the *Immanuelian People*, because they are to be the People of our *Immanuel*, and *God with us*, is to be their peculiar Character. In my Treatise of, *Things to be more thought upon*, I sett myself to serve all these Designs.

5. G. D. I am writing to my Friend, the Agent of this Countrey, at *London;* [1] and I would sett myself to think on as many services to good Interests as I can, whereto I may excite him to apply himself. And indeed, I would have this Intention to be prosecuted in all my Correspondences. When I write unto any Person of any Capacity, I would often think, *what good may this Person be capable of doing if he be minded of it?* and putt him in Mind of it accordingly.

6. G. D. A poor Child going to be cutt for the Stone, I must contribute unto the Expence of the Operation; and be as helpful as I can, on the Occasion.

The Minister going to be settled at *Needham,* [2] is in very needy Circumstances; and needs Encouragements. I will procure a Present unto him.

7. G. D. There is one Point in my Conversation, wherein I must press after much greater Sanctity and Purity; and have my Behaviour in it more governed by that Reflection, *The Eye of the Great God is now upon me; Am I guilty of no Irregularity, which He may be displeased at?* And I must go mourning to my Grave, in the Sense of the Miscarriages, in this Point, wherewith His Holy Eyes have seen me chargeable.

1. [*April* 5.] G. D. I shall have an unhappy Occasion this day, to bring the Censures of the Church, on a poor

---

[1] Jeremiah Dummer.

[2] The meeting-house at Needham was not yet constructed. March 16, 1713, David Deming was invited to settle, but he does not appear to have accepted, as two months later a like invitation was extended to Samuel Terry.

Man, fallen into a Trade of Drunkenness.[1] On this Occasion I may speak many Things unto the Brethren of the Church, which may be of great Consequence unto them: especially, dispense faithful Warnings unto some others, whom the same Vice may have ensnared.

2. G. D. When any domestic Affair is carrying on my Family which takes up so much of our People's Time, as to make it fall under a little Notice, I would be led unto some spiritual Meditation and Supplication, which I may profitably putt into the Family-Sacrifices.

E. g. When BREWING; *Lord, lett us find in a glorious Christ, a provision for our thirsty Souls. And, Lord, bring us to drink of the River of thy Pleasures.*

When BAKING. *Lord, lett a glorious Christ be the Bread of Life unto us. And, Lord lett us not Labour for the Food that perisheth, but for that which endures to everlasting Life.*

When WASHING. *Lord, lett us be washed and made clean, by the Blood of a glorious Christ applied unto us; and in the Methods of a repenting Faith be cleansed from the Sin, which would not by Sope and much Nitre be cleansed away. Oh! wash us throughly from our Sin; Oh! Take away our filthy Garments from us!*

Thus, when Gardening; when laying in Provisions, etc., etc., etc.

3. G. D. My Kindred at Charlestown, do need some Advice that they may not sin against God and one another. I must visit them, and advise them.

4. G. D. I have now litt upon an hopeful young Man, who is willing to travel into the southern Colonies, and labour for Christ in any Field that shall be assign'd, for him there. This is what I have much wished for. Accordingly, I accommodate this young Man, with my Letters and Commendations thither, and help him to bear the Expences of his Journey.

[1] "*5 d. 2 m. Ezekiel Needham*, having been convicted of being scandalously overtaken with Drunkenness and of being accustomed unto a Trade of excessive Drinking, he was this Day laid under the Admonition of the Church and suspended from the Communion." *Cotton Mather's MS. Records Second Church*, II.

5. G. D. I am writing home to *London* those Things, that may be of great Service, to our Indian Comissioners and the evangelical Affaires among the Indians.

I am also of the Opinion, that if the English Preachers to the Indians, would supply me with Information concerning any notable Efforts of Piety among them, and their dying Speeches that may have in them something Extraordinary, I may do some Good therewithal. I would therefore ask them for such Things.

6. G. D. I can't insert (nor is it worth while) all the poor Objects, that call for my Compassions and Contrivances. They grow upon me. But one poor, sickly, honest Man, that is out of Employment, requires my more than ordinary Care for him.

7. G. D. Many things look, as if I were under peculiar Obligations to spend my Time this year, as if (I might immediately Dy, but) very probably I have at most but little more than one Year to live. My God, Give me Wisdome to spend my Time, exceeding Fruitfully!

1. [*April* 12.] G. D. In my Conversation with the People of the Church, whereof I am the Servant, I would often enquire of them, what Service more they would wish me to do for the Church. And entreat them to think, and then give me the Result of their Thoughts upon that Article.

2. G. D. I would now scarce lett a Day pass me, without obliging my Son *Increase*, to transcribe neatly and fairly, into a blank Book, some instructive Passage, and mostly such an one, as may have a Tendency to animate a Principle of Religion in him.

3. G. D. My Kinsmen, that are prentices, must have my frequent Counsils and Charges, to shun the evil Doings by which young Men undo themselves, and to serve their Masters with all possible Fidelity.

4. G. D. I have thoughts of reviving my Purpose, of publishing my Discourse, about *Evil Customes;* with a

Collection and Catalogue of the Evil Customes, with which the Countrey is threatned, and a Proposal of Methods to prevent them.[1]

5. G. D.   A religious Society of Young Men, at *Milton*, having desired me to accompany with a Preface, a Sermon of their Pastors to them, which they are publishing, it gives me an opportunity, to address them, and other such Societies, on points of the greatest Importance in the World.

15 *d.*/16 *d.* 2 *m.* [*April.*] *Wednesday*/*Thursday*.   I addressed Heaven this Night, in the way of a *Vigil*, and I carried several Petitions unto the Lord!

Among the rest, I especially insisted on this; that my Book of, *Things to be more thought upon*, may prove exceeding serviceable to the Kingdome of God; and that particularly, the *Maxims of the Kingdome* therein exhibited may be much considered and entertained in the World.   I also entreated of the Lord, that I might understand the Meaning of the Descent from the Invisible World, which nineteen years ago produced in a Sermon from me, a good part of what is now published.   And I bewailed before the Holy One, all my Impieties and Impurities; particularly under this Aggravation of them, the Grief I have thereby given to His Holy Angels.   My Psalm-book then being opened, it fell at Psal. XCI. end,[2] which I now sang unto the Lord.

16 *d.* 2 *m. Thursday*.   This Day was kept as a general Fast thro' the Province.[3]   I Enjoy'd much Assistence from Heaven, in the Duties of it.   I made it, (as I use to do) a Day for Alms, as well as for Prayers.

6. G. D.   There are some aged Widowes of the Church, poor and in languishing Circumstances, whose Condition calls me, to do what I can for them.

---

[1] See pp. 122, 128, *supra*.

[2] "With long life will I satisfy him, and shew him my salvation."

[3] The proclamation, issued "with particular reference to the important negotiations on foot for the establishment of a lasting and happy peace," is printed in the *Boston News-Letter*, March 30, 1713.

7. G. D. As whatever Trouble befalls me in general, I would presently fetch and form out of it, a pœnitent Confession of some Sin, which the Trouble may lead me to take notice of; so if I particularly suffer any troublesome Circumstance in my Health, I would be led thereby, presently to think on some analogous Distemper in my Soul, or Miscarriage in my Life, which I should make an Article of Repentance before the Lord.

1. [*April* 19]. G. D. In my Catechising, I would not only upon each of the Questions, putt the Children in Mind of a Prayer which they should make unto God. But I would also in the Conclusion of the Exercise, in a catechetical Way single out great Points of practical Piety, and go thro' the same with such of the Children as I may single out, and require a great Attention from all the rest. Such as, the Improvement of the Baptismal Covenant. The way of entring into Covenant with God. The Nature of a true Conversion. A thorough Preparation for Death. And the like.

I would also consider the peculiar Vices of the Children, and employ my Warnings and Charges agreeably upon them.

2. G. D. I will have the *Maxims of the Kingdome of God* readd over in my Family, and having explained them and propounded them unto my Family, I will invite them all to declare their Consent unto them; that so my Children may all be the Subjects of the Holy King, and enjoy His peculiar Protection in the evil Day.

3. G. D. Taking my Leave of the Governour of Connecticut who is my Kinsman, (returning to his Government, after His having here lately married one,[1] who is also my Kinswoman,) I come into an Agreement with him, for Communications from time to time, about such Things as

---

[1] Gurdon Saltonstall, who married for his third wife Mary Clark. He left Boston April 21. Sewall, *Diary*, II. 376, 377.

may be for the Kingdome of God, and for the common Good.

4. G. D. I am entertaining a Projection of more than ordinary Consequence, for the Formation of that People, who are quickly to become a great Mountain, and fill the whole Earth. Tis, to propose the, *Maxims of the Kingdome of God*, and that *Societies* be formed upon those Maxims, uniting in them, and promoting of them, and studying of Methods to draw Mankind into their Association.

5. G. D. I must use a more particular Care about supplying the religious Societies with proper Materials, to be read among them, in their Exercises. Look out suitable Books for them!

6. G. D. A miserable Child, this week undergoing the grievous Operation of Lithotomy, my Compassions must be many wayes Expressed on this Occasion. Particularly, in enabling the Parents to undergo the Expence of it.

7. G. D. One of my Studies, has been to have suitable Thoughts, Wishes and Prayers excited in my Mind, on all such recurring Occasions as my Life is filled withal.

I find, that among these Occasions, there often occurs one, which I have not hitherto taken a due Notice of. I am often putt upon *Mending of my Pen*. I would make this Action, an Occasion of my sending up to Heaven some Desire of this Importance, *Lord, Mend me, and fitt me for thy Service*.

25. *d. 2. m. Satureday.* This Day I sett apart for Prayer with Fasting in the Religion of the Closett. My Spirit underwent considerable Anguish in Reflecting on and Confessing of, my horrible Sinfulness before the Lord. But for my Pardon, I made my Flight unto my Saviour; not without Hopes of obtaining it. I also besought of the Lord, that I might be indeed Blessed of Him in many Instances, and I again left in His wise, and gracious and faithful Hands, the critical Affair of our new Church, which

has been for some Time carrying on. I likewise called my
Son *Increase* unto me, and had his Promise, that he would
no longer persist in a prayerless Life, and I pray'd with the
Child, and cried unto the Lord, that He would give unto
my Son a Perfect Heart: entreating therewithal for Direction about the Disposal of him, the Determination whereof
now drawes near unto us.

1. [*April* 26.] G. D. Perhaps, by preaching on, *the
Vain Thoughts*, which are hated by the Soul of a Godly
Man, the Flock may [be] exceedingly edified. I would
look up to Heaven for Assistence, and proceed upon the
subject.

26 *d. 2 m. Lord's-Day*. My first Action, at the Table
of the Lord this Day, was to consider the Pardon purchased
for me, by the Punishment of my Sin laid on my Saviour,
and profered to me by the Sovereign and marvellous Grace
of God, tho' my Sins have been such, and so aggravated,
as I know no Man's in the World beside me. To receive,
and embrace, and beleeve this Pardon ; and then to study,
and resolve, the Methods of glorifying the God who has
pardoned me ; particularly, in the Hatred of all that I
judge to be a Sin : And in my rejecting alwayes every
Thought that has a Tendency towards my Sin, with as
direct a Contradiction to it, as is possible : and in my
Endeavours to excell in the Piety and Purity, that shall
be most contrary to my own Iniquity : And,

My second Action, was, to behold the Blood of a Sacrificed Jesus ; and rely on that great Sacrifice for all the
Blessings of Goodness, and Reconciliation with God. And
then, to make an eucharistical Sacrifice, and as a Thank-
offering, to present unto the Lord, myself, and my All :
First, that my All, may be actively employ'd in the Service
and for the Kingdome of the glorious Lord. Then, that
I may readily part with all my Enjoyments (which I now
particularly thought upon,) if the Lord please to call for

them; and that my Will may suffer Death, and be extinguished, and that the Will of God, may be my perpetual Satisfaction.

2. G. D. Being determined at length, to have my Son *Increase* applied unto sæcular Business, I must be much in cries to Heaven for Direction thereabout; and I must now come to alter diverse Points of his Education, especially to have his Writing and Cyphring perfected; wherein I shall need also to be directed of God.

3. G. D. My aged Mother growes very infirm and feeble. I must study all the Wayes I can to suit her Condition with my best Assistences.

4. G. D. I may do good, by advising our Booksellers, what Books, they should send to *London* for; that from their Shops, there may go forth into the Countrey, such things as may best serve the Interests of Truth and Piety.

5. G. D. I would take my Opportunities, mightily to insinuate into the Tutors at the Colledge, and inculcate upon them, how much it concerns them, to instill good Principles into their Pupils, and be concerned for their orthodox and religious, as well as learned Education.

6. G. D. A poor Youth in my Neighbourhood, has the King's-Evil upon him, and languishing under this Malady, a lingring and a grievous Death, is likely to be his Portion. I would visit him, and instruct him, and pray with him and for him, and see that no needful Releefs be wanting to him.

7. G. D. I take notice of an Error, I too easily fall into; the foolish, uncivil, and ungrateful Carriage, in the People of the Town, and my own Vicinity towards me, I am too ready to express my Resentment of it; and my Opinion of them as being an ill-spirited People. There would be more Wisdome and Virtue in it, if I less follow'd the Dictates of the Splean in this Matter; but with Silence and Patience kept rejoicing in every ill Usage that augments my Conformity to my admirable Saviour.

1. [*May* 3.] G. D. For the Restraining of Profaneness in a considerable Number of unruly Children on the Lord's-day in our Congregation, I have litt on a Person, to look after them, whom I accordingly employ and reward for that Service.

2. G. D. It is time for me to resume certain Points of polite and pious Education in my Daughters, which of late have somewhat languished; especially as to their Use of their Pens.

3. G. D. Cloathe one of my Nephews, who is an Orphan.

4. G. D. I have Thoughts of writing a Letter, as well and as soon as I can, unto the famous *Arian*,[1] who is now making a violent and various Attempt on the Faith of Christianity; which Letter, may be of some further use unto the Church of God.

5. G. D. I have considered the marvellous Accomplishments and Performances, of Mr. *Wm. Jameson*,[2] the professor of History, in the University of *Glasgow;* who tho' he has been totally Blind from the Cradle, has published admirable Composures to serve the Cause of Truth in the World. I am writing unto this Gentleman, to take the learned *Arian* into his hands, and particularly undertake the Detection and Confusion of that Imposture, the *Apostolical Constitutions*,[3] which he would have to be what their Title pretends unto. For the *Philistines* to have their Temple pull'd down about their Ears, by the Hand of such a *Sampson*, will render the Victories of Truth still the more Triumphant and Illustrious.

6. G. D. A Gentleman complains to me, of his Daughter taking to very wicked Courses. I must in the wayes of Prudence and of Goodness endeavour the reclaiming of her.

[1] William Whiston.
[2] See *Dictionary of National Biography*, XXIX. 235.
[3] The title of one of Whiston's volumes, printed in 1711.

7. G. D.   Upon reading some Funeral-sermons on some excellent persons lately dead, with some Accounts of their Lives,[1] I find the Dispositions to do good, in a way of Liberality, and to watch all Opportunities of exciting others in like Manner to do good, and provide a faithful Account of our Stewardship, exceedingly inflamed and increased in me. My glorious Lord, give me yett more of thy Direction and Assistence![2]

1. [*May* 10.] G. D. The critical Affair of a new Meeting-house carrying on among us, calls yett for much Prayer, and Prudence, and Patience in my Conduct; that so the Devices of Satan may be disappointed.

2. G. D. I think, I must now no longer delay, my Choice of Patrons, for the children whom I may shortly leave as Orphans; but prepare the Letters, to be after my Decease delivered unto them.

3. G. D. To my Kindred of *West-Hampshire*, I am sending things, that may enlighten them, and edify them, and comfort some of them under some grievous Articles of Adversity.

4. G. D. It is desired by some Gentlemen at *Marble-head* that I would make a Visit unto that Place and preach unto the People there; especially unto the poor Fishermen. I will seek the Direction of Heaven about this Proposal; and if it be found likely to do much Good, I will endeavour further to prosecute it.

5. G. D. I would renew my Sollicitations in the Society for the Suppression of Disorders, that some good Men may take their Walks among the Children, in the Time and Place of their Playes, and observe the wicked Language

---

[1] Probably Thomas Reynolds' *Practical Religion exemplify'd in the Lives of Mrs. Clissold, and Mrs. Mary Terry: with their funeral Sermons and Passages from the Diary of the former.* It was printed in Boston this year by John Allen, and was recommended by Increase Mather.

[2] On May 5 Mather made "an excellent Dedication-Prayer in the New Court-Chamber." Sewall, *Diary*, II. 381.

heard among them, and employ the best Methods to nip the Impiety of their Language in the Bud. As also to walk in School-time, and observe what Children are at play, and see that they be sent unto some School or other.

6. G. D. I have a little Money in my Hands to be dispersed unto the poor. I must again remember *Cambridge*.

7. G. D. I know not, but such may be my Barrenness and Senselessness, that in a little Time, I may grow to be at a Loss, what further Answer to give unto the Question of the Morning, or what further Service I have to do for the Kingdome of God abroad or within. If it should be so, I will then spend some Time, in mourning over my barren and senseless Mind, and crying unto Heaven that I may be more enlightened. But I will then in the following Day, be often pressing after further Thoughts upon the Question, and make no doubt, that before Night, I may light upon something worthy to be prosecuted.

1. [*May* 17.] G. D. Insisting on the evil Thoughts, that should be hateful to us, I rank them under three Heads : base Thoughts, and false Thoughts, and vain Thoughts. Under false Thoughts, it will be a part of seasonable Fidelity unto my Flock, to warn them in a very particular Manner, against three Systems of Error, which they may be in danger of ; the false Thoughts of *Popery*, and of *Quakerism*, and of *Arminianism*.

2. G. D. Such of my Children as are able to write, I would oblige to entertain with a written Answer of their own, to these two Questions.

Q. 1. *What is it, that I am to make the principal End and Care of my Life?*

Q. 2. *What are the great and chief Things that I should address my Saviour to do for me?*

3. G. D. I must, by the Means of my Kinsman at *Say-brook*, find out all that are akin to me in the Colony of *Connecticut*, and lodge Books of Piety in the hands of

them all.   For, I suspect, there are some, whom I have not yett come at.

4. G. D.   My Book of, *A confirmed Christian*, has been destroy'd by the Avarice and Perfidy of the Men in whose hands the Copy was fallen.   But a strange Providence has ordered it, that a Scholar would needs transcribe it in Short-hand, before I sent it away.   He has now written it out in Long-hand from his Copy; and I incline to review and cor-rect what he has done, and again fitt it for the Press, and render it more agreeable than it was before, and make fresh Attempts for the Publication of it.   Direct me, O my God!

5. G. D.   There are some Physicians in this Countrey, whom I would sollicit, to obtain for me, as much as may be, of the Knowledge of the Botanicks of the Countrey; as also, of rare cures or cases occurring to them.

6. G. D.   There is an aged Woman in my Neighbour-hood, poor, and lame, and sick, and in miserable Circum-stances.   I must not only myself releeve her, but also summon together her several Relatives, that they agree to have her well-provided for.

7. G. D.   I would make it my Endeavour, with as much Ingenuity as ever I can, that whatever my Neighbours entertain me withal, whether an Eatable or a Drinkable, it may afford me some Instruction of Piety, by way of occa-sional Reflection raised from it.   And this Instruction I would Communicate unto them, which if it prove profitable to them, will also be some Retribution for their Civility.

(III.)   We had promised unto our glorious Lord (I and my Friend,) that if He would look upon our Enemy, and bring a Change of Mind upon the Wretch, it should en-courage us, to go on with special Services for His Kingdome; and particularly, a Testimony against evil Customes.   But it has been one of my Customes, to anticipate the Per-formance of my Voice, and to do before my Prayers are accomplished, the Things which I intended after their

Accomplishment. There is an evangelical Ingenuity in such a Method of proceeding. Accordingly with the Assistence of my Friend; in hopes to do some remarkable Good, and sett good Men all about the Countrey on thinking how to prevent Evil, and with a design particularly to present one of the Books, unto each of the Representatives in the General Assembly, I sent unto the Press about this Time, a composure entituled; ADVICE FROM THE WATCHTOWER; *In a Testimony against Evil Customes, A brief Essay, to declare the Danger and Mischief of all EVIL CUSTOMES, in general; And offer a more particular Catalogue of Evil Customes growing upon us. With certain METHODS, for the prevention and suppression of them.*[1]

23 *d.* 3 *m.* [*May.*] *Satureday.* This Day I sett apart for Prayer with Fasting before the Lord, on such Occasions, as use thus to employ me. It was a Day not altogether uncomfortable. I enjoy'd some Communion with Heaven in it. Some heavy Mischiefs impending over the Town, called for my special and solemn Supplications.

1. [*May* 24.] G. D. Some in the Flock having lately mett with great Losses, I would endeavour that they may glorify God with a most sacrificing Resignation, and in such a contented and sanctified Mind, enjoy something better than all that they have lost. Some that go abroad into other Places, I would fortify with Admonitions, even with written ones, against the Temptations of the Places to which their Travels carry them.

24 *d.* 3 *m. Lord's-Day.* At the Table of the Lord, my main Intention was, to make sure of having the Gates of the Heavenly World sett open for me, and finding an open Entrance at the strait Gates, when I leave the World. My Endeavour was therefore to express, and obtain the Grace, which distinguishes the righteous Nation which keeps the Truths.

But in the Prosecution hereof, I had my Mind exceed-

[1] Printed by J. Allen, for N. Boone, 1713.

ingly comforted, at my coming to two or three Points of
Piety. First, I sett open the Doors of my Soul unto my
Saviour. So I concluded, He would open the Gates of
His Holy City to my Soul.

Secondly. I saw myself devoted unto the Service of
my Saviour, and delighted in it, and resolved on it. I concluded now, that He would not shutt the Gates of His
Holy City, on a poor Servant, that loved alwayes to be at
Work for Him. Thirdly, I found myself determined for
the narrow Way, which leads to the Gates of Life. Thence
I concluded, that I should not find the Gates at the End
of the way barr'd upon me.

2. G. D. I must revive this Point of domestic Piety,
and improve in it, that whenever my Consort comes to me
in my study, or I go to her in my Lodging, I speak to her
something or other, that may be Instructive; something
whereby she may grow in knowledge or in Goodness.

3. G. D. I have a Kinswoman at *Dorchester*, of whom
I may do well, to take more notice; and convey suitable
Books of Piety unto her.

4. G. D. The Ministers of the Province now coming
together, at their anniversary Convention,[1] I would promote
the Consideration of this Case among them, *What are those
Points of a good and wise Conduct, which the Pastors of our
Churches may, from the Circumstances of the Day, apprehend themselves more peculiarly call'd unto?*

5. G. D. I propose to write as moving a Letter as I
can, unto the Governour of *N. York;* that the Instruction
of the Indians on *Long-Island*, in Christianity, may be
countenanced and encouraged by him.

28. *d.* 3. *m. Thursday.* This Day I enjoy'd a precious
Presence of the Lord with me in my Discourse unto the
Ministers, on the Case which I had præpared for them; and
in my Prayers among them.

[1] See note in Sewall, *Diary*, II. 386.

6. G. D.   There is a poor, distracted man in my Neighbourhood, for whom and for whose Family, I must contrive to do what Kindness I can.

7. G. D.   When in passing the Streets, or elsewhere, I am so unhappy as to hear any wicked Language used, I would not only lift up a Prayer to Heaven, for the Pardon of the Evil-speaker, but also make it a Provocation, and Invitation unto me, to form some agreeable Acknowledgment of the Great God, in my Mind, with which I will address the Glorious one immediately.

1. [*May 31.*] G. D.   I must sett apart more than ordinary Time, to pour out my Supplications before the Lord, for a good Issue to that critical Affair of the People swarming into a new Meeting-house; and that I may have the Direction of Heaven for a wise and good Conduct in it. And I must use particular Methods to preserve a good Understanding with some Gentlemen, that are Violently sett on prosecuting that Undertaking. Some other Bones of Contention in the Neighbourhood, I must also endeavour to remove as well as I can.

2. G. D.   I would putt my Children upon chusing their several Wayes of Usefulness, and enkindle in them as far as I can, a mighty Desire of being useful in the World; and assist them unto the uttermost.

3. G. D.   I have a Kinsman at *Windsor*, who is an ingenious Man, a gracious Christian, and an excellent Physician. I would many Wayes employ him to serve the Interests of Piety. I would also communicate unto him Curiosities in Medicine, as I happen to meet with them.

4. G. D.   My, *Testimony against Evil Customes*, I would procure to be sent into all Parts of the countrey.

I have now also a further opportunity to do Good. I take my Week, in going every morning to the Governour and Council, at the Council-chamber, for daily prayers. I would exceedingly fill my Prayers; with the most suitable and impressive Passages; and such as may quicken and assist the Government, unto the doing of abundance of Good.

5. G. D. I have some Thoughts of Writing to the B[isho]p of *Salisbury*,[1] a Remonstrance against the Missions that are sent over by the Society, to hurt the Churches in this Countrey.

6. G. D. Some contentious Neighbours, I must give my best Assistences, towards the Reconciling of them.

7. G. D. I am obliged unto the Writing of many Letters. My Correspondencies are many, and some of them with the politer sort of Persons. As I would in all my Letters endeavour to lett fall something, that may be serviceable unto those whom I write unto, so that what I write may be the more acceptable and serviceable, I would have my Letters ever sprinkled with some taking Flowres on them: To this purpose, I would read, with Attention the Epistles of learned Men, and in a blank Book, I would insert from thence, those Passages, and Flourishes and Witticisms, which may be a continual Store for my ready Supply on all Occasions.

1. [*June* 7.] G. D. I am reading over the, *Pastoralis Cura*, of *Gregory M.*[2] In hopes to find there some Hints, for the good Conduct, with which I desire to serve my Flock.

I am using a particular Method of Mediation, that my Father may be reconciled unto that Part of the Flock, which are swarming into a new Church; and have dissatisfied him about the Place of their Building.

2. G. D. My poor Son *Increase!* Oh! the Distress of Mind, with which I must lett fall my daily Admonitions upon him, even with a continual Dropping, especially on

---

[1] Gilbert Burnet.

[2] He may refer to the *De Cura Sacerdotali*, of Gregory I. surnamed "the Great."

those two Points; Conversion to God, with a sincere Compliance with His Covenant! And, the Care of spending Time so as to give a good Account of it. I would also have read over in the hearing of my Children in the Family, a brief Discourse about coming into the Covenant of God, and then bespeak their Consent unto it.

3. G. D. Make certain Presents for the Releef and Comfort of an aged Relative.

4. G. D. I am now upon a peculiar Projection, to form Societies in the World, upon the Design of Entertaining and Propagating the, *Maxims of the Kingdome of God.* Who can tell, what may be the Issue of it? or how great a Matter a little Fire may Kindle? Glorious Lord, I resign all to thy Direction.

10 *d.* 4 *m.* [*June.*] *Wednesday.* This Day I preach'd to, and pray'd with, the Brethren, who are building a new Edifice, in order to their Swarming into a new Church among us. I enjoy'd such an Assistence from above, that my courteous and candid way of treating them, had a great Impression on the Brethren, and they not only sent Thanks to me for my poor Sermon, but also (tho' I were hardly six minutes preparing it,) they desired a copy of it for publication.[1]

5. G. D. It has been a time of great Scarcity for corn with some Towns in the Countrey, especially in *Plymouth, Colony;* where some Families have not seen a bitt of Bread for many Weeks together. I would propose it, in some Societies of good Men, whereto I am related, whether we may not procure a good Quantity of Corn, to be sent for a charitable Distribution among those distressed Families.[2]

6. G. D. There are some very poor Children in the

---

[1] But it does not appear to have been printed.

[2] Sewall, *Diary,* II. 384, mentions a "bread riot" at Boston, May 20, 1713. Only the night before the members of the Council, Justices of the Peace and selectmen of Boston agreed to "walke in their Turns by Night to Inspect and prevent disorders in the Towne" after June 1; and on June 2 the selectmen fixed the assize of bread at seven shillings and six pence. *Boston Record Commissioners,* XI. 185.

Neighbourhood which our over-stockt *Charity-Schole* will not well entertain; I would myself pay for their Schooling.

7. G. D. When any Persons, and much more, when any Orders of Persons, fall into Errors and Evils, and great miscarriages, I must keep a Guard of Meekness and Wisdome, on the Expressions of my Zeal on such Occasions; violent, boisterous, intemperate Expressions on such Occasions will not work the Righteousness of God. I am afraid lest I am sometimes too vehement.

1. [*June* 14.] G. D. The Lord is very gracious unto me, in helping me, to treat our swarming Brethren, in a suitable and obliging Manner; the best Thing I can do, to prevent the Wiles of Satan, and procure the Smiles of Heaven, is to hold on this Conduct; for which therefore I must continually look up unto God.

2. G. D. I would have a strict Enquiry instituted among my Children, and each one of themselves to prosecute the Enquiry, *By what evil Custome any of them, in any Point may have their welfare incommoded or endangered?*

3. G. D. I have a Kinsman, who is a Member of the General Assembly. I would make use of him, as an Instrument of Good, as well there, as at home.

4. G. D. It will be a Testimony for God, and for Truth, and it will be for the service and Honour of the Countrey, if I bear the Testimony, to take my late Lecture on Fidelity, and in the way of the Press publish it and scatter it.

(IV.) Accordingly, I give the Sermon to the Bookseller; entituled, A MAN OF HIS WORD. *A very brief Essay on Fidelity in keeping of Promises and Engagements; Declaring How and Why a Good Man will be as Good as His Word. With a Touch upon some weighty Cases relating to it. Uttered at Boston-Lecture.* 11 d. 4 m. 1713. *And now published, that it may be employ'd among other Instruments, to keep Truth alive in the Land.*[1]

---

[1] Printed by John Allen for N. Boone, 1713.

5. G. D. I have several Services in View, for the Indians at *Punkapoag*, which I would prosecute at my next Interview with the Commissioners.

6. G. D. Just as I was going to look out and write down an object for Compassion, a Woman of *Windsor* comes to me, with Extreme Distress, for a little Money, to redeem her son out of miserable Circumstances; with which accordingly I accommodate her.

7. G. D. Rise earlier!

Last Night, in a wicked Book, I readd a fling at Clergymen, as a revengeful Generation of men, who never forgive such as have offended them. I do not remember, for my own part, that ever I designed the Revenge of an Injury in my Life. However, this venemous Fling, shall quicken my Watchfulness, upon this Article.

20 *d.* 4 *m. Satureday.* I sett apart this Day, for Prayer with Fasting before the Lord, on the usual Occasions.

But especially to cry unto God, for His poor Church in *Scotland;* which is in a miserably distracted Condition.

1. [*June* 21.] G. D. I would preach a Sermon to my Flock, wherein I may collect and offer those Maxims of Piety, which People of the lowest Capacity and even *little Children* may take notice of. The Death of such in the Neighbourhood, will cause the more Notice to be taken of them.

21 *d.* 4 *m. Lord's-Day.* At the Lord's Table, I first beheld the Lord, as purchasing and præparing an Heavenly Kingdome for His People. Then I look'd unto His great Sacrifice, for the Pardon of the Sin, which is the only Thing that can shutt me out of the Kingdome; and look'd unto His Righteousness to be pleaded by me, as my Claim unto it. Hereupon, I took up Resolutions to have a Conversation in Heaven, and think very often about it, and also do all possible Services for the Kingdome of Heaven, and bring as many as I can into it.

My second Action, was, to behold the Blood of my Saviour, as purchasing Abundance of Grace for me. Which I was now willing and wishing to receive. I begg'd it of Him, as being furnished with it for me; especially the Grace of much Patience under Sufferings from God, and much Meekness under Injuries from Men. I therewithal reflected on the Exemple of such Grace, in the Life of my Saviour. And I particularly sought for the Grace that might enable me, wisely to encounter the Difficulties and the Temptations, of the new church arising in my Neighbourhood.

2. G. D. Preaching a Sermon, on Lessons relating to the Fear of God, which People of the lowest Capacity, and our very Children, might soon be sensible of, I instil these Maxims into my own Children, and expressly take their consent unto them all, and charge them never to forgett them.

(V.) I now sent unto the Press, a little Book of Lessons relating to the Fear of God, adapted unto Children, and People of the lowest Capacity; with a Design to disperse it in Schools and Families. Tis entituled, THE A. B. C. OF RELIGION. *Lessons relating to the Fear of God, fitted unto the youngest and lowest Capacities; And Children suitably instructed in the Maxims of Religion.*[1]

3. G. D. I am informed of some Relatives, about *Hadley*, which I was not aware of. I would endeavour, with Books of Piety, to discharge my Duty to them.

4. G. D. I propose to do some good, in a Journey to *Maldon*, and a Lecture there.

24 *d.* 4 *m. Wednesday.* And I took this Journey, and enjoy'd a most gracious Presence of God in it; all the Circumstances of it, having much Mercy and Comfort in them.

5. G. D. There are knotts of riotous Young Men in

[1] Printed by Timothy Green, 1713.

the Town. On purpose to insult Piety, they will come under my Window in the Middle of the Night, and sing profane and filthy Songs. The last night they did so, and fell upon People with Clubs, taken off my Wood-pile. 'Tis hightime, to call in the Help of the Government of the Place, for the punishing and suppressing of these Disorders.

6. G. D. A poor Family at *Cambridge*, which I am acquainted withal; wanting a Supply of Corn.

7. G. D. In walking to a Funeral, I would be forever careful, that the Gentleman whom I walk withal shall be Entertained with some Communication, that shall be instructive to him, and assist our Præparation for the future State.

1. [*June* 28.] G. D. Two young Persons have newly died in our Neighbourhood, and were buried within half an Hour one of another: a young man, who had been a candidate of the Ministry, and was become the M[aster] of our Grammar Schole; and a young Woman, who had been one of a sober and vertuous Character.[1] I would on this Occasion renew my public Discourses with the greatest Pungency, on a early Mortality, and on early Religion.

2. G. D. Before my Evening-Prayer in my Family, I would still consider, what remarkable Occurrence of Providence has happened in the Day; either in Mortality or on any other Account; and make my Remarks upon it in my Discourse unto my Family, and in the Prayer also take notice of it.

3. G. D. I have a Kinswoman at *Dorchester*, to whom I would convey some Instruments of Piety.

4. G. D. To procure that suitable Books be gott into the Hands of the Students at the Colledge, may be a Service of great Consequence. I would endeavour it.[2]

[1] Recompence Wadsworth and Mrs. Sarah Smith. A "Short Memorial" of Wadsworth is appended to Mather's sermon *Golgotha*, p. 222, *infra*.

[2] Doubtless his presence at commencement on the previous day reminded him of the field that demanded his attention.

The Case of *Newbury*[1] also calls for a speedy and earnest Consideration.

5. G. D. Several Proposals of good Consequence, to be laid before the Commissioners for the Indian-Affaires. Particularly, the publication of an Instrument, for the Maintaining of houshold Piety among the Indians.

6. G. D. One that once lived in my Family, is now sick, and very poor. I must endeavour to releeve her, and make her Condicõn comfortable.

7. G. D. 'Tis a Question, which I would require of myself a most serious and exact Answer to; *What is necessary to render me ripe for the heavenly world? And what Points of Ripeness am I most sensibly defective in?*

4 *d.*/5. *d.* 5 *m.* [*July.*] *Satureday.*/*Lord's-day.* I kept a *Vigil*, and prostrate in the Dust before the Lord, I did, with extended Supplications cry unto Him; on sundry and pressing Occasions; After that I had exceedingly humbled and loathed and judged myself, on the Account of the abominable Impurities, which my Life had been filled withal, and pleaded the Blood of my Saviour, that I might obtain my Pardon. From the Depths I cried unto the Lord, for His Grace to be given unto my Children; particularly my Son *Increase;* and the Direction of Heaven in disposing of him: For a Recovery to be granted unto a dear Youth in my Neighbourhood who lies dangerously sick: For a Smile of Heaven on all the Circumstances of a Journey for the Service of the Glorious One, to *Marblehead,* which I propose the next Week; For gracious Assistences to be given me, in the Work of the next ensuing Lord's-Day, and Lecture; For some happy Returns from *England,* of the Packetts I have sent thither several Months ago; the Miscarriage whereof I have some Reason to fear; but entirely submitted

---

[1] These references to Newbury probably concern the attempt to set up an Episcopal Church in that place. Sewall's *Diary* II. and *Letter Book,* I. 416, contain not a little on the controversy.

and resigned all unto the Lord; Finally; For the Conversion of the poor Jew, who is this Day returned once more unto *New England*, and who has now for nineteen years together been the Subject of our Cares, and Hopes, and Prayers. My Mind seemed singularly satisfied in the success of my supplications on that one Article; the Recovery of the Young Man I am so concerned for.

When my long Supplications were over, I took my Psalter, to sing unto the Lord. And the first Place that opened in it, was a little surprisingly that where it is said: Psal. CXIX. 55, 62. *I have remembred thy Name, O Lord, in the Night; and have kept thy Law.* And, *At Midnight I will rise to give Thanks unto thee, because of thy righteous Judgments.*

1. [*July* 5.] G. D. I have sometimes given my Hearers, a Sermon of *Winter-Piety*.[1] It will be seasonable, and it may be serviceable, for me now to give them a Sermon of *Summer-Piety*. I would endeavour to speak as penetrating Things as I can, and exhibit the Truths of the Gospel, under the Advantage of such a Text as that; Amos. VIII. 2. *A basket of Summer-fruit.*

2. G. D. I would observe, when the *Birth-dayes* of my several Children arrive; and I would make it an Opportunity, not only to discourse very proper and pungent Things unto them, relating to their eternal Interests, but also oblige them, to consider, first, *What is their main Errand into the World;* and then, *What they have done of that Errand.* And such of them as are old enough to write, shall give me some written Thoughts upon these Things.

3. G. D. I will encourage and animate my aged Parent, for to bestow some holy and useful Visits, on some *aged* people; that so he may with his wise Discourses, do something to prepare them for the better World.

4. G. D. The divine Providence having by Mortality

---

[1] See p. 148, *supra.*

made a Vacancy in our Grammar-Schole, I shall do a Service for the public, if I procure the Succession of a good Master in it; which accordingly I have in my Eye, and Prosecution.

8 d. 5 m. Wednesday. Proposing a Journey to *Marblehead*, in the latter End of this Week, that I may there do some Service to the Kingdome of God; I sett apart this Day, for Prayer with Fasting before the Lord, that I might obtain a Blessing on my Journey; and that Satan may not hinder me, or injure me in it; and that a good Number of Souls may be enclosed in the Netts of the Gospel, where I am going to cast them forth.

I also besought the Lord, that I may enjoy a precious Presence of His with me, in my Lecture to-morrow; And for the many other Favours, which I had now an Opportunity to make the Matter of my Supplications.

(VI.) About this time, considering the horrible Confusions come upon the Nations, and the prospect of a new Face ere long to come upon the World, I thought it might now be a Time of Day, to publish the *Maxims of the Kingdome of God*, and invite the unsettled Minds of men to unite upon them. So I prepared for the Public, a brief Essay, which I propose to send over into *England*, that it may there, in as convenient Circumstances as may be, pass thro' the Press, into universal Consideration. It is entituled. THE THINGS THAT CANNOT BE SHAKEN. *Proposed unto most serious and general Consideration, at a Time when the World under the most shaking Dispensations, is hastening into the greatest Changes that ever came upon it. With* THE MAXIMS OF THE KINGDOME OF GOD, *offered as the only uniting Maxims, and the most unexceptionable* TERMS OF UNION *for that people, who from small Beginnings will certainly and speedily become a great Mountain, which the whole Earth shall be filled withal.*

5. G. D. Among the Ministers, I would sett forward

the Design of putting the Wheel of Prayer into Motion, by Dayes of Prayer, sett apart publickly in our Churches, under the dismal Aspect which the Times have upon us.

6. G. D. A poor young Man belonging to the Family next unto me, in danger of being ruined, by an indiscreet Amour, calls for my Essayes to save him.

10 *d.* 5 *m. Friday.* I went unto *Salem,* very favourably accommodated in all the Circumstances of my Journey; and I was kindly entertained there.

7. G. D. I would mightily improve in that Grace which inclines me to rejoice in the Favours which I see God bestowing on any of my Neighbours where I come; tho' they may be such Favours as are denied unto myself. At the same time, I would think on some spiritual Blessings, analogous and preferrible unto those Temporal ones; and look up to the Glorious One for these; expressing my Satisfaction in the Enjoyment of them, tho' the other should never be bestowed upon me. And I would ask for the like Mercies to be bestow'd on my prosperous Neighbours too.

11 *d.* 5 *m. Satureday.* I went over unto *Marble-head,* and lodged there; surrounded still with the Mercies of God.

1. [*July* 12.] G. D. Being at *Marble-head,* I would consider the state of the Flock here, instead of my usual Thoughts about my own. If their aged Minister [1] dy before another Minister, and a good and wise and faithful one, be settled among them, there will be extreme Hazard of their falling into miserable Confusions, and a wretched Crue declaring for the Ch[urch] of E[ngland] prove a mischievous Majority unto them. I would therefore press the Principal Inhabitants, to consider what they have to do on this Occasion, and speedily to exert themselves.

12 *d.* 5 *m. Lord's-Day.* In the Morning, prostrate on

---

[1] Samuel Cheever, who began his ministry in that place in 1684. In July, 1714, John Barnard was appointed to assist him. Cheever died in 1724.

the Floor of my Lodging, I resigned myself up to the Possession of the Holy Spirit, and implored His Influences also to fall on the Assembly, to which I am this day to carry His glorious Gospel.

I then enjoy'd a mighty Presence of the glorious One with me, in my public Ministrations, both Parts of the Day. And I hope, a very great Impression is left on the Minds of the People in the great Congregation, which was now convened.

2. G. D. My Negro-Servant, is one more Easily govern'd and managed, by the Principles of Reason, agreeably offered unto him, than by any other methods. I would oftener call him aside, and assay to reason him into a good Behaviour.

13 d. 5 m. Monday. I returned home in Safety, having been wonderfully blessed of God in all the Circumstances of my Journey.

3. G. D. Having observed the Condition of things in the Countrey, I would prepare certain Articles of solemn Advice and Warning unto this People, about the Interests of the Kingdome of God among them. I would then prevail with my aged Parent, if I can, to form these things into an agreeable Instrument, and leave them as his Testimony and Legacy to the Countrey, or, if he decline it, I will see, what I may do myself.

(VII.) About this time, to do a further service for the Cause of Piety, I sent unto the press, a Treatise of this Title; GOLGOTHA; *A lively Description of Death; with such Thoughts as are to be Entertained by Men, that they may not perish in that very Day, when the Thoughts of Men do perish. Occasion'd by some fresh Instances of Early Mortality, with a more particular Memorial of One of them.*[1]

4. G. D. The Publication of some things I find in the reserved Papers, of the pious young Man, who was lately our Schole-master, may serve the Cause of Piety.

[1] Printed by B. Green, for D. Henchman, 1713.

And some adapted Letters going from hence to *New-bury*, may be of some service to Religion.

(VIII.) About this Time also, considering that I had formerly entertained the Churches of God, with some Essayes of *Winter-Piety*, I thought, it would be some service unto Religion to do something at *Summer-Piety*, and make the Objects of the *Summer* subservient unto the the Interests of *Piety*. I therefore sent unto the Press, a Sermon I lately preached; under this Title. A PRESENT OF SUMMER-FRUIT. *A very brief Essay to offer some Instructions of Piety which the Summer-season more particularly and Emphatically leads us to; But such also as are never out of Season. Being the short Entertainment of an Auditory in Boston, on a Day distinguished with the Heat of the Summer.* 5 *d.* 5 *m.* 1713.[1]

5. G. D. A young Gentleman, being lately recovered from Sickness, I would consult and concert with him, what special Return, he may make unto the glorious Lord, by way of Gratitude for his Recovery.

6. G. D. Some aged and bed-rid Widow's in the Town, call for my Compassions to them.

7. G. D. I find, that I have shown too much Respect unto wicked Men in my Conversation; I have treated them with more of Complaisance than I should have done; Tho' my Intention has been to shew all Gentleness to all men, and recommend the Maxims of Religion unto them, and do the Part of a Physician upon them; yett I doubt, less Freedom with such Wretches, less Familiarity with such Divels, would have been better; And I have been accordingly punished for it, in the Providence of God. I desire to make a due Improvement of what I have in this Matter mett withal.

18 *d.* 5 *m. Satureday.* This Day I sett apart for Prayers and Alms, with Fasting, in secret before the Lord; On the

---

[1] Printed by B. Green, 1713. See Sewall, *Letter Book*, II. 22.

usual Occasions. My soul this Day received some Impressions from Heaven, which filled my Mind with satisfaction, in Assurances of Mercies intended for me.

There are Mercies and Comforts coming to me from *England*.

I renew'd my Sacrifice of my Flock, if the Glorious One, shall in the unhappy Affair of our new Meeting-house call me to it.

I carried my son *Increase* unto the Lord, having him with me in the Action; to obtain a new Heart for him, and the Direction of Heaven for the disposing of him.

1. [*July* 19.] G. D. There are diverse particular Subjects, to be handled for the special Service of my Flock, which I have in View. But I would with all Solemnity look up to the glorious Lord, that He would point me out, unto the next Portion and Paragraph of the Sacred Scripture, to be in the Course of my public Ministry insisted on; that it may be such an one; as the Flock may receive a singular Edification from.

19 *d. 5 m. Lord's-Day*. At the Lord's-Table, I considered the great Number of no small Mercies, which are there exhibited, and I thankfully and earnestly made my Claim unto them. And I very particularly admired the Favour of God, in that what we are doing in the Worship of God the Lord here, is a joining in Consort, with what they are doing in the Heavenly World.

2. G. D. There is fallen into my Hands, the Life of Mr. *Tho. Beard*, an incomparable young man, who died at Seventeen; but before he died, wrote the Dispositions and Experiences of his Piety. I will oblige my Son *Increase* to read this Composure; and I will confer with him upon it. I would also procure the Publication of it. And I would likewise transcribe into the Book I have now in the Press, a Passage of it, relating to Societies.

3. G. D. Sollicitous for the Health of my aged Parent,

I would perswade him to a frequent Use of the *Sal volatile*, which God has blessed unto me for more than ordinary Benefit; and I would present him with a Bottel of it, and keep him ever supplied with it as long as we both do live.

4. G. D. I apprehend, it would be a Service unto the Kingdome of God, if under the form of a Letter to the Hæretical *Whiston*, I should prepare for the public, a fuller Testimony to the Doctrines of the Trinity in the Godhead, and the Godhead of our Saviour. To this, therefore, with many supplications to Heaven for Direction and Assistence, I now apply myself.

5. G. D. Unto some that have Coaches, I would much recommend this Consideration; what Service they may do with them to that God from whom they have received them.

6. G. D. There is a poor Lad, but one of uncommon Capacity for Learning, to whose Education at the Colledge, I would contribute, and stir up the Charity of others. (Μεσεγγερ)[1]

7. G. D. The use of the *Sol Volatile*, having recovered much Health and Strength unto me, beyond what I have sometimes enjoy'd, I apprehend, that among other Expressions of my Gratitude unto the glorious Lord, I ought mightily to double my Diligence, especially in afternoon-Studies, for the Dispatch of those Things, which I would fain finish before I dy.

1. [*July* 26.] G. D. There is no one point, which my Hearers need so much to be warned about, as the Folly of setting the Heart on an earthly Treasure with a Neglect of the Heavenly. Wherefore I would insist on this Point unto them with much vehemency of Inculcation.

2. G. D. My Son *Increase!* My Son *Increase!* I am now seeking a Merchant who may be his Master, yett would I have him to preserve and increase his Learning. But

---

[1] Probably Henry Messinger, who graduated in 1717.

among the Questions which I daily putt unto him, one must be, *Have you this Day made your secret Prayers unto God?*

3. G. D. Having published a Treatise, which I call, *The A. B. C. of Religion*, it will be an agreeable Present for me to make unto the Children in the several Families of my Relatives.

4. G. D. The miserable Flock at *Newtown*, calls for abundance of Cares and Pains, to heal the Discomposures in it, and procure a good Settlement of a Minister. Their more particular Applications to me, lay me under more particular Obligations to do for them.[1]

5. G. D. *Quære*. Whether some of our Schole-Masters, may not order my *A, B, C. of Religion*, to be read over in the Schools, by Parcels, and then inculcate upon the Scholars, their Attention to the Maxims of Piety?

6. G. D. An unhappy Youth in my neighbourhood, tho' a Pretender to Religion, yett will curse and swear, and speak very profanely. I must talk to him.

7. G. D. When I have readd thro' a Book, at any time, I would make a Pause; and first, give Thanks to the Father of Lights, for whatever Illumination He has by this Book bestow'd upon me. Secondly, If the Author be in his Book an useful Servant of the Church, I would give Thanks to God, for His Raising up such an Instrument, and Inclining and Assisting of him to this Performance. Thirdly. If the Book be of an evil Tendency, I would bewayl the Corruption and Misery of the World, in such an Instance, and I would pray unto the Holy One to prevent the Infection. Lastly, I would enquire, what special Point of Piety or Usefulness may I, by this Book be minded of?

1. [*August* 2.] G. D. A wonderful deal of Care must be taken, that the Part of the Flock, which are swarming

---

[1] Nehemiah Hobart, after a pastorate of more than forty years, died August 25, 1712, and a petition was sent to the General Court that Newton be divided into two precincts. The request was denied, and in 1714 John Cotton was chosen to be minister.

off into a new Church, may not make themselves, and others, unhappy, by a Choice of a very unsuitable Minister; which they are greatly in danger of.

2. G. D. I must with the Help of Grace resolve upon it, that it shall be my Custome, to be at home with my Family, about Nine aClock in the Evenings; and employ an Hour, in Instructing of the Children, and Conversing with them, on the several Points, wherein I should be desirous of their becoming Excellent. The Time so spent with them, will turn to much better Account, than what I have sometimes allow'd in sitting with my Neighbours.

3 d. 6 m. [*August*.] *Munday*. I took a Journey to *Newtown*, in Company with several other Ministers. I did it with much Aversion, and with a Despair almost æqual to my Desire, of doing any Good. But, as the main Work to be done there, was imposed upon me, so I was not without some hope, that the Glorious Head of the Church would make me feel His Influences in that Hour. An Experience I have heretofore enjoy'd, was now wondrously renewed unto me; and the Glorious One supplied me with agreeable Thoughts and Words for the many difficult Occasions that were before me. So we managed the Brethren of a divided Church, and carried them thro' their Choice of a Pastor. We then call for the obstreperous Inhabitants, and spoke unto them such Things, as, I hope, have left a good Impression upon them. In the Evening I returned with a good Hand of God upon me.

3. G. D. I have some aged Relatives, to whom I would present my *Golgotha;* and some younger ones, to whom I would also commend the Early Piety, exemplified in the End of it.

4. G. D. Perhaps, by sending some agreeable Things, to the Author of, *The Spectator*, and, *The Guardian*, there may be brought forward some Services to the best Interests in the Nation.

5. G. D.   I would, in a Society, move to have some charitable Assistencies from their Bounty, communicated unto the necessitious Minister at *Endfield*.

6. G. D.   There is an old Man in the Town, who was a Souldier in the Army of my admirable *Cromwel*, and actually present in the Battel of *Dunbar;* He is now come to eighty-eight; an honest Man, and in great Penury. I must releeve him, and look after him.

7. G. D.   The Crowing of a Cock was a Monitor, whereby Peter was awaken'd unto Repentance. And why should not I, improve the Voice of such a Monitor, for my Awakening? 'Tis a very notable occurrence of Nature, and has in it what is a little Surprising. When I hear it, I would have Wishes of this Importance raised in me; *Lord! Quicken me Watchfully to observe the Times, and be aware of approaching Changes!*

1. [*August* 19.] G. D.   A miserable young Man, who has been received into the Covenant of God among His People here, has proved a notorious Instance of Apostasy, and fallen into very scandalous Crimes. The Discipline of the Church must be exerted on this Occasion; But I would make it an Occasion of inculcating in a very cogent way, the Admonitions of Piety on such as are in the Covenant of God, and on the young men in the Congregation.[1]

2. G. D.   Oh! why don't I in my Family, more livelily keep up the Temper and Conduct of a Parent expecting to be speedily taken from his Family! To drop Instructions of Piety on my Domesticks, as often as I come near them.

---

[1] "9 d. 6 m.   Richard Woods, one in the Covenant of God among us, having been guilty of a very disorderly Life, in his Master's Family, and of many Crimes, terminating in this, that the last Week he drank to the Damnation of them who do not love him. He was brought before the Church. But because he appeared very pœnitent, his Church agreed only to his having a solemn Admonition, at this time dispensed unto him, which was at this time done accordingly. With Assurance given him, that if he did not in due Time come to us with great Expressions and full Testimonies of Repentance, the Censure belonging to him should be publicly passed upon him." *Cotton Mather's MS. Records of the Second Church,* II.

To Examine them very often, whether they do and have the
Things that accompany Salvation! To see that they all spend
their Time in a very accountable Manner; and to dispatch
their Education as fast as I can, and enrich them with useful
Knowledge. I do something at all these Things. But I
ought to awaken myself unto the doing of more, than I do.

3. G. D. Among my Relatives, there are several
Youths to whom I present, my *Golgotha;* at the End
whereof there is an Exemple of early Piety.[1]

4. G. D. And that Exemple of early Piety in a Scholar
I would have to go into the Hands of the Students in our
Colledges; both that at *Cambridge* and that at *Say-brook*.
I would send it also unto *Glasgow*.

5. G. D. I am informed of several Houses in this
Town, where there are young Women of a very debauched
Character, and extremely Impudent; unto whom there is
a very great Resort of young men, which are extremely
poisoned by such conversation as these entertain them
withal. I must address our Society, that by suitable Admonitions, and some other Methods, this Mischief may be
extinguished.

6. G. D. There is a young Gentleman gone to sojourn
at *Jamaica;* of whose Morals there, his Friends and I,
would be very sollicitous. I would write unto him; and
send Books of Piety also to him.

7. G. D. When I have in my Eye, any Service wherein
I would fain be employ'd, I would first seriously consider,
by what Sins I have more especially rendred myself unworthy to have the Honour of such an Employment, and
obtain the Pardon of them; I would then also consider my
own Foolishness and Feebleness and Incapacities, which
will render the powerful Grace of Heaven the more conspicuous in it, if ever I go thro' such an Employment. And
in this way præpare to be serviceable.

[1] See an amusing entry in Sewall, *Diary*, II. 392.

15 *d.* 6 *m. Satureday.* This Day I sett apart for Prayer with Fasting before the Lord. My Occasions and Intentions and Petitions, were the same that I have had of later Time, when I have been thus engaged. I had my Son *Increase* also with me, and on the like Account, as formerly. I pray'd likewisely for encouraging Advice to me from *England.* And, for the Lord's accepting, and assisting, and instructing of me, to do Him Service in relation to a poor young Man committed for Murder;[1] that it may prove an Opportunity for Good unto many; and that I, notwithstanding my Unworthiness, may be employ'd in it. And, for a Smile of Heaven on the Confutation of the *Arian* Hæresies, which with the Help of Heaven I have præpared for the Public.

(IX.) For with the good Hand of God upon me, I have, not without some Study, and contrivance, elaborated a Testimony for the Cause of Truth, which has not been given by some that had singular Abilities and Obligations for it. I have entituled it; GOLIATHUS DETRUNCATUS. *The Trinity of Persons, in the One most Blessed and Glorious God; And the Eternal Godhead of our Great Saviour; briefly asserted. and clearly explained, and victoriously defended; both by the Infallible Scriptures, and by the Antenicene Fathers. In an American Letter to the Learned* Mr. William Whiston.

I have thoughts of having this Essay transcribed, and so transmitted for *London.*

1. [*August* 16.] G. D. My pastoral Visits to the Flock must be revived; enquiries into the State of every one must be proposed; one Afternoon in a fortnight must be sett apart for this Purpose. I must not be weary of this Work for the Lord.

16 *d.* 6 *m. Lord's-Day.* At the Lord's-Table, first, beholding the blessed Jesus as purposing and purchasing a wondrous Glory for His People, and publishing His Will,

---

[1] David Wallis. See p. 240, *infra.*

that they who are given to Him, should be with Him, to
behold His Glory; I endeavoured then to putt it out of
Doubt, that I am one of those who are for that Intent given
unto Him. I gave myself unto Him; and I chose it as
the Delight of my Life to study His Glory; the Design of
my Life, to proclaim it.

2. G. D. I have an Opportunity to gett my Son
Increase cultivated, with many Points of a polite Conversation, in his Evening-Hours; and I desire it may be
husbanded unto the best Advantage.

3. G. D. A late Marriage has added unto my Relatives, a new Kinsman, who is of the Sea-faring Tribe. Unto
him I would apply myself, with suitable Books of Piety,
and such Discourses as may have a Tendency to produce
in him the Fear of God.

4. G. D. The Condition of the poor Malefactor committed for a Murder,[1] I would endeavour so to consider,
that the Kingdome of God, and the Interest of Piety, may
have considerable Services from it. *Newbury*, still calls
for more Care.

5. G. D. In my writing of Letters to very capable
and eminent Persons, I would still think of notable Services, which they may be putt upon doing of. Thus, now
particularly writing to that miraculous Man, Mr. *Jameson*,
blind from his Nativity, but an Author of wonderful Books;
I would putt him upon writing a Book for blind People.

6. G. D. Some that are fallen into dreadful Snares
of Sin, and of Death, must have Means used upon them
to recover them. Especially, the Indian Youth, at the
Colledge.

I would also write a Letter of Consolation unto a young
Gentlewoman, uneasily circumstanced, at *N. London*.

One likewise at *Windsor*, having borrowed a sum of
Money of me, I would empower a Minister there to call

[1] David Wallis.

for it,[1] and to divide it between himself and the Minister of *Endfield*.

7. G. D.   The Case of a poor Criminal in the Prison, to dy shortly for a Murder, will oblige me to bear solemn Testimonies against various Miscarriages to be found among our People.   I ought in order hereunto, exceedingly to examine myself, how far I may have been myself chargeable with any Degree of those Miscarriages, and with a renew'd and thorough Repentance obtained the Pardon thereof.

22 d./23 d. 6 m. Satureday night.   Something of a Vigil.

1. [*August* 23.]   G. D.   Will not the cxvith Psalm, in likelihood be a Portion of Scripture, which I may with much Advantage to the Flock, in a course of Sermons insist upon?

And some other Subjects I have my Eye upon.

2. G. D.   My Prayers for my Consort must be quickened, and so must her own by my Advice, from some present Circumstances.

3. G. D.   I have a Nephew at *Roxbury*, who is one of ripe Abilities, and of great Expectations, designed for the evangelical Ministry.[2]   I would now make a very particular Notice of him, and in all the Wayes I can, contribute unto his future Serviceableness.

4. G. D.   The Condition of several Churches, calls for my most exquisite Care, to gett them delivered out of their Temptations.

Moreover I must gett that Matter well settled; the ordaining of Ministers, whom we send unto places destitute of the Gospel; and empowering of them to act as Ministers. *Freetown* particularly should be accommodated in this matter.[3]

---

[1] Rev. Timothy Edwards was then over the church at Windsor, but Mather speaks too indefinitely to identify him as the man. Rev. Nathaniel Collins was at Enfield.

[2] Thomas Walter.

[3] Rev. Joseph Avery had ceased his duties in 1711, and after some contention Recompence Wadsworth had been called, but declined the offer. In 1713 Rev. Jonathan Dodson, a citizen of the town, received a temporary appointment (June 2), and held the pulpit for more than two years.

5. G. D. Besides my drawing up Instructions for Agents to go from the Indian-Commissioners to *Martha's Vineyard*, I must prevent some indirect Proceedings in *Connecticot*, whereby our Attempts to Christianize the Indians there, may meet with Obstruction; and Letters must be written for that Purpose. There are several other Intentions of Piety, to be sett forward among the Indians.

6. G. D. There are several Miserables in the Prison, whose conditions call for my Kindnesses.

7. G. D. It will mightily illuminate and invigorate my walk with God, if I entertain a right Notion of that *Return to God*, wherein lies both Religion and Felicity. That ceasing to seek Satisfaction in Creatures, and to aim at my own Satisfaction exclusive of the Glorious *God:* That aiming at the Glory, and Service, and Pleasure of God in all that I do, and in all that I have; and that pressing after a most near Communion with God, and Enjoyment of God, and Acquiescence in His Will, that may render Him All in All unto me. And a View of our glorious JESUS taken up into God, as the Cause and Way of our being brought home unto Him. A clear Notion of this illustrious Matter, which indeed, I have now for many Years lived upon, yett needs to be more thoroughly concocted into my Soul.

29 *d.*/30 *d.* 6 *m. Satureday-night.* I enjoy'd a Vigil, wherein I had some intimate Conversation with Heaven. My Visits thither, were for pardoning Mercy; and for purifying Mercy; and for a successful Ministry; and for something from *England* that may Encourage me in my work; and for a Blessing on what I have sent thither; and for a Blessing on my Family, especially in the Disposal of my Son *Increase;* and for the Conversion of the Jew, for whom I have been so long and so much concerned! My God will hear me! (Psal. XXII. 2.)

1. [*August* 30.] G. D. In my Catechising, as among the Jews, it is expected every Child should betimes learn that Verse, Deut. XXXIII. 4. So I would now and then single out some notable Verse of the Gospel, and command and perswade all the Children to learn it. Such as, Joh. III. 16. and 1. Tim. 1. 15. and Eccl. XII. 14.

2. G. D. Two of my children, *Cresy* and *Lizzy*, have newly been scorched with Gun-powder, wherein tho' they have received a most merciful Deliverance, especially of their Eyes, yett they undergo a Smart that is considerable. I would improve this Occasion to inculcate Instructions of Piety on them and the rest; especially with Relation to their Danger of eternal Burnings.

Cresy, must also imploy the Liesure which this has occasion'd for him, in the most profitable Manner.

3. G. D. I have an Aunt at *Northampton*, whom in regard of her Piety, and her Affliction, I ought to take much Notice of.

4. G. D. The Condition and Repentance of the Prisoner under a Sentence of Death, may afford me some notable Opportunities to serve the Kingdome of God, and the Cause of Piety; which accordingly I would cultivate unto the best of my Capacity.

2 d./3 d. [*September.*] *Wednesday/Thursday.* In a Vigil, I humbled myself before the Lord exceedingly. Being anon to preach probably in a very great Auditory, with the condemned Malefactor there; and an Eye had unto the Use to be made of his Condition, and being also thrown into a feeble State of Health, which makes me afraid whether I shall be able to do any Thing at all; prostrate in the Dust, I loathed and judged myself before the Lord, for my Miscarriages, wherein I had not been willing to be witheld from sinning against Him, and wherein I was worthy to be so left, that I should have been as miserable a Spectacle, as he that is now to appear in the Congrega-

tion. Especially my Impurities, and my Hatred and Malice towards other Men, wherein I have been a Degree of a Murderer. I received the pardoning Mercy of God, and pleaded the Blood of my Saviour for it; and I entreated the gracious Presence of the Lord with me, in the Service now before me, for which I apprehended myself utterly insufficient. I then also sought for the Mercies propounded in some former *Vigils* (Psal. XLIV. 25, 26.)

5. G. D. I have now gott a Catalogue of young Men, who visit wicked Houses. And I will improve it in their Service as much as I can. Especially laying it before the Society for Suppression of Disorders; from whence we will send Admonitions to them.

3 *d.* 7 *m. Thursday.* It has pleased the Holy One, this Day to humble me; and I entertained the Humiliation with a sweet Satisfaction in the Will of my Father and my Saviour. Having been these two Dayes wasted with a *Diarrhœa*, and grown very sick at my stomach, my Spirits utterly failed, before I had stood an Hour, in my Sermon, so that I was forced to break off. There was a vast Auditory, and the poor condemned prisoner was a part of it. But I was defeated of saying a very great part of the Things which I was desirous to have declared on this Occasion. But I am satisfied. I improve this Dispensation to further a Work of Repentance in me. And the Holy One saies unto me, *What I do, thou knowest not now, but thou shalt know hereafter!*

6. G. D. There is in this Town the Son of a Minister; in danger to be led away with Temptation. I would seasonably apply myself to his Rescue.

7. G. D. I am oftentimes on Satureday towards the Evening, engaged in an agreeable Conversation with some young Gentlemen, on the *Christian Asceticks*. I hope, to make this a precious Opportunity, of my Improving in the clear Knowledge of many Points relating to the more vital

Piety; and confirming and strengthening my Dispositions for a walk with God.

1. [*September* 6.] G. D. A religious and a desirable Schoolmaster, now being brought into the Grammar-School of my Neighbourhood, I hope to concert many things with him for the Good of the Flock, and see him an Instrument of doing many Services.

2. G. D. My youngest little Daughter is a marvellous witty, ready, forward Child; I would oblige every Child in the Family, to teach her each of them Sentences of Piety, that so she may betimes and apace have her mind filled with Maxims of Piety.

3. G. D. I would encourage my aged Parent, unto as many Services by the way of the Press, as may be; where his Bow yett abides in Strength. Particularly, to write a Book for *aged People*.

4. G. D. The more I think of it, the more it appears unto me, a most seasonable and profitable Service, to revise and prepare for the Press, my, *Ratio Disciplinæ* an Account of the Methods and Customes used in our Churches. It will have a mighty Tendency, to præserve our Discipline, and procure a Beauty to the Exercise of it in all Administrations. And it may also be our Vindication to the World, and a Satisfaction to our Brethren.[1]

5. G. D. There is a multitude of Services, in the School for the pious and learned Education of the Children, whereto I would propose to advise our Schole-Master.

10 *d*. 7 *m. Thursday*. And now I see the Glorious Goodness of my dear and sweet Saviour. Oh! that I may love and serve my most gracious Lord, with a most marvellous Reliance upon Him! The Balk which I suffered in my Services a week ago, was but only to find me an Opportunity for further and greater Services. The Minister who should have succeeded in the Lecture, was importunate with me,

[1] Printed in 1726.

to take his Lecture. I did so; and in a great Auditory, with mighty Assistences from above, I bore my Testimonies for Piety, and made large Additions to what I intended a Week ago, and was heard with much Attention, and I hope, with much Impression; my Sermon extended unto about an hour and three Quarters, and my Strength held out unto the Last; tho' I was tired with my Catechising yesterday, and had something of my last Week's Distemper then also upon me. The Prayer-hearing Lord, in a way of sovereign Grace, dealt wonderfully with me.

6. G. D. I must renew my Enquiry's into the Condition of poor Prisoners; It is possible I may find among them, some Objects of Charity, whom I may releeve in many Instances.

7. G. D. I would most accurately Study the Description of a lukewarm Christian, and most impartially enquire, wherein, and how far, I may myself answer the unhappy Character.

12 d. 7 m. Satureday. This Day I sett apart for Prayers and Alms, with Fasting before the Lord. The Occasions were such as I have had heretofore; and so were the Exercises. I had also an Eye to some special Services that are before me.

1. [September 13.] G. D. One of the best Things that I can do for my Flock is, to give them a Description of *lukewarm Christians*, with a Disswasive unto them to avoid the unhappy Character. The Neighbourhood is full of them.

13 d. 7 m. Lords Day. Having preached a Sermon as full of divine Flame, as I could, that I might bring the Flock out of the lukewarm Frame, that so generally prevails upon them, I carried them, as in my Sermon I told them I would, unto the Lord's-Table for the Care of it. Here in the Prayers I proposed such Considerations from the object before us, as might quicken us to Religion in earnest; and

pleaded also, that the Death of our Saviour had purchased
for us the Life of Piety in our Souls, and that He lived as
the Prince of Life, to bestow it upon us. I presented myself with the Flock, as a Sacrifice before the Lord, as a
People willing to be the Lords; entreating, that a Ray shott
from the glorious Lord upon us, might sett us on Fire; and
inflame our Hearts with a Love to Him, and a Zeal to serve
Him, that should be a Fire with a vehement Flame.

2. G. D. I have now a various Prospect, for the
Improvement of my Son *Increase,* in a good Education,
and I would prosecute it unto the uttermost.

3. G. D. I have a poor little Kinsman under an unaccountable Malady, in much Danger of Death; I must
endeavour the service and the comfort both of the Child,
and of his Mother, as much as I can.

16 *d.* 7 *m.* 4. G. D. An Ordination is this Day sol-
emnized in this Town, at which a great Confluence of
People are like to be present. And I may be called unto
some of the public Actions in it, I would make it an Opportunity to declare such Things, as may leave a manifold
Impression [of] Religion; especially, with the Candidates of
the Ministry.[1]

5. G. D. Something must be done, to prevent the
Division and Confusion of the Christian Indians at *Sandwyche.*

17 *d.* 7 *m. Thursday.* As the Lord accepted me yesterday
to glorify His Name, in a principal part of the public Action,
that was carried on with great Solemnity, in a very great
Auditory, so He this day, allowed me and assisted me, notwithstanding the weak State of my Health, to Glorify Him
in the Lecture; Three Lectures together have now been
devolved upon me; and tho' I was humbled with Sickness,
that obliged me to some Abruptness in the first of them, I

---

[1] Rev. Joseph Sewall was ordained colleague of Rev. Ebenezer Pemberton.
See Sewall, *Diary,* II. 397.

have in the Rest, enjoy'd a very sensible Presence of God with me. What shall I render to the Lord!

6. G. D. Some Servants of God arrived unto us from other parts of the world, are in Circumstances of Difficulty, which call for my charitable Contrivances and Assistences on their behalf.

7. G. D. My Skill and Care in this Point, ought to be improved into a greater Degree of Brightness; in Writing of Letters, I would with more ingenuity contrive, be the Business what it will, how to bring in something that may glorify my dear Saviour, and contribute unto the grand Intentions of Piety.

1. [*September* 20.] G. D. I think to transfer my Catechising at which the Lads are very numerous, from my own House unto the School; where I may have a greater Opportunity to edify others that may be Spectators. For the Catechising of the Females, I yett need further Direction.

2. G. D. I have a Prospect of a religious Family, of a Merchant in good Business, to which I apply myself, that my Son *Increase* may be disposed there. But I would still ply him with all possible Methods for a most liberal Education in other Points; that he may be a man very useful in the World.

3. G. D. I have some Kindred at *Mistick*, whom I incline, as soon as I can recover an Afternoon for that purpose, to visit with Endeavours to serve the Cause of Piety among them.

4. G. D. The poor young Man, who is to dy this Week, I obtain from him an Instrument of pertinent and penitent Passages, which, I hope, will be applied unto many good Purposes, when I come to publish it.

(X.) And this is what I purpose to do. For to serve the Interests of Piety, with the Engines wherewith I am furnished, from the Condition of the young Man, who is condemned to dy for a Murder, I give to the Bookseller, what

I have preached on his Occasion; with some further Account
of the young Man, and his Repentance. It is entituled,
THE CURBED SINNER, *A discourse upon the Gracious and*
Wondrous Restraints, Laid by the Providence of the glorious
God, on the sinful Children of men, to withold them from
Sinning against Him. Occasion'd by a Sentence of Death,
passed on a poor young man, for the Murder of his Com-
panion. With some Historical Passages, referring to that
unhappy Spectacle.[1]

23 *d.* 7 *m. Wednesday.*   With a Mind full of Discouragements, I took a Chaise, and rode unto *Dedham,* where, (as
it uses to be, and after my Mind is very much discouraged)
I enjoy'd a mighty Presence of the Lord with me, in preaching the Lecture.

5. G. D.   I observe diverse, especially Elder, men in
the Town, who have little Business to do; I would insinuate myself into their Conversation; and project with them,
and suggest to them, those Methods, with which they may
improve their Liesure-time in doing Abundance of Good.
Especially in visiting and counselling and comforting the
Afflicted, and finding out the Indigent.

6. G. D.   I must make the poor Indians as well as the
poor English, the Objects of my poor Dispensations. I
hear of an aged Indian, thirty miles off, under Languishments nigh unto Death, and cast off by those that should
have more Compassion. I would send, Releefs unto this
destitute Creature.

7. G. D.   Whenever I do any Services for the Lord,
and for His Kingdome, tho' I am not on such Occasions
a Stranger to Thoughts on the Points, which render me
singularly unworthy to be honoured with being employed
in such Services, yett I must grow more explicit in them,

---

[1] Printed by John Allen for Nicholas Boone, 1713, with a sermon by Benjamin Coleman, and a *True Relation of the Murder.* The *Relation* was probably
prepared by Mather, and on Wallis's narration.

and more effected with them. So will sovereign Grace be glorified; and this on continual, and observable Occasions.

(XI.) The Sermon which I preached at the Lecture, a little above a Week ago, I was much at a Loss in my Mind, whether I should preach it or no, or what I should preach upon, if I did preach at all. In the Night, while my mind was thus dubious, I dream't that I did preach, and I had my Text also assigned me in my Dream. I proceeded, and all fell out, unto good Acceptance among the People of God. Some of my Neighbours desired a copy of the Sermon, that they might give it unto the Public. The Subject is the most important in the World; and the Sermon will be an agreeable Engine for me to employ on many Occasions, when Books of Piety are to be dispensed. So I fitt the Discourse for the Press; and give it unto the Bookseller, under this Title. WHAT SHOULD BE MOST OF ALL THOUGHT UPON. *A brief Essay to awaken in a Dying Man (that is to say, in every Man,) a proper and lively Concern for, A Good State after Death. With some Direction, how the Good State is to be obtained and Ensured.*[1]

1. [*September* 27.] G. D. Why should not the Ringing of the Bell, on the Lords-Dayes, ever awaken in me some suitable Upliftings of Soul unto the Lord, on the behalf of the Flock, which the Bell·thus calls together!

2. G. D. Great Reason have I to suspect, that I shall by Death be taken from a large, and a poor Family; and that I may leave a numerous Family to conflict with many Difficulties, in a barbarous Neighbourhood. I ought with all possible Prudence and Vigour, to take my Measures accordingly: To treat my children every Day, as one quickly going from them; To bring them into such Methods of Piety, from that Consideration, that they may be sure, God will be their Father; To cultivate such Points of Education in them, as may enable them to subsist them-

---

[1] Printed by T. Green, for D. Henchman, 1713.

selves; and to bespeak such Friends for them, as may do friendly Offices for them, when I shall be gone from them.

3. G. D. I have a Sister, in many other Afflictions, and in Hazard of losing her Sight. Her Condition calls for my Compassions and Assistences, in all the Wayes that I can think of.

4. G. D. I am informed, that the Minds and Manners of many People about the Countrey are much corrupted, by foolish Songs and Ballads, which the Hawkers and Pedlars carry into all parts of the Countrey. By way of Antidote, I would procure poetical Composures full of Piety, and such as may have a Tendency to advance Truth and Goodness, to be published, and scattered into all Corners of the Land. There may be an Extract of some, from the excellent *Watts's* Hymns.

5. G. D. An aged and a pious Matron, the First-born of this Town, died yesterday.[1] It may glorify God, and promote Godliness, if I this Day in the Lecture, preach a Funeral-sermon for her; it may putt many women upon the Exercise of all Goodness.

6. G. D. A Wretched man, who is a Justice of Peace lives in detestable Adulteries. I would write unto him, a solemn Letter, and by such Faithfulness endeavour his Recovery.

7. G. D. In reading over Dr. *Calamies* Accounts of the *Bartholomæan* Sufferers, I hope to make sensible Improvements in Piety; And especially in those two Points; First, much Industry in the Business, of my great Master;

[1] Mary, daughter of Rev. John Wilson, was born September, 1633. She married November 5, 1651, for her first husband Rev. Samuel Danforth, who died in 1674; and for her second, Joseph Rock, whose first wife was Elizabeth, daughter of John Coggan. In a sermon delivered upon her death Mather says: "one of the First-born, if not the *Very First* of her Sex that was born in this famous Metropolis of the English-America: and who deserves to be honourably mentioned as long as *Boston* shall endure, which, I hope, will be unto the Second Coming of our Saviour." She died September 30. The text of the sermon is given on p. 288, *infra*.

Secondly, much Reliance on the Providence of the glorious One, to have my Family well provided for. Moreover, many historical Passages will be of great Benefit unto me, in my Endeavours after a fruitful and useful Conversation.

1. [*October* 4.] G. D. Some very remarkable Deliverances at Sea, have been lately granted unto some in this Place; May not I do well to collect and publish them; and from thence also take Occasion to address the Seafaring Part of my Auditory, with new Admonitions, to make a right Use of the divine Dealings with them?

2. G. D. I am now proceeding in the Choice of *Patrons* for my Children, to treat each of them with a particular Tenderness; especially, which I leave them *Orphans*.

3. G. D. The Departure of that aged and pious Matron, who was buried the last week, affords me an Opportunity to discourse with my Mother, upon her præparations.

4. G. D. I would with mature Advice, prevail on our Booksellers, to become furnished from *England*, with certain Books, that our Candidates of the Ministry ought in the first place, to be supplied withal. And then see that the said Candidates do therewith supply themselves. This may prove a Service of no little Consequence.

Especially *Ravanellus, Turretin. Ushers* Body of Divinity. *Alstedii Turris David, Edward's preacher And, Theologia Reformata.*[1]

5. G. D. There are some wealthy Persons, who have no Children; and by consequence are capable of doing much good with their Estates. I would address Letters to them, with as much Artifice and Insinuation as I can, to obtain from them, all the Good that they can be mov'd unto.

[1] These names are written in the margin.

Three generations of Turretini wrote upon theology as then understood — Benedict (1588–1631), François (1623–1687), and Jean Alphonse (1671–1737). Ussher's "Body of Divinitie" first appeared in 1645; Johann Heinrich Alsted (1588–1638) wrote much on divinity, and always in Latin, long holding a favored place among the educated. His *Turris Babel Destructa*, 1639, may have been the book intended by Mather in this entry.

6. G. D. A poor Man who has liv'd in credible Circumstances, but fallen into Decay, putt himself into a Red-Coat, that he might receive the Kindnesses of the Governour at *N. York*, who advised him to it. But missing what he Expected, he elopes to N. E. Where our Governour at the desire of him at N. York takes him up, and keeps in prison, to send him home. Here, his ungodly mind has been so enraged at his Evil circumstances, that with all his force and fury, he stab'd at his Heart with a Pen-knife. God strangely prevented the Wound's proving mortal. He is very pœnitent, and in wonderful Distress. Tis possible he may be brought home to God, on this woful Occasion. However, I write as nice Letters as I can, unto the Governours both of N. E. and of N. York, to obtain favour of him; and his Rescue from the Circumstances, that procure him his Temptations.

(XII.) That I might serve the Interests of Piety, and do Justice to the Memory of a religious Matron, and provoke the Imitation of her Piety, I now fitted for the Press, a sermon, I lately preached at the Lecture. It is entituled, NEPENTHES EVANGELICUM. *A brief Essay, upon a soul at Ease, in what Piety will bring both Parents and Children to. A Sermon occasioned by the Death of a Religious Matron, Mrs. Mary Rock; who having Entred the Eighty first year of her Age, withdrew from us; 30 d. 7 m. 1713.*[1]

7. G. D. It is time for me to enquire into the Errors, that may attend the Dayes of Prayer, I keep from time to time in the Religion of the Closett.

I must not leave too much of my Study for my Sermons, to be prosecuted on these Dayes; whereby my Application to the more special Work of the Dayes has been sometimes too much interrupted.

I must more particularly consider the more enormous Transgressions of my Life, and renew my Repentance for

[1] See p. 242, *supra.*

those Enormities; remember against myself my former Iniquities.

I must conclude the Services, with more explicit, new and strong Resolutions, for a Walk with God.

10 *d.* 8 *m.* [*October.*] *Satureday.* This Day I sett apart for Prayer with Fasting, as has been usual with me. The Occasions were the same, that I have of late had for my former Dayes; The Experiences also much the same.

1. [*October* 11.] G. D. I would again look into Gregories *Pastoralis Cura*, and consider the several Classes of people in a Flock, by him enumerated; and how each of them are to be admonished. And I would endeavour as great a Variety of both public and private Admonitions, unto the various People of my Neighbourhood.

11 *d.* 8 *m. Lords-day.* My Father's Illness, cast upon me the Administration of the Eucharist. At which my main Endeavour was, to obtain a Deliverance from the chief Trouble and Sorrow of a dying Hour, which lies in the Pains of Hell then getting hold on the Sinner; and this I did, especially by pleading of this, that our Great Saviour had suffered these on our behalf.

2. G. D. May not I humbly plead it with the glorious Lord, on the behalf of my poor Children, and for their being well-provided for, when I am dead and gone; that the considerable Interest, (by this Time, it would have been many hundreds of Pounds,) which I should have laid up for them, has been employ'd in their Subsistence and Education, when I might have justly expected the Supplies for that, from the Flock; but have waved that Expectation, that so I might not be burdensome to them, or hinder the Success of my Ministry! There is not the Least of Merit in this my Self-Denial; But yett, may it not encourage me to hope, that the gracious Lord will retaliate this unto my Children?

12 *d.* 8 *m.* This Day, in Ships arriving from *London*, I

receive Letters from the Secretary of the Royal Society, who tells me, that my *Curiosa Americana* being readd before that Society, they were greatly satisfied therewithal, and ordered the Thanks of the Society to be returned unto me; they also signified their Desire and Purpose, to admitt me as a Member of their Body. And, he assures me, that at their first lawful Meeting for such Purposes, I shall be made, A FELLOW OF THE ROYAL SOCIETY; Whereof he Expects then to send me the Advice, and some other Entertainments.[1]

This is a marvellous Favour of Heaven to me; A surprising Favour; One that will much encourage me, and fortify me, in my Essayes to do Good; and add unto the superiour Circumstances, wherein my gracious Lord places me above the Contempt on [of] envious Men. Oh! what shall I render to the Lord? I entertain these things, prostrate in the Dust before the Lord, with all humble self-Abhorrence, and cry from thence unto Him, that He would enable me to make a due Improvement of the Things in which He smiles upon me; and hereby quicken my Diligence in His Holy Service.

3. G. D. Still my Concern is for my aged Parents; Inventing all possible Wayes, to make them comfortable. And unto some of my Relatives that are at this time sojourning in my Neighbourhood, I would give some agreeable Books of Piety.

13 *d. 8 m.* This Day an Ordination was carried on at *Charlestown:* and thro' the Favour of God, so carried on, as to testify His presence among us, and exhibit something of His Glory, and as honourable Solemnity in the Order of

---

[1] The doubts, which have surrounded the election of Mather to the Royal Society, have been solved by Sir Arthur Herbert Church, who finds that he was elected F. R. S. on April 11, 1723. He had been proposed for membership some years before, and this entry in the *Diary* probably fixes the time of the first submission of his name. He certainly used the usual letters of a member before his election was actually held.

our Churches. But, by the Singular Providence of the Lord, a great part of the work was devolved on the unworthiest Person in the Great Assembly. I made the Prayer before the Sermon; and I gave the Fellowship of our Churches, in a large Speech, wherein I enjoy'd the signal Assistences of God.[1]

4. G. D. I would consider, what Subjects in Philosophy may peculiarly need cultivation, and I would improve my Correspondence with the Secretary of the *Royal Society*, to sett afoot among the Members thereof, such Studies as may be for general Benefit, and have hitherto been but little prosecuted.

5. G. D. I would send a Copy of my, *Goliathus detruncatus*, unto *Cambridge*, to be perused by the principal Members of the Colledge there; supposing it may be seasonable to fortify them with such Things against the Error of the wicked. I would also send thither, to be read, the Books of my Friend Mr. *Jameson*, etc. against Episcopacy.

6. G. D. An aged Gentlewoman, whose Milk I suck'd, when I was an Infant, is now in another Town, lying a poor Clinic under a Palsey, and in indigent Circumstances. I must send Releefs unto her.[2]

7. G. D. The *Maxims of the Kingdome of God*, which I have studied, and præpared, and published, I would successively take each of them, into yett a more solemn and thorough Consideration, and so study them, as to have my Heart and Life exceedingly conformed unto them, and to render it evident that they are the Maxims of my whole Conduct in the World. I would propose hereby, not only

---

[1] Rev. Joseph Stevens, who was ordained as colleague of Rev. Simon Bradstreet. Sewall describes Mather's speech as "august, shewing that the Congregational Churches early declar'd against Independency, that all the Reformation of the Continent of Europe ordain'd as New England did; shew'd that their Ordination had no other Foundation. Declared what was expected of the Ordained person, what of the church, and then gave the Right Hand of Fellowship." *Diary*, II. 402.

[2] Probably Mrs. Gale. See p. 160, *supra*.

to assure my part in the Kingdome of God, but also to be a more qualified Instrument from the advancing of it.

1. [*October* 18.] G. D. The Measles coming into the Town, it is likely to be a Time of Sickness, and much Trouble in the Families of the Neighbourhood. I would by my public Sermons and Prayers, endeavour to prepare the Neighbours for the Trouble which their Families are likely to meet withal.[1]

2. G. D. The Apprehension of a very deep Share, that my Family may expect in the common Calamity of the spreading Measles, will oblige me to be much in pleading the Great Family-Sacrifice, that so the Wrath of Heaven may inflict no sad Thing on my Family; and to quicken and augment the Expressions of Piety, in the daily Sacrifices of my Family; and to lay hold on the Occasion to awaken Piety, and Preparation for Death, in the Souls of the children.

3. G. D. I am now furnished with Opportunities, which I would make use of, to convey Books of Piety, in discharge of my Duty, to Relatives, whom I have never seen, in *Connecticot*.

4. G. D. The Island of *Nantucket* greatly wants, to have a Minister afforded unto it; and I would Employ my best Enquiries and Endeavours, that this want may be supplied.[2]

5. G. D. There are several fresh Occasions, for service to be done unto the Interests of Religion among our Indians; which I am to prosecute among the Commissioners.

6. G. D. A decay'd Gentleman of *Youghal* in *Ireland*, is here; to whom I am to dispense many Kindnesses: and make some Disbursements for him.

[1] See Sibley, *Harvard Graduates*, III. 113, for a printed letter on the measles, attributed to Mather. Also pp. 252, 272, *infra*.

[2] Of the early history of the Congregational Church in Nantucket little or nothing is known. About 1711 a church was gathered, and presumably under one of the Mayhews.

7. G. D. For my more effectual Supply with good Thoughts and that my Mind may not ly fallow as I am walking the Streets, or in the Intervals of Business, I would have the Sceletons of Sermons on several Subjects, præpared, with Blanks left for good Thoughts to be entred thereupon, and have my Mind applied this Way, when I have nothing more suitable to think upon.

On the 18 *d.* 8 *m.* a week ago, my Son *Increase* fell sick; about the Middle of the Week, the sickness appeared to be *Measles*. God graciously carries him thro' a gentle Visitation. But now, what Uneasiness is my Family to look for?

1. [*October* 25.] G. D. The grievous Unsuccessfulness of my Ministry, ought to be unto me, the most pungent Matter of Grief in the World. It should be with me, a Matter of more Concern, more Study, more Prayer, and very deep Abasement of Soul before the Lord. I ought to be more concerned about it, more affected with it; and to do more that I may find out the Cause of it, and if it be possible obtain the Removal of it, and a greater Success of the Gospel in my Neighbourhood.

2. G. D. The spreading Malady of the *Measles*, which to many proves a Grievous one, having entred my Family, I must in my Family-Sacrifices have an Eye to the Condition of my Family.

I must quicken the præparation of my Domesticks, for the unknown Issue of their Calamity.

And now, my Son *Increase* is on his Recovery, I must oblige him unto it, as his first Work, to draw up in writing, some special Resolutions, for the future Conduct of his Life.

3. G. D. I have some Relatives at *Medford*, especially one Kinswoman languishing under incurable Sickness. If I can accomplish it, I would give them a Visit; and instruct them, and comfort them, and pray with them.

My desireable Daughter *Nibby*, is now lying very sick of the *Measles*.

4. G. D.   Since a very sensible Calamity is begun upon the Town, and such as will not be without some Degree of Mortality, I may do well to glorify my Saviour, with a Discourse at the Lecture, on the Methods of consulting the Safety and Welfare of our Families, by getting the Blood of the Great Passeover sprinkled on our Houses.

5. G. D.   The Time of the year arrives for me, in my prayers, at the Lecture as well as on the Lord's-day, to animate the Charity of the good People in the Town, and their Compassion to the Poor for their Difficulties in the approaching Winter.

6. G. D.   The Spreading of the Measles in the Town, which will prove an heavy Calamity, and is much worse to us Americans than it is in Europe, it adds exceedingly to the Difficulties of the Families, where they conflict with Poverty.   I must have my Eye much upon these miserable Families, and do my best, that they may be provided for.

30 *d. 8 m. Friday.*   This Day, my Consort, for whom I was in much Distress, lest she should be arrested with the Measles which have proved fatal to Women that were with child, after too diligent an Attendence on her sick Family, was no doubt something before her Time, surprized with her Travail; But God favored her with a very easy Time; and about the middle of the Afternoon graciously delivered her, of both a Son and a Daughter; perfect and likely children, wherein I receive numberless Favours of God.[1]

My dear *Katy,* is now also down with the *Measles;* in somewhat more favorable Circumstances, than those that have gone before her.

7. G. D.   The Glorious God, in the surprising Increase of my Family, rebukes my sinful Fears of having them all well-provided for.   Thro' the Assistence of His Grace, I

---

[1] Mather had a taste for the unusual.   Only a fortnight before he had piloted Sewall to see a "portentous birth" of twins, at the North End in Prince Street. Sewall, *Diary,* II. 403.

find those Fears gloriously vanish, as my Family increases. I find my soul rejoicing in the View of my having in my Family, more Servants born unto my Saviour. And I triumph in an Assurance, that his fatherly Providence will take a marvellous Care of them. I must watch against the least Motions or Tendencies of Unbeleef.

1. [*November* 1.] G. D. There are People in my Flock, who have arrived unto a considerable Age, and are of good Esteem for their Piety. And yett these People, never have come to the Table of the Lord. Nay, some of them are not baptised unto this Day. In public Sermons, about the Things, which it will trouble one in a dying Hour, to have left undone, I would bestow some terrible Awakenings, on these dilatory Christians.

1 d. 9 m. [*November.*] *Lords Day.* This Day, I baptised my new-born Twins; and first secretly, then publickly, gave them up unto the Lord, and laid hold on His gracious Covenant for them. My Wife's vertuous Mother having worn the Name of *Martha*, the Relatives were fond of having the Daughter called so; which name also signifying, *Doctrix;* may the better suit (as my Father said) a *Doctor's* Daughter. I then thought, who was *Martha's* Brother; and that *Eleazar* was the same with *Lazarus;* and a priestly Name; and the Child must be led to look for the *Help of God*, which is in the Signification of the Name. I had also an excellent Uncle of that Name.[1] So I called them, ELEAZAR and MARTHA.[2]

2. G. D. I will now teach my Son *Increase*, (and others of my Children,) the way of raising a *Lesson* out of every Verse, in his Reading of the Bible; and of turning it into a *Prayer;* and engage him (and them) unto a daily Course of Reading the Bible in such a Way.

[1] Born in Dorchester, Mass., 1637, and died at Northampton, 1669. He married Esther, daughter of Rev. John Warham. He also kept a diary, from which his nephew makes an extract, in the *Magnalia*, Book III. 131.

[2] Both died in November. They were the last born of Mather's children.

3. G. D.   The Languishments of my Parent supply me with fresh Occasions to serve him, and help him, and study Wayes of making his Condition easy to him.

4. G. D.   I would consider, whether I may not do well, to print a little Sheet, of Advice for sick persons, and Houses, and lodge it in the sick Families, as the Malady spreads, which is now likely to prove so grievous unto the Town.   I am afraid, whether I shall gett Time, or no.

In my poor Family, now, first, my Wife has the *Measles* appearing on her; we know not yett how she will be handled.

My Daughter *Nancy* is also full of them; not in such uneasy Circumstances as her prædecessors.

My Daughter *Lizzy*, is likewise full of them; yett somewhat easily circumstanced.

My Daughter *Jerusha*, droops and seems to have them appearing.

My Servant-maid, lies very full and ill of them.

Help Lord; and look mercifully on my poor, sad, sinful Family, for the Sake of the Great Sacrifice!

5. G. D.   The Corporation in *London*,[1] having refused to dismiss me, (as I desired,) from sitting with the Commissioners for the Evangelical Affaires among the Indians, I would more than ever sett myself to serve them.   And I would now particularly, write unto one who is very capable of doing it, that he would project and offer a Plan, to be prosecuted, for a good Settlement of Things at *Natick*.

My little Son *Samuel* is now full of the Measles.

[1] That is, the Society for working among the Indians in New England, or that for the Propagation of the Gospel in Foreign Parts.   In a privately printed volume, prepared by the existing New England Company, which holds the records of the earlier company for missionary work among the Indians, will be found some interesting letters written by Mather and others on its operations.   It is entitled: *Some Correspondence between the Governors and Treasurers of the New England Company in London and the Commissioners of the United Colonies in America . . . 1657–1712.*   Mather in his references is not very clear as to the particular society intended, but the Society for the Propagation of the Gospel in Foreign Parts was an agency of the Church of England, to which Mather, of course, could never have belonged in any capacity.   See p. 327, *infra*.

6. G. D. An aged Man in my neighbourhood, letts me know that he wants a Garment for the Winter. I must provide him one.

7. G. D. Those Words of my Saviour do much run in my mind; *The Cup which my Father gives me, shall not I drink it?* I would endeavour all possible Imitation of such a patient Submission unto the Will of God, in the Difficulties which are at this Time exercising of my Family. But then I would in my most serious Meditations extend this Piety much further than so. I would sett myself, (and sett apart a due Portion of Time for it,) seriously to consider, on every *Cup*, that I may suppose possible to be given me; and on each *Cup*, I would very distinctly consider the divine Principles which ought to produce my Submission to it, and I would humbly and with all possible Resignation express my Submission accordingly.

7 *d.* 9 *m.* I sett apart this Day, as I had much Cause, and it was high Time, to do, for Prayer with Fasting before the Lord. Not only are my Children, with a Servant, lying sick, but also my Consort is in a dangerous Condition, and can gett no Rest; Either Death, or Distraction, is much feared for her. It is also an Hour of much Distress in my Neighbourhood. So, I humbled myself before the Lord, for my own Sins, and the Sins of my Family; and I presented before Him the great Sacrifice of my Saviour, that His wrath may be turned away from me, and from my Family; and that the Destroyer might not have a Commission to inflict any deadly Stroke upon us.

1. [*November* 8.] G. D. The most seasonable Instruction I can give unto the Flock, at this Time of uncommon Affliction, will be, in a Discourse, upon a patient Submission to whatever *Cup*, our heavenly Father shall order for us.

8 *d.* 9 *m. Lord's-Day.* My Errand unto the Table of the Lord, was to obtain a Pardon, for whatever Sin, might embitter whatever Cup shall be ordered for me; that it

may come from a reconciled Father; and to obtain the Grace to take in a suitable, and submissive Manner, every Cup that my Father shall please to give me.

This Day, I entertained my Neighbourhood, with a Discourse, on Joh. XVIII. 11. *The Cup which my Father has given me shall not I drink it?* And, lo, this Day, my Father is giving me a grievous and bitter Cup, which I hop'd, had pass'd from me.

For these many Months, and ever since I heard of the venemous Measles invading the Countrey sixty Miles to the Southward of us, I have had a strong Distress on my Mind, that it will bring on my poor Family, a Calamity, which is now going to be inflicted. I have often, often express'd my Fear unto my Friends concerning it. And now, *the Thing that I greatly feared is coming upon me!*

When I saw my Consort safely delivered, and very easy, and the Measles appearing with favourable Symptomes upon her, and the Physician her Brother[1] apprehending all to look very comfortably, I flattered myself, that my Fear was all over.

But this Day we are astonished, at the surprising Symptomes of Death upon her; after an extreme Want of Rest by Sleep, for diverse whole Dayes and Nights together.

To part with so desireable, so agreeable a Companion, a Dove from such a Nest of young ones too! Oh! the sad Cup, which my Father has appointed me! I now see the Meaning and the Reason of it, that I have never yett been able to make any Work of it, in Prayers and Cries to God, that such a Cup as this might pass from me. My Supplications have all along had, a most unaccountable Death and Damp upon them!

Tho' my dear Consort, had been so long without Sleep, yett she retain'd her Understanding.

I had and us'd my Opportunities as well as I could,

---

[1] Dr. John Clark, prominent as a politician as well as a physician.

continually to be assisting her, with Discourses that might support her in this Time, and præpare her for what was now before us.

It comforted her to see that her children in law were as fond of her, as her own could be![1]

God made her willing to Dy. God extinguished in her the Fear of Death. God enabled her to committ herself into the Hands of a great and good Saviour; yea, and to cast her Orphans there too, and to beleeve that He had merciful and wonderful Things to do for them.

I pray'd with her many Times, and left nothing undone, that I could find myself able to do for her Consolation.

On Munday, 9 *d.* 9 *m.* between three and four in the Afternoon, my dear, dear, dear Friend expired.

Whereupon, with another Prayer in the melancholy Chamber, I endeavoured the Resignation to which I am now called, and cried to Heaven for the Grace that might be suitable to the calamitous Occasion, and carried my poor Orphans unto the Lord.

It comforts me to see how extremely Beloved, and lamented a Gentlewoman, I now find her to be in the Neighbourhood.

Much weakness continues on some of my other Children. Especially the Eldest. And the poor Maid in the Family, is very like to dy.

2. G. D. Oh! the Prayers for my poor Children, oh! the Counsils to them, now called for!

The particular Scriptures, I shall direct them to read! And the Sentences thereof to be gotten by heart.

3. G. D. My Relatives, especially those of my deceased Consort, I will entertain with Books of Piety, that shall have in them a Memorial of her.

10 *d.* 9 *m.* This Day, in the midst of my Sorrowes and Hurries, the Lord helped me to præpare no less than two

[1] This paragraph is written in the margin.

Sermons, for a public Thanksgiving, which is to be celebrated the Day after to morrow.

But I am grievously tried, with the threatning Sickness, on my discreet, pious, lovely Daughter *Katharin*.

And a Feavour which gives a violent Shock to the very Life of my dear pretty *Jerusha*.

Fresh Occasions of Supplication and Resignation!

11 *d*. 9 *m. Wednesday*. This Day, I interr'd the earthly part of my dear Consort. She had an Honourable Funeral.[1]

4. G. D. On the Occasion of my Consort's Funeral, I considered, that it would be a sensible Service to the Cause of Piety, if the Rules of Piety to be observed [at] a Funeral, were more understood, embraced, and practised.

(XIII.) For which Cause, I now gave unto the Printer, a Discourse, which I had lying by me, præpared some while ago, on that Intention. And I propose to annex unto a Convenient Number of them, a Memorial of my Departed Consort, which I would present unto her particular Friends. It is Entituled; A CHRISTIAN FUNERAL. *A brief Essay on that Case*, WHAT SHOULD BE THE BEHAVIOUR OF A CHRISTIAN AT A FUNERAL? *or, Some Directions, How to Regulate a Funeral, by the Rules of Religion; and how to enliven Religion from the Circumstances of the Dead, at the House of Mourning*.[2]

5. G. D. The epidemical Malady begun upon this Town, is like to pass thro' the Countrey. A good Regiment of the sick under it, might save many Lives, which are like to be lost thro' mismanagement. I am thinking, whether it would not be a service unto the public, to insert in the News-paper, a brief Direction for the managing of the sick. I will advise with a Physician or two, whether I had best offer such a Thing or no.

---

[1] "Bearers, Col. Hutchinson, Mr. Em. Hutchinson; Mr. Dallie, Wadsworth; Pemberton, Colman." Sewall, *Diary*, II. 407. Daillé was minister of the Huguenot congregation in Boston.

[2] Printed by B. Green, 1713.

12 *d.* 9 *m. Thursday.* This Day I am called unto the Services of a public Thanksgiving.

I rose early; In the Retirements of my study, I spent some Time, in my Thanksgivings to the Glorious Lord, for the Favours of the divine Conduct, which I have seen in the former Part of my Life; and then for the favourable Circumstances with which I am at present revived, while walking in the Midst of Trouble; my Life and some Degree of Health and Strength praeserved, my Family of desireable Children, and comfortably provided for; my Ministry, and in so considerable a Station, and so enriched with Opportunities to do Good; And the Reputation which I enjoy abroad in the World: but above all, my Acquaintance with, and Interest in my dear Saviour, and the sanctifying Effects of His Grace upon me.

I was then carried thro' all the public Services in both Parts of the Day; and enjoy'd a marvellous Presence of the Lord with me, assisting, enlarging, strengthening of me.

This very Thing, is a precious Article for Thanksgiving; that in the midst of so many Hurries and Sorrowes, and grievous Disadvantages, I should be enabled to go thro' so many and so heavy Services, and in such a Manner!

The Subject on which I preached my two Sermons, was, Psal. cxxxviii. 7. *Tho' I walk thro' the midst of Trouble, thou wilt revive me.*

6. G. D. I hear of some aged and bedrid people, which I design speedily to visit, with the most suitable Consolations and Assistences.

14 *d.* 9 *m. Satureday.* This Morning, the first Thing that entertains me, after my rising, is, the Death of my Maidservant, whose Measles passed into a malignant Feaver, which has proved mortal to her.

Tis a Satisfaction to me, that tho' she had been a wild, vain, airy Girl, yett since her coming into my Family, she became disposed unto serious Religion; was awakened unto secret and fervent Supplications; gave herself to God in His Covenant: (upon which, a few Weeks ago, I baptised her:) and my poor Instructions, were the means that God blessed for such happy Purposes.

7. G. D. And now, as I am called still unto more Assiduities in my Præparations for my own Death, and unto more exquisite Projections and Contrivances, how a Family visited with so much Death, may become an Exemple of uncommon Piety: So, I must have my Repentance for my Miscarriages in my Behaviour towards my Servants, very much excited and promoted.

Oh! the Trial, which I am this Day called unto in the threatning, the dying Circumstances of my dear little *Jerusha!* The Resignation, with which I am to offer up that Sacrifice! *Father, Lett that Cup pass from me. Nevertheless —*

The Two Newborns, are languishing in the Arms of Death.

1. [*November* 15.] G. D. Tis a Time of much Calamity in my Neighbourhood, and a Time of much Mortality seems coming on. My public Prayers and Sermons must be exceedingly adapted for such a Time.

15 *d.* 9 *m. Lord's-day.* I am this day called unto a great Sacrifice; for so I feel my little *Jerusha.* The dear little Creature lies in dying Circumstances. Tho' I pray and cry to the Lord, for the Cup to pass from me, yett the glorious One carries me thro' the required Resignation. I freely give her up. Lord, she is thine! Thy will be done!

16. *d.* 9 *m.* Little *Jerusha* begins a little to revive.

2. G. D. Having my Family in a new Condition, and under many Calls for a great Improvement in Piety, I would now form a new Projection, for Exercises of Piety to be maintained in my Family, that shall be attended with more exquisite and heavenly Circumstances than ever, as

soon as ever the restored Health of my little Folks, will putt us into a Capacity.

3. G. D. I have a Family of remote Relatives, not far from me in this Town; a Family from which I am treated with so much Love and sincere and hearty affection, that I owe great Returns of Love unto it. I will endeavour to multiply my Kindnesses to that Family, and the Expression of my Concern for the Welfare of every part of it.

The Cross is a dry Sort of Wood; but yett it proves a *fruitful Tree;* and I shall see much Peace in those Fruits of Righteousness, which I shall find growing upon it.

(XIV.) The Sermon, which I preached on the Lord's-day when my Consort lay adying, and which I intended for the Instruction of my Neighbours in a Time of sore Affliction and Calamity, but Heaven intended it for my Own, is now in the Press, and, I hope, will be serviceable to the Interests of Piety.

It is entituled, THE WILL OF A FATHER SUBMITTED TO. *The Duty of Patient Submission to Every Condition, which the Providence of God orders for the Children of men: Enforced from the Glorious Pattern of the Blessed JESUS, readily and cheerfully submitting to take the Cup, which His Father had given Him. In a very brief Discourse, made with a special Regard unto a Religious Family burrying an only Son. And at a time of much affliction in the Neighbourhood.*[1]

(XV.) And then, the Sermon which I preached this Week, on the Occasion of my Consort's Funeral, partly to do Justice unto her Memory which is of precious Esteem in the Neighbourhood; but chiefly that I may still have the Happiness to do the more Good for every Evil that befalls me; I have sent this also to the Press, with a Design to make a Present of it, unto such as it may be proper for me to treat with it, on her Account. It is entituled, THE RELIGION OF THE CROSS. *A brief Essay upon the CROSS,*

[1] Printed by T. Fleet, for D. Henchman, 1713.

whereof our Great Saviour, who was crucified for us, will have every Christian to be a Sufferer. With some Instructions unto the Christian how to bear the Cross appointed for him. Occasion'd by what was encountred in the Death of that Vertuous Gentlewoman, Mrs. Elizabeth Mather; *who expired,* 9 d. 9 m. 1713.[1]

17/18 *d.* 9 *m. Tuesday, Wednesday.* About Midnight, little *Eleazar* died.

4. G. D. A considerable Interest, bequeathed in an ancient Legacy, for pious Uses, is lately and strangely recovered, for the Encouragement of Literature and Religion, in this Countrey. The Master of Chancery, who has it lodged in his hands, waits for Directions from some Gentlemen, here, to whose Number I belong. The Gentlemen are very dilatory; and therefore I would speedily move in this Affair, and putt it into motion, and see it accomplished.[2]

5. G. D. I am now writing for *London.* I would send certain little Books which have been published here, and may prove acceptable and serviceable there, unto certain Booksellers, who, if they please, may give them a new Edition.

I am the rather encouraged unto this, because newly, in the midst of my domestic Troubles, perusing the public Prints, I find in the Advertisements, that sundry little Books of mine, have been lately reprinted at *London,* with Prefaces of eminent Persons to them.

6. G. D. The distressed Families of the Poor to which I dispense, or procure needful Releefs, are now so many, and of such Daily Occurrence, that it is needless for me here to mention them.

20 *d.* 9 *m. Friday.* Little *Martha* died, about ten a clock, A.M.

---

[1] Printed by John Allen, 1714.

[2] The legacy of £800 left to Harvard College fifty years before by Edward Hopkins. Quincy, *History of Harvard College,* I. 205, 521.

I am again called unto the Sacrifice of my dear, dear, *Jerusha*.

I begg'd, I begg'd, that such a bitter Cup, as the Death of that lovely child, might pass from me. *Nevertheless!* — My glorious Lord, brought me to glorify Him, with the most submissive Resignation.

7. G. D. My glorious Lord has not only brought me into a State of widowhood, but I must also look upon myself, as obliged unto a Continuance in that State, all the rest of my little Time in this World; And this after I have been very agreeably circumstanced in the married State. I must now, not only quicken, and most religiously observe, a Rule heretofore practised with me, that if an impure Thought start into my Mind, I must presently reject it, and rebuke it, and make it a Provocation to form an holy Thought in Contradiction to it: but also, I must with the most heavenly Methods of Meditation, Supplication, and Resolution, endeavour to obtain from Heaven, the Grace of the most unspotted Purity; that so, I may not grieve the holy Spirit of God, and provoke Him to be my Enemy; the consequences whereof would be beyond all Expression miserable.

21 *d.* 9 *m. Satureday*. This Day, I attended the Funeral, of my two: *Eleazar* and *Martha*.

Betwixt 9 h. and 10 h. at Night, my lovely *Jerusha* Expired. She was two years, and about seven Months, old. Just before she died, she asked me to pray with her; which I did, with a distressed, but resigning Soul; and I gave her up unto the Lord. The Minute that she died, she said, *That she would go to Jesus Christ*. She had lain speechless, many Hours. But in her last Moments, her speech returned a little to her.

Lord, I am oppressed; undertake for me!

1. [*November* 22.] G. D. It will be a great Service unto my Flock, for me to exemplify, a patient Submission to the Will of God, under many and heavy Trials, and a

most fruitful Improvement of my Crosses. But besides this; finding some excellent Passages in a Manuscript written by my deceased Consort, I will publish them, at the End of her Funeral-Sermon: since they may be of uncommon Consequence to serve the great Interests of Piety, not only in my Flock, among whom I design much to disperse the Book, but also among all the People of God.[1]

2. G. D. My poor Family is now left without any Infant in it, or any under seven Years of Age. I must now apply myself with most exquisite Contrivance, and all the Assiduity imaginable, to cultivate my Children, with a most excellent Education. I have now singular Opportunities for it. Wherefore I must in the first Place, earnestly look up to the glorious Lord, who gives Wisdome, for Direction.

Our Diet at the Table, shall be mighty handsomely and usefully carried on. There shall be the Rules of Behaviour nicely given and used there. And some instructive Subject, alwayes be discoursed on.

23 *d*. 9 *m*. *Munday*. This Day, I followed my dear *Jerusha* to the Grave. But having a Mind, full of Resignation; with Resolutions, more than ever to glorify my dear Saviour; especially in what I may do for my own and other Children.

I putt a printed Memorial for her, in a Number of my little Books about, *A Christian Funeral;* which I design to give away.

3. G. D. I am writing and sending such Things, unto my Brother in *Witney*,[2] as may be of use to him in the Service of God, and may be an Introduction to the Benefit of my own Family.

4. G. D. It is a Time of much Adversity with the Town; several Things may I do for the Service of the Town in its Adversity.

---

[1] An Appendix of six pages contains the results of her "Self-examination."
[2] Rev. Samuel Mather (1674–   ).

First, I may give to the Town, an Exemple of bearing Adversity after a suitable Manner, and of not Fainting in the Day of Adversity. The Eyes of the People are much upon me. O my dear Saviour, Assist me to glorify thee! Secondly, my Sermons may be suited unto this Day of Adversity. On the Lecture to morrow,[1] I design one particularly.

Thirdly. I may do something to awaken the Spirit of Prayer, which the Day of Adversity calls for. This I would propose among my Brethren, particularly for applying the Lecture that way.

Fourthly. Charitable Distributions among the Poor, are now very seasonable. I will procure, and I will dispense, as many of these, as I can.

5. G. D. The grand Intention of my Life is, *to Do Good*. These poor Memorials are far from containing all the Projections which I have of such a Tendency. And it comforts me to think, that when I am, tho' with much Imperfection, yett with some Sincerity, thus engaged, my gracious God will fulfil that Word unto me, *I will surely do thee Good*.

On this Day of the Week, when I am not thinking on what Good may be sett forward in the several Societies, to which I stand related, I think, what Good may I excite other Men unto the doing of.

I am writing to an ingenious and accomplished Friend in *London*, who maintains a very general Conversation, with great Men, and men of Capacity. I will mightily insinuate into him, that his Conversation brings him Opportunities to Do Good, which are Talents to be accounted for; and press him, to cultivate that Subject mightily in his Conversation, what good he may move these Persons to.

6. G. D. I am now furnished with Money to be distributed among the Poor of my Flock. I need not here

[1] November 26.

mention who they are, that come under that Character with me, the objects of present Charity. But in public, I will go on to cherish this Beneficence.

(XVI.) That so my Cross may still yield more of that Fruit, by which my Saviour who has ordered it, may be glorified and His People edified, I send unto the Press, the Sermon which I delivered at the Lecture yesterday. I entituled it; HEZEKIAH. *A Christian armed from Above with the Strength, which keeps him from Fainting in a Day of Adversity. In an Essay made at Boston-Lecture; At a Time of much Adversity upon the Author, and his Neighbourhood.*[1]

7. G. D. Breathing in the midst of so many Deaths, what can there be so needful and so proper for me, as for me to *Die Daily*, and become a Man dead unto this World; crucified unto all worldly Enjoyments and Impressions! I resolve exceedingly to study this Mystery and Attainment of practical Christianity, and live in the daily Practice of it, and be restless until I find a very sensible and powerful Mortification brought upon all my Inclinations for this World, and every Thing that is in it.

(XVII.) Because I thought it would contribute unto the Intentions and Interests of Piety; and because it may particularly render my dear little *Jerusha*, a living Instrument of Good after her Death, I sent unto the Bookseller, the Sermon I preached on the last Lord's-Day while the Child lay Dead in my House. It is entituled; THE BEST WAY OF LIVING; *which is, To Die Daily; Briefly described and commended, in a plain Discourse, at a Time when the Author had newly seen Repeted Strokes of Death on his own Family; And the Publisher had his Family also struck with a Death upon a Vital part of it.*[2]

1. [*November* 29.] G. D. I think, One of the best Ser-

---

[1] Printed by B. Green for Benjamin Eliot, 1713.
[2] Printed by J. Allen, 1713.

vices I can do for my Flock, will be to reprint my little Essay of, *Wholesome Words*,[1] for Families visited with sickness; and not only now disperse it among our many sick Families, but also hereafter (if I should live,) in my pastoral Visits of the sick, to leave it for their Tenders and Watchers, to read unto them.

2. G. D. My Family is now getting into a Model extremely to my Satisfaction. I have an Opportunity to pursue numberless and exquisite Projections, for the Growth of my Olive-Plants, in all that is excellent. Every Week will produce new and fine Essayes to render my House a School of Piety.

First, Now, to be very exact in my stated Hours, for the Devotions of the Family.

And, next, to reform our Hours of Rising to work in the Morning, and going to Rest at Night. To be earlier in both.

3. G. D. It will add unto the Honours and Comforts of my aged Parent, and unto his heap of Services, if I take a Copy of the Sermon he lately preached on the Death of my Consort, about Living to Christ, and Gaining by Death, and publish it.[2]

4. G. D. The Lord exhibited me unto all the Countrey, for One whom His People are to take as an Exemple of *suffering Affliction;* I shall glorify Him, if they have in me an Exemple of *Patience* also. For this purpose, the best Thing I can do, will be to disperse thro' the Countrey, the little Treatises which I have now on the Press; all Four composed in the Three Weeks of my Adversity. By this Action, I may serve the Interests of Religion in the Countrey exceedingly.

5. G. D. I am collecting some Curiosities, to transmitt unto the Secretary of the *Royal Society* by which I hope to make some valuable Accession unto their Treasures.

[1] First printed in 1703.
[2] *The Believers Gain by Death*, printed by B. Green for S. Gerrish, 1713.

But I will use my most exquisite Contrivance, That [full] Testimonies to the Glories of my Saviour may accompany them.

6. G. D. I will propose and forward a Collection for the Releef of the Poor in this Town; and procure a Day of Supplications, to be kept, by the four Churches in the Town, under the heavy Calamity that is now upon us; on which Day, the Collection may be attended.

7. G. D. My glorious Lord, having of late so much called me unto the Work of *Sacrificing*, I desire that the Skill and Will for that Work, may have a mighty Improvement with me. I would therefore mightily use myself to such an Exercise as this; I would look on åll my Enjoyments, and very often cast such a Look upon the dearest and most valuable of them, with a *sacrificing Thought* of this importance, *O my dear Saviour, If thou shalt be most glorified, by my having this taken from me, I resign it, I forego it, I am content and willing to be without it.* I feel a vast Army of Reasons conquering of me, and reducing me to such a Submission. By using myself to such *Sacrifices*, I shall become a *weaned Christian.* And I shall be prepared for *all Events.* I shall have my Life all filled with Acts that will be unspeakably pleasing to my Saviour. I shall have upon me a joyful Token of my Share in the *royal Priesthood;* an Evidence and Assurance, that I shall walk with my Glorious JESUS in *white Robes* among them, whom He will make *Priests unto God.*

5 *d.* 10 *m.* [*December.*] *Satureday.* Tis high Time for me to be, at my ancient Practice, of setting apart whole Dayes, for Prayer with Fasting before the Lord. I am sure, the Occurrences of the last Month, (a *Month* which *devoured* my Family,) sufficiently oblige me to it. Accordingly I sett apart this Day, for Supplications; that I might confess and bewayle the Sins that have procured such a Desolation, as has been lately made upon my Family, such as

exhibits me to all the Countrey, for an Exemple of suffering Affliction: (May I be so, of Patience!) And that I might have the Pardon thereof seal'd unto me; which I think I had this Day: And then, that I might obtain Grace to behave myself well and wisely under my Adversity; and that I may mightily improve in Holiness and Usefulness; and that I may be left unto nothing in my Widowhood, that may be dishonourable to my Character and Profession. And, finally, that my Family may be putt into an agreeable Condition, and every Thing in it be comfortably carried on, and the Exercises of Piety, and the Accomplishments of a fine Education, be more than ever prosecuted in it. Other Petitions, I had also to carry unto the Lord.

1. [*December* 6.] G. D. The Strokes of Heaven on my Family, methinks, call me to do more for the Service of my glorious Lord, in the Families of my Neighbourhood. As far as Weather and Liesure, and Strength, will admitt of it, I would make more Visits to my Neighbours. But in these my Visits, I would with all possible Sanctity, and Gravity, and Pertinency, not only address the Heads of the Families, on Points of the greatest Concernment, but also call for the Children and Servants, and with as exquisite Artifices of Insinuation as I can be Master of, engage them to serious Piety.

6 *d.* 10 *m. Lords-Day.* My Errands to the Table of the Lord, were first, for that Grace that may render me holy in all manner of Conversation. And, then, for a Disposition to enquire much into the glory of my dear Saviour; and the Blessedness of arriving to very clear Apprehensions of it.

But, what shall I say? My Life is almost a continual Conversation with Heaven, and more particularly, in my Attendence on the divine Institutions, my Intentions of Piety, and my Applications to Heaven, are so many and so various, — it becomes impossible for me to keep Records of thousands of them.

2. G. D. The quiet and easy and unhurried Condition which my Family (by sad Things) is bro't unto, gives me new Opportunity to examine more distinctly my Children every Night; especially, on these two Points; *Whether they have observed the Religion of the Closett in the Day?* And, *How they have spent their Time, what good Thing they have done in the Day?*

3. G. D. I have a Kinsman, the Son of my Sister, at *Roxbury*, who designs the Evangelical Ministry.[1] Besides other wayes of serving Him, I will bestow certain agreeable Books upon him.

4. G. D. I greatly incline to the Study of Sermons on Subjects, adapted unto several Occupations, which are follow'd by great Numbers of People; and when I have prepared such Sermons, I would procure them, to be transcribed; perhaps with annexed Meditations; and then send them unto my Bookseller in *London*, to be published there, with Prefaces of the best men unto them.

5. G. D. Our Neighbours, that are forming a new Church, have begun a private Society which invites me to visit them. I would with all possible Candor give my Visits unto them, and make it a precious Opportunity to prevent Abundance of Sin, and produce Abundance of Good.

6. G. D. The poor and miserable, are so multiplied and so manifested by the epidemical Sickness, that it is needless for me, to insert as yett, any particular Objects of my Care in that Rank; there is a Number of them, which this Morning I am thinking of.

7. G. D. I will pursue the Thoughts of this Day se'n night and mention a sweet Experience thereupon, wherein I desire to grow exceedingly.

If I happen to think on any desireable Enjoyment, which I have not sacrificed, with a cordial and explicit

---

[1] Probably Rev. Thomas Walter (1696–1725), son of Rev. Nehemiah Walter, and Sarah Mather.

Resignation of it, my Soul falls a Trembling at the Idolatry
and Rebellion I am in danger of, and presently forms an
Act of Resignation. Every Relish I take in any Enjoyment, shall produce a Thought of this Importance, *O my
Saviour, If thou wilt have this thing to be denied unto me,
that so my knowing and Loving and Serving of thee; may be
the better accommodated, I consent, I consent that it be denied
unto me; I am willing to be deprived of it.*

One happy Effect of this Exercise is, that tho' the Idea
of having my Desireables taken from me, and much more
the suffering of the Bereavement be for the present not
Joyous but Grievous, yett afterwards I find my soul fill'd
with Peace, in a Reflection upon it. If any Desireables
be continued unto me, I behold them with a singular Pleasure in that Notion of them, *this is one of my Sacrifices.*
And, if I call to Remembrance the Wormwood and the
Gall of the Time when I underwent the Loss of my Desireables, I have my Mind presently and wondrously refresh'd
with this Consideration: *My God help'd me then to offer
Sacrifices that were well-pleasing to Him.* I find a *Sacrificing
Life,* to be fuller of strong and strange Consolations, than
can be imagined by one, who has made no Trial of it.

12 *d.* 10 *m. Satureday.* It is with me a Time that calls
for more than ordinary Supplications. Wherefore I sett
apart this Day, as I did this Day se'nnight, for prayer with
Fasting, before the Lord.

I had, besides the usual and general Intentions for such
a Day, especially two Things intended with me.

The one was, to obtain the Grace, that I may behave
myself with all possible Discretion and Purity in the Widowhood, in which I must propose to spend the Rest of my
Dayes. The other was, to obtain a new Heart for my
Son *Increase,* and then the merciful Direction of Heaven,
for a Matter and a Business, that he may be assign'd unto.

1. [*December* 13.] G. D. My Contrivances must not be

over yett, nor have I yett litt upon them all, to render
the grievous Visitation in the Sickness on the Flock, useful
unto the Interests of Piety among them. The public
Prayers and Sermons, afford me, an ample Field for these
Contrivances; and indeed what I have continually there,
are too many to be here enumerated.

2. G. D. I have my Family now in such a Tranquillity, by a Release from the Hurries, which the Number of
Infants in it, formerly alwayes gave unto it, that we are
at Leisure to prosecute many excellent Purposes, which
were formerly projected, but could not be much proceeded
in. One of them is, for the Children to become furnished
with a Closett of Remedies, for very many Cases, in which
we may releeve the miserable. This I would now immediately apply to. I would præpare my Catalogue. And
scarce lett a week pass, without præparing of something,
till we have gone thro' the Catalogue.

3. G. D. I am sending some Instruments of Piety, to
a new Relative, at *Say-Brook*.[1]

4. G. D. I would send unto several Booksellers in
England, and in *Scotland*, several Treatises which have
been published here, and which they may with Gain to
themselves, by a new publication there, send forth to serve
the Interests of Religion in those Parts of the World.

5. G. D. I would encourage the Physicians of this
Place, to do all the Good that may be. But among other
Methods for it, I will putt into their Hands, numbers of my
little Essay of, *Wholesome Words;* to be left by them, in
sick Families, where they may see it Convenient.

17 *d.* 10 *m. Thursday.* This Day was kept as a Day of
Prayer in the several Churches of *Boston*, because of the
heavy Calamity on the Town. And a liberal Collection
was made, for the Releef of the Poor, under the Calamity
of Sickness, and growing Scarcity. It was a most bitter

[1] Mrs. Gurdon Saltonstall?

season, in regard of the Cold. But I enjoy'd a gracious Presence of God with me, in the Services of the Day, both publickly and privately.

6. G. D. I will contribute my best Informations, to perfect the List of the Poor, to be considered in the charitable Collection, that is now made for them.

7. G. D. My Thanksgivings to the glorious Lord, for the Mercies of the foregoing Day; in my last Exercise for every Day, before my going to my Lodging, ought to be invigorated, and expatiated. I am too formal, and straitned in the Acknowledgments of what has been done for me in the Day.

But there is especially one Favour of God, whereof when I have had much Experience, the Praises wherewith I glorify Him, ought to have Raptures in them; I ought with a mighty Sense of my Obligations to the free Grace of God my Saviour for such a Blessing, to confess his admirable Goodness to me. That is, when I have been preserved from Sin, and assisted unto a watchful, fruitful, humble Walk with God.

1. [*December* 20.] G. D. Quickly, it may be a Time for me, in the most solemn and earnest Manner, to call upon that Part of the Flock, that have lately had a Share in the healing Mercies of God, that they endeavour to glorify Him, with suitable Returns of Obedience to Him. I would prosecute this Intention as powerfully, as tis possible.

And when I again receive the Children unto the Catechising, they having had a singular Share in restored Health, I would very particularly adapt unto them, the Admonitions of Piety, suitable to the Occasion.

2. G. D. There are several Points, relating to the Instruction and Management of my Servant *Onesimus*, which I would now more than ever prosecute. He shall be sure to read every Day. From thence I will have him

go on to Writing. He shall be frequently Catechised. I would also invent some advantageous Way, wherein he may spend his Liesure-hours.

3. G. D. My pious and worthy sister *Walter*,[1] with Tears in her Eyes, entreats me, to cry mightily unto God, that her Two Eldest sons, may have a Principle of His Grace given to them.

4. G. D. That which I have proposed unto my Physicians, I have now done myself, upon their Declining (tho' highly Approving) of the Action. I have given to the Printer, a Letter about the *Right Management of the Sick under the Distemper of the Measles;* which is now spreading and raging in the Countrey.[2] I purpose to scatter it into all parts, and propose with the Blessing of Heaven, to save many Lives. Tho' doubtless my Action may expose me to some Invectives, yett my Conformity to my dear Saviour, in what He did for the sick, will be my inexpressible Consolation.

5. G. D. A Minister lately ordained in this Town, I would move, that he may be brought into a share in our weekly Lecture.[3]

6. G. D. A Gentlewoman in my Neighbourhood, in her Age reduced unto great poverty and Misery; I will immediately concern myself, to have her well provided for.

7. G. D. No doubt, the glorious Lord will call me to spend the little Remainder of my Dayes, in that single State, which He has now with a second Shipwreck bro't me to.

That I may glorify the Lord in such a State, I would in the first Place make it my daily Prayer unto Him; *Grant,*

---

[1] Sarah. Her two sons were Increase (1693–1718) and Thomas (1696–1725).

[2] See p. 248, *supra.* It is to be noted that an epidemic pestilence prevailed at this time in parts of Europe and the East. In Austria and Hungary it was a spotted fever, which gradually changed to the plague; and in England it took the form of the sweating sickness. Even cattle and horses perished in Italy.

[3] Rev. Joseph Sewall.

O God of all Grace, that I may glorify thee, with an exemplary Prudence and Patience, and Purity, in the Widowhood which thou hast call'd me to!

But this is not all. I must not humour the Discourses of silly People, inviting my Return to the married State; which it is unaccountable to see, how much they have already begun upon. (Even the last Night, I have a foolish Message from a Gentlewoman bro't unto me.)

More than so. I must watch against all internal Temptations of such a Tendency.

Wherefore, first, I would by no means indulge my Soul, in reviving to my Thoughts, any Idea of those grateful Circumstances which I have heretofore enjoy'd in the married State; I would not so much as think upon the old and past, *Maritales ineptiæ*. But if such Thoughts happen to begin at any Time in my Mind, I would presently rebuke them, and retund them. They shall provoke an Ejaculation to Heaven, of this Importance; *O my dear Saviour, I freely Sacrifice to thee, whatever, thy Holy Hand has taken from me!* I will immediately change them into Wishes of this Importance; *O, that I may have the unspeakable Pleasures of knowing my dear Saviour, and of doing very great Services for His Kingdome, and good Offices for Mankind!*

And who can tell, what my Glorious Lord may do for me!

1. [*December* 27.] G. D. It may now be a Time for me to revive my Exercise of Catechising. A Multitude of restored Children coming to this Exercise, I would make it a precious Opportunity, to inculcate mightily upon them, the Lessons and the Duties, which they ought now to be exceedingly mindful of.

2. G. D. May I not further modify the Evening-Sacrifices in my Family, and make some edifying Addition to the Exercises in them? Yes; my two younger Children, shall before the Psalm and Prayer, answer a Question in

the Catechism; and have their Leaves ready turned unto the Proofs of the Answer in the Bible; which they shall distinctly read unto us; and show what they prove. This also will supply a fresh Matter for the Prayer that is to follow.

3. G. D. A Marriage of a Sister, has produced me a new Brother-in-Law,[1] and several new Relatives, for whose Welfare I must be concerned. I Bestow agreeable Books of Piety upon them.

4. G. D. In my Letters to *London*, I am to do some Service for our Churches, as an Advocate against some false and foolish Accusations, that are said or fear'd to be going home against us.

5. G. D. I will accelerate the Publication of an Instrument for *Houshold-Piety*, among the Christian Indians.

6. G. D. A poor Woman belonging to the Church whereof I am a Servant, is languishing under an horrible Cancer, as well as conflicting with oppressing Poverty. I will visit her, and relieve her, and much concern myself that her Miseries may be mitigated and sanctified.

7. G. D. In my Prayers to God for the Pardon of my particular Miscarriages, (and such Prayers, as I make every Night, with relation to the foregoing Day,) I would not only consider the Sacrifice of my blessed JESUS in general, as cleansing from all Sin: but I would also more particularly consider, what there was in the spotless Heart and Life of my lovely JESUS, most contrary to the Points wherein I have miscarried; and consider how admirably that holy, harmless, undefiled One, was qualified, in regard of His perfect Obedience unto the divine Law, to be a Sacrifice for the Disobedient. And having thus glorified my sacrificed Saviour, then will be my Time to come in with my Supplications for the Grace which he has purchased

---

[1] Maria Mather (1665–1746), widow of Bartholomew Green, married Richard Fifield in this year.

for me; the Grace that shall bring me into the highest Conformity that is possible unto His Obedience.

2 *d.* 11 *m.* [*January,* 1713-14.] *Satureday.* I sett apart this Day, for Prayer with Fasting before the Lord, on the same Occasions, that I had, when I was last thus engaged. And I enjoy'd a precious Presence of the Lord with me, in my Supplications.

This Day I had a notable Experience.

1. [*January* 3.] G. D. I have not yett gott into a Way that pleases me, for Catechising the female Children of the Flock. But since I have translated that Exercise unto the School-house, I see agreeable Accommodations for both Sexes there. I would propose it unto Consideration, whether I may not order both to come together, into that Place. And if they be so numerous, that they can't all be heard at once, they may be heard alternately: But all have Opportunity to attend the Admonitions then dispensed.

2. G. D. It is high time for my dear *Katy,* to proceed with her Intentions of joining herself unto the Church.

3. G. D. I have a young Kinsman, who is entring upon the evangelical Ministry. I would apply myself to him, with my best Instructions and Assistences.

4. G. D. In my Book of, *Pastoral Desires,*[1] there is to the Quantity of about a Sheet, employ'd upon the Methods of præparing for, and Approaching to, the Table of the Lord; with agreeable Motives unto the Duty. Such a brief Engine of Piety, lodg'd in the Hands of the People about the Countrey, may prove serviceable to Religion. I would move it unto the Ministers of a neighbouring Association, to unite in the Publication of such a thing, with an Attestation of theirs unto it.

5. G. D. The General *Society, for the Suppression of Disorders,* having been dissolved by the Calamities of this Winter, I would advise with a Number of Gentlemen,

---

[1] Printed in 1712.

about the Reviving of it, and the leaving out of some
unworthy and improper Members.

6. G. D.   There are several Persons, to whom the Discipline of our Church is extendible; especially some that
by Recommendations from abroad, have a transient Communion with us; of whom I hear a very evil Report. I
must concern myself in all proper Wayes, that these Persons
may not go without the Admonitions, which belong unto
them.

7. G. D.   I apprehend, The holy Spirit of God, is not
in an explicit Manner enough pray'd unto; He is very
GOD; a distinct Person in the eternal God-head. When
I am crying to Heaven for those Blessings, which do more
peculiarly and conspicuously proceed from Him, I would,
after a Recognition of His being that God, who is the
Father, and the Son, and the Holy Spirit, very distinctly
make my Addresses to Him. And very particularly if an
impure Thought should be at any time thrown into my
Mind, I will immediately address Him, with such a Groan
as this; *O Holy Spirit of my God, of my Father, and my
Saviour; purify me, purify me, purify me! Dwell in me,
as in an Holy Temple!*

1. [*January* 10.] G. D.   I hear of no less than four
young Men, in the Covenant of God, and under the Watch
of the Church whereof I am the Servant, who take very
vicious Courses. I must use the most proper and speedy
Methods I can, that the Discipline of the House of the
Lord may reach unto them. This may be a Service, not
unto them only, but also unto all the Flock.

2. G. D.   My Daughters must live in the daily use of
their Pens, on Subjects that I shall direct for them.   And
besides this; I would, when I sitt with my Family at nine
a clock in the Evening, have one of them to read a little
on some or other of the Sciences, and then in a way of Discourse convey unto them agreeable Instructions thereupon.

3. **G. D.** I have a good Kinsman at *Suffield*, from whose brotherly Civilities and Assistences, I expect a considerable Accession to the temporal Interest of my Family. I ought to use more than common Endeavours for His eternal Interest. And then also, I would project with him, how to make a new Plantation, wherein we are together concerned, a Seat of Piety.

4. **G. D.** I much incline to resume the Consideration of the *Maxims of the Kingdome of God*, which I have heretofore more briefly offered unto the Public; and with many Illustrations and Demonstrations, in a Treatise upon them, show how reasonable and how honourable they are, and how serviceable they would be; and what would be the excellent Consequences of it, if they were made the *Uniting Maxims*, for all Good Men to concur upon, with a Resolution to associate upon them, and prosecute them, and establish them, and lett fall Things that are unworthy of so much Esteem as to divide the World upon them.

5. **G. D.** I would write a Letter unto a Gentleman at *Connecticot*, who was of the same class with me, when I was a student in the Colledge. He is a rich Man, and I fear, not a very good Man; and he hath also no Family. I would so manage my Address unto him, as to win upon him, first to be good, and then to do good.

14 *d.* 11 *m. Thursday.* A general Fast, thro' the Province. I enjoy'd a very gracious and precious Assistence from God, in the Services of the Day.

6. **G. D.** There are some very aged Women in my Neighbourhood, by old Age and Weakness, for a long while confined from coming to the House of God. I would visit them; and bestow suitable Instruments of Piety upon them.

7. **G. D.** I desire, that when in my Library, or elsewhere, I take up a Book, which is a very useful Performance, and an Effect of much Learning or Labour or Piety, I would usually lift up my Soul to God, with some Acknowledgment

of Him, and of what He has done, in disposing and assisting a Writer to such an Undertaking.

1. [*January* 17.] G. D. The poor Flock, the poor Flock, whereof I am the Servant; a poor, foolish, senseless People; how unfruitful, and how ungrateful! How abandoned of Heaven to the neglecting and even confounding of their own Interests!

I am so strangely at a Loss, what to do further for them! I am daily serving them in all the Methods my barren Mind can think of! And when the Article of, *what is to be done for them*, returns upon my Meditations, I am not so long plodding upon any Article, before I find out some Invention to do further Good. This Morning, after long Deliberation, I can think of nothing to purpose, but this; I will enlarge my Prayers, that the Wrath of God may be turned away from the poor Flock.

And I will be more explicit, and exquisite, and full of Resignation in my making a Sacrifice of it, as well as in pleading the great Sacrifice for it. And I will also spend more Thoughts, in projecting Petitions and Expressions for the public Prayers, in those Points which are of more common Concernment among them.

2. G. D. I foresee an Advantage to *Cresy*, of his being accomplished in certain mathematical Sciences, (as well as those of the fencing and music Schole) namely, Geometry, Trigonometry, Navigation. His Genius also stands much that Way.

There are two or three Points in *Lizy*'s Education, to be likewise prosecuted.

3. G. D. I have a Widow-sister, who greatly needs to be putt into a Way of subsisting herself, and to be animated unto the use of her own vigorous Endeavours for that Purpose.[1]

4. G. D. It is now time for me to address the Town

---

[1] Elizabeth Mather, whose second husband, Josiah Byles, died March, 1707–08.

and especially the young People of it, with such Admonitions as the late Calamity on the Town,[1] and Recovery from it, have rendred seasonable. May the Glorious Lord accept me, and assist me in this Essay; for I am able to do nothing.

5. G. D. There is yett another Society, which I am introduced into. The Lord Chancellour [2] has by his Decree, made me one of the Trustees, for the applying of a Legacy left many years ago, by Mr *Hopkins*, unto our Colledge, and lately recovered. As a Member of this Society, I would watch all Opportunities to serve the Good Interests, which are to be served in it.

21 *d.* 11 *m. Thursday.* After previous Humiliations and Supplications, wherein I resigned myself up unto the holy Spirit of God, that I may be as His Mouth unto His People, I received a sweet Satisfaction in my Mind, that I should be accepted of the Lord. Then I went forth into a vast Auditory; where the glorious Lord was mightily present with me, in my beginning to discourse the Things, which I thought seasonable for the Town, relating to the late Calamity and Deliverance. What I purpose, to conclude, with His Leave and Help, on the next Opportunity.

6. G. D. There are two men under much Discomposures of Mind, and very negligent of their Duty, to whom I would apply myself, with my best Endeavours to serve them, and help them.

7. G. D. There occur certain Occasions on which I would use myself, to turn my Eye, unto God, and His holy Spirit, with such an Ejaculation as this; *O Glorious Lord, Pardon my past Impurities; and now purify me wonderfully!*

1. [*January* 24.] G. D. I am still upon this Thought; that I will endeavour to have Passages, and Petitions, and Expressions in my public Prayers, which may suit the several Tribes and States of the People, in a copious

---

[1] The measles.   [2] Simon, Lord Harcourt (1661?-1727.)

Distinction of them; and find out such Variences, and such Pungencies, upon each of them, as may much affect them, with a Sense of their own Circumstances, and also direct them, how they shall themselves call upon God for themselves.

2. G. D. I must not give over, till my three elder Children, have given themselves up to the Lord in the Covenant of His Church, and sealed it at His holy Table. I would keep seriously, frequently, continually conversing with them, on such Points, as may prepare them for so excellent an Action.

3. G. D. I must cry mightily to the God who forms the Spirit of Man within him, that my aged Parent, may have his Mind made easy, with relation to the new Church swarming in our Neighbourhood. His Uneasiness is the worst, and in a Manner the only, part of mine; and his placid, and pleasant Encounter with the Occurrences of this Affair, will glorify God, and be an Honour to our holy Religion, and a great Comfort unto me.

4. G. D. I have in view, a great Service, to be prosecuted, not only for the Colony of *Connecticot*, but for our Province also, — some Letters of Mine to principal Persons in that Colony, may be of great Consequence.

5. G. D. A worthy Minister of this Town, has, with too much Reason, his Apprehensions of being speedily taken off by Death. I would be his Monitor, for his præparing a short Instrument, which he may leave behind him, in Writing to serve this People, and the Church of God, with several Important Admonitions, relating to their great Interests.

6. G. D. There is a Candidate of the Ministry, in my Neighbourhood, who has now waited for Settlements and Improvements, till he be gott beyond Thirty; is at last like to be disappointed in his Expectation, to be invited by the new Church in this Neighbourhood. I am in dis-

tress for him; full of Sollicitudes, that he may find acceptance with the People of God, and be serviceable. I do for
him all that I can; but I would particularly endeavour to
reconcile his Mind unto Serviceableness at a further Distance, and procure him an Offer of Opportunities.

7. G. D. *The Snuffing of my Candle* is a very frequent
Action with me. I have provided a great Number of Per-
tinent *Thoughts*, and *Wishes*, and *Prayers* and *Praises*, to
be form'd upon the Occurrences in my Life, which afford
Occasions for them. I have not yett made so particular a
Provision for this, as I now do. In the Doing of this Action,
I would often think, and wish, and say, *Lord, Lett me shine
the brighter, for all my afflictive Diminutions!*

30 *d.* 11 *m. Satureday.* This Day, I sett apart for Fasting, with Prayers and Alms. I renew'd my Flight unto
the Sacrifice of my Saviour, for the Pardon of my Sins;
particularly, of those which have brought upon me all the
Desolations of my second Widowhood. The Lord comforted me, with some Assurance, that He has pardoned
me. I cried unto the Lord, for the Aids of His Grace,
that I may glorify Him in my Widowhood; and that I
may be preserved from all Steps that may wound my Profession, or hurt my Family. I look'd up to the holy Spirit,
that He would guide my Studies, and prosper my Writings
as well as my Labours, for the Service of His Kingdome;
especially One, which I have my Heart much sett upon.
I had some domestic Distresses; particularly one, relating
to the Disposal of my Son; which I carried unto the Lord.
The State of His People, was also with me.

I bewayled the Impieties which fill the English Nation
at this day; from a vile Generation of men, that keep this
Day unto their Lord, an abominable Tyrant; and besought
of the most High, that He would putt an End unto their
Abominations, and mercifully deliver the Nations once
again from that which depraves them wonderfully.

1. [*January* 31.] G. D.   I sett myself this Morning, to think; what Account can I give to the glorious Judge of the world, concerning my Discharge of my Ministry to the Flock, whereof He has made me an Overseer.

When my Mind is barren of wise Thoughts, on that Question, What further to be done for my Flock? I would still retire to this Meditation.

2. G. D. My Servant burying of his Son, it gives me an Opportunity, to inculcate agreeable Admonitions of Piety upon him.

3. G. D. I must proceed with further Contrivances and Assistences, that my Widow-sister may be well provided for.

4. G. D. Having a Variety of extensive Services for the Church of God before me, it is of consequence, that I use a good Order in prosecuting of them, and that I determine which I shall first of all take to and stick to. For this I humbly look up to the Direction of Heaven.

5. G. D. There are many Points relating to *natural History*, and Improvements in Philosophy, wherein to gain some Information, would enable me to do some Good. I would form a Catalogue of those Points, and then employ many suitable Hands to prosecute the Enquiries.

6. G. D. Having some further summs of Money, to distribute among the Poor, I shall be as careful as I can to find fitt objects for the Distribution.

7. G. D. My Mind is buffeted with horrible Temptations to the *Paulician* Heresy.[1] I must use more than ordinary Methods, to quench these fiery Darts of the Divel.

1. [*February* 7.] G. D. The Swarming Part of the

---

[1] It would be difficult to express the precise heresy here named, for even to this day the Paulician tenets are somewhat vague. Attempting to model their lives and cults on Christ and his apostles the followers of this cult fell under condemnation of the council of Nice in 325, and ceased to have any material influence upon the development of Church traditions.

Flock, are in danger of running themselves into Disorders and Confusions. I must with the Prudence and Patience, and Charity, that may be, give them what Help I can.

2. G. D. Would it not be many Wayes a profitable Exercise, if I should on a Satureday Evening have the Notes of my Sermon for the Day following, readd over in my Family, by one of the Children, in the Hearing of the rest, and my own?

3. G. D. I have a very wicked Brother-in-Law, for whom I must use the best methods I can, (and consult with his Brother,) that he may not persist in his Wickedness, and be abandoned unto all Confusion.[1]

4. G. D. It seems now high time for me, to come into Action, and to do what my Hand finds to do, that the, *Biblia Americana*, may be brought forth into the World. Lett me therefore publish a Sheet, entituled, *A New Offer, to the Lovers of Religion and Learning*, therein giving an Account of the work, and so an Opportunity for Subscriptions towards the Encouragement of it; and not only spread Copies of that *offer*, thro' this Countrey, but also send them to *Europe*.

5. G. D. I must in the Society for such Purposes, bring on an Enquiry, what may be done, for the Suppression of some very wicked Houses, that are the Nests of much Impiety.

I must also assist the Booksellers, in addressing the Assembly, that their late Act against Pedlers, may not hinder their Hawkers from carrying Books of Piety about the Countrey.[2]

And, thus, the Goodness, and Mercy, and Patience of the glorious Lord, has brought me to the End of another Year. The fifty first Year of my Age is terminated.

My most faithful Saviour has at length brought me to a continual

---

[1] Probably John Oliver.
[2] *Province Laws*, I. 720. It was published November 14, 1713.

Stroke at *Sacrificing*. And I will here briefly relate the Sum of my Experiences concerning it.

I much use myself to this *Exercise*. I endeavour to look on all my Enjoyments, and very often cast a pausing Look, upon the dearest and most valuable of them, with a Thought of this Importance; *O my dear Saviour, If thou shalt be most glorified, by my having this taken from me, I Resign it, I forego it, I am content and willing to be without it.* I feel a vast Army of Reasons, conquering, and reducing of me to such a *Submission;* especially when I consider how *Sovereign*, how *just*, how *wise*, and how *good* a Lord, I am to submitt unto.

But, by using myself to such *Sacrifices*, I do more especially propose, to become a *weaned Christian*, and one præpared for all Events. I propose, to have my Life all filled with *Acts* that will be unspeakably *pleasing* to my lovely Redeemer. I propose, to have upon me a joyful Token of a Share in the *royal Priesthood;* an Evidence and Assurance, that I shall walk with a Glorious JESUS, in *white Robes*, among them whom He will make *Priests unto God.*

If I happen to think on any desireable Enjoyment, which I have not sacrificed with a cordial and explicit oblation of it, my distressed Soul falls a trembling at the Rebellion and Idolatry I am in danger of; and I presently form, *an Act of Submission,* for its being made a *Sacrifice.*

Every *Relish* I take in any Enjoyment, produces in me a Thought of this Tendency, *O my dear Saviour, If thou wilt have this thing to be denied unto me, that so my knowing and loving and serving of thee may be the better accommodated; I consent, I consent, that it be denied unto me; I am willing to be deprived of it.*

One happy Effect of this Exercise, is; that tho' the *Idea* of having my Desireables taken from me, and much more the real *Suffering* of the Bereavements wherein they are actually taken from me, is, *for the present not Joyous but Grievous*, yett *afterwards* I find a Soul filled with *Peace* in a Reflection upon it.

If my Desireables are continued unto me, I behold them with a singular Pleasure in that Notion of them; *this is one of my Sacrifices!* And if I call to Remembrance the Wormwood and the Gall of the Time when I underwent the Loss of my Desireables, I have my Mind, presently and wondrously refreshed with this Consideration; *My God helped me then to offer Sacrifices that were well-pleasing to Him!* Tis impossible for me, to express the marvellous *Peace* and *Joy* that irradiates my Mind, while I am thus walking in the *Love of God*. I find a *sacrificing Life*, to be fuller of strong and strange Consolations, than can be imagined by one who has made no Trial of it.

THE COURSE OF MY MINISTRY THIS YEAR.

15 d. 12 m. [February.] 1712. I preached on, Luk. 23. 39. The best of Men railed upon, and by the worst of Men; And People suffering of Calumnies, without being the better for them.

19 d. 12 m. Thursday. I preached the Lecture, on Rev. 2. 19. Love and Charity, what it is, and how known (if we have it) unto our great Saviour. (Designing to blow up that holy Fire in the Town, on some great Occasions.)

22 d. 12 m. I preached on Luk. 23. 39. Ungodly people, demanding unreasonable Proofs of the Gospel; and preferring temporal Benefits to Spiritual; and questioning whether Jesus be the Christ of God. And, that the Christ of God is the Saviour of men.

1 d. 1 m. [March.] 1713. I preached on, Luk. 23. 40. The converted Man seeking the Conversion of others; and Repentance for Sin inclining a Man to the Rebukeing of Sin.

8 d. 1 m. I preached, on Luk. 23. 40. The Fear of God in true Religion; how destitute of it they are, who gett no Good by Afflictions; how dreadful a Thing it is to dy without it.

15 d. 1 m. I preached, on Luk. 23. 41. The Demerit of a suffering Sinner, and the Innocence of our suffering Saviour.

19 d. 1 m. Thursday. I preached the Lecture, on Gal. 6. 3. Whence and how, men deceive themselves.

22 d. 1 m. I preached on Luk. 23. 42. The Reason which dying men have to be concerned for a good State after Death.

29 d. 1 m. I preached on, Jer. 31. 3. The Peculiar and everlasting Love of God unto His People. (And administred the Eucharist.)

5 d. 2 m. [April.] I preached on, Luk. 23. 42. The Kingdome of our Saviour, at his coming; and the Happiness of those whom He will remember at His coming in His Kingdome.

12 d. 2 m. I preached, on Luk. 23. 43. A Paradise for the departed Souls of the Regenerate.

16 d. 2 m. Thursday. A general Fast. I preached on Zech. 11. 9. The Misery of a People, when the Glorious Lord refuses to feed them.

19 d. 2 m. I preached on, Luk. 23. 43. That the greatest of Sinners may arrive to Conversion and Salvation. And so, in eleven Discourses finished my Essayes on the History of the Convert on the Cross.

26 d. 2 m. I preached on 1. Chron. 4. 10. Who are indeed blessed, and how the Request to be so, is to be managed.

3 *d.* 3 *m.* [*May.*] I preached, a second Time, on 1. Chron. 4. 10, and finished what I began the last Lord's-Day.

10 *d.* 3 *m.* I preached on Psal. 119. 113. The *base* Thoughts, these are hateful to a godly Man.

14 *d.* 3 *m. Thursday.* I preached the Lecture, unto a vast Auditory, on the Return of the ancient Lecture, unto the former Place, in a stately Edifice now erected and finished, in the room of that which was laid in Ashes.[1] The Vicinity, being rebuilt with it, I preached on Isa. 65. 21. The favour of God shining on His People, when they *build Houses* and *inhabit* them; and yett more, when they *rebuild Houses,* and *reinhabit* them.

17 *d.* 3 *m.* I preached on Psal. 119. 113. The *false* Thoughts, to be hated and shunned by a godly Man.

24 *d.* 3 *m.* I preached on, Isa. 26. 2. The *Gates* of the holy City opened unto the righteous Keepers of Truth. (And I administred the Eucharist.)

31 *d.* 3 *m.* I preached on Psal. 119. 113. The *vain* Thoughts to be hated and shunned by a godly Man.

7 *d.* 4 *m.* [*June.*] I preached, on Luk. 5. 6. A *great Multitude* enclosed in the *Netts* of the Gospel; which I now threw out, with great Assistences from Heaven.

11 *d.* 4 *m. Thursday.* I preached the Lecture, to a great Assembly and with a great Assistence, on Psal. 15. 4. A good Man as *good as his Word;* bearing my Testimony against Unfaithfulness in *Promises;* a vice too epidemical.

14 *d.* 4 *m.* I preached, at *Charlestown,* on 1. Chron. 29. 19. The Concern of Parents to seek a perfect Heart for their Children, and of Children to ask it for themselves.

21 *d.* 4 *m.* I preached on Psal. 34. 11. Such Lessons relating to the *Fear of God,* as may be learn't, even by Children, and People of the lowest Capacity.

24 *d.* 4 *m. Wednesday.* I preached the Lecture at *Malden,* on Ps. 21. 9. A Good State after *Death.*

28 *d.* 4 *m.* I preached, on Psal. 146. 4. The Circumstances of Mortality, Man's *Breath* going forth; Man returning to *his Earth;* Men's *Thoughts* then perishing. (On the occasion of several Instances of early Mortality, in my Neighbourhood.)

5 *d.* 5 *m.* [*July.*] I preached, on Amos. 8. 2. A *Basket of summer-Fruit.* Instructions of Piety, fetched from the Summer-Season.

[1] In 1711 the meeting house of the First Church had been burned, and on the same site a brick church was built and came to be known as the "Old Brick."

9 *d.* 5 *m. Thursday.* I preached the Lecture, on Prov. 14. 10. *Secret Sorrowes*, embittering the Lives of People.

12 *d.* 5 *m.* I preached both Parts of the Day at *Marblehead.* A. M. on Act. 10. 44. The Spirit of God falling on His People in their Hearing of His Word. P. M. on Luk. 5. 6. The *Netts* of the Gospel enclosing a Multitude.

19 *d.* 5 *m.* I preached on Psal. 5. 7. The great number of no small Mercies, to be considered in coming into the House of God. And how He is to be worshipped in His Seat, and with what Eye to his holy Temple. (And I administred the Eucharist.)

26 *d.* 5 *m.* I preached on Matth. 6. 21. An *earthly Treasure*, and an *heavenly Treasure;* and the Consequence of setting the Heart on each.

2 *d.* 6 *m.* [*August.*] I preached, on Matth. 6. 21, and finished what I began the last Lord's-Day.

6 *d.* 6 *m. Thursday.* I preached the Lecture, to a very great Auditory, and the Assembly sitting, on Eccl. 2. 14. A Wise man having his Eyes in his *Head;* concluding, with what was to be seen at this Time.

9 *d.* 6 *m.* I preached on, Psal. 22. 11. The Interest and Wisdome of having a *good God near unto* us, when *Trouble* is near.

16 *d.* 6 *m.* I preached, on, Prov. 14. 25. A *true Witness* delivering Souls. And, having first applied it unto Testimonies born about Matters of Fact in the Neighbourhood; I then exhibited, our *Great Saviour* as the *true Witness*, who is also the Deliverer of Souls. And, finally, urging those who are employ'd by Him, as his *Witnesses*, to *deliver Souls* by their Testimonies, I endeavored, particularly to do so.

23 *d.* 6 *m.* I preached on Joh. 1. 39. To *come and see*, the Way to be satisfied, whether the Gospel of the blessed Jesus be the Truth of God, or no; a Trial of Religion, both in a way of *Enquiry*, and in a way of *Experience.*

30 *d.* 6 *m.* I preached, on Job. 10. 15. What a *woful* Thing it is to be a *wicked* Man.

3 *d.* 7 *m.* [*September.*] *Thursday.* I preached the Lecture, in a vast Auditory; on Gen. 20. 6. The Mercy of being *witheld from Sin.* But by Sickness and faintness, was forced to break off, before I could finish what I intended.

6 *d.* 7 *m.* I preached on Psal. 119. 28. What there is to be found in the Word of God, for the *Supporting* and *strengthening* of a *Soul melted* with *heavy Loads* upon it.

10 *d.* 7 *m. Thursday.* I preached the Lecture again, in a vast

Auditory; on Gen. 20. 6. And, with a gracious and mighty Assistence from Heaven, finished what I began a week ago.

13 *d*. 7 *m*. I preached, on Rev. 3. 16. The Character of a *lukewarm* Christian; with some Endeavour to cure his Malady. (And I administred the Eucharist.)

17 *d*. 7 *m*. *Thursday*. I preached the Lecture, on Psal. 116. 4. The Concern lying upon them that are to dy, for a good State after Death.

23 *d*. 7 *m*. *Wednesday*. I preached the Lecture at *Dedham;* on 1. Chron. 29. 19.

27 *d*. 7 *m*. I preached on Psal. 116. 1. The *Love of God;* and how the *Success of Prayer* should animate it. Beginning a Course of Sermons on the CXVIth Psalm.

1 *d*. 8 *m*. [*October*.] *Thursday*. I preached the Lecture, on Psal. 25. 13. A Funeral Sermon for a religious Matron, who died yesterday [Mrs. Rock].

4 *d*. 8 *m*. I preached on Psal. 116. 2. The Use to be made of the divine Condescension in *hearing our Prayers;* therefore to call upon the Lord *in all our Dayes.*

11 *d*. 8 *m*. I preached on Psal. 116. 3. The *Trouble* and *Sorrow* of a dying Hour; and the *Pains of Hell* then getting hold on Men; and the Way of repairing to our Saviour, (who underwent these,) for our Deliverance from them. (And I administred the Eucharist.)

18 *d*. 8 *m*. I preached on Psal. 116. 3, and finished what I began a Week ago.

25 *d*. 8 *m*. I preached on Job. 7. 3. About enduring *Nights* of Weariness and possessing *Months* of Vanity, to prepare the Neighbourhood, for the Calamity of the spreading *Measles.*

29 *d*. 8 *m*. *Thursday*. I preached the Lecture, on Exod. 12. 7. How we should consult the Safety and Welfare of our Families, by getting the Blood of the great Passover, sprinkled on them. (To præpare the Town for an Encounter with the Difficulties of the Spreading Malady.)

1 *d*. 9 *m*. [*November*.] I preached on, Psal. 116. 4. How the *Name* of God is in Prayer to be called upon; the Necessity of *Prayer* in them that expect Salvation; the *prayerful Piety*, whereto they are obliged, that are near to Death; and what *Religion in Earnest*, must be found in them that would be saved.

8 *d*. 9 *m*. I preached on, Joh. 18. 11. The *Cup* of Sufferings given to our Saviour; His glorious Exemple of submissive Patience under it; pressing our Imitation of it. (Some of my Neighbours

having mett with sad Things; and my own Family being in great Affliction. And I administred the Eucharist.)

12 *d.* 9 *m. Thursday.* A Day of general Thanksgiving, I preached both Parts of the Day, on Psal. 138. 7. The People of God walking in the Midst of *Trouble,* but meeting with *Revivals* in it; which they should be thankful for.

15 *d.* 9 *m.* I preached on Luk. 9. 23. The Christian a *Cross-bearer.* (A funeral Sermon for my dear Consort.)

22 *d.* 9 *m.* I preached on, 1. Cor. 15. 31. *Dying daily.* (Having in less than two Weeks had *five Deaths* in my Family.)

26 *d.* 9 *m. Thursday.* I preached the Lecture, on Prov. 24. 10. Not *Fainting in a Day of Adversity;* and gave the Reverse of it, in the Description of an unfainting Beleever under Affliction. (The Occasions obvious.)

29 *d.* 9 *m.* I preached on Heb. 5. 8. Our Saviours learning *Obedience by the Things which He suffered,* and our Imitation of Him.

6 *d.* 10 *m.* [*December.*] I preached on, 1. Pet. 1. 15. *Holiness in all Manner of Conversation;* what it is, and what our Obligations to it.

13 *d.* 10 *m.* I preached on, Job. 21. 17. A *Distribution of Sorrows,* made by God, among the Children of Men, and unto the wicked, in His *Anger.*

17 *d.* 10 *m. Thursday.* A Fast kept by the Churches of *Boston,* because of our Calamity in the Malady of the Measles, and a growing Scarcity. I preached on Exod. 15. 26. Our *Saviour* to be glorified, as the *Healer of* our Disease.

20 *d.* 10 *m.* I preached on, Psal. 116. 5. The Glorious God a most *righteous* God.

24 *d.* 10 *m. Thursday.* I preached the Lecture, on Mic. 6. 13. People smitten of God for their Sins in their Sufferings; especially when smitten with Sickness. (To suit the present Case of the Town with a seasonable Word.)

27 *d.* 10 *m.* I preached, in the Forenoon, on 1. Chron. 29. 15. No *Continuance* in this World, or *Expectation* from it.

In the Afternoon, on Psal. 116. 5, and finished in agreeable Flames [Frames], my Discourse on the *punitive Justice* of God.

3 *d.* 11 *m.* [*January, 1713-14.*] I preached on, 1. Chron. 29. 3. An *Affection* placed on the *House* of God. (And I administred the Eucharist.)

10 *d.* 11 *m.* I preached on Psal. 116. 5. The *Justice* of God, in *Rewarding* of our Piety, and in *Fulfilling* of His Covenant.

14 *d.* 11 *m. Thursday.* A general Fast. I preached on Ezek.
15. 7. People delivered from one Calamity, but for their Misbe-
haviours quickly thrown into another, and a more devouring one.

17 *d.* 11 *m.* I preached on Ps. 116. 5. The *Goodness of* God as
operating, first in His *Love* unto His Creatures.

21 *d.* 11 *m. Thursday.* I preached the Lecture, on, Joh. 5. 14,
calling upon the Town, whereof there was now a vast Auditory, to
make a due Improvement, of the late Calamity and Deliverances.
Reserving the rest of my Discourse for the next Opportunity; which
will [not] now be, till six Weeks hence; A sixth Lecturer coming in to
settle this Period.

24 *d.* 11 *m.* I preached on, Psal. 116. 5. The Goodness of God,
shining in His *Mercy.*

31 *d.* 11 *m.* I preached on, Psal. 116. 5. The Goodness of God,
shining in His *Grace,* and in His *Patience.*

7 *d.* 12 *m.* [*February.*] I preached, on Psal. 116. 6. The *simple*
preserved, and the People of God *helped* in a *low* Condition.

[On the last sheet is recorded:]

Abigail, William, [Katharine,] Mary, Joseph, Abigail, Mehetabel,
Hannah, Increase, Samuel, Elizabeth, Samuel Nathanael, Jerusha,
Eleazar, Martha.

Of 15, Dead 9, Living 6.

Quos nubi Indignissimo Deus dedit Filii Filiaeque.

To Samuel Penhallow.   M.H.S.

Boston, 21 *d.* 8 *m.* [October.] 1713.

Sir, — Tis more than Time for me, to return my own and my
Consort's, thanks to you and yours, for the *Hyblaean* Present wherewith you lately obliged us. This I now do, with my hearty Prayers,
that you may be satisfied with that out of the Rock!

I wish my Pen were able to entertain you with any thing like what
the Poet saies dropt from the Lip of Nestor; whose Greek Verse I
have turned into *this* English Hexameter;

His Lip dropt Language, than Sweet Honey, Sweeter abundance.

But such as it is, I pray your Acceptance of my last Publication.

Our Friend,[1] for whose Arrival, we made so many smokes above a
weeke ago, has now exhibited his Commissions, and Instructions; in
which, *Nihil invenio bonis moribus contrarium,* or that has any hurtful Aspect on these Colonies or Churches.

[1] Francis Nicholson.

The next Day after his Arrival, he (with an Army of the same Religion) was present at an Ordination in *Charlestown* where, among other Things, a Speech was made, that asserted the Validity of our Ordination, and the legitimate Vocation and Investiture of our Ministry, with great Freedome and Assurance; and affirmed, that all the Churches of God on the Continent of *Europe* do subsist on an Ordination received from an Order not superiour to that of our Pastors.[1]   Nevertheless he declared afterwards, not without Appearance of some Impression, that he *had never seen such a Spectacle before; and it was a solemn, serious affecting Transaction.*

His Commission relating to these Provinces, is, I suppose only to examine Accounts; which, I hope, you Gentlemen Treasurers, etc. are not afraid of.

I was going on with my Intelligence; but at this moment your lovely Children stop at my Gate, calling for my Letter.

So that I am under a necessity to break off here; Purposing a very speedy Appendix.   I am, Sir, Yours alwayes

                                                  C. MATHER.

The Measles is gott into my Family and is like to prove an heavy Calamity to all the Town.

To SAMUEL PENHALLOW.   M.H.S.

BOSTON, 24 *d.* 10 *m.* [December.] 1713.

SIR, — To the Letters and Packetts, which I have this Week already directed for you, I have nothing to add; but only pray your communicating of these two printed *Letters of Charity*, as Providence may afford Occasion.

Yes; — there is one Thing more.   In your Conversation with my aged Parent, when you were last in this Town, you mentioned a surprising Curiosity, of *two very sympathizing Sisters at Hampton.*[2] We both of us, pray the Favour, that you would obtain for us, a particular and a well-attested Relation of that Curiosity.   There is a Society in the World, who, I perceive, expect from me, what may be curious, in these American Regions.

The *Letters of Charity*, I now send you, may no doubt be censured, as every Thing of mine is, by some of your Neighbours, whose Envy (and Folly) uses to be at least a equal to their Learning.   But the Imitation of our dear, dear Saviour, in helping the sick and miserable

[1] Sewall, *Diary*, II. 401.
[2] Bridget and Jane Moulton.

yeelds a Consolation, which will weigh down against all their Impertinencies. I am, Sir, Your hearty Friend and Serv't.

Co. Mather.[1]

To Sir William Ashurst.   A.A.S.

Boston, N. E. 12 d. 8 m. [October.] 1714.

Sir, — Your grand Revolution on the first of *August*, has affected
these Plantations in a very uncommon Manner; and we comfort
ourselves with Hopes, that our King, will extend his benign Rayes, to
his American Colonies, where he has diverse hundreds of thousands
of Subjects; but none more loyal and faithful than those of N. E.

Our Governour,[2] with whom I have of late Months lived in Good
Correspondence, commands me to give you his Service.

Many (whereof your Servant who now writes was one,) were of
the Opinion, in the Reign of the late Ministry that we should be much
easier and happier in him, notwithstanding some Dissatisfactions,

---

[1] "22 *d.* 1 *m.* [*March.*] 1713–14. The Committee who served the Church the
last Year this Day received the Thanks of the Church for their faithful Service,
and were desired and empowered by the Vote of the Church, to act another Year
in the same Capacity.

"This Vote was also passed : There having been passed in the Year 1676 a Vote
of this Church, *That in case any that should build Pewes in the Meetinghouse, should
see cause afterwards to leave them, the Pewes should be disposed of, not by them, but
as the Church should see cause:* which Vote has not been regarded and executed,
as it ought to have been; by reason whereof many Inconveniences have arisen
to the Church :

"For Prevention thereof for the time to come, is now Voted and agreed, that
the former Vote be confirmed, and henceforth putt in Execution; and that in
Explanation thereof, when any Owner or Owners of Pewes shall remove out of
this, to inhabit in another Town, or shall desire and obtain a Dismission from this
to another Church; or shall absent themselves (except on a Voyage at Sea, with
a Prospect of their Return) from their Attendance here, and neither by themselves
nor some of their Family generally or frequently contribute towards the Mainte-
nance of the Ministry, and the Charges of the Church. In such cases, they shall
be deemed to leave their Pewes, and the Church, or their Committee for the time
being, may at their Discretion offer and return to them ten Pounds in Money,
out of the Church-stock in satisfaction for their Pewes, and in convenient Time
after such a Tender made to them, shall be authorised to dispose of said Pew or
Pews to some other suitable Person; the former Owners being at Liberty to accept
of their Money, either before or after such Disposal."

"2 *d.* 3 *m.* [*May.*] 1714. Nath: Henny dismissed to join with the fourteen
Brethren, that are forming a new Church in the Neighborhood.

"16 *d.* 3 *m.* John-Lately Gee, dismissed unto the new Church in our Neighborhood." *Cotton Mather's MS. Records of the Second Church,* II.

[2] William Tailer.

than in any such disbanded, boisterous, terrible *Flanderkin,* as we fear'd might come into the Succession; and therefore heartily desired his Continuance in the Government; and so much the rather, because all agree him to be a Gentleman of fine Accomplishments. I perceive, that some are even still of the Opinion, that we had better still have him for our Governour, than some that may be *Strangers to us;* or *not of our Nation.*

And I myself cannot well shake off a certain Principle which obliges me, to wish him all the good that may be obtained for him; and particularly as much quiet as may be, when his, *Quietus est,* shall be granted him.

Nor have I forgotten what *Chrysostom* did for *Eutropious.*

While I was in the midst of these Contemplations, I was entertained with the comfortable Advice of the safe Arrival of our former Friend Sir Ch. H [obby] yea; and a fresh Prospect which he might now have of a Succession to our Government.

As my whole Conduct in relation to the Friend of ours, has for many Years, been a perpetual Series of Civilities to him, and Wishes and Essayes for his Prosperity; nor can any one living tax me with one Act or Word inconsistent with the Friendship I have ever treated him withal: (tho' some things have sometimes happened that look'd a little discouraging, — especially when the Publication of my Letters to him, did so extremely expose me to the Revenges of our Governor).[1] So, I am still full of all due Regards unto him. And, Syr, you will not be the less so, for my informing you, that I never knew him take more Delight in speaking of any Person, than of Sr. W. A [shurst] which he very often has done to me, and alwayes with an uncommon Veneration.

If the Divine Providence bring into the Hands of that Gentleman, the Royal Commission for our Government, I hope, the many and severe Afflictions wherewith God has exercised him, will have a Tendency only to render him the more Serviceable in the World, and the more capable and the more disposed to be a generous Benefactor unto the People that shall be comitted unto him. I hope, likewise that all old personal Animosities between him, and our present Governor will be so laid aside, that nothing shall be done in any Point, but what public Welfare shall call for. Behold the most unlikely and improper Person in the World, interposing as a most unexpected Mediator.

I have broken my præscribed Measures, in writing you a Letter without one Indian Curiosity. But the Occasion must be my Apology.

[1] Joseph Dudley.

May the Glorious God our Saviour, grant you His continuall Direction, and Protection; and multiply His Blessings to Your honourable Family.

Tis the unceasing prayer of, Your Honors, Most sincere and humble servant.

To Sir Charles Hobby.   A.A.S.

15 d. 8 m. [October.] 1714.

Sir, — Tis just now, that I have had the Pleasure of hearing that you are safely arrived; the Captain of the Ship saies, at *New-Castle;* but private Letters say, at *London.*

I may truly say, you never had a Friend upon Earth, more sincerely, and assiduously concerned for your Prosperity; and more heartily sympathizing with you in every Article of Adversity; or that preserved a more inviolable Friendshipp under Circumstances that perhaps might have shock'd it in some other Person. When I have been diverse Times told, that you have spoken to my Disadvantage, my constant Answer has been, that Gentleman knowes me so well, I am sure he never spoke an ill Word of me! You might therefore justly wonder at it, if I should lett slip, an opportunity of expressing to you my Satisfaction in the good Providence, which has thus watched over you.

Our Governour desires me to do him all the good Offices, which my poor pen may serve him in. And you may be sure, that the fifth Chapter of Matthew will compel one of my Principles, to do all good Offices, for one to whom I am so obliged.

I know nothing that I am capable of doing; but only to entreat of you, that when a certain Point, the Revival whereof, you have been long since apprised of my Apprehensions and Expectations is accomplished, you do him what good may ly in your way.

He has powerful Enemies (as well as Friends,) and some that are gone from hence, no doubt, carried terrible Representations of him; And, I wish that he had given them less occasions.

But tho' Governor *Eutropius* had very much maligned *Chrysostom,* and loaded him with Indignities, yett, when *Eutropius,* likely to be overwhelmed with his Enemies fled unto *Chrys:* to defend him, the honest old Man spoke, as far as his Conscience would lett him, if no farther, on his Behalf.

That for which I am still more sollicitous, is, that a generous Disposition to do all the good that is possible unto my poor Countrey may alwayes inspire you, and that your Opportunities for it may be

multiplied, and that all Vanity and Vexation you have seen embittering this evil World may raise in your Mind those noble and holy
Ideas of a better world, which may assure you of a Portion in it.

Think on these Things; and I shall be content, tho' you never
employ one Tho't on, Your Honours, most sincere Friend and humble
servant.

TO SIR PETER KING.[1]   A.A.S.

BOSTON N. E. 22 d. X m. [December.] 1714.

HONOURABLE SIR, — So well acquainted have you been with our
uncontroleable Maxim, *that no man can at once acquire a great Esteem
and enjoy a great Repose;* as to render it no Surprise to you, if the great
Esteem which you have in these *American* Colonies, procure you the
Trouble of Addresses from them on many Occasions.

If one of the Things addressed unto you from this side of the
Atlantic, be what you have here enclosed, it is not from one who
cherishes any fond or vain Expectations from the Action, but it is
because it might be thought some Gratification unto the Curiosity of
so illustrious a Literator, to be inform'd, whether any good Letters are
cultivated on the *American* Strand; whether any light ever shines in the
American Regions; and what Studies are prosecuted in the Western
Haemisphere, which Antiquity condemned unto perpetuall *Darkness.*

Nor had this Preesumption been committed, if it had not served
as an Introduction to another Matter, wherein it is desired that I
should give your honour the Trouble of reading a Petition on the
Behalf of these Plantations.

It cannot but recommend my Country unto your Favour, when
you consider the Churches, which illuminate it, as the nearest Counter-
pane upon Earth unto these *primitive Churches,* unto whose Constitution, you have made such exquisite and impartial Enquiries. But
it will be a sufficient Recommendation, that it is a Country full of
honest people, whose Distresses may bespeak your Concern for them;
to be distressed is ever to deserve your favour!

New-England is now grown a populous Country; and by Consequence the Business therein carried on must be considerable. But
for some well known Causes tis come to pass that it may say, *Silver
and Gold have I none.*[2]

[1] This is a copy of a letter, but not in Mather's writing, to Peter King (1669–
1734), who had defended William Whiston.

[2] An undated fragment in the American Antiquarian Society, written by
Mather to Sir William Ashurst reads: "Our Countrey is now growing full of

The Main Subsistence for our Business these many Years has been, upon *Bills of Credit,* issued out from the publick Treasury of the Province, the Fund whereof has been in our immense Debts contracted by our grievous Wars; for the Payment of which the Faith of our General Assembly has been engaged, that certain heavy Taxes should be annually levyed on the People, untill the whole sum in the Bills of Credit thus emitted, should return into the Treasury. The Debts of the Province have thus been the Riches of it, and in the Circulation of these Bills, a Medium of Trade and a Method for our Conveyence of Credit unto one another has been kept in Motion.

But our extraordinary Debts are hastening, we hope to a period. Our *Bills of Credit* are apace going into the Treasury; where having done what they have to do, they expire, as the Theatre on which they have done their part, at length is to do, in *Flames.* What Number and Value of them we have now circulating, is, as our Gentlemen of Business express it, no more than a *Spratt in a Whale Belly;* and bear little Proportion to the Business of the Country, that our People are plunged into inexpressible Difficulties. The most uneasy of the four grand Jewish pains, *Vacuitas Marsupis,* is come upon us. The Blood in our Veins is much of it exhausted; and what little is left, is by some wealthy and hoarding People, stagnated. We find the Name of *Truckland* (which your Honour knows is that Name of *Germany*) will scarce do for *New england;* but throws us into inextricable Difficulty's. For the Releef of these Difficulties, not a few of our more ingenious Gentlemen, form'd a Projection of a BANK in Partnership among themselves the *Bills* whereof might somewhat answer the Necessities of the Country. The Persons concerned in it are many of them such as in all Ac'tts are in superior Circumstances. From all Parts of the Land they pray to come into the Partnership; their Interest is very potent, and very much carries the new Elections for our Generall Assembly.

I forbear to give your Honour the severale Articles of the Pro-

People and by consequence full of Business. But a Medium of Trade almost wholly failing among us, we find ourselves plunged into inexpressible Difficulties. For the Releef of these Difficulties a great Number of our best Gentlemen, began to form a Projection of a Bank, which your Honour finds in the Packett that now waits upon you. The Projection meeting with Opposition from some who can do what they will in our Government, the Gentlemen prostrate themselves before the King, for His Royal Favour to it. It is now humbly desired by the Gentlemen concerned in this Affair, that our Honourable and most Valuable Friend, Sir *William Ashurst,* will please to bestow a few Thoughts on their projection; and that, if a Person [   ]" See also Sewall, *Diary,* III. 27.

jection because it will be laid before you by certain Gentlemen who
will wait upon you with it. What I have to relate is, that some
gentlemen (for some Reasons which in the Monarchia Solipsorum are
very passing ones,) have appeared violently against this Projection;
and partly by their Share in the Government, and partly their way
of gaining their Points upon it, they have drawn upon it a Discountenance from the Government. At the same time the Government
has been drawn into an Action which many think to be not advisedly,
and hardly justifiable. Even to order the making more Bills of
Credit like our former, and letting fifty thousand pounds of them out
upon Interest unto such as will borrow them; the Principall with the
Interest to be paid in five Years, or the Mortgaged Lands are seiz'd
by the Government. However many who dash hard and with much
noise against the projected Bank, do it really from a publick Spirit,
and from a real Perswasion that the Public will be best served in the
way whereof the Government is now making an Experiment. In this
[torn]   [experience the Gentleman   Bank humbly]
prostrate themselves before the Throne for the Favour; And what I
have to request of your Honour, is, that if in your deep Penetration,
you see their Proposals to be wise, and just, and allowable, you will
please to cast a benign Aspect upon them. Your excellent Character
assures us, that if you see what is proposed, will be for the service
of the Crown, and for the Encouragement, and Consolation of a well-
disposed People, willing in all Things to live honestly, it will be made
Partaker of your favourable Influences.

I shall not make the Trouble of my long Letter an endless one;
but with hearty Prayers, that you may long shine, which you have
hitherto done, as One of the bright Glories of our Nation; and that
when you retire, your precious Memory may be celebrated in more
Languages, [than] the Obsequies of the renowned Counsellour *Peires-
kius;*[1] I take leave, and subscribe, Your Honour's Most sincere, and
Humble Servant.[2]

[1] Perhaps the French scholar and antiquary, Nicholas Claude Fabri de
Peiresc (1583–1637), is intended.

[2] "*December* 23. Dr. C. Mather preaches excellently from Ps. 37. Trust in
the Lord etc., only spake of the Sun being in the centre of our System. I think
it inconvenient to assert such Problems." Sewall, *Diary,* III. 31.

"26 *d.* 10 *m.* 1714. Also [admitted], Isaac Pearse, one of the fourteen Brethren, dismissed unto the new Church, returned unto it."

"9 *d.* 11 *m.* 1714-15. Dismissed unto the New Church in our Neighborhood,
Lydia Alexander." *Cotton Mather's MS. Records of the Second Church,* II.

To John Frizzell.[1]　　　　　A.A.S.

January 25, 1714–15.

Honoured Sir, — The constant Kindness you express to my Father's Family, makes me fly to you, with some hopes that you will also be my Father.

Tis too well known, that my Inclination is more for Business than for Learning.

And being inclined unto the Business of the Sea, my Friends have a prospect of my arriving sooner to some figure on that Element, than on the Long wharf or the Dock.

I have pretty well perfected myself in the Theory of Navigation. And it is now Necessary that I take a few Voyages for the practick part. I must go aboard some ship, as a school for my Education; and some very good Commanders who have been advised withal, think it is not absolutely necessary, nor perhaps convenient, that I should enter at the Cook-room door.

I confess my desire, that the ship whereof your son is the Commander, may be my School.

Here, I would most heartily submitt unto my Father's Expectation, that I apply my Hand unto Every Action aboard, whereof the Master and Mate shall judge me capable, and yeeld an exact obedience to all their orders.

And that when I come to *London*, I should stay aboard, stick to the ship, and attend both the unlading and Loading of it, and only ask one Fortnights Leave to visit my Uncle; I hope, I am every way so disposed, that there will be no Difficulty in my obedience to the Commands, of those aboard whom I shall acknowledge as my Superiours.

My Father is willing to have me under all the Government of a sailor, and to do all possible Duty and service aboard; and yett to pay for me, as a passenger.

Sir, I cast myself upon you, in this matter, and pray to be considered, as your younger Son; who, by consequence, must pay obedience to the Elder.

But, I do it with submission, that, if you think any better Advice can be given to prepare me to do some Good in the world, I shall be sensible that it ought to be complied withal.

So I take Leave; Sir, Your most obedient Servt,[2]

---

[1] A letter written by Mather, but intended for the signature of his son Increase Mather, now destined for a commercial life.

[2] "16 d. 1 m. [*March*], 1714–15. At a Church Meeting. The Church desired

To Sir William Ashurst.   A.A.S.

[1715.][1]

Sir, — By the next Opportunity, I hope to entertain your Honour with something that may be more pertinent than what this Packett can pretend to.

Tis but just now, that I have had the Satisfaction of receiving your Letters, which were dated as long ago as the tenth of August, the Ship on board whereof they were, having been blown off the Coast, in the beginning of the Winter. You will easily beleeve, that we partake and rejoice with you, in the Blessings, which the first of August introduced. In my Letters, I have still taken care to treat you, with some Indian Curiosity. But [ ] that I have at th[is instant] for you, is the hand [that] brings you a small parcel of our squash-seed, from our worthy Friend Mr. *Sewal*. It comes by a tame Indian; for so the Europeans are pleased sometimes to denominate the Children that are born in these Regions.

More plainly, tis my own Son; a Youth not sixteen years of Age; but one who having pass'd thro' the learned and polite Education of our Schools, chose a Life of Action; and having been so long with an acute Merchant as to acquaint himself with Business, the Death of his Master, opened a new Scene and Hope to him, of arriving more speedily to significant Business by the Sea, than in any other way. Accordingly, he is aboard, in the Quality of a Passenger, but with a Design to accomplish himself in the practick Part of shortly comanding a good Ship, whereof he has already gott much of the Theory. I have been perhaps too willing to indulge and follow the Genius of a Child, in the Choice of a Business for him; as knowing that if that be not very much considered, a Child will never prove considerable.

and betrusted *John Clark*, Esqr. *Thomas Hutchinson*, Esqr., Mr. *Adam Winthrop*, Mr. *Edward Hutchinson*, Mr. *John Ruck*, Mr. *John Frizzel*, and Mr. *Samuel Greenwood*, to act as a Committee on the behalf of the Church, for the Year ensuing, in such Methods and Affaires as were assigned unto such a Committee, for the five former Years.

"A Copy of a Vote then passed by the Brethren, after the Withdraw of the Pastors. (Drawn up by Col. *Winthrop*.)

"At a Meeting of the Brethren of the North-Church in *Boston*, duely notified, Voted, *Nemine contradicente*, that the House of Mr. *Thomas Hutchinson* in Ship Street, now vacant, be hired, for the Accommodation of the Reverend Dr. *Cotton Mather*, at the Charge of the Church, until some further Provision be made for him." *Cotton Mather's MS. Records of the Second Church*, II.

[1] Young Mather was in London in May or June.

Tis an Alleviation to my Dissatisfaction in this Choice, that it may give the Lad an Opportunity of waiting on your Honour; and bringing to your Lady, the enclosed little Treatises; With my repeted Wishes of all Prosperity to your Person and Family. Wherewith I am, Your Honours, Most affectionate Servt.

To Dr. Williams and Others.   A.A.S.

Boston. N. E. 14 d. 2 m. [April.] 1715.

Reverend Sirs, — The Ministers of the Gospel, in two Provinces of N. E. had the happy Tidings of the Arrival of our lawful and rightful King *George* to the British Throne, whereof we are not the least joyful, tho' some of the most remote Subjects, no sooner brought unto them, than the Disposition of addressing His Majesty with our most hearty Congratulations was operating in them.

The long and strong Bands that a new English Winter, laid upon them, are no sooner taken off, than they have mett by their Delegates from their several Associations in the Countrey, at our Capital Town; where they have unanimously agreed upon an Address unto His Majesty, on the behalf of themselves and of their Churches.

What they first of all desired was, that there should go two Persons of their own order from hence, personally to wait upon the King with their Address; and there were two accordingly chosen for that purpose. Not without hopes, that also by their Means a better Correspondence with the Churches of the Dissenters in England, and with the Church of Scotland, might be obtained for the Churches of New England, which are in reality their most united Brethren, and have the Difference between Congregational and Presbyterian, very little known, and not at all mentioned or considered among them.

Unexpected Encumbrances have stopped the Voyage of our intended Messengers. But the Ministers at their Convention made a provision, that if any such thing should happen, we should on their behalf apply our selves unto you, with our humble Request, that you, (or as many of you as may see cause to attend it) would accept the Trouble, of presenting our Address unto His Majesty, and say what you shall think proper on that occasion.

But we have generally thought it a decent Circumstance, that the polite Gentleman, and our very good Friend who is the Agent for N. E. should accompany you in this Action; for which Purpose, he is also written to.

What has procured you this Trouble, is, not only, that we are

well-apprised of your gracious and generous Disposition to serve all
the Churches of God on all opportunities, but also that your Names
are very particularly known and precious, throughout these American
Churches, and your Books are justly and highly valued, yea, some of
them also reprinted, and have done great Service to the Kingdome of
God in these distant Parts of the World.   One of you is likewise a
Son of New England, and no Stranger to the Circumstances of his
native Countrey.

To our Address, we have annexed a *Memorial;* which is to be
entirely left unto your Discretion; either to present it unto His
Majesty, or (taking off the Inscription,) to publish it unto the World,
or to suppress it altogether; what you shall judge most for the Interest of those on whose Account we thought the Pen of a *Justin Martyr*
or a *Tertullian* thus employ'd, might be not unserviceable.

So entire is the Confidence we repose in your Wisdome, and your
Goodness and your hearty Affection to a numerous People of God,
and a little Nation sprung from your old Puritans, in these American
Colonies.

The Trouble we have already imposed on you, is enough, without
adding to it by Extending our Letters unto too large Dimensions.

We therefore conclude them, with our Supplications to our glorious Lord, that He would continue and multiply your Opportunities
to glorify Him, according to all your holy Desires; and that He would
particularly give you, and the People for whom you are now to be
concerned, a favourable Acceptance with the Throne, which is to
be addressed on their behalf.

And subscribe, Honoured Sirs, Most affectionately yours, In the
Name of the Ministers of our Two provinces.

To the Reverend, Dr. Daniel Williams,
Dr. Edmund Calamy,
Mr. Thomas Reinolds of London
Mr. Samuel Mather of Witney.

ADDRESS TO MINISTERS.   A.A.S.

[February or March, 1714-15.]

HONOURED SYRS, — The happy Accession of a King[1] so much
wish'd and pray'd for, as Him whom we now with unspeakable Satisfaction, see sitting on the Throne of the British Empire, opens to us

[1] George I, who became king August 1, 1714.

a fair prospect of considerable Services to be done for the Churches
in these American Colonies.

Our Brethren in the Kirk of *Scotland*, have sent five of their
most eminent Ministers, to wait upon His Majesty, with proper
Congratulations, and the Dissenting ministers about *London* have
also personally addressed the Throne, on this great Occasion. And it
is thought by men of Sense among ourselves, that we shall be exceedingly and scarce excusably wanting to our selves and unto the best
Interests, if we do nothing after their Exemple.

Tis to be feared, there will be those who will take all Opportunities
to misrepresent us; and as we have already felt some ill Effects of the
Misrepresentations which have hereto fore been made of us unto our
Superiours, thus we cannot but rationally look for more, if we do
nothing to rectify them.

If His Majesty might have in his royal View, the true State of
our Countrey in regard of the Religion and the Disposition which
prevails among His loyal Subjects here, and His great Ministers of
State, be duely apprised of our Condition, and at the same time such
a good Correspondence established between us, and our united Brethren, in the Church of *Scotland*, and the Dissenters in *England* that
they may look on what is done unto us, as done unto themselves; it
would no doubt be followed with a long Train of desireable Consequences; too many to be at once enumerated.

For this Cause, the Ministers of this Town, have had serious
Thoughts of desiring that an Address may be presented unto the
King, on the behalf of the Ministry and of Churches in the countrey;
to Congratulate His Accession to the Throne; and the Succession of
the Crown in the illustrious House of *Hanover;* And humbly to pray
His royal Protection, in our peaceable and undisturbed Possession
of our sacred Liberties; and in prosecution of the main End of these
Plantations; to have Churches Established on those Terms of Communion which our great Lord-Redeemer has instituted, and wherein
all good Men ought to be united. We have made the Proposal unto
the Honourable Council, at a very full Board, and the Return we have
had from thence is, that it is very Acceptable to them and that they
desire, it may be proceeded in.

But we cannot proceed in this Matter, till we have obtained the
Judgment of our Brethren throughout the Countrey upon it, and their
Consent unto it.

We do therefore humbly entreat, that the Brethren in your Association, or, Vicinity, would as soon as tis possible, procure an Inter-

view, and Communicate from thence unto us, (either by Letters or Messengers) your Apprehensions about the important Matter that is now proposed; in the several Points of the Desing and the best Method of prosecuting it; particularly whether by any Hands that may be sent from hence, of our own Order, which is by some thought worthy of consideration.[1] We say, *as soon as tis possible*, because tis an Affair which requires Expedition, and there should be no Time lost about it.

It is more particularly desired, that on the second Wednesday in *April* next, we may enjoy an Interview with such Delegates from you as may think fitt to afford their presence at the House of Dr. *Mather* the Elder on this Occasion.

We commend your whole Ministry, and more particularly this Grand Affayr, unto the Conduct and Blessing of the glorious Lord. And subscribe, Syrs, Your affectionate Brethren & Servant.[2]

To Mrs. Lydia George?[3]   A.A.S.

MADAM: A person of your good Skill at making Inferences, having a little Considered what you know, of Him who now addresses you, will easily Infer some things, that will be very much to his Advantage.

If he be one who looks upon Love to his Neighbor, as a very essential Article of his Religion; and who so loves every man, that the Offer of an Opportunity for the doing of Good unto any one, is the sweetest pleasure that can be given him, and his Life is entirely spent in the doing of Good unto all sorts of people, in all the wayes imaginable; yea, if upon any peoples Abusing and Injuring of them, he presently prayes for them, and sets himself to do good offices for them, it will be very reasonably inferred from hence, that the Gentlewoman who comes one day into the nearest Relation unto him, will be lov'd by him, as much as can be wished by her.

Especially, if he be one of a singular Fondness in his Temper; fond to a Fault, and never more obliged, than when the objects will give him Leave to lett them know how fond he is of them.

[1] Mather wished to be the messenger.

[2] Written on back of this sheet:
"Letters to, Mr. Sparhawk, Mr. Roland Cotton, Mr. Little, Mr. Danforth, Mr. Baxter, Mr. Whiting, Mr. Noyes, Mr. Rogers, Mr. Stoddard."

[3] The following four papers seem to relate to Mather's wooing of his third wife, Lydia Lee, widow of John George, who died November, 1714. Mather married her July 5, 1715, and Sewall visited him "and his new wife at the house that was Mr. Kellond's" on July 14.

Were the Gentlewoman one of no more than common Circumstances, yett might she expect here to be honourably and comfortably treated; but how much more, when he shall have the sense of all the World concurring with his own, that she is a Gentlewoman of Endowments and Endearments, exceeding what can any where else be mett withal!

Madam, The person, to whom you have done the Honour of admitting him sometimes to your Tea-table, has that high opinion of your wisdom, that he hopes never to be guilty of taking a step, which may not have your Approbation.

He will entirely wait the Allowances of your wisdom, for the more finishing strokes of the Conversation which has been begun, and will press for no public Appearance, or proceedure, that you shall judge unseasonable.

Nevertheless, He begs your Leave, that it may not be thought too soon for him to tell you, that your bright Accomplishments, your shining Piety, your polite Education, your superiour Capacity, and a most refined Sense, and incomparable sweetness of Temper, together with a constellation of all the perfections that he can desire see related unto him, have made a vast Impression upon him.

If ever he should be so inexpressibly happy, as to enjoy you, he could not but receive you, as a wondrous Gift of God unto him; a Token that the unworthiest of Men, had yett obtained Favour of the Lord.

Such an Idea, he has conceived of you, that every Thing you shall be or say or do, will forever please him; and the pleasing of you, will be his continual study and Rapture.

His Tenderness for you, will be the Effect not only of the natural Sense he must have of your Merits, or of a Disposition in him always to oblige; But also, of a strong Apprehension he will be ever under the Power of, that the more of Love and of Goodness he shall express in his carriage to you, the more his conformity to his Great Saviour will be Exhibited.

It will be yett augmented, by the strange and kind Providence of God, which has been at work, to bring about what is proposed. Especially the Answers of prayers, which alwayes bring Blessings with them.

Truly, Madam, as it happens, that the Gentleman is one, whom the Eyes of all the Countrey, and many more, are much upon, so the General Vote and Voice of the Countrey has been that way, which he is now agoing. His purposes (which [   ] have eagerly waited for) are already a common subject of Discourse; but with universal satisfaction. Especially among the more praying people, whereof there have been many concerned for him, and those now begin their praises for the prospect which they have of a precious Harvest.

I know not what is in the enclosed Letter; but, I beleeve, it may be something of such a Tendency; tis from a Mother and Sister of yours, and one of the best of Women.[1]

What remains, is, to entreat, that it may be no offence unto you Madam, if hereafter, I may take the Liberty to speak unto you, such Things as I have now written, and that such Talk in our Interviews may not be grievous to you, as will be an unspeakable satisfaction to, madam, Your most affectionate serv't.

MEMORANDUM.

21 d. 1 m. [March.] 1715.[2]

In the Evening. — After some words of decent Respect unto Mrs. G[eorge] she said, she had thought fitt, to have one Interview alone with me, that I might fully know her Mind, about the matter I had propos'd unto her.

She remonstrated the Reproach that she had suffered in the Talk of people, about that affair; And therefore she thought it time, to lett me know her Desire, that she might hear no more of it, and that I would speak and think no more of it.

She said, there were other persons that would be more agreeable to me; and in whom the prayers of many good people for me, would be more likely to be answered.

She gave me to understand, that if it were not for a Regard she had unto my Character as a Minister, she should forbid my ever making any more Visits unto her. She said, my Visits would have been a consolation and satisfaction unto her, if I had mentioned nothing of this affair.

But she peremptorily forbad my writing any more Letters unto her.

She many times insisted on it, that, I would say to all persons, As for the matter talk'd of, there is nothing in it.

[1] The will of Rev. Samuel Lee (Waters, *Genealogical Gleanings in England*, 70) mentions wife Martha, and four daughters, but Mather may have referred to Mrs. George.

[2] That is, 1714-15, as he was married in July, 1715.

I offered, that I would say to all persons, Tis a matter which Madam is not at present disposed to hear of.

She then said; But people will say, why does she entertain him? if she have no purpose hereafter to allow of his Intentions? This she express'd herself desirous, that there should be left no occasion for.

I represented unto her, some fatal consequences likely to follow on this Conduct. But she would not admitt any Apprehension of them.

The conversation lasted for several Hours. On my Part, it was as calm, and as pertinent, and as obliging, as my dull Witts could render it. With as full answers as could be made unto the Things that were objected unto me; and just Reasons for every step of my Conduct.

At last I said; *Madam, To give you a full Testimony of my Honour and Esteem for you, my Satisfaction shall be entirely sacrificed unto yours.* She answered; *Say, and Hold.*

To Thomas Craighead.   A.A.S.

Wednesday, 23 *d*. 1 *m*. [March. 1714–15.]

Sir, — Tis with a grateful surprise that I reflect upon it, that one so much a stranger and so lately arrived as he to whom I am now applying myself should be admitted into such an intimate Acquaintance with us and with our most important and reserved affaires. But since the divine providence has brought you into Circumstances of so much Friendship and Freedom with us, I take the Liberty of entreating you do your good office, wherein this letter terminates.

The best of Women having in express and severe Terms repeted her prohibition, that the Hand which now writes, (and which has written some few things in its time that have been of a little use to others,) should at all write unto her, I am under a Necessity of writing to you, what I desire she may be acquainted withal.

A worthy Relative of hers, just now gives me to understand, that nothing will satisfy her, but such a conduct in me, as will put a total stop, unto the Discourse of the people, about my Intentions to pursue a Reception with her. And he seems to be of the Opinion, that the Method I am now taking, is the most proper that can be taken.

For my past Conduct, I thought, I follow'd such Advice, as would præscribe no wrong measures to me; But I perceive I have hitherto done just nothing that is Right. And it is a killing thing to me, to think, that I have been led into Steps, that have been so very offensive, and have occasion'd so much Trouble, to a person for whom I must alwayes have so great a veneration.

Some of my Last Words to her were, *That I would Sacrifice all my satisfaction unto hers.* And I know not how tis possible for me, to give a fuller Demonstration of my vast value for her, than by saying it over again, and keeping her charge unto me upon it, *Say and hold!*

Wherefore, tho' the Earth could not afford me a greater pleasure, than her most agreeable Conversation; and I envy you, the Fœlicity that you enjoy in it; yett I will totally Deny myself of it, for as many Months, as her Wisdome, to which I pay all the Deference imaginable, shall order me.

You were proposing to me, one Interview more, with our Incomparable Friend. But, this will prove, perhaps, to both of us a Disadvantage.

First, to her. Because, it will be impossible for me to come there unobserved; And the Least observation of my being there, will keep alive the Talk, which gives her so much uneasiness. And I cannot be guilty of any thing that shall have any Tendency to make her uneasy; tho' I never so much cross my own Inclinations in forbearing it.

Secondly, to *me.* Because as I gather from what I just now meet withal I cannot but expect from her, over again such afflicting passages, as I receiv'd when I last waited on her.

And I must from Experience confess unto you, my weakness to be such, that they will make too deep an Impression upon me; My tender Spirit and Health will suffer so much, and I shall be so unhinged for my Employments, which are what they are, by wounds from an Hand, I so much admire, that I am lothe to have them renew'd upon me.

If the people, that are to govern us, knew, how cold a Reception I have hitherto had, and what a perpetual care Madam has used in all her Expressions to discountenance any thing that I might hereafter propose relating to her, and how she did at last, when I came to speak more plainly, as plainly signify her wish that I would come no more; there would be no room left for the Censures whereof she is afraid. It would indeed be sufficiently for my Dishonour, if this ever come unto their Knowledge. (whereof, I hope, I shall be very patient.) But, it is enough, that I omitt the Visits, which are, thought so obnoxious to misconstruction. And that I say no more than this to my Friends; *That Gentlewoman is too discreet, to allow of any unseasonable overtures.*

What I have to request of you is to assure, that excellent Person, that my Resolutions to keep out of sight, (even until those two very precious Friends to both of us, Mr. C. and Mr. B. whose Good will to me I very much value myself, and unto whose Prudence, I can entirely refer myself, shall direct me to do otherwise,) oppress my own mind with violence, which could be well born, by none but one of my Age and one so much used unto Sacrifices; But they are formed meerly to gratify her; whom I can undergo anything to oblige, even while I have never yett received one favourable word or Look from her; and it may be naturally inferr'd, how much more I should do so, if ever any thing Reciprocal should invite unto it.

And then, give her Assurance of this also; that my vast Regards for her will continue inviolable. She may depend upon it, (tho I know not, whether a total Deliverance from me, would not make her yett more easy,) that I can by no means lay aside those vast Respects but must renew my Endeavours one Day, to make her yett more sensible of them.

However, to be free with you, I have strong Apprehensions, That my dying Hour will Intervene, which, oh! join with me, in my praises to our dear Saviour for it, I often even long for, and hope it will be the best Hour that ever I saw. I leave all with Him, and am, Sir, Your affectionate Brother and Servt.

To Mrs. Lydia George?   A.A.S.

My — (Inexpressible!) I am a fraid you been't well, because my Head has aked pretty much this Afternoon.

The pain of my Heart, will be much greater than that of my Head, if it be really so.

But I imagine, you are growing well, because my Headake is going off.

Your Little Daughter waits upon you, to bring me the agreeable satisfaction.[1]

May you tomorrow, (and praeparatory to it,) have sweet Interviews, with Him, whom your soul Loveth!

What is He, more than any other Beloved! O infinitely more! All others, pretenders in your esteem and I among the rest, are black and base and vile things, yea, and the brightest Angels in Heaven,

[1] The only child of John and Lydia George was named Katherine, who married, August 11, 1708, Nathan Howell, and had two children, both sons, when this letter was written. "Your little daughter" was, therefore, hardly applicable to her.

are mean Things in Comparison of Him. O Sun in the Firmament; Thou too art all Blackness, before that sun of Righteousness.

Think so, my dear, grow in such Thoughts; And Lose the sight of all things but Him.

I mightily wish, That you may Love nothing that is Mine. My wishes are, That I may be so Happy as to exhibit unto you some Reflections of His Image. If you can discover any thing of [*illegible*] in the meannest of men, tis well. Every thing else, Dislike it. And the more will you be Lik'd and Lov'd by

One who Loves you Inexpressibly (and *placilla*[1] most affectionately and compassionately.

To Thomas Reynolds.[2]   A.A.S.

Reverend and very dear, Sir, — The generous Friendship wherewith you have treated me, is like to bring an unknown Trouble upon you.

There is an *Opus Ecclesiæ* præpared, which is waiting to be at some Time or other published; whereof the enclosed, *New offer to the Lovers of Religion and Learning* will give some Advertisement.

I know very much of your Love to do good, and of the ready Mind wherewith you embrace Opportunities to serve the Ch: of God in its most valuable Interests.

And I know something of the unmerited Respect which you bear to the Person who now addresses you.

This has emboldened me, to committ unto you, and unto two more, the Direction, and the Management, of this important Affair.

But who those other two shall be, I have left unto your Determination; because I might ignorantly have putt in such, as you might have less approved of. I have therefore left Blanks, entreating you to fill them up with such Names, as you think most suitable; which you may do, with what Reservation you please; for your Satisfaction will be entirely my own.

My Request is, that you three, will condescend unto the Care, which is now betrusted with you; and this, not only as from the Author, but also as from the Churches and Pastors in all these Colonies, which you have no little Value for: and among whom, Syr, the Reprinting of your excellent Book of Mrs. Terry and Mrs. Clissold, by my means, has made you to be particularly considered.

[1] The MS. is clear, but the word has not been identified.

[2] Written in the spring of 1715, as the reply of Dr. Reynolds follows.

I should be glad, that your Bookseller, Mr. *John Lawrence*, may be one of mine.

I make no doubt, that many of our Brethren, with you, may have a very mean opinion of every ones capacity here, to do any service that may be worthy of your Notice. And I do not expect that my own having, near two hundred and forty times, entertained my Friends with publishing by the way of the Press, Treatises and Composures on various Arguments, and in various (living as well as dead) Languages, will obtain for me with some, the Favour of being thought capable of any valuable Performance. However, I am willing that you who have perhaps more favourable Sentiments of me, than some others have, should make some Trial on my Behalf, whether my *New offer* may not meet with some Subscriptions and Encouragements.

And, I will now keep looking up to the glorious Lord, for such an Answer from you, as may shew me, what I may have to do, about sending the Manuscripts of the *Biblia Americana*, over the Atlantic. In Him, I am, Sir, Your Brother and Servt.

[ENCLOSURE]   A.A.S.

To the Reverend _____, and the Reverend _____, together with my Reverend, and most Honoured Brother, Ministers of the Gospel, in the City of London.

My most Honoured Brethren, — It is a Consolation of God, which cannot be small with you, that you have American Colonies, who have an Ambition to be acknowledged as your *United Brethren;* are ambitious to be bound up with you in one Bundle, of Life and of Love. We beleeve, we enjoy the Benefit of your Prayers for us; and are sure, our Prayers for you, our sollicitous Concern for your Prosperity, and our sympathizing Distress in all your Adversity, are such as well become our declared Brotherhood. And if any Service for the Church of God, worthy of any Notice, be performed by His Grace granted unto any Person here, it recommends itself unto you, under that Consideration; Tis done by *One of you;* Tis One of *your own* Performances.

Behold, now laid before you, *A New offer to the Lovers of Religion and Learning*, made by one of yours, at a Thousand Leagues distant from you, which will, no doubt, sufficiently explain itself in the Perusal.

That the Things promised in this offer are indeed prepared, I suppose, will be unquestionable, unto such as may think the Author

could not otherwise be so senseless as to make a Tender of them;
For, I can assure you, there will be found rather more than what the
Bill of Fare has mentioned.

It has not been any Disadvantage unto your particular Profession of Dissent from the Irregularities in the Worship imposed on
the Nation, or unto the Cause of pure and undefiled Religion in
general, which is your Cause more than any Peoples, that so many of
our Way, have had their Pens used by the glorious Head of the
Church, to do things that have proved advantageous and acceptable
to the reasonable Part of the World. And more particularly, what
has been done by such Men, as our Pool,[1] and some others, in their
Annotations on the Sacred Scriptures, will be a living and a lasting
Testimony for you, in the Consciences of them who pay any Respect
unto the heavenly oracles; It will testify, that you are not such a
People, as deserve to be hated and cast out from among those, who
would say, lett the Lord be glorified.

Such diligent Servants, as you have at this Day among you;
your *Williams's*, your *Calamies*, your *Henries*, and others, whose
Works ought to be their Praise in the *Gates*, (the Place where a true
and just Judgment of Things is pretended to;) These doubtless find
their Labours encouraged, as well as their Persons had in due Esti-
mation, among all those of your People, who understand the best
Interest, and their own. He that now waits upon you, is not so vain
as to expect a place in that superiour Class; but yett he hopes, that
your favourable Aspect upon his poor Essayes to do some good, may
do no hurt unto that which you reckon your common Interest.

When *Diodati* had prepared his useful Works, Annotations on the
Bible, the Prejudices which many of the Reformed Churches in *France*
had unaccountably conceived against that Work, obliged him, to address
the National Synod of *Alanson*, that he might be more equally treated
with them. And the plea for himself, which he began withal, was;
'That it was a Labour of pure, innocent, confessed Orthodoxy, done
by a Man who never ministred the least occasion to have the Sincerity of his Faith quæstioned, and who for many Years hath given
to the Public, an Essay of his small Talent in this kind of Work.'

That your American Servant may obtain some Share in the candid
Sentiments of the Churches pursuing the Reformation, in *London*, and
wherever you may see Cause to commend the Essay which he now
tenders you, he might plead, that as far as the publishing a Variety
of some lesser some larger Treatises and Composures, on various

[1] Matthew Poole or Pole (1624–1679).

Arguments and in various Languages, may secure him, the Reputation (if not of having Talents rendering him in some Degree capable of his undertaking, yett,) of his pure, innocent, confessed Orthodoxy, you may depend upon it, that no Disservice will be done to the Kingdome of God, by your Encouraging of what you find thus undertaken.

Some eminent Persons in the Church to the Rites whereof we are Non conformists, have given me such a Prospect of Encouragement from them, for our, *Biblia Americana*, that if you should wholly cast it off, it may happen by their Means to make its way into the World. But, I think my Duty to you, obliges me to chuse, that it should rather be by yours.

If you, my dear Brethren, (and those who meet you, on the common Affaires to whom you may if you please, communicate these my Letters,) do judge it worth your while, to concern yourselves for the forwarding of this Work, I shall request, that you Three accept the Trouble of advising, directing, ordering what shall be done about it.

That you single out the Booksellers, whom you would have to go thorough with it.

That you give effectual Injunctions, for the Press-work to be well done; fairly, neatly, correctly, and according to the Directions I may in time give concerning it.

That you exert as full Power in agreeing upon Terms, for every Thing about the Work, as if it were your own.

Only, I would entreat that my dear and only Brother, Mr. *Samuel Mather* of *Witney*, may interpose his Sentiments with yours, if there may be occasion.

I delay sending over the Copy, till I have some Returns from you, to make my Way more plain before me. When you say, *lett it come*, we will do our best that it may be no longer detained here.

In this Countrey, my Friends begin to send me in such *Indefinite Subscriptions* for the Work, as the Proposals have spoken of; supposing, that the two Volumns will not cost much more than five Pounds of our Money, to the Subscribers. And your Booksellers may have a rational Expectation, of having Subscriptions for many more than one hundred setts of the Work; to be paid in upon their Arrival here; if they will run the Risque thereof.

I add no more, but with an Eye to our glorious LORD, for His continual Conduct and Blessing to be vouchsafed you, I take Leave, to subscribe myself, Much Honoured Sirs, Your Sincere Brother, and most humble Servt.

C. M.

To Jeremiah Dummer.

A.A.S.

4 *d.* 3 *m.* [May.] 1715.

My dear and most valued Friend, — As you are sure when you are opening my Letter, which by the hand in the Superscription, you know to be mine, that you shall find nothing to render you uneasy in it, so, I perceive my Task sometimes must be, to find you uneasy, and cure it.

First and foremost, it will be in vain for any evil Instruments or any trivial Occasions to break that generous Friendship, which has hitherto been cultivated between us. No body shall perswade me, that my *Pamphilus* [Dummer], is not a person of bright Accomplishments, and one of a singular Goodness in his Temper and ready forever to do good Offices, and a Lover of his Countery and an Honour to it.

No body can perswade him, that his *Usebius* has not an high Esteem for him, and is not of those Principles, which will cause him to do him good and not hurt all the Dayes of his Life.

Whoever tells you, that I have ever spoken any Thing to do you the least mischief in the World, is a Talebearer, and wrongs me unaccountably.

If *Adoni Avi* [Increase Mather], should happen to express any Dissatisfaction at any thing, it is an Injustice to make me responsible for it.

The only Thing, that I have ever spoken, that can have the least Aspect of what you may dislike, is, that I have expressed, (and this but very privately,) a concern, lest the open Appearance of *Irenæus Americus*, to blanch the late Ministry, might prove some Disadvantage to him with the present. But, I know not that ever I have heard that matter spoken of, without my adding, *I am sure, that his Countrey ought to love him for it; for it was nothing but a noble zeal to secure his Capacity of serving them that caused him to appear so far on that side; But I am not much afraid; He will have sense enough to make a good Retreat.* And how often have I added; *We are too much at a distance from Europe, to be competent Judges of a Friend's Conduct there.*

And suppose, I should once take the Liberty, to express myself not mighty well satisfied in one Book of yours; Does not my dear *Pamphilus*, without the least offence to me, lett me know, concerning some Hundreds of mine, *he likes not my writing of them!*

I am not so Vain, as to say, that no man alive has contributed more, than the least of men, has done unto the good Esteem with which your Countrey has devolved upon you the Agency, wherein you are now serving them. The Trouble it gives you, will make you owe little Thanks to them that procured it.

But I will say this upon it; it would be an unreasonable Inconstancy in me, to disserve, or desert, one whom I have so openly asserted on all Occasions.

Beleeve me, my Friend: one cannot live on the Edges and in the Suburbs of the heavenly World, without a mighty Conscience of those two Rules, Do as you would be done to; and, Do good unto all men. But is it possible for me then, to do anything that shall wrong or harm, one to whom I am under so many distinguishing Obligations?

My simple Essay on, *The Balances of Equity*, was designed by me for the Public, with the more of Alacrity, because I proposed in it; a very public, solid, lasting Testimony of my Value for you. I cannot be of the Opinion, that the raising of Envy, was any Objection at all against my doing the Part of a *Justin Martyr*, for my Countrey, who have deserved it, indeed as little of me, as of any that serve it. I am very willing to encounter that Envy; and shall count it my Glory. But I entirely resign my own Opinion to yours. Do as you please, about it. Only, don't think, to proselyte me unto that Perswasion, that my writing so many Books, procures me any Damage, which is to be esteemed so much as the light Dust of the Balance, when weigh'd against the Service done by them to the Kingdome of God.

Nor is it easy to beat me out of that Perswasion, that our *Biblia Americana*, must be an Amassment of most valuable Treasures; and that it has not been amiss to make an offer of it, unto the Lovers of Religion and Learning. I am uncapable of determining the Price of two large Folio's with you. But, I have lett my Countreymen know, that I suppose, subscribers may have a Sett of the Work, for 5 lb of our Money. And I am some what sure of having above an hundred Setts taken off. However, I have laid aside all Expectations of the Work Meeting with any Countenance, where according to common Sense, I might most justly have expected it. I have addressed my worthy Friend Mr. Th. R[eynolds] once and again, in the most expressive and engaging Manner I could imagine, that I might know the Dispositions of my Brethren, the Dissenters concerning an Essay thus made, which, I supposed might not be disreputable or disadvantageous for them in particular, as well as the Cause of religion and Learning in general. But the best part of a Year is passed, without his taking the least Notice of me; which if you see that valuable Person, you may inform him, that I somewhat wonder at. An Eminent N. C.

Minister in the Countrey, wrote me only that silly Condemnation upon the work; If it were for Mr. *Baxter*, a great part of the N. C's would sett them against it; if it were against him, a greater part would do so. As if the, *Biblia Americana*, had anything to do with Mr. B. But, my Friend, I am very easy, if the rest of the World, be as indisposed unto a Work of this Nature, as my Brethren the Dissenters. I can easily resign the Disposal of it, unto the glorious Head of the Ch: who knowes how and when His Interests are to be served; and I would have none of my *own*. I only add, you will not in the least Measure disoblige me, if you never take one Thought more about this Work; while you have such a ponderous Load of other Cares upon you.

To have done. If you will bestow some Study on the Characters of true Love, in the 13 chap. of the 1 Ep. to the Cor's you will find, the Points, wherein I endeavour as a dying Man to approve myself unto God, in my Conduct unto my Neighbour. But then how much may you depend upon a true Love with such Characters, upon it, in the inviolable Frames of my Soul, toward my dear *Dummer!* Who shall never find me any other than [

To Dr. Daniel Williams. A.A.S.

10 *d. 3 m.* [May.] 1715.

REVEREND SIR, — Since I had the Honour of your obliging Letters and Packetts the last Summer, I have diverse times made some small American Returns which I hope, have reached you.

And I have also more lately joined with the Ministers of these Provinces, who upon my Nomination, have made choice of your venerable Hand, for the presenting to the King an Address, and a Memorial, on the behalf of near two hundred Churches, among whom your Name is precious.

To these things, all that it may be proper for me to add, at this Time, is, to pray your Acceptance of two or three of our latest Publications.

It is not very long ago, that an unknown Author published, an Instrument of this Title, *Ter mille querelæ de corrupto Christianismo.* I find my Excellent and Illustrious Friend, Dr. *Franckius*, lately making on that Instrument this Reflection, *At verò Myriadem ea facile aliquis dederit.*

Alas, that in the British Nations, yea, and among our dear Brethren the Dissenters, there is found so great a Share for the Occasions of the Complaints, which good Men are making over the corrupt State of the Christian World.

God has made you a faithful and famous Witness against the epidemical Corruptions, may He still preserve you, and give a great success to your Holy Essayes for the abating and removing of them, I am, Sir, Your most affectionate Friend and Servt.

To Dr. Daniel Williams. A.A.S.

1715?]

Rev'd Sir, — It is not long ago, that the Ministers of our two adjacent Provinces, at my Motion imposed upon you, the Trouble of presenting their Address and Memorial, unto the King; which it is hoped, have long since reached you.

Since then, there has little occurr'd in these plantations worthy of your Cognisance.

The deplorable State of wick'd and ruin'd Carolina, has doubtless reached you.

You will pardon me, if I repeat my humble Wishes, that my Brethren, the Dissenters, would please to take it into their consideration, whether it may conduce unto the best Interest, and their own, for our *Biblia Americana*, to meet with some countenance among them. I have diverse times addressed my excellent Friend Mr *Reinolds*, for his Advice on that Head; and I have waited a Year and half, without the least Word of Return; which has held me in a little suspense, as to some other Applications.

Our Friend, Mr. P.——[1] who is the Bearer hereof, has behaved himself so as to preserve a Good Reputation with our Godly People.

I pray your Acceptance of a few of our latest Publications.

May the Glorious Lord, multiply the Blessings of a fruitful and joyful old Age, and anon an open and abundant Entrance into His Rest.

To ——. A.A.S.

Boston N. E. 20 d. 4 m. [June.] 1715.

Reverend Sir, — My good Friend Mr. *James Sherman*,[2] is he, who brings you my Letters. And the Design of the Letters, is, to bespeak your kindness to him.

---

[1] Joseph Parsons.

[2] See 1 *Collections*, x. 87. The letter may be addressed to some one in Elizabethtown, New Jersey, where Sherman settled.

His Desire is, to do what Good he can, the Little Time he has to continue in the world.

He is desirous to do good, both to Bodies and Souls, as he may have Opportunity.

We are so plentifully supplied for both in this Countrey, that he thinks more Opportunity may be expected abroad than at home.

And perhaps he may meet with some in your Vicinity.

Tis true, Age is coming upon Him; and as I remember, in the Levitic Law, one after sixty has not a third Part of the Value sett on him, that one had before. But the older he is, I hope, he will be the wiser, and the more serious; and more sollicitous to redeem all the little Time that remains, for the best of Purposes.

He has mett with some Troubles and Rebukes in former Years; But he stands right in the Communion of our Churches, and has been for diverse Years improved in occasional Preaching of the word.

I must confess myself to be touched with a sensible Compassion for him, and am so concerned for his being brought into some comfortable Circumstances, that I must assure you, whatever Kindness you show to him, I shall gratefully acknowledge, as done unto myself.

I know you will at all times favour him with your Directions and Assistences.

May the Glorious Lord graciously continue and multiply the Tokens of His Good will unto you; especially in His employing you still to do excellent Services for His Kingdome. I am, Sir, Your True Brother and Servt.

FROM REV. THOMAS REYNOLDS.   A.A.S.

June 9th, 1715.

REV'D D'R., — A few days since I rec'd a further Testimony of your kind remembrance and Affection in a parcel of books which I esteem as a vast present. They are upon useful Subjects. Your thots are proper, and delivered in [words] that must make them profitable with Gods Blessing to such as read them with [a] serious Spirit. You have mine and my wives thanks for them, who do's particularly approve of them and hopes to receive Benefit by them. With these I have also been favoured with a Letter from you, which has given me some trouble becaus of the dissappointmts you are under with respect to your B[iblia] Americana. I have spoken about it, but am sorry I am not able as yet to give you the Encouragemt you have wished and do deserve. The design you propose is in all respects great and worthy of yourself but Circumstances are really such with us and have been so for these twelve Months past and more, as very much dishearten persons from an undertaking that will be attended with so much Charge; besides, Mr. Lawrence the only Bookseller in whom I had Interest sufficient to entrust a Matter of such a Nature died several months ago, and we under whose direction you have left this matter [are] not yet able to get Subscriptions that might answer yours or the Booksellers Expectations. The Dissenters by the Schism Bill of which I gave you an Advice (tho' I don't hear you have received it) and by other intervening Accidents has been under great discouragements, and at present the publick Affairs are in such Distraction that we scarce know where we are, and how matters are like to issue. No longer than Saturday last was a Week, and the day [   ] the first King George's birthday, and the other that of the Restoration [   ] by some Schollars riffled and pulld down three, (which were all [   ] Oxford. And this day which is appointed by the House of [Commons to enquire] into the late mismanagemts, the Govern[ment   ] and Insurrections, so that the City and [People] are obligd to be in Arms. Were you here yourself you would not blame your Friends as guilty of culpable Neglects but would advise them to await some more fitt Opportunity for the publishing your Bible. This is the State of the Case. I shall add no more than that if hereafter [we] through the merciful Providence of God shall be in a better posture and a more favorable opportunity present, I shall be ready to contribute what I can with the Rest of my Brethren to recommend your book that the publick may be obliged with the Benefit of it.

I must now acquaint you that Mr McNish has not been forgott by me, who have upon all Occasions, endeavoured to sollicit the [Board] of the foreign plantations, and have stirred up my Brethren to [aid] the designs of the Missionaries. Endeavours have been usd [and] much Time spent for this purpose, I am sorry to say it [has not] been with that Success as has been wished. I formerly gave you [an] Acct. of this Affair. And I must now with sorrow of heart tell [how] the Society proceeds, and are not without hopes of gaining Bishops to be sent into his Majesties Plantations. We are attempting afresh to represent the Case to the Society. I am directed to write to you and acquaint [you] that we think it would be of service to have some Person or persons [sent] over on purpose with power to represent to the Governm't, the State of yr Affairs with respect to the Missionaries. I desire you will please acquaint Mr McNish, and that you will take this matter into your [consideration.] If Mr. McNish or any others can send any thing that may afford matter of further Remonstrance to the Society we pray they will do it with all expedition, and with authentique Testimonies. I was in hope by your Letter to have had an Opportunity before this of paying my respects to your Son, but inquiring after him I find he is gon to pay his first Visits to his Uncle your Brother at Witney in Oxfordshire. Upon his Return he will favour me I doubt not with [   ] let him know my readiness to show him ail [   ] to his worthy Character and to a Son of the [   ] May God preserve you long for the Interest of his [has made use of] you for further eminent [services]. Go on to honour your Posterity [   ] Gifts and Graces to brighten their Father and [   ] may the Name of Mather be in everlasting Remembrance in the Churches of [   ], I am with much affection, Rev'd Sir, Your respectful Brother and humble Servt.

THO: REYNOLDS.

To ———.   A.A.S.

BOSTON, 20 *d.* 4 *m.* [June.] 1715.

HONOURED BRETHREN, — Before ever we were any of us addressed from you, on the late Occasion, we were many of us fill'd with distress for the dear Church of Newhaven, under your very great Bereavement;[1] we were concerned that you might be supplied with a Pastor who might in some Degree be a suitable Successor to that excellent person of whom you have been bereaved; and we were employ'd even to Agony, in Supplications to our ascended Lord that He would graciously provide such a supply for you.

You may then well wonder at it, that after such an Address as we have received from you, there should roll on so long a Time, ere any of us return any thing of an Answer to it. But for the same Reason that all Answer hath been hitherto delay'd, what now comes, is not from us in Conjunction, nor any other than my own single Report. What I have to report unto you is, that I cannot find we are any other, than very much at a Loss, for any Candidate of the Ministry among ourselves, who may be of a Character promising enough to prove such a burning and shining Light as the conspicuous Candlestick at New-haven may call for. Except perhaps those who may be under some Engagements, already lying on them.

[1] The death of Rev. James Pierpont, which occurred in November, 1714.

We have not laid aside our most sollicitous Look-out on your behalf; and if any thing occur worthy of your Notice, before you are otherwise determined, you shall hear of it.

Some of us, have been very much of the opinion, that if your Church can see a Person of Eminency, already station'd in some lesser Charge, he might with the Advice of a Council from the Neighbouring Churches, be translated from his present Station, and the Church whereof he is now the Servant, may do well to hearken unto the Direction so given them, that a general Interest may be accommodated.

If this method be not thought adviseable, we are not without Hopes, that you may find sons of your own Education, who may prove rich Blessings unto you.

A young person really a Candidate, who evidently is filled with the Love of God, and the Faith of the Son of God, and a Zeal to do Good, and an hearty Desire to advance the Kingdome of God, and is of competent Abilities, tho' short of what you have lost: such an one, embraced in the Arms of your tender Affection, and carried by you continually unto the glorious Head of the Church who gives Gifts unto Men; would, no doubt, so improve in all that belongs to a faithful and able Minister of the N. T. that it would not be long before you should be sensible of cause to bless God, that ever you saw one another.

In the mean time, it is impossible for us to express the Sollicitude upon our Mind that you may not fall into Contentions, which will produce Confusions, and every Evil work. Satan your grand Adversary, is doubtless watching and waiting for leave to break in upon you, and raise those Disturbances among you, which will be Bitterness in the latter End; but being once begun, tis unknown when they will come unto an End.

It is hoped, that you will be much in prayer to the God of Peace, that Satan may be kept bruised under your Feet; and that whole Dayes of prayer for that purpose, and for the obtaining of the mercy you want from the Lord of the Harvest, will be repeted among you.

It is also hoped, that every man will be afraid of being drawn into any one rash Act or Word, which may bring him under the Mark of them that cause Divisions: but that you will all unite in a Resolution, that you will take no Steps of Importance in your Affair, without first Consulting certain men of worth in your Vicinity, whom you shall jointly pitch upon, as your Counsellours; for most certainly, with the well-advised is Wisdome.

At this time, I add no more, but my hearty Wishes, that you may be of one mind, and live in Peace and have the God of Love and of Peace to be with you. And that in all your Proceedings, the twelfth to the *Romans* and the Tenth, may be alwayes remembred with you. I am, Honoured Sirs, Your Brother and Servt.

To ———.   A.A.S.

27 *d.* 4 *m.* [June.] 1715.

Sir, — A week ago I did myself the Honour of writing to you. At which time I was not apprised, as I now am, that you have a Son of your own Colony and Colledge, of whom it is hoped by some that he may prove a considerable Blessing unto N. Haven, if the glorious Lord incline you to him, and bestow him upon you.

The person intended is, one whose Name is, Mr. *Noyes;* [1] the Son of that excellent Man of God, who has been such a long and rich Blessing to *Stonington.*

If he may in his Day, be like his valuable Father, you will have a precious Gift of Heaven in him; and tho' I am a stranger to him, I have heard what is very Encouraging to hope that he may be so.

I now write, only on my own separate Sentiments, not having Lately discoursed with any of my Brethren on the Subject. But you will give me Leave to shew you mine Opinion; which is, that if you can have a Son of your own Education, it will be very much to your Advantage; and a zeal to overlook such, with a præference to others perhaps not superiour to them, at a greater Distance from you, is either unintelligible, or, too easy to be understood.

What I write, I show to the Doctor, whom I still have the Honour and pleasure to call my Father, and he allowes me to tell you, that he has the same Sentiments.

Now may the great Shepherd look in much mercy on His dear Flock among you, and give you a Pastor after His own Heart, by whom you may be led in the Pathes of Righteousness, I am, Sir, Your sincere Friend, and hearty servt.

To Thomas Craighead?   A.A.S.

[July, 1715?]

Sir, — I am now *There.*

But remembring my vast obligations to you, for the many good services you did me with so much sincerity and Alacrity in my grand

---

[1] Rev. Joseph Noyes, son of Rev. James Noyes. He was chosen in July.

affair, and believing the share of satisfaction, which your hearty Friendship will dispose you to take in my Fellicity; I thought it my Duty to inform you, that the fifth of July is the brightest Day in my Kalender.[1]

Then it was, that one whom you love, saw himself invested with a constellation of Blessings, which you do not imagine me capable of Language Enough, to sett off in their proper Lustre.

Instead of making a vain Essay to declare my just Sentiments of Gratitude unto Heaven, upon so illustrious an occasion, I shall only ask, that you would go on to oblige me with your supplications to the glorious One whom I have in this most Joyful Experience found, a prayer-hearing Father, that I may by a Vast Improvement in Sanctity and Industry and usefulness, walk in some degree worthy of the Great Things which have been done for me, when I have so obtained Favour of the Lord.

I Long to take a Walk with you in an upper-room of an House, which I hope to see illuminated the next week, with the presence of one that shines forever with a thousand Lovelinesses.

In the mean time, I am præparing to entertain on the Lord's-day approaching a Church which I am robbing of an Invaluable Treasure and Beauty, with a Discourse on, 1. Sam. 1.27.

And I am at all times, my dear Friend, Yours in Bonds never to be forgotten.

FROM SAMUEL MATHER.   A.A.S.

DEAR BROTHER, — An undesigned courtesie has put me to a great Expence, I mean my name being mentioned with some London Ministers, has occasioned a needless journey to London.

Your son is with me I must keep a pretty strict eye over him for if left to himself he will not escape sinne in a place of Temptation. He told me his grandfather was coming over and that you intended to send him a remittance by him which made me the more willingly invite him to stay with me till the next spring. His Grandfather's not coming makes his affairs to be in a puzled state. He came with but ten shillings in his pocket to Witney. I sent to Capt. Pamele to remitt what he had also to answer a Bill that he drew upon them which I doubt not but that you would have paid at sight, and Coz. Increase was positive would be paid by the Capt'n. But 'twas rejected. He had but one shirt and was so bare in every respect that I was perfectly ashamed. I take care to let him have credit with

---

[1] His marriage with Mrs. George.

our Countrey Shopkeepers at Witney that he may have Linnen and Woollen suitable and handsome. I propose that you make a genteel remittance to Him, but let the Money come into Mr Sodens hands to manage it for him. I perceive he is infected with the disease which is the blemish of the Family viz. to spend inconsiderately and take no thought about providing against future unavoidable occasions. If I can I will cure him. I design to keep him at Witney 'till just the Instant of his going off to N. England again lest the Snares of London should occasion his returning to His Father with a worse Character then he had when he came. I enclose a three and six penny piece of paper. I am afraid some packets which have come from N. England to some of your Friends have cost them as much.

I have enquired concerning Vertues price for an head   He has five guineas and an half guinea for Engraving such an octavo picture as White Engraved for my Father.[1]   I am

[SAMUEL MATHER]

London, July 23, 1715.

TO INCREASE MATHER.   A.A.S.

[August, 1715.]

CHILD, — Sollicitous I am, that you may return unto me, as fast as you can: and come into new Methods as soon as may, to qualify you for usefulness in the world:

But much more sollicitous, that you may Return unto God, and be witheld from Sinning against Him.

A Thing, for which it is impossible for me, to express the pain of mind, wherein you have long held me distressed.

You know not the Child upon Earth, which has been more pray'd for, and more talk'd to, that he might be converted unto God and unto all the former means for your Good; there have now been added the Admonitions of a pious uncle.

God forbid, that you should be so infinitely unhappy, as you must be, if all these be lost upon you.

I hope, you lett not a Day pass you, without prayers to the glorious God; And that all the Vices of Dishonesty, Debauchery, and False-speaking are abominable to you.

[1] Robert White (1645–1703), who made some four hundred prints, comprising most of the public and literary characters of the day. His plate of Increase Mather may have been intended for one of his printed volumes. A coarse woodcut was made from it by Thomas Emmes, in 1701, and appeared in Increase Mather's *Ichabod*, issued by Nicholas Boone, in 1702.

To Samuel Mather.   A.A.S.

[August, 1715.]

My dear Brother, — The first Advice, that I had of the Circumstances wherein my Son has been detained with you, was the last Week, and a few minutes before the Departure of a Ship, just ready to sail.

I had then an opportunity only to render you my Thanks for your [   ] Civilities to the Child; which I now repeat: and assure you of my speedy care to make the Remittances you direct me to.

I am since advised, that it is much easier to obtain Bills of Exchange from England hither, than from hence to England.

If with no body else, yett the masters of ships coming over hither, it may be easy to find those, who will disburse what shall be necessary on this occasion, and accept your Bill drawn upon me for it.

I am also at a loss, what sum will be necessary on this occasion, and my condition won't invite me to superfluous Expences.

What I therefore chuse to do, is, by a Vessel which is to touch at *Plymouth*, to hasten my Direction to you that whatsoever sum you order me to advance, for my son Increase, that so his Return to me, may be hastened, you would please to draw your Bill upon me for it, and it shall be punctually answered.

I confess, I flatter myself, that you will use all prudent Frugality, in assigning what shall be judged necessary on this occasion and that it will not much exceed Twenty pounds.

I again and again renew my Thanks to you and my sister for your Civilities to the Child; especially for the Admonitions of piety which you have been continually distilling upon him; and, which oh! that they make a due Impression!

I hope, I have putt you out of pain, as to the Library, about which you seem to have such an uncommon Tenderness.

I renew my Request, that you would not lett my *Christian Virtuoso* be lost, but, if you know no better way to make it public Lett it pass thro' *Dr. Woodward's* [1] hand, into the Repository of the Royal Society.

May the Glorious Lord multiply your precious Opportunities to be serviceable and your generous Dispositions to value them and improve them.

---

[1] John Woodward (1665-1728), geologist and physician, is probably intended, who had some difficulties with the Royal Society in 1710, of which Mather could hardly have known.

To Mrs. Samuel Mather.   A.A.S.

[1715–16.]

MY DEAR SISTER, — My value for you has been very great, ever since I understood, that you made my only Brother, one of the happiest men in the World.

I have thought, that Madamoiselle de *Gournay* the Lady, who a while since wrote an Essay to demonstrate, the *Equality of women to men* might victoriously enough defend her problem, (tho' that learned and famous and wondrous Lady A. Maria Schurman, had the modesty to disallow it) while she had such as you, as friend, who help so notably to render your Husbands useful and considerable.

It was the Acclamation made by Spectators in the primitive Times of charity, *What rare women are to be found among the Christians!* By such as you the occasions for it as continued in our Dayes.

Go on to love him, and serve him, and felicitate him; and become accessary to all the Good which he may do in the world; and consider him as a valuable minister of God; and one of whom our Lord will say, of what you have done for him, you have done it unto me.

As you have obliged me, in all you have done for him, so you have made a vast Accession to those obligations, in what you have done for my Son, in the many months of his residing with you.

Your maternal Tenderness for him, in the Time of his long Illness and the many Civilities he at all times received from you; as well as the excellent Accomplishments wherewith he saw you adorned; he never mentions without a sense of passion of Gratitude and admiration.

I return you my most hearty Thanks, for all your Kindness to the Lad; and, if God bless him, he will one day be able to return you his own Thanks in a manner, more significant, than meer verbal Acknowledgments.

May you have goodness and mercy following of you all your Dayes and may the Great Saviour who has Espoused you, forever take delight in you.

The best of women in the American World, accompanies me, in the most affectionate Remembrances which you have in the heart of, Your obliged Brother.

To Rev. William Brattle.   A.A.S.

19 *d*. 6 *m*. [August.] 1715.

Sir, — Among the many who heartily condole with you, in the sorrows of your late Bereavement, there is none more sincerely affected, than he who now tells you so.[1]

But you that have been for so many years an excellent and experienced Comforter of the Mourners, need not so all Assistences, as the best of Mine, to comfort you.

You are a Sacrificer. The Signs and Hopes and Joyes of your share in that priesthood, which must be our future Blessedness, ly in your skill and stroke at Sacrificing. It is a great Sacrifice to which the Holy One has lately called you. But your oblation will be so managed, as to have in it, imcomparable Tokens for Good.

May you yett see Dayes of Service, in a World, which I make no Doubt, by its late Embitterments makes you more willing to leave it, than ever since you came into it. Very relishable Comforts here make some Servants of God but the more willing to dy. For they argue, If there be any thing here below so very desireable, what is there Above? Where ——

Great and sore Troubles, will have the same Effect; and make us long to be, where the weary are at Rest. God that hath shown you such by His admirable Discipline præpares you for it.

A small Instrument of Piety, which I hope, will a little answer some Designs that your Heart is more than a little sett upon, is now humbly tendered unto your Acceptance.

To which I have added, *The Religion of the Closett*, which I present unto your hopeful Son,[2] whom I pray God, to spare, and bless, and use; and give you much consolation in him. I am, Sir, Your affectionate Brother and Servt.

To Robert Wodrow.[3]   A.A.S.

17 *d*. 7 *m*. [September.] 1715.

Sir, — When the distance of the huge *Atlantic*, separates Brethren from one another, one Method unto which we must resort for Maintaining, *the Communion of Saints*, is the Epistolary.

[1] Elizabeth, his wife, and daughter of Nathaniel Hayman, of Charlestown, died July 28, 1715.

[2] William Brattle.

[3] Robert Wodrow (1679–1734), ecclesiastical historian, and professor of divinity in the University of Glasgow.

You have so often obliged me, and so sweetly by your communications in that way, that I cannot be guilty of so much Ingratitude, as to endeavour no Returns; tho such are our Circumstances on this side the water, that you can expect but very small ones.

A Little of what we are and of what we do, after which your brotherly charity towards your most united Brethren here disposes you to be inquisitive, you will perceive a few composures of the latest publication among us, in the Packett which I now humbly tender to your Acceptance. To which I will add; that the Churches of N. E. at this time, enjoy much Tranquility, and are continually, but very peaceably, multiplying into new Societies.

No remarkable Disturbance is offered unto them; only that a furious Man, called John Wise,[1] of whom, I could wish he had, *Cor bonum*, while we are all sensible, he wants, *Caput bene regulatum*, has lately published a foolish Libel, against some of us, for presbyterianizing too much in our Care to repair some Deficiencies in our Churches. And some of our People, who are not only tenacious of their Liberties, but also more suspicious than they have cause to be of a Design in their pastors to make abridgments of them; are too much led into Temptation, by such Invectives. But the Impression is not so great as our grand Adversary doubtless hoped for. And his Devices are disappointed, by or taking the Course, which I find a celebrated University in *Europe*, preferr'd on a late provocation.[2]

We are not without some Inconvenience, from the Missionaries of the Church of England sometimes arriving among us. It seems to us a little surprizing, that the *Society for propagation in foreign parts*, should Leave so many English plantations in the most paganizing Circumstances, and at the same time, chuse to send their Missionaries where they can only serve as Tools of Contention for perhaps about a dozen wretched and sorry people, who merely for mischief declare themselves for the Ch: of E. in Towns, where there are faithful and painful pastors, and flourishing Churches, wherein the meanest Christians understand Religion and practise it, better than the Ministers whom they send over to us.[3] But by the marvel-

---

[1] John Wise (1652–1725), of Ipswich, printed at New York, in 1713, *The Churches' Quarrel Espoused*, a "satirical" production. It was reprinted in Boston in 1715, with a commendatory letter signed by Samuel Moodey and John White.

[2] On August 2, Mather preached, "censured him that had reproached the Ministry, calling the Proposals Modalities of little consequence, and made in the Keys; called it a Satanick insult, twice over, and it found a Kind Reception." Sewall, *Diary*, III. 51. [3] A glance at the troubles at Newbury.

lous Providence of God it comes to pass, that the Ministers whom they send over, have been such ignorant, vicious debauched Creatures that their Hearers have soon grown weary of them, and the Ch: of E. has been in a Countrey of Religious People, rendred, (and how should it be otherwise?) to the Last Degree Contemptible. No Remonstrances have hitherto signified any thing to cure this Infatuation upon the Society; But even this week another Blade of the Mission keeping up the Character of his predecessors, is arrived, for a litigious Vicinity in one of our Towns, where the parson who went before him, so disaffected his own crue of pretenders for the Ch. of E. that they generally deserted him. God will one day putt an End unto these things.

The Colony of *Carolina*, to the Southward of us, is newly destroy'd by the dreadful Judgments of God, for which an uncommon measure of Iniquities had ripened it. The unhappy people, in carrying on their Trade with the Indians, had greatly Injured them and provoked them: And the scandalized salvages at Last, conspired, and broke in upon them, and with a massacre of the people, whom their first Fury fell upon, among which were fourscore of the Traders, they laid the Countrey waste; so that they are generally driven into Charlstown, their Capital Town; where tis thought, they cannot be long subsisted.[1] In the prosecution of this Descent upon the miserable *Carolinians*, the Barbarities perpetrated by the Indians are too hideous to be related. There were a sort of Inhumanity in the Relation of such things, But yett I will venture to mention one Instance, that *Crimine ab uno*, you may apprehend the rest.

One major Cockrain,[2] a very honest man, had been a Trader with these Indians: yea, their Leader in Expeditions against the Spaniards and their Feeder very often at his Hospitable table; and they had a Reciprocal Esteem for one another: Nevertheless, he was one of the first, siezed by the Indians; who bound him, and then strippt his Lady, and abused her with all possible and infamous prostitutions before his Eyes. Then they stuck her Flesh with Splinters of that oily wood which they burn for Candles; and sett them on fire. In this condition she was two or three Dayes broiling and roasting to Death; In which time they roasted her Sucking Infant, and Compelled her to Eat of it. And when these diabolical operations were gone thro', they finished all by Barbikueing of the Gentleman.

It is very much feared, that the Combination of the Indians, is more general, than meerly for the Destruction of Carolina; and

[1] See Ramsay, *History of South Carolina*, 1 159.   [2] John Cochran.

under a French and Spanish Instigation. And that some other Colonies, which, alas, are too obnoxious, may shortly suffer grievous Depredations from them.

In this Countrey, we are not free from our Share with the rest if them that profess the reformed Religion abroad in the world, in a lamentable Decay upon the power of Godliness. Nevertheless, the Countrey has in it a Number of prayerful, watchful, Fruitful Christians, and something more is to be said, than meerly this, that it is generally filled with a sober and an honest people. And it is impossible for me to express, how dear the Ch: of Scotland is, unto their Brethren here tho' it be a little Express'd in the Civilities, which its Ministers happening to come hither, do commonly meet withal.

I join with you in expecting, that the Kingdome of God will quickly be seen, in some Appearances and Advances of it, beyond what have been in the former Ages. But very much of my Expectation is, that God will raise up some Instruments, who from the Mines of the Sacred Scriptures, will dig and run the Maxims of the everlasting Gospel; the glorious Maxims, wherein all the Children of God really are united, and whereinto all that come are to be esteemed and embraced as the Children of God. The children of God and of His Kingdome, under various professions will arrive to a declared and explicit union on these Maxims; and lesser points will be depressed into their due subordination. Disputations on these Lesser Points may be continued; but managed with that mutual Justice, and Candor, and meekness, which becomes the Children of God. The Brethren thus becoming sensible that they are so, will associate for the Kingdome of God, in such methods, that the Things to be consumed by the Stone cutt out of the mountain shall be all broke to peeces before them. Glory to God in the Highest, with peace on Earth from Good-will among men, will be the grand Characters and Intentions of the Kingdome; and the Tokens and Effects of the divine Presence among this people of our Immanuel, will be wonderful, wonderful! *Joels* prophecy is also to receive its full Accomplishment!

I confess myself to be at Work upon those Maxims; not without hopes, that some Fruits of my Studies may ere long reach unto you; In the mean time, I was comforted with Letters from the most illustrious University in the world, which much animated my studies, whereof I have here enclosed you a short memorial, under the Title of, *Nuncia bona.*[1]

[1] Printed by B. Green for Samuel Gerrish, 1715. Mather adds to his name on the titlepage the letters "F. R. S."

I entreat you to remember me most affectionately to the best of men, my Lord of *Pollock*, unto whom I wish always the best of Blessings. You will treat him with the sight of all that this packett containeth in it.

My long letter terminates in my earnest Supplications to our glorious Lord, That His Church with you, the dearly beloved of His soul, may be preserved from the High flying Birds of prey; on whom *Obadiahs* prophecies will be spedily executed; and that you particularly may be many years an useful Instrument of much service to His Kingdome in the world. With such Prayers, and all possible Brotherly affection, I am, Sir, Your Brother and Serv't.[1]

TO SIR WILLIAM ASHURST.   A.A.S.

BOSTON, 18 *d.* 8 *m.* [October.] 1715.

SIR, — In the last Letters, which I had the Honour of receiving from you, there were some Intimations of your Desire to receive some Account of the *Biblia Americana*, a work waiting to see its publication encouraged.

In obedience to your command, I have here enclosed, a, *New offer*, which exhibits a brief Account of the Work. And therewithal assure you That altho' the Author has all this while even ever since his being seventeen years of age, had lying upon him the ponderous Load of the Evangelical service which the greatest, Church in these Colonies has expected from him; and tho he has in this while undergone the fatigue of publishing more than 250 Books of sundry Dimensions, on various Arguments, in diverse Languages; yett, thro' the most gracious Assistence of God our Saviour, there is performed in the *Biblia Americana*, more than all that is promised in the Advertisement.

I have sometimes flattered myself, with an Imagination, that if the Treasures wherewith our B. A. are enriched, were so acceptable in their separate States, as to render many copious and costly volumes Vendible, certainly there would be at some time or other so much common sense operating in the world, as to beleeve, that a close Amassment of these Treasures, refined from Superfluities, with an Addition of many never before exposed, would be not unworthy of some Acceptance.

---

[1] "16 *d.* 8 *m.* Dismissed unto the new Church at Romny-marsh three Stasseys, two men and a woman." *Cotton Mather's MS. Records of the Second Church,* II.

I did not know, but that a Composure, which may pretend without Vanity to be the richest collection of the most valuable Treasures, in so little a Room, that ever the Ch: of God was entertained withal, might hope for a favorable Reception, with people of Religion and Ingenuity.

But I find, and I do not wonder at it, that I do so, the work labouring under Discouragements.

The Booksellers are generally such, that a celebrated Author, thinks the most opprobrious Term he can give unto them, is to say, in one word, they are Booksellers.

It is complained unto me, I know not how truly, that our Dissenters do not seem to over-value Literature; and that a public Spirit among them is much lost by their unusual Emulations; nor do they seem to think, that it is much for their Interest or Honour, to have any of their Number, do things of much consideration in the Common-wealth of Learning. It has been surprizing unto me to read the little, absurd, ridiculous exceptions, which have been made against this work among some of my Brethren. Indeed the good-spirited Mr. *Henry*, several times, in his Letter to me express'd his Good-will to this undertaking; but, he is dead.[1]

The Surviving seem to be of the opinion, that a poor *American* must never be allow'd capable of doing any thing worth any ones regarding; or to have ever look'd on a Book. And the Truth is, we are under such Disadvantages, that if we do any thing to purpose, it must carry in it a tacit Rebuke to the sloth of people more advantageously circumstanced.

I have done expecting anything, from my Brethren in the City; upon the Reasons whereof, I know not, whether or no I am right in my Conjectures.

I am not without importunate sollicitations, from other parts of England, and from Scotland, and from Ireland, that the work may be proceeded in; and promises of Subscriptions, which I beleeve would be Numerous.

And some very Eminent persons in the established Church, lett me understand by kind Letters that they will be Benefactors unto it.

I no sooner published the *Advertisement* here but I had about an hundred Subscribers in view: whereof three are Governours of the Colonies; many of them Gentlemen of uncommon Erudition.

I have been this year and half, begging my Brethren, the Ministers of the City, to lett me know, what they would have me to do, in

[1] Matthew Henry died of apoplexy, June 22, 1714.

pursuance of the proposal, at the End of the *Advertisements*. But they have never to this Hour thought fitting to take the least notice of my Request.

I am sensible, it has been an extraordinary Time with them; and I would make no misconstructions.

However, I am wholly at a Loss, what further to do, in the affayr.

It is no unlawful or immodest or imprudent Thing for me, to make unto the world, a Tender of my poor Studies to serve it; in wayes wherein wiser and greater men have gone before me.

But if the Tender be rejected, I am sure I ought to be humble and patient, and with all possible Resignation, leave unto the glorious Lord, the Disposal of my Essayes to do Good in the world.

Had not the work been in the English Tongue, my Correspondents in the most illustrious Frederician University[1] who have putt great Marks of their Favour upon me, would soon bring it into the Light.

One considerable Article in the work, namely *The Christian Virtuoso*, one would think, might procure some subscribers to it, among the members of the Royal Society, which have allowed my Relation to them.

It may be, God our Saviour will in His Time, dispose the Minds of some eminent and opulent persons, to cast a benign Aspect upon a work which may hand down their Names with lasting Acknowledgments unto posterity.

Be it as it will, I do with the greatest Acquiescence of Mind in the holy Dispositions of His Providence Leave all in His glorious Hands.

To which your Honourable person and Family is also most affectionately comended by, Sir, Your Honors, Most affectionate servant.

To ANTHONY WILLIAM BOEHM.   A.A.S.

2 d. X *m.* [December.] 1715.

MY MOST HONOURED FRIEND, — Several Months are passed, since by way of Return, for the Favours, which accompanied those of our dear *Franckius*, I addressed you with a large Number of Packetts, which had in them some scores of American Treatises, besides a few small presents of Gold, unto the Orphanotropheum. All which I hope, have long since reached you.

I am extremely desirous of maintaining a correspondence, with a person of your excellence, spirit, and Intention; And therefore you

[1] Founded in 1694, by the elector Frederick III of Brandenburg.

must give me leave to lay hold as frequently as I can on opportunities to entertain you, with such Books of Piety as are published in our Countrey: In which, perhaps you will find, something of the spirit of that vital Religion which you have so wisely chosen to cultivate and inculcate.

But of the Things, which the mean hand that now writes has published, since the last that I have tendered you, there is none that has more of my Heart, than the Enclosed, *Lapis Excisus;* upon which I will freely declare unto you my Apprehensions.

A small spark, will sett fire to a mighty Train, when it is already praepared: He was wondrously exemplified, in the Successes of *Luther's* Essayes, which if they had been made some years afore, would have been insignificant enough, and have succeeded but very poorly.

I apprehend the Time is now coming on apace, for the Empire of Antichrist and Satan (whereof, there are too sensible Remains, even in the most Reformed churches;) to come unto its promised period, and the Kingdome of our Saviour to be Exhibited wth glory to God in the Highest, and on earth Peace, thro' Good Will among Men.

But if it be so, that the Time to Favour the sett Time, is come, who can tell, how far such a small Thing, as our *Lapis Excisus,* may operate, for the Introducing of the Things, which the soul of my dear Boem, is with weary anhelations, looking and longing for!

God will shake all Nations, that He may bring them to the Ms[1] of the everlasting Gospel, which are the Things that cannot be shaken. And, I am altogether of the same opinion, with our excellent Ludolf, that the world is already deeply entred into the Distresses, that are designed for such a purpose.

My Request therefore is, that you would please, to disperse these little Engines of Piety, as fast and as far as you can; send of them, to our invaluable Friends at Halle; send of them, to the *Malabarian* missionaries; And if you can do it, send of them into *France;* yea, excuse me, if I say, procure them to be translated into as many Languages as you can. *Magna est veritas, et prevalebit.*

By the next, I may furnish you with more of them; and then more fully acquaint you with the Reasons that have emboldened me to impose at this rate upon you.

In the meantime, and alwayes you will continue your Loves and Prayers for, Sir, Your most affectionate Brother and Serv't.

[1] Mercies or Messages?

1716

THE LIV YEAR OF MY LIFE.

12 *d.* XII *m.* [*February.*] 1715–16. *Lord's-Day.* *12.[1]
G. D. What! And is the *fifty-third* Year of my Life this Day
finished? A Life so forfeited; a Life so threatened; such
a dying Life; yea, and such a barren One! My God, I
praise thee; the Display of thy sovereign Grace, is my
Admiration, my Astonishment! My SAVIOUR, I bless
thee, I love thee, I resolve to serve thee.

I will this Day glorify my SAVIOUR, with Meditations
and Acknowledgments, of His having the *Keys* of the *invisible World*, and of *Death* in His glorious Hands, and His
having the Souls of Men, and very particularly their *Lives*,
at His Disposal. Yea, I will communicate my Meditations
unto my Flock this Day, and invite them to join with me
in my Acknowledgments.

13. G. D. I am reviving my Cares to visit the Flock,
and I would as soon as I can, gett furnished with my *Echo's
of Devotion*,[2] (which is not yet published,) that I may lodge
the Book in all the Families where I come.

14. G. D. Unto each of my Children, present my
Utilia,[3] with my Charges unto them, to make the Book
very much their Companion and Counsellor.

15. G. D. There are some Relatives at a further Distance from me, to whom the like Present of my *Utilia*,
will be an agreeable Expression of my Concern for them.

---

[1] He now alters his entries, so as to follow the days of the month instead of
the days of the week. The * marks the first day of the week.

[2] Printed by T. Fleet and T. Crump, 1716.

[3] Printed by the same, 1716.

16. G. D. If I could redeem the Time, now and then to dress up sublime Thoughts in an agreeable Metre, I might in Time, have a Collection, which may prove a profitable and an acceptable Entertainment, unto the Church of God.

17. G. D. A Society of Christians in our Neighbourhood, being disposed for the publishing of some Discourses, I will propose as advantageously to them, as I can.

18. G. D. Releeve a poor Man clothed with Rags, at the South End of the Town: At the same time, rebuke him, and exhort him.

* ☞ 19. G. D. Tho' I have been after a poor Manner *living unto God*, these many Years, yett methinks, I am not frequent and vigorous and explicit enough on those *Thoughts*, with which the *Life of God* is to be carried on.

I would therefore now endeavour a greater Frequency, in forming those *Thoughts* upon every Turn, which being applied unto my *Actions* and my *Enjoyments*, will bring such a Respect unto GOD upon them, that I shall indeed *live unto Him*.

Upon my ACTIONS. *In this Action I propose an Obedience to the glorious GOD; animated with an Apprehension that He knowes what I now do, under the Eye of His Glory; and that on the Account of my beloved JESUS, it will find Acceptance with Him.*

Upon my ENJOYMENTS. *What gives a Relish to this Enjoyment, is, that the glorious GOD, showes to me something of His Glory in it; and that by this good Thing I am assisted and comforted in serving of Him.*

These Considerations will often require to be made with a particular *pause*, that shall examine, wherein these *Ends* are more particularly answered in my *Actions*, and my *Enjoyments*. And then, I am so to take my Measures therefrom, that if I do not find the *Ends* answered, I am to desist from them.

20. G. D. A Sermon of *Tokens for Good*, may be of good use unto the Flock, whereof I am the Servant.

21. G. D. It may not only be a Service to myself, but also greatly serve the Interests of Piety in my excellent Consort, if I should use, every Morning before I rise, to

read a Chapter in my dear *Arndt;* and communicate unto her the principal Thoughts occurring on it.

22. G. D.   Send the *Utilia,* and some other Things to an aged Relative, at *Medford.*

23. G. D.   There being some Settlements begun at the Eastward, (particularly *Arowsick* and *Brunswick,*) and some devout Persons applying themselves, while they yett want a minister to carry on Exercises of Religion among the people there, I would supply those Christians, with Instruments of Piety, suited unto their Occasions.

And since the Instruction of the Indians has been begun by some good Men there, I would particularly furnish them with Instruments, for that excellent Purpose.

24. G. D.   Procure a good Justice, if it may be, to be commission'd, for a destitute place in the countrey, on the behalf whereof I am applied unto.

25. G. D.   A poor Drone, must have something done for him, and Employment provided.

And a crack-brained Youth in my neighbourhood, (who also belongs to our Church) must be look'd after.

25 *d.* XII *m. Satureday.* This Day I sett apart for Prayer with Fasting, in Secret before the Lord.

My Errands to Heaven were, to obtain the Pardon of my Miscarriages; greater Measures of Piety and Sanctity; the divine Conduct and Blessing to my Ministry in every Part of it; a Smile on the Offers made by my Pen unto the Public; the good State of my Family; the Welfare of my Son abroad; the Rescue of my Daughter-in-Law from her unhappy Circumstances; the comfortable Disposal of my Daughters in the married Life; the Favour of Heaven to my Flock, to the Land, and to the British Nations, and my dear Brethren, that are at work for God in the Lower *Saxony;* — and other Matters.

I enjoy'd most gracious Visits from Heaven to me, in my Devotions.

I pray'd in the Name of my Saviour, and even with a Nature and a Temper conformed unto His, and I prevailed.

When I perceived by the Breathing of my Soul, that I began to live unto God, oh! the Triumphant Joy, that I was filled withal, to think, that now I am assured of everlasting Life. This Life of God, is what never can be killed!

March. 1716. 1. G. D. It may be of great Use to our Ministers, and our Colledges, if I can procure the *Medicina Mentis*, of the Excellent *Langius*,[1] to be much studied among them. I would use all due Methods to bring it about.

2. G. D. I would exhibit a little Summ of Money, to be bestow'd upon such Lads at the School, as gett by heart, the *Maxims of the Everlasting Gospel*, in the, *Lapis e Monte*.

3. G. D. A miserable Man in the Prison, cries to me for my Compassions. I must clothe him, and help him, what I can.

* 4. G. D. That Sort of prayer or that Elevation of the Mind in Prayer, which is in the *Verus Christianismus* called, *Supernatural Prayer*, is what I would exceedingly aspire unto, and grow more experienced in. I would soar towards it, in great Essayes at the *sacrificing-Stroke*, which with a Self annihilation will bring me on towards an Union with God, and an Acquiescence in Him, and in His Will; and when I feel in this way GOD becoming All in All unto me, I would be entirely swallowed up in Him.

5. G. D. Lett the public Prayers, in the Hearing of the Flock, take a pathetic Notice of the Value and Longing which our People gone abroad, express in their Letters to us, for the *New England-Sabbaths*. Manifold may be the good Use of this Intimation.

6. G. D. Very much inculcate on the Children the Lessons of Thankfulness to the glorious God, for His having provided so marvellously for them, when He had made them Orphans; and now bestowing an excellent Mother upon them.[2]

7. G. D. Not only must Relatives abroad be prayed

---

[1] Johann Lange (1485–1565), of Silesia. See p. 405, *infra*.

[2] Mather had married July 5, 1715, Lydia, daughter of Rev. Samuel Lee. See pp. 302, 322.

for, but also their Wives at Home, in their Absence, have the Duty of Resignation much recommended unto them, and so a Preparation for all Events.

7 *d.* 1 *m.* [*March.*] *Wednesday.* This Day I devoted, (and what sinner on Earth has more Cause to do so?) unto the Exercises of a Secret THANKSGIVING unto the glorious GOD.

I began the Day with considering and acknowledging my answering the Character of a meer *Shadow* before GOD; sensible that I am nothing, have nothing, do nothing, but in an entire Dependence upon Him.

I confessed before the Lord, my exceeding Unworthiness of all His Favours; and how unworthy I am to be accepted or assisted in His Praises. I went over the Articles of my Vileness, with all Self-Abasement.

I entertained my Family with Meditations on the CXXXVIII Psalm. And with them I celebrated the Favours of Heaven to my Family; especially in the excellent Mother that He has bestow'd upon it.

Ah! quam deceptus! [1]

I distinctly adored the divine perfections; and breathed after such Dispositions and Behaviours in myself, as they call for.

I beheld each of the three Persons in the Godhead, shining with all those Perfections; and very particularly the God-man, who is my Saviour; and I triumphed in the Enjoyment of such a Saviour.

I made Recognition of my Obligations to live unto this glorious GOD; and be entirely for Him; and I proposed the Methods, wherein I desired forever to glorify Him: ascribing at the same Time unto my Saviour, the Glory of accomplishing my Desires.

Having expatiated upon these Things, in the Afternoon, I went on to recapitulate the former Vouchsafements of a gracious God unto me, in the Course of my Life; and then the Enjoyments wherewith I am this Time favoured of the Lord; more particularly; the strange Prolongation of my Life, with my Health restored and Strength renewed; my Employment in the Ministry of the Gospel, and in so large an Auditory, (yea, notwithstanding the late Swarm therefrom:) And with an Utterance bestow'd in such a wondrous Manner upon me; my marvellous Opportunities to be serviceable unto the King-

[1] These words were written in the margin.

dome of God by the Way of the Press: all the good whereof the sovereign Grace of Heaven has made me the Instrument; the Accessions made unto my Library, and of late some very precious Ones; my Correspondences abroad, especially with the universities of *Glasgow*, and of *Glaucha:* and giving me, tho' I am a sorry and an obscure Creature, a Name among the great Men of the Earth; the credible and plentiful Circumstances wherewith I am accommodated in my Habitation; The good Condition of my Family; especially in regard of the Excellent Consort in which I have strangely obtained Favour of the Lord. For these and such Things, I offered my Praises unto the glorious God, with humble Confessions of my own Unworthiness on the several Articles, and the Triumphs of sovereign Grace in them: and seeing the Purchase and Power of my Saviour operating, in my Arrival to these Blessings of Goodness.

But, oh! the Joy of Soul, wherewith I then beheld, what the Lord has done for my Soul! His Revealing of His Christ unto me, His uniting of me unto His Christ; His pardoning my Sins; and making me one of His children; and a Temple of His holy Spirit; on beginning that Life in me, that shall never, never, never be extinguished!

After this, I carried my lovely Consort with me, into my Library; and there we together offered up our Praises unto God, for His Blessings; especially spiritual Blessings; and for His bestowing us upon each other, with surprising Dispensations of His Providence.

I concluded with Praises to the Lord for His good Angels; and all the unknown Good, which He had by their Ministry convey'd unto me.

My finishing Dispositions and Resolutions were; to grow more frequent in direct, express, explicit Acts of living unto God; with Reflections on the Reason of my doing what I do, and of my Relish in my Enjoyments.

To be more sollicitous about a real and vital Communion with God, in the Prayers which I make unto Him.

To be more Industrious in my Studies, that I may dispatch apace, what my Hand finds to do.

And visit the Flock with more Assiduity, and Edification.

8. G. D. Is there no Possibility, for me, to find the Time, that I may contrive a System of the Sciences wherein they shall be rescued from Vanity and Corruption, and become consecrated unto the glorious Intention of *living unto God*, and the real and only Wisdome?

If I see, that I cannot obtain the Liesure for it, I will address my Friends in the *Frederician* University.

9. G. D.   In conversing with a Society of Gentlemen, I would move it.   There is a Youth at School whose Parents are capable of bestowing on him the Education, whereof he is desirous and capable.   The Master of the School recommends him, as an agreeable Object for our Charity.

10. G. D.   A miserable Man under Distraction, must have Kindness done for him, and his Family.

Another destitute Family also.

*11. G. D.   Those interval Spaces of Time, about the well-filling whereof I have been sollicitous, I will endeavour now more than ever to fill with *Acts of Consecration to GOD*, formed upon the various *Actions* and *Enjoyments*, wherein I may be at the Time concerned.   How gloriously will this fill my Life with *Sacrifices!*   In what a *marvellous Light* will my Walk be carried on!   What *Influences* from Above will my Mind be revived continually!

12. G. D.   A number of Persons qualified for church Fellowship, who have hitherto delay'd it, must be call'd upon.

But, oh! how seriously am I to consider the great Flock, as consisting of a People, for whom I am to do my best, that they may live unto God, and be directed, and quickened and strengthened in the Life of God!   With what Sollicitude am I to beg of the glorious God from time to time, that He would lead me to insist on such Subjects among His People as may be most adapted unto the Intentions of Piety, and most suitable unto their Circumstances!   And when I have my Subjects under my Cultivation, how industriously must I prosecute them, as if I were immediately to give an Account of my Conduct therein unto God the Judge of all!

13. G. D.   Animate the Visits of my dear Consort unto the Poor of the Neighbourhood.

14. G. D. Further Engines of Piety, to be convey'd unto my Kinsman at *Windsor;*[1] for him to do Good with them.

15. G. D. Is there no Possibility for me, to gett the Prosecutions and Operations of Piety into the Schools; that the Education there, may not only have Piety intermixed with it, but become the principall Intention of it. This would I make a Point of much Consideration, and be restless till I see a good Progress made in the Design.

16. G. D. The expired Charity-School, in the Middle of the Town, I would gett revived.

17. G. D. Several poor affected Ones, I have in View, to be releeved.

And a poor Gentleman in the Prison for Debt.

*18. G. D. My Reading a Chapter in the *Verus Christianismus*, every morning, to my Consort as well as myself, before I rise, and then turning it into Prayer upon my Retirement into my Library, — of how much Advantage may it be, to the Interests of Piety, in my Heart and Life!

19. G. D. There are certain Strains and Flights of Devotion which being brought into the public Prayers, may have Impressions on the Flock, full of admirable Consequences. I have elsewhere some Hints of them.

(I) Oh! *What shall I render to the Lord?* For me to *glorify* my admirable SAVIOUR, and be an Instrument for inviting others to behold and confess His *Glory;* This is the very Top of my chosen Felicity. How strangely am I gratified in it! And yett, I hope, what now befalls me, is but the Beginning of the Gratifications wherewith I shall be favoured. I began to be suspicious, whether this Year, would prove to me such a bearing Year, as was the last. But I know not what may happen. I am already entred upon Fructifications that sweetly Comfort me. A Society

[1] Samuel Mather (1650–1728).

of young Men, in the more southern Part of this Town, sollicit for a Sermon from me. I give them one. And the Publication of it, is proposed. The Title of it is, THE RESORT OF PIETY: *our SAVIOUR considered and Exhibited, as a Tree of Life, which all may and must resort unto. And an Early Flight unto it particularly called for. An Essay offered unto a Society of Young Men, united in the Intentions of Early Piety.*[1]

20. G. D. My Servant has newly buried his Son; (*Onesimus* his *Onesimulus*). Lett me make this an Occasion of inculcating the Admonitions of Piety upon him.

21. G. D. A Kinsman, to be now putt upon joining to the Church.

22. G. D. What can I do more for the Church of God, than what I am to endeavour this Day?

In as affectionate a Representation, as I can make, of its Condition, in solemn Supplications before the Lord.

22 d. 1 m. Thursday. A general Fast, in the Province. I enjoy'd a gracious Presence of God with me, in the Services of the Day.

This prevented, my keeping a Day in secret this Week, as else I should have done.

23. G. D. I would sett forward good Motions among the Ministers; but there is one humoursome, furious, boisterous Man among us, who confounds all my Intentions that way. I am utterly dispirited for doing any Thing among the Ministers in our Vicinity, or indeed for going among them. Yett I desire to be armed with Patience; and watch Opportunities for Good. And what I cannot obtain among the Ministers nearer at hand, I would observe and enquire, whether it may not be obtained at a further Distance.

24. G. D. Several old Men, in wants, to be look'd after.

[1] Printed in 1716, without the name of the printer. The sermon was delivered March 18, 1716.

* 25. G. D. O what a marvellous Consideration is there, whereof I am to feel the Sense grow more and more powerful upon me, that my Endeavours to pray without ceasing may be animated!

All my Prayers made according to the Will of God; are the Dictates of the Holy Spirit. Tho' I forgett the Prayers which I have made, and I receive not immediate Answers, that infinite One perfectly remembers all His own Dictates. When I arrive to the heavenly World, where I shall reap the rich Harvest of all my Devotions here, the holy Spirit having all my Prayers in a most perfect Remembrance, will then heap in upon me the Answers of them with Blessings of Goodness, far beyond all that I can ask or think. Oh! Lett the strong Faith of this, produce in me a very praying Life, and give Life to my Prayers, and make my sowing Time to be very diligent and plentiful.

26. G. D. Cannot I possibly procure a Number of good Men, in our Church, to combine, as a little Society, for the Consideration of that Question, *What Service may be done for the Church?* I would propose this, first among the Deacons.

27. G. D. Oh! that my House may be more an *House* of my SAVIOUR'S *Glory!*

Shall it now be a Care more punctually prosecuted with me, that I will never sitt down at my Table, without pointing my Family, to some *Glory* of my SAVIOUR!

In my *Thanksgiving* at the Table, I would more particularly than ever, ascribe to my SAVIOUR, the *Glory* of purchasing and bestowing the Comforts of the *Table.*

28. G. D. Make a profitable Visit, among my Relatives at *Charlstown.*

Assist my Father, in writing a Book for old Men.

29. G. D. Can there be no Projection; that the Ministers meeting at the Election, may spend their Time together, to better Purpose than heretofore?

30. G. D. Procure the dead Charity-Schole in the Middle of this Town, to be revived.

31. G. D. An aged Handmaid of the Lord, in Poverty, to be provided for.

April. * 1. G. D. Among my Essayes to glorify my SAVIOUR, this may be one. I will consider the Gods of the ancient Pagans; the several Glories, which the poor Idolaters did ascribe to them, and the several Favours they did expect from them. Then my Soul shall make my Boast in my SAVIOUR. In Him, I will see all of these; all united in Him.

2. G. D. I have Proposals to make, for the better Accommodation of our Meeting-house.

3. G. D. My Children shall do more than they have done, to comfort their aged Grandfather; and therefore visit him.

4. G. D. I find Relatives at *Hadly,* which I did not think of. I would convey to them, some Expressions of my Care of their best Welfare.

5. G. D. *Barmudas* cries to me, to provide a good Minister for them. A Service of good Consequence. Help me, my God, in prosecuting this Care!

6. G. D. Being furnished with Proposals of Good, for the Comissioners of the *Indian*-Affairs to proceed upon; lett me animate their Proceedings all that is possible.

7. G. D. I will take a poor fatherless Child, to lodge and feed in my Family; and watch Opportunities to do him further Kindnesses.

A strange Thing befalls me. A Monster of a Man, and one of the Wickedest of Men, and one who went away to *London* many Months ago, full of Malice against me, and against the Countrey, and one from whom I expected the Publication of bitter Libels against me, and one whom I have often carried unto the Lord, with Desires of divine Restraints upon him; addresses me with Letters full of

Respect; bewayling his former Disaffection; protesting that he has not spoken one diminutive Word of me since his going away; and entreating my favourable Opinion of him; and assuring me, that I shall suffer no Incivility from him. At the same Time, he sends me over, an Instrument that he has published for the Service of the Countrey.

Doubtless, God has brought him to feel some Occasion for his being on good Terms with me. There is in this Thing, *the Finger of God*.

* 8. G. D. I fear, I suffer by two Distempers. First, I may be too quick and hard, in my Resentments of Things, that look like Judgments cast upon me. Secondly, I may too easily give way to Discouragements, and make my Recess from Opportunities to do good, upon Apprehensions of People's Aversion for me. O my SAVIOUR, Deliver me from these Distempers.

9. G. D. I have several Subjects, in View, the Cultivation and Inculcation whereof, may be of great Use to the Flock.

10. G. D. My Son *Samuel*, is taken ill of a Feavour. An Occasion for me to endeavour much Good, unto him, unto myself, and unto all the Family.

11. G. D. A Kinswoman that is near her Travail, should have my Counsels and Comforts.

12. G. D. As soon as I can, I would prepare certain Proposals, about the Methods of a religious Education, in Schools, and Universities; the Methods to be used, that the young ones may be taught and brought to live unto God.

The Publication and Inculcation of these Proposals, I would then labour in.

Vast, vast may be the Consequences.

13. G. D. I would move it among the Comissioners of the Indian-affairs, who have a strange Dullness upon all their Managements, that they would appoint two or three

of their Numbers, persons of a singular Activity and Capacity, to receive Proposals, for the good proceeding of our Affairs, and to prepare and offer what they think proper for the Board, and have their Times of consulting with one another upon that Intention.

14. G. D. A miserable Woman, that wants to be releeved on many Accounts, and also to have Passage to *London* paid for I must be at Expenses for her.

* 15. G. D. That I may yett more distinctly walk in the Light, I would make a Catalogue of my chief Enjoyments, and I would upon each of them, see how they are to be Enjoy'd in GOD, and for GOD, and with an holy Reference to GOD. And I would make it my care, to place my Delight in them upon those considerations.

16. G. D. The Children of the Flock, I would Endeavour more exquisitely than ever, in my Catechising to teach them the Skill of Living to God. In the next Catechising preach to them, on the dead Child raised by the Prophet.

17. G. D. My religious and excellent Consort meets with some Exercises, which oblige me, (and, oh! how happy am I, in the Conversion of so fine a Soul, and one so capable of rising and soaring to the higher Flights of Piety!) to treat her very much on the Point of having a Soul, wherein GOD alone shall be enthroned, and all the Creature that have usurped His Throne ejected and banished, and having a Will utterly annihilated before the Will of God!

18. G. D. A Sister in Law, in hourly Expectation of her Travail, should be visited and addressed with suitable Admonitions.

19. G. D. Quære, Whether the *marvellous Footsteps of the divine Providence*, in what has been done, in the *Lower Saxony*, have not such a Voice to the World, that I may do well to think of some further Methods to render it more sensible unto these American Colonies.

The Voice is mainly that; Matth. VI. 33.

20. G. D. A Society of pious and praying Youths, at the Colledge, I will study which way I may be useful to.

21. G. D. A poor distracted Youth in my Neighbourhood must be look'd after.

21 *d. 2 m. Satureday.* I sett apart this Day, for the Sacrifices of a Fast in Secret before the Lord. And the holy One helped me to offer up a Variety of *Sacrifices.* Yea, with His Help, I singled out my most valuable Enjoyments, and the Things which my Heart is most of all sett upon, and I turned them into *Sacrifices:* I consented, unto the *Will* of my dear SAVIOUR, if He will have those Things to be denied unto me.

My Errands unto Heaven this Day, were much the same, with what I had on my former Dayes of later Times.

But I have one special and bitter Concern, to carry not only on this Day, but every Day unto the Lord. I have advice, that my poor Son *Increase* lies very sick of a *Rheumatism,* at his Uncle's in *Witney,* having lost the Use of his Limbs. Oh! The Anguish with which I am to cry unto God, that He would yett be gracious to this poor Child, and make him a new Creature and an useful Man, and return him to me! Oh! the Resignation to which I am called on this Occasion! My Father, I committ this poor Child into thy Fatherly Hands!

* 22. G. D. I would now more than ever, employ the Minutes I can recover for such an Exercise, in forming the Acts of a *Sacrificer,* upon all my dearest and most valuable Enjoyments; and snatch at all opportunities for *Sacrificing,* with a Soul full of unspeakable Satisfaction.

God will wondrously dwell with me, and in me, while this is my way of Living.

23. G. D. In conversing with the People of the Flock lett me find out what Subjects they most want and wish to hear publickly insisted on.

24. G. D.   My Prayers for my poor Son *Increase*, and my Letters to him, on the Occasion of the sorrowful Advice I have received concerning him!

25. G. D.   New Applications must be made unto my Kinsman, T. W[alter] that he may now in good earnest come into the Life of God.

26. G. D.   I forsee an Opportunity for me to do some notable Services, in my Correspondences with the Danish Missionaries at *Malabar*.

27. G. D.   I will make a Present, unto our poor Colledge, of certain Books, that are of great Improvement and Influence in the famous *Frederician* University, and of a Tendency to correct the present wretched Methods of Education there; As the works of, *Arndt*, and *Franckius*, and *Langius*, and *Boehm*.

28. G. D.   An aged Handmaid of the Lord, in Want, must have Kindnesses bestowed on her and procured for her.

A poor Woman of *Malden* also in dark Circumstances.

*29. G. D.   The more perfect Work of Christianity will very much appear in that Strength of Piety, which carries us well thro' our Duties towards our Neighbours. I would therefore spend some Time, in considering, what are those Points of Piety, wherein my good Carriage towards my Neighbours, will argue a great and high Improvement in the Love of God, and Conformity to my SAVIOUR! And be restless until I come unto them.

30. G. D.   The Manner of managing the Collections in the Flock, should come under some further Considerations.

May. 1. G. D.   For my Table-talk in my Family, I would oblige my Kinsman in the Morning to read a Portion in the *Verus Christianismus* of my *Arndt*, and at the Table, I would call for, some Repetition of it, and make it one of the Subjects, which I would inculcate on my Domesticks.

2. G. D.   An aged Relative at *Fairfield*, should be considered by me, with Presents of suitable Books unto her.

3. G. D. I have had many Thoughts, about writing a Book, of, The *Christian Asceticks*. My Experience therein has been of so great Variety, that I may do well to consider what Account should be given of the Talents.

4. G. D. I would among the Trustees of the *Hopkinsian* Charity, procure a Letter of Thanks to be written unto the Lord-Chancellor whose Prudence and Justice procured our Enjoyment of it.

5. G. D. There is a Lad, who is an Orphan; an hopeful Child; I would become sollicitous for his Education. Yea, I will take him, and feed him, and lodge him in my own Family.

6. G. D. A wondrous Thing is come to pass; My Consorts only Daughter, has had an Husband, who has proved one of the worst of Men; a sorry, sordid, froward and exceedingly wicked Fellow.[1] His Life would have kill'd the Child; and have utterly confounded, not only her temporal Interest, but my Wife's also. I was a Witness of their Anguish. And almost a year ago, I began to have some Irradiations on my Mind, which I communicated unto them, that before a Year came about, they should see a Deliverance. However, I could not bring about my Purposes, to beseech the Lord thrice, until towards the Beginning of the Winter. But then, I kept *three dayes of Prayer*, in every one of which, a principal Errand unto Heaven was, to putt over this wicked Creature into the Hands of the holy God, that in His Way, and in His Time, the poor Child might be delivered from his insupportable Tyrannies; but above all, that it might be by his becoming a new Creature, if that might be obtained. The Supplications were made on these, and on other Dayes, with a proper Spirit of Charity towards the miserable Man, and with all possible Resignation to the Will of GOD. And my excellent Consort often went up with me to my Library, to make a Consort in them.

[1] Nathan Howell, son of Matthew Howell, of Southampton, Long Island.

Well; I had no sooner kept my *third Day* but God smote the Wretch, with a languishing Sickness, which no body ever knew what to make of. He was a strong, lively, hearty young Man; a little above thirty; But now, he languished for *six Months;* nor were any of our Physicians, tho' he successively employ'd no less than five of them, able to help him. In this while, our Faith, our Love, our Patience, and our Submission to the Will of God, underwent many Trials more precious than Gold. But on the last *Wednesday* the glorious GOD putt a Period unto the *grievous Wayes* of this wicked Man.

Now, what remains, is for me to make a very holy Improvement of these Dispensations. In what an holy, humble, trembling Manner, am I now to walk before the Lord! How much must I watch over my own Heart, lest any undue Frame should come upon it! How much must a praying Life be more than ever encouraged and animated with me!

O my God, I will call upon thee, as long as I live!

7. G. D. Some Things of Importance for good Order in the Church, must be settled; I will speedily appoint a Meeting of the Church for that purpose; and look up to God for His Direction.

8. G. D. My dear Daughter *Katharine*, is ill, and in much hazard of going into a Consumption. I must have her Condition seasonably look'd after. Much Prayer must be employ'd for her. Her Mind must be comforted.

9. G. D. I find a Relative at *Medford*, which I had forgotten. I must give some Testimony of my Care to serve the Cause of Piety in her.

10. G. D. What Service may I do the Countrey, by my Letters to eminent Persons at home?

11. G. D. I will gett certain Books, which I think may be of great Use for the Interests of Piety and Orthodoxy in the Colledge, into the Hands of the Students there.

12. G. D. A young Man, who is in the Care of the School at *Sudbury*, addresses me, as an object of Charity, in singular Circumstances.

A poor Negro in the Prison, condemned to dy for Burglary.

* 13. G. D. My Morning-Prayers, are not so managed as to carry me into a sufficient Communion with GOD. I must think of some Way to bring more Fire from Heaven into the Sacrifices of the morning. But I am nothing; and must entirely resign myself up to the Conduct and Quick'ning of God.

14. G. D. I have an Opportunity this Day, at a Meeting of our Church, to propose and utter many Things, which have a Tendency to serve the Intentions of Truth, and Peace, and Holiness, in the Flock.[1]

15. G. D. I have my Dayes of prayer. Why should I not allow such of my Children successively, a singular Share in the Supplications of the Day? But then, on the Day, take that Child which is more peculiarly concerned in the Supplications and have the Presence of that Child with me in part of the Day; to be a Witness of my Desires for them, and to hear the Counsils and Warnings I may on this Occasion give unto them!

16. G. D. A remote Kinsman, who is a Scholar at the Colledge, must have some Cultivations from me, upon the Intentions of Piety and Usefulness.

17. G. D. I propose now speedily to resume, the Cul-

---

[1] "14 *d.* 3 *m. Monday.* The Church by their Vote requested the Committee, which were chosen the last Year, to continue their Care of the Affaires committed unto them, for another Year.

"*Nathaniel Gill,* having brought a Scandal on our communion, by being disguised with Drink, which had been by some ill Men imposed upon him, and by an idle sort of Life, which exposed him to many Temptations: but his Impertinencies at the same time appearing such as to argue a Degree of Distraction in him, the Church voted, that he should be suspended from the Communion until he should be found so regular in Mind and in Life, as to be again thought qualified for it." *Cotton Mather's MS. Records of the Second Church,* II.

tivation of my, *Ratio Disciplinæ*, for the Service of our languishing Churches.

18. G. D. To the Grammar-Schole in my Neighbourhood, I would send a Version of the Ten Commandments, in Latin Verse, to be recited by the Scholars.

19. G. D. A very poor Family upon *Fort-hill*, must be look'd after.

Satureday. This Day I sett apart for prayer with Fasting, on such Occasions, and with such Exercises, as my former Dayes.

But especially, To committ the Case of my poor Son *Increase*, unto the fatherly Care of God.

And obtain a Return of Health to my Daughter *Katharin*.

And a Direction in some weighty Affairs before me.

* 20. G. D. It is a marvellous Point of Piety, for me in my Dealing with my Neighbour, to exhibit a Resemblance of the Benignity express'd by the glorious GOD, in His Dealing with me.

I would pursue the Contemplation of this Point, until I have understood it and obtained it.

21. G. D. Visit, visit, visit, — more frequently, more fruitfully. Redeem Thursday's Afternoons, for my own Part of the Town.

22. G. D. This Day my Son *Increase* returns to me; much polished, much improved, better than ever disposed; with Articles of less Expense to me than I expected; and, which is wonderful, with an excellent Business prepared for him immediately to fall into. I am astonished at the Favours of the prayer-hearing Lord. O my Father, my Father, how good a thing it is to trust in thy fatherly Care!

But, oh! what shall I now do, to fix the returned Child for the Service of God!

23. G. D. A sick Brother-in-Law should be visited with my seasonable Admonitions unto him.

24. G. D. I am not without Hopes, of getting a Congregation of Dissenters revived at *New York*. Prosecute the Design.

25. G. D. I entertain Thoughts, of beginning a *Society*, in the Methods, and on the Designs, of my, *Work of the Day*.

26. G. D. A sober young Man, out of Employ, I would bring into some Employ, about an Estate I am related to.

* 27. G. D. In the last Week, thro' the Spite of one particular Man,[1] I had the Indignity putt upon me, of being putt by from a public Service, which People generally expected from me. On this, and the like Occasions, I would glorify my SAVIOUR, with a sweet Acquiescence in His Wisdome and Justice, and His having all my Opportunities of Service, at His Disposal. And with Rejoicing in every Stroke of my Conformity to Him, who was despised and rejected of Men; and with a Pleasure, as well as Patience, in seeing my Brethren preferr'd before me.

I shall find, that the Lord is only preparing me for His Favours.

28. G. D. Those of our Church, that are gone off to the New for Seats, ought not to continue undismissed unto it; that they may have a regular Station and Attendence there.

29. G. D. A Week of many Play-dayes. I will have *Sammy* turn into Latin some Sentences I prepare for him, about the true and right Intent of Play, and a good Use of it.

30. G. D. Something more must be done, to rescue my Kinsman T. W[alter] from fatal Entanglements.

Present a Memorial to the General Assembly, on the behalf of my aged Parent.[2]

31. G. D. A Variety of Services to be done.

Tis the anniversary Convention of the Ministers. They putt upon me, the Honour of being their *Moderator*. In

---

[1] Governor Dudley?   [2] See p. 407, *infra*.

II · 23

my repeted Prayers with them, I have an Opportunity to utter impressive Things. I carry thro' the Affair of an Address to the King, which may be of use to our united Brethren, as well as ourselves. I propose a Motion in the Assembly, that no Family in the Countrey be without a Bible and a Catechism; and that all Children of a fitt Age, be found able to read; and that there be Inspectors for this Purpose.

June. 1. G. D. A miserable Negro, is to be executed this day, for Burglary. Instruct him, how to do good, as well as find good, in his Death.

2. G. D. A poor Man in Prison for Debt; I must be concerned for him.

A poor woman of *Lyn*, under Confusions.

* 3. G. D. The jejune Performances with which I find the People of God sometimes entertained by some of our Ministers, afford me an Opportunity to labour for some suitable Dispositions.

I must beware of despising my Brethren. I must value the least Savour of Piety in them, when I perceive the Absence of other Excellencies. I must consider myself as more worthy to be despised than they, on Accounts unknown unto the World. I must apprehend all Men, and myself, to be no other than what the sovereign God of all Grace does please to make us.

All Expressions and Sentiments of a most profound Humility are proper on these Occasions.

4. G. D. Oh! that more of *Religion in Earnest*, were to be found in the Flock! what shall I do to produce it?
   Publickly. Privately.

5. G. D. Oh! my dear Daughter *Katharine;* what shall I do for thee!

Cresy must be so fixed in the Business of the Store-house, as anon to be taken into a Partnership, with his intended Brother-in-Law.

6. G. D. An hopeful young Gentleman, a Merchant, proposes to marry my *Nibby*. His Acquaintance with my Family has already been a marvellous Advantage to him, and brought him into a Business, which is likely to prove superiour unto what any young Man in the Countrey pretends unto. But I must now endeavour that it may be to his Advantage, in regard of his better Part. This must be, by the continual Admonitions and Inculcations of Piety. Thus I already begin to reckon him among the Relatives that are the Objects of my Cares.

7. G. D. I am to gett ready a Memorial for the General Assembly, relating to Piety in Families.

8. G. D. Among the Commisioners for the Indian-Affairs, there are several Things to be prosecuted.

Especially, a translated, *Monitor for Communicants*.

9. G. D. A miserable poor Family in my Neighbour-hood, calls for some Releefs.

10. G. D. It will be a proper Vigilance in me, to make ready for some *Events* and *Changes*, which may suddenly come upon me; and gett an *Heart established* and fortified for an Encounter with them.

11. G. D. For this Purpose, I prepare a Discourse, to be also tendred unto the Flock, whereof I am the Servant.

12. G. D. My two elder Daughters, are sick; the Fever and Ague takes the second, convey'd perhaps from the first, who has them for one of her Symptomes. God calls me to consider, what may be His Voice to my Family, in this Dispensation, and bring my Family to a Compliance with it.

13. G. D. A Sister-in-Law, in *London*, is poor, low, miserable.[1] My Letters and Bounties, must be sent unto her.

14. G. D. My Letters for *Europe*, give me fresh Oppor-tunities, for extensive Services to the Kingdome of God.

[1] Mrs. Henry Wyrley.

15. G. D. A Memorial of great Consequence for the Christianized Indians, must be laid before the General Assembly.

16. G. D. Occasions for Charity to the Poor, multiply upon me.

16 *d.* 4 *m.* [*June.*] *Satureday.* I sett apart this Day, for Prayer with Fasting, as I use to do. Alas, that I may say with Grief and Shame for the mean Performance, *as I use to do.* The sick State of my two elder Daughters, was a special Article of my Supplications. I hope, I have obtained Mercy for them.

* 17. G. D. Stepping into my Library every Morning, for a Version of the Psalms into blank Verse, I would make this Exercise, exceedingly subservient unto my Devotion. And particularly fetch Lessons and Wishes out of every Verse as I go along.

This may not only have a Tendency to purify my Mind, but also, to prepare the Work for Use among the People of God.

18. G. D. The Death of some young Persons, must be pungently improved, on the survivors in the Flock.

19. G. D. My Son *Increase*, must be supplied with proper Books, to employ him in the Intervals of Business at the Store-house, and furnish his Mind with valuable Treasures.

20. G. D. My Parent just finishing seventy seven, I must now more than ever treat him, as one taking Wing immediately for the heavenly World.

21. G. D. The General Assembly now sitting, I would improve the Opportunity, to deliver in their Hearing, a Discourse about the due Improvement of Advantages for good; And especially insist on two Articles; the Advantages which our People in general have, to be the best People in the World; and, the Advantages that men in public Stations have to be public Blessings.

22. G. D.   Several Things to be prosecuted among the Commissioners for the Indian Affairs.

Especially, care for *Punkapoag.*

23. G. D.   Bestow a Bible on a poor Family.

A poor tempted Man in my Neighbourhood must be look'd after.

* 24. G. D.   The astonishing Mercies of God unto me, in a Constellation of happy Circumstances, oblige me, not only to maintain a very heavenly Frame of Mind, ready and willing to take Wing for the heavenly World at the first Call of God, and prepared also for afflictive Changes in my Pilgrimage thro' this World; but also to study mightily; how I may improve these Days of my prosperity, in a very uncommon Industry and Fruitfulness.

I have not so many Opportunities to do good, by the way of the Press this Year, as I have had in some former Years. I must look up to the glorious Lord, who has all my Opportunities at His Disposal, that He would not permitt any abatement of them.

25. G. D.   Draw up a more complete Catalogue of *Enquiries* to be made, and of *Directions* to be given, and of *Articles* to be insisted on, where I make my pastoral Visits in the Flock.

26. G. D.   I must think of some exquisite and obliging Wayes, to abate *Sammy's* inordinate Love of Play. His play, wounds his Faculties. I must engage him in some nobler Entertainments.

27. G. D.   Another Visit, unto an aged Father-in-Law. Treat him, as if never to see him any more.

28. G. D.   There are some very unwise Things done, about which I must watch for Opportunities, to bear public Testimonies.

One is, the Employing of so much Time upon *Ethicks*, in our Colledges. A vile Peece of Paganism.

Another is, the commending of Ch[urch] of E[ngland]

Authors, without proper Cautions and Antidotes against the corrupt Things, which come with what may be valuable in them.

29. G. D. Make more significant Visits to the Charity-School.

30. G. D. A poor young Man, labouring under a Fistula, with Poverty; something must be done for his Releef.

July. *1. G. D. That so my care of holy and useful *Meditation*, may be invigorated, I would have alwayes ready, a sett of Subjects; and, in the Intervals of Business, especially as I walk the Streets I would have Recourse to one or other of the Subjects, and so prosecute it in my Thoughts that I may be able on the first Opportunity to write down the Heads of them.

A perpetual Treasure this may produce, for my public Performances.

2. G. D. Several special Cases of Calamity in the Flock, I am to consider with suitable Applications; especially in the public Supplications.

3. G. D. My Son *Samuel*, I entertain yett fresher and riper Thoughts, for an exquisite Improvement in his Education.

4. G. D. My Consort, has two Sisters in *England* that are in great Affliction, and one of them in very singularly afflictive Circumstances. I must be concerned very much to comfort both of them, and support one of them.[1]

5. G. D. I take Notice of several very considerable Devices of Satan, operating to do very much hurt among the people of the Countrey. Will the Lord enable me to take a nice and a wise Observation of them, and then bear my Testimonies!

6. G. D. Move diverse Things to the Indian Commissioners.

[1] Anne Wyrley was one, and the name of the second was Mrs. Peacock or Mrs. Bishop. Sewall, *Diary* I. 149.

Especially; the Education of some Indian Youths, for the Ministry, in a better Way, than has been yett practised.

And furnishing the Catechisers with Bread, to be distributed unto their Catechumens.

7. G. D. Some Families in my Neighbourhood, that have distracted people in them, call for my singular Compassions.

* 8. G. D. Methinks, Opportunities and Inventions to turn my Enjoyments into Sacrifices, grow more and more acceptable to me. Oh! Lett me be very much dissatisfied with myself, until I find an incomparable Pleasure in the Exercises of a sacrificing Soul.

I find a Progress, (but I must make a much further yett,) in the Experience of growing dead unto the World; and I more feel the Meaning of being alive unto God. I will study upon the Subject.[1]

9. G. D. The Humours of many in the Flock, who easily withdraw from the Assembly, afford unto me, such an Exercise for a patient Sacrificer, as may have happy Consequences.

10. G. D. I have been guilty of an Oversight, in my not making the *Birth-dayes* of my several Children, at the Arrival thereof, a more useful Occasion, of inculcating the most lively and pungent Admonitions upon them. Tho' I have said something to them, on these Dayes; yett not enough.

11. G. D. I don't know what to do, about my Kinsman, T. W[alter]. My Expectations from him, seem to suffer a grievous Disappointment. I will once more admonish him; and if no Impressions be made, I will then cast him off.

12. G. D. It is a Time of wonderful Disturbance be-

---

[1] "8 *d.* 5 *m.* Dismissed Mr. John Barnard to the Church at Marblehead, in order to his Ordinance for the pastoral Charge of that Church." *Cotton Mather's MS. Records of the Second Church*, II.

yond-Sea. May not I take this Time to do very extensive Services.

I am thinking to write as exquisite Letters as I can, to some of the most eminent Members of Parliament; and inclose my, *Lapis Excisus* in them, and, — [1]

13. G. D. Something more must be done, for another Charity-school, in the Heart of this Town.

I will fix upon the Town, the Name of, *a City*. And therewith, animate the Inhabitants, to consider more for the Good of it.

14. G. D. Some in Affliction, to be visited and comforted.

14 *d.* 5 *m.* [*July.*] *Satureday.* This Day, I sett apart for Supplications, *as I use to do.*

My Occasions, and Exercises, were much the same, as a Month ago.

Especially, the sick, and low State of my dear *Katy.*

A Journey to *Marble-head* the next Week, where and when the Services of an Ordination will be expected from me : I particularly entreated for the Divine Presence with me in what is before me.

* 15. G. D. Except it be in the Sickness of my two elder Daughters, I enjoy upon all Accounts, a most wonderful Prosperity. A most wonderful Prosperity! A valuable Consort! A comfortable Dwelling! A kind Neighbourhood! My Son *Increase*, vastly to my Mind, and Blessings without Number. Together with my own Health and Strength, strangely recruited.

I must be very sollicitous to hear what the Holy One speaks to me in my Prosperity; and sett apart some Time to think on the more special Improvement I should make thereof!

16. G. D. Some foolish and froward people in the Flock fall out, about their Seats; I must use the Methods

1 Unfinished sentence.

of Prudence and Piety, to manage such Roots of Bitter-ness.

17. G. D.   Some Occasions arise, of a more than ordi-nary Concern, relating to the Education of my Son *Samuel*.

And in releeving of him, I may provide for the Releef of other Children.

But, oh! what a Work am I putt upon! The Sacri-ficing of my Daughter *Katharin*.

This Day, I travelled, with manifold Smiles of Heaven on my Journey, unto *Salem*.

18. G. D.   A great Variety of Services may be done by me this Day, for the Churches in the Neighbourhood.

This Day, I went over to *Marblehead;* and with extraor-dinary Assistences of Heaven to me, in the Variety of Ser-vices, wherein I was concerned, I ordained Mr. *John Barnard*, a Pastor to the Church there.[1]

In the Evening I returned unto *Salem*.

19. G. D.   In my Return home, I visit and comfort an aged Mother-in-Law at *Medford*.

This Day I returned home; having seen wonderful Smiles of Heaven on my Journey.

20. G. D.   I would concert, with two Gentlemen, for a better Proceedure of all Things among the Indian Com-missioners.

21. G. D.   A pious Woman in my Neighbourhood, under great Affliction, must be comforted all the Wayes I can think of.

(II.) Having lately delivered unto some young Men associated for the Purposes of Religion, a Discourse upon the Resolutions of Piety, I gave them the Copy of it, which they are publishing. Tis entituled; PIETY DEMANDED. *A very plain and brief Essay, to demand Piety from all People;*

---

[1] He had entered upon his duties as assistant pastor of the First Church in Marblehead, in the previous November. In April, the Second Church was organized with Rev. Edward Holyoke at its head. This division resulted from a difference between the two men as the successor of Dr. Cheever.

more especially from young People; And to direct the Answers that are to be returned unto the Demands. Offered unto a Society of young People associated for the Intentions of early Piety; In the City of Boston. 8 d. V m. 1716.

* 22. G. D. My Thoughts about a Return to God. See the Sermon I preach on 1. Cor. IX. 26.

23. G. D. I have some very agreeable Subjects in View, for the Flock to be entertain'd withal.

24. G. D. I will have my Son *Samuel*, out of School-time, to turn into Latin, the Questions and Answers, in my Book of, *Supplies from the Tower of David.* Proposing a manifold Service unto the Child; Yea, and anon unto many others; in this Exercise.

25. G. D. My Relatives now going to Sea, What shall I do, to prepare them for their Voyage?

25 *d.* 5 *m. Wednesday.* The languishing State of my Daughter *Katharin*, brings me into the Dust before the Lord.

I sett apart this Day, for Prayer with Fasting, to carry the Condition of the Child unto God her Saviour. I took all the Methods of the most successful Petitioner, and managed the Cause in such Wayes, and with such Frames, as are most likely to be followed with Answers of Peace.

And, now, I am waiting for thy Salvation, O Lord.

I took the Opportunity, to prosecute other Matters of Supplication.

26. G. D. If my *Supplies from the Tower of David,* should be turned into the Latin Tongue, accompanied with some other Things that may be joined with it, who can tell what an Engine it may prove, of Service to the Churches of God!

27. G. D. I am employing some Hands, to make agreeable Collections of such Things in the Countrey, as may give some Entertainment unto men of Ingenuity.

28. G. D. A very pious Woman in my Neighbourhood,

has a very froward and wicked Husband. What shall be
done for her?

* 29. G. D. I am afraid, lest the Multiplicity of my
Affaires, and my easy Circumstances, procure some Abatement of those Ejaculations towards Heaven, with an Eye
continually unto the Lord, which I am used unto. Oh!
it must not be so! It must not be so!

30. G. D. To single out a Number of special Cases,
wherein the Combates of Christianity, are most usually
called for, and in a Sermon briefly and plainly show the
Flock, how to manage their Combates in these Cases.

31. G. D. My Servant *Onesimus*, proves wicked, and
grows useless, Froward, Immorigerous. My Disposing of
him, and my Supplying of my Family with a better Servant
in his Room, requires much Caution, much Prayer, much
Humiliation before the Lord. Repenting of what may
have offended Him, in, the Case of my Servants, I would
wait on Him, for his Mercy.[1]

August. 1. G. D. Miserable T. W[alter], abandoned

---

[1] In the American Antiquarian Society is the following memorandum in the
writing of Cotton Mather:

"My servant *Onesimus*, having advanced a Summ, towards the purchase of
a Negro-Lad, who may serve many occasions of my Family in his Room, I do by
this Instrument, Release him so far from my Service and from the claims that
any under or after me might make unto him, that he may Enjoy and Employ his
whole Time for his own purposes, and as he pleases. But upon these conditions.
First, that he do every Evening visit my Family, and prepare and bring in, the
Fuel for the day following, so Long as the Incapacity of my present Servant,
shall oblige us to Judge it necessary: As also, in great snows, appear seasonably
with the help of the Shovel, as there shall be occasion.

"Secondly, that when the Family shall have any Domestic Business more
than the Daily affairs, he shall be ready, upon being told of it so far to Lend an
helping Hand, as will give no Large nor Long Interruption to the Business, of his
own, to which I have dismissed him; As particularly, to carry corn unto the mill,
and help in the fetching of water for the washing, if we happen to be destitute.
And in the piling of our wood, at the season of its coming in.

"Whereas also, the said *Onesimus* has gott the money which he has advanced
as above mention'd, from the Liberties he took, while in my Service, and for some
other Considerations, I do expect, that he do within six months pay me the sum
of Five Pounds, wherein he acknowledged himself Endebted unto me."

by the Wrath of God, unto unaccountable Stupidity! What shall be done for thee?

2. G. D. In the astonishing Things done at *Hall* in the Lower *Saxony;* under the Influences of my incomparable *Franckius,* our SAVIOUR has preached a loud and a living Sermon, on His own precious Text, *the Sixth of* MATTHEW *and the thirty third,* which doubtless He would have the whole World every where take notice of. I beleeve, I shall do a Thing pleasing to Him, and a sensible Service to the Kingdome of God, if I preach a Sermon on this famous Text, in the hearing of the General Assembly of the Province, and conclude it with a Relation of those marvellous Occurrences.

Oh! that my glorious Lord, would when this is done, by His gracious Providence, bring about the Publication of my Essay!

3. G. D. Excellent and extensive Services, may I putt my incomparable Friend *Boehm* upon, in my next Writing to him.

4. G. D. An aged Widow in Poverty, must receive Kindnesses.

*5. G. D. My Morning-Exercise of Translating the *Psalms,* must be a Devotionary and Sanctifying Exercise. I must accompany every Verse, with Prayers darted up unto the Heavens. Precious Effects will there be, of my thus conversing with God in this Exercise.

6. G. D. I would send for the *Negro's* of the Flock, which form a religious Society; and entertain them at my House, with suitable Admonitions of Piety.

7. G. D. The Methods of *seeking first the Kingdome of God,* in the Management and Government of my Family, ought more distinctly to be thought upon; and further Improvements must be made in them.

8. G. D. Has my poor Kinsman languishing for many years at *Windsor,* had my prayers enough concerned for him?

9. G. D. I will go on with my Proposals for the religious Education of Schools, and Colledges; and, if I can, bring n the other Ministers to favour them.

10. G. D. It shall be considered, whether the *Religious Societies* of young Men, may not have their Quarter-nights all together; and whether they may not on those Nights hold their Meetings in one or other of our public Meeting-houses; and, whether a Sermon preached on that Occasion by one of our Ministers, may not be a great Service to Piety among the Youth of the Town.

11. G. D. A gracious Woman in my Neighbourhood, almost kill'd with a froward Husband, and other abominable Relatives; her Case calls for much Commiseration with me.

11 *d.* 6 *m.* [*August.*] *Satureday.* This Day, I sett apart for secret Supplications, as I use to do, preparing for the Eucharist.

The Occasions, and the Exercises, were what have of late been usual.

But then, I went unto the Lord, with my humble Memorial, concerning the State of His Kingdome, the Approaches whereof are by His faithful Servants greatly look'd and longed for.

I represented, that there were Servants of His, industriously at work for His Kingdome in the World. Among these, I particularly mentioned those of the *Frederician* University, and those of the *Malabarian* Mission. But we can do very Little. Our Encumbrances are insuperable; our Difficulties are infinite. If He would please, to fulfil the ancient Prophecy, of *pouring out the Spirit on all Flesh*, and revive the extraordinary and supernatural Operations with which He planted His Religion in the primitive Times of Christianity, and order a Descent of His holy *Angels* to enter and possess His Ministers, and cause them to speak with the Tongues of Men under the Energy of *Angels*, and fly thro' the World with the *everlasting Gospel* to preach unto the Nations, wonderful Things would be done immediately; His Kingdome would make those Advances in a Day, which under our present and fruitless Labours, are scarce made in an Age. I pleaded, that His Word had given us Reason to hope for a Return of these Powers, and for the making bare the Arm of the Lord before the Nations; and He has promised His holy Spirit unto them that

ask Him. I pleaded, that His diligent Servants, having preferred
the *sanctifying Influences* of His holy Spirit, above any *miraculous
Powers*, and been humbly willing to undergo any Fatigues for the Service of His Kingdome, seem'd somewhat prepared for these Favours
of Heaven. And having made this Representation, that Orders may
be given by the glorious Lord, for a Descent of His mighty Angels,
to give wonderful Shakes unto the World, and so sieze upon the Ministers of His Kingdome, as to do Things which will give an irresistible
Efficacy unto their Ministry; I concluded with a strong Impression on my Mind; *They are coming! They are coming! They are
coming! They will quickly be upon us; and the World shall be shaken
wonderfully!*

* 12. G. D.   Temptations arise, relating to some little
Points of Church-order among us.   I must keep a mighty
Watch upon my own Spirit under these Temptations.   I
must be silent, patient, humble.   I must continually wait
upon the holy One for His Direction.

13. G. D.   My God, Shew me, shew me; what Subjects I shall next endeavour to suit and serve thy Flock
withal!

A Revival of Care, to spend the *Lord's-day Evening*,
religiously and advantageously.

14. G. D.   My Thoughts must be intensely bent, on
the Improvement in Piety, which ought to be the Effect of
the divine Dealings with my two Children, who have lately
been sick, and now are in a Way and Hope of Recovery.

This Day, a singular Thing befel me.   My God, Help
me to understand the Meaning of it!   I was prevailed withal,
to do a Thing, which I very rárely do; (not once in Years)
I rode abroad with some Gentlemen, and Gentlewomen, to
take the countrey Air, and to divert ourselves, at a famous
Fish-pond.[1]   In the Canoe, on the Pond, my Foot slipt,
and I fell overboard into the Pond.   Had the Vessel been
a little further from the Shore, I must have been drown'd.
But I soon recovered the Shore, and going speedily into a

---

[1] Spy Pond, Cambridge.

warm Bed, I received no sensible Harm. I returned well
in the Evening; sollicitious to make all the Reflections of
Piety, on my Disaster, and on my Deliverance. But not
yett able to penetrate into the whole Meaning of the Occurrence. Am I quickly to go under the Earth, as I have
been under the Water!

My Consort had her Mind, all the former part of the
day and all the day before, full of uneasy Impressions, on
her Mind, that this little Journey would have Mischief
attending of it.

15. G. D. I discover a new Relative, at *Rehoboth*.
What may I do for her?

16. G. D. What if I should in my Letters to the *East-
Indies*, propose and pursue the Thoughts which I had on
the *eleventh* day of this Month.

17. G. D. I would on the approaching Lord's-day,
speak some Things, to animate the *religious Societies* of
the *Lords-day Evening*.

18. G. D. A Family in much Distress, with Sickness
and Poverty, must be releeved and comforted.

* 19. G. D. A Drowsiness, upon the Activity of my
living to God, is growing upon me.

My Soul, Awake immediately!

20. G. D. I will try, whether my Discourse on the
Methods of spending the *Lord's-day Evening* religiously and
advantageously, may not be spred into the Families of my
Neighbourhood.

21. G. D. I will take more effectual Care, that the
first Work of my Children, in the Morning of every Day
next their Hearts, be to converse with God, and His Word.

22. G. D. I am in View of having shortly a Family
of new Relatives; I would begin betimes, my Essays to
do good unto them.

23. G. D. Considering the two great Principles asserted
in that *Protestation*, which was the Original to the Denom-

ination of *Protestant*, I am apprehensive, that the Defending, the Restoring, the Reviving of the *Protestant Religion*, is very much the Work of this Day. And the Bringing of those Principles into their Operation, will be a vast Service to the Church of God; have a mighty Tendency, to destroy the Kingdome of Antichrist, and advance the Kingdome of our Saviour.

I. That the Sacred Scriptures are the Rule, and a sufficient Rule, for Faith, and Worship, and Manners, to the People of God.

II. That there are plain Scriptures enough to explain the obscure ones, and every Christian has the Right of Explaining for himself.

I will think, how to propagate these Principles.

23 *d.* VI *m. Thursday.* A Day of general Thanksgiving, for the Victories over the Rebels.

I enjoy'd precious Assistences from above.

24. G. D. I may putt Judge *Sewal*, upon several Services.

25. G. D. A poor Creature under dreadful Temptations, calls for my Compassions and Assistences.

* 26. G. D. In my Methods of *Living to God*, I must endeavour still more explicitly, and with more clear, direct, proper Declarations for GOD, exactly to state the Aspect of my several *Actions*, and *Enjoyments*, upon Him. I will therefore distinctly consider the *Actions* and *Enjoyments;* and putt into Shape the Thoughts which I would shape upon them for the *Life of God*.

27. G. D. It has been my Custome, to do several Things, as my first Exercises in the Morning; — all of a Tendency to Piety, and Usefulness. But I am resolved now upon altering my Method. And my first Work every Morning, upon the Prayers that I make, in my Retirement, (whereto a passage of the Scripture, or some holy Subject, on which I will think, while I am rising, shall be a Nourish-

ment). It shall be to prepare something for my Sermons!
At which I will continue, until I am called unto my little
Breakfast; and our Family-Sacrifices. And the other usual
Things I will try to do, in some following Hours of the
Day. I am apprehensive, that the chief Work I have to
do is to preach the Gospel of my Saviour. And it calls
for my first Thoughts; the clearest, and brightest Exercises
of my intellectual Powers. And by thus ordering my
Studies, I may not only have my Sermons very seasonably
prepared and finished, but I may also gett ready before-
hand a Collection of Treasures for all Occasions. My Flock
may find the Benefit of my coming into such a Method for
my Studies.

28. G. D. A new Servant in my Family, must be putt
upon the Exercises of Piety.

29. G. D. An holy and an aged Servant of God, the
Minister of *Bridgwater*, who has not been in this City, since
above seven and twenty years ago, is come to sojourn with
me, till the latter End of the next Week.[1] And his principal
Intention is to enjoy the Consolations of my Family. I
must now allow much of my Time to this excellent Friend
while he staies with us. But I would redeem the Time, to
render him as useful as may be in the City before he goes.
And study to be as useful to him as ever I can.

30. G. D. I begin to discern Opportunities of preaching on some Subjects, the Sermons, which being transmitted
unto *London*, and published there, may greatly [be] accommodated unto the Work of the Day, and have uncommon
Influences.

31. G. D. I shall take particular Care, to have some
of the religious Societies, well supplied with proper Entertainments.

My Friend shall also on the next Lord's-day Evening,
preach at one of them.

[1] Rev. James Keith (-1719). Mather deals with him in the *Magnalia*.

II · 24

(III.) That I might serve the Cause of piety, and accommodate well-disposed People, with an Instrument for the pursuing of pious Intentions, on the Lord's-day Evenings, I gave to the Public, a little Treatise, entituled, A GOOD EVENING ACCOMMODATED WITH A GOOD EMPLOYMENT. *Or, some Directions, How the Lords-day Evening may be spent Religiously and Advantageously. With perswasives to spend it so.*

September. 1. G. D. I am now again furnished with a Number of Bibles, to be dispensed in a way of Charity among poor Families that want them. This opens for me a new Sett of Opportunities to do good among the Poor.

* 2. G. D. A very distinct Operation of Piety, for the *Return of the glorious GOD unto His Throne in my Soul,* which has been usurped by Idols; would be of excellent Consequence to me, in the Life of Christianity.

3. G. D. And the Cultivating of that Subject, the Exhibiting of Piety under that Notion, may be a precious Food for the Flock to feed upon.

4. G. D. Ah! My dying Daughter! My dear dying Daughter! What shall I do for thee, that thou mayst in thy Death glorify God!

5. G. D. My Sister at *Roxbury*, in several Regards, may need my Comforts and Counsils.

6. G. D. The Condition of Religion on the Island of *Nantuckett* calls for some speedy Essays, to retrieve it.

7. G. D. It is Time for me again to visit the Charity-school, and bestow Rewards on such as have learnt some good Things that I have assigned them.

8. G. D. Two Daughters of a worthy Minister, sometimes of *Middleburgh* in *Holland*, are now arrived here, in the Quality of Servants. They are Objects of much Compassion, and Charity. And I shall treat them accordingly.

8 *d.* 7 *m. Satureday.* This Day, I sett apart for secret Supplications, on the usual Occasions.

But One very singular and very distressing Matter of Supplications, was in the Condition of my dear *Katy*, who is in dying Circumstances. Oh! what a Sacrifice am I now call'd unto!

At the same Time, I have cause to rejoice exceedingly in this Favour of God, that the Child enjoyes an admirable Serenity, and gloriously triumphs over the Fear of Death!

In the Close of the Day, I went up to my Library, and prostrate in the Dust, after deep Humiliations, I saw God restored unto His Throne in my Soul.

I felt some Newes coming to me from the other Side of the Water, that will encourage me in the Service of God.

I learnt that in the State of dear *Katharin*, God will deal wonderfully.

I discerned, the Angels of the God, of whose Armies there is no Number, making a speedy Descent, for the producing of mighty Changes in the World.

*9. G. D. Go to the Table of the Lord, with earnest Petitions to thy SAVIOUR, for the Influences, that may render thee a Man very diligent in the Business, wherein thou standest before the eternal King.

10. G. D. Entertain the Flock, with a Discourse on the *Speech* of *Solomon*, that pleased the Lord. Win them into the making of it.

11. G. D. *Nibby* is near her Marriage. There are several Steps of Prudence and of Piety, of which I am to be sollicitious on this Occasion.

12. G. D. What shall I do, to render my Kinsman at *Newtown*, considerably useful?

Employ my Kinsman at *Roxbury* to make a Collection of *Plants*, peculiarly *American*.

13. G. D. There is extreme Hazard of a mighty Flame arising in the Town, from the Proceedings of the new Church in the south Part of it, unto the Choice of a Minister,

unacceptable unto the Rest.   I would seasonably interpose, as far as may be, to prevent the Devices of Satan.

14. G. D.   Several Affairs among the Christian Indians, call for Consideration.

Particularly at *Yarmouth*.

15. G. D.   Revive the Care of getting more Medicines into the Family, to be dispensed unto the Poor, for various Maladies.

* 16. G. D.   It must be more than ever my Endeavour, when I ask for any Blessing from God, which it may be my Duty to be content, in His Denying to me, then in the first and cheef Place, to ask a submissive Heart, that shall be Patient in case it be deny'd unto me, and therewithal to Express my Submission unto God, and my Satisfaction in His Wisdome, and Justice, and Sovereignty, and fatherly Love.

I would therefore look back upon those Favours of God, which I request in my daily Supplications, and employ particular Pains, to bring my Mind unto Resignations of them; and to take up with the glorious GOD, as a sufficient Portion for me, tho' all of these Things were witheld from me.

17. G. D.   Having lately exhibited real and vital Piety, under the Notion of *GOD in the Throne of the Soul*, or, *GOD reigning in the Heart*, I hope, it would much edify the Flock, to have another Exhibition of it, under the Notion of *an healed Soul*.

18. G. D.   Of my two elder Daughters,

The one, I am giving up to GOD, and preparing for the Finishing Stroke of the Sacrifice, which the Death of the dear Creature putts me upon.   My God, carry both me and her, thro what is before us.

The other, I am giving away to an hopeful young Gentleman, who is tomorrow to become her Husband.   But I am in several Wayes to give her up also unto God; and do the best I can to render her a Blessing to her Husband, and in the City.

19. G. D. Ah! Poor T. W[alter].

19 *d.* VII *m. Wednesday.* My *Nibby* was married (by my Father) to *Daniel Willard.* GOD be gracious to them!

20. G. D. Can I think of no Subjects to preach and write upon, which may be sent over to *Europe*, and contribute unto the Work of the Day?

Methinks, a Discourse on the true Notion of a *Protestant*, might be highly seasonable and serviceable.

21. G. D. Promise the Gift of a Bible, to such of the Children at the Charity-Schole as become able readily to read a Chapter in it.

22. G. D. A poor Woman in my Neighbourhood, a strange Instance of Prayer, and Faith, and Communion with GOD, and Heaven, must be a singular Object of my Cares that she may be well provided for.

* 23. G. D. The Angel of Death, stands with a drawn Sword over my Family, in the dying State of my dear, good, wise, and lovely *Katy.* I am called unto uncommon Exercises of Piety and Submission on this Occasion. Lett me sett apart some Time extraordinary, that I may obtain the Dispositions which are now called for.

24. G. D. The Psalmody in our Assembly must be better provided for.

25. G. D. My lovely Daughter *Katharin*, drawes now near unto her End. I must use all possible Methods, to render the Period of her Life, not only comfortable to her, but also profitable to the People of God.

26. G. D. Another Kinsman at *Roxbury*, must be warned against certain Miscarriages.

26 *d.* VII *m. Wednesday.* My dear *Katy* is utterly given over. Physicians can do no more for her; a Consumption does waste her, wherein the Assaults of a Fevor in the Shape of a quotidian Ague exasperates the Malady.

Her Life drawes nigh to the Grave. But her Soul is not full of Troubles.

I cannot but wondrously rejoice, in the Favours granted unto the Soul of the Child, which is from above so irradiated that she triumphs over the Fear of Death; Death is become easy, yea, pleasant unto her;

She rather chuses it, and has a Contempt for this World, and a most satisfying Vision of the heavenly World. It is very strange to me; the Child feels herself a dying; but has a strong and bright Perswasion of her own Recovery. I have none. I expect the speedy Approaches of Death upon her.

I sett apart this Day, for Prayer with Fasting, in secret, on the Behalf of the Dying Child.

And it was a Day of inexpressible Enjoyments unto me.

I obtained Pardon for all the Sins, that may have had a share in procuring my present Sorrows.

I resigned the Child unto the Lord; my Will was extinguished. I could say,

My Father, Kill my Child, if it be thy Pleasure to do so!

But yett I interceded, that if it might be so, the Cup of Death might pass from me.

27. G. D. I would look out for some Assistence, to encourage the Publication of a Work, which I am now sending to *London*, on *The Work of the Day*. Whereof I have great Expectation.

28. G. D. Several affairs of Consequence, to be moved among the Indian-Commissioners.

29. G. D. A young Man, a Schole-master at *Spring-field*, needs my various Assistences unto him, to render him further serviceable; which I purpose to give him.

* 30. G. D. I am to study yett more perfectly the Notion and Practice, of being *dead* unto all Things here below; The Meaning of a *Death* to all the Things of this Life. T'wil be of mighty Consequence unto me, to be well-acquainted with it.

October. 1. G. D. A Discourse on the *purged Floor*,[1] may be of as great use unto the Flock, as any Thing I can think upon.

2. G. D. Alas,[2] God sanctify to him, the Rebukes which I bestow upon him. I must humble myself before God, in that He has not accepted and favoured my Intentions.

I know not whether this unhappy Youth, may not at length go off to High-Church, and then make me the Object of his malicious Calumnies; For I have seldome obliged any one with uncommon Kindnesses, but they have afterwards proved Monsters of Ingratitude, and I have received singular Injuries from them. I do therefore here arm them that survive me with this true and brief Account.[3]

3. G. D. My new Relatives, will afford an ample Field for my projections to do good unto many.

4. G. D. Some young Students at the Colledge have lately died; Especially one, who was a notable Exemple of early Piety. I would consider, whether I may not make the Death of these young men, and the Life, of at least one of them, serviceable to the Interests of Piety; especially among the younger Students.

5. G. D. Our new Governour [4] arrives this Day. As I would improve my Acquaintance, which I am like to have with him, for all the good Purposes imaginable: So, because there arrives with him, a new Commission for our Indian-Affaires, which constitutes him one of the Comissioners,[5] I would prosecute some further good Purposes in that Relation.

6. G. D. A Gentlewoman in very disconsolate Circumstances, for the Death of an hopeful Son, may be a fitt Object, for my doing the part of a Comforter to the Mourners.

---

[1] Matt. 3. 12.
[2] Five lines obliterated at this point.
[3] Thirty-two lines struck out.
[4] Samuel Shute. Sewall, *Diary*, III. 105.   [5] See Sewall, *Diary*, III. 106.

6 d. 8 m. Satureday. This day I sett apart for Prayer with Fasting, in Secret before the Lord.

The Occasions and Exercises were the same, with those of the former Dayes, which in the later months I have so devoted.

I glorified the Lord this day, with the sweetest Acquiescence and Resignation, in the Case of the *Biblia Americana*, whereof I receive Advice this day, that the publication thereof, is to be despaired of.

I still kept sacrificing my languishing Child; not without Hopes, that the Lord may deal yet wonderfully with her.

I have some special services the next Week before me, for which I implored the divine Assistences.

I poured out my vehement Supplications, that *Joels* Prophecy might be accomplished; and the Spirit of God be poured out upon all Flesh; and the holy and mighty Angels, make their Descent, and possess and inspire Instruments to serve the Kingdome of God, and spread the Maxims of the everlasting Gospel in the World.

* 7. G. D.   I would every morning, before I rise, read certain Paragraphs, in the *Enchiridion precum*, of my *Boehm;* and have my Consort hear the same in English: until I have gone thro' the Book.

8. G. D.   Some in the Covenant of God among us, I hear by the Edges, have miscarried, and live not according to their Obligations. I must find them out, and in suitable Manner deal with them.

9. G. D.   In and to my Family, I would cause to be readd over, on some Lord's-day Evening, the last Accounts of God providing for the *Orphan-house*, at *Hall*. And make remarks upon the Story, that shall be incentive to Piety.

This Day was kept as a Day of Prayer, by the First Church in *Boston*, preparatory to their Choice of a Minister. I enjoy'd gracious Assistences from above, in preaching to the Congregation on this Occasion.

10. G. D.   Yett one Essay more to recover T. W[alter] whose Return into my Family, I have permitted.

11. G. D.   Being to preach this Day in the Audience

of our new Governour, and with much Expectation from
the Auditory, I contriv'd, a Recapitulation of *Tokens for
Good*, as the whole Protestant Interest, and our own Countrey has to Comfort us. And with as much Insinuation as
may be, I gave our Governour to understand what sort of
Conduct in him, we hoped for.

GOD was graciously with me, in the Action, and it
found much Acceptance, both with the Governor and the
People.

12. G. D. Is there nothing to be done for the miserable
Colledge? Yes; I will commend some Things unto the
Perusal of the more serious Youths associated for Piety
there.

13. G. D. An honest, godly, needy Man, lying alone,
Bed-rid with the Gout; I must look after him.

* 14. G. D. I have been endeavouring to glorify GOD,
with elaborate Preparations of my Pen, to serve the Cause
of Piety in the World. The Composures, which with the
Help of GOD, I have prepared for that Purpose, I have
offered up for Sacrifices unto Him. It pleases Him, to
reject them from the Service for which I have intended
them. Strange Frowns of Heaven have defeated the Publication of those things, which it has cost me a World of hard
Study, to gett ready for the Church of GOD. Now, what
shall I do on these Occasions? I would be entirely satisfied in the Wisdome, the Justice, the Faithfulness, and the
Sovereignty of my great SAVIOUR, who knowes what the
Interests of His Kingdome call for, and when to bring them
forth. And I would satisfy myself in my Oblations to the
Kingdome of my SAVIOUR, and consider my sweet Acquiescence in His holy Pleasure to reject them, as a sweet
Addition to my Oblations, and His Delight in them; and
give a Demonstration, that the acquiring of a Name to
myself (a Vile Idolatry!) is no End of my Oblations, in my
patient and easy Bearing of it, that they should be lost as

to this World, and known unto Him alone. And I would go on with all possible Industry to present as many Oblations to the Work of God, as I can; cheerfully leaving to Him the Disposal of them.

(IV.) That I may invite serious Minds, to glorify GOD, in the *Tokens for Good*, which He gives to His people, I gave to the Bookseller, my late Sermon, at the Lecture. It is entituled, MENACHEM. *A brief Essay, on Tokens for Good; wherein, together with the Good Signs which all Good Men have to Comfort them, there are Exhibited also some Good Things of a Late Occurrence, and of a great Importance, which have a comfortable Aspect, on the protestant Religion in general, and on a particular countrey of distinguished protestants.*[1]

15. G. D. A late and a strange Impression of Grace, on the Jewish Children, in the City of *Berlin;* may I not improve it, for an Excitation of Piety in my Flock, and among the young People of it.

16. G. D. To have the Footsteps of God, in what is done for the *Orphan-house* at *Hall*, read over in my Family, with agreeable Remarks thereupon, may be of great Use to my Domesticks.

17. G. D. My Relatives at Sea, ought more than ever, to make a distinct Article in my daily Supplications.

17 *d.* 8 *m. Wednesday.* One Day more, must I sett apart for Prayer with Fasting on the Behalf of my dear *Katy;* who continues in her Languishments, and yett unto our Astonishment, grows not feebler under them.

My Endeavours, and my Enjoyments, on this Occasion, were much the same, with what I had three Weeks ago, on the same Occasion.

Having thus *besought the Lord thrice*, besides what I have done, on my monthly Dayes, and every day, I now wait to hear what God the Lord will say.

[1] Printed for Benjamin Gray, 1716.

The Child shall be wondrously dealt withal!
The Lord will *shew Wonders to the Dead!*

18. G. D. May it not be a service unto the Kingdome of God, if I address our numerous Tribe of *Whale-Catchers,* with some suitable Meditations, that may have a Tendency to make them sensible of their Obligations to live unto God?

(V.) That I might serve this Intention of Piety, I send unto the press, a Treatise entituled; THE THANKFUL CHRISTIAN, *An Essay upon those Thankful Returns of obedience to the Glorious GOD, in which there Lies the most acceptable and ingenuous Thanksgiving for His Benefits. Address'd unto all that have received the Favours of Heaven; But more especially unto them, who after the Good Successes of a Whale-catching Season, would Express their Gratitude unto God their Saviour.*[1]

19. G. D. I would yett again see whether I cannot produce and support a *Charity-Schole,* for Negro's in Evenings, to learn to read, and be instructed in the Catechism.

20. G. D. A young man a Bookseller, poor and low, needs Encouragement.

* 21. G. D. That great point, of, *Doing as I would be done unto,* It must be more exactly conform'd unto. I will not only study it; but make it a most frequent Subject of Self-Reflection.

22. G. D. Who can tell, what Effects it may have upon the Flock, if two Sermons were preached on the Promise of the Holy SPIRIT! (Luk. XI. 13.) In preaching of them, I would use all possible methods of Devotion, to obtain the Influences of the holy SPIRIT, suitable unto the Occasion.

23. G. D. It may have a good Effect upon my Son *Samuel,* if I hear him sometimes read unto me, into English, the *Adspirationes,* in my *Boehm's, Enchiridion precum.*

24. G. D. Is there nothing further, possible to be

---

[1] Printed by B. Green, for Samuel Gerrish, 1717.

done, for the Recovery of a wretched Brother-in-Law, become so far a Castaway, as he at *Charl[e]stown!*

25. G. D. Our new Governour appears to have a singular Goodness of Temper, with a Disposition to do good, reigning in him; He also favours me with singular Testimonies of Regard. Oh! Lett me improve these unexpected Opportunities to do good, in such a Manner that God may have much Glory and His People much Service from it.

26. G. D. Speak to the new Lieut. Governour of *New Hampshire*, to do all he can, for the restoring of Peace among the People there.

27. G. D. A Gentleman that has a considerable Quantity of Grain, to dispense among the Poor, employes me to find the Objects, and send them with Notes of Recommendation to him.

*28. G. D. The secret and vitious Workings of *Self-Love*, I must labour exceedingly to grow more aware of them, and become thoroughly acquainted with that Mystery of Iniquity, and victorious over it.

29. G. D. And can I do a better Service for the Flock, than by finding out for them this their Enemy, and warning them of it!

30. G. D. *Liza's* Education, — several Points to be prosecuted in it.

31. G. D. Relatives at *Glocester*, must have some Expressions of my Care for them.

With very much Study and Prayer, I have been by the Grace of GOD, carried thro' a very large Preparation for the Public. I have considered the Condition of the World; and I have prepared a Book, wherein the greatest Affaires, that are like to be agitated among the Nations, are more than a little accommodated. I have considered what the service the Kingdome of GOD calls for, and I have prepared a Book, as much adapted unto the Intentions that most call to be prosecuted, as I can contrive it. I have considered, the *Signs of the Times.*

My Book is a large Treatise of many Sheets; Entituled;

(VI) BOANERGES. THE WORK OF THE DAY. *A Tender made (which has never till Now been so clearly and fully done) of those Evangelical and Everlasting MAXIMS, wherein All Good and Wise men are united, and All men become Good and wise, when they come into that Union with them. An IN-STRUMENT of PIETY tendered, wherein the vast purposes of Truth and Peace in the Church of GOD, are to the Satis-faction of Reasonable and Religious Minds accommodated. With Demands made thereupon, which the Distresses of the Nations, will compell them anon to hearken to. And Millions of People in the world, who are groaning, and will daily be more so, after* ANOTHER AND A BETTER STATE OF THINGS, *are furnished with PROPOSALS, to obtain the Accomplish-ment of their Desires. With Just REMARKS upon the present and Future State of the Distressed Nations.*

If this Work may come abroad, it will make some Little Reparation for my unfruitfulness, in the Number of Lesser Composures, which I have published in the Year that is now passing over me.[1]

I committ the Work unto the glorious Head of the Church; and entirely resign it unto Him, for Him to do according unto His own good Pleasure with it.

I was not willing to lett the year 1716 pass, without sending it over the *Atlantic.*

November. 1. G. D. I may do the Countrey consider-able service by some seasonable Hints unto the Governour. And by preventing what I can, the countermining Inten-tions of some Gentlemen among us.

2. G. D. Now bring forward, the Affair of Guardians, for the Christian Indians. Now is the Time.

---

[1] It does not appear to have been printed. Mather again used the leading word, Boanerges, in 1727, in the title of an essay on the earthquakes of that year.

3. G. D. A poor, feeble, gouty Man, in a solitary Widowhood, must be look'd after; that he do not suffer, in being alone.

3 *d.* IX *m. Satureday.* I sett apart this Day for Prayer and Fasting, on the usual Occasions, and with the usual Exercises.

The dying State of my dear *Katy,* was a special Article of my Supplications.

I presented the State of several sick Ministers in the Countrey, before the Lord.

I cried unto Heaven for Direction about my *Boanerges,* and resigned the Work unto the Glorious Head of the Church, for Him to do as He should please with it.

I offered up Sacrifices to God.

* 4. G. D. Of my Errands to the Table of the Lord this Day, a principal one must be, for the Destruction of that *Self-Love,* which has carried away my Soul from God.

5. G. D. Call upon the Flock, to express their zeal for the House of GOD, in more effectual Considerations, upon that Point, What Good they may do for the Church.

6. G. D. My Daughter-in-Law, and her children, shall be entertained in my House, until she marries; and I will endeavour, to serve her in all her Interests, and also to befriend the pious Education of the Children.

7. G. D. My Brother *Walter,* being indisposed, I will preach for him, and otherwise also study for his Comfort; especially in a Point, which I suppose grievously exercises him.

8. G. D. There is hazard of much Disorder and Confusion and Iniquity in our General Assembly; by reason of three unhappy Men, who are the Representatives of this Town.[1] I would procure a considerable Number of the

---

[1] The representatives from Boston, elected in this year, were Oliver Noyes, William Payne, Elisha Cooke, and Anthony Stoddard. Stoddard was a new member of the House of Representatives. Payne alone seems to have been of the Second Church. See p. 417, *infra.*

Representatives to visit me at my House; where I would endeavour their Illumination in the Things of our Peace. I would also endeavour to reduce our own Frowards from the Error of their Way.

9. G. D. Visit a Meeting in the Neighbourhood, whereof several have lately buried Relatives, and encountred Afflictions; and preach an agreeable Sermon unto them.

10. G. D. Our late Lieutenant Governour,[1] going to *London*, desires me to do him some Kindnesses.

* 11. G. D. More distinct and affectuous Contemplations on, CHRIST my ALL, are to be endeavoured.

12. G. D. A Sermon to the Flock, on the Man cured of his withered Hand, perswading People to try, what they may find God helping them to do, may be very useful to them.

13. G. D. That my Family may be blessed with another and a better Negro-Servant, I must look up to God, in the wayes of Repentance, and Supplication.

My dear *Katy* being brought now so low, that she cannot attend the family-Sacrifices with us, I must pray daily with her, in her Chamber.

14. G. D. Several Ministers in the Countrey are languishing in Sickness. I would look on them, as being so much my Brethren, that when I consider my Relatives I will here enter my Purposes, to pray particularly and continually for them.

15. G. D. There has lately been in the Town, an Apparition of a dead Person. It is a Thing so well attested that there can be no Room to doubt of it. It may be a service to Piety, and serve many good Purposes, for me to obtain a full Relation of the Matter; and have the Persons concerned therein, to make Oath unto it, before a Magistrate.

16. G. D. Call upon those that are most capable to look out for a Minister to be sent unto *Barmudaz*, from

---

[1] William Tailer.

whence I have repeted Cries, for one to come over and help them.

17. G. D. A poor Man that wants a good Employment; what shall I find for him?

*18. G. D. The Life of my Spirit lies in a *Death* to Fear the *Things which are seen and are temporal*. In what Regards, am I to become Dead unto the World?

I must look on all things here below with the eye of a Dying man; and when I look on all my enjoyments, consider them as a Dying man, and as one immediately going from them.

I must be ready to sacrifice all those things, and if God call for them I must be willing to be striped of them all, and be left as Naked as a man that is dead who cannot take them away with him.

If any of these Things, particularly invite me to [do] any thing that may be a sin against the Glorious GOD, their Invitation must make no more Impression on me, than a Speech unto the Dead.

(Note) I could never learn, how or why these Blotts were made.[1]

Finally, To the Saints that are dead, God is become All in All. A Respect unto GOD, must be the Thing that shall Influence me in my addressing to, and my [   ]. them all of my [   ].

I can't be ready to dy and leave the World, until I become thus dead unto the World.

19. G. D. Several Proposals for the Advantage of the Flock, must be made unto the Committee.

20. G. D. A new Negro Servant, (a little Boy) is come into my Family. What, what shall I do? what Cares must be used, that GOD may have Service from him?

21. G. D. Do some very good Offices for one that is going to marry my Daughter-in-Law.

[1] This page of the MS. is badly blotted.

22. G. D. Poor *Barnstable;* what shall be done for thee? Give the best Advice that may be, to the afflicted and oppressed young Minister there.[1]

23. G. D. I hear of a Minister, grievously negligent in the Discharge of his Ministry. Write lovingly, and faithfully to him.

24. G. D. An unhappy Man in the Prison, cries to me for some Kindnesses.[2]

26. G. D. I have often seen it, that my Exercises, Temptations, Calamities, are made singularly, serviceable, to the Edification of the Flock, whereof I am the Servant: they lead me to discourse on Subjects, and communicate Meditations and Experiences, which God makes useful to His People. I must exceedingly and exquisitely contrive, how the terrible Trial come upon me in the Condition of my lovely *Katy,* may be made profitable unto the People, whom I am to instruct in the Wayes of God.

27. G. D. Such is the Condition of my Family, in regard of my dear *Katy's* dying Circumstances; that I am called of God unto more than ordinary Methods for the Quickening of Piety in my Family. Oh! That I may be directed of God, what I am to do upon this Intention!

28. G. D. Some related unto me very far off, by an Affinity contracted in a Marriage with my Neece. Lett me present Books of Piety unto them.

29. G. D. Lett me renew my Thoughts upon that Enquiry; Whether I may not employ Part of my public Ministry, on Subjects, which may be very serviceable and very entertaining to the Church of God, in an ultramarine Publication of my Discourses upon them.

But I despair of any good Acceptance for any thing of mine.

---

[1] Rev. Jonathan Russell, Jr. The parish was about to divide.
[2] Some lines that are illegible follow.

However, there are two or three Subjects, which I design to cultivate, with brief Essays upon them.

30. G. D. We are now getting on towards the clearing and settling of our Estate. I would propound unto my wife, what special Service for God and His Kingdome, she will do, in Case the Administration be well finished, and she find any Estate remaining, that may render her capable of doing any thing.

(VII) That I might further serve the Cause of Piety, and help to bring on the Reign of Righteousness, I gave to the Bookseller, another little Treatise, entituled; THE GOLDEN RULE. *A very brief Essay on the Grand Maxim of Good Morality*, TO DO AS WE WOULD BE DONE UNTO: *The true Universal Medicine for all the Disorders in the world. Exhibited at Boston Lecture. 25 d. VIII m. 1716.*

December. 1. G. D. A most pious and praying Widow, who strangely lives by Faith on the divine Providence, must receive some fresh Benignities from me.

1 d. 10 m. Satureday. I sett apart this Day for Supplications as I use to do. And Things were in it, as they use to be. I am sorry, that this Expressiye must imply but a mean Account. However, it was a Day wherein I enjoy'd some Communion with Heaven.

The dying State of my dear *Katy*, made a grand Article in the Supplications of the Day. It was this Day fourteen Years ago, that her Mother expired, (on a Tuesday.) I hope, a great Improvement in Piety, will be the Effect of the Exercises to which I am called on this Occasion.

I made this a Day of other and many Sacrifices.

* 2. G. D. God calls me to wait upon Him, in all the wayes of Piety, for those Influences of His Grace, which may render me very low and vile in my own Eyes, and very patient under Contempt, and satisfied in His not allowing the most laboured Effects of my Studies to be published and accepted in the World; and exceedingly

afraid of aiming at a great Name for myself, in my Offers to serve the best Interests.

3. G. D. A Gentleman was last Night complaining to me, that he observed, that many Pretenders to be justified by Faith in the Righteousness of our Saviour, yett lived in a very unjustifiable Neglect of many known and plain Duties commanded by our Saviour. I pray'd him to furnish me with the Instances, that I may faithfully serve the Flock with the Warnings of God.

4. G. D. *Liza's* Education, must have some new Thoughts and Cares exercised upon it.

I must allow as much of my Time, as I can, to my dear dying Child; her Consolation and her Preparation.

5. G. D. I have some Relatives in *Ireland;* and I spend some time this Morning, in transmitting to them a considerable Number of Books of Piety; as Expressions of my Loves and Cares for them.

6. G. D. I grow very strong in the Perswasion, that the Kingdome of God will be brought on, and the great Revolutions expected in the Dayes approaching be accomplished, by a Return of the Prophetic Spirit in Angelical Operations; and a Revival of the Supernatural Powers; which planted the Christian Church in the primitive Times. Wherefore I will now make it an Article of my daily Supplications, *Lord, Pour out thy Spirit upon all Flesh, according to thy Promise.* See Luk. XI. 13.

6 *d.* x *m. Thursday.* A Day of general Thanksgiving.

7. G. D. Move my dying Child, that she speak such Things, especially unto her two Brothers, as may leave a precious and lasting Impression upon them.

8. G. D. I will gett a Number of my *Pascentius's*[1] and Scatter them among the Poor.

*9. G. D. Oh! That I were more frequent, more exact, in examining the Principle of my Designs, my Pas-

---

[1] Printed in 1714-15.

sions, my Actions; and lett me be forever dissatisfied, except I find the Principle to be, the Love of GOD, and a Care and an Aim to please Him. When, when shall I be entirely swallow'd up in the Life of GOD?

10. G. D. Among the Poor of my own Flock, the Deacons will now be putt upon many Dispensations of Charity. I would furnish them with a Number of my *Pascentius's* to dispense therewithal.

11. G. D. My lovely *Katy*, desires mightily that her Death may glorify God!

Oh! the Variety of Projections which my broken Heart is forming, that it may do so!

12. G. D. My Kinsman, T. W[alter] gives Hopes of his yett coming to Good; has begun to preach publickly. What shall I do for him?

And something I will propose, to recover the Health of his Father.

13. G. D. I am resuming the Design of preparing my *Ratio Disciplinæ* for the Public. I foresee and project many exquisite Purposes to serve the Kingdome of GOD, in the Progress of the Work.

14. G. D. Wait upon the Governor this Evening; and propose to him some Services for the Public.

15. G. D. I will perswade some of our Physicians to bring the *cold Bath* into fashion; Whereby many poor, sick, miserable People may obtain Releef under various Maladies which now remain otherwise Incurable.

16 *d.* x *m. Lords-Day morning.* A Little after 3 *h.* A.M. my lovely Daughter *Katharin* expired gloriously.

The Things which her dear Saviour has done to her and for her, afford a wonderful Story. But because I relate it in other Papers, I shall here insert nothing of it.

Much of my Time, of late, has been spent in sitting by her with Essayes to strengthen her in her Agonies, wherein God graciously assisted me.

* 16. G. D. I have been for many Months a dying in my feeling the dying Circumstances of my lovely *Katy*. And now, this last Night, she is actually dead; but how triumphantly did she go away!

Certainly, Heaven expects in me, a vast Improvement of Piety, under what I have mett withal.

I must sett myself, in a most exquisite Manner, to consider, how I should improve what has befallen me, unto the best of Purposes, and beg the divine Directions. One thing very particularly look'd for, will be this; that after so many *Deaths*, I should be a man *dead* unto every thing in this World. And therefore, I will this Day preach a Sermon, upon *Dead with CHRIST*.

17. G. D. And now what can I do for my Flock, more agreeable, or more serviceable, than to preach to them a lively Sermon, on the Death of my lovely Child, and on the Text that she has left them as her dying Legacy, with such Admonitions of Piety, as she desired me from it and from her, earnestly to commend unto them!

18. G. D. Oh! What Endeavours must I use, that my living Children may improve the Death of their lovely Sister, to their best Advantage!

Especially *Creasy*. For whom I would now draw up certain Rules of Conduct, unto which I would expect his daily Conformity.

19. I shall very sensibly discharge Part of my Duty to my Relatives, if I convey as far as I can, to every one of them, the Memorials of my dear *Katy* which I am now preparing for the Public.

20. G. D. And will it not be a very comprehensive Service to the Kingdome of GOD in the World abroad, if I procure to be dispersed a published Account of my dear *Katy's* exemplary Piety, and of the Joy, which in the End it brought her to.

20 *d*. x *m. Thursday.* This Day, my dear *Katy* had her Funeral with a very honourable Attendence upon it.[1]

21. G. D. Would it not be a Service to the Cause of Piety in the Colledge, and so yett more extensively, if I should procure some late Exemples of Piety, which have been given by several Youths, who have lately died there, to be published unto the World?   I am endeavouring of it.

22. G. D. A Soul in particular Snares, must be warn'd, charg'd, recovered.

* 23. G. D. And what special Improvements in Piety, does the Death of my lovely Daughter call me to?

1. A renew'd and increas'd Repentance, for the Sins, which the Stroke of GOD upon me calls me to think upon.

2. A patient Submission to abasing Dispensations, wherein my GOD will humble me.

3. A Stronger Apprehension of my own Death approaching and Preparation for it.

4. A more frequent and fervent Inclination of Piety on my surviving Children; and particularly of the Religion of the Closet.

5. New Projections to have all Things in my Family, under an excellent Regulation. Especially for the Strain of Sabbatizing.

6. Fresh Endeavours to recommend early Religion unto the young People of my Flock, and throughout the Countrey.

7. More communion with the Spirits in Paradise; by Meditation on them.

Help me, my GOD, thus to answer thy holy Expectations.

24. G. D. Such Subjects, as the Death my dear *Katy*, leads me to insist upon, will be of great Use to the Flock, which I should be a prudent and faithful Feeder to.

That I with the Child which God had given me, may glorify Him. With Testimonies to the pleasant Wayes of

---

[1] Sewall describes her as a "vertuous, pious Gentlewoman."

Piety, and that my dear *Katy*, may outlive her Death, and
continue gloriously to do good among the living after she
is Dead, I give to the Bookseller, the Sermon which the
excellent Creature desired me to preach after her Decease;
and accompany it with such Memoirs of her, as I hope,
will prove exceeding serviceable.

(VIII) It is entituled; Victorina, *A Sermon preach'd
on the Decease, and at the Desire, of* Mrs. Katharin Mather;
*By her Father. Whereunto there is added, A further Account
of that Young Gentlewoman; By another hand.*[1]

25. G. D. Oh! For a Family now, better ordered in
every point, than ever heretofore!

26. G. D. Perhaps it may have a tendency to confirm T. W[alter] in Piety, if I employ his Hand, in drawing
up the account of his Kinswoman, which is to see the public.

27. G. D. I have a new Prospect of providing a Minister for the eastern Parts; particularly for the Instruction
of the Indians there. A Thing of extraordinary Consequence. Lett me prosecute it.

28. G. D. The Society that are forming a new Church
in the south Part of the Town, must have Services done for
them. Several I have before me.

Particularly, when I preach to them, on the first Day
of their opening their Edifice.

29. G. D. I have Money in my hands, to be dispensed
unto some needy, aged, praying Women.

29 *d.* x *m. Satureday.* I sett apart this Day, for prayers
before the Lord, as I use to do. But have cause to mourn,
bitterly before the Lord, that it was with me little otherwise than as it use to be.

I humbled myself before GOD, from the Sense of His Rebukes
upon me, in the Case of my departed Child. And I cried unto Him,
that the Fruit hereof might be, a sensible Improvement of Piety, in
me, and the Rest of the Children.

[1] Printed by B. Green for Daniel Henchman, 1717.

I asked the divine Conduct and Blessing, for what I am now publishing, of the deceased Child.

Other Matters, I carried unto the Lord, as usually.

Especially, I implored Him, for such a Descent of His holy Angels, as may bring an astonishing Revolution on the World.

For myself, I asked these three singular Favours of GOD.

First; that I may have the *Spirit of Prayer* in a greater Measure poured out upon me,

Secondly; that I may be more *diligent* in the Work of GOD, and be rescued from the *Sloth* which is the grand Burden of my Soul.

Thirdly; that I may grow up to an high Degree of *Sanctity*, in the most explicit Wayes of *living unto GOD.*

The Health of my lovely Consort, who is the greatest of all my Temporal Blessings, is a particular Matter of Concern unto me.

*30. G. D. Lett me go to the Lord's-Table this day, on the three Errands, mentioned for yesterday.

31. G. D. God speaks to the Sea-faring part of the Flock, in many late Shipwrecks; Lett me, mightily urge upon them their hearkening to the Voice of God.

January. [1716–17.] 1. G. D. In my Supplications this Day, with my Family, I would render singular Thanks to the glorious One, from whom having obtained Help, we continue to this first Day of another Year: and implore His Blessing for the new Year that we are now entring upon.

2. G. D. I have a Sister in some domestic Afflictions, to whom I must endeavour a Particular Serviceableness.

3. G. D. Our Governour going to *N. Hampshire*, I may putt him upon doing his best, for the reconciling of the Contentions there.

I have some Thoughts of presenting him with our *Church-History*, that so he may not only know the Countrey; and how to serve it, but also have before him the Exemple of our former Governors.

4. G. D. I would prevail with some, to send unto *London*, for some Remedies, whereby the Lives of People

here may be preserved and sweetened, if the Promises in the Advertisements are answered.

5. G. D. A Minister in the Countrey, who conflicts with Straits and Wants is to have my poor Charity dispensed unto him. [Mr. καπεν.] [1]

*6. G. D. Why may not I be more diligent, more vigorous, more explicit than ever, in this point of Piety! Before every new Action in my Study, to make still a short Prayer which may relate unto it; and in this Prayer form an Act of consecration to God, wherein what I do, shall be directly aimed at the serving of Him! And this may be also done, at my going forth out of my Study; upon Designs which I have before me. [2]

7. G. D. I will use particular Methods to find out very taking and useful Subjects for the Flock to be entertain'd withal; *Seek out acceptable Words.*

8. G. D. My Family is now, by the Death of one dear Creature, and the Removal of six or seven more, coming unto a mighty Diminution. What Opportunities will this give me to contrive, that it may be a Family exemplary for all that is holy, and just, and good.

8 *d.* 11 *m.* [*January.*] *Tuesday.* The People that are forming a new Church, in the south Part of the Town, this Day enter into their new Meeting-house. The Ministers of the Town, kept a Day of Prayer with them. And I had Opportunity to preach unto them, with gracious Assistences from above. A vast Auditory. [3]

9. G. D. My Father-in-Law at *Charlestown*, has great Symptoms of his Death, just ready to sieze upon him. I must visit him, assist him, strengthen him.

---

[1] Capen. Probably Joseph Capen, of Topsfield (d. 1725).

[2] "6 *d.* 11 *m.* Dismissed Joseph Hill and Benjamin White that they may bear their part in laying the Foundations of a new Church, in the South part of the Town." *Cotton Mather's MS. Records of the Second Church,* II.

[3] See Sewall, *Diary,* III. 116. This church, known as the "New South Church," was located on the "Church Green."

10. G. D.   The Direction of the new Church in this Town, for furnishing themselves with a Minister that may be a Blessing to the Town and Countrey, is a Thing of great Consequence, I would earnestly look up unto Heaven, to direct them.[1]

11. G. D.   I have in view, some services to be done, for the scholars at the Colledge.

12. G. D.   There are certain Ministers in a broken state of Health, whom I would by Name remember before the Lord in my daily Supplications.

*13. G. D.   Being to day to preach on that Subject, I will sett myself this Day, to glorify GOD, with forming, Acts of Acknowledgment and Resignation to His uncontroleable Sovereignty.   I will consider this divine Perfection, and not only as actually display'd in the Things already done unto me, but also as it may be exercised in Cases which may be supposed by me, and in Sorrows which I may suppose to be the Things appointed for me.   And I will endeavour to express all possible Acquiescence in the Will of the glorious GOD.

14. G. D.   Some Contrivances for the Accommodation of people in our Meeting-house, must be speedily prosecuted.

15. G. D.   My Son-in-Law, Mr. *Willard*, offers himself to our Church.   I rejoice to see him thus early disposed for a walk in the Truth.   Oh! Lett me take all possible Methods to animate him unto Piety, and Usefulness!

This Day there come to me a Number from the Undertakers of the new Meeting-house in the South Part of the Town in the Name of the rest, with their unanimous Desire, that I would give them a Copy of the Sermon, which I preach'd unto them this Day se'nnight.   So wondrously does the Sovereign God, and glorious Head of the Church, multiply my Opportunities to serve His Kingdome.

(IX) So, I gave it unto them; Entitled: ZELOTES.

[1] See p. 426, *infra*.

*A zeal for the House of GOD; Blown up, in a Sermon preached
unto an Assembly of Christians, in the south part of Boston;
on 8 d. XI m. 1716–17. A Day of prayer kept by them, at
their first Entrance into a New Edifice Erected by them for the
public worship of God our Saviour.*[1]

16. G. D.   The Lord pitty my poor Kinsman, J. W.
bound to sea.   What shall I do for him!

17. G. D.   To entertain the Public at the Lecture with
the Description of real and vital PIETY given with the
loud Voice of an ANGEL; (Rev. xiv. 7.) and make such
Remarks as are to be made upon it; may prove a notable
Service to the Kingdome of GOD.

18. G. D.   Consult with my Society of Gentlemen, that
combine for Projections to do good; Whether it be not
possible to project Methods, for the Introducing of good
Orders into our Vessels.

19. G. D.   A miserable Fellow in Prison for Debt, must
be delivered; and Admonitions of a better Life given to
him.

20. G. D.   Three Dayes ago, I gave to the Public, a
Description of real and vital PIETY. As I would be
alwayes making Essays, to live unto GOD, according [to]
the Methods and Maxims I then delivered, so I would this
Day, have a particular Exercise, wherein I would examine
my Conformity to them, and procure a new and strong
Impression of them upon me.   And Read, *Egardus*, his,
γνῶθι σεαυτόν.

21. G. D.   A Sermon upon GOD *hiding His Face*, may
be of great use, to many Souls in the Flock.

22. G. D.   Ought I not every Day now to insert that
Clause in my family prayers; *And may the Families that
are sprung from us, have the Light of GOD shining upon them!*

23. G. D.   New Relatives made, by the late Marriages
in my Family, call for Expressions of my Concern for their

[1] Printed by J. Allen, for Nicholas Boone, 1717.

welfare.   One shall be my presenting of my *Victorina* among them.

24. G. D.   The affair of procuring a Missionary to our Eastern Indians, is now devolved much upon my Care. Tis of great Consequence.   Lord, Give thy Direction and Assistence!   I first write Letters to *Martha's* Vineyard, on this Occasion.

25. G. D.   I must procure an Attorney to be made for the Christian Indians on *Martha's* Vineyard.

26. G. D.   A poor Boy tortured with the Stone, must be made an Object of my singular Compassions.   The Expence of the *Lithotomie*, must be Part of my Care.

26 *d.* 11 *m. Satureday.*   I sett apart this Day for Prayer, with Fasting; on the usual Occasions; and with the usual Petitions.

But especially, I besought of the Lord, that He would assist me to a wise, holy, fruitful Improvement of His Dispensations towards me, in what has befallen my lovely *Katy*.

I besought Him also, for the Fulfilment of *Joel's* Prophecy among the Nations; and the Return of that Spirit which introduced and erected and managed the Kingdome of God in the primitive Times of Christianity; and a Descent of His mighty Angels, whereby His kingdome would rule over all.

* 27. G. D.   Why may not I take a Catalogue of the Books that I have published; and in the Perusal (perhaps repeted) of it, upon the Title of each Book, seriously consider, *what point of excellent Piety, am I, by this Publication singularly oblig'd unto?*   And aspire accordingly.

28. G. D.   I will read with Attention, *Egardus*, on the Duties of a Preacher.

29. G. D.   A Maid escaped from a Servitude in a very vicious Family, coming to sojourn in my House, already feels many Impressions of Piety upon her.   She may be so

mated as to have cause forever to bless God, for his bringing her into my Family: And I will endeavour that she may.

30. G. D. My Kinsman at *Newtown* must be help'd under some of his Difficulties and his Temptations.

31. G. D. My Thoughts about the great Things to be done for the Church, and in the World, by the Return of the *prophetic Spirit.* I am in distress, how far I may improve them, to raise in the People of God, Supplications and Expectations for such a Matter. *Direct me, O my God!*

February. 1. G. D. There are Numbers of Persons, whom I should advise and quicken to join unto the religious Societies among us.

2. G. D. A very abusive Creature, in whom the three parts of the Satanic Image, Pride, Malice, and Falsehood, are very Conspicuous, must be pittied and pray'd for. [I. Κολμαν] [1]

* 3. G. D. My Heart is exceedingly affected with my most comfortable and undeserved Enjoyments in my domestic Circumstances. I can scarce desire to be better of it, than I am, upon all Accounts. An amiable Consort, agreeable Children, most accommodated Habitation, a plentiful Table: the Respects of kind Neighbours, a flourishing Auditory.

I am even distressed, that I may render unto the Lord, according to the Benefits which I have received from Him. Full of Thoughts, what shall I do in a way of extraordinary Thankfulness and Fruitfulness: Full of Cries to Heaven, that I may be directed, quickened, assisted unto a right Behaviour.

4. G. D. And especially, much Industry for the Good of my Flock!

5. G. D. O my dear SAVIOUR, instruct me, assist me, strengthen me, more and more to imitate thy Goodness,

---

[1] John Colman, well known for his writing in the controversy over the bank and currency.

and Wisdome, in my treating all my domestic Relatives, on all Occasions.

6. G. D.   And the rest.

And by the Hand and Pen of *Creasy*, send some very agreeable Things to his Aunt at *Witny*.[1]

7. G. D.   Make yett a further Trial, whether a Body of good Orders, may not be contrived for our vessels; and the Owners be brought into a Combination and Resolution, for the obliging of the Masters to Execute them.

8. G. D.   Renew a Motion for the visiting of the Prison by the Ministers of the Town.

9. G. D.   A Fellow in Prison, for a Murder, should be seasonably now, diverse Months before his Trial, under proper cultivations.

* 10. G. D.   On my Birth-day, which arrives two Days hence, Lett me seriously sett myself to consider the further Improvements in Piety; which are expected of me.

11. G. D.   Having Occasion to spend good Part of this Day in Prayer with the Ministers of the Town, on the behalf of some sick Ministers,[2] I would cry earnestly to God with them, for Grace to double our Diligence in our Cares of the Flocks, committed unto our Charge.

THE COURSE OF MY MINISTRY THIS YEAR.

12 *d.* 12 *m.* [*February.*] 1715–16.   I discoursed on, Rev. 1. 18. the *keyes* of the *invisible World*, and of *Death*, in the Hands of our SAVIOUR.   And His having under His Government particularly the Circumstances of the *Death* by which Men pass into the *invisible World*.   Meditations for a Birth-day.

16 *d.* 12 *m. Thursday.*   At the Lecture.   On Jam. II. 5.   The *Lustre* of true *Piety*, or a Principle of Grace, even in people of the *lowest* Circumstances.

20 *d.* 12 *m.*   On, Psal. LXXXVI. 17.   *Tokens for Good;*   In our State, and, on what befalls us, and on our Prayers, and, in the Sacraments.

---

[1] Mrs. Samuel Mather.   [2] For Mr. Pemberton.   Sewall, *Diary*, III. 119.

26 *d.* 12 *m.*   On, 2. Cor. III. 18. the *Glory of the Lord*, Exhibited in the Gospel and Ordinances of it; and the Effects thereof, in a *Change*, yea, a *growing* one, introduced with the *Image* of God, the most *glorious* Thing in the World. (And I administred the Eucharist.)

4 *d.* 1 *m.* [*March.*] 1716.   On, Ezek. XVII. 23. Our Saviour, a *goodly Cedar*, where *all Fowl of every Wing* may find Shelter and Repose.

11 *d.* 1 *m.*   On, Rom. XV. 5.   Our God, in the usual Order of His Dealings, first a God of *Patience*, and then a God of *Consolation*.

18 *d.* 1 *m.*   On, Joh. XVI. 14.   The holy *Spirit* of God, *glorifying* our Saviour; and therein acting as the *Comforter* of His people.

22 *d.* 1 *m.* *Thursday.*   A General Fast.   On, Joel II. 13.   An hearty *Conversion* to God, with an hearty *Contrition* for Sin, the Way to obtain the Favours of Heaven.

25 *d.* 1 *m.*   On, Joh. XVI. 14.   Going on with the Subject of the last Lord's-Day; we are to *glorify* our SAVIOUR.

29 *d.* 1 *m.* *Thursday.*   The Lecture.   On 1. Cor. X. 14.   The *Idolatry*, to flee from which, is the Duty, and Safety, and Mark of Christianity.

1 *d.* 2 *m.* [*April.*]   On, Joh. XVI. 14.   Going on with the Subject of the last Lord's-Day.   How our Saviour is to be *glorified*.

8 *d.* 2 *m.*   On, Joh. XVI. 14.   In a fourth Essay, finishing my Directions, how to *glorify* our SAVIOUR.

15 *d.* 2 *m.*   On, Jon. IV. 6.   The Effects of taking an undue Satisfaction in temporal Enjoyments.

22 *d.* 2 *m.*   On, Judg. XIII. 19.   The *Wonders* attending the *Sacrifices* offered for and by the People of God.   (And I administred the Eucharist.)

29 *d.* 2 *m.*   On, Isa. XXX. 18.   The glorious GOD, *waiting* for *fitt Opportunities*, to make His People find Him *gracious* to them.

6 *d.* 3 *m.* [*May.*]   On 1. King. XVIII. 21.   People *unresolved*, what *Answers* they shall make to the Demands of the glorious GOD.

10 *d.* 3 *m.* *Thursday.*   The Lecture.   On 1. Joh. III. 20.   The awful *Inferences* to be drawn from the *Condemnations* of *Conscience*.

13 *d.* 3 *m.*   On, Matth. XIII. 44.   *Heavenly Blessings*, a *Treasure;* and tho' *hid*, yett *found*.

20 *d.* 3 *m.*   On, 1. Tim. I. 1.   CHRIST our *Hope*.

27 *d.* 3 *m.*   On, Eccl. XII. 10.   *Acceptable Words*.

3 *d.* 4 *m.* [*June.*]   On, Mar. VII. 37.   Our Saviour *doing well* in all that He does.

10 d. 4 m. On, Jam. V. 8. An *established Heart*, looking and ready for the Coming of the Lord, in Death, and in other Events and Changes.

17 d. 4 m. On, Lam. III. 58. Our Saviour *pleading the Causes of our Souls*, and redeeming our Life. (And I administred the Eucharist.)

21 d. 4 m. *Thursday*. The Lecture. On, Prov. XVII. 16. Advantages for good; the Improvement that is to be made of them.

24 d. 4 m. On, 1. Pet. II. 7. CHRIST *precious;* and how prized by the Beleever.

1 d. 5 m. [*July*.] On, Luk. X. 20. The *Joys* and the *Signs* of a *Name written in Heaven.*

8 d. 5 m. On, Mal. IV. 2. The *Sun of Righteousness*, with His *Healing Rays.*

15 d. 5 m. On, Phil. IV. 13. Our SAVIOUR *strengthening* the Beleever, to do *all Things*, that are to be done in living unto God.

22 d. 5 m. On, Phil. IV. 13. Concluding what I began the last Lord's-Day.

29 d. 5 m. On, 1. Cor. IX. 26. The *Combates* of Christianity; what and whence they are; and how to manage them.

2 d. 6 m. [*August*.] *Thursday*. The Lecture; On Matth. VI. 33. The Methods of *seeking first the Kingdome of God;* and the Blessings that follow upon it. Concluding with a Relation of the great Things occurring in the Experience of Dr. *Franckius.*

5 d. 6 m. On, 1. Cor. IX. 26. Finishing what I began, the last Lord's-day.

12 d. 6 m. On, Cant. V. 10. The Mixture of *White* and *Red*, in the Aspect of our SAVIOUR; the Mystery of it. And His Glory as a *Standard-bearer.* (And administred the Eucharist.)

19 d. 6 m. On Act. XX. 7. Methods for spending the LORDS-DAY EVENING religiously and advantageously.

23 d. 6 m. *Thursday*. (A Day of General Thanksgiving, for the Defeat of the Rebels, in Great Britain.) On Psal. XLVII. 7. The *Praises* of God, on the Occasion of our Saviour's *Kingdome* extending and prevailing in the Earth.

26 d. 6 m. On, Psal. XLVII. 7. Finishing what I began three dayes ago.

2 d. 7 m. [*September*.] On, Psal. XXXVII. 31. God returning to His *Throne* in the Soul of Man, and reigning there.

9 d. 7 m. On, Psal. XXXVII. 31. Finishing what I began the last Lord's-day; and giving the Signs of *God reigning in the Heart.*

16 d. 7 m. **On,** 1. King. III. 10. Chusing and asking the *spiritual Blessings of Wisdome*, with a *Speech* that shall please the Lord.

23 d. 7 m. **On,** Rev. XXII. 2. The Properties and Benefits of *an healed Soul*. Religion exhibited under that Notion, *the healing of the Soul*.

30 d. 7 m. **On,** Matth. III. 12. Our Saviour *thoroughly purging of His Floor*.

7 d. 8 m. [*October*.] On Cant. II. 14. The *sweet Voice* of Piety, which our SAVIOUR desires and expects to hear from His People. (And administred the Eucharist.)

9 d. 8 m. *Tuesday*. A Day of Prayer, kept by the First Church in *Boston*, præliminary to the choice of another Pastor. On, Isa. LX. 7. A *Church*, an House of our SAVIOUR'S Glory, and glorified by Him.

11 d. 8 m. *Thursday*. The Lecture, in the room of another; It being the first Appearance of our new Governour in one of our Assemblies. On, Psal. LXXXVI. 17. *Tokens for good;* Especially, for the Protestant Interest; and for our own Countrey.

14 d. 8 m. **On,** Matth. VII. 27. The Fate of the disobedient Hearer in the *Storm* to be looked for. (It being a violent *Storm*, at the Time of preaching it.)

21 d. 8 m. **On,** Luk. XI. 13. The Heavenly Father giving the holy SPIRIT, unto them that *ask* Him.

25 d. 8 m. *Thursday*. The Lecture. On, Matth. VII. 12. The *golden Rule*, of, *Doing as one would be done unto*.

28 d. 8 m. **On,** Luk. XI. 13. Finishing what I began the last Lord's-day.

4 d. 9 m. [*November*.] On, Joh. II. 17. The *Zeal of the House* of GOD.

6 d. 9 m. *Tuesday*. The Lecture at *Roxbury*. On Cant. II. 14. The *sweet Voice* of Piety.

11 d. 9 m. On 2 Tim. III. 2. The Mystery of Iniquity operating in *Self-Love*.

18 d. 9 m. **On,** Matth. XII. 13. The Duty of People, to make a *Trial*, whether they do not find GOD enabling them to do what He calls them to, tho' they are not of themselves able to obey His Calls.

25 d. 9 m. **On,** Job. XXIII. 14. Acquiescence in the Will of GOD, who in all our Circumstances performs the Thing appointed for us.

2 d. 10 m. [*December*.] On, Cant. VIII. 6. The Soul of the Beleever, desirous to be found as a Seal on the Heart and Arm, of our glorious High-Priest. (And I administred the *Eucharist*.)

6 *d.* 10 *m. Thursday.* A General Thanksgiving. On, Psal. CXXXV. 3. The *Pleasure* to be found in the *praising* of GOD.

9 *d.* 10 *m.* On, Prov. XX. 4. The ill Effects which both the *natural Cold*, and a *spiritual Cold* also, has upon the works [of] Piety. (A cold, as well as a short, Lord's-day.)

16 *d.* 10 *m.* On, Rom. VI. 8. *Dead with CHRIST.* The *Death* which the holy and happy, must aspire, and will arrive unto. (My lovely *Katharin* dying in the Night before.)

23 *d.* 10 *m.* On, Prov. III. 17. The *Pleasures* to be found in the *Ways of Piety.* A Subject which my dying Child asked me to preach upon; and from her, bear a Testimony thereunto. A vast Auditory come together.

30 *d.* 10 *m.* On, Isa. XXVI. 20. The *Chambers* of the Grave for our Bodies; and of a *Paradise* for our Spirits, at our Dissolution. And such Thoughts thereof, as may render our Death easy to us.

6 *d.* 11 *m.* [*January, 1716–17.*] On, Matth. XIV. 30. Our Eye and our Cry to our Saviour, when we are in danger of *Sinking.*

8 *d.* 11 *m. Tuesday.* At the new Meeting-house, in the South part of the Town. A Day of Prayer; at the People's first opening the House. On, Joh. II. 17. *The Zeal of the House of GOD.*

13 *d.* 11 *m.* At the New-North, A. M. On Matth. XIV. 30. At the old-North, P.M. On Job. IX. 12. The divine *Sovereignty*, how to be adored. Particularly, in bereaving Dispensations.

17 *d.* 11 *m. Thursday.* The Lecture, on Rev. XIV. 7. A Description of the real and vital PIETY, which men are by the *loud* Calls of Heaven oblig'd unto.

20 *d.* 11 *m.* On, Job. XIII. 24. God *hiding His Face* from His People; and the dreadful Condition of them, whom He holds for His *Enemies.*

27 *d.* 11 *m.* On, Cant. VIII. 7. The *Love* of our Saviour to His People, *strong as Death.* (And I administred the Eucharist.)

3 *d.* 12 *m.* [*February.*] At the old South, A.M. on Matth. XIV. 30. At the old North, P.M. on Matth. XX. 34. On People *receiving their Sight*, and then seeing sufficient Cause to be the *Followers* of our great SAVIOUR.

10 *d.* 12 *m.* On Matth. XII. 35. The *precious Treasure* of a *good Heart*, laid up and laid out, by a good Man.

To ATHERTON MATHER.   A.A.S.

21 *d.* 12 *m.* [February.] 1715-6.

DEAR COUSIN, — To all the other Inconveniencies which I have of late suffered in my temporal Interest, there is this added, that my Brother having detained my son in England, I have been thereby putt upon such Difficulties as are not yett known unto me; but this I know that I have already a Demand of more money made upon me, to defray my son's Charges there, than all that you have borrowed of me.

And now, after all the wrong Things that you have imposed upon me, what is it that you design to do.

I have many months ago, freely told you my Thoughts, about your Conduct, and the Rules of Charity and Discretion violated in it.   But I now again desire you to pay your debts unto me, without which I must be putt unto extreme Trouble, to discharge mine unto other men.

If you refuse to do this; I have then another Proposal to make. Never till the last Night, had I any Discourse with *Mr Oliver Noyes* concerning you and your affaires.   And now, I perceive that he has the same Account of you, that I have had from every Quarter.

However, for your Debt of an hundred pounds unto him, you have invested him in two Thousand Acres of the Land, in your New Plantation.   If you deal no worse with me, than with him, you can do no less than invest me in six hundred Acres, of as good Land, in your plantation, if it be not all disposed of.

I desire you, to lett me know, by the first Opportunity, what you will do, and what you would have me to do, and no more Deal with me, as you have done hitherto.

The Eighth Comandment, will oblige me to do some Justice unto my Family, as well as the Fifth, to approve myself, Your kinsman, and servt.,

If you don't give me quickly to hear from you, I must putt over my Business, into the hands of our Attorney, in your parts of the Countrey.

To REV. ROWLAND COTTON.   A.A.S.

BOSTON, 23 *d.* 12 *m.* [*February.*] 1715 [-16].

REVEREND SIR, — The pastors of this Town have been this day address'd by two persons [1] appearing on the behalf of the aggrieved

---

[1] William Cowell and Thomas Atkins.

Majority of the Rateable Inhabitants of the Town of Chattam, and requesting our Advice, whether Mr. H[ugh] A[dams] may do well to preach unto them, until the calling of a Council, which they intend, for a further hearing of their Case, which has been already under some Cognisance of a former. And, whether another Council may do well, to vouchsafe such a further hearing unto it.

We are very far from offering our opinion on the Case, that has been heard by our reverend and honoured Brethren, of whom we have such an Esteem, and from whom we are at such a Distance; nor indeed are we so much as willing to Enquire into the Reason of their Judgment. Yett, we hope, we may without offence, in general, say, that an Appeal unto a further Hearing, seems to be a common Right, which cannot well be denied unto an aggrieved Party, who may have many things to offer, which at the first Hearing there might not be opportunity to consider of. And for this further Hearing, it seems to be most natural and rational and suitable, that for the most part (and in the present case,) it should be by them who are as near as may be to the seat of the Difference; It will be but a Brotherly peece, of Charity, for these Neighbours, to accept the Trouble of doing what they can, for the Healing of what is out of order in their Vicinity. And if this Council should happen in any thing to vary from the Judgment of the former, they have the Wisdome and Goodness to carry things with such a Christian Temper, Moderation, and Condescension, that it may be hoped, it will not at all interrupt a good Correspondence between them. All second Hearings must have an everlasting Obstruction upon them, if a variety of Sentiments arising from them should necessarily infer a Disaffection between the Judges. Wherefore, we cannot but wish, that you, Syr, and your adjacent Brethren, would as soon as may be, answer the importunate and irresistible cries of the poor People at *Chattam*, to take some notice of their Circumstances.

About Mr. H. *Adams's* preaching in the meantime, we are much at a Loss, what can in Prudence be said unto him. In Justice, it seems, that while the Appeal is depending, and the cause for Suspension is not very criminal, and very evident, a preacher so concerned, may go on in his business. And if a Majority of the Christian Inhabitants, in *Chattam*, or any other Town, should ask, such a Person to carry on the Exercises of piety among them, we suppose, the Intention of the Civil Government would not be absolutely to forbid it. And it may be, they will not interpret it, as a Transgression of any Law, if such a person, do modestly serve the religious Desires of the Neighbours.

But we apprehend ourselves to be not so proper Directors to him, as you, that are more fully apprised of what may be most prudently proposed unto him.

Upon the whole; if it should be, as those that have been with us do understand it, and represent it, that the Rise of Mr A.s Troubles, is principally owing to the Zeal, with which he has born his Testimonies, against some real Mischiefs,[1] his case may deserve the more deliberate and favourable consideration, and the Indiscretions with which it may have been exercised (if there have such) not be too far aggravated.

We commend you to the Conduct of our glorious Lord, and entreat you to communicate these our Thoughts, as you may see Occasion; and subscribe, Sir, Your affectionate Brethren

To Harvard College.[2]   A.A.S.

[March, 1716.]

Sir, — Finding myself enabled by an unexpected occurrence, to entertain your Library with a present I now send you a small packett of Books, upon that Intention.

I do it, with an humble Tender of my opinion, that if you would procure, the Medicina Mentis, of the Excellent Langius, to come under the perusal of the Students, and Numbers of the Books to be for that purpose brought into the Shops of our Booksellers, you and they would find their Account in it.

Yea, for the Tutors to expect from their Pupils, an Account of what they have read from time to time, in so rich a Mass of the truest Erudition, I am humbly of opinion, would be of greater use to them, than some other Articles of Study, wherein Time is thrown away.

I am well aware, how impertinent a Thing, it will be for me to offer my Judgment or Advice in your Affaires. But I will not lay aside my Perswasion, that the more effectually the glorious Design of living to God is prosecuted in our Schools, and the more nearly subservient all our Literature is made unto that End, without which is but exalted Folly, and mischievous Madness, the more the Schools are made the true Seats of wisdome.

One of the best of men, in Letters which I have within these few Hours received has a passage, which I heartily subscribe to.

[1] It was a dispute over money. Freeman, *History of Cape Cod*, II. 593, 595. See the advertisements in the *Boston News-Letter*, May 28 and June 11, 1716. Adams had been indiscreet in speech and in writing. Sewall, *Diary*, III. 76.

[2] See p. 337, *supra*.

I should be glad, if in my next Communications, unto the most illustrious and flourishing University in the world, whereof Langius is one of the professors, I may be able to say that in *America* we have Colledges, that very much Espouse their Sentiments, and pursue their Intentions. Perhaps I make too bold with you; but having this occasion; I Praesume so far; and with my humble service to your Praesident and Corporation subscribe,

To Anthony William Boehm.   A.A.S.

[1716?]

Reverend Sr., — It was a great Consolation of God, that I received, when I was favoured with your most obliging Letters, and those of the Incomparable *Dr. Franckius* that accompanied them, and the most acceptable Treatises which were bright satellits to them.

The amiable Piety breathing in your excellent Writings, has endeared you to me beyond Expression; and by the Communications which I have made thereof, your Endearment unto other Servants of God in this Countrey, is what, I hope, you will take pleasure to find me mentioning. For, tho' you have dy'd unto self, and you behold and enjoy every thing, as in relation to the Glorious GOD, yett, when we perceive that God makes us the Instruments to convey something of Himself unto His people, tis what may very well be very pleasing to us.

Happening to be just now in some uncommon Hurries, my Letters to my excellent *Franckius* are more unpolished and unfinished than otherwise they should have been. However such as they are, I leave them and the Packetts which I have enclosed them, open for your Perusal; and I entreat that when you have perused them, you would seal them up, and send them away with the bitts of Gold in them, unto the Marvellous Man, unto whom I have directed them.

In the Packetts, there are some Duplicates; with which I happen to be furnished, at the time of my writing, and on such, you will find your dear Name inscribed, that you may reserve them, for your own Disposal.

My lovely Friend, will give me leave to observe unto him, that, it is vital Piety embracing the Maxims of the everlasting Gospel, (and your *Arndtian* and *Franckian* Charity,) which must unite the People of God. And a more explicit union being produced on those Maxims, the Papal Empire will fall before it, and the Kingdome of

God will come on. Until this Union be accomplished, and for the accomplishment of it, God will go on to Distress the Nations, and vex them with all Adversity, and make them suffer Concussions and Convulsions, and Confusions to be trembled at.

I was just thinking, — while I was in the Midst of these Thoughts, your Letters, with those of my admirable *Franckius*, arrived unto me, and with an agreeable Surprize give me a Confirmation of my Apprehensions, and a Demonstration of the Terms, which will forever produce the closest Union among the true Children of God.

For the rest I need only to refer you unto what you will find in my Packetts, for a full Information in all those Points, wherein you would have expected any satisfaction from us. Having done this, I have nothing at this time to add, but my hearty Prayers that your Life and Health may be prolonged, and your holy Studies to advance the Kingdome of God, graciously directed and prospered.

In these Prayers, and in the most friendly Salutations, there concurr, my valuable Collegues. But in a very particular manner, my highly esteemed Friend and Brother, Mr. *Benjamin Coleman*, who has been singularly gratified and edified, with your holy Writings, which I have communicated unto him.

MEMORIAL.[1]   A.A.S.

[May-June, 1716].

To the Honourable, the Lieutenant Governour, and Council and the Representatives in the General Court now assembled; A memorial of Cotton Mather.

He that now humbly offers this Memorial, has been informed that the last General Assembly gratefully ordered the Summ of Three hundred pounds, for some of their Agents, who were employ'd for two years in the public Service, as in Acknowledgment of their Endeavours to serve the Countrey: and he takes a share in the Satisfaction that good Men have to see them who lay themselves out for the public Service, duely acknowledged.

But he does not understand, that any such Notice was then taken of the Person, who served with very much Toil, a much longer Time, in the Affaires of the Countrey, that were then in very difficult and critical Circumstances, and is well-known to have been the principal Instrument of obtaining the valuable Priviledges of the present

[1] See p. 353, *supra*.

Charter, when the Recovery of the former was no longer to be hoped for.

We read of one, *That God Extended favour to him, before the King and his counsellours.*

And he hopes, he may without any Trespass upon Modesty, say that it is well-known, that his Parent was bless'd of God, with Favour before King William, of glorious Memory, and before His great Ministers of State, and that the Effects were such as turned unto the Advantage of his Countrey; yea, in one Article thereof, the Countrey received of a royal Bounty upon his Petition, as much as the Expence of all his Agency. It is well-known that with indefatigable Industry unblemishable Fidelity and unexceptionable Discretion, he employ'd all his Talents and Interests four Years together, for the good of his people. Heaven and Earth were Witnesses: He returned with ample and honourable Testimonials.

He counts it but a filial Duty, to represent it on the behalf of his Parent, that tho' he never asked any Reward in this World, yett for him to be rewarded with a total Neglect when others are not so may carry an Imputation upon him, and may neither be pleasing above, nor contributed unto the Esteem of the Country, with many that wish well unto it, abroad in the World as well as here at home.

Having been led into this Action, by what has been so generously done on the behalf of other Agents, one who never did ask any thing for himself of any Society since he came into the world, apprehends it but a proper Thing, that he should on the behalf of his aged Parent, ask to have this Matter taken into a just Consideration.

C. M.

To ———. A.A.S.

SIR, — It will doubtless be an Honour unto our Countrey, that it has been equal to the best in the World, for the Justice exercised in paying the Debts of the public; and a sensible Addition is made unto its honourable Character, when there are done such things as are done in the present Session, and unto Justice there is added Gratitude.

Good men are pleased, when they see the Countrey grateful, unto those worthy Gentlemen, who ventured over the Atlantic Ocean in a dangerous Time, and underwent the Inconveniencies of an Absence from their Families and Businesses, in an Agency for us.

But I perceive, many good Men, do express their Wishes with

some concern, that there may not be at the same time a total Neglect of a Person who bore a part in that Agency, with some distinguishing Circumstances of Service, when all the Gentlemen concerned for us, found the Prosecution of the former Charter become hopeless and united in its Petition for another, which produced what we now enjoy. Many are concerned, lest such a total Neglect of that person, may carry an Aspect with it, which I make no doubt would be far from the Intentions of Gentlemen of such Consideration, as we have the Happiness to see both Houses fill'd withal.

To confess the Truth; some very considerable persons in both Houses, have given me to understand that if the motion be brought forward on his behalf, they beleeve the Assembly will readily give to that Person also, some Testimony, that they accept with Thankfulness, the Pains which he also took, to obtain for us the Things by which we have enjoy'd great Quietness. And I am very sure, that if any Objections happen to be offered, a very little Discourse with him, will presently sett Things in so true and clear a Light, as to remove them all, and render his Merits incontestible.

Tis true, when the first Great and General Assembly of this Province, offered him a Recompence, at his Arrival; he, considering the Grievous Debts then lying on a distressed People, answered, he would have his Recompence adjourned unto the Resurrection of the Just. But, certainly, the Sentiments of the Province act this Day, and under the Influence of the generous Dispositions, which are now operating, will not be the less favourable to him, for so noble, and christian an Answer.

Tis' also true, that he now declines to take any Step himself, in this Affair. But you will be so far from censuring, that you will rather commend a Son, for thus doing the part of a Remembrancer, and stepping in with a Memorial for his aged Parent.

Briefly; it will not seem strange, if the Assembly hear a Proposal of this Importance. Tis their own Goodness towards two worthy Persons, that has introduced the Thoughts of not leaving a third forgotten. But it might very well seem strange, if a Son, so advised, and so directed, as I have been on this occasion, should not have address'd you, as I now do; with an Action, the like to which, I never did in my Life before. For I never in my Life ask'd any Beneficence unto myself, from any Society in the World; and verily if I had now been on my own Account, you should not have Syr, Your most hearty servant

To Mrs. Ann Wyrly.[1]   A.A.S.

[June, 1716.]

My dear Sister, — While yours, does by the favour of God, render me one of the happiest men in the World, I should be very inexcusable, if I should not with her, have your Condition very much at heart and consider it with all the brotherly Tenderness imaginable.

In the first place, we do most affectionately remember you in our Prayers, when we are together pouring out our Supplications unto the Lord.

And then we would comfort one another with Hopes, that the holy Discipline under which you have been kept, by many humbling Circumstances, are intended by our faithful Saviour, to conform you more unto His, glorious Image, and produce your more consummate Obedience unto Him and render you a great Sacrificer, and so prepare you for the Blessedness of the heavenly World;

At your Arrival whereunto you will see, that God has meant all unto good; and in the mean time, O Child of God, accept this Consolation from Him, what I do, thou knowest not now, but thou shalt know hereafter!

But a few Good words must not be all the good, that you are to expect from us.

Our Daughter *Howel*,[2] (who has two Sons, *George* and *Nathan*,) was yoked unto the worst Husband upon Earth. Had he lived, he had soon brought a Noble to Nine-pence; and your excellent Sister's Interest also, which was unhappily in his hands, would have been all confounded. But she was two months ago delivered from him. And you may assure yourself, that as soon as the Estate is gott into any such settlement, as to lett us know, what we can command as our own, I shall do all that you can expect from a Brother, full all due affection for you.

In the mean time, I do now pray your Acceptance of a small present of five pounds Sterling, which we have ordered Mrs. *Blerso* to pay unto you.

And I do return very hearty Thanks, to dear Mr. *Nesbett*, for all the compassion and Benignity, wherewith I am informed, that he has treated you. May the glorious Lord reward him?

I purpose to make unto you, and unto our sister *Clark*, by the

[1] Daughter of Rev. Samuel Lee, and wife of Henry Wyrley.

[2] Katharine Lee George, married (1) Nathan Howell, who died May 2, 1716; (2) Samuel Sewall, nephew of the diarist.

first safe hand, I can find for conveyance, a small present of certain
Books adapted unto your present Circumstances, and expressive of
my fraternal Regards, Wishes, and Counsils, for you under them.

I am, with a Tender of my Wife's most affectionate Remembrances
to both of you, My dear sister; Your true Brother.

Dear Mrs. *Pitson*,[1] approves herself, a Lovely and a gracious
Ctian; one of an Excellent Spirit and Carriage. And, if any have
written a word amiss of her, they are some unworthy People. Tell
Mr. *Nisbet* for his Comfort; A church of such Christians, as Mrs.
Pittson would be a glorious Thing. I wish, I could say, . . .

To ANTHONY WILLIAM BOEHM.   A.A.S.

6 *d*. VI *m*. [August,] 1716.

REVEREND SIR, — Your Letters, dated about ten Weeks ago,
accompanied with our dear *Ziegenbalgh's*,[2] and a most obliging present
of Books, have arrived unto me; and are as *cool Waters to a thirsty
Soul*.

It is among the singular Felicities, with which the good Hand of
Heaven has favoured me, that I enjoy a Correspondence with my
invaluable *Boehm;* (which alone, is to me an inestimable Treasure;)
yea, and that by his Meditation I am lett into a Correspondence,
which carries my precious Opportunities to serve the Kingdome of
God, into a vast Extensiveness.

I rejoice to find the *Magnalia Christi Americana*, fallen into
your hands; and I verily beleeve, the *American Puritanism*, to be so
much of a Peece with the *Frederician Pietism*, that if it were possible
for the Book to be transferr'd unto our Friends in the Lower *Saxony*,
it would find some Acceptance, and be a little serviceable to their
glorious Intentions.

Your Enquiries, after the History of the Introduction of Christianity into the other English Plantations of *America*, must meet
with a short and melancholy Answer.

For one must make very free with that worthy Name, if it
be said, that Christianity is yett, well introduced into them. Our

---

[1] Elizabeth Pittson joined the second Church, September 18, 1715.

[2] Bartholomew Ziegenbalgh, "pastor of the Indian Church, and an indefatigable Missionary, and most faithful and famous Servant of Christ, among the
Malabarians in the East Indies." Some information concerning him is given
in the reply to Mather's letter of December 31, 1717, printed in Mather's *India
Christiana*, 62.

Islands are indeed inhabited by such as are called Christians. But, alas, how dissolute are their Manners! And how inhumane the way of their Subsistence, on the sweat and Blood of Slaves treated with infinite Barbarities! What little Worship of God they have, as it is confined unto the English Liturgy, so it is too commonly performed by Parsons, of a very scandalous Character.

On the Continent, the Colony of *Carolina*, was in a fair Way to have been filled with a religious people; until your *Society for the Propagation of Religion in foreign Parts*, unhappily sent over some of their Missionaries thither; and, I am informed, that with them and from that time, a mighty Torrent of Profaneness and Wickedness carried all before it; and every thing that might be worthy to be called Religion is very much lost in that woful Countrey.

The other Colonies, have such a Religion as your Ch: of E. maintains, in many parts of the Realm at home; and is, as your Neighbours usually are, afraid lest the Dissenters break in, to show men the true Methods of living to God, and instruct them in a Religion that shall not wholly consist in lifeless Forms and Ceremonies, Expiations for a vicious Life. In *Pensylvania*, and the *Jersey's* and some adjacent Places, a Congregation of more serious Christians, is now and then formed, under the Conduct of a godly Minister. But then presently some of those Missionaries whose Bigotry for their High-Church Follies is usually more conspicuous than their piety, presently pursue them, with all possible Disturbances. *New England* is the only Countrey, in *America*, which has much of real and vital Religion flourishing in it; and here also, your Missionaries, who are of little use, but to propagate Impiety, come to disturb well ordered Churches of God. In many of the other Colonies there are Numbers of ungospellized Plantations, which have no public Worship of God among them. Your Society sends not its Missionaries, unto these. But a Countrey fill'd with holy Churches and Pastors, cannot have a dozen litigious Families in a Village, where the Name of the Ch. of E. pretended by odd People, who know nothing of the matter, may be of Use, to serve their political and vexatious Purposes, but presently the Society dispatch their Missionaries hither. However, by a strange Infatuation from Heaven upon them, the Missionaries which have been sent hither, have been generally men of such a Behaviour, that it was impossible to take a more effectual Course for the prejudicing of this religious Countrey against that sort of men, or the begetting an Horror for the Ch. of E. in the New English Colonies. If a true History of the Missions from the Society were published,

Mankind would be convinced, that Charity was never so abused in the World.[1]

But Sir, if you would have an Account of the American Colonies[2]

It gives me a great Satisfaction, that our, Lapis' e Monte does agree so well with you; as indeed, I was well assured it would.

I continue my Instances, that you would, if it be possible, gett the Instrument into *France;* and, I pray, convey one of them, if you can, to the Marquess of *Langallen's.* Tis this everlasting Gospel, that must carry all before it.

When I readd the preface of our excellent *Frankius* to his Greek New Testament, it revived in me some Hopes; that our glorious Lord, may in His Time inspire and incline some capable Persons to bring our, *Biblia Americana,* into the World. There being so little of my own in that Work, I may use the more Freedome, in giving you some Account of it. Yea, I may venture to say this: I can without Vanity assure you, that the Church of God, has never yett had so rich an Amassment of the most valuable Things together tendered unto it. But after all, the most valuable Things, are those which such men as your *Arndt,* and *Franck,* and others of the like truest Erudition, have led into. I expect no distinguishing Favour from any distinguished party of Christians. And, the Dissenters in London have particularly treated me, and the offer of this Work after such a manner, as I have ever expected, from men of their narrow Spirits; and among whom, I wish, learning were more esteemed and exemplified. If this work ever see the Light, I expect, it will be from the Countenance and Contribution, of men of our *Universal Religion;* who will every way appear more and more in the several Forms of Christianity. And among such I entreat of you, that my, *new offer,* may be communicated.

I purpose, that, if I live, you shall suddenly hear further from me. In the mean time, I pray your Acceptance of a few of our latest Publications; whereof, I shall be glad, if you send some to our Friends in the Frederician University.

May the glorious Lord, graciously continue, and multiply your Opportunities to serve His Kingdome, and bring on the Reign of Piety, I am, Sir, Your most affectionate Brother and serv't.

[1] Such a history did appear in 1730, as *An Historical Account of the Incorporated Society for the Propagation of the Gospel in Foreign Parts,* prepared by David Humphreys, Secretary to the Society.

[2] He probably here inserted a sketch of the state of religion in America.

To Jeremiah Dummer.   A.A.S.

Sir, — If many Letters of mine, can bring you into the Debt of so much as one you are certainly at least so much in mine.

This hinders not my adding this to the Number of my Letters, wherein I shall (and alwayes,) keep close to the two Rules, on which, I have heretofore told you, that when you saw my hand in a Superscription, you might go on, and open, with a perpetual Dependence.

There is not that man upon Earth which will charge me, with ever speaking one injurious Word of you on any Occasion. And, tho' I have perhaps mention'd *Irenæus Americus*, it has alwayes been with the candid Sentiments and the very Expressions, which have been employ'd on that Occasion, by our incomparrable Sir Wm. Ashurst, whom you know to be one of the best of men, and I know that you have not a better Friend upon the Earth.

If you find an odd sort of a Treatment among us, you will not wonder, that one who has the ill hap to have a certain Man whom you know very well, to be his Adversary should be treated so.   Mr. *Mather* has been formerly as much maligned and abused by that man as Mr. *Dummer;* but the one has outlived it, and so will the other.

I have my just share in the common Joy, of your Deliverance from the Brand which threatned you, and have signalized it in a more significant way, than any Person in the Countrey.

But, Oh! may the precious Effects, both of the Trouble, and of the Rescue be with such a conspicuous Improvement in Piety and all Goodness, that it may be said, God has meant it unto good.

Your Circumstances upon many accounts, expose you to wondrous Temptations; and the Trial which has befallen you, comes upon an Errand from Heaven, whereof, may our gracious God make you wisely sensible.

Your not being assign'd a share in the Presentation of an Address from our Ministers, was, I suppose, entirely a Complement unto one, who is now succeeded by a person, whose excellent Character, fills us with praises to our merciful God, and thanks unto our King, and unto them, who have made him appris'd of our Condition.

There will be no doubt of your being again desired to continue in your Agency and I desire you to continue in your Generosity.

I do not use to nauseate you, with any of my published Composures; but there is one which I will now impose upon you.   Behold.

To Henry Walrond.   A.A.S.

31 d. 8 m. [October.] 1716.

My dear and most valuable Brother, — One Infelicity among the Consequences of my not meeting with you at *London*, is, that I am afraid the Oportunities for Correspondence will have an uneasy Abridgment upon them. We shall not have so many Opportunities to hear from one another.

But what I can lay hold on, I will embrace with all the Alacrity of a Brother, hoping to converse with a Friend, than whom no Brother can be more endeared.

Our Countrey affords little matter of Intelligence to entertain and gratify an *Europaean* Curiosity. But, because it will be a satisfaction unto you, I will inform you, that our Churches are continually, and peaceably multiplying and as in the rest of the Countrey, so in our City of Boston, tis remarkably exemplified.

The Church which I serve, has mett in an aedifice, no less than seventy foot long, sixty six foot wide, and three Tires of Galleries one over another; but yett so throng'd an Auditory that they proposed a swarm. I approved and assisted their Motion; help'd them to build another Meeting-house, and gathering their Church, and ordaining their Minister. So, I have a flourishing Society drawn off from me, but subsisting in the very midst of my own, and such a strange Blessing on my own, that our Congregation hardly misses any of its Numbers, and the Lord's-day-Collections (which in this City bear all our ecclesiastical Expences,) are larger than they were before the Secession. Within a Month or two, another new Church will be formed in the South part of our City. And then we shall have seven Churches, of our *United Brethren*, belonging to this Town; besides a Synagogue of High Church and another of the Baptists, and another of the French with whom we live in all decent Agreement.

The Ch: of E. is become exceeding lothesome in these Colonies, by the Scandal they have taken at your *Society for the Propagation of the Gospel*, (as they are pleas'd to call, Episcopacy,) *in foreign Parts*. For, first, it hath seem'd strange unto them, that, while they left many Places in the more Southern Colonies utterly ungospellized and without any social Worship of God, at the same time, if half a score or a very few sorry People in the well-instructed Towns of N. E. that they might serve some litigious Purposes, declare for the Ch: of E. presently the Society dispatch and support their Missionaries, to strengthen these People, in their Wayes, which are alwayes grievous.

But, secondly, it has happened, that the Missionaries for the most part have been men of such a vicious and horrid Character, that the worst People we have are not near so bad, as they that should have been their Instructors in all Goodness. You may easily apprehend, what Ideas of the Ch. of E. must be produced in the sober Christians of this Countrey, by such a Conduct, and how much they must look on what is done by the Society for the Molestation of the Gospel in foreign Parts, as the greatest Prostitution of Charity, that ever was in the World.

But so much for that ungrateful Subject!

You have been pleased, Syr, to lett me know, that you are willing to afford a place in your Library, unto the poor Composures, which the mean hand that now writes, has published. About forty of these, you have lett me understand, that they have already reached you. But indeed there are above two hundred more; belonging to the Catalogue; which have already pass'd the Press; Altho' some, which are longer than any of these, (except the *Magnalia*,) and the *Biblia Americana* also (which are more than three times as big as the *Magnalia*,) and have cost me exquisite Elaborations, ly by unpublished. A great Part of these are already so out of print, that I despair of recovering them. Such as I can recover, I shall endeavour, as I do so, to croud into such Packetts, as I may (if I live,) transmitt from Time to Time unto you.

Tho' I am, from very many parts of the world, sollicited for the *Biblia Americana*, yett, I have no Prospect of its being undertaken by the *London-Booksellers*, until the present Storms are over; which, I am so far from expecting, that I beleeve, the Times must grow yett more tempestuous.

But, it becomes me, with all possible Resignation, to submitt unto the Disposals of Him, who is the Head of the Church, and I have no Eyes but what are in that glorious Head. Lett Him do with us, and our Essayes to serve Him, even what, and when He pleases!

Among the Composures in a Packet which now visits you, there is a very little Thing, entituled, Lapis etc. which is of greater Expectation with me, than anything that I have ever yett been concerned in, you shall give me leave to say, —

After all this, I have been informed, that when the Consideration of it, has been offered unto the General Meeting of your Ministers, it has been treated after such a manner, as much to confirm such Thoughts as I had before Entertained of my honoured Brethren, being yett, scarce ready to see, and much less to do the great Things wherein the Kingdome of God is to come on. The Truth is, it looks as if *Lutherans* in *Germany* had righter Sentiments of, and were like to greater Services for, the Kingdome of God, than my excellent Brethren, the Dissenters in Gr. Britain, seem disposed for.

But my *Walrond* is a person of more Catholic Spirit, than many in the world. I throw the *Lapis Excisus*, into his hands. I beg him to bestow a deep Consideration upon it. I beg him to penetrate into the vast Tendencies of it. I beg him, to do what he can, that it may be shott into the Bowels of *France;* and communicate it, wherever else it may serve the Intentions of it. Pardon me, Syr, if I say to you.

But it is time for me to conclude my long Letter. I do it, with earnest Supplications to our glorious Lord, that your precious Life may be prolonged, and that all your Holy Studies to serve the best of Interests may be directed and prosperity continue your Loves and Prayers for, Sir, Your most affectionate Brother.

To Oliver Noyes.   A.A.S.

[November? 1716.]

My honoured Friend, — When some Gentlemen of your honourable House, lately, (that is to say, the last Thursday Evening) obliged me with a visit, I did offer my present sentiments on two Articles, after which there was made some Enquiry.[1]

First, Concerning our Governour, I declared, that I took his Candour and Goodness to be such, that, we may be happy in him, and should be thankful for him, and that we shall do well to do every thing, that may have a Tendency to make his Government an easy Station to him. To this purpose, I read certain passages in Letters from our Friends abroad. And added, my hopes, that the faithful Methods used continually to rescue His Excellency from some Dangers our People were afraid of would not be ineffectual. And I intimated that I also hoped, all wise Men would avoid every thing that should give the least Occasion of Suspicion, that they could prefer before him a Person of a much less agreeable Character for us.

Secondly, Concerning our Agent, I declared, That I was most inclinable to the opinion, that we should not be too sudden in laying aside Mr. D[umme]r, from his Agency, with any Indignities, inasmuch as all our powerful and more distinguished Friends at home were his; and had copiously and vehemently recommended him unto

---

[1] See p. 383, *supra.*

us; and I fear'd, a Contempt cast upon him, would be such an affront and Offence unto them all, as would be greatly to our Damage. And tho' that Business of *Brand* had a very odd Aspect,[1] yett there were come over such legal vindications of Mr D—r, under the Seal of the Lord-Mayor and otherwise that it seemed not at all proper publickly to insist upon it. So that, some remarkable Indescretion or Unfaithfulness in his mismanagement seemed the only just Cause, at this time to lay him aside, which, if it were found, there could not one word be spoken for his Countenance. But in the mean time, so very great a Number of considerable Persons in the Place, were so strongly possess'd of his being a great Sufferer for his doing a great Service for us, they would espouse his cause to such a Degree, as to make a very uncomfortable Clash, which would be attended with much Iniquity among us. For which Reasons, I could not but think, such a Matter ought very deliberately to be proceeded in.

This was the Summ of my Discourse; in all which, as I spoke, *ut qui suum Dominum* [   ], so, I wish you could have heard it all. I don't remember, that one disrespectful Word was uttered of the Gentlemen who might have other Sentiments; but all possible Deference paid unto their Merits, (tho no Persons particularly mentioned.)

Our late Lt Governour's Name,[2] did not once occurr, that I remember, in all our Conference.

And whereas you have had Intimations as if I declared some relinquishments of my former Thoughts, about our private Bank, tis, *cujus contrarium.* I have never done so, to any one man in the world. And at this time, I expressly said, I may be as qualified as another man, to say what I am going to speak; because I suppose, I differ from the Generality of the Gentlemen present, in the Matter of the Bank. I cannot but hope, the different Views of wise men about that matter, will be so temperately maintained, as not to affect the public Tranquillity.

This is the Summ and Aim of what I have spoken.

And I now speak it all over again, unto you, my particular Friend, perswaded, that I serve the cause of Piety, as well as of Peace, in praying you, to allow the Points, a very calm, and just Consideration.

And I do now add some further Thoughts, which nothing but a pure Friendship could move me to.

First; I beseech you to do nothing which they that are most of all jealous of you, may have any pretence to construe, as a Design to

[1] See Sewall, *Diary*, III. 78.   [2] Tailer.

give any Uneasiness, unto our sweet spirited Governour and provoke his Return, that we may be unhappy in an unknown successor. As His Excellency's Interest at home is not easily to be abated, so it will grow among our selves. And they that shall be thought his Enemies will mightily hurt themselves. I much desire, that your valuable Accomplishments, may be ever improved for the Benefit of your Countrey.

Secondly, I entreat you, to keep your Stops, in your Opposition, to what may be the prevailing Inclination for Mr. D—r. I take not Mr. D—r, to be a personal Friend of mine; He has given me cause enough to reckon him very much otherwise. It is very seldome that he has written to me of late years; and when he has done it, I think it has alwayes been with an Acrimony, that I take little pleasure in. But I cannot imagine, an outrage upon him just done to be seasonable. You sufficiently discharge your Conscience in a moderate Manifestation of your Judgment; and so leaving of it. If the Wrath go on, you sacrifice to his numerous Friends, what your usual purdence in other Cases, would not so liberally throw away. *Sic causeo*.

You will give my service, to my vertuous, and highly esteemed, Mr. A. *Stoddard*, and lett him see all that now comes to you from Sir, Your most sincere Friend and Serv't.

To Elihu Yale.   A.A.S.

November 12, 1716.

Sir, — Your honourable Kinsman returning for *London*, gives me an agreeable Opportunity, of congratulating the Satisfaction, which you cannot but enjoy, in having a Kinsman so worthy of your best Regards.

He has not only been so much my particular Friend, but the public has also been so obliged and gratified, in his candid, generous, uncorrupt Administration, while he possessed the chief Seat of our Government that I owe him all the Expression of a friendly Respect, that I can give him.

I am very much a Stranger to the clashing of particular Interests, and I have none of them to serve; but, I think, I may, without Prejudice to anybody, say, that it is a rare thing for a Person to recede from a Post of public service, more generally esteemed for a gentlemanly Behaviour in it, than Col. *Tailer*.

The End of my writing this, is purely to add a Grain or two, unto the Pleasure, which the first Interview of such Relatives, after long Distance, is to be fill'd withal: And therewith to pray your Acceptance of two or three small American Productions, which only for the sake of a Countrey, which has not lost your affectionate Remembrance of it, may hope for your favourable Eye upon them.

Which I do, with hearty Prayers to our glorious God and Saviour for His Blessings to be multiplied on your Person and Family. And with many Thanks to Heaven for the excellent Governour, whom you have lately sent over to us. And subscribe, Sir, Your most hearty servt.

To Sir William Ashurst? A.A.S.

Sir, — Having a few Dayes ago, written to your Honour, by C[olonel] *Tailer*, I have nothing to add, but a short Report of what occurr'd in our G[eneral] A[ssembly] about the Time of his going off; because it will be an Article of your more particular Sollicitude and Satisfaction.

Three or four of the Representatives, (those particularly that act for the city of Boston,) have been extremely disaffected unto our Agent Mr. D—r and better affected than they should have been unto one whom he had made his Enemy by his doing for us the greatest of Services. These Gentlemen being sufficiently noisy and subtil and Master of all the Arts which were necessary on such an Occasion, caused much Distemper in the G. A. at their first coming together. About nineteen or twenty principal Members of the House, together did me the Honour of a Visit, before three Dayes of their Session had passed over.

At what time, I had an agreeable Opportunity, first of all, to expatiate on the excellent Character of our Governour, and our vast Obligations unto you particularly, for the share you had in obtaining so rich a Blessing for us. And then, I sett before them, in as engaging a manner as I could, what Reasons there were for our publick Respects to be still continued unto Mr. D—r. How amply and fully he had been vindicated from Aspersions; and how copiously he had been recomended unto us, by our best Friends, with you, for his Fidelity and Assiduity, in our Service.

The Effect of this Conference, was beyond what I could have had the Vanity to have look'd for;

A conspicuous Change in the Tempers and Measures of the House Ensued. And the House quickly came to very much of what was desired from them. If they do not in the present Session come up to all that should be done, it is expected that the men who have been so troublesome, will be dropt in the next Election, and then the Spirit of the People, which appears full of zeal for our Governour, and for our Agent, will doubtless more fully exert itself.

To Mr. Ward.   A.A.S.

Boston, N. E. 20 d. IX m. [November.] 1716.

Sir, — It is, I suppose, hardly a month ago, that I gave myself the Satisfaction of writing to you; and you may be sure, tis a Satisfaction, which I shall on all Opportunities be grasping at.

The only subject of this Letter, will be a Matter somewhat foreign from what I usually treat you withal: but not altogether Foreign to the Friendship, wherewith our whole Conversation is to be maintained.

I grow somewhat sensible, that the Trade between *Holland* and *New England*, is on the growing hand, and that on both sides it proves pretty much to the Mind of those concerned in it.

You are now addressed by a young gentleman, Mr *Samuel Sewal*, with Tenders of his best Services to you, if you see cause to favour him with any of your Consignments. Perhaps, by giving you some Account of him, I may do something to introduce him into the way of being serviceable to you, if you may judge it proper that he should be so.

He is an acute and polite Merchant; one of distinguished Ingenuity, and of a very worthy Family: But what is best of all, he is a person of unspotted Probity, and excellent Piety; nor do I know a young Gentleman, whom I could with more assurance recommend for his Capacity and Fidelity.

And I beleeve it will be no Prejudice unto the Recommendation which I have given of him, when I add this Article to it; That before this comes to your hands, he hopes to be a Son-in-Law to your American Friend, who now mentions him.

I will confess to you, that I also hope for one Advantage to myself, if ever the Correspondence now proposed, should be produced, which is, that I have a mighty Thirst after the Sight of Books, now and then published in *Holland:* which may upon sending you the *Titles* be transmitted with the Goods that you may send hither, and I pay here the Price at which you charge them. In this literary Trade, our candid and precious Friend Mr. *Loftus*, may be of use, to procure, what I may write for. And the Truth is, I will now already begin the Trade; with a Request upon it.

There is one *Thomas Crenius*,[1] who had published above a dozen little Duodecimo Volumes, of Collections of small Treatises, full of Erudition, which have been heretofore exhibited in Separate and scattered Editions. Our dear Mr. *Loftus*, will explain what they are; and will direct how to come at them. If you thought fit to procure these for me, and send them, in what way you please, I should immediately pay to your order here, the Price at which they may be charged.

What remains is, to repeat my Supplications to the Glorious God our Saviour, that He would multiply His Blessings on your Person and Family, and subscribe, Sir, Your most affectionate Friend and Serv't.

FROM SAMUEL PENHALLOW.   A.A.S.

PORTSMOUTH, Decbr. 27th, 1716.

REVD. AND DEAR DOCTOR, — I need not I presume tell you that our friend Capt. Wentworth[2] is in Nomination att home for being Lt. Governour of this Province, but the King's absence did put a stop unto the Methods then used to effect it; and it being hoped that he is now returned; and for as much as interest with some great person is needfull to obtaine such an End; I would pray the favour of you to write a letter on his behalf with Sir Wm. Ashurst, with whom I well know you Entertain a constant correspondence. I need not tell you that he is a deserved member of our councill, and a gentleman every way qualified as to Estate, vertue, and loyalty, who studies the interest of the Country, and an upholder of the constitution of our churches; a true friend to the present Governour,[3] and universally beloved among us; whereas our present Lt. Gov'r[4] is on the reverse, of which I have writt att large unto your honoured father. Mr. Dummer I am well assured will Second every thing that you write on this head.

And whereas we have a ship hence bound for England in a few days, would pray you to send over the letters unto Sir Wm, or any else you are interested in, that I may send accordingly. Your favour herein, will be of greatest interest unto our poor Province, and a particular interest unto Revd Sir, Your truly affect. and most obliged servt.

SAMLL. PENHALLOW.

---

[1] His real name was Crusius (1648–1728). His *Historical and Critical Dissertations*, in ten volumes, appeared in 1691.

[2] John Wentworth. See Belknap, *History of New Hampshire*, I. 187.

[3] Shute.   [4] George Vaughan.

To Rev. John Squire.   A.A.S.

[January, 1716-17.]

Sir, — When you (and the Brethren with you) arrived here, we did with unspeakable Pleasure, lay hold on the Opportunity, to express our Communion with the dear Church of *Scotland*, and the precious Sons of *Zion* therein, whom we valued as our most *United Brethren*.

Accordingly we have all along treated you, with all the Civilities imaginable, as we have always done other Ministers of your Nation, upon their Arrival among us.

You are the first, that ever we have known to decline and renounce Communion with the Churches of God in this Countrey. Albeit, I am very certain, that for you to have held an occasional Communion with them, would have been very grateful to your excellent Mother, the Church of *Scotland*: the *Elect Lady*, I am very certain, would have been pleased with it; And your treating of it, in such a manner as you have done, has much reproached her.

You must not wonder, if Declarations that it would be a Wrong unto Conscience, to hold Communion with our Churches; and Insinuations thrown among the people, that our Ministers can admitt you no otherwise than as Lay-men; and that our Baptism is little better than none at all; should be Things, at which we are dissatisfied. Nor can it, without a Folly equal unto the rest, be called, *a Persecution for Righteousness Sake*, if in our Discourse with you will tell you so.

This does not hinder me from telling you, that I am afraid your hasty Leaving of the hospitable and religious Family, where you have alwayes been honourably treated, may expose you to some Inconveniencies.

Wherefore I do in the most brotherly Manner, invite you to my own Habitation; where your Diet and Lodging shall cost you nothing, while you stay in the Countrey, if you see Cause to accept thereof; or are not provided more to your Satisfaction. Your Accommodations here, will be Inferiour to few in the Town; and, in respect of the Library superiour to any. To which this easy Circumstance will be added; that all the while you stay, you shall not hear those Things, which we take to be your Weaknesses, uneasily insisted on. Do what you please, I shall alwayes endeavour to approve myself, your Friend and Servant.

                                              C. M.

BOSTON, January 10th, 1716.

SIR, — I received your letter by Mr. White, In which you seem to express your great affection towards the Church of Scotland, which, you say, you took pleasure to express to us upon our arrival at this place. In my judgement that Church deserves esteem and regard of all about here, whatever others may think; but really if she be tory in her government, I think at least in that she ought to be discountenanced, for my part were it not that I know better, I should disown her from being an honest and Creditable mother, and avouch it before the world that she had played the harlot since I left Scotland. However If you think her such an Elect Lady as you profess, I do confess that I don't see upon what grounds, or with what consistency you call her Government Torism.

As for the Civilities you have treated me with, I can say, I never designed to return any other than civilities for them, and I think there is no Just ground given for to alleadge, that I have done otherwise. However your Civilities Savour the worse to me that they are cast so frequently in my teeth; and I think If my poor preaching of the Gospell was not as much worth as your civilities, you and I both were beyond the bounds of Civilitie in acting as we have done.

You alleadge that we are the first that ever declined Communion with you, but If I be not mistaken by Information there have been of ours, that have declined to go so great a length as we have done, tho perhaps others have gone further; But supposing it to be so, I reckon it no cause of upbraiding us, For Mens practices one way or other is no argument to me.

And I'm sure of this that you seemed to decline Communion first, as to Ministerial acts in dispensing Sacraments tho I never quarelled it, as Judging it consistent with your principles. And I think you have as little ground to be offended at us, If we act consistently with ours, as far as our present condition will allow.

As for its being acceptable or unacceptable to the Church of Scotland, is unknown to me, and never consulted them on the head, nor did I ever think of it untill I came to New England; but this I'm sure of that upon our arrival here, it was told us either by your Selfe or a friend of yours, If not both, that one, upon his return home, was challenged for Joining in Communion with you. Whether it was so or not is no matter to me, I desire to have Clearness in my own mind in what I do, but this is certain that it looks not like Civilitie to treat us after such a manner, as to drive us to that which may give the least ground for such treatment when we return home. And for my part If there had been no other thing than your way of treating me on this head, I should think it would occasion thought before I could Join with you; for If it was my weakness as you alleadge, other treatment than open insults became you towards a weak brother, but these I can easily forgive, and pray for more of a gospell spirit to all of us than we have.

Its realy a matter of wonder to me, to think, what can be the reason you seem so violent against us on this head, when you trouble your selfe so little with hundreds that live by you, who never Join with you; but the reason of this is best known to your Selfe, and you must allow me to make conjectures about it. As for my being a reproach to the Church of Scotland, I suppose, you would neither have said so nor thought so, If I had turned to be of your mind, but I can leave any to Judge, whether those that forsake her principles and practise or those that would gladly keep to them be a reproach to her. Sir, I must tell you that She does as great duty to her Children, as any Mother in the world, and, If her Children prove disobedient, they deserve reproach, not She. As for Conscience what I do, God is my witness, and I think for any to go beyond their sphere in Judging me as to this matter, discovers want of due consideration. And as for Insinuations amongst your people, that your Sacraments were no better than non, is a groundless Calumnie, I do put to a defiance any one in Boston, to prove, that ever I spoke one word as to your authority to your people, and when I spoke on that head in Mr Frizels, that which was extorted from me (after declining several times to give an account of this matter) I did expressly distinguish myselfe from your Flock, and told with all the modestie I was capable off, what seemed to Me Wherein you were not concerned with me according to your principles. And truely I'm surprized to find, that you alleadge, I sued so to you. Sir, If you draw consequences, pray, Father them your Selfe for they are non of mine, and beware of spreading abroad, that which I never thought it my bussiness to question, for I think it not fair.

You accuse me of folly and weakness in yours, and particularly in calling it persecution which I have mett with from you. I will not return railing for railing, you know, Sir, that persecution lies not in buffeting, Scourging, &c; but also in persecuting with the tongue, and to give me such names as are certainly very Infamous and represent me to others as guilty of that, which I never designed, If it may

not Justly gett the name of persecution, I'm at a loss to know what
the Spirit of God means by persecuting and Smiting with the tongue.
Sir, I have that wisdome God has thought fitt to bestow on me, and
desire to seek more from him who will not upbraid with my follies,
but truely, Sir, you are the first that ever called me so; and I cant
forbear to tell you, that I'm not the only person that thinks, you need
much more wisdome than you have, and I pray God you may obtain
it, that you may know better how to medle with things that concern
your Selfe.

In the Close of yours, you express your kindness to and Concern
for me. I thank you heartily for your offers, but tho I have mett
with many Inconveniences since I left Scotland (and it seems my
difficulties are not yet at an end) yet I bless the Lord that he hitherto
helped, and I hope will do it alwayes, so that I shall not need to be
troublesome to others as of late I have been. I'm sensible of the
respect that Mr. Frizel and his Lady showed to me, and can assure
you, that it was not out of any disregard to them, that I left their
family; but for reasons that your letter has abundantly confirmed
me in I shall add no more, only, whatever has been your Carriage
towards me, I hope, (thro' grace) shall be enabled to cary Christianly
towards you, I'm Your real friend and most humble Servant

JOHN SQUIRE.

As for your Illustrations they are safe and I shall take care they
be delivered safely unto your hands.

TO JOSEPH PARSONS.   A.A.S.

22 *d.* XI *m.* [January.] 1716[-17].

SIR, — Since it is a critical Time with you, it appears unto me,
the best Thing that I can do for your Service at this Time, to sett
before you in as true a Light as I can, the true cause of those dark
Difficulties and Encumbrances, which attend your proposed Settlement in the Service of the Church now forming in the South-part
of *Boston.*

While the Ministers of the Town are so generally prejudiced, as
at present they seem to be, against your being taken into their Number, such a Settlement seems unto me for a thousand Reasons to be
despaired of.

But what shall be done for the Removal of that Prejudice? Tis
fitt you should first of all know the Resons, why those faithful Servants of GOD have entertained it.

They seem to fear, that you are a Person who have sometimes indulged yourself in a *Way of Lying*, and invented very black Slanders of innocent and vertuous Men which is the worst Sort of Lying, and therewithal improved the Arts of Insinuation for the sowing of *dangerous Discords*.

Upon this Fear, tho' their *Charity* be such that they wish well to a good Improvement of your Talents, yett their *Conscience* of Duty to GOD, and His Churches, will not suffer them to recommend you to a Flock of such Importance, as what is now to be provided for.

The Things that have produced a *Terror of GOD* upon their Minds about you, are such as these.

You did once and again, assert very horrid Things, concerning Mr. *Bulkly;* and concerning Mr *Whiting*. But the papers lodged in the hands of one of the Ministers in this Town will doubtless compell all of them, and any others that shall see them, to beleeve, that there was no Truth in your Assertions.

It is affirmed, that you uttered Scandals, of the same Tendency concerning Mr *Woodward*, while it was thought he did not favour your Interests at *Lebanon*. But afterwards Mr. *Woodward* was a better man.

You did report several Things much to the Defamation of some Candidates of the Ministry; which were very false; and you never could produce any Author for them.

While you pretended the greatest Respect unto the two Ministers of the North-Church, and received nothing but such from them, you did, (hoping thereby to ingratiate yourself,) at the Table of a Minister of the South, bestow indecent Flings and Flouts upon them; for which the Mistress of the Table severely rebuked you, and told you, that you took the wrong Way to be ingratiated there; you also know, what you said of that Gentlewoman, when you were afterwards told of this.

You may remember, some other mischievous Tale-bearings, wherein you were, about that time detected.

My Father then wrote unto you his Dissatisfactions. And you never answered his Letter.

It is very certain you went into Families in our Neighbourhood, and there sett yourself to poison them with all possible Disaffection to their two Ministers. Your practise raised an uncomfortable Discord between Husband and Wife. They that loved us and our Ministry, found their Souls hurt unto such a Degree, that they desired never to see you more, and obliged your withdraw from them.

I know something of your way to speak unto my Disadvantage: which exposed you to the Resentments of some serious People, more than you were aware of. All that while, and in all my life, never had I done you any Wrong or Harm. I now also overcame the Evil so far, that I discouraged not our private Meetings from using of you, tho' one word of mine would have done it. And I now perfectly forgive it all; judging myself obliged above others, to Do you good.

You associated yourself with some of our Brethren, to form a New Church at the North, upon the Foundation of an Aversion for the two Ministers. The Defamations, with which you fly-blow'd the Minds of those Brethren have not unto this Hour worn off their ill Impressions. But you know, what passed between you and Mr. *Gee*, on that occasion. And if Mr. *Gee* be compelled now, to exhibit the Particulars of that Story, which he can in part justify, (tho' Deacon *Atwood* be dead,) it will make some Impressions on many that hear it. The design of our *New North*, was delay'd a Year, upon the Defeat of your making yourself an Interest in such a Way.

It is greatly suspected, that the Troubles in the old Church were much owing to your blowing of the Coals on the Intention of having a new Meeting-house built for you.

I have mett with some other unintelligible Things in your Conduct. But being personal, they are forgotten. And I am as willing as any man living, that all that I have mentioned, should be charitably thrown into the Heap of *Unintelligibles*.

Now, my Friend, what Method can you take, to satisfy the Discreet Servants of God, and Watchmen of the Churches, either that such Errors have not been committed; or that if they have been committed, they have been duely repented of, and that you have no such *habitual Inclination* unto these crooked Paths, as to keep them still afraid of you?

Can any proper Address to them, give them the Satisfaction?

If by Pretensions of your Friends, to make an Interest for you, they be putt upon demanding an *hearing of their Objections*, before any persons of superior Consideration, how will this terminate?

I pray GOD, graciously to direct you; I confess myself much at a Loss what I should offer for your Direction.

I can only say, that if your Case were my own, I should not have Courage enough, to try whether a way could be forced for me into a Church in this Town, with a Dislike of it [on] the most [part] of the Ministers and with a Division and Contention raised in the place, and a Fire, in which I should undergo the utmost hazard of being incinerated. I would much rather accept of Opportunities to do Good, where I should meet with, *Rixae multo minus, Invidiaeque;* Which you may have the offer of, and which being offered, such is the Tenderness of the Ministers for you after all, that they would leave you undisturbed in them.

For my own part, were my Assurances of your Integrity, aequal to my Dispositions of doing you no Hurt, yett I should not think myself *strong* enough, or *bound* at all, to engage in any Wars, to bring about by Force of Arms your Establishment in an uneasy Station; and fight the way thro' an Army of Contradictions for it.

It may not be amiss for me to add, that some eminent Persons in the Place, are of the Opinion, that you have been so far from having, in your Abilities and Performances, your profiting appear unto all Men, since your first coming hither so many years ago, as to lay them under much discouragement in their Hopes of your shining with such a Lustre as ought to be for a City sett upon an Hill; the Capital City of these Colonies.

These are the Things which I would calmly and humbly leave, to your wisest Considerations; and if you purpose any Answer to them, I would not have it meerly *oral*, and I would have it address'd rather to the rest of my honoured Brethren, than to, Sir, Your Thoughtful, Friend and Serv't.[1]

To Rev. John Squire.   A.A.S.

[January, 1716-17.]

Sir, — In answer to what I this moment received from you, I have at present nothing to say, but only desire you to forbear filling the Town with a false Story, that I have said, the Government of the Church of *Scotland* is a *Tory-Government.*

All that ever I said, (as the Gentlemen in the Company can Witness,) was, that I doubted a great Part of the Church-Government in the world, had a little Touch of (what I called, in a way of perfect pleasancy, and all the company took me so,) *Ecclesiastical Torism.*

I said nothing of the Ch: of Scotland; it was you ran upon *that.* And I explain'd myself, that my Meaning was, the People in some things seem'd to want the due Exercise of their Liberties.

If you go on to traduce me, on this Occasion, you will persist in

---

[1] Parsons was not accepted, and the church remained without a pastor until September, 1718, when Samuel Checkley was unanimously called.

a Violation of the Ninth Commandment. No man in *America*, has a juster Veneration for the Ch: of *Scotland*, than I must alwayes maintain, and shall do so.

And I am sorry for the Wrongs that you have done to that venerable Body.

I pray God forgive you all the Sins of your abusive and virulent Letter. As well as your Endeavours to sow Discord in a Town, that ought to be more gratefully treated.

I have something else to do with my Time, than to spend it in Altercations with a Person of your Disposition.

More Humility, Meekness, and Wisdome, would render you more amiable and more serviceable.

You will Expect nothing further, from Your abused Friend.

To Benjamin Colman.

1 *d.* XII *m.* [February, 1716-17.]

Sir, — Your Candour and Goodness towards little *Ereskin*, very much obliges me: and I pray you to continue it.

You will allow me to transcribe a part of your Letter, which may be very much to the Childs Advantage, if I live to write unto Mr. Woodson.

But how full of Little mistakes are our Neighbours on all occasions! I wish Mr. P—s[1] could tell, who told him, that the New-South Society had a copy of my poor Letter to him. I never spoke one word of it, unto any one man of them.

I never gave the sight of that Letter to any but *Adoni Avi*, and you, and Mr. W—b.

The last had it a little while in his hands, with my Desire that no one might see or hear any thing of it.

He so far forgott, as to read it unto one Intimate Friend of his; who has no Relation to that Society; nor would make any Talk of it.

He seems to be of the Opinion, That Mr. P—s himself, told *Boone* of it. And *Boone* is most certainly that man, that has made the Discourse of such a Thing, which has proved something to Mr. P—s's disadvantage. This he understands from Mr. *Adams*.

For Mr. P—s, as I do forever entirely forgive and forgett all personal Injuries; He has for them, long been to me, as if none of them had ever been at all; so, for the more General Heads of Dissatisfaction, he has (in an Act of Attrition last night particularly)

---

[1] Parsons.

express'd himself much in the Language of a Christian. This I am willing to report, if there be occasion.

I am desirous to do nothing that may hurt him. Yett I have Repeted this to him, That I cannot be drawn into *Wars* for him, and make myself Responsible for a World of Iniquity, which the Tongues engaged in Strife, will soon run into. And, I think, he said, He could not desire it of me.

My Brother Web this Evening assures me, That if all the Ministers of the Town should write in Recommending of Mr. P—s to our *Austrians*, it would only break them all to peeces; The prejudices imbibed are so strong, and Lately increased and confirmed, by what has passed in his own conversation with them.

I cannot but be displeased at a great Stickler for him, to whom I Lately in commendation of Mr. *Foxcroft* said, That I understood he could freely subscribe the Doctrinal Articles of the Ch. of E. professing at the same time, that if he were an Armenian, he could not on any Terms prevail with himself to do so. And I am told, this Blade has mischievously frighted some of his Neighbours with affirming, that Mr. F—t can freely subscribe all the Articles of the Ch. of E. The meaning of which they take to be, that he is a Ch. of E. man. Such perversions, how shall one shield against them.

But enough of these Things.

If I Live till *Munday*, I hope to see you at your House in the forenoon, and go with you to Mr. *Wadsworth*, about *Barnstable*.

Your excellent performance in your Letter to *Martha's Vineyard* Last week, (so much superiour to what accompanied it,) is Reason enough, besides many others, for me to entreat you, that you would prepare a Letter of Excuse and Advice, unto the contentious people who have been so weak as to expect our Travelling Fourscore miles in the Depth of Winter to them. I am, Sir, your Brother and Servant

Co. MATHER.

To JOSEPH PARSONS.

21 *d.* I *m.* [March.] 1717.

SIR, — It is to do the part of one who wishes well to your Interest, that I now would offer you an Advice, which a Regard unto an Interest infinitely greater than yours or any Man's, does extort from me.

I cannot but earnestly advise it, and propose it, that you would not encourage those who call themselves your Friends, to make a struggle for your Settlement in the New South Church, but putt a period unto all the painful prospect of such a Struggle by your accepting an Invitation to Labour, where you will not meet with such Embroilment and Encumbrance, as will anon prove too hard for you.

Be sure, if you have sollicited the Votes of any, or importuned them to act for you, (which I am told, you say, you never did,) this would be so unevangelical a Thing, that it were alone enough utterly to disqualify the Election of a Minister.

Instead of this, I find, that in the primitive Times, when there was a Division among a People, about the Election of a Minister some excellent Men of God, whom the Votes of many ran upon, cried out, *O People of God, we will throw ourselves overboard, rather than the Church of the Lord shall suffer any Storms for our sakes.* This was the true Spirit of the Gospel; well worthy of a *Nazianzen,* and a *Chrysostom!*

It is most certain, that your settlement in this Place, cannot be prosecuted, without so much Contention, and so many evil Works, that the Fear of God in its due Exercise, would make a good Man chuse to dy, rather than be accessory unto such grievous Things.

You so far know the Disposition in the Majority of the inchurched Brethren towards you, that you cannot but foresee, your Introduction there cannot be accomplished, without a Dissolution of the Church, or a disorderly overwhelming of the Rights, which the Church has a claim unto. Are these your Pretensions? If they be, all the Churches in the Countrey, and all the Christians that wish well to the Order of the Gospel, will concern themselves in the Quarrel. And, how will this terminate at the Last?

Finally. In a former Letter, I laid it before you, that the Ministers of the Town "were apprehensive of your being a Person who have indulged yourself in a way of false speaking and inventing very black slanders of innocent and vertuous Men, and improving the Arts of Insinuation for the Sowing of dangerous Discords." I recited unto you many of the Things, which produced such a Terror of God upon their Minds, that they could not *recommend* you unto Service, especially in such a Place as this; while yett their Compassion to you, join'd with some Hope that such Things might be repented of, made them willing to *leave you undisturbed* in what Opportunities for service, the divine Providence might cast upon you.

You did upon this, address me with many Expressions of Repentance, for the wrong Steps you had taken. And tho' they were only in general Terms, yett I was willing to declare, that so far as they went, they were in the Language of a Christian: and at the same time I was, yea, ever have been, willing to do the Part of a Christian, in entirely forgiving and forgetting all personal Injuries.

In the short Letter, wherein I declared this, tho' I intimated, that I should leave the South Church to the Direction of God, and acquiesced in it, there is no Intimation that I could recommend you to their Choice: much less, that the other Ministers could do so: tho' being Men of peaceable Spirits they have not been ready to appear against you.

And the Letter has been improved beyond its Intention, when this Construction has been made of it: for it expressly renounces all *Activities* for you.

But, while a Number of People distinguish themselves by their Zeal for your being here, they run you into the Hazard of a Ruine, which I am now to inform you of.

One of them whose Name is *Dorby* has lately written a Letter to my aged Parent, requiring of him an Account of the Dissatisfactions, which have hindred him from recommending you unto that Service.

And under this Compulsion, he has praepared an Answer to it, which, if it be sent, will be very little to your Advantage. When you wrong'd me tother day, with a false Report, that I had communicated unto the people of the *New South*, my Letter to you, you were pleased to distress a very valuable Friend, with saying, *that I had utterly ruined you*. To obviate which, and because I desired nothing but your Good, that other Letter was drawn from me of which an use has been made, that good Men are troubled at. If the Letter which your Friends do force the Doctor to, should be sent, all the Damage that you fear'd from what I sent unto you, and what I have been so desirous to save you from, will be unavoidable. But the Servant of God, out of Tenderness to you, suspends the sending of his Letter, until the Man who addressed him has first spoken with you.

The rest of the Ministers, as well as he, are sensible, that they have been much reproached, for their Lenity, in forbearing to have matters brought unto an Hearing. But if the Party that push for your being here, go on to more Violence in their Proceedings, the Gentlemen will certainly be under a Necessity to demand an Hearing; and some honourable Persons in the Government already press them to it, and will expect that they shall have their Share in them passing a Judgment, on the Quaestion, whether you are to be recommended unto the Station that is now aspir'd unto.

My Letter to you, of 22 *d*. XI *m*. gives you as good as a thousand Reasons, why you should by no means bring things to this Extremity.

I earnestly protest unto you, that if you were my own Brother,

I would now perswade you, to drop all Pretensions here, and be humbly thankful to God, that He mercifully opens to you Doors of service where you may have more undisturbed Opportunities to spend your latter Dayes, in a Correction of those Errors, which have created you so much Trouble in all the former Stages of your Action. I am, Sir, one that wishes you very well.

1717

THE LV YEAR OF MY LIFE.

12 d. XII m. [*February.*] 1716.–17.   The fifty-fourth Year of my Life is now finished.   And the Glorious Lord of my Life, has with marvellous Displays of sovereign Grace, prolonged it, how much beyond my Reasonable Expectation!

In the former part of the Day, I sett myself to give Thanks unto the Lord, for His Favours which I have seen in His hitherto preserving and variously sweetening of my Life.

In the latter Part of the Day, I humbled myself before Him, for the Errors of my Life: and especially bewailed the cursed Sloth, which has been such a Crime and such a plague unto me; and made my Flight unto the great Sacrifice for the Pardon of all my Miscarriages; and I entreated of Him, that He would spare me this Year also; and make it a fruitful year; and prepare me for all the Events and Changes, which in this year I may, meet withal.

G. D.   My Son *Samuel,* must be made more the object of my Conversation, and my Cultivation.   As often as the Lad comes in my View, I must think, *What Good shall I now do to the Child?* or, *What Good shall I putt the Child upon?* or, *What shall I now enrich his Mind withal?*   Especially, teach him to live unto God, in what he does, both at School, and at Home.

13. G. D.   I would look on certain sick Ministers, as my Brethren.   My Prayer shall be in their Calamities.   I will study to do for them all the acts of a Brother born for their Adversity.   Tho' I must overcome Evil with Good, in doing so.

14. G. D.   Yesterday in the Afternoon, there died the elder Minister of the old South Church in the Town; one

who was eight or nine years younger than myself.[1]   He was
a man of greater Abilities than many others : and, no doubt,
a pious man : but a man of a strangely choleric and envious
Temper, and one who had created unto me more Trials of
my Patience, and more Clogs upon my Opportunities to
do good, than almost any other Man in the World.   The
younger Minister of that Church,[2] a dear Son, and one of
an excellent Spirit, should have preach'd this Day; but in
his Distress he flies unto me to take his Place in the public
Services.   I cannot easily reckon up the Opportunities to
do good, which I find concurring, in this one Invitation to
public Performances on such an Occasion.   And the glorious
Lord helped me to glorify Him, in the speaking of many
Things to serve the general Interests of Religion, as well as
in the Testimony which I gave to what was laudable in
the Character of the departed Minister.

There was a vast Auditory ; and I was greatly assisted
of God.

Præliminary to my public Performances, as I had my
Humiliations, thus I humbled myself before the Lord,
bewayling all the Distempers which the ill Carriage of the
Deceased Neighbour may at any time have thrown me
into ; and admiring the divine Goodness and Patience,
which has given me to outlive so many of my younger
Brethren.

15. G. D.   In Conversation with our excellent Governour, I am now proposing of several Services.   But
very particularly to forward the Publication of the, *Biblia
Americana*, by the Help of his Brother[3] in *England*.

16. G. D.   Some foolish and froward Peoples have by
very disingenuous Misrepresentations, done me much harm.
I must overcome Evil with Good.

[1] Rev. Ebenezer Pemberton (1672–1717).

[2] Rev. Joseph Sewall.

[3] John Shute Barrington, first Viscount Barrington (1678–1734).   See *Dictionary of National Biography*, III. 290.

*17. G. D. Two ministers of Note in the Countrey, one if not both, of them younger than myself, are now lying Dead.[1] What Improvement should I make of the Spectacle?

Be sure, a most Quickened Industry, a strong Vigour, a swift Despatch, in the Work which my Hand finds to do.

My God, Help me to abound, and make haste in the Work of the Lord!

18. G. D. The Admonitions of Piety from such a Text as Eccl. IX. 10. on these Occasions, may be such as the Flock may receive good Impressions from.

19. G. D. So many of my Family are now so taken off one way or another, and the rest are so indifferent at Singing, that I am afraid, I must often omitt, the Singing, which makes a part of the Evening-Sacrifices in our Family. When at any Time I do omitt it, what shall I substitute in the Room of it? I am thinking, on Reading one of *Luther's* Meditations, on the, *Insignes Sacrtae Scripturae Sententiæ*, whereof there is a published collection, or else [2]

20. G. D. Propose to my Brother at *Witney*, a Retreat unto *New England*, in Case any Storms arise in *England*.

21. G. D. Direct the, *Lapis e Monte Excisus*, to *Geneva*. It may be a seasonable Action, and attended with marvellous Consequences.

22. G. D. Some Care must be taken, to find a convenient Place, where the Ministers of the Town may meet after the Lecture; where I may be an Instrument of some good.

23. G. D. A poor Man sick, whom nobody takes notice of, must be the Object of my Kindnesses.

23 *d.* XII *m. Satureday.* This Day, I sett apart for Prayer with Fasting in my Study.

---

[1] Rev. Mr. Pemberton and Rev. William Brattle, the latter dying February 14. Sewall wrote, "That Two Divines so eminently usefull, should ly dead in their Houses at once, is what I have not before observed, and wish it be not portentous." *Letter Book,* II. 66.

[2] Left unfinished.

It was with me a Day of sorrowful Contritions, and Sacrifices.

At length, I obtained some encouraging and comfortable Symptoms of my having the Sentence of Death upon me for my sin taken off, in my having my soul quickened unto Acts of living unto God.

A wretched Family in my Neighbourhood, having hurt me, with cursed Lyes raised upon me, revenging on me a Provocation which they had received from the Zeal of my Father, against an Error committed by them. This was a Matter of my Supplications; that my conduct may be wise, good, humble, patient, and fruitful, on such an Occasion.

I carried all my Concerns unto the Lord: especially, the Præparations which He has helped me to make for the Press; and particularly, what I have sent beyond-sea.

And I cried unto Him, for His Fulfilment of that gracious Word, *I will pour out my Spirit upon all Flesh.*

I also beg'd of the gracious God, that He would communicate those Things to me, which might render me a Great Benefactor to Mankind.

But so managed my Petitions, that they may not still terminate in *Self.*

* 24. G. D. And this is a Point of Piety, which I would grow exceeding accurate and circumspect in the Study of. I would examine my Petitions unto God; and see to it, that God and not *Self*, be the Chief end wherein they terminate.

25. G. D. There are some Cases, which I do well more particularly to consider, in the public Prayers wherewith I serve the Flock, in the weekly Sacrifices.

26. G. D. For a Bed-Book, out of which to read some Entertainment for my Consort, in the Morning, I propose, the *Suspiria* in *Egardus.*

27. G. D. Another Visit unto an aged Father-in-Law at *Charlestown.*

28. G. D. As mighty a Snow, as perhaps has been known in the Memory of Man, is at this Time lying on the Ground; and as mighty a Thaw must be look'd for. Would it not be a seasonable, may it not be a serviceable Action, to entertain the People of God, at the Lecture, with a Discourse on Psal. CXLVII. 18. *He sendeth forth His Word, and melteth them.*[1]

(I.) Having preached a Sermon by which a gracious God made Impressions on the Minds of many Hearers, the Publication of it was by some desired: but very particularly by one who was willing to make a little Reparation for some Drowsiness which overtook him in the Hearing. I considered, that the Discourse might be of use to me, in my dealing with a Multitude of People. So the Press exhibits it under this Title. THE CASE OF A TROUBLED MIND. *A brief Essay, Upon the Troubles of a Mind, which apprehends the Face of a Gracious God hidden from it; The Symptoms of the Troubles, and the Methods of preventing them.*[2]

March. 1717. 1. G. D. Why may I not resume the Consideration, I have sometimes had, of having a Delegate or two, from each of the religious Societies belonging to my Flock; who may together have Interviews with me, at proper Times, and concert with me Projections to serve the Kingdome of God among them?

2. G. D. A poor Student in Divinity, at some Distance, from me, must be helped with Books and some other Assistences.

* 3. G. D. I would speedily draw up an Exhibition of those Things I apprehend the principal and most elevated Points of Piety and Sanctity, and of living unto God; And have my Soul unspeakably restless, until I find myself arriv'd in some good Measure unto them.

---

[1] "Apply'd it also to the Conversion of the Jews." Sewall, *Diary,* III. 123.
[2] Printed by B. Green for S. Gerrish, 1717.

4. G. D. Probably in reading the *Theologia Mystica* of *Harphius*,[1] I may meet with many Thoughts and Flames, that may furnish me to serve the Flock in those Points and Wayes, which I most of all desire.

5. G. D. To read a Chapter of *Egardus* unto my lovely Consort, every morning before we rise, may be an acceptable Entertainment unto her, and a profitable one to both of us.

6. G. D. Mr. *Craighead*[2] has been so near to me on many Occasions, that I will assign him a Place in my Memorials among my Relatives. I will every Day mention him in my secret Prayers, that he may be *kept holy and made useful.* I have Thoughts of getting him translated unto a comprehensive Service at the East-ward.

7. G. D. Tis a Time of much Rebuke from Heaven upon us, in the Season. Such Storms and Heaps of Snow, visit us in the approach of the Spring, as were hardly ever known in the Depth of Winter. A great part of the Assemblies in the Countrey have been inter[dic]ted their public Sacrifices. A Multitude of Cattel have perished. The Business of the Countrey has an uncommon Stop upon it. Many Difficulties grow upon us. I would procure a Day of Humiliations and Supplications to be kept on these occasions.

8. G. D. Many People are thrown into Straits and Wants, by the Difficulties of the Season; I would both express and excite all suitable Expressions of Charity on these Occasions.

9. G. D. There is a poor Widow in this Neighbourhood, who, with her son, is exposed unto Difficulties. I would make my House to become an Home unto them.

* 10. G. D. I feel a very sensible Rebuke from Heaven upon me, in shutting me out from the Service of the Flock. On the last Lord's-day I was compelled unto sitting still,

[1] Henricus Harphius (-1478), a Flemish mystic theologian. This work was published in 1611.   [2] Thomas Craighead. See p. 306, *supra.*

out of a Complement unto a Person who had been asked
by my Father to preach for him, and yett arrived not so
soon but that my Father fearing his Failing had gott another
to supply his Room. The young Man, to whom I thus in
civility gave away, was also one, whom for the Vanity of
his Character, I did least of all desire to see in our Pulpitt.
This Lord's-day I am arrested with a Cold, and a Cough,
and am therewithal so hoarse, that I am laid by from all
public Ministrations.

On these Occasions I humbled myself before the glorious
God. I renewed my Importunities for the Pardon of the
Miscarriages, which had provoked Him thus to deal with
me; and repaired unto the great Sacrifice. I entreated,
that I might know, and hear the Calls of the divine Providence, in what had befallen me. And I requested, that I
might yett be employ'd in the Service of my Glorious Lord.

11. G. D. I hope, the ill Turn upon my Health; which
has thus confined me and exil'd me, from the Service of the
Flock, will prove a mighty Animation unto my Endeavours,
to serve the Flock, more painfully, faithfully, skilfully, than
ever in my Life before.

12. G. D. Nor would I under the Admonitions which
my Illness gives me, delay to settle in a testamentary Way,
what may be for the Good of my Family, and to dispatch
what Things I should leave in writing, that they may be
well-circumstanced, when I am gone from them.

13. G. D. My Kinsman T. W[alter] gives great Hopes,
of his proving an useful Man. Behold, a revived Subject
for my Cares, and Considerations!

14. G. D. I have been desirous, that good may come
out of all the evil that befalls me. A foolish Calumny has
been rais'd upon me, and spred thro' Town and Countrey,
as if I had encouraged the making and sending of an Idol,
for the Papists at Cape *François*, to make an Object of their
Adoration. This may awaken me to do some special Ser-

vice for God; what if it should be, to publish an Essay upon the *Spiritual Idolatry*, by which the Souls of Men are generally endangered?

The Lecture was this day turned into a Day of Prayer, upon my Proposal; and handsomely attended by the People of the Town.[1] I should have preached unto them this Day, but my God humbles me with Illness that confines me. However at the Time when the People of God were in public attending on Him, I harmonized with them, in Humiliations and Supplications at home.

Sollicitous to know, why the Lord thus contends with me.

15. G. D.   There is now a Prospect of a more grateful and easy Harmony than ever among the Ministers of this Town. I would project, our coming into a more stated Way of Meeting at one anothers Houses, at proper Times; to consider, what may be done for the best Interests.

16. G. D.   I resolve to unite in bearing the Expenses of a Schole, to be opened every Evening, two or three Hours, for the Instruction of poor Negro's, and Indians, in Reading the Scriptures, and learning their Catechisms.

* 17. G. D.   It appears to me, that the Holy One requires me to employ as exquisite Thoughts as I can, upon that Subject; *How my last Works may prove my best Works?* I do it accordingly; and first, prepare a Sermon on the Subject.

18. G. D.   And all of my Flock, that are more than forty years of Age, will be deeply concerned in the pungent Sermon which may be preached on this Occasion.

19. G. D.   In sitting with the People of my Family lett it be a frequent Practice with me, to demand of them, an Account, *Why they do* such and such Things, as I see them engaged in; and on this Occasion, instruct them in the Methods of Piety, for living to God in all they do.

20. G. D.   I have Relatives in much Exercise about

[1] Sewall (*Diary*, III. 124) credits the suggestion to his son, Rev. Joseph Sewall.

theirs abroad. I should on this Occasion, advise and comfort them.

I would putt a Friend of mine, on doing some Services for his Relatives.

21. G. D. The Condition of the People in the Southpart of the Town, is in Danger of being very miserable by a Division arising among them; and the Interests of Religion in the whole Town, are likely to be deeply affected therein; my Thoughts and Prayers are to be much exercised on this Occasion.

22. G. D. Lett me in the public Prayers more frequently have a Petition of this Importance. *And lett the Work of Christianity among our Indians be prosperously carried on, that among these also our SAVIOUR may be glorified.* Perhaps my Exemple may bring others to the like.

23. G. D. A miserable Woman in our neighbourhood, is like to be destroy'd under her Temptations. I am to do what I can for her Succour.

23 *d.* 1 *m. Satureday.* This Day I sett apart for secret communion with Heaven, as I use to do.

In the former Part of the Day, with a Soul full of Contrition and Confusion, I considered, the strange Work of God, in making so foolish and filthy a Creature as I was before Him, to become a Servant of His Kingdome in the World. I considered the amazing Attempts of Satan, to destroy this Work of God, and how near they have often been to the accomplishing of it. I considered, that many of the Advantages which Satan had against me, lay in my own Indiscretions, wherewith I have continually exposed myself to be despised and reproached: but much more in my secret Impieties and Impurities, which have provoked the Holy One to chastise me with many Scorpions. In the Sense of these Things, I humbled myself before the Lord, and confess'd my Vileness, and justified the Holy One in all the sad Things, that ever did or could befall me. I durst not utterly despair of a Pardon, but made my Flight unto the great Sacrifice. And then I begg'd of the Gracious Lord, that He would not Reject me; but still preserve and increase my Opportunities to be serviceable.

On this Day I again singled out the desireablest Things, which I enjoy, or could wish for, and with the humblest Resignations thereof, I made Sacrifices of them.

I went on with the many Supplications, which my own present Circumstances, and those of my Family and Relatives and the People here, and the whole World called for.

I enjoy'd more Help from Above, than I have done in some former Days.

Yea, I seem to feel the Approach of Something, that will very much encourage me in the Service of God.

*24. G. D. My dear SAVIOUR, what a Frame hast thou brought my Soul unto? I am willing to be slandered, reviled, lessened; patient of being despised and rejected of Men. This proceeds not only from an Acquiescence in the divine Sovereignity, and from a Submission to the just Punishment of my Iniquity; but also from a secret Pleasure in Conformities to my SAVIOUR, and from an Horror of being thought a considerable Man by People who terminate in Man, and sett man up in the Throne of GOD, and make an Idol of whatever Man they ascribe any Grandeurs to!

25. G. D. My Hearers ought to be more powerfully and pathetically than ever, treated upon that Point, that so few make *thorough Work* of it in turning and living to GOD, and so many leave the Condition of their Souls in a woful Uncertainty. Give them the Proofs of this their Stupidity: and sett before them the Acts of Piety, that must putt an End unto it.

26. G. D. A Servant that sojourns with me, is preparing for Admission into our Communion. My Assistences must [be] given her in the great work before her.

27. G. D. I have two Nephews[1] in this Town, (the Sons of a wretched Father,) to whom I would extend the Eye of my Care, and send Books of Piety which may suit their Circumstances.

---

[1] George and Nathan Howell. See p. 410, *supra.*

28. G. D. I have in view some very important Projections, for the Good of our Eastern Plantations, and for the Evangelizing of the Indians there.

29. G. D. I would study Ways to assist an honest Man, who is willing to go an hunting with our Eastern Indians, and lodge Months among them, that he may instruct them in our holy Religion.

30. G. D. Two poor Persons, Objects of my Care, I would endeavour by bringing them into an Intermarriage, to bring into better Circumstances.

* 31. G. D. I find the glorious One, dethroning my Idols, in several Articles of Adversity; and I would have my Spirit sweetly reconciled unto such Dispensations. But then, I want more clearly to see God assuming the Throne. Wherefore, on each of my Troubles, I would still think; *Well, what is the Homage to be paid unto the glorious God on this Occasion?*

There has been an Image of St. *Michael* carved in this Town, to be sent unto Cape *François*, by one of our Traders thither, from whom they desired it. Whether it be only an ornamental Business, or an Idol to be worshipped by the bruitish Papists, I know not. But our People suppose the latter; and a mighty Cry has been made about it. I only spoke a transient and pleasant Word on that Occasion, (distinguishing between an ornamental Business, and an Idol) unto the foolish Woman, who is the wife of the Trader, many Months ago. That wretched and bruitish Family improved that Word, in their own Favour, and made a formal, a lying, Story out of it. It is incredible, what a vile Representation is made of me all the Countrey over. On this Occasion, I take little Pains to vindicate myself; I feel myself dead unto the World, in regard of my Reputation; and rather pleas'd than vex'd at any Diminution. But sett myself to consider first, *What Good I shall gett*, by the Storm of Calumnies and Obloquies, now beating upon me. And then I go on to consider, *What Good I shall do;* and I would be awakened unto taking of some notable Revenge upon Satan and his Kingdome, from the Insults which he makes upon me.

(II.) Under these Dispositions, the best Thing I could think of, was to publish a little Treatise about *Idolatry,* that may serve all the Interests of practical Piety: and in a Præface to it, exhibit the Temper and Conduct proper for the faithful Servants of God, when they have a Tempest of Reproaches falling on them, from the Spirit working in the Children of Disobedience. God graciously hears Prayer, in assisting the Publication. Tis entituled, ICONOCLASTES. *An Essay upon the IDOLATRY too often committed under the profession of the most Reformed Christianity; and a Discovery of the IDOLS, which all Christians are every where in danger of.*[1]

April. 1. G. D. The grievous Losses and Sorrowes, my Neighbours have lately suffered by the Way of the Sea, oblige me to Meditations peculiarly adapted for them.

2. G. D. I fear I have not been so frequent and fervent and particular, as I should have been, in my Prayers for the converting Influences of Heaven, on the Soul of my Servant *Onesimus.* Who can tell, what may be done for him, and what a new Creature he may become, if more prayers were employ'd for him!

3. G. D. A young Man at the Colledge, who is my Kinsman, shall be taken by me under my poor particular Consideration, that he may be præpared for Service. [N.C.][2]

4. G. D. Lett me entertain some deep Thoughts, Whether I may not handle some further Subjects and perform some further Actions, that may have a Tendency to serve the grand Interests of the Kingdome of God in Europe.

4 *d.* 2 *m.* This Day was a general Fast, thro' the Prov-

---

[1] Printed by John Allen for Daniel Henchman, 1717.
[2] Nathaniel Cotton.

ince. I enjoy'd precious Assistences from Heaven, in the Services of the Day.

5. G. D. Tho' the strange and odd Humour in the Relatives of the deceased youth, forbidding me to publish the useful Memorials of his Piety, and their killing their Child a second Time, has delay'd my Publication of what I proposed, for the enkindling of early Piety from the Patterns of the Youths dead at the Colledge, yett I would resume an Endeavour for one of them, and see how I can proceed in it.

6. G. D. The late Calamities on our Vessels and Neighbours abroad, afford me Objects enough to engage my Compassions at home.

* 7. G. D. O my Soul, Beware lest thy Temptations, (which are wonderful!) discourage thee, from any suitable Activities in serving the Kingdome of God, and good Interests.

There is extreme Danger of it!

Lett *Moses* also make thee afraid of *speaking unadvisedly with thy Lips.*

8. G. D. The *Love of God*, considered as the *Root* of all Piety; all being only diversified Love; only variegated Love; This notion well-cultivated; and now at the Time when we are all hands filling our Gardens with pleasant Plants. The Flock may hereby be singularly edified.

9. G. D. I hope, I have now found one whom I may recommend unto *Cresy*, to be made very much his Companion, and very much to his Advantage. But, Oh! my unceasing Inculcations on the Child!

10. G. D. I have a kinsman, a Candidate of the Ministry, at this time a Chaplain on our *Isle of Wight;* whom I have not hitherto took Notice of. I would now take a particular Cognizance of him, and furnish him with Books, and advise him about his Conduct.

11. G. D. A great Opportunity shall I have this day,

to bear my Testimony to everlasting MAXIMS of PIETY, and make my Demands on the Behalf of those MAXIMS.

I will beg of the glorious Lord, that He would accept me, by the Way of the Press, to extend my Testimony.

12. G. D. Having a Prospect of publishing Memoirs of a young Student, who died at our Colledge, may I not consider what agreeable Addresses and Instructions, to the surviving Students, may accompany them?

13. G. D. A poor distracted Youth in my Neighbourhood, must be look'd after.

*14. G. D. Should not my monthly Practice of setting apart a Day for Prayer with Fasting, be brought under a further Consideration?

15. G. D. It is a very *dark* Time with many of the Flock. Especially in regard of Relatives and Interests abroad. It may be a seasonable Action, for me to preach on, the *Light* of God, by which we may *walk thro' Darkness*.

16. G. D. In my Family I will renew my Cares, that the Satureday-Evening may [be] rescued from all sæcular Encumbrances, and be entirely devoted unto Piety.

17. G. D. A new Kinsman offers to my View, that I may consider, What may be done for him, to render him serviceable.

18. G. D. The deplorable State of our New South-Church, calls for Cares and Prayers.

19. G. D. A new Offer for the Reviving of Religion at the Eastward, is to be considered and cultivated.

20. G. D. The Prison is to be visited.

A Bible to be bestow'd, for the use of the Prison; and such Prisoners as may want it.

20 *d.* 2 *m. Satureday.* This Day, I sett apart, for Supplications and Humiliations, with Abstinence, as usually.

I enjoy'd some comfortable Influences from above; some Tokens, and Effects of the divine Life in my Soul.

Especially, when submitting to whatever Punishments

of my Sin, the infinite God may glorify and vindicate His Holiness upon me withal. But, then assured, that the Punishments of my Sin, had all fallen on my blessed Saviour. And when turning all my Enjoyments into Sacrifices.

Ardent my Cries, that the *Spirit* of God may be *poured out upon all Flesh*, and that glorious Troops of mighty and Holy *Angels*, may make their Descent upon the World.

'(III.) About this time, that I might serve many Good Purposes, and especially give one Stroke more for the advantage of early Piety, I sent unto the Press a Treatise of this Title. THE VOICE OF THE DOVE. *The Sweet Voice of PIETY, and more particularly that of EARLY PIETY, articulated. And some Notes of it Exhibited, in certain Memoirs of Mr.* Robert Kitchen, *a desireable Youth, who expired at* Salem. 20 *d.* VII *m.* 1716.[1]

* 21. G. D. There are Errands upon which I would this Day go unto the Table of the Lord, and unto my Saviour who is there to be mett withal. But this especially. My glorious Lord sees and knows, what is yett lacking in my Soul, to render me a brighter Instrument of Good in the World, and to ripen me for the Blessedness of another World. I would apply myself to Him, with ardent Cries, that He would carry on the Work of His Grace in me, unto Perfection, and help and heal what is defective in me; and I would proceed as far as my own Observation will carry me, unto much Particularity in my doing so.

22. G. D. The Cases of the many afflicted in the Flock, require me, to be very particularly concerned both in my Prayers, and in my Sermons for them?

T'were proper to preach on, Psal. CXIX. 92. Many afflicted ones to be visited.

23. G. D. I must lay all possible Charges, and use all possible Methods, that the Families which spring from this, whereof I am the Father, may live in all possible Accord

---

[1] Printed by John Allen for D. Henchman, 1717.

with [one] another. The least Appearance or Beginning of Discord, I would forever provide for the immediate Extinction of it.

24. G. D. I have a miserable and an ill-humoured Sister, who may be in danger of hurting herself, as well as creating Disturbances in our Families. I must, with all Meekness of Wisdome contrive, that she may use a more discrete Conduct, and that all Mischief may be obviated.

25. G. D. Should not I take into Consideration, what may be done for the Service of the Ministry and Religion and the Churches, throughout the Land, that the Poison of Wise's cursed Libel may have an Antidote?[1]

26. G. D. I hope, an Association of the Ministers, is now formed in this Town; for the Regulating and Entertaining of our Society, I hope now to be full of agreeable Projections. The Field will be copious.

27. G. D. Grievous Calamities befall several in my Neighbourhood, which oblige me, to do among them the Part of a comforter to the Mourners.

* 28. G. D. The Notion of our Soul being formed with a Principle of *Re-Union to God*, by Him originally implanted into it, if well-cultivated, may prove of great Use, first unto my own Soul, and then unto many others. Dr. *Cheines*[2] Reflections on this matter, should be exquisitely considered.

29. G. D. One of our Deacons, is a man more ingenious, more agreeable, and more active than the rest. I must needs have him unite more intimately and particularly with me, in Projections for the Good of the Church.

30. G. D. The temporal Interest of my Family must be consulted, in my seasonable Cares, to secure a Farm at *Connecticut*, which is made over to me.

May. 1. G. D. I must oftener invite the Presence of

[1] John Wise published this year *A Vindication of the Government of New England Churches.*

[2] George Cheyne (1671–1743). Mather probably refers to his *Philosophical Principles of Religion*, printed in 1715.

my Aged Father, at my Table — one of the most grateful Spectacles in the World.

2. G. D. Writing to *Scotland*, I have several Designs to prosecute for the Kingdome of God.

Among the rest, the Introducing of *Langius* to be read in the University of *Glasgow*.

I will also try, what the, *Lapis e Monte* may do amng them.

I send likewise Books of Piety unto the aged Master of the great Schole, to be read among the Scholars.

3. G. D. A good Settlement of Minds and Things, in the South Part of the Town, and the Prevention of Contention and every evil Work, is mightily to be laboured in.

4. G. D. The Liberty of two young Women, who are the Daughters of an Eminent Minister, once living at *Middleburgh*, and who rashly bound themselves in a Servitude for five years unto one coming from *London* hither, is to be purchased, and the poor Creatures are to be cared for.

* 5. G. D. The two comprehensive Points of our corruption, are an Ambition of sæcular *Grandeur*, and an Affection for sensual *Pleasures*. My Soul must be deeply engaged, in prosecuting the cure of these two Maladies.

6. G. D. The Sea-faring part of the Flock, tho' degenerated into all possible Stupidity and Malignity, yett since the late Judgments of God upon them, are come to such a tremendous Degree of Desolation, there must be more attempts to awaken them unto some due Notice thereof.

7. G. D. Oh! when! when shall I see my Son *Increase* converted unto serious Piety!

More clear and close Discourse with him on that important Matter, must be repeated with unceasing Assiduities.

8. G. D. What shall I do, that my Relatives mourning under the Fate of theirs abroad, may have a right Behaviour in, and make a right Improvement of, their present Adversity!

9. G. D. The difficult Case of our New South Church.

I have certain Projections, which if prosecuted, may cure all that is amiss.

10. G. D.   *Barmudas*, Renew applications, that it may be provided for.

11. G. D.   Malefactors in the Prison, call for my fresh Endeavours, to do good unto such miserables.

* 12. G. D.   There is a way of living, how sweet, how high, how holy! For me to beleeve and behold the Love of God my Saviour to me, in all the Circumstances and Occurrences of my Life, still as they arrive unto me; and perswaded and sensible of His Love unto me therein, for me thereupon to have my Heart enflamed with Love to Him, and formed into Dispositions and Resolutions to praise Him, and please Him, and serve Him, and shun every thing that may [be] offensive to Him, and study what I shall do for His Kingdome and Interest.

O may I gett more into it!

But may I take it for granted, that there is the Love of my Saviour, in all that is done unto me! If I find it inflaming my Love to Him, I cannot question it.

13. G. D.   Can I do a more useful Thing for my Flock, than to sett before them the grievous Demonstrations of it, that few, few of them are in earnest about the grand Business of Religion!

14. G. D.   There are diverse Things, which may have a singular Tendency to nourish the Flame of Piety in my Family, if I would cause them to be read over there;

15. G. D.   My Brother-in-Law at *Roxbury*, is in a state of Health, which very much threatens his Life, and has laid him aside from Service; a *Vertigo* growing towards an Epilepsy. I would not only pray for him continually, but also animate his Flock to sett apart a Day of Supplications for him, and bear my part in it.

16. G. D.   A wretched Man[1] is under a sentence of

---

[1] Jeremiah Fenwick.

Death for a Murder. He dies a Sacrifice to ungoverned Anger. To entertain the Public, on this Occasion, with a Discourse on the Folly and the Danger of Ungoverned Anger, may be a Service to the Cause of Piety.

17. G. D. I would propose, unto the Master of the Grammar-Schole in my Neighbour-hood, that he would cause the Memoirs of the Pious Lad, in my, *Voice of the Dove*, to be readd over at the Schole, and then follow it with suitable Exhortations; as also advise the Scholars to gett the Book. I would entreat likewise, the Gentlewoman[1] the mother of the Lad, that she would bestow the Book, on each of the Scholars, in the Schole at *Salem*.

18. G. D. I have an excellent Friend in my Neighbourhood, who is under some Degree of Alienation of Mind, left by a late Fever upon him. I must use exquisite Methods, to preserve him from an unhappy Conduct.

18 *d. 3 m. Satureday.* The Perswasion grows upon me, that *Joel's* prophecy yett remains to be accomplished, yea, that the Time shortly comes on for its full Accomplishment: that the Kingdome of God, which we are to look for, and long for, will not come on without a Return of the prophetic Spirit, in such Operations as planted Christianity in the primitive Times; that the Mighty Operations of the prophetic Spirit, are from Angels whom our ascended Lord having received the Command of them, sends with their various Gifts to possess the Children of Men; that all other Wayes to introduce Piety into the World, or establish Unity among the People of God, are by sad Experience found ineffectual; but if the Holy One will please to take this Way, all Things will give way before it, and also the Lord alone will be exalted in that Day: that the plentiful Rain with which the Lord once comforted His Heritage, has been stopt by the Ingratitude of Mankind; and so, for

---

[1] Bethia, daughter of Daniel Weld, married Robert Kitchen, merchant, who died October 28, 1712.

three Years and an half, (the M. CC. LX Dayes of Antichrist) it has not rained; but these now expiring there will
be a Sound of Abundance of Rain.

Under the Influence of this Perswasion, and a strong Anhelation
to see the World made happy, and GOD and His CHRIST, owned
and served and reigning in the world, I resolved upon devoting some
Dayes for Prayer with Fasting before the Lord, that this Favour
may be obtained, and the Dove be sent forth the third Time, and
abide with us, and the Flood which overwhelms all our Foundations
be carried off.   My Encouragement is in Luk. XI. 13.

It may be, I am the only Man upon Earth so engaged; but I
hope that my Gracious God will preserve me from Delusions.

This is one of the Dayes that I sett apart for this Purpose.

And I take the Opportunity to ask for such other Blessings, as
in my Soul, and my Family, and my Ministry I have Occasion to
think upon.

While I am doing these Things, I do not in any Measure ask,
that I may myself enjoy any Share in the Gifts of the prophetic
Spirit.   I desire nothing extraordinary for myself, but extraordinary
Holiness.   All that I desire for myself is a strong Descent of the
sanctifying Spirit on me, to fill me with the Love of God.

* 19. G. D.   I am exceeding sensible, that the Grace
of *Meekness*, is very defective in me.   I would now more
than ever study to excell in that gracious Ornament.

I would particularly resolve on these Maxims for my
Conduct.

I. Upon a Provocation to Anger, I would make a Pause, and
think, *Is it a Sin that now calls for my Anger?* and, *How must I manage
it, that I may not sin in my Anger?*

II. I would then also think, *I have the Eye of a glorious, gracious,
righteous God now upon me.*

III. I would then likewise think, *What would my patient SAV-
IOUR have done on such an Occasion?*

IV. Every Night at my going to Rest, I would be able *to say, my
Mind is in an easy Frame towards all the World.*

V. I would especially keep a Guard upon my Spirit, when I
think on the base Treats I suffer from the ungrateful and abusive
people in general; that I do not *speak unadvisedly with my Lips.*

20. G. D. I would from a Principle of Gratitude be quickened, unto doing for my Flock all possible Services. My Salary from them, is considerably more, than ten Shillings per day. Lett it then be a Shame and a Grief unto me, if any Day pass me, wherein I shall not be able to say, *I have done something for the Flock to day, which may be an honest Consideration of the Wages I have received from them!*

21. G. D. Now I will not only pray for all my Children by Name, every Day, as I use to do; but single out suitable Blessings, to be asked for each of the five by Name every Day.

And for my Children in Law, I would particularly ask, that they may live in all Harmony and Agreement with one another.

22. G. D. My Relatives returned from a Captivity among the Spaniards, must be address'd with Admonitions agreeable to their Circumstances.

23. G. D. A poor Man under a Sentence of Death for a Murder, dies a Sacrifice to *Ungoverned Anger*. A Sermon about, *Ungoverned Anger*, preached at the Lecture on this Occasion, may be a great Service to Piety, and a good Improvement of the Spectacle we have before us.

24. G. D. I would make some useful Collections of the rare Occurrences, which were in the Storms and Snows, that we had in the Conclusion of our Winter. I may make a good Use of them. And communicate them [to] the Royal Society.

25. G. D. A gracious Woman afflicted with a froward Husband, must be directed and comforted.

* 26. G. D. A sweet Acquiescence in the Will of God, on several Occasions, is what I am now sensibly call'd unto.

27. G. D. Some under the Discipline of the Church, have miscarried, and must be look'd after.

28. G. D. Some Things particularly to be recommended unto the Perusal of my Children.

Onesimus's Recovery from a dangerous Fitt of Sickness, must be improv'd for his Awakening to Piety.

29. G. D. Repeted Visits and adapted ones, unto my aged Father-in-Law, at *Charlston*.

30. G. D. A Variety of Services, to be done in the general Convention of Ministers, who allow me to be their Moderator.

Methods to preserve and promote Piety, proposed.

An Address to the King agreed upon.[1]

The Convention ordered me in their Name, and with them attending on me, to make a SPEECH unto the Governour; which God helped me to do, so as to find much Acceptance. I suppose, it, with his Answer to it, will be published unto the World.[2]

31. G. D. What shall I do, to make the miserable Man under Sentence of Death, and his Case, yett more serviceable!

My dear *Franckius* tells me, that when the Servants of GOD, have projected any Thing, that will be evidently a Service to His Kingdome, they should go on with a lively Faith in Him, to carry them thorough, tho' they have at present little Prospect of accomplishing their Designs; He will doubtless do wonderfully for them.

I beleeve, it is hardly possible for me, to do a greater Service for the Kingdome of God, than to give unto the public, a little Treatise which I have now prepared. When I had prepared it, there was a Sentence of Death upon the Publication of it, in the Avarice of our Booksellers. But after I had expressed the Resignation to the sovereign, wise, and just Will of God my SAVIOUR, in the matter, He putt it into the Hearts of some, to make those Offers, which will revive the Design.

(IV.) It is Entituled, *MALACHI. or, The Everlasting Gospel to be preached unto the Nations; and those MAXIMS*

---

[1] See p. 300, *supra*.   [2] Printed by B. Green, 1717.

f PIETY, which are to be the Glorious Rules of Behaviour, he only Terms of Communion, and the Happy End of Con- roversy; among all that would meet and serve those Advances which the KINGDOME of God is now making on the World; and What the Distressed Nations must see their Distresses go on till they are brought unto.[1]

That which animates me the more to bring forth this Treatise is, in that I hear nothing, what is become of my BOANERGES.

June. 1. G. D. A poor, young, ungodly and ungrateful Wretch, must have something done for him, to prevent his quick perishing under the Judgments of God.

* 2. G. D. I would study to excell, in every Point of Piety; press after what may be call'd, *heroic Piety.* Methinks, there is a yett more excellent Behaviour which I may endeavour as a Neighbour, towards those who are in my nearest Neighbourhood. Wherefore I would not only treat all of them always lovingly, and courteously, and be ready to do them all good Offices, but I would visit them with greater Frequency, and in my Visits I would study to lay Obligations of Goodness upon them.

3. G. D. What can I do better for the Flock than make a solemn and awful Improvement, of the sudden Deaths which have newly happened in the neighbourhood?

4. G. D. In the evening Entertainments for my Family, I would particularly go over the eight Beatitudes; and urgently press upon my Domesticks the Pursuit of the Characters.

5. G. D. A Minister of *Windsor*, somewhat remotely related unto me, is under peculiar Difficulties and Temptations;[2] A Variety of Services and Kindnesses, I propose to do for him.

6. G. D. By the Publication of my late SPEECH to

---

[1] Printed by T. Crump for Robert Starke, 1717.
[2] Rev. Timothy Edwards?

the Governour, and his Answer to it, I propose a Variety
of Services to the Public; various and comprehensive
Services.

7. G. D. At the Wharfs, which ly a little below my
present Habitation, and belong to the Owner of it, there
are usually many Vessels. I will take my Time to walk
down upon the Wharfs, and lovingly talk to the People
belonging to the Vessels, about their greatest Interests; and
lodge Books of Piety in their Hands. Not knowing, whether
the Glorious God may not send some of His Elect thither,
for His Grace thus to meet with them.

8. G. D. Several Objects for my Compassion, do I in
the Prison meet withal.

*9. G. D. I see a strange Effect of a modest, humble,
self-denying Satisfaction, in the Improvements of my
younger Brethren.

The poor Man, under Sentence of Death, having visited
the other Congregations, was to have been executed on
the last Thursday; which was the Lecture of another.
My private Labours for his good, were what they were;
and such a Success thereof began to appear, that I obtained
a Reprieve of one Week longer for them; which had a
strangely happy Consequence on the Soul of the Malefactor.
All this while, I had no Share, in those public Appearances,
that might give me Opportunities to do good unto many
on this Occasion. My mind sweetly acquiesced in the Will
of God, and I took Pleasure, in His using of whom He
pleased, and how.

But, behold, without any seeking of mine, the greatest
of all the Opportunities to do good, from the Circumstances
of the Man, which are now grown very remarkable, are
thrown into my Hand. The man has a distinguishing
Regard unto me above all Men. And he desires to be on
this last Lord's-day of my [his] Life, in my Auditory; which
proves one prodigiously vast; and the gracious Lord can

-ies me comfortably thro' the Services before me. The Man also by his Desire procures it, that I must be the Man, who must preach the last Sermon he shall hear, on -he next Thursday just before his Execution; yea, and he -ssigns me a tremendous Text then to preach upon; even -hat, Matth. x. 28. *Fear Him who can destroy both Body -nd Soul in Hell.* Such Things as these, animate me more -nd more to study the Temper of Mind, which introduced -hem.

10. G. D. I hope, what I have preached yesterday, -bout improving a *Space to Repent,* is what the Flock will -are the better for.

11. G. D. What shall be done, for the raising of -ammy's Mind, above the debasing Meannesses of Play!

12. G. D. My Brother languishing at *Roxbury,* and -ny Nephew lying dangerously and dubiously sick, at *Ded--am,* call for my most earnest Cries to Heaven, and other -ares on their behalf.

13. G. D. What a surprising Opportunity to do good -nto many, have I thrown into my hands this day, by the -esire of a poor Man,[1] who procures my preaching on a -ext that he has chosen to hear handled before his Death, -vhich is to be this Afternoon.

My Glorious Lord graciously carried me thro' the hard -ervice before me, in a very vast Assembly.

(V.) The Sermon is immediately desired and expected -n the Way of the Press. I give it unto the Bookseller -nder this Title. *The Valley of Hinnom. The Terrors of -ELL demonstrated, and the Methods of Escaping the Ter--ible Miseries in the punishment of the Wicked there, declared; -n a SERMON, preached in the Hearing and at the Request, -f a Man under a Sentence of Death for a Murder; Just -efore the Execution of the sentence, and upon a Text by him-*

---

[1] Jeremiah Fenwick, of Boston, who had in November, 1716, killed one Ralph Moxtershed, a ropemaker. Sewell gives the name Phenix.

self assigned for the Sermon to insist upon. At Boston, 13 *d.* IV *m.* 1717. *To which there is his Dying Speech annexed.*[1]

14. G. D. Deeply engaged, in Writing many Letters to England, of a public Importance, I am Contriving many and special Services for the Public.

15. G. D. More Objects for Compassion in the Prison.

15 *d.* 4 *m. Satureday.* This Day, I sett apart for Prayer with Fasting in Secret before the Lord.

I had many Concerns to spread before the Lord in my Supplications.

Particularly the deplorable State of the new South Church in this Town.

But, what I most of all designed and pursued, was, the Accomplishment of *Joel's* Prophecy.

Whereof I have expressed my Sentiments, on, 18 *d.* 3 *m.*, a month ago.

* 16. G. D. I would not only resolve the Frames and Acts, which belong to a Life of Piety, but still as I take up the Resolutions, I would pitch upon *particular Times*, wherein I will express those Frames and exert those Acts, and so make sure of obtaining my Purposes.

17. G. D. And I will mightily insist upon the like Advice to the Flock, that so the Exhortations to Piety may not be lost upon them.

18. G. D. *Nancy's* Health calls for a timous Consideration.

19. G. D. With what Solemnity must I call upon my Kinsman, T. W[alter] to make a right and a great Use, of his Deliverance from the Jawes of Death, which the God, who hears Prayer, has lately given?

20. G. D. The miserable Condition and Contention, of the People in the South-part of the Town, very much takes up of my Time and Thought for them.

[1] Printed by J. Allen for Robert Starke, 1717.

21. G. D. Our excellent Governour who has delivered
he Countrey from a Flood of Corruption, which was introduced by the selling Places, is to be encouraged, and a
course must be taken, that he may be vindicated from the
Aspersions of a cursed Crue in this Place, who traduce him
as guilty of that Iniquity.

22. G. D. Some in our Church, fallen into Sin, must
be recovered.

* 23. G. D. I am defective, I am not enough explicit
and enlarged. In the Morning, to lay the Plan of the
Work to be done in the Day for God; In the Evening, to
reflect particularly, upon all the Passages of the Day.
Mend.

24. G. D. By doing more about my Sermons, in the
former part of the Week, I shall render myself more useful
to the Flock, on many Accounts, as well as in the Study
of my Sermons.

25. G. D. My Children must be obliged oftener to
wait upon their two aged Grandfathers, with dutiful Visits.
They may help to sweeten and prolong the Lives of their
Grandfathers, and also receive efficacious Instructions from
hem.

26. G. D. I have a very wicked Brother-in-Law, whom
is high time for me to think of more effectual Methods
or the reclaiming of.

27. G. D. Diverse ungospellized Plantations, destitute
of Ministers, must be exceedingly cared for.

28. G. D. Some Care must be taken that the Loss of
Time at Funerals in this Town, may be prevented and
redressed. I will present a Memorial to the select Men,
on this Affair.

29. G. D. Some in great Affliction to be visited.

30. G. D. My SAVIOUR sais, *a Corn of Wheat, if it
dy, it bringeth forth much Fruit.* In all my Essays to do
Good, I still find a Sentence of Death written upon what

I have undertaken, before it comes to any Thing. Wherefore, when I see a Sentence of Death on any of my Essays I would entertain it, without froward and sinful Discouragements, and have a lively Faith awakened and exercised in my Soul, for a good Issue of all.

How strangely does the glorious Lord continue to make use of me! I gave to the Bookseller my Essay upon, *The valley of Hinnom*. I was desirous at the same time, to have had him taken another Discourse for the *Cure of Ungoverned Anger*. He declined it, and I was easy; my Discourse must ly by under a Sentence of Death; my Labour be buried.

(VI.) But in five Dayes time, the Bookseller sells off an Impression of near a thousand which he printed of the former Essay; and now he comes to me for the Latter. So it comes abroad, for the service of Piety under this Title. FEBRIFUGIUM. *An Essay for the Cure of ungoverned Anger, In a Sermon preached at the Proposal, and on the Occasion of a Man under a Sentence of Death, for a Murder committed by him in his Anger*, At Boston, 23 *d*. III *m*. 1717.[1]

July. 1. G. D. A severe Expostulation, with such of the Flock, as by neglecting to approach the Table of the Lord, plainly declare themselves yett *Minors* in Christianity.

2. G. D. My dear *Nibby*, draws near her Time.

3. G. D. I have a Kinsman, to be advised against the prevailing of Slothfulness, and the Neglecting of his Business, which threatens to grow upon him.

3 *d*. v *m. Wednesday*. This Day, being the *Commencement*, as they call it; a Time of much Resort unto *Cambridge*, and sorrily enough thrown away, I chose to spend this Time at home, and I sett apart a good Part of it, for Prayer with Fasting before the Lord.

And besides the usual Matter of Supplications, there were especially three Errands, which I now went unto Heaven upon.

[1] Printed by J. Allen, 1717.

One, that the Spirit of God may be poured out upon all Flesh, according to His Promise; and the Kingdome of God introduced with a fresh and large Rain of the Gifts which refreshed the Heritage of the Lord in the primitive Times.

For this, I have now besought the Lord thrice.

Another, that our Colledge, which is on many Accounts in a very neglected and unhappy Condition, and has been betray'd by vile Practices, may be restored unto better Circumstances, and be such a Nursery of Industry, and Piety, and all Erudition, as that our Churches may therein see the Compassion of the Lord unto them.

A Third; that my dear *Nibby,* may be carried well to and thro' her Time, and see a gracious Deliverance.

4. G. D.   Care to be taken for the Recommendation of some fitt Persons to the Governour, for public Places, who may be likely to be Blessings in their Stations.

5. G. D.   This Day, I prosecute several Designs among the Commissioners for the Indian Affairs, that may be for the public Interest.

6. G. D.   A poor man in our Church, must be recommended unto Charity.

* 7.   G. D.   I propose a sensible Improvement in Piety, by my Perusal of Mons'r. *Placettes, La Morale Chrétienne abregée.*[1]

8. G. D.   A Sermon upon *Secret Sorrows,* may be of marvellous use unto the Flock.

9. G. D.   My two youngest Children, of their own Accord, incline to learning the French Tongue; and visit master for it.   I would cherish the Inclination.

10. G. D.   A Kinsman, of whom I have hitherto taken little Cognisance, appears to me, capable of Service in our Eastern Plantations.   I would propose and pursue the Matter.

11. G. D.   I have in view, a sensible Service for the Kingdome of God; by forming for some Students, who have taken their Degree, a Method of Studies which may

[1] Jean La Placette (1639-1718).

prepare them for great Service in the World; and keeping
them under my Inspection in my Neighbourhood; and
having them to attend upon me, with frequent, perhaps,
daily Applications. This Design requires a little further
Cultivation; and the Direction of Heaven must be asked
for it.

11 *d.* v *m. Thursday.* This Day, was kept as a Day of
Prayer thro' the Province. The Drought threatning of us,
was the principal Occasion.

I was graciously assisted. But this Day releases me,
from a secret Fast, this week; with which I should else
have prepared for the Communion.

12. G. D. I begin to have something in View for poor
Barmudas; which I would prosecute.

13. G. D. A poor man languishing of a Consumption,
must be visited, assisted, comforted.

* 14. G. D. Examining my *Love to GOD*, I find, I have
an unspeakable Delight in Obedience to Him, yea, in sacrificing to Him.

Yett, I find, there are some Exercises of Communion with GOD
wherein I take not so much Delight, as I ought to do. Especially
secret Prayer.

Examining my *Love to my Neighbour*, I find, I am afraid of doing
him the least Wrong; afraid of doing him the least Harm; ready
with Alacrity to do him all the good Offices imaginable, Yett, I find
a secret and sudden Inclination to be pleased, when I see God revenging my Cause upon a personal Enemy with bringing them into
humbling Circumstances.

Examining my *Faith in my Saviour*, I find, my Mind so sensible
of His Glories, that I desire nothing so much as to live unto Him.

· Yett, I find, a Suspicion sometimes working in my Mind, whether
His Great Sacrifice be a sufficient Security for me.

Examining my *Repentance of Sin*, I find an hearty Sorrow for
my Offences unto the Glorious GOD, and an hearty Design to avoid
every Thing, which the Light of God in me shall condemn as an evil
Thing.

Yett, I find that the odious and horrid Nature of Sin, appears not unto me, so livelily, and so frightfully, and so efficaciously, as it ought to do.

15. G. D. Such Things prosecuted in the public Prayers, may serve the Cause of Piety in the People to whom I am to Minister.

16. G. D. Concert with *Sammy's* Master, Methods for his further Improvement.

Lett him, and his Brother *Cresy*, read a Book lately published, *The Young Mans call to his Brethren.*

17. G. D. A Kinsman, who is a Sailor, must come into very more particular Care, for the Animation of Piety in him.

And I would send some Instruments of Piety, to his Relatives.

18. G. D. The main Intention of my Studies, wherein my Spirit is deeply and strongly engaged, is, to awaken the Zeal of an Union for all good Men upon the Indisputable Maxims of the everlasting Gospel.

I must sett myself with frequent Meditations, to find out witty Inventions, beyond all that I have hitherto used, for the Service of this Intention.

19. G. D. By some of the young Men learning to read well my Notes of my Sermons I may be yett more useful to their Societies.

20. G. D. Go to the Prison, and find out special Objects for Charity and Compassion.

* 21. G. D. Suppose that a Child of my singular Love and Hope, should so fall into Sin, and be after wondrous Means of Recovery, yett so abandoned of God, and so ensnared in Vice, that there may [be] terrible Cause to fear lest he prove a Cast-away; If the Glorious GOD should order such a Trial for me, what should be my Behaviour under it?

First, I must watch over my Spirit that the Grief and Wrath arising on such Occasion may not proceed from the Vexation of my missing the Reputation and Satisfaction which a Child of more honourable Behaviour might bring unto me. Here *self* would operate. Perhaps, I have carried the Supposal, beyond any real Occasion for it. Yett, my GOD would have me come up to all the Piety, which the Supposal would call for.[1]

Secondly. I must adore the divine Sovereignty; and endeavour an unmurmuring Acquiescence in the Thing that is appointed for me.

Thirdly. I must pœnitently see my own Sins chastised in what shall thus befal me, and humbly accept the Punishment of my Iniquity.

Fourthly. Yea, I must mourn for the Sins of my Child, as for my own; and walk softly before the Lord.

Fifthly. Yett I must not give over Crying and Weeping to the Lord, and using the Methods which are effectual for the Dispossession of an Evil Spirit.

GOD will anon say to me, *Concerning thy Sin, I have heard thee.*

22. G. D.   Would not the call of our Saviour over the Grave of the dead *Lazarus*, agreeably insisted on, be a proper Engine, with which I might hope, that the Spirit of Grace may cause many sinful Ones in the Flock, to come forth from their evil Circumstances?

23. G. D.   My Son *Increase!*   I am distress'd for him: I hear, I fear, what is amiss concerning him; Snares which threaten him.

With what Plainness, with what Vigour, but yett with what Prudence, must I dispense and repeat my Admonitions to him!

I take him into my Library; there I renew my Importunities; I obtain from him Expressions of Repentance, and fitt Answers to the Demands of Piety. I pray with him there, and make him see and feel my Agonies for him.

I give him fresh Directions for his Evening-hours.

Methinks, I hear the glorious One saying to me, *Concerning thy Son I have heard thee!*

24. G. D.   I have a transcendently wicked Brother-in-

---

[1] The last two sentences are written in the margin.

Law, to whom I owe a Duty. I must advise with some wise Friends, about the doing of it.

25. G. D. I would make a fresh Essay, to draw up in a plain and brief manner the Points of Religion and Liberty, which the several Parties of them, who agree in opposing the Plotts to make the Nations miserable, may and should unite upon.

26. G. D. I design to make an handsome Treat at my House, for two excellent Governours: Our own, and him at *Connecticot;* that so I may strengthen my Opportunities to do Good, to them and by them.

27. G. D. Several bereaved Families, to be visited and comforted.

* 28. G. D. The Acts wherein the Love of God in the Soul is expressed and exerted, I not only make Enquiry whether I have experience of them or not, but I put it out of Doubt, by my doing of them.

This [is] the more seasonable, because this Morning I sitt down at the Lord's-Table, with the Old South Church.

29. G. D. The Flock must be advised withal, about an Assistent, in the work of the Ministry, which Providence now sends into our View.

30. G. D. The last Night, my dear Daughter *Abigail,* is delivered of a Daughter.[1] I am to quicken the Consort of her Praises with my own, to the Prayer-hearing Lord, who has most graciously appeared on this Occasion, with some singular Circumstances of His fatherly Goodness. As a Grandfather, I would ask Blessings for the new-born Infant; and have my Concern to express all the Piety, Gravity, and Expectation of approaching Death, which such a Relation calls me to.

31. G. D. A Brother-in-Law, wants the Assistences in his Affaires, which I may give him, and make them an Handle for doing more Good unto him.

[1] Catherine Willard, baptized August 4.

August. 1. G. D. I have now in a more brief and plain Essay, drawn up an INSTRUMENT OF UNION, which may render the several Parties of Protestants, more capable of holding and acting together, as true *Eleutherians* against the common Enemy: *A Bond of Peace*, in the Incontestible Maxims of *Piety* and *Liberty*, upon which all that come into the *Unity of the Spirit* ought to look upon themselves, as bound Charitably to bear with one another in their *Differences* about more *Disputable Matters*, and help one another only in the right and sweet Methods of Illumination for the gradual Cure of them, and firmly stand by one another, in the most glorious CAUSE that ever was asserted in the World. I purpose to be at the Expence of publishing this *Instrument*, and sending it abroad, and seeing how it may operate.

2. G. D. I would send some Instruments of Instruction, for the Assistence of one who is labouring among our Eastern Indians.

3. G. D. I am desired to enquire after a poor prodigal Son of a Scotch Minister, and to do him good Offices.

* 4. G. D. This being the Day, on which the first of my Grand-children is Baptised, the Exercises of piety proper for a Grandfather, will be this Morning seasonable for me. Wherefore, I now, first, give Thanks to the glorious GOD, with much Admiration of His Goodness, from whence having obtained Help, I am continued unto this Day:

And, secondly, give up unto the Lord, my whole Offspring; particularly, the new-born: entreating that she may be the Lord's.

And, thirdly, rejoice in the Favour of God, that the immediate Parents are His Children; with Resolutions to animate them, that their Offspring may be brought up for Him.

5. G. D. And on this Occasion, I thought, a Sermon of, *Conspicuous Blessings* to [be] obtained of God, for the Children of His Covenant and of His People, might con-

spicuously serve the Interests of Piety in the Flock, both
the old and the young.

6. G. D. My dear *Sammy;* I must consult with his
Master, about Employments for him, at the School; His
Ingenuity making him to dispatch his ordinary Task there,
sooner than his Companions.

But, oh! what shall I do, effectually to sett him a
Praying!

7. G. D. A Kinsman going to Sea, and one that has
formerly mett with grievous Difficulties and uncommon
Dangers, at Sea, should now be much advised by me about
getting into good Terms with Heaven.

8. G. D. Having præpared my, SURE FOUNDATION
for Union, I now send it unto such hands in *London,* as I
may hope will disperse it thro' the Nation.

9. G. D. Advise with a Gentleman capable of such
Services, about redressing and preventing some of our
public Inconveniencies.

10. G. D. I hear of a Jew in this place. I would
seek some Conversation with him.

10 *d.* 6 *m. Satureday.* This Day I sett apart for more
special Communion with Heaven; mourning exceedingly for
that Mark which I have of the divine Displeasure upon me,
in my having so little of that Blessedness granted unto me.

In the morning, I found myself raised unto such Annihilations of
myself before the glorious GOD, and such Compliances with His
Will, as were very comfortable to me.

I presented before the Lord my usual Matters of Supplication.
And, my fresh Essay for Union.

My Purpose about a *Collegium Precatis* in my neighbourhood.

My design of Conversing with a Jew, in this Place.

But especially, a Return of the Showers which first introduced
and propagated Christianity in the World.

* 11. G. D. My Mind wants a better præparation for
my approaching Dissolution, and for all the Encounters

which in the mean time I may be call'd unto. Now that I may be prepared for these things, it is requisite, that I have a clear Idea and a strong Perswasion, of that World, into which I am to go, at my Departure out of this. For this purpose, I would now apply myself to more fixed and frequent and thorough Meditations on the heavenly World. And I would particularly, every Night fall asleep, in the midst of such Meditations. Every now and then also, take a Walk in my Garden for them. Never be satisfied, until I see, what it is to be there.

12. G. D. To entertain the Flock, with a Discourse on the enlivening Voice of our SAVIOUR, over the Grave of the dead *Lazarus*, may be an useful Action. Who can tell, how far He may breathe in it?

13. G. D. I will putt *Sammy* upon the Translating of some Things into Latin, which may prove of use, not unto him only, but also unto many others.

14. G. D. Some Advice to be given unto the Minister of *Newtown*, about giving himself to reading, and ordering his Studies.[1]

15. G. D. A Lecture upon the *purged Floor*, may very sensibly suit and serve the public Edification.

16. G. D. Write unto our Agent, what may encourage and animate, his Agency for the Countrey.

17. G. D. A Person in my Neighbourhood, having his Affaires brought under grievous Difficulties, and some evil Instruments having made some disadvantageous Representations of him to his Friends in *England*, I will of my own Accord, write home unto his Friends on his Behalf.

How strangely does the Providence of my SAVIOUR still employ me to serve His Kingdome, and bring forth of the Fruit by which He may be glorified! The Things my Heart has been most sett upon, have a Sentence of Death

[1] John Cotton (1693-1757), son of Rev. Roland Cotton, had been ordained at Newton, November 3, 1714.

upon them. Such Things as I have least projected, are what my Sovereign Lord will putt Respect upon.

A well-disposed Gentlewoman among my Neighbours, died the last week.[1] On the Satureday, under a strong Impression on my Mind, I laid aside what I intended of the Sabbath. I finished another Discourse, the Beginning whereof I had lying by me. I thought, it would afford me an Opportunity to introduce a short, but just mention of the Departed Gentlewoman. I enjoy'd a precious Presence of the Lord with me, in my public Ministrations. The Husband of the Deceased presently asked me for a Copy of the Sermon, so its published under this Title.

(VII.) ANASTASIUS. *The Resurrection of LAZARUS improved; In a brief Essay, on what our great SAVIOUR will do, for the Dead Bodies of His People hereafter; and for their Dead Spirits now, in order to it, Preached upon the Interment of a well-Esteemed Neighbour.*

* 18. G. D. My secret Prayers, must be so regulated, as to afford more of Room, for the New Matter, which I would still with affectuous Meditations prepare for them.

19. G. D. I would so contrive the short Meditation with which I preface my Morning-prayers in my Study, that by entring the Minutes thereof in my Papers, I may prepare a Stock of rich Materials, to entertain my Auditory.

20. G. D. I grow more and more sollicitous, for the Welfare of my dear *Sammy*. And I shall sollicitously pursue it in several Articles.

21. G. D. Certain Hints of Piety, may be seasonable and serviceable, to my desireable Daughter-in-Law.

22. G. D. A vast Service might be done for the Plantations to the South-ward of us, if there could be obtained a couple of itinerant Ministers for them. I would, by the first Opportunity, importunately write home to *Scotland*, upon it.

---

[1] Sewall (III. 135) mentions the death of a Mrs. Bant. John Bant, a ship captain, is frequently mentioned by him.

23. G. D. The Master of our Schole needs to be advised, about a good Conduct, that the Scholars may love him, and may profit under him. I would join with my Father, in writing to him.

24. G. D. A poor Man rescued lately from Death and Hell, I would earnestly take him into my Hands, and do what I can, that of a great Sinner he may become a true Convert.

* 25. G. D. If any froward and foolish Person become disaffected unto me, and abusive and injurious, I would more than ever consider him as a Preacher of Repentance and Piety, that God sends unto me, and I would sett myself to consider what Improvements in Repentance and Piety God by that Person calls me to. And all my Prejudices against that Person shall be swallow'd up in the grateful Sense of that Good, whereof God makes him the Instrument.

26. G. D. The Life of men is full of Labour; and it is generally a Labour in Vain. A Discourse offering to my Flock those Maxims, the Pursuance whereof will rescue them from the Unhappiness of Losing all their Labour, may be of excellent Use unto them.

27. G. D. The Good of my Children may be consulted, by my publishing for them, as well as for others, the Sermon lately preached on the Baptism of my Grandchild.

(VIII.) The Father of that Child putts himself to the Expence of publishing that Sermon; which now comes abroad under this Title; THE TRIBE OF ASHER. *A brief Essay on the Conspicuous Blessings, with which the People of GOD, and their Offspring, are known to be the Blessed of the Lord. A Sermon preached, on the Baptism of a Grandchild.*[1]

28. G. D. That my Kinsman T. W[alter] may be well-improved and well-station'd, for service in the Church of God, my Cares are particularly called for.

[1] Printed, without a printer's name, 1717.

29. G. D. A Congregation of Dissenters is forming at N. *York;* I must endeavour in several Ways to assist them. Letters must be written unto *Haverhill.*

30. G. D. A foolish and profane Custom, of a Mock-Baptism, in the launching of a Vessel, I would rebuke it; and prevail with our Builders, to disswade their Masters from it.

31. G. D. A Minister in distress for an Employment. My Cares must be employ'd for him.

September. * 1. G. D. That so I may more effectually have the Kingdome of God sett up within me, I would exquisitely study the full Meaning of that *Righteousness* and *Peace* and *Joy*, in which it consisteth. And by lively Meditations thereupon, obtain the Experience of them.

2. G. D. And then entertain the Flock with the Effects of my Meditations, and Experiences.

3. G. D. Entertain *Sammy* betimes, with the first Rudiments of Geography and Astronomy, as well as History; and so raise his Mind above the sillier Diversions of Childhood.

4. G. D. My Kinsman at *Newtown* must be assisted in managing some ecclesiastical Difficulties arisen upon him.

5. G. D. Some Towns groaning under wicked Officers, may be delivered, by my Representations to the Governour.

6. G. D. If it be possible, procure a Cabinet, for — [1]

7. G. D. A poor Man, come from *Ireland*, wants to be Employ'd, as a Schole-master.

7 d. 7 m. *Satureday.* I sett apart this Day, as usually; and upon such Occasions as have lately most employ'd my Supplications.

And I made it a Day of Sacrifices as well as of Supplications.

My Mind was this Day raised unto such Expressions of Love to GOD, and such Communions with the heavenly

[1] An unfinished entry.

World, that I am sure I am alive; I am sure I begin to live; And so, I am sure, the Sentence of Death once passed on me is taken off; and the Life begun in me, will never dy.

*8. G. D.   Oh! For a wise, a meek, an humble, and a patient Conduct, under the Venome and Malice which the disaffected Rulers of our Colledge, treat me withal!

My Resolutions are —

9. G. D.   A Sermon on the *Reproaches* of a guilty Conscience, concluding with advice to such as are sensible of them; how serviceable may it be to my Auditory!

10. G. D.   O! My Son *Increase*, my Son, my Son! *Sammy's* writing.

11. G. D.   My aged Father is ill; His Comfort and Releef, must be studied every Way in the World.

12. G. D.   The Church at *Newtown*, wants the Assistences of a Council.

The Church at *Haverhil*, torn all to peeces.[1]

13. G. D.   Now, for Letters to the East-Indies!

14. G. D.   A very miserable Object in the Prison must be visited and releeved.

*15. G. D.   My Sentiments about the angelical Ministry, have been more clear and full and strong, than many other Men's.

But I feel so much of it, in the Conduct of the divine Providence toward myself; and the vast Consequence of it appears to me in such a lively Manner, that I must more than ever heretofore consider it in my Supplications unto

[1] Rev. Joshua Gardner died March 21, 1715-16, and the church at Haverhill could not agree upon a successor. Various candidates came before it — Jonathan Cushing, Robert Stanton, ——— Fiske — and finally Joseph Parsons, of Lebanon, the same to whom Mather wrote in January, 1717, (p. 426, *supra*). He did not succeed in winning the suffrages of the people, and the church remained without a pastor until February, 1717-18, when Samuel Checkley was unanimously called, but declined to accept. The congregation turned to John Brown of Little Cambridge (now Brighton), who was ordained May 13, 1719. His wife, Joanna, was daughter of Rev. Rowland Cotton of Sandwich, and thus this minister came to be entitled to Mather's care as a relative. Chase, *History of Haverhill*, 247.

God, and in my Endeavours to regulate my whole Conversation in Methods of Piety, proper to prepare me for the
Enjoyment of it.

Some singular Methods, must, as soon as I can, be
thought upon.

16. G. D. Our Church is now in a mighty Motion,
towards inviting unto the Assistence, and Succession, in
the Work of the Ministry among us, a desireable Person,
offered by Heaven unto us. I must serve the Flock, in
this important Matter, with all the Discretion and Industry,
I can.

17. G. D. Diverse beautifying Ornaments for his Mind,
must I now recommend unto the Studies of my dear *Sammy*,
instead of his more useless Diversions.

18. G. D. A very wicked and froward Relative, having
Sickness in his Family, I must visit them, and overcome
Evil with Good.

18 *d. 7 m. Wednesday.* This Day I travelled unto *Newtown;* where a Council of Five Churches, chose me their
Moderator. And with a very gracious and precious Assistence of Heaven, I was carried thro' the Service imposed
on me; not only in the Dispatch of the Result, in which
the whole Council united, but also in the public Speeches
which the Occasion called for.

In the Evening I returned, with a good Hand of God
upon me.

19. G. D. Yesterday.

20. G. D. I have now something in View for *Barmudaz.*

Gett the Story of the Difficulties and Deliverances
attending the Ship from *Ireland.*

21. G. D. More of the poor Men from *Ireland*, want
Employment.

* 22. G. D. I behold myself in the Condition of one
that is nailed unto a *Cross.* A Man that is *crucified*, endures

very *uneasy Circumstances*, and has all possible *Indignities* heaped upon him, and finds himself stript of everything he had in the World. I live, or I may rather say, I *dy daily*, in a continual Expectation of all these Things; I actually suffer much and am in a Condition that obliges me to look for more, of these Things. My Spirit is reconciled unto this Condition; tis welcome to me, in regard of the glorious Designs which my SAVIOUR has, in ordering for me such a Conformity unto Himself.

Am I not now *crucified* with my SAVIOUR? But now, — Oh! the Wondrous Consequences!

23. G. D. The Flock whereof I am the Servant, have in view, a desireable Person, for an Assistent and Successor in our public Sacrifices. The best Service I can do the Flock, is to lead in their Motions; and particularly, to begin with a public Day of Prayer on the Occasion.

24. G. D. Heap a great Library on my little *Samuel*. *Nibby* is in a difficult and a declining State of Health.

25. G. D. My aged Parent, is to be served with all possible Tenderness and Discretion in the Affair now before the Church.

25 *d.* VII *m. Wednesday*. A public Fast, at the Old South-Church, to seek the divine Direction, for the inviting of another Minister. I preached at it.

And yett had strength, with the divine Assistence, to preach the Lecture the day following.

26. G. D. *Barmudaz*, I hope, I have now provided for thee!

27. G. D. Speak to the Ministers, concerning Days of Prayer, for a Spirit of Piety to be poured out upon our Children.

28. G. D. Some very poor Ministers in *Ireland;* something must be done for them.

* 29. G. D. O Thanks be to my gracious Redeemer! I find, that I grow in skill and strength for Sacrifices on

all Occasions: and when any Exercise of Patience occurs to me, I presently sett myself to form those Acts of Resignation to the will of God which are proper for the Occasions: The Love to the Glorious GOD, which I express in preferring His Will to my own, soon fills me with Joy. But, O what a joyful Thought have I lately had shott into my Mind; *If the Will of the great God be mine, shall not His Power be so too?*

30. G. D. I am still at Work for the Flock, in that important Matter, which is now in Motion among them.

October. 1. G. D. A strange Providence of GOD, has brought into my Family a new Servant; A Negro Boy of promising Circumstances. Oh! Lett me use all possible Projections and Endeavours, to make him a Servant of the Lord. That this may be kept in Mind, I call him, *Obadiah.*

2. G. D. In the Management of what is now adoing in our Church, I must peculiarly study, for the Repose, Comfort, and Satisfaction of my aged Parent.

2 d. 8 m. Wednesday. The old North Church, kept a Day of Prayer, for Direction, in the Choice of an Assistant and Successor for the evangelical Ministry. I began the Day with a Prayer. In the Afternoon I preached a long Sermon. I enjoy'd very great Assistences of Heaven in the Services of the Day. We had a vast Auditory.[1]

[1] "7 d. 8 m. At a Meeting of the Brethren of the Church. In consideration of the great Age to which our venerable Pastor is arrived by the good Hand of God upon him, and his many services to the Public, whereof we have a grateful Remembrance; and from our Desire to have his life prolonged, and rendered comfortable, and that we may enjoy his public labours in such a way as may be most easy to him: the Church is disposed to proceed, as God shall please to make our way plain for it, to provide a further supply for the public services of the Gospel, in a more constant way among us, by a well-qualified Person; and this in order to a Settlement in the pastoral Charge, when upon mature Satisfaction, there shall be judged the most proper Season for it:

"Voted, with much Unanimity, the Church propose to meet on the next Munday, at ten o'clock in the Forenoon, to proceed upon what has been there proposed as may be judged convenient.

"Voted with a general Concurrence, John Clark, Thomas Hutchinson, Adam Winthrop, Edward Hutchinson, Esquires, and Mr. John Ruck, Mr. John Frizzell,

3. G. D. Obtain a clear and full, and well attested Account of some remarkable Providences, which are of a late Occurrence.

4. G. D. I would animate our Societies of young People, by preaching another Sermon to them.

5. G. D. One fallen into Sin, must be wisely laboured with.

A Student of the Colledge lies in the Town sick, like to dy.

* 6. G. D. The Points, wherein I am to be *sacrificed wholly*, (offered in my Sermon to day.)

7. G. D. Treat the Flock, with a short Course of Sermons, on, 1. Thess. v. 23.

8. G. D. I am very defective in the Degree of exquisite and assiduous Cares, which I should use for the Education of my desireable *Samuel*. Take it into the strongest Consideration.

9. G. D. What, what shall be done for my languishing Brother-in-Law at *Roxbury?*

9 *d.* 8 *m. Wednesday.* A Minister ordained at *Cambridge.*[1] A great Part of the Work was by a singular Providence devolved upon me; the Prayer before the Sermon; and, the giving of the Fellowship of the Churches. Wherein I enjoy'd the special Assistences of Heaven, and bore my Testimonies for Truth and Piety, in a very great Assembly.

10. G. D. I hope, I have also provided now a Minister for our Eastern Plantations.

11. G. D. Revive the Charity-Schole for Negro's.

12. G. D. I want a little Book, to lodge in the hands of the afflicted, when I visit them. I will now take some care for such an one.

The gracious GOD, oh! the Praises due to Sovereign

Mr. Samuel Greenwood, were desired to accept the care of a Committee for the Church as formerly, for a Year from this Time." *Cotton Mather's MS. Records of the Second Church,* III.

[1] Rev. Nathaniel Appleton, chosen to fill the vacancy caused by the death of Rev. William Brattle. See Paige, *History of Cambridge,* 289.

Grace! continues unto the most unworthy Sinner in the World, Opportunities to do Good, yea, and bring forth Fruit that shall remain, after he has left the World.

(IX.) A Society of young Men in our Neighbourhood, requested a Sermon from me; which they are willing to offer unto the Public, in the Way of the Press. But my Essay upon the *Golden Rule*, having lain by unpublished by the Follies of the Bookseller, the same young Men are willing to add that unto the former. So they come forth together, and make a bound Book, under this Title. PIETY AND EQUITY UNITED. *In Two Essays. I. The Desires of Piety; Breathing after the Blessings, which our Great Saviour and High-Priest has to bestow upon His People. II. The Measures of Equity; In the Golden Rule, to be observed by all People in their Dealings with one another.*[1]

* 13. G. D. A Thought visits my Mind, which I hope, will grow upon me, and have blessed Consequences. The holy Spirit of GOD who inspired His Chosen Servants to write the Oracles He has given us in the Scriptures, made heavenly Impressions on the Minds of the Writers, which raised Heavenly Affections in them. When I take a Passage of the Bible under my Consideration, I will nicely observe, what Affection of Piety appears in the Passage, and press after the raising of the same Affection in myself, and not count that I have the full Meaning of the Text until I have done so. I would also, when I would more particularly propose to have my Mind suitably affected, fly to some agreeable Paragraph of the Scripture, with Essays to raise in my own Soul, the Affections which I may apprehend it written withal.

This Course in the Singing of *Psalms*, will make a Melody in my Heart unto the Lord. And I would for so sanctifying a Purpose employ the Book *Psalms*, with a singular Application.

[1] Printed by J. Allen, for R. Starke, 1717.

This Design must be pursued. It will be elsewhere more largely spoken to.

14. G. D. Our Church is this Day defeated, of what they had in View, for the Choice of an excellent Minister. On this occasion, I make a Speech unto the Church, as well-contrived as I can, to prevent the Devices of Satan, from operating among our People.[1]

15. G. D. Such [is] my Distress for my Son *Increase*, that I think, I must sett apart three Days, (*Beseech the Lord thrice!*) with extraordinary Supplications, that he may not go on in a Course of Impiety. But first, before I come to such a *critical* Proceedure, lett me repeat my more usual Methods of bringing the Child home unto GOD.

16. G. D. A furious, venemous, rancorous Man, has, for no Reason in the world, insulted me, with a base Libel written to me, full of Slanders. I call in such injurious and abusive Wretches, for the same Kindnesses that I show to my Relatives. I would first, bury with Patience and in Silence, the Indignities which this false Man has offered me. I would forgive and forgett his Follies, and pray for him, and be willing to do him and his any Good, and overcome Evil with Good. I would rejoice in the Conformity to my SAVIOUR, which my Usages from this Man bring me to and study an Imitation of His Meekness. I would humble myself before the holy GOD, for the Occasions which He sees in me, that there should be sent such Messengers to buffet me. And receive such Informations for my Conduct, from the Malice of disaffected Men, as may be an excellent Fruit of the Things, which are for the present Grievous, that I may have Cause to bless them, and bless God for them.

Think, what my SAVIOUR means, in these Things; and what *Satan* means; and accordingly take my Measures.

---

[1] "14 *d*. 8 *m*. At a Meeting of the Church. Upon a due Consideration, the Church agree to delay the Proceedings proposed a Week ago, until a more convenient Opportunity." *Cotton Mather's MS. Records of the Second Church*, III.

17. G. D. Tho' Satan by frequent Assaults upon me, designs and labours to discourage my unceasing Projections to serve the Kingdome of God; for I am satisfied, I should not suffer what I do from him, and his Instruments, if my continual Contrivances to do Good were not such as they are: Yett, I will in this way make myself much more vile; and be stedfast and immoveable, alwayes abounding in the work of the Lord: beleeving a good Issue of all.

What I now think of, is; how to render the Condition of the poor Pyrates, who are coming on their Trial, serviceable unto the Interests of Piety in the World.

18. G. D. Some further Views I have, of encouraging some, to do good abroad.

I also provide a Schole-master for *Bridgwater*, who [is to] be anon an Assistent, and a Successor to my aged Friend there.[1]

19. G. D. Judge *Sewal* this day loses his Wife; and I do the Part of a Comforter to the Mourners.[2]

* 20. G. D. By reading the *Manuductio* of my dear *Franckius*, I hope, greatly to improve in the Piety, which I had so much in View, a week ago.

21. G. D. I would entertain the Flock, with a Discourse agreeable to the sad Occasion given, in a Number of wicked Pirates, who are speedily to be destroyed among us. A Discourse on the Folly, of getting Riches, and not by Right.

22. G. D. The State of my dear Consort's Health, calls for my wisest Conduct.

But, oh! Lett me also, and above all, help her forward and upward all I can, to those Attainments in the *royal Priesthood*, wherein the Life of my own Spirit lies.

23. G. D. To some Relatives at *Salisbury*, hitherto

[1] The "aged friend" was Rev. James Keith, now in his seventy-fifth year. He died July 23, 1719.

[2] Sewall, *Diary*, III. 143, 144. He makes no mention, however, of Mather's sermon, although he doubtless defrayed the cost of printing.

not much thought upon, I would no[w] apply myself with agreeable Books of Piety.

24. G. D. The Transplantation of great Numbers of good People from *Ireland* hither, is a Concern, whereto I would give my helping Hand.

25. G. D. In our New South church, there is now a Door opened, for bringing their Confusions to a Period.

26. G. D. The condemned Prisoners!

* 27. G. D. To assist the Designs of Piety, in Conversing with the Word of GOD, lett me read, *Franzius*.[1]

(X.) A Sermon which I preached yesterday, at our Old-South Church, (a sensible Providence of my Glorious Lord leading me to it) is desired for the Press; and I immediately send it thither, under this Title. THE VALLEY OF BACA. *The Divine Sovereignty displayed and adored; more particularly in Bereaving Dispensations of the Divine Providence. A Sermon preached on the Death of* Mrs. Hannah Sewal; *the Religious and Honourable Consort of* Samuel Sewal Esqy *which befell us on, 19 d. VIII m. 1717. In the Sixtieth year of her Age.*[2]

28. G. D. Lett me watch exceedingly against ill Impressions on my Mind, from the Temptations which any foolish and froward People in the Flock, may cause unto me.

29. G. D. My dear *Samuel*, is dangerously sick of a Feavour. Oh! what a Sacrifice am I now call'd unto! But the Life of the hopeful Child, how must it be wrestled for! And his future Improvement in all that is good, if he recover, studied for!

---

[1] Wolfgang Frantz (1564–1628), whose *Tractatus de Interpretatione Sacrae Scripturae* was held in high repute.

[2] Printed by B. Green, 1717. On this day the *Church Records* contain the following entry: "*Sarah Gould* (formerly *Cock*) appearing before the Church with poenitent acknowledgements of the Crimes for which a Censure was passed upon her, near twenty years ago, and with Testimonies of a Behaviour becoming a poenitent, and of the Readiness of the Church in *Hull* to receive her into their Fellowship, the Church agreed she should be released from her Censure, and be dismissed unto the Church at *Hull*, where she now resides." See Vol. I. 244 *n*.

30. G. D. New Relatives at *Salem*, have I done enough yett for their best Interests?

31. G. D. Some Representatives in our General Assembly must be talk'd unto.

November. 1. G. D. I, with some others, were to have bore our Part, the next week, in ordaining a Minister at *Brooklyn*. A very strange Providence, by some very trivial Accidents, leads us to a Knowledge of some very disqualifying Circumstances, in the Person to be ordained. We are distressed; But upon Enquiry into Things, we find that we cannot proceed; and signify so much unto the Church accordingly.[1]

But our Duty to the Church, and the young Man, and my own unto myself (in the deepest Humiliation for my own Miscarriages) on this Occasion! What is it?

2. G. D. Obtain a Reprieve, and if it may be, a Pardon, for one of the Pyrates, who is not only more pœnitent, but also more innocent than the rest.

2 *d.* 9 *m. Satureday.* I sett apart this Day, for Prayer with Fasting, on the usual Occasions. The Humiliations befalling the young Preacher at *Brooklyn*, in the inflicting whereof the holy and sovereign Lord, makes me a principal Instrument, gave me singular Calls to humble myself before the Lord, for those Miscarriages, which render me also, worthy to be rejected from serving of Him.

* 3. G. D. One Trial is no sooner over with me, but another comes on; I am for ought I know, as tempted a

---

[1] June 27, 1716, the town of Brookline voted to refray the cost of James Allen's entertainment on the sabbath days out of the town treasury. He gave such satisfaction that in December he was chosen to be the settled minister. Some further negotiations between him and the town intervened, and it was not until October, 1717, that an appropriation was made to pay for his ordination, and November 13 was named for the occasion. The action was delayed for a year, as he was not placed in full charge of the church until November 5, 1718. See p. 566 *infra.* The nature of his disability cannot be determined; but his death in 1747 is said to have been hastened by the effects of the "great awakening of 1735." *Muddy River and Brookline Records,* 107, 109; Lyon, *First Parish in Brookline,* 13.

Man, as any in the World. I have on this Time, a strong Impression on my Mind, that some very trying and grievous Thing is near unto me. The Lord præpare me, by furnishing me, with a great Strength for Sacrificing. I never can be safe, until the Love of God shall so far cause my Will to be swallowed up in His, that I can take part with GOD against myself, and entertain any Condition which He shall order for me with a sweet Acquiescence in the Pleasure that He takes to perform the Thing that is appointed for me; and then to look upon such a Disposition as a greater Favour of GOD, than any Thing that it pleases Him to Deny unto me.

4. G. D. Have I not in view, a Person who may prove, (if God please, and in His Time,) a wondrous Blessing to the Flock, whereof I am the Servant? [1] One, whose Improvement in the Church of GOD, has had formerly with me, a Sentence of Death written upon it! Oh! Lett me pray for him; and give the Flock an Opportunity of hearing him!

5. G. D. The Evil that I greatly feared, is come upon me. I am within these few hours, astonished with an Information, that an Harlot big with a Bastard, accuses my poor Son *Cresy*, and layes her Belly to him. Oh! Dreadful Case! Oh, Sorrow beyond any that I have mett withal! what shall I do now for the foolish Youth! what for my afflicted and abased Family? My God, look mercifully upon me.

The most sensible Judges upon the strictest Enquiry, beleeve the youth to be Innocent. But yett, oh! ye Humiliations! [2]

6. G. D. Send unto my Brother in *England*, something that may excite him, and assist him, to great Services.

7. G. D. One Mr De la Phillonnière, a French Jesuite,

---

[1] In the margin are written the letters "T. W.," that is, Walter.

[2] This paragraph is written in the margin.

becoming a Protestant and a Refugee, appears to me, from what I just now read of his, a Person to whom I may do much good, under some Temptations which I see scandalize him; and by whom, as by one many ways qualified, I may do great Services for the Kingdome of GOD. I therefore now write largely unto him; and send unto him, our *Malachi*, and some other Composures.[1]

7 *d.* ix *m. Thursday.* My Lecture this Day (which proves a dismal stormy Time,) I have under a gracious Direction of Providence, changed for an Opportunity to preach in the room of him the next Week, who preaches for me to Day.

This Day I sett apart for the Devotions of Prayer, with Fasting, in Secret before the Lord.

I considered the Sins of my Son, as being my own; and as also calling to Remembrance the Sins of my former Years; For all which I renewed my Repentance, with all Abasement of Soul, in the Sight of GOD. And I have some lively Symptoms of their being pardoned. Especially, in my living to God, I have Tokens for Good, that the Sentence of Death upon me is taken off.

I carried the Case of my sinful Son before the Lord: And arrived unto an holy Acquiescence of Mind, in the Will of the glorious GOD, whatever it may be concerning him; Resolving that if after all, he do not prove a Lover of GOD, my Love shall be utterly taken from him. God help'd me in the sacrificing Stroke, to go as far as any of His children commonly go in the present State of Mortality.

But my grand Concern was, for the conversion of the young Man unto serious Piety, and the effectual Embitterment of all Sin unto him, and of such evil Company as has been a Snare unto him.

For this Purpose, I not only applied my proper Discourses unto him, with Directions for the spending of his Time, while he must remain confined and retired with me, until the Storm shall be blown over: but I also cried unto GOD for him, with all possible Importunity, that the almighty Arm of Heaven may be bare, for the changing of his Heart, and the holy Spirit entirely renewing of him. And if this blessed End might be obtained, I was reconciled unto the holy Ones taking such a dreadful Way, as is now taken for it.

[1] See p. 563 *infra.*

I also pray'd with the poor Youth in my Study, as affectuously as I could.

And I afterwards called my Consort also, to join with me, in my Supplications.

Adding, our Petitions for a good Issue of the prodigious Difficulties, which this Affair has brought upon us.

I purpose, in this Way to *beseech the Lord thrice,* as soon as I can.

8. G. D. Several Services there are to be consulted among our Ministers.

Am not I as tempted a Man as lives in the World. Some that know very much of me, do think so.

Behold, a new Trial! My dear, pleasant, hopeful Son *Samuel,* is relapsed into the Feavour, from which we hoped, he was recovered; and lies in threatning Circumstances.

But still, my Gracious GOD helps me to make my Sacrifices. I acknowledge Him; I glorify Him, with the profoundest Resignation.

9. G. D. A poor and sick Family in my Neighbourhood, must be releeved.

This Day, my little Son's Feavour goes off, with a critical Bleeding.

What shall I render to the Lord!

* 10. G. D. *My GOD humbles me* exceedingly in the Circumstances of my poor son *Increase.* My Concern and Study must now be, above all things to gett my Spirit conformed unto the Humiliations, and ly low in the Dust before the Lord; and above all, the Extinction of my Will must be brought unto as much Perfection, as may be here arriv'd unto.

11. G. D. A dreadful Feavour is gott into the Town, and the other Churches in the Town, have been dreadfully wounded by the Death of desireable Men, whom this Feavour has carried off. My poor Flock is yett spared; tho' Sickness upon some has threatened it. I would endeavour to make the Voice of GOD in this work of His

Providence, as intelligible and effectual to the Flock, as I can.

But I would also employ the most fervent Intercessions, that the Flock may be spared, and the destroying Angel have no Commission to make any Spoil upon it.

11 *d.* IX *m. Munday.* In pursuance of my purpose to *Beseech the Lord thrice,* on the distressing Occasion, which caused me the last Thursday to be so Employ'd as I was, I sett apart this Day, for Prayer with Fasting, that my poor Son *Increase* might be effectually brought home unto GOD, and that we may also see a good Issue of the Trouble which threatens Ruine unto him.

Now, as well as then, I pray'd with the poor Youth in my Study.

And anon associated my Consort with me in my Supplications.

I think, my weeping Faith is arrived unto this Assurance, *my God will hear me.*

12. G. D. Among other Methods of bringing my Son *Increase* home unto GOD, I would ever now and then assign him, a proper Sermon to be read by him, and oblige him to turn the principal Points of the Sermon into a Prayer, which I will have to be written by him in his reserved Memorials.

13. G. D. I have a Sister-in-Law, in *England,* Mrs. *Clark,* of whom I have never taken yett so much Notice, as I think now to do, in sending some agreeable Instruments of Piety unto her.

14. G. D. Now I see the Design and Conduct of the divine Providence, in disposing of me, to change my Lectures.

My Honourable Friend, M[ajor] G[eneral] *Winthrop,*[1]

[1] Wait Still Winthrop (1643–1717) died November 6. He was, says Sewall, "for Parentage, Piety, Prudence, Philosophy, Love to New England ways and people very eminent." *Diary,* III. 146. Sewall's tribute will be found in *Letter Book,* II. 86.

is to be interr'd this Day. A service to Religion may be
done, as well as what may be for the good of the Countrey,
by my preaching a Sermon this Day, which may celebrate
the Glories of my SAVIOUR, who has the *Keys* of *Hades*
and of *Death* in His glorious Hands, and also bear a due
Testimony unto the Character of one who has been such a
Lover and Servant of his Countrey, as my departed Friend,
in the Hearing of the General Assembly now sitting.

I enjoy'd a gracious Presence of God with me, in the
Work before me.

(XI.) And my Sermon being immediately desired by
the only Son[1] of the Deceased, I give it, under this Title;
HADES Look'd into. *The Power of our Great SAVIOUR
over the Invisible World, and the Gates of Death which lead
into that World; Considered in a Sermon preached at the
Funeral of the Honourable WAIT WINTHROP Esqr. who
expired, 7 d. IX m. 1717. In the LXXVI year of his
Age.*[2]

15. G. D. There is good this Day to be done, on a
very solemn Occasion.

Six Pirates were this Day executed. I took a long and
sad Walk with them, from the Prison, to the Place of Execution. I successively bestowed the best Instructions I could,
upon each of them. Arriving to the Tree of Death, I
pray'd with them, and with the vast Assembly of Spectators, as pertinently and as profitably as I could.

16. G. D. Some lately recovered from the Jaws of
Death, and especially one Gentleman, for whom GOD has
remarkably heard us, must be address'd by me, as pungently and cogently as may be, that they may be confirmed
in Resolutions for the Service of GOD.

16 *d.* IX *m. Satureday.* I have now *besought the Lord
Thrice*, on the distressing Affair of my Son *Increase.*

---

[1] John Winthrop, F. R. S. (1681–1747).
[2] Printed by T. Crump, 1717.

I repeated the Exercises of the two former Days, with agreeable Varieties.

And now, *I will hear what God the Lord will say.*

I am ready for the Will of God. My God, I am ready for it.

I am now perswaded, *My God will hear me.*

*17. G. D. No Apology can be made for me, if I be not now,

A Man always abstaining from all Appearance of Evil.

A Man ever proposing to serve and please the glorious GOD.

A Man full of continual Projections to do good unto all that I am concerned withal.

A man full of Meekness under Provocations, and watchful against all ungoverned Anger.

A Man full of Patience under Calamities, and of a Spirit sweetly reconciled unto Humiliations.

A Man forever studious in my Dealings with my Neighbours, to do as I would be done unto, and forever afraid of harbouring the least evil Frame towards any Man in the World.

And a Man, Repairing still to my SAVIOUR for all that is good, with perpetual Studies to be in all Goodness conformed unto Him.

Finally, a Man dead unto the World, and having my own Will entirely swallowed up in the Will of GOD.

18. G. D. The Flock ought to be better advised, about, *Sending for the Elders,* to the sick, and not expecting them to come without *sending* for.

19. G. D. Alas, I have this Day, an heartbreaking Intimation, that *my God has not heard me,* in the main Point of my late Supplications; tho' I am heard with regard unto one remarkable Distress in the Case upon me. My poor Son, has made a worse Exhibition of himself unto me this Day, than I have ever yett mett withal. O my God, what shall I do? what shall I do? I will not yett utterly cast off the wretched Child. But I will still follow thee with Supplications, for what nothing but an almighty Arm can accomplish. There may [be] yett unknown Reserves of

Mercy, when the work of Repentance on me, intended in my Trials, is accomplished.

20. G. D.   Study to overcome evil with good, unto one who has greatly wronged me.[1]

21. G. D.   May not I do well to give the Bookseller, something that may render the Condition of the Pirates, lately executed, profitable?

The people of *Bridgwater* publishing a Sermon of their aged Pastor, I wrote a PREFACE to it, whereto my Father also signs; containing some things that may be of lasting Use to the People there.[2]

22. G. D.   The Ministers used much conduct in the affair of *Brooklyn*.

23. G. D.   Not only am I to dispense my own Releefs to the Poor, but the Season arrives for my public Hints unto the Liberal of the Flock, to do what is to be done for the Poor, against the approaching Winter.

* 24. G. D.   The good Providence of my SAVIOUR has brought me the Devout *Spener's* Treatise, *De Natura et Gratia:*[3] By a serious Perusal whereof, I hope, to make desireable Improvements in Piety.

My dear *Sammy* again fallen sick of a Feavour.

25. G. D.   Some Affairs of Discipline in the Church must be wisely managed.

Late Instances of Mortality in the Church must be improved for the Animation of Piety, in the Survivers.

Endeavours must be used, that the Loss of the Church may be recruited.

26. G. D.   The sick State of my dear *Sammy*, must quicken my Resolutions, upon the more exquisite Methods of prosecuting his Cultivation, first in Piety, and then in

[1] On this day he took part in the ordination of Rev. Thomas Foxcroft, as pastor of the First Church.   Sewall, *Diary*, III. 148.

[2] Two sermons were thus printed, *Bridgewater's Monitor*, by James Keith and Samuel Danforth, preached August 14, upon entering the new meeting house.

[3] Philipp Jakob Spener (1635-1705), the "father of pietism."

ll useful Accomplishments, if God will graciously spare
im to me.

(XII.) I had sometimes made a Prayer, that the Condi-
ion of the late *Pirates*, might be so ordered, as to furnish
ne with some special Opportunities, to do Service for the
Kingdome of GOD. After the Execution of the Criminals, I
ad some Thoughts of writing down the Conference I had
vith them in the way from the Prison to the Gallows:
dding the strange Story of their Capture, and the Sermon
preached unto my Flock on their Occasion. But my
Thoughts were so feeble and flitting, that I laid them aside.
However, I resumed them; and remaining still entirely at
Loss what to do, I betook myself unto the *Lott*. I wrote
on one Bitt of Paper, *Proceed*, on another, *Forbear;* and
after a solemn Invocation of the glorious Lord, I drew the
Lott; which fell to be *Proceed*. I sett myself to the Work,
and in a few Hours I made a strange Dispatch of it. The
Bookseller for whom I intended the Work, declined it;
which caused me to wonder at my Direction to *Proceed*.
But some other Booksellers, from whom I least expected
it, without any offer of Mine to them, accepted it, and
print no less than twelve hundred of them; and the Cause
of Piety, is likely to be more than a little served. The
Book is entituled; INSTRUCTIONS TO THE LIVING FROM THE
CONDITION OF THE DEAD. *A brief Relation of Remarkables,
in the Fate of more than one hundred Pirates, that were ship-
wreck'd on the Coast of* New England; *and in the Death of
Six who after a fair Trial, were convicted and condemned at*
Boston, *and were Executed,* 15 d. IX m. 1717. *With an
Account of the Discourse had with them on the way to their
Execution. And a SERMON preached on their occasion.*[1]

27. G. D. I have a poor Brother-in-Law out of Employ,
and froward enough; What shall I do for him?

28. G. D. I entertain serious Thoughts of reprinting

[1] Printed by John Allen for Nicholas Boone, 1717.

here, the Account I have lately received of some Jewis
Children at *Berlin*, strangely converted unto our SAVIOUR
adding some Remarks thereupon, to serve the Cause o
Piety. What if I should annex to it as a Present unto th
Jewish Nation, my brief Confutation of Judaism, in m
Book of, *Things to be thought upon?* I'l advise.

28 *d.* 9 *m. Thursday.* Twas a Day of Thanksgivin
thro' the Province. I enjoy'd very gracious Assistence
from Heaven, in the Work of the Day; and preached bot
parts of the Day.

29. G. D. I would send my Account of the Jewis
Children at *Berlin* unto the Master of our Grammar-Schole
with my Desire that it be readd publickly unto the Chil
dren in the Schole, and that he make suitable Remark
thereupon unto them.

30. G. D. A poor Woman under both Guilt and Want
must receive sundry Kindnesses from me.

Because of the Day sett apart for Exercise of Piet
two days ago and my Labours thereupon, I do not set
apart this Day for a secret Fast, as else I should have done

December. * 1. G. D. Most certainly there is no Con
sideration in the World, more sanctifying and more ani
mating, unto all the Tempers and Actions of Piety, tha
that, Gal. II. 20. *The Son of GOD has loved me.* I woul
as far as tis possible, gett into the way of entertaining thi
Consideration upon all Occasions, and experiencing the
holy Efficacy of it on me. I need not quæstion the Love
of my SAVIOUR to me, if I entertain the Beleef of it, upon
this Intention; to render all Sin odious unto me, and t
quicken myself in pleasing of God and in doing of Good.
But if I entertain this Beleef, how wondrous will be the
Force of it, when I apply it, unto the Services, whereto 1
am called; unto the Sufferings which are dispensed unto
me; unto the Relations wherein GOD shall station me;
and unto all the Enjoyments which are bestow'd upon me

purpose very much to exercise myself unto this Godliness; and anon to entertain the People of GOD with a
Treatise upon it.

2. G. D. And can I entertain the Flock, on a better,
or more useful Subject!

3. G. D. I must use many Methods of Instructing,
inclining, enriching my restored *Samuel.* Among the rest,
I would putt him upon composing of Prayers out of Books
of Piety, which I would putt into his Hands.

4. G. D. A Brother-in-Law at *Charlestown*, in a feeble
State of Health, must be visited, and assisted.

5. G. D. Writing Letters to *Scotland*, I would prosecute several public Services; especially, those designed in
our *Malachi.*

6. G. D. Procure two Things among the Christian
Indians, at *Martha's Vineyard*, First, a Tutor, to bring up
Indians for the Ministry; Secondly, a Visitor for the Schools,
to see that their Ends be answered.

7. G. D. One who lived many years in my Family,
is, in regard of a sick Husband, and on other Accounts, in
a very poor and sad Condition.

*8. G. D. The Proposal made a week ago, about my
Keeping myself in the Love of GOD, and acting under the
Influence of a Perswasion, *that my SAVIOUR has loved me*,
(than which there can be nothing more sanctifying, or more
comfortable) I have now digested into a clear and plain
way of proceeding; and I hope, to live in a continual Conformity unto it.

It is done in the Sermon, which I this day deliver to
the People of GOD.

9. G. D. Mortality has lately taken off some that
belong to the Flock. I must be concerned, that the Flock
may be recruited, with the Addition of such as may fill up
the Room of those that are taken off.

10. G. D. My Duty to my Family, will oblige me to

hasten the Settlement of Affaires, relating to the Adminis
tration, upon which I entred a year and half ago.

11. G. D.   More must be done for my Brother-in-Law
at *Roxbury.*

And for some Relatives in *England.*

12. G. D.   I incline to think, that the Reprinting o
the strange Relation which we have of the Jewish Children
at *Berlin*, with some Remarks upon it, may sensibly serve
the Kingdome of GOD.   And, what if I should therewitha
reprint, my Address to the Jewish Nation, which is in my
Book, of, *Things to be more thought upon.*

(XIII.) I do accordingly give these things unto the
Bookseller, under this Title; FAITH ENCOURAGED. *A brief
Relation of a Strange Impression from Heaven, upon the
Minds of some Jewish Children at the City of Berlin, (in the
Upper Saxony.)   And an Improvement made of so marvellou.
an Occurrence.*[1]

13. G. D.   I will sett myself to think, how the Meetings
of the Ministers in this Town, may be made serviceable
unto many precious and glorious purposes.

And move them, to take the Point into consideration.

14. G. D.   Some young Scotchmen recommended unto
my Care and Love, I would make special Objects of my
Care and Love.

* 15. G. D.   That part of the divine Image, which
lies, in a right Frame of Love towards our Neighbour; is
what I resume into my Consideration, for a more special
and exquisite Cultivation of it.

For this Purpose, I would speedily draw up the Maxims
of Love, by which I would be entirely governed, in my whole
Conversation; and gett my Mind exactly formed according
to them.

16. G. D.   And can I do my Flock a greater Service,
than by the Communication thereof unto them!

[1] Printed by J. Allen for T. Fleet, 1718.

17. **G. D.** There is a Projection relating to my poor son *Increase*, that may have a Tendency, not only to his temporal Prosperity in the World; but also to his Preservation from various Temptations, to which he may be obnoxious.

18. **G. D.** A Relative going to sea, comes under my fresh Cares for his Welfare.

19. **G. D.** GOD speaks to the Place, the Voice of the Lord cries to the City, in the Sickness which has carried off many pious and some useful Persons; and is yett smiting and wasting, (more in some neighbouring Towns than in this.) To render the Voice of Heaven articulate and intelligible, and also to obtain from Heaven a Return of Health unto the Town, and serve many good Purposes, my Lecture is this day turned into a Day of Supplications.[1]

20. **G. D.** There is a young Gentleman of a Great Estate who is lately recovered from sickness, which brought him to the very Gates of Death. He seems much affected with the Goodness of GOD unto him in his Recovery, and inclined unto the making of suitable Returns. I would cultivate an Acquaintance with him; and therein move him to such Things as may be of great Consequence for the Service of GOD, and the Comfort of others as well as his own.

21. **G. D.** An Hopeful Child at the Colledge is become an Orphan; and his Mother a very poor Widow. I would endeavour to procure a Subsistence for him.

*22. **G. D.** The Aspect that some Occurrences have upon me, tells me, that I have not sufficiently repented of some former Iniquities. The Language of the Occurrences is, that I ought to renew the Repentance due to the Occasions, with the most frequent and bitter Exercises. Perhaps, in my doing so, very much of the End, which may be intended in some very grievous Dispensations will be attained.

[1] Sewall, *Diary*, III. 155.

My GOD, Help me, Help me, to conform unto thy Dispensations, and ly in the Dust before thee:

23. G. D. One good way for me to do good in the Flock will be to supply the private Meetings, with proper Instruments of Piety, to be readd in them.

I have lately preached six Sermons on the *Thessalonian* Benediction, wherein real and vital Piety is described and assisted.[1] These Essays on, *The best of Blessings*, are so written, as to be ready for the Press, if they should be called for. But this I cannot look for. However, I have Thoughts of depositing the Treatise in the Hands of one who reads to a religious Society; that by its being readd there, it may serve the Cause of *Piety*.

24. G. D. For the more effectual Formation of my Son *Samuel*, and to furnish him with uncommon Erudition, but especially with Religion, I would speedily sett apart some time, to invent, and project, and form certain Proposals of a Method which may be for that Purpose proceeded in.

25. G. D. A Relative, whom I have not yett thought upon, I would employ singular Cares to render a pious and an useful Person.

26. G. D. I am sollicitous about the Gospellizing of paganizing *Tiverton*. I light on a proposal for it; moving that Elder Ministers may in their Turn visit the Place, (wherein I also, if I live till a good Season for it, may be willing to take my Turn,) and a younger supply their vacant Places, until the Gospel be received with them.

27. G. D. There are certain Books, lately published beyond-Sea, which if they were more common in this Countrey, might have an happy Influence upon us. I would prevail with an honest and a wealthy Man here to send for some Numbers of them, and scatter them about the Countrey.

28. G. D. A young Minister, who has lately refused

[1] I Thess. v. 23.

Motions and Offers from our Ch[urch] of E[ngland] has therein rendred himself worthy of all possible Cares to be used for his Promotion and Encouragement.

28 d. 10 m. *Satureday.* This Day I sett apart, as I use to do, before the Administration of the Eucharist; for the Exercises of Prayer with Fasting before the Lord.

The Occasions and the Exercises, were what were usual.

But there was nothing that my Cries to Heaven did more insist upon, than this; that the glorious GOD would pitty His poor Creature Man, and not cast off Mankind forever; but visit the World, with the sweet Influences of the Saviour, who is God become a Man; and rescue the miserable Children of Men, out of their Ignorance, and Corruption, and Slavery, and most miserable Circumstances and graciously please to dwell with them and in them, and make them His holy Temples.

From this I argued, how particularly ought I to prosecute such Desires for my own Children, and most particularly for my ungodly Son! Certainly I am now prepared for some Success in my Petitions.

* 29. G. D. The distinguishing Acts of true, real, vital Piety, are so curiously described in my *Spener's* Treatise *De Natura et Gratia*, that I cannot but repeat my Proposal, in the Perusal of this Treatise, to gett such Acts continually formed in my own Soul, as I go along. Will anything tend more to render me a finished Christian.

But I propose also to employ my Studies on that Subject, *a Meetness for the Inheritance of the Saints in Light.* And in so doing, to gett my own Soul raised up unto every Article.

30. G. D. And what better, what fitter, what more useful Subject can I entertain the Flock withal!

31. G. D. Good may be done in my Family by much inculcating the Grace of Dependence on the fatherly Providence of God for a Subsistence in the World, and Patience

under Disappointments of our Expectations from the world.[1]

January. [1717–18.] 1. G. D. It being a tolerable Day for such a Walk, I this Day go over to *Charlestown*, and visit some aged Relatives, who in all Probability are not far from the eternal World; and endeavour in my Conferences with them, to prepare them for that World.

2. G. D. What shall I do for the Welfare of the Colledge at *New-haven?* I am inclinable to write unto a wealthy East-India Merchant at *London*,[2] who may be disposed on several Accounts, to do for that Society, and Colony; and solicit his Bounties unto such an Interest.

3. G. D. Our Governour must be talked withal, on several important Affairs.

4. G. D. A very poor and a very old Man in my Neighbourhood must be looked after.

* 5. G. D. This Morning I sett myself to consider, What are the principal Articles of Adversity, which I have afflicting of me. Now every Affliction is an Invasion upon some Enjoyment. Wherefore on each Point wherein I am Exercised, I thought, *What is the Enjoyment whereof I am called now to make a Sacrifice?* Accordingly, I applied myself unto the Acts of Sacrificing thereupon. I found a sensible Improvement in Piety.

6. G. D. Lett my Flock be entertained, with a Discourse on *Patience.* Many have great Occasion for it.

Read Mr. *Baxter's Gildas Salvianus* again, to animate a due Care for the Souls of the Flock.

7. G. D. One thing I will do for my Son *Samuel*, shall be, to teach him the Way of reading the Scriptures that may prove of the most impressive and eternal Advantage unto him. I will oblige him to take certain Portions of the Scrip-

---

[1] This paragraph is written in Greek characters.

[2] Elihu Yale. Mather's letter to him is in Quincy, *History of Harvard University*, I. 524.

tures, and write what Maxims and Lessons of Piety, he can find in them, and add, what Wishes and Prayers, he would form thereupon.

8. G. D. Entertain my aged Parent, with Dr. *Spener*.

9. G. D. Writing to the West of *England*, I have in view, several Services for the Kingdome of God.

10. G. D. Encourage the new Lieut. Governour of *Hampshire*,[1] to such Things as may be for the Peace and Good of his Province.

11. G. D. A family in my Neighbourhood, fallen into wretched Circumstances of Sin and Strife; can't I recover them into better Circumstances?

*12. G. D. I draw up three Resolutions, that I may keep clear of damnable Idolatries; and that I may not come into the multiplied Sorrows of them that hasten after another GOD.

They are to be seen, at the End of my Sermon, on Psal. XVI. 4.

13. G. D. And, oh! what more important Service can I do for my Flock, in the fulfilling of my Ministry, than to warn them of the Idolatries, daily committed, but rarely considered.

14. G. D. *Sammy* is united with a Society of sober and pious Lads, who meet for Exercises of Religion. I will allow them the Use of my Library, for the Place of their Meeting; and give them Directions, and Entertainments.

15. G. D. The Gentlewoman which my Father has married,[2] is, upon the Death of a Kinsman, very much discomposed. I will do the best I can, to assist and strengthen in her the Dispositions of Sacrificing.

But, Oh! What a Stroke of Sacrificing am I putt upon! My dear, amiable valuable Consort, is arrested with the

---

[1] John Wentworth (1671-1730).

[2] Anna Lake, daughter of Captain Thomas Lake, and widow of Rev. John Cotton of Hampton.

Fever, which has made such an horrible Slaughter both in Town and Countrey.

God calls me, to Repentance for my Miscarriages, and Submission to His Will in whatever shall be the Thing appointed for me, and earnest Supplications for the Life of the dearest Enjoyment I have in the World, and holy Contrivances that in her Soul as well as my own, this Visitation may produce the Improvements in Piety, by which the Errand of it shall be answered.

16. G. D. Something extraordinary must be done by me, (tho' under as much covert as may be,) to preserve the Town from going into a dreadful Day of Temptation, which the Contentions and Confusions in the South part of it, seem to threaten and hasten upon it.

17. G. D. I am this week entertained, with surprising Advice, concerning the *Jew*, with and for whom we were so much concerned, three and twenty years ago. A matter for some revived and renewed Supplications.

18. G. D. I have now a *Charity-Schole* erected for the Instruction of Negros and Indians, whereof I am at the sole Expence. God prosper it.

*19. G. D. What Improvement in Piety, shall I make, of the Sickness and Fever, which my dear Consort now labours of?

Being thus tried unto the uttermost, I would even in this Point also, do the Part of a *Sacrificer*.

My Conversation with her, shall have in it, a yett more shining Sanctity; and very much turn upon those Things wherein we shall both of us be brought nearer to GOD, and grow in our Obedience and Conformity to Him, and Communion with Him.

Even for the most free and most mean Part of our Conversation, it shall still be, not only with an Eye to the Indulgence of Heaven, but also with explicit Regards to some good End, which Heaven will be pleased withal.

20. G. D. Our Church having lost by Sickness within a few Months, many more than twenty of our Communicants, I would make my Remonstrances unto the Church, and the rest of the Neighbours on this occasion; unto the Church, for due Improvements in Piety; unto the rest, that in the Ways of Piety they recruit the Losses of the Church.

21. G. D. In pursuance of what I was thinking two Days ago, I would strengthen my Resolution, that I will not ordinarily come and stay any number of Minutes, where my Consort is, without speaking of some valuable Thing, which it may be worth her while to remember, or consider. And I will desire her, to call upon me, for the Performance of this Resolution.

22. G. D. There are diverse Points of Consequence, that I should mention to my Son-in-Law, Mr. W[illard], relating and conducing to his Welfare.

23. G. D. I entertain Thoughts about the forming of a Society here, upon the design of cultivating and propagating the Maxims in the Reign whereof there is to come on the Kingdome of GOD.

I might have mentioned it, that yesterday,

22 *d*. XI *m. Wednesday*, was kept, a Day of Prayer with Fasting, by the Ministers of the Town, with some other Christians, at the House of Judge *Sewal;* occasion'd by the late Humiliations on his Family.

I preached at his Desire on Psal. LXXXIX. 8.

It was a good Day; And perhaps it may supersede, what I would else have attended in my Study, on the next Satureday.[1]

24. G. D. An unknown Hand, on the last Lord's-day convey'd into one of the Boxes at our Collection, the Sum of Ten Pounds; with a Letter unto me, to distribute it unto the Ministers in the Proportions which it mentions.

This gives me an Opportunity, in writing unto the Min-

[1] Sewall, *Diary*, III. 162.

isters to animate their Diligence in the Discharge of their
Ministry as well as their Dependence on the Faithfulness of
our Saviour in the Care of His Providence for them.

25. G. D.   Several Miserables I have in View, to be
cared for.

* 26. G. D.   My Spirit getts on somewhat comfortably
unto the Frames and Acts, which discover the *Life of GOD*
beginning there.

I particularly find, that when some afflictive Thing is approaching me, I have a secret and serene Satisfaction arising in my Mind,
from the View it gives me, of an Opportunity for the Sacrifices with
which the great GOD will be now gratified and glorified.   My Sacrifices will be acceptable to GOD, because of what his CHRIST has
done, and will do, to make them so.   I am glad beyond all Expression,
when I can come to any Thing, which I think will be well-pleasing to
GOD, and will find Acceptance with Him, who is infinitely worthy
of my dearest LOVE.   The Adversity which putts me upon the Sacrificing of the Enjoyments for which I have a Kindness, furnishes
me with an Opportunity therein to do that, which the great God will
with Pleasure look down upon.   And now, that Grace of GOD, which
enables me to make Sacrifices of all my desired and valued Enjoyments, and acquiesce in His wise, just, sovereign Will, which denies
them to me, becomes to me a better Thing than any of the Enjoyments, which are thus made my Sacrifices.   Indeed sometimes the
sacrificing Stroke must be upon power wherein I cannot have the
Enjoyments witheld from me, without the great GOD leaving of
them to *Sin*, in whom I am to lose my Comforts.   But here, while I
retain the Horror of *Sin*, which causes me to deprecate it wonderfully,
and say, *oh! lett such a Cup as this pass from me!* Yett even here
also, I do in an holy Darkness annihilate my Will before the Lord;
and Conclude, *O my God, I submitt unto thy Will forevermore!*

But then, in Projections for advancing the Kingdome of GOD,
in my Heart and Life, I shall invent yett a more copious Way of
proceeding.

27. G. D.   I entertain the Flock, with as moving a Discourse as I can, of the Numbers taken from us, wherein
we are a People *consumed by the Anger of GOD*.   I putt
them upon an Examination of what may have provoked

this *Anger* in several Articles. I propose methods for diverting this *Anger*. I press for the doing of what may be done for the Repairing of our Breaches; especially, in Peoples joining themselves to the Church after a due Preparation for it.

28. G. D. Exquisite Methods are contriving with me, that my dear Consort may recover out of her Sickness, with unspeakable Advantage to the Interests of Piety, in her Heart and Life.

29. G. D. The Widow, of my transcendently wicked Brother-in-Law, who has just now died very suddenly, must be visited and instructed.

30. G. D. It has been a Time, wherein Sickness has made many Visits and Ruines, both in City and Countrey; Many noted People are taken off; and the Sickness is taking still its Round thro the Land. Many have been restored; and [those] preserved also have had their Health, a matter of great Concern unto them. A Sermon at the Lecture, on the *Blessings of an Healed Soul*, might be very seasonable, and very serviceable.

This Day I preach the Sermon, to a great Assembly, with a great Assistence and Acceptance.

31. G. D. My, *Faith Encouraged*, being published, in which the strange Conversion of the Jewish Children at *Berlin*, is accompanied with an Address unto the *Jewish Nation;* I propose to send it, unto as many of the Jews, in several Places and Countreys as I can.

How strangely does the sovereign Grace of GOD still favour me, the vilest of Men, in regard of the Fruits, which He enables me to bring forth for the Service of His Kingdome! And it is a little surprising unto me, to see how in the Things which I have most of all projected, I am still disappointed; but the Things, wherein there has been the least of my own Projection, are those which the holy One employs to do Good among His People.

(XIV.) This Day there come some young Gentlemen to me, desiring the Notes of the Sermon I preached yesterday, for Publication; as, what may be very seasonably diffused thro' the Land, at such a Time as is now upon us. I give it under this Title. RAPHAEL. *The Blessings of an HEALED SOUL considered: In a very brief and plain Essay, made at a Time, when Sickness had been making many Visits, with an uncommon Mortality, especially upon more noted People both in City and Countrey.*

February. 1. G. D. There are some distracted Creatures, for whom I would consult with the Physicians.

I would move some Physicians, to unite in setting up a *Cold-Bath*, by which the difficult and even desperate Cases of many poor Miserable might be releeved.

* 2. G. D. I entreat of my discreet Consort, that she would plainly discover it unto me, if she see in me any Thing that needs to be mended, or that she would have to be otherwise. As yett she tells me of nothing.

An Healed Soul, is the grand Thing that I am to Labour for.

I doubt, I have one Distemper hanging about me, in my being too ready to take up an Apprehension of Peoples being generally Disaffected unto me, (Tho' I must be blind indeed, if I do not see enough of that!) because I meet with very odd, absurd, and froward Usage from some of the People. I must beware of Jealousies that shall be Injuries. I must watch against the Entertainment of too much Leaven in my Spirit against a People, whose Behaviour towards me, is very unrighteous and ungrateful. I must enjoy a sweet Satisfaction of Mind, if I find myself conformed unto Him, who was despised and rejected of Men. I must beware of speaking unadvisedly with my Lips.

3. G. D. An evil Instrument or two, is doing Mischief in the Church, which with the Exercise of a little Wisdome, and Patience, and Meekness, I hope to putt a stop to.

4. G. D. Oh! What Return of Obedience and Gratitude shall I make unto the Lord, in a well-ordered Family,
for His Mercy in restoring unto it, so rich a Blessing as I
and all of us enjoy in my Consort. I will contrive some
special Thing.

5. G. D. A good Providence orders it, that my aged
Parent shows me, what he intends for his last Will and
Testament. This gives me an Opportunity to do Service
for him, and for others, by proposing some very necessary
Alterations.

6. G. D. There are some Things to be proposed for the
Quieting of the raging Follies in the South-part of the
Town.

7. G. D. By Encouraging of Mr. *Prence* [1] to accept
the Invitation of the Old South Church, I may have a
Companion with whom I may unite, more than any one
upon Earth in doing services for the Kingdome of GOD.

8. G. D. A religious Woman under total Blindness,
meeting with uncivil and indecent Usage from froward
Relatives, is exposed unto grievous Difficulties. I must
contrive what may be done for her.

* 9. G. D. Looking over a Catalogue of the Books, pub-
lished, whereof the Grace of GOD has made poor me the
Writer, I must in the first place loathe and judge myself
exceedingly before the Lord, for the sinful Corruptions, and
especially the selfish Intentions, which have defiled all these
Publications. And I must exceedingly watch against all
Vanity of Mind, even the least Motion that way, from the
Number of the Publications, which amounts to near two
hundred and fourscore, so I must admire the Goodness and
Mercy of a sovereign GOD, who has herein distinguished the
Chief of Sinners, and might have employ'd any one else, as
well as this Vilest of Men, in this Variety of Services. But
then how exceedingly must I labour, that my Publications

[1] Thomas Prince.

may not be my Condemnations; and that there may therefore be as much Piety in my Practice as in my Paper! For which Purpose, I would in a deliberate Perusal of the Catalogue, upon each of the Titles form such Wishes of Piety, as they would naturally lead me to, and send them up in Prayers and Cries unto the Lord!

10. G. D. A Catalogue must be taken of such as may be hopefully prepared for the Communion of the Church; and they must be severally called upon.

11. G. D. Temptations to be wisely encountred and improved.

The Course of my Ministry this Year.

14 *d.* 12 *m.* [*February.*] 1716[–17]. *Thursday.* On Isa. XXVI. 20. The *Chambers*, entred by the People of God, at their Death. (A Funeral Sermon, for a Minister of the Town who died Yesterday. Preached in the Room of his Collegue.)

17 *d.* 12 *m.* On, Eccl. IX. 10. On the *Vigor* and the *Dispatch*, wherewith we are to do the *Work* which God has assign'd us to do; because it cannot be done after we are gone to the Grave. (Occasion'd by the Death of two noted Ministers, who ly dead, one of *Boston*, t'other of *Cambridge*.)

24 *d.* 12 *m.* Never such a *Snow*, in the Memory of Man! And much falling this Day, as well as fallen two Dayes ago, that very many, of our Assemblies had no Sacrifices. This Day, I preached on, 2. Sam. XXIII. 20. The Mystery of *Benajah* killing a *Lion* in a Pitt, in a Time of *Snow*.

28 *d.* 12 *m. Thursday.* The Lecture; on Psal. CXLVII. 18. The melting Efficacy in the Word of God suiting the great Thaws now looked for.

1717. Two Lord's-dayes, to my Sorrow, were intermitted.

17 *d.* 1 *m.* [*March.*] On, Rev. II. 19. The Happiness of the Christian, whose *last Works* are his *best Works*. (To awaken my own Attention unto the Calls of GOD, in my own Age and Health.)

24 *d.* 1 *m.* On Cant. VIII. 6. The *Love* in the Heart of the Beleever to His lovely SAVIOUR, strong and glorious. (And I administred the Eucharist.)

31 *d.* 1 *m.* On Luk. XIV. 23. The *Compelling* of people to *come* unto our Saviour and His Religion.

7 *d*. 2 *m*. [*April*.] On, Prov. XII. 12. The *Root of the Righteous*, in the LOVE of GOD.

11 *d*. 2 *m*. *Thursday*. The Lecture. On, Rev. XIV. 7. The Everlasting MAXIMS of PIETY. Finishing what I began on a former Lecture.

14 *d*. 2 *m*. On, Job. XXIX. 3. The Light of GOD, by which we may *walk thro' darkness*.

21 *d*. 2 *m*. On, Psal. CXIX. 92. The *Delights* in the Word of GOD, by seeking whereof, our *Perishing* in our *Affliction*, may be prevented.

28 *d*. 2 *m*. A. M. At the New South Church, on Psal. CXIX. 25. P. M. At the Old North Church, on 2. King, XXII, 19, The Proofs and fruits of a *Tender-Heart*.

5 *d*. 3 *m*. [*May*.] On, Joh. VI. 21. Our *Immediate* arriving to the best of Circumstances, by *receiving* of our SAVIOUR, and obtaining His gracious Presence with us.

12 *d*. 3 *m*. On, Isa. LXIV. 7. *Few* people in earnest, about the *grand Business* of Religion.

19 *d*. 3 *m*. On, Col. III. ii. CHRIST, the true Christians *all*. (And I administred the Eucharist.)

21 *d*. 3 *m*. *Tuesday*. A Fast at *Roxbury*, on the behalf of their sick Pastor. On Lam. III. 57.

23 *d*. 3 *m*. *Thursday*. The Lecture; On Eccl. VII. 9. The Follies and Mischiefs of *ungoverned Anger*. On the Occasion of a poor Man under the Sentence of Death, (now in the Auditory,) for a Murder committed by him in his Anger.

26 *d*. 3 *m*. On Job. XV. 21. The *dreadful Sound* in the Ears of a wicked Man.

2 *d*. 4 *m*. [*June*.] On Eccl. IX. 12. Man's *not knowing his Time*. On the Occasion of several sudden Deaths, and some of them very tragical ones, the Week before.

9 *d*. 4 *m*. On, Rev. II. 21. The Improvement, that should be made of, *a Space to Repent*.

This being the last Lords-day of a poor condemned Malefactor appearing in any of our Assemblies. A vast Auditory!

13 *d*. 4 *m*. *Thursday*. The Lecture, devolved on me, by the Desire of the poor condemned Malefactor; who is to dy this Day; and has desired me to preach, on, Matth. X. 28. The Terrors of HELL. The gracious Lord, mightily assisted me, in addressing a vast Auditory.

16 *d*. 4 *m*. On, Prov. XI. 11. Men of a right Character Bless-

ings to the public, and in all Societies. (Our Governour this day beginning to appear in our Assemblies.)

23 *d.* 4 *m.* On, Isa. LV. 8. The Divine Dispensations full of *glorious Transcendencies*.

30 *d.* 4 *m.* On, Joh. XI. 29. An *immediate Compliance*, with the Calls of our Saviour.

7 *d.* 5 *m.* [*July*.] On, Joh. XII. 26. Who the true *Servants* of our SAVIOUR and what the *Honours*, which He will bestow upon them.

11 *d.* 5 *m. Thursday.* A general Fast. On, 1. King VIII. 38. The Course to be taken under *Secret Sorrows*.

14 *d.* 5 *m.* On, Cant. II. 3. The comfortable *Shade*, and the agreeable *Fruit*, wherewith we are accommodated in our SAVIOUR. (And I administred the Eucharist.)

21 *d.* 5 *m.* On, 1. Pet. III. 13. CHRIST, the *good One*, and the good of being His *Followers*, in His *Goodness*.

28 *d.* 5 *m.* On, Cant. VIII. 6. At the Old South-Church. (Where I also enjoy'd the Benefit of the Eucharist.)

4 *d.* 6 *m.* [*August*.] On, Isa. LXI. 9. *Conspicuous Blessings*, bestow'd by GOD, on the *Children* of His People, and of His Covenant. (My first Grandchild, being this Day Baptised.)

11 *d.* 6 *m.* On, Joh. XI. 43, 44. The Resurrection of *Lazarus*, applied unto the Intentions of Peoples being Raised from a *State of Sin*, to *live unto GOD*, by the enlivening Voice of our SAVIOUR.

15 *d.* 6 *m. Thursday.* The Lecture. On Luk. III. 17. The *purged Floor*.

18 *d.* 6 *m.* On, Rev. III. 19. The *Rebukes* and *Chast'nings* of the Lord, on the Objects of His *Love*.

1 *d.* 7 *m.* [*September*.] On, Isa. LXV. 23. That Case, what is to be done that so our Labour in this world, may not be a *Labour in Vain*, and all thrown away.

8 *d.* 7 *m.* On, Isa. XXXIII. 17. A Sight of our SAVIOUR, as a glorious *King in His Beauty*. (And I administred the Eucharist.)

15 *d.* 7 *m.* On, Job. XXVII. 6. The *Reproaches* of Conscience; the Good, and the Way of a Deliverance from them.

22 *d.* 7 *m.* On, Psal. LXXXIX. 15. The *Blessedness* of a People who *know* the *joyful Sound* of the Gospel. (Our People having a strong Motion among them, to provide an Assistent and Successor, in the work of the evangelical Ministry.)

25 *d.* 7 *m. Wednesday.* A Fast, at the Old South Church, to ask the Direction of Heaven, about their Choice of another Minister. **I**

preached on Joh. VI. 11. Our Saviour distributing *Bread*, by the Hands of His Disciples.

26 *d*. 7 *m. Thursday*. The Lecture. On, Joh. IV. 6. An undue Satisfaction in temporal Enjoyments.

29 *d*. 7 *m*. On, Amos. VIII. 11. A *Famine* of Hearing the Word of God. Advice to them who see the Reverse of it. On the same Occasion, that the last Lord's-day.

2 *d*. 8 *m*. [*October*.] *Wednesday*. A Fast at Old North-Church, to seek Direction about Calling a Minister. On Joh. X. ii. The *good Shepherd*.

6 *d*. 8 *m*. On, 1. Thess. V. 23. Being *sanctified wholly*, by the *God of Peace*.

13 *d*. 8 *m*. On, 1. Thess. V. 23. Being *præserved Blameless*.

20 *d*. 8 *m*. On, 1. Thess. V. 23. The *Spirit Sanctified*, and *preserved Blameless*.

27 *d*. 8 *m*. A. M. At the Old South. On Job. IX. 12. The Sovereignty of GOD, particularly in *taking away*. A funeral Sermon for Mrs. *Sewal*.

P. M. At the Old North; on Jer. XVII. 11. *Getting Riches*, and not *by Right*. That the Condition of the six condemned Pirates may be rendred profitable.

3 *d*. 9 *m*. [*November*.] On Cant. V. i. The Provision, whereto our SAVIOUR invites His beloved Friends, in His Institutions. (And administred the Eucharist.)

10 *d*. 9 *m*. On 1. Thess. V. 23. The *Soul Sanctified*, and *preserved blameless*.

14 *d*. 9 *m. Thursday*. The Lecture. On Rev. I. 18. The Power of our SAVIOUR over *Hades*. (A funeral Sermon for Major General *Winthrop*.)

17 *d*. 9 *m*. On Prov. I. 31. Wicked People dreadfully punished in their own Wickedness. (On the Death of the Pirates, two days ago.)

24 *d*. 9 *m*. On, Eccl. IX. 5. The *Knowledge* which the Living have, that they shall Dy: And what sort of Knowledge it should be. (A Funeral-sermon for a Sister-in-Law.)

28 *d*. 9 *m. Thursday*. A general Thanksgiving. On Heb. XIII. 15. Offering the *Sacrifice* of Praise to God continually by our SAVIOUR. Both Parts of the Day.

1 *d*. 10 *m*. [*December*.] On, 1. Thess. V. 23. The *Body sanctified*, and *preserved blameless*.

8 *d*. 10 *m*. On, 1. Thess. V. 23. Powerful Considerations to animate *blameless Holiness*, the *Coming* of our Saviour, the *Eye* of

our Saviour, and the *Love* of our Saviour.   The sixth and finishing Sermon on the *Thessalonian Blessing.*

15 *d.* 10 *m.*   On, Rom. XIV. 7, 8.   Our being the Lords; and therefore both *Living* to Him, and *Dying* to Him.   (A Funeral-sermon for Col. *Hutchinson.*[1])

19 *d.* 10 *m. Thursday.*   The Lecture was turned into a Day of Prayer with the Inhabitants of *Boston;* on the [*torn*] of our late Losses by Mortality, and the Sickness yett visiting and threatning of us.

I preached both parts of the Day on Job. XXI.   *Sorrows distributed* in the *Anger* of GOD.

22 *d.* 10 *m.*   On Psal. CXIX. 107.   What is to be done by those who are *afflicted very much*, that they may be *quickened* under it.

29 *d.* 10 *m.*   On, Cant. i. 4.   *Desires* to be *drawn* to and by our SAVIOUR; and *Resolves* to *run* after Him; and the *Chambers* wherein He gives a kind Reception to those who have such *Desires* and *Resolves.*   (And I administred the Eucharist.)

5 *d.* 11 *m.* [*January.*]   On, Jam. V. 7.   The *Patience*, to be exercised by the Christian in a Course of Christianity

12 *d.* 11 *m.*   On, Psal. XVI. 4.   The *Idolatries* being committed, but rarely considered.   And the *Sorrows* in the Consequences.

19 *d.* 11 *m.*   On Psal. LVII. 7.   An *Heart fixed*, in a due watch against *wandring Thoughts* in Devotions; and in a due *Preparation* for troublesome Events and Changes.   (Not knowing how GOD may deal with me, or mine, in the Sickness now come into my Family.)

27 *d.* 11 *m.*   On Psal. XC. 7.   A People *consuming by the Anger of GOD.*   Entertaining the Church, with Reflections on the Lessening of our Numbers, by Mortality; twenty-four of our Comunicants having died in a few Months; and half of these our Brethren.

2 *d.* 12 *m.* [*February.*]   On, Psal. LVII. 7.   An *Heart fixed* in RESOLUTIONS for the Service of GOD.   Earnestly bespeaking it, and finishing what I began a fortnight ago.

9 *d.* 12 *m.*   On Isa. XXVI. 9.   The *Desires* of GOD, which in a *dark Time*, the Soul should be filled withal.

To Sir William Ashurst.   A.A.S.

5 *d.* I *m.* [March.] 1716–17.

Sir, — Four Winter Months have rolled away, since my last; wherein I applied myself to answer the Commands which I had received, with much Satisfaction, to exhibit some Account of our,

---

[1] Colonel Elisha Hutchinson.

Biblia Americana, and of my Prayers and Hopes concerning a Work
of that Importance.

I am unhappy, if the Packett have not arrived. But in some
Expectation that it has, I now grow so much in my encroaching
Boldness upon you, as to add this unto it. The *Opus Ecclesiæ*, which
is now waiting for the Light, is a Work, wherein all sorts of Persons
will find themselves accommodated with Entertainments, which, if
they have been agreeable and acceptable in a separate Exhibition,
how much more will common sense tell any man, they must be so in
a refining Amassment of them! In these Varieties, none of all the
Readers, will be more gratified, and edified, then the more curious
Philosopher, who is on all Occasions here treated with such Things,
as would be for the Palats of a *Christian Virtuoso*. I may without
Vanity be of the Opinion, that if two or three able and (if there be
such) honest Booksellers, exhibiting the *new Offer*, and making their
Proposals, would soon find Subscriptions enough to encourage their
procedure with the Work. My own Countrey subscribe for at least
one hundred, *Scotland* and *Ireland*, as well as many parts of *England*,
offer me to subscribe, as soon as they shall know where and how.
And therefore, will your Honour forgive my rudeness, if I presume to
say; that should a Person of your great Esteem and Figure, prevail
with two or three more Persons of Quality, to appear as Patrons and
Favourers of a Work, so evidently Calculated for the Service, of the
Interests, which the best of men have been valued for serving of;
and thereby obtain the Monuments and Memorials of their generous
Goodness which would be therefore due to them, and rais'd for them;
the thing desired, would be soon accomplished.

I am dismissed from any Expectation of much Encouragement,
from the Dissenters. And the Truth is, I have dismissed and even
divorced myself in a great measure from every Party, but one which
is now going to be formed; and in the Formation whereof, the mean
hand that now writes, has a Prospect of being somewhat concerned.
My Correspondence with the most illustrious *Frederician University*
in the Lower Saxony, where the most glorious Design that ever was
managed in the World, is now under a notable Prosecution, has been
a Circumstance of great Use to me, in this grand Intention. Your
Honour shall give me leave, to think, that you are of it; and indeed
all good men are so, tho' sometimes they are not aware of their being
so. Those Distresses upon the Nations, which may perhaps for a
while retard the Publication of our B. A. will doubtless be so hott,
as ere long to melt all good Men down, into a Compliance, with the

Sentiments, in an Instrument, which I now humbly tender to your Acceptance and which is getting into the Heart of distracted *France*, as well as of *Germany*.

Sir, I may not break off, without a Word upon the evangelical Affairs among our *Indians*. After I had ineffectually sollicited the Governor of N. Y.[1] who was too much encumbered with High-church, to do the Good he wished for; The Ministers on *Long-Island* have promised me, to do their best for Christianizing the Pagan Indians there, whose Children are now generally in *English* Families. And for their Assistence in that work, I have prepared for them, an Essay which is enclosed in this Packett. But the same Essay, is like to have a much more extensive Usefulness; not only for the Indians in the Eastern as well as the Southern Parts of *Massachuset*-Province, but also in many of our Families, where we have *Negro's* as well as Indians; and perhaps in some other Countreys.

In the Packett, you find it accompanied with some other small Things, which are humbly tendered unto your excellent Lady. My Wife by whom a good God has made me one of the happiest of men, has the Honour to be known to her; and the Book entituled, *Utilia*, consisting of Sermons on Subjects, which were at her Desire preached upon, she tis that with her most humble Service, presents that Book to your Lady's Acceptance.

That the Blessing of our glorious Lord, may rest upon your Person and your honourable Family, is the hearty Prayer of, Your Honours, most sincere servant

To Rev. Thomas Prince.   m.h.s.

Satureday Morn.   26 *d*. VIII *m*. [October.] 1717.

Sir, — Having first repeted my Thanks to you, for your Goodness, in the hopes you have given us, of your Assistence for the public Sacrifices in our Church on the Morrow in the Forenoon; I take the Freedom to request, that it may be rather before than after *Nine o'clock* in the Morning, that you lett our Patriarch[2] have the sight of you; and this, (not only because, *Aspectus viri boni delectat*, but also) because I would have him to be wholly out of the Pain; which my Absence always gives him.

I have nothing further to add, but only a matter of deep Contemplation. A late Candidate for the place, from whence you lately received a Letter, *hoping you were in good Health*, does, as I under-

---

[1] Robert Hunter.   [2] Increase Mather.

stand, express a great Aversion for a Compliance with an Invitation thither, on this account, that they are a People so peculiar and irregular in their Principles about ecclesiastical Matters, that he (who is for the true, old, N. E. Principles,) could never be easy with them, in the ecclesiastical Circumstances they would impose upon him.

The Glorious Lord will give you His Direction, and the Blessings of the XXV Psalm, I am well-assured.   I am Syr, Your Brother and Servt.

Co. MATHER.

1718

THE LVITH YEAR OF MY LIFE.

12 *d.* XII *m.* [*February.*] 1717 [-18.] *Wednesday.* Entring this Day upon the unexpected as well as undeserved fifty-sixth Year, and I really beleeve, the last, of my Life, I sett apart the Day for Devotions, with Fasting, before the Lord.

It was with me a Time full of most bitter Contritions and Confusions, in a Review of the Sins, which my wretched Life has been filled withal: and unspeakable Agonies in the Flights I made unto the infinite Mercy of God, and infinite Merit in the Sacrifice of my SAVIOUR, for a Pardon: and importunate Supplications for the Grace to be a more diligent Servant of the Lord and of His People, in the small Remainder of Time that may be yett allow'd me.

But these were follow'd with my Thanksgivings to the glorious Lord, for His many and marvellous Favours to me, all my Dayes until this very Day; and for those Wonders of Goodness, which at this day I am surrounded withal.

I made the best Preparations I could this Day, on more Accounts than one, for my dying Hour.

G. D. I hope, I putt my Parent in the best Way, to provide well, for my widow Sister and her Orphan.

So dead am I grown to this World, and so willing to disappear unto it, and so dispos'd wholly to be swallow'd up in God; that among other Effects of this Frame, I am inclined wholly to destroy all these Memorials of my Life, and proceed no further in Writing of them. As I am determined, that I will never have my Picture drawn; and I repent, that I have heretofore satt for some Draughts of it;

So I would go on in daily Projections to do good, but am content that they be observed and remembred by the glorious God alone.

But when I consider, that my writing down of my GOOD DEVISED, contributes unto the more effectual Execution of my Purposes, and that it is possible, my Son may learn how to do good, from the Things that are suggested in his poor Father's Memorials, I am inclined still to do, as I use to do.

13. G. D. One of the best Things that can be done for my poor Countrey is, to extinguish as far as tis possible, that cursed, and senseless Party-Spirit, which is now among us, in a most abominable Operation. Lett me contrive to do all that I or others can towards the Extinction of so comprehensive a Mischief.

I procure an Interview with a Number of the Assembly this Evening on that Intention.

14. G. D. A Method for introducing the Gospel, into miserable Tiverton, I have now brought into its Operation. It may produce no little Travel and Labour to me, in the Prosecution of it, But ——

15. G. D. A poor young Man of the Neighbourhood in danger of Distruction calls for my Consideration.

* 16. G. D. In working about my own Salvation, my Work must be, to gett my Soul cured of all the Maladies, which by my Departure from God, I am fallen into. The Blessings of an healed Soul, not only fitt me for, and bring me to, the Blessedness of the heavenly World, but also are the very Blessedness. I would therefore successively consider the several Maladies of my Soul, and what is lacking in the divine Image, which is begun to be restored in it. And so enquire after the Methods of a Cure for them.

The first of my Maladies, which I do this Morning take notice of, is; My Barrenness in regard of those exquisite Inventions, which Wisdome would find out, for the Service of GOD in all my several Relations, and particularly for an

Improvement of Piety in my own Heart and Life. I am
strangely dull, stupid, senseless when I come to consider
the Quæstion, *What shall I do for God?* I bewayle this Distemper before the Lord; I look up to my Saviour, as the
Lord my Healer; I resolve to compel my mind unto close
Thinking on the noble Quæstion, and at the same Time,
resign my Mind unto the Conduct of Him, without whom I
am not sufficient for so much as one good Thought, or for
any thing in the World.

17. G. D. The Widows of the Flock are numerous;
They make about a fifth Part of our Communicants. A
Sermon full of Counsils and Comforts, unto that part of
the Flock, is what I am now giving to them. And, I hope,
God will also enable me to publish it, that it may be
lodged with them.

18. G. D. Among my Returns of Gratitude and Obedience unto Heaven, for the Restoration of my invaluable
Consort, I would use an effectual Care, that all our domestic
Business be over before the Satureday Evening, and that the
whole Evening be devoted unto Exercises of Piety, with
more Care than ever yett has been used with us.

19. G. D. I would invite my afflicted Brother-in-law,
Mr. *Walter*, (who has been a year laid by from his public
Preaching,) that he would come and sojourn some Weeks at
my House, to be under the Cure of some Physicians in my
Neighbourhood.

20. G. D. I am this Day writing Letters to the *East-
Indies*, in my Correspondence with the Danish Missionaries
at *Malabar*. And I project the Proposal of several Things
unto them, which may be of the greatest Consequence.

21. G. D. I have Opportunity to do another Service, by
the Instrumentality of some in our Neighbourhood.

On the Lord's-Day, I preached a Sermon unto the
WIDOWS of the Flock. It proved so acceptable to them,
that a Number of them join to bear the Expence of the

Publication. I hope it will prove a sensible Service to the Cause of Piety, among the *many Widows in Israel*, who are greatly multiplied, and exposed unto grievous Temptations.

(I.) I give it unto them, and unto their Tribe throughout the Countrey, under this Title: *MARAH spoken to. An Essay to do Good unto the Widow; Dispensing those Lessons of Piety which are the Portion assigned for the Widow, in the House and Word of God.*[1]

22. G. D. A poor Family, under long Affliction by Sickness, calls for my Consideration.

22 *d.* 12 *m. Satureday*. This Day I sett apart, for Prayer with Fasting, as I use to do, in my Approaches to the holy Table.

I exceedingly humbled myself before the Lord, for the manifold Wickedness of my Heart and Life. And I made a fresh Flight unto the pardoning Mercy of God, and the atoning Sacrifice of my Saviour. Not without Hope, that my Transgression is forgiven, and my Sin is covered; and that I have a Token of my being released from the Sentence of Death upon me, in my Living unto God.

There were many special Matters of Supplication this day carried unto the Lord.

Especially, a Smile of GOD upon what is doing for Him at *Glaucha*, and at *Malabar*.

* 23. G. D. *Sloth*, wicked *Sloth*, cursed *Sloth*, is the Distemper, which I cannot but in the first Place think upon, when I come to consider the Maladies of my Soul. *Have I found thee, O mine Enemy!* There does not a Day pass over me, but I ly down mourning at Night for the Mischiefs that I have suffered from this hateful Enemy.

But what shall be done for the Cure of this evil Disease!

First with a repenting Soul, I fly to my SAVIOUR, and with Faith and Hope, all the Ardours of the greatest Importunacy I cry unto Him, that He would be my Healer.

[1] Printed by T. Crump, and contains a preface by Increase Mather.

And then, I will consider with as powerful and impressive Thoughts as I can, those Things, which may animate my Diligence. Particularly read Mr. *Baxter,* what he writes upon *Idleness,* in his, *Christian Directory.*

24. G. D. I will take a Catalogue of such as are now, to be invited into our Communion as prepared for it; (that so our Losses may be recruited:) and both publickly and privately pursue the Invitation.

25. G. D. I would in family Sacrifices, make a very thankful Acknowledgment of the divine Goodness and Mercy, which has restored my Consort unto me. But I would particularly propose, that all the Ministers in the City, meet at my House, to give Thanks with me, and then to taste the Bread of my Table: or, some way assist me in my Thanksgivings.

26. G. D. Our Church now pursuing a strong Motion, towards the Inviting of my Kinsman T. W[alter] unto the Assistence and Succession of the Ministry here, I have opening to me, a thousand Occasions of being useful to him.

27. G. D. Supplications for the Public, are one way of my being serviceable unto it; with Admonition unto my Flock how to manage their Supplications.

This Day, being a Day of Prayer thro' the Province, it gives me an Opportunity for them.

28. G. D. There is extreme Danger of *Boston* going into much Temptation, and Contention, and Confusion. The Ministers of the Town must be seasonably advertised of the Danger.

March. 1. G. D. An hopeful Youth, who is a poor Orphan, at the Colledge, I must subscribe, and procure Subscriptions, for to subsist him there.

*2. G. D. Another Distemper, which troubles my Soul, is that of, *sudden Anger.*

Now for the Cure of this Malady, and that I may grow in the Wisdom of Meekness I would, first, make my Flight unto my SAVIOUR; that all my froward Follies may be pardoned, and that He would bestow upon me, the Meekness, whereof He has given such a glorious Pattern.

And then, I would mightily inculcate upon myself the *Maxims*, for my Government under Provocations to Anger, which I drew up, 19 *d*. III *m*. 1717.[1]

3. G. D. It looks, as if our poor Church were dreadfully under the Wrath of God; and as if it were in danger of going into Confusions that are not without Horror to be thought upon. All the Brethren of the Church, except four or five Gentlemen, who must always be the Rulers of all, are fond of Inviting Mr. *Walter* unto the Assistence and Succession in the Ministry.

Last *October*, an excellent Gift of our Ascended Lord, who was tendered unto the Church, and much desired by the most of our People, was thrown away to please these Gentlemen. There is now a more general Desire, and a very vehement One, for this Person, who is one of rich and rare Accomplishments, and such another cannot presently be hoped for. But from I know not what Principle, these Gentlemen clog all our Motions; and *Roxbury* is like to sieze upon him. On this, besides the Loss we are like to suffer, the Ferment of the People is like to rise unto a prodigious Heighth, and we are like to be the most miserable Church in the Land. Oh! the Wisdome! Oh! the Patience! Oh! the Prayerfulness, which I am on this Occasion call'd unto!

I am afraid, Sin lies upon us, in the Neglect of the holy Discipline, whereof some objects have not been duely considered.

4. G. D. There are affairs of great Importance to *Creasy's* carriage and comfort, which I am this Day to advise him upon.

5. G. D. Something is to be done, that the domestic

[1] See p. 454, *supra*.

Circumstances of my aged Parent may be very easy to him. There is nothing more in my Wishes, than to be the *Helper of his Joy*.

6. G. D. Sending to the *East-Indies*, I would send several Pieces of Gold, for the Support of the Charity-Schole at *Malabar*.

7. G. D. I would committ some Numbers of my *Raphael's*, into the hands of pious Physicians, entreating them to bestow them upon their Patients, as they find them to recover of their Maladies; that so corporal and spiritual Healing may go together.

7 *d.* 1 *m.* [*March.*] *Friday.* Tis with me a Day of strange Occurences. I have a strong Impression on my Mind, impelling me, to sett apart this Day, for Prayer with Fasting, with a singular Eye to the Ministry of the holy Angels, for the Enjoyment whereof I have more than ordinary Occasion to be sollicitous.

I begun the Day with forming due Thoughts of the glorious Object, unto whom I am to address my Prayers, and of the devout Manner wherein I am to do it; and with Confessions of my Inability to do anything, and Contritions for the miserable Defects and Errors, which have attended my former Days of Supplications, and Cries to Heaven for Assistences and Influences from Above.

After this, and after suitable and affectuous Meditations on the ANGELS of GOD, I did on my Knees, glorify Him, as the Creator of those wonderful Creatures; and if the Multitude of the heavenly Host, were composed of Creatures, who were so full of Power and of Wisdome, and of Goodness, and of holy Love to God, (for which I loved them and would exceedingly and perpetually do so, tho' they should be employ'd, as the Inflicters of the saddest Things upon me!) I argued how glorious must be the infinite GOD, their Maker before whom they are but Shadows, and very Nothings. I considered my admirable SAVIOUR, the Son of GOD incarnate in my blessed JESUS, as now on the Throne of God, as having all these mighty ANGELS under His Dominion; and I resolved upon paying an Obedience, as far as I can, like unto theirs, unto this glorious Lord. I considered, the Ministry of the mighty Angels, as extended unto Societies of

men in general, and unto all Individuals among the elect Heirs of
Salvation in particular; and I gave Thanks to the Lord, for His
Benefits therein done unto the sinful Children of Men. But, then,
I considered the Praises which the holy ANGELS rendred unto the
infinite GOD. I was glad, I was glad, that the Infinite God has the
Gratification of having such Praises paid unto Him, as He hears from
these marvellous Creatures. Tho' I am the vilest Thing in the World,
yett I so far putt in for a share in the Homage which these marvellous
Creatures yeeld unto the infinite GOD, as to rejoice with an inexpres-
sible Gladness, at His having the Pleasure of His Praises from them.
I went on, with an Heart fixed in these Dispositions, that if I should
be forever banished from the innumerable Company of the holy
Angels, yet I would even in my outer Darkness, be pleased with the
Apprehension of it, that the infinite GOD had such Praises as these
would forever pay unto Him. Astonishments filled my Soul, in the
Flights, which I thus took among the holy ANGELS. I find my Pen
unable to write the Things, and the Terms, to which my Soul mounted
up as with the Wings of an Eagle. But I became assured that I
should be hereafter associated with the lovely Creatures, unto whom
I united myself in these Contemplations.

In my family Sacrifices, I expressed unto the Lord, the Regards,
which as a Family we owe unto the ANGELS.

I also sang in my Study, Portions of the Psalms, relating unto
these Morning-stars.

I proceeded then, to humble myself before the glorious GOD, for
the Sins of my Life, and especially the sinful Tendencies of an Heart
that is desperately wicked. This I did chiefly on the Account of
the Dishonour and the Displeasure done unto the glorious GOD, in
my Offences. But then it became a sensible Article of my Grief, that
I had grieved the holy ANGELS and basely treated their Ministry
with a monstrous Indignity and Ingratitude: but at the same Time
had complied with the evil Ones. I more particularly mentioned
some Instances, wherein I had rendred myself singularly loathsome
unto the holy ANGELS, and as a *Beast* before them: especially, my
slothful and selfish Conduct in the Discharge of my Ministry, wherein
I have had the Work of ANGELS assign'd unto me: But, Oh! how
unlike have I been unto them! I owned, how just it would be, if the
holy Angels were made the Instruments and Inflicters of all dreadful
Judgments, in both Worlds upon me. But I made my Flight unto
the pardoning Mercy of God, and the Fountain sett open for Sin
and Uncleanness, in the Blood of my SAVIOUR: And with a

strong Faith herein, I obtained some Assurance of my Pardon. And whereas formerly I have often feared that all the Favours that Heaven hath shown to me, and all the Uses that Heaven hath made of me, would only be, to prepare me for a more horrid Vessel of a Wrath unto the uttermost, I now became assured, that all my crying Sins, wherein I have been upon some Accounts worse than any Man in the World, would be only made Scaffolds, for the greater Triumphs of sovereign Grace to be seen upon. But oh! The Love of God, which I now felt filling of my Soul! And now, being at Peace with GOD, I know, that His holy ANGELS will be at Peace with me. Tho' they have been highly offended at me, yett from their Love to God, and their Obedience to my SAVIOUR, they will now be ready to take me under their Wings, and to do unspeakable Kindnesses for me. I still find my Pen unable to write what occurr'd; it can only give a general Report of the Matter.

Anon I went again unto the Lord; and cried unto Him, that the Ministry of His holy ANGELS might now more than ever be allowed unto me. And that I might be rendred the more meet for it, I came with the Acts of a consenting Soul into the Covenant of God, wherein He becoming mine, His ANGELS will be so too. I annihilated myself before the Lord; resolving that GOD alone shall be owned, as the Doer of all the Good, that is done for me, or by me, and whatever His ANGELS do, about me, He alone shall have the Glory of it all. I passed on to the sacrificing Stroke, and with the Exercises of the royal Priesthood, I made Sacrifices of all, even my dearest Enjoyments: hoping that the ANGELS drawing near to me, would now do wondrously. I uttered my Aspirations after all possible Conformity to the holy ANGELS, in their Hatred of all Sin, their Activity and Alacrity in the Service of God, their Submission to the Will of GOD, their Goodness, and perpetual Delight in doing of Good; and whatever may maintain an Harmony with them in the Work of GOD. I entreated of the Lord, that He would order the Agency and Influence of His holy ANGELS, to befriend my Health, to supply my Wants, to direct my Studies and all my Motions, to strengthen me against my Temptations, to raise up such as may be powerful Friends unto me and my Designs; and especially to touch the Minds of some suitable Persons, with Inclinations to bring into the Light, several great Works, which I have prepared for the Church of God in the World. I then also entreated, that the holy ANGELS, may make their Descent, and the Kingdome of the Heavens come on, wherein they shall possess the Children of men, and preach the ever-

lasting Gospel unto the Nations. I finally entreated, that my poor
Family may fare the better for the angelical Ministrations; in some
Instances particularly then enumerated.

8. G. D. A poor Widow, greatly oppressed for speaking the Truth, must have me concerned for her.

* 9. G. D. The Diseases of my soul are not cured until
I arrive to the most unspotted Chastitie and Puritie.

I do not apprehend, that Heaven requires me utterlie to
lay aside my fondness for my lovelie Consort.[1]

But I must mourn most bitterlie and walk humblie all
my Daies for my former pollutions. I must abhor the
least tho't of regard unto anie other Person but this dearlie
beloved of my soul. I must be temperate in my Conversation with her. And I must alwaies propose a good and an
high End in it; something that mai be an Expression or an
Evidence of my Obedience to God.[1]

10. G. D. My Conduct in the Management of the
Church, on the critical Occasion that is now before us, must
be full of Patience and Meekness, with a Satisfaction in the
Will of GOD ordering all Things. I must permitt nothing
to be driven, but endeavour that all things may proceed,
lento Gradu. And I must in all the ways that are possible,
sweeten the Spirits of the Brethren towards one another.

11. G. D. *Liza* and *Sammy*, must return to their
Improvements at the writing School. *Sammy* has abundance of Spare-time at the Grammar-Schole; I must concert with his Master some Employments for him.

12. G. D. What Good shall I do in a Family of Relatives, where I am sometimes very kindly entertained.
Prayers, and Books of Piety.

13. G. D. Our excellent Governour is in danger of
some Steps inconvenient for himself and us; No body will
advise him. I must.

A Testimony to the Kingdome of our SAVIOUR and

---

[1] These two paragraphs were written in Greek characters.

some Glances at the Displays and Openings of it, which are now appearing may have its Efficacy.

This Day I offer it.

14. G. D.   Encourage some Schole-Masters, to have the Story of the Jewish Children at *Berlin,* read in their Schools, with Application.

15. G. D.   It is desired of me to do something for the Interest of a young Gentleman labouring under Disadvantages at *Connecticot.*

* 16. G. D.   For the Cure of what is amiss in my distempered Soul, one of the best Things that I can do, will be this : I will use to examine, what lies at the Bottom of my Designs, my Studies, my Sorrows, and my Angers, and my Comforts ; and if I discover, that an undue Respect unto myself, or unto any Creature does therein usurp the Throne of the glorious GOD, I will immediately dethrone it, and endeavour that a due Respect unto HIM shall entirely govern me.

17. G. D.   The Temptations which my poor Flock is going unto! I must cry to GOD, for His conduct, both unto it, and unto myself.   And guard mightily against the Devices of the Grand Adversary.

18. G. D.   *Sammy's* Association with a Number of serious Lads, for the Exercises of Religion, opens to me a View of many and precious Projections, for the Drawing of him on to do much Good in his day, and for the infusing of great Sentiments into him.

19. G. D.   I must, if it be possible, find out some Relatives at *Connecticot,* of which I have never taken yett sufficient Notice, and send Books of Piety unto them.

20. G. D.   I am writing to the famous *Franckius* and the *Frederician* University.

May Heaven direct me, what I may propose to them for the Kingdome of GOD!

21. G. D.   Poor *Brooklyn!*   I am in extreme Distress

I know not my Duty! I must cry to GOD for His Direction.

22. G. D. Several very poor in the Flock, are objects for my further Cares.

And unto Widows also, I would convey my *Marah*.

22 d. 1 m. Satureday. This Day I sett apart, for Supplications, as I use to do. And my Exercises on it, were such as they use to be.

Upon a renewed Repentance, with a Flight unto the Sacrifice of my admirable SAVIOUR, my poor, dark, distressed Soul, received some Assurance of my Pardon. And an infinite load lying upon me, was taken off.

Some very uncommon Trials of Patience even to Longsuffering and such as GOD orders to lay me and keep me under the greatest Abasements, oblige me to be much in crying to Him, that He would strengthen me with Strength in my Soul.

I repeted my Supplications and Præparations, to have the Ministry of the good Angels employed for me; for the Accomplishment of such Petitions, as I insisted on. Especially the bringing forth unto the Public, such Things as I have gott ready to serve the Kingdome of God.

* 23. G. D. The Characters of One *dead with CHRIST*, and willing and striving to dy unto all this World; will not these assure me, that I have a claim to the Benefits which the *Death of CHRIST* has purchased for His chosen People? I think, I feel the Power and the Sweetness of this Consideration. But it must be further prosecuted.

24. G. D. There are some Acts of Discipline, to be exercised in the Flock, wherein I very much need the Direction and Assistence of Heaven; Oh! may I so go through them, that God may be glorified, and the Flock may be edified.

25. G. D. *Sammy* shall daily bring me, his Version of, *Supplies from the Tower of David.* And I will make the

Exercise, an Occasion to instil into him the Documents of Piety; and what may strengthen and adorn him.

26. G. D. A Kindness is to be done for a Kinswoman at *Roxbury*.

27. G. D. The better People, at *Pensylvania* fly to me, that I would serve them with Repræsentations at home, that may divert great Mischiefs from the Jacobite party among them.

28. G. D. Sollicit my Brother, and some others beyond-sea, to fall in more vigorously, with the Design of prosecuting and propagating the Maxims of the everlasting Gospel, as the grand Basis of Union among the People of God.

29. G. D. The Physician, who is my next Neighbour, is an Object of my special Thoughts and Cares on several Accounts.

*30. G. D. I am afraid of some Decay upon my sabbatizing Stroke. I must fill the Lord's-day with higher, and more numerous and labourious Elevations towards the heavenly World.

31. G. D. Satan is watching to insinuate into the Flock and make his Devices operate; Oh! may my prayerful and watchful Conduct, anticipate them!

(II.) Wanting a Book to be lodg'd in the Hands of the Afflicted, when I visit them, I now give unto the Public a Treatise entituled, THE OBEDIENT SUFFERER. *A brief Essay, upon that Obedience to GOD, which his Children are to Learn, in and from the sufferings which are the Things appointed for them.*

April. 1. G. D. Be not satisfied until *Increase* be prevailed withal, to read more, and spend his Evenings to better Account.

On the Lord's-day Evenings, I will have him, and *Sammy*, to read unto the Family, Books of Piety; particularly, Mr. *Janeway's* Treatises.

2. G. D.   More Prayers as well as other Means, must be used for the Recovery of my Brother *Walter*.

3. G. D.   Prevail with my dear Governour, to befriend the Interests of Religion in the Southern Colonies, for which I am this Week applying to *England;* and gett him to engage his Brother in the Cause.

4. G. D.   Lord, How barren am I!

Engage my ultramarine Friends to do what they can, for the rendring of my poor Treatises, as extensively useful, as they can.

By a young Gentleman going thither, make a present of *New English* Treatises, to the Ministers of *Londonderry* and Parts adjacent.

5. G. D.   A foolish and froward old Man, who has been a great Professor of Religion, is in a very wicked Frame and way; which there must be some care taken to stop him in.

* 6. G. D.   My dear SAVIOUR has raised my Soul, to such a Frame as this.   The Approach of great Calamities, finds a sort of welcome with me, from the View it gives me of Opportunities to glorify God with Sacrifices.   I feel my Heart pleas'd and glad, at the Thoughts of being putt upon Sacrificing.   And, is not the Love of GOD, now sensibly at work in my Soul?   Yea, what will the glorious One do with one, whom He has thus made a Sacrifice?   I must keep myself in this Love of GOD.   And I must grow more frequent and expert in the Acts of applying to myself the Love of my Saviour on all Occasions, in all Occurrences.

7. G. D.   The Commitee of the Church, must have certain Points of care commended unto them.

My List of them, who are to be putt upon joining to the Church, is to be prosecuted.

8. G. D.   *Liza's* Education, further Articles of it.

9. G. D.   Relatives at *Concord*, and *Hampton*, to be considered with fresh Presents of Piety.

10. G. D.   Having præpared and finished a great Work,

entituled, *Psalterum Americanum,* which is an Essay to render the Book of *Psalms* (in *Blank Verse,* with Illustrations,) more accommodated for answering its End, and being the most glorious Book of Devotions in the World. I will now with the Help of Heaven, seek after the best Methods for the Publication; as apprehending therein a singular Service to the Kingdome of GOD.[1]

11. G. D. Several Things of great Importance, to be communicated unto our Governour.

12. G. D. Do good Offices for a Candidate of the Ministry, who has deserved well of us, but is under Discouragements; (now on a Journey to *Pensylvania.*)

* 13. G. D. I am this Day to preach a Sermon on the Things which render men *meet for the Inheritance of the Saints in Light.* The best Thing I can do for myself is to gett a deep Impression of those Points on my own Soul, and immediately make sure that I am arriv'd and attain'd unto them.

14. G. D. I must again come to consider distinctly the several Tribes and Sorts of People in my Flock, and have my more explicit Contrivances for each of them.

And now, if I begin with the Sea-faring. Oh! what an horrible Spectacle have I before me! A wicked, stupid, abominable Generation: every Year growing rather worse and worse, under the Judgments of Heaven; drowned in all Impiety and Perdition. All the Prayers, and all the Pains I have employ'd in a distinguishing Manner for their Good, they requite with making me above any Man living the Object of their Malignity.

But yett I must continue crying to GOD for them, and I must watch all Occasions to drop suitable Admonitions upon them, and I must scatter Books of Piety among them.

15. G. D. Poor *Cresy,* is in more Snares.

---

[1] Proposals for printing were issued in 1718. See p. 540, *infra.*

Ah, Lord, when shall that poor Child be in surprizing Mercy look'd upon?

My Faith yett seems to be quicken'd for him!

16. G. D. My Kinsman at *Newtown*, may need some of my careful Advice unto him.

17. G. D. I begin to have in View some comprehensive and considerable Services, which I may do for the Church of *Scotland*.

Lett me ask Direction, and use Diligence in the Matter.

18. G. D. I am getting the Countenance and Assistence of some eminent Persons, towards the Publication of our *Psalterium Americanum*.

19. G. D. What shall be done for a poor Child in the Neighbourhood; whose Education I am concern'd about?

19 d. 2 m. *Satureday*. This Day, I sett apart for Supplications.

The Occasions and Exercises were with me much the same, that they were a Month ago.

My Prayer and Faith for my poor son *Increase*, is what I feel some strengthening Revivals on.

* 20. G. D. I feel, I feel the Death of my SAVIOUR in me. I feel myself dying to the world; grown very much Dead both unto the Comforts of it, and the Troubles of it; willing to be stript of all things, and pass into the Condition of the Dead. In this, I enjoy a Disposition which the Death of my SAVIOUR has purchased for me; and I endeavour a Conformity to His Death, and such a Sense of Things in this World, as He had in the Hours of His Crucifixion. Is not this now a sure Sign, that my SAVIOUR had Dyed for me, and that I have a share in the Benefits of His Death! Most certainly! But, oh! the glorious Consequences!

To prosecute this Consideration, will very much befriend the Life of Piety.

21. G. D. I am in hopes that a Sermon, on an *Heart*

which the Lord has opened, may be exceedingly blessed of God for the Good of the Flock, whereof I am the Servant.

22. G. D.   Points of Piety to be in my Conversation with my dear Consort, much insisted on.

23. G. D.   What are those Things, that I would speak to my aged Parent, if I were to see him only once more in the World!

24. G. D.   I may glorify God, and may do a public Service if I entertain the Auditory at the Lecture, with just Remarks upon the Voice of Heaven to the World in the tremendous Inundation which has lately brought such Ruines on the Dutch and German Coast.

25. G. D.   Can I think of nothing to communicate, that may be of Service to the Kingdome of God, at the anniversary Convention, to be shortly at *Hartford?*

26. G. D.   A godly young Man, perfidiously and barbarously used, for telling the Truth, when he was called unto it, must have my cares exerted for him.

* 27. G. D.   I expect some Improvement in Piety, from Reading of the, *Saintes Conversations d'un Chrestien* of M. *Pictet.*[1]

28. G. D.   A Sermon of Expostulations, to conclude my Sermons, on Col. 1. 12.

29. G. D.   With much Prayer, and Patience, and Imitation of my great and meek and merciful SAVIOUR, I must encounter Temptations, which the Wisdome of Heaven orders for me.

30. G. D.   Some Relatives of *Hampton*, coming in my Way, I must endeavour to serve them in the ways of Piety.

May. 1. G. D.   A very desireable Opportunity offers, for my bearing a Testimony to the grand Intention of an Union for good Men upon the *Maxims of Piety*. The *Baptists* in our Neighbourhood, ask me to come and act in the Ordaining of their Pastor, and preach on that Occa-

---

[1] Benedict Pictet (1655-1724), a Swiss Protestant minister.

sion.[1] My Action will cause much Discourse and Wonder; but methinks, I see the Kingdome of God opening in what is now adoing.

2. G. D. Renew Applications to the Government of *Connecticot*, about Christianizing the Indians there.

3. G. D. Some good Offices to be done for the Schole-Master, in my Neighbourhood.

3 *d. 3 m. Satureday.* A very wicked Woman is found in the Church whereof I am the Servant. She not only had an unlawful Offspring a few Years ago, which is now discovered, but her Impenitence has provoked her Neighbours to come in with Testimonies of a very lewd Conversation, that she has carried on. The Work of God in bringing forth her Wickedness is to be wondred at, to be trembled at. But her Father, who is an old and great Professor of Religion, does most grievously misbehave himself on this Occasion. He, and his foolish Family do not only treat me very ill, and with a strange Malice and Revenge for the doing of my Duty, and the poor Man is dreadfully forsaken of God: but also, they use violent Wayes to sow Discord among the Neighbours, and the Peace of the Church is threatened.[2]

I think it my Duty to fall down before the Lord, with extraordinary Humiliations and Supplications on this Occasion: as I have still used formerly to do, upon great Miscarriages in any of our Communion.

I would bewayl my own Sins, with a Renewal of the deepest Repentance, that so I may be qualified for Testifying against the Sins of others.

Especially considering the share which my Sins may have in the Displeasure of Heaven breaking forth against the Church, whereto I am related.

Yea, I would bewayl the Sins of my People, as being on some Accounts my own.

I would cry to the God of all Grace, that He would help me and

[1] See May 21, p. 535, *infra.*   [2] See p. 538, *infra.*

His People to a good, and a wise, and a right Conduct in managing the Discipline, which is now called for.

I would entreat the glorious Head of the Church, that He would Interpose with His Providence, to rebuke the raging Impiety of this unrepenting Harlot, and of her discomposed Father.

I would committ the whole Affair into the Hands of Him, who is the King of *Jacob*, and who ruleth to the Ends of the Earth.

At the same Time, I am attended with various Difficulties, and marvellous Temptations, (whereof one is, I hope, this day happily conquered,) that call me to ly in the Dust before the Lord.

And some things relating to my public Services and Intentions, do also call for my Cries to Heaven.

I was not without some Consolations as well as very great Contritions, in the Exercises of the Day, which I now sett apart for Approaches to the Lord.

* 4. G. D.   Rising much earlier on the Lord's-dayes, than on other Days, I find therein so much Advantage to the Intentions of Piety, that I resolv'd with the Help of Heaven, to be yett more Industrious in the Practice.

5. G. D.   I have a Number of black Sheep in my Flock, which it is time for me again, to send for; and pray with them, and preach to them, and enquire into their Conduct, and encourage them, in the ways of Piety: a Religious Society of Negros.

6. G. D.   My Mind is visited with dark Thoughts, lest my Children should, thro the just wrath of Heaven upon me, prove a miserable Offspring.   Oh! lett these Fears produce in me, that Repentance, those Prayers, those Tears, those Flights to the Covenant of a gracious GOD, which may issue in this, that my poor Children may be known to be an Offspring which the Lord has blessed.

7. G. D.   I have a Relative who does not so well as he ought to do.   The Lord help me to do what is wise and right in my treating of him!

8. G. D. My Advice is asked and needful, for the good Settlement of the evangelical Affairs at *Barmudas*.

9. G. D. A fresh Visitation of our Schools, will give me now some Opportunities for the Doing of Good more Wayes than one.

10. G. D. A poor young Man, perishing with the Kings-Evil, must be an object of my Charities and Kindnesses.

10 *d.* 3 *m. Satureday.* On the same Occasions and with the same Exercises, that I was this Day se'nnight before the Lord, I sett apart this Day also.

I find in my soul a strange Experience. I meet with very breaking and killing Things, which are the Chastisements of the holy GOD upon me, for my manifold Miscarriages. In the sad Things that befall me, the glorious GOD is gratified : it pleases Him, to behold His Justice thus inflicting Strokes upon me. Now such is my Love unto my God; and so united is my Soul unto Him, that I have a secret Pleasure in my Thoughts of the Gratification which is done unto Him, in the sad Things which tear me to Pieces before Him. I fly away from even my very self into Him, and I take part with Him against myself: and it pleases me, that He is pleased, tho' I myself am dreadfully torn to Peeces in what is done unto me. By this I know, that now my GOD will return unto me, with astonishing Expressions of His everlasting Love; and that the Bruises given to my dear Saviour are accepted for me, and my GOD will no more delight in bruising of me, but the Punishment of my Sin having been laid on my SAVIOUR, I shall now have my God reconciled unto me, and rejoicing over me to do me good.

It is also an Encouragement unto me, to hope, that my Repentance may be sincere inasmuch as the most unjust and bitter things, that have a Tendency to quicken, and renew and increase my Repentance, are welcome to me.[1] The God of Peace, will shortly do Wonders for me. But much Prayer must prepare me for it.

I have now a World of Reason to beleeve, that my Death is very near, very near, unto me. One special Request of this day was, that I might finish well; and that my Death might be attended with comfortable Circumstances; not in the Dark; but with holy Triumphs over the King of Terrors.

* 11. G. D. I ought yett more clearly to state the *End* of the several Actions, which often recur in my Life, that

---

[1] Three lines, struck out, follow.

so there may be an explicit Living to God in them, and that so I may from a Design to please and serve God therein, be after an holy Manner more animated for the doing of them.

12. G. D. A Sermon upon the Methods of going to our Saviour for Succour under Temptations, may be of singular use to many in the Flock.

13. G. D. Exquisite Wisdome and Patience and Prayerfulness, will be requisite, that some Devices of our great Adversary, to disturb the sweet Course of Piety and Strain of Harmony, in my Family, may be conquered.

My God will give me a glorious Conquest over them.

14. G. D. Further Considerations for the Welfare of my Kinsman at *Newtown*.

15. G. D. My public Endeavours to gett our Schole-Masters encouraged, may be attended with good Consequences, on more Accounts than one.

Particularly, in their being disposed, the more to hearken unto my Projections and Proposals for the Kingdome of GOD, in their Schools.

16. G. D. I am now again sending to the Lower *Saxony*, for the Encouragement of what is doing at *Hall*, by my dear *Franckius* there. I must gett some Assistences of Money here, on the Occasion.

17. G. D. A very poor Widow in the Neighbourhood must have her Condition enquired into.

17 *d.* 3 *m. Satureday.* Not only on the same Occasions, and with the same Exercises, that was this Day Se'nnight, I was this Day also before the Lord; but also fresh Troubles full of Darkness and Horror, caused me to be again upon my Knees.

Things appear'd unto me, as if the holy GOD, were coming forth, to take a terrible Vengeance on me, for the Sins which my Life has been filled withal; yea, and as if my Death being at hand, I am to dy in ill Terms with Heaven, and have the dreadful Portion of the Hypocrites assign'd unto me.

Oh! the inexpressible Agony, wherewith I now cried unto the Lord; and at length pressed and passed thro' the Points, that bring a Sinner into a Reconciliation with GOD, and render one meet for the Inheritance of the Saints in Light. So that I durst not cast away my Hopes, of my being yett in Favour with God. Yea, if He please forever to cast me away, I shall yett carry something with me, that will be an everliving Root of Love to Him in my Soul.

In one of these Transactions, I had my Consort with me.

Something has been done this day, to bespeak a Return of Kindness from the good ANGEL of the Lord unto me.

*18. G. D. There are especially four Exercises of PIETY of which I would every day that passes over me, make a most frequent Repetition.

The First is; To form in the most explicit Manner that may be, Designs for the Serving and Pleasing of God, in what my Hand finds to do, and find the Life of my Hand in doing so.

The second is, to abound in Sacrifices, and while I am sacrificing those Enjoyments which my GOD calls me to part withal, to look upon a sacrificing Heart as a better thing than any of those Enjoyments.

The third is; to behold and beleeve the Love of my SAVIOUR to me, in every thing that befals me, and by this perswasion to animate the Dispositions and Resolutions of Love to Him, and my Essays to glorify Him.

The fourth is, to be Devising of Good continually, contriving that all about me may be the better for me.

19. G. D. A Sermon on the Lord Jesus Christ with our Spirit.

20. G. D. The Conquest foretold, on 13 d. is happily obtain'd.

But fresh Assaults must be look'd for.

21. G. D. I must use the hand of a Kinsman at *Saybrook* to find out all my Kindred at *Connecticot*, and convey Instruments of Piety from me to them.

21 d. 3 m. *Wednesday.* This Day, I do a very uncom-

mon Action, and what will occasion various Discourse in the world. I visit the Church of the Baptists in my Neighbourhood, and ordain a Pastor to them.[1] On this Opportunity I preach a long Sermon, on the Duty of Receiving those, whom our SAVIOUR does receive unto the Glory of GOD ; and bear a Testimony to the Union of good Men on the Articles of their Goodness.

22. G. D. The Exceptions taken against my Action yesterday, will oblige me to publish my Sermon to the World.

And yett I should not proceed unto that, if I had not therein a View, of doing a very sensible Service to the Kingdome of God.

23. G. D. Consult with some good and wise men, about Services to be done, at the approaching Election.

24. G. D. A poor Woman of our Church, ensnared in rueful Circumstances of Sin and Confusion, calls for my Cares about her.

And a man, who has neglected Family-prayer.

* 25. G. D. Several Customes relating to the constant and lively Exercise of PIETY, are in danger of languishing with me.

Examine what, in order to the Invigorating of them.

26. G. D. Ah! what shall I do? Lett me place myself before the Judgment-seat of GOD, and suppose myself called unto an Account before the glorious Lord, about my Conduct in feeding the Church committed unto my Care.

27. G. D. I would ordinarily not lett a Day pass, without calling my Consort, unto the Holy Fellowship of praying with her, about eleven a clock in my Study.

I propose, inexpressible Advantages unto myself, as well as unto her, in such an Exercise of PIETY.

Elisha Callender (1692–1738) was ordained, as colleague to his father, Rev. Ellis Callender, who served that church from 1708 to his death in 1728.

28. G. D. There is a Relative unto whom an Hint about Sobriety and Vigilancy, may be a Service.

This Day, I act as Moderator, among the Ministers, at their General Convention; and pursue some Services.

29. G. D. Among the Ministers, I cultivate the Consideration of that Quæstion; *What Proposals may be offered, of things to serve the Kingdome of GOD, and promote the great Interests of Religion?*

30. G. D. New Essays must be made for the gaining of the Eastern Indians.

Tiverton must also be still cared for.

31. G. D. A poor dying Man in my Neighbourhood, under long Languishments.

(III.) I give the Bookseller, in hopes of some Service to be thereby done for the Kingdome of GOD, my Discourse, Entituled; BRETHREN DWELLING TOGETHER IN UNITY. *The True Basis for an Union among the People of God, offered and asserted, in a Sermon, preached at the Ordination of a Pastor, in the Church of the Baptists, at Boston, on 21 d. III m. 1718.*[1]

June. * 1. G. D. What a glorious Triumph, will the Grace of our God give unto me, if those very Things, wherein I discern my great Adversary trying to hurt me, may become serviceable to me, for Purposes of Piety and Fruitfulness, and Watchfulness, and my comfortable Enjoyment of my Blessings, directly contrary to those, which he is aiming at! This is what I have a glorious Prospect of.

2. G. D. I grow sensible, that my public Prayers may omitt some Articles, which might very well have more Notice taken of them. I would very exquisitely consider and examine what those Articles may be, and proceed accordingly.

3. G. D. My God, my God!

A very wicked Servant, putting on a Face of Religion,

[1] Printed by S. Gerrish, with a preface by Rev. Increase Mather.

is detected in my Family, and banished from it. What Holy Improvement shall I make of such a Dispensation?

4. G. D. The desolate Condition of my kinsman at *Windsor*, should be resumed into my Consideration; and more lively Prayers be made, that a Period may be putt unto it.

5. G. D. May it not be a Service unto our good Interests, if I entertain our General Assembly, with a Sermon, on that *Self-Love*, which does inexpressible Mischiefs unto us, as well as unto the rest of Mankind?

6. G. D. Some Services for the public, are concerted with the Governour of *Connecticot*.

7. G. D. In visits to credible Families, I will bespeak little Studies and Book-shelves for the little Sons that are capable of conversing with such things; and begin to furnish their Libraries and perswade them to the Religion of the Closet.

* 8. G. D. My Sermon this day, which is on, *Soul-Prosperity*, expresses those Points, which I would pursue, that my *Soul* may *prosper*.

9. G. D. A Discipline to be this day managed in the Church — which I have made many Prayers about.[1]

May the glorious Lord help me on this Occasion, to

---

[1] "9 *d.* 4 *m.* At a Meeting of the Church. Mrs. *Katharin Russel*, having had an unlawful Offspring in the Time of her Widowhood, which long remained a secret, and was by her too much denied before the full Discovery of it.

"Her Confession was this Day read unto the Brethren of the Church, which foolishly insisted on her total Ignorance of any thing done unto her to give her any Impregnation, the Church unanimously voted, that they could not accept of her Confession.

"There being brought in also five or six Testimonies of her lewd Carriage towards diverse Men at sundry Times, and she utterly denying the whole of those Testimonies; and refusing to own what the Church required, of some sense that she had not observed the strict Rules of Chastity and Modesty.

"The Church with much Unanimity voted, that it should with a solemn Admonition be declared unto her, that she is to be shut out from the Communion of the Church, until the Lord bring her to more satisfactory Expressions and Evidences of Repentance, than have yett appeared to her." *Cotton Mather's MS. Records of the Second Church*, III. See p. 531, *supra*.

speak such Things as the Flock may fare the better
for.

The Church proves unanimous.

10. G. D. Oh! what Cries, what Cries to the glorious
God of all Grace, am I call'd unto!

11. G. D. My two aged Fathers, I am in Agony to
render their Condition comfortable, in all the Ways that I
can imagine for it.

And, how much Prayer must be made, that anon, they
may finish well!

This Day I was row'd in the Castle-barge, with some
good Company, unto an Ordination at *Hingam*.[1] Contrary
Wind and Tide would not lett us gett home, till the next
Morning.

12. G. D. A Projection for the Restoring of Peace to
miserable *Wenam*.

13. G. D. In Letters directed beyond-sea, several good
Motions to be prosecuted.

14. G. D. What? Am I at a Loss for objects of Compassion? Comfort one of our Deacons, in a singular
Affliction.

14 *d.* IV *m. Satureday*. This Day I sett apart, for such
Exercises and on such Occasions, as employ'd me, when I
was last in the Way before the Lord.

O Thou glorious Forgiver of Iniquity, Transgression and
Sin; O Thou gracious Hearer of Prayer; From the Depths
I cry unto thee!

*15. G. D. I would immediately draw up an Instru-
ment, that shall truly represent the State of my Spirit before
the Lord, and the several Points of my Præparation for the
Death, which I am now to be daily looking for. It is impossible for me to be too solemn or too exact in my forming
of this important Instrument. May my glorious Redeemer,
and He who has wrought His Works in me, assist me in the

[1] Rev. Ebenezer Gay (1696–1787). See *History of Hingham*, I. Pt. ii, 24.

Action, which is now before me, in order to my having my Heart established for His Coming.

16. G. D. A Sermon to the Flock, on the Marriage of our SAVIOUR unto His People, may be attended with many happy Consequences.

17. G. D. I would renew that Practice of Piety unto which I have sometimes obliged my Children: to write some Desire of Piety, fetched and formed out of some Sentence in the sacred Scriptures.

But especially, I would bring my dear *Samuel* into the Practice.

(IV.) After many Deliberations, I now at length putt into the Hands of the Book-sellers, a large Book, from whence I expect a sensible Service to the Kingdome of God, if ever it shall be published. In order to the Publication, the Booksellers print Proposals for Subscriptions; that so the Impression of a Book, which will be five Shillings price, may be courageably carried on. I am now waiting on my glorious Lord, that I may see how far He will please to accept my poor Offerings to serve His Interests; humbly and wholly submitting to His glorious and sovereign, and wise and just Will concerning all.

The Work is Entituled;

PSALTERIUM AMERICANUM: *The Book of PSALMS, exhibited in* BLANK VERSE, *fitted unto the Tunes commonly used in the Churches of God; But with a Translation so Exactly Conformed unto the Original, as neither to leave out anything dictated by the Holy Spirit of GOD, nor to putt in any thing that belongs not unto His Holy Dictates: With both of which Inconveniencies, every other Version in Metre heretofore has been Encumbred. And ILLUSTRATIONS added, which discover in the PSALMS, Rich Treasures not commonly apprehended: With Directions to employ the PSALMS on such Intentions of Piety, as to render this Divine Book yet more than ever, the most glorious Instrument of Devotions that*

*ever was in the World. For which Purpose also, some other
Portions of the Sacred Scriptures, as exactly translated, are in
the like metre offered.*[1]

18. G. D.   In the Family of my Daughter-in-Law, there
is her little Son under Languishments.   As my Prayers and
Cares for the child, are on this Occasion called for, so my
seasonable Discourses with the Mother, to præpare her for
the Events of Providence.

I began to sett apart this Day, for Prayers and Cries
to God.   But in the Forenoon of the Day, I had so gracious
and precious an Answer to what I had begun to ask, that I
desisted, at the Desire of my Consort, with whom I offered
up thankful Praises to God.

19. G. D.   A new Prospect opening to terminate the
Confusions, in the South-part of this Town: which I would
prosecute.

How strangely does the divine Providence deal with the
Chief of Sinners!   Oh! The Triumphs of sovereign Grace,
over the vilest and blackest Unworthiness in the Chief of
Sinners!

(V.) About nine Years ago, I formed a brief Treatise,
which I entituled, *A Man of Reason.*   One who pretended
much Friendship to me, carried it for *England,* with a
declared Purpose to, publish it there.   The French took
him, and he lost all that he had with him.   Only one day
at his Lodgings in *France,* his Landlord brought this Manuscript unto him, telling him, *I can gett no good by it; it might
do you some Good:*   He carried it over to *Bristol* with him:
and there left it carelessly in an Hand unknown unto me.
After some Years, it was by the Mediation of my Friend
Mr. *Noble,* returned unto me.   Here it remained some
Years, until a religious Society of young men, asked me

[1] Printed by S. Kneeland, for B. Eliot, S. Gerrish, D. Henchman and J.
Edwards.   In spite of his good intentions, Mather did not succeed in making his
book acceptable to the worshipper.   A casual reading will explain why it did not
displace the versions then in use.

lately to give them a Sermon; and this was the Sermon, which with some other strange Circumstances, that at the Instant brought it into my hand, tho' I had lodged it with one that was now gone a Voyage from us, I gave unto them. The young Men at last committ it unto the Press; and it looks as if it were designated for some good in the World. It is entituled,

A MAN OF REASON, *a Brief Essay to demonstrate, That all men should hearken to Reason: And, what a World of Evil would be prevented in the World, if men would once become so Reasonable.*[1]

20. G. D. My Prayers with the Governour and Council, furnish me Opportunities to utter such Things in the Council-Chamber as the whole Province may fare the better for.

21. G. D. Several wretched Creatures are found, unto whom the Discipline of the Church belongs. Lett me study what is to be done, that they may be brought unto Repentance.

* 22. G. D. I find myself greatly improved in a Disposition of Piety; in which I must yett pursue further Improvements.

Instead of courting a great Honour and Esteem in the World; a great Name among Men, I have rather some Horror of it; and have a great Aversion for the Sacriledge commonly committed by them who see no further than the Creatures; who terminate in Man; who do not carry up their Acknowledgments unto the Glorious GOD. I decline many Things that might gett me a great Name in the World; merely because while Men make something of me, the glorious GOD will be forgotten.

And hence, when I suffer Defamations and Diminutions, I find my Spirit sweetly reconciled unto them, from this Consideration; now an Idol is dethroned; now there will

[1] Printed for John Edwards, 1718.

be no Fear of my being Idolized, and having those Regards,
which the glorious GOD alone has a claim unto.

23. G. D. Entertain the Flock, with at least three Sermons on the three famous Articles; Rom. XIV. 17. Wherein
the *Kingdome* of GOD, is exhibited.

24. G. D. *Miserere mei, Deus!*

I sett apart this Day, for extraordinary Supplications
unto the glorious GOD.

Great Improvements in Repentance, and Piety, and
Patience, being at this Time called for.

25. G. D. The sudden Death by Drowning, which
befalls a young Man, that lived with my Son-in-Law, and
was like one of my own Family; I must endeavour, that
an holy Improvement be made of it, in both Families.

26. G. D. And it may be a Service to the Cause of
Piety, especially among the young People of the Town, and
more especially among the Prentices, if I preach a suitable
Sermon on this mournful Occasion.

27. G. D. The excessive heat of the Season, indisposes
us for every thing.

Yett, in a Letter to the Governour, I attempt some
good.

28. G. D. A poor Man, by odd Means, detained many
years an Hostage, in *France*, and in miserable Circumstances, calls for my Compassions, and Endeavours.

* 29. G. D. What, Oh! what should be the Conduct
of a great Sinner, under grievous Punishments and Chastisements from GOD, for his manifoed Miscarriages?

What the Repentance? What the Submission? What
the Flight unto the great Sacrifice? What the Union with
the Will of an holy GOD? What the Improvement in
Piety, that may answer the End of the Dispensations?
What the Returns of Service to a gracious Lord, who is
ready to Pardon? To præpare for, —

30. G. D. O my God, I am troubled, I am troubled,

that I am no more fruitful in Inventions for the Service of the Flock, whereof I am the Servant. Oh! what shall I do, that I may more imitate the glorious Exemple of the good and great Shepherd! I will with a Soul full of zeal for the Welfare of the Flock, not only go on doing, what I am doing for it, but cry to God more than ever, that He would show me what I shall do.

July. 1. G. D. My dear *Sammy,* now appears within a year of his Admission into the Colledge. I must immediately putt myself into a Method, of more closely plying his Education than ever; I would within a day or two, draw up the Method I would proceed upon.

2. G. D. A Kinsman at *Hampton,* would I do good unto, and animate unto the doing of good.

Wednesday. This Day, I sett apart for extraordinary Supplications before the Glorious GOD.

And this being the Day of the senseless Diversions, which they call, *the Commencement* at *Cambridge,* one of my special Errands unto Heaven, was to ask Blessings for the Colledge, and the Rescue of it from some wretched Circumstances in which it is now languishing.

My God and Saviour makes wonderful visits unto me!

3. G. D. I am sending to my Friends in the *Frederician* University, many things that may have a Tendency to serve the Kingdome of GOD. Among the rest a Copy of my Letter to *Malabar,* may be of some good Consequence.

4. G. D. The lovely Society of Pious Children, whom I allow to meet in my Library, I am to take under my Instruction and Protection, with special Endeavours for their Encouragement.

5. G. D. A poor young Man, in the Hands of a wicked Master, from whom he suffers barbarous Things, for speaking the Truth; Pains must be taken to rescue him.

*6. G. D. Oh! The wondrous Favour of a most gracious God unto the Chief of Sinners! I am enriched and refreshed, with a Disposition of PIETY grown to a great Strength upon me, whereof it is impossible for me to express the blessed Consequences.

Having entertained a right and clear Apprehension of my great SAVIOUR; and, His glorious Person, as the Eternal SON of GOD incarnate and enthroned in my Jesus; being somewhat understood with me, the Thoughts of Him are become exceeding frequent in my Mind. I count it a Fault, if my Mind be many waking Minutes together without some Thoughts that have in them a Tincture of PIETY; but I have learnt the way of Interesting my SAVIOUR in these Thoughts; and I feel an Impatience, raised in me, if I have been many Minutes, without some Thoughts of Him. I fly to Him, on Multitudes of Occasions every Day. I find the Subject infinitely Inexhaustible. And my thus conversing with my SAVIOUR, has the most sanctifying Impression upon me, of any Exercise that ever I have been used unto. After I have been in the Day thus employ'd, I fall asleep at Night in the Midst of a Meditation on some Glory of my Saviour; so I sleep in Jesus. And when I wake in the Night, still in the Night, the Desires of my Soul carry me unto Him.

The Holiness and Happiness, whereunto I am introduced by my great Improvement of late in this Way of Living is Better to me, than all the Enjoyments of this World. But certainly, My SAVIOUR is preparing me for something or other, which I am not yett perfectly aware of.

I am very willing to be,——

But, my Life is hid with CHRIST in GOD!

Some years ago, I wrote an Essay, of this Tendency: and I have essay'd some Conformity to the Maxims of Christianity, then communicated. But I never have arrived unto such a Degree of Love unto my SAVIOUR, as now I am; to be uneasy if many Minutes have passed without some Recourse unto Him.

7. G. D. And shall not my Flock feel the Influences of this Disposition in me? Yea, I shall doubtless be disposed by my Saviour, to find out new, rare, exquisite Ways, of leading them unto Acknowledgments of Him, and of His Glories.

8. G. D.   A poor, weak, helpless, young Woman, but the Daughter of an eminent Minister beyond-Sea, and One of the Orphans which the Ministers here formerly rescued from a Servitude, is taken into my Family, from a Principle and with an Intention of Charity; wherein, may the gracious Lord assist us, and accept us.

9. G. D.   Sickness in the Family of my Wife's Daughter, calls for my Prayers and Thoughts, that there may be a good Conduct in it, and a good Issue of it.

10. G. D.   I am sending to *Scotland*.   And I propound the doing of several Services in the Church of *Scotland*, and so unto the whole World.   Especially this; that more of the *Scotch* Ministers may have a Liesure and Pleasure for the writing of such Books, as may be for the general Good of the Church.

11. G. D.   The wretched Condition, which our Colledge is in, requires Prayers and Thoughts concerning it.

12. G. D.   Several new Objects, full of Poverty and Misery, offer themselves unto my Cares.

Satureday.   This Day I sett apart for extraordinary Supplications before the glorious God.

The Occasions and Exercises were such as have in the later Weeks employ'd me.

My glorious Lord fills me with Assurances of His Love unto me.

* 13. G. D.   The Disposition of PIETY, which I mentioned this Day Se'nnight, my Soul improves in it at such a rate, and I find such blessed Consequences of it, that I count myself more favoured of the Lord in my being brought unto it than if all the Riches in this World were bestow'd upon me.   But very particularly when I meet with such Things as have a Tendency to Trouble me, I find here a strong Anodyne, a strange Cordial under all my Troubles; a Soul rendred almost insensible of them.   The best Thing that I can devise to serve the Kingdome of God in my Soul,

is to go on with the Methods of getting my SAVIOUR to be thus Reigning there.

At the Lord's Table this Day, I gett this Disposition strengthened.

14. G. D. In Conversation with the People of the Flock, ask more frequently, what it is, that they desire to hear preached on. I may in this way receive a notable Direction. And be sure, the Persons whose Desire I gratify, will give a singular Attention.

15. G. D. My Servant *Obadiah:* — his Religious Education.

16. G. D. Putt my Brother at *Witney*, upon several Services.

17. G. D. I am disappointed this Day, of the Help that I expected for my Lecture. I am suddenly putt upon preaching it. But my Good God leads me to a Subject, which proves in an uncommon Measure acceptable and serviceable unto a Multitude; How to manage Combats against special Temptations.

18. G. D. I have a Projection for a Revival of the Interview, which the Ministers use to have just after the Lecture; and how to make it more useful than ever.

19. G. D. A miserable Person, that has long lain under dolorous Languishments.

* 20. Oh! Blessed, blessed be my glorious Redeemer. There are many temporal Enjoyments, which my Heart is willing to ask of a gracious GOD. But my Heart has now such a Bias upon it, and is now so wean'd from this World, and so turn'd unto GOD, that instead of asking for such Enjoyments, I much more ask for an Heart willing to go without them. There is not any one of these Enjoyments, but when I go to ask it, I pass rather to a sacrificing Heart, and pray rather for an Heart able and ready to make a Sacrifice of it; this I esteem a Blessing preferrible to any Thing that can be denied unto me.

21. G. D. A Sermon upon the Desires of PIETY, may have a Tendency to enkindle and animate the Desires, in the People.

22. G. D. New Distresses about my poor Son *Increase!* To find Employments for his Pen, at the Store-house, may be many Ways of use to him.

23. G. D. The People at *Brooklyn* sett apart this Day for solemn Humiliations and Supplications. I go to them, and preach to them, this Day; and so have an Opportunity to serve the Work of God among them.

24. G. D. I have a Kinsman at *Brooklyn*, for whom I would employ my very particular Thoughts, what should be done, that he may be rendred an useful Man.

25. G. D. A Minister arrived from *Ireland*, with Instructions to enquire after the Circumstances of this Countrey, in order to the coming of many more, gives me an Opportunity for many Services.[1]

26. G. D. The many Families arriving from *Ireland*, will afford me many Opportunities, for Kindnesses to the Indigent.

* 27. G. D. That I may go on with my continual Resort unto my SAVIOUR, I would employ my Pen, as soon as may be, to draw up the various Methods of it, and Subjects of Contemplation in it.

28. G. D. Some Sermons on Col. III. 3, 4, may do notable Service to the Designs of Piety among the People of the Flock, to which I am a Servant.

29. G. D. My GOD! My GOD!

30. G. D. Directions to be given for the Service of some related unto me.

31. G. D. Letters and Packets, which I am sending to the other side of the Atlantic, have their Projections for Good in them. Great Projections and a Variety of them.

August. 1. G. D. A special Occasion of Advice to the

[1] Rev. William Boyd of Macosquin. Bolton, *Scotch Irish Pioneers*, 91, 132.

Schole-master, about some horrid Things, which the Children at the Schole, may be in danger of.

2. G. D. A poor Man in our church, an old Professor of Religion, horribly out of Frame, what shall be done for him?

*3. G. D. I am greatly concerned, that I may keep a most holy, watchful, exact Guard upon my Spirit, that not the least Beginning of any evil Frame arise on any Occasion there.

O my GOD, my SAVIOUR; From the Depths I cry unto thee.

4. G. D. A public Notice taken of an excellent Character to be found, in some obscure and retir'd Christians, which the Public takes no notice of, may have a tendency to animate an excellent Piety, among the Poor of the Flock.

5. G. D. My GOD! My GOD!

6. G. D. Animate my Brother *Samuel*, to begin the Work of Associating, to serve the Kingdome of God, and propagate the Maxims of it.

7. G. D. And write unto others beyond-Sea, on the like Intention.

But what shall be done for the great Numbers of People, that are transporting themselves hither from the North of Ireland? Much may be done for the Kingdome of GOD in these Parts of the World by this Transportation.

8. G. D. A Variety of new Services to be done for the Kingdome of GOD among our Indians, now occur unto me.

8 *d*. 6 *m. Friday*. This Day I sett apart, for secret Supplications unto the Lord.

Unspeakable Occasions have I to cry unto Heaven.

As an Addition to the Occasions for Supplications this day, there is a sad Occurrence in my Family. A Spanish Indian Damsel, who was a very useful Servant in my Family, died very suddenly the last Night, of Bleeding in her Lungs.

Her Death administers many calls to solemn Humiliations; with Prayers that a good Servant may [be] sent into the Family, and that our Sins may be pardoned.

She was buried this Evening. And I made as pungent a Discourse as I could, unto the many Indians and Negroes that came unto the Funeral.

9. G. D. A worthy Servant of the Gospel among the Indians, needs my Endeavours to do several important Kindnesses for his Encouragement.

* 10. G. D. Blank Books may for this purpose be præpared by me, and I may make daily Entries into them. Since the Thoughts of my great and my dear SAVIOUR, do so grow upon me, and have such precious Effects of them, and the further I go, the more expert I am in my conversing with the inexhaustible Subject, these blank Books, will help to methodize my Heads of Meditation, and increase my Supply for it, and be a Repository for such Stores, as I may afterwards bring forth for the public Entertainments in the House of God.

11. G. D. Methinks I do not enough use a Variety of Artifice, in my Catechising.

12. G. D. What Methods am I to take? Direct me, assist me, succeed me, O my SAVIOUR that there may be nothing but the Comfort of Love, always reigning in my Family.

13. G. D. And in the Families that spring from it, and have Relations to it!

14. G. D. Divisions and Confusions in the Church at *Framlingham*, call for my best Endeavours to bring them unto a Period.

15. G. D. I am getting ready, with some Gentle-men, certain Proposals for the præserving and promoting of the evangelical Interests among the Indians at *Martha's* Vineyard.

15 *d.* 6 *m. Friday.* Tho' I am somewhat spent with

having preached every other Day this week, in public Assemblies, yett I sett apart this Day for Prayer with Fasting before the Lord on such Occasions, as thus employ'd me a Week ago.

16. G. D. A noted Neighbour, now in years, is fallen into an uncomfortable Distraction. I must be greatly concerned for him.

*17. G. D. I propose to consider my admirable SAVIOUR, more distinctly and more exactly than ever, in the several Articles of His *holy Pattern*. I would putt the Subjects into Order; and then on a Lord's-day Morning, successively employ my Meditations and my Supplications upon each of them, until I have gone thro' them, and felt, a very deep Impression from them upon me. My Work this Morning, shall be a general Introduction, with mighty Cries from the Depths unto the Lord, that His Image may be most livelily apparent in me.

18. G. D. And my Flock shall feel it.

The House wherein I entertain them, shall be the House of my SAVIOUR'S Glory.

19. G. D. My Operations on the Mind of my hopeful Son, *Sammy*, must every day be various and exquisite.

But the more promising Hopes I have of the desireable Child, the more obliged am I to look upon him with a sacrificing Eye.

20. G. D. I am sending Books of Piety, to my Relatives at *Lime*.

21. G. D. I will be no longer putt off; but will try whether I can't form a Society, to consider and prosecute that Enquiry, *What may be done to bring on the Kingdom of God ?*

22. G. D. I must project and pursue a more intimate Correspondence and Conversation with our good, wise, generous Governour. It may issue in unknown Services and Benefits to the Kingdome of God.

The extreme Heat of the Weathers, etc, hindred my setting apart this Day, as I intended.[1]

23. G. D. A poor, weak, helpless Orphan, by the Providence of God cast into my Family.

* 24. G. D. This Morning, that I may come at the Glory of the Lord, and be transformed into His Glorious Image, I consider;

How did my dear SAVIOUR, seek the Glory of Him that sent Him?
After I have Thought on the Pattern of so living unto GOD, which He has given me, with Resolutions of Imitation, I cry to Heaven for the Grace to conform unto it; And I plead the Purchase which His Blood has made of this Grace for me.

These were the Heads of my Desires.

My GOD, I desire to consider myself, as being sent into the World by thee, to be an Instrument of thy Glory; And I heartily close with it, as the chief End of my Life, to *render* and *procure* those *Acknowledgments* to Thee, wherein thou wouldest be glorified. It shall be the principal and perpetual Business of my Life, thus to conform unto the Exemple of my SAVIOUR; And I will forever abhor, avoid, rebuke, whatever would be a Dishonour to Thee. O my SAVIOUR, Thou hast purchased this Grace of GOD for me. O holy Spirit of my SAVIOUR, apply it, bestow it; enter me; Take possession of me.

25. G. D. I am now in quest of another Subject, which the Flock may most unto Edification be entertained withal. Among the rest, why not the endearing *Titles* of our SAVIOUR.

26. G. D. Two sickly Persons coming to sojourn in my Family, afford me some Opportunities, to consult the Welfare of my Family.

At least, my Charity and Compassion to them, will in the Rewards of Heaven prove so.

27. G. D. Some Discords to be prevented, and redressed.

28. G. D. Of later Months, my Sermons are so fairly

[1] This sentence is written in the margin.

and fully written, that they may be ready for the Press without any more adoe. I propose to form little Books of them and give Titles, to them, so that they may be ready, for any Publication, which before or after my Death, any unexpected Providence of GOD may [my] SAVIOUR, may order for any of them. Whether the Lord accept these Essays or no, yett it is not amiss for me to præpare and offer them.

29. G. D. A good Service to be done, by settling an Attorney for the Indian Commissioners at Marthas Vineyard.

30. G. D. A miserable Daughter of a Minister in very indigent Circumstances, must be cared for.

* 31. G. D. This Morning, I consider;

How did my dear SAVIOUR, make it His Meat and His Drink, to do the Will of His Father?

And I propose to imitate Him, with a Delight in Obedience to God, and in doing of good unto all that are about me. Yea, if I do any delightful Action, the chief Delight of it, shall be the Obedience to GOD in it.

September. 1. G. D. I have some Thoughts, of entertaining the Flock, with a Course of Sermons, on the Transfiguration of our Saviour.

2. G. D. Dear *Nancy,* —

3. G. D. My continual Prayer for my Brother at *Witney,* must be, *Lord, accept him, and employ him, to do great Things for thy Kingdome.* And I must be more free in suggesting such Things unto him.

4. G. D. Write unto the Governour of *Connecticut,* that he would make the Interview of the Ministers at their Commencement more significant and serviceable to the best Interests.[1]

And some important Things for the Welfare of their Colledge.

[1] Mather had written on this very subject, August 25, 1718. The letter is in Quincy, *History of Harvard University,* I. 526.

5. G. D.   Procure a Meeting of the Indian Commission ers that something may be effectually done, for the Introduc tion of Christianity among the Pagan Indians at *Connecticot*

5 *d.* 7 *m. Friday.*   I sett apart this Day to present my Desires before the Lord, and obtain Mercies from Him.

The Occasions and Exercises were, as formerly.

6. G. D.   A Scotch Scholemaster arrived here from *Ireland*, wants Employment.

Poor Mr *Eliot*, lies languishing.[1]

* 7. G. D.   This Morning I consider;

What was the Diligence of my SAVIOUR in dispatching of the Work, which was given Him to do, before the Night of Death came upon Him?

And I cry unto the Lord, that my Sloth may be pardoned and the Grace of a very diligent Hand, and the Skill of Redeeming the Time wisely, may be bestowed upon me.

8. G. D.   *The unsearchable Riches of CHRIST;* A noble Subject!   Very particularly for the Poor of the Flock

9. G. D.   My daily Discourses with my Son *Samuel* in the Latin Tongue, will notably help to cultivate him.

10. G. D.   An hopeful young Man in my Neighbour hood, and one of a learned Education, do's with much Affection, in many Instances do the Part of a Son unto me Especially in the Affairs of my Library, whereof he is now taking a Catalogue.   I must make him such an one; and study all possible Wayes to cultivate him, and accomplish him, for great Services.

11. G. D.   If the French Priest, who is an Instructor to the Indians in our Eastern Countrey, might be brought over to the Protestant Religion, it would be a wonderful Service to the Countrey; wonderfully contribute unto the Tranquillity of the Countrey.   Some are not without Hopes that this may be done: I would make an Essay towards it by writing largely in the Latin Tongue unto him.

[1] John Eliot?   See p. 647, *infra.*

12. G. D. I renew my Request unto the Societies to consider, what Subjects they more especially would propose to hear handled in my public Ministry.

13. G. D. Among the Families arrived from *Ireland*, find many and wondrous Objects for my Compassions. Among other Methods of helping them, I would enclose a Sum of Money with a nameless Letter unto one of their Ministers, to be distributed among them.

*14. G. D. This Morning I consider,

What was the Submission to the Will of GOD, with which my SAVIOUR took every Cup that was assigned unto Him?
And in conformity to Him, I desire that I may with a patient, silent, easy Frame of Mind, entertain all the Troubles which a soverign GOD may order for me.

Satisfied in this, that as He does all things well, so He will be gratified in beholding my Obedience to Him; And that this Resignation will be but a Præparation for the Blessings of the Joy sett before me; the Cross going before the Crown.

15. G. D. To the House where I live, a large Wharf belongs. At this Wharf there usually ly Vessels, which I would look upon as a singular Part of my Flock and Charge. I would therefore often take my Walk down on the Wharf, talk with the People of the Vessels, and lodge Books of Piety in their hands.

16. G. D. There is an unhappy Discord, between some; for the Curing whereof I would use all exquisite Methods of Prudence and Goodness.

It is a grievous Burden to me.

17. G. D. There do arise little Discords also among some Relations, at a further Distance from me. I would in all dulcifying Wayes bring them to be well-disposed unto one another.

18. G. D. The wretched Condition of our College; can I do nothing towards the mending of it.

Be sure, Cries to God, that it may bere covered into

a Condition, which may have a good Prospect on the
Kingdome of GOD, and the Service of His Churches.

19. G. D. I have had some Thoughts, whether i
might not have good Effects, if once in two Months, o
so, I should preach at one or other of the Congregation
in my Neighbourhood; changing with the neighbourin
Ministers.

Hereby I shall have Opportunities to preach the Gospel
unto the whole City. And it may be some Releef unt
my weary Studies.

20. G. D. A forlorn, froward, wicked old Man, perish
ing in an helpless old Age, and the want of every thing
I must look after him.

* 21. G. D. This Morning I consider;

*What was the Conduct of my SAVIOUR in the Repelling of Temp
tations, when He was assaulted with them?*
And in Conformity to Him, I resolved upon a vehement anc
perpetual Hatred of all Sin;
A constant Recourse to the Word of GOD; wherein, *It is written*
what forbids and condemns the Sin I may be tempted to.
A Repetition of earnest Cries to Him, who succours the Tempted.
I now particularly thought on the Passages of the Sacred Scrip
ture, which fulminate the Faults I may be most in danger of.

22. G. D. A Sermon on the Espousal of a Soul unto
a SAVIOUR.

23. G. D. Further Points of *Liza's* Education.

24. G. D. A young Man in *London*, my wife's Nephew,
a Letter and a Present, that may have a Tendency to engage
him in the Ways of Piety.

25. G. D. I am thinking on a Catalogue of great
Services and Benefits to be done for Mankind in general;
and for the British Nations. Which if I can finish and
publish, it may in Time have blessed Effects in the
World.

26. G. D. Letters must be written unto the General

.ssembly at *Connecticot*, about Christianizing the Pagan
ndians in their Colony.

27. G. D. A Family in Affliction, calls for my
:ompassion.

*28. G. D. This Morning I consider,

*What was the Carriage of my SAVIOUR under provoking Injuries
nd Abuses from them that were about Him?*
And in Conformity to Him, I Resolved,
That I would see the Hand of GOD, in all the Provocations that
ny Children of Men may offer me.
That I would most religiously and circumspectly forbear all
.evenges, and avoid so much as a revengeful Wish in my Soul.
That I would suppress all Ebullitions of sinful Wrath and Rage;
ll wrathful and raging Expressions, and unadvised Speeches.
That I would endeavour to overcome Evil with Good.
And for this Purpose I look'd up unto Him.

29. G. D. Something more must be done, (in private
:onversation particularly,) to animate and awaken the
eople, that they would more seriously and earnestly pro-
ect for the Good of the Flock, to which they belong.

30. G. D. Certain Points of *Manliness* there are,
vhereto my Son *Samuel* must now be raised apace.

And my daily Discourses with him are to be in the Latin
ongue.

October. 1. G. D. I am this Day concerned in the
)rdination of a very hopeful young Gentleman,[1] to the
,astoral Care of the old South church. I will here enter
.im as one of my Relatives; hoping to enjoy a Brother in
.im, and a Friend more useful than a Brother.

2. G. D. I have been some Occasion of the Visits
vhich many Ministers have made unto miserable *Tiverton*.
 have not had Strength, to bear my part in those Visits.
3ut yett, that in my poor Manner and Measure I may do
omething to serve the Kingdome of God, in that wretched

[1] Rev. Thomas Prince (1687–1758). Sewall, *Diary*, III. 198.

Place, I am at the Charge of reprinting my little Book, o
THE GREATEST CONCERN IN THE WORLD; and sending
Number, to be dispersed in the Families there.[1]

3. G. D. Encourage the People of *Draycot*, unto th
Inviting of a worthy Scotch Minister lately arrived her
to settle among them.[2]

3 *d*. 8 *m. Friday*. This Day I sett apart for the Devo
tions of a Day of Prayer.

The Occasions, and the Exercises, were the same tha
[as] on some former such Days.

But my SAVIOUR was, alas, this day very much with
drawn from my Soul. I have not had Heaven opened t
me and visiting of me, as at some other Times.

I suspect some heavy Trials may be near unto me. (
my SAVIOUR, do thou return unto me.

4. G. D. A poor Man, whose Debts have a consider
able while confined him, is an Object for my Compassions

* 5. G. D. This Morning, I sett myself to consider,

*What was the Conduct of my SAVIOUR, in His Management o
His Family?*
And in Conformity to Him, I Resolved,

That I would keep continually Instructing my Domesticks in the
Things that concern the Kingdome of GOD.

That I will faithfully advise them of the various Temptations
whereto I may apprehend them obnoxious and lovingly Rebuke all
that I see amiss in them.

That I will without ceasing pray with them, and for them.

And, that I will do what I can, to guard them against the Mis
chiefs which they may in an evil World be expos'd unto.

The Grace to do these things, I implored as having been pur
chased by Him for me.

6. G. D. I am sensible, that I am too defective in
my pastoral Visits; with Cryes to the Lord for Forgive-

[1] Printed at New London, Conn., by T. Green. It had first appeared in 1707
[2] Rev. James McGregor, of Aghadowey. Bolton, *Scotch Irish Pioneers*
106, 199.

ess and Assistence, I will sett upon the Reforming of
iis Defect. And scatter in the Families, besides other
ooks, of Piety, my little Treatise of *The Greatest Con-
ern in the World.*

7. G. D. Some Things occurr in my Family, which
quire in me, exquisite Prudence, Patience, Goodness, that
) Sin may not be committed, but GOD and His Gospel
iay be glorified: Exquisite Projection for a Good Issue;
nd, oh! continual, and uncommon cries, unto the glorious
ord, for His gracious Conduct.

8. G. D. I have my youngest Sister, brought unto a
Vidowhood; I am to take a brotherly Care of her, and to
o in every thing the Part of a Brother born for Adversity.

8 *d.* 8 *m.* Because of some singular Circumstances
hich call me to more than ordinary Humiliations and
upplications, I sett apart this Day for them.

At length I obtained some Assurances of a gracious GOD
econciled unto me.

My main Request was, That I might not by any Temp-
ation whatever be overcome to Sin against the glorious
iOD, nor admitt the least ill Frame, or the least ill Thought,
nto my Heart.

But then with the same Intent, and with the same
Irdour, I requested for, *a Soul full of a CHRIST;* that I
nay mightily improve in the Blessedness which I am in
he daily and mighty Pursuance of.

My GOD has heard me.

9. G. D. Sending to *Scotland* this day, I project sev-
ral Services for the Kingdome of God.

10. G. D. Some Things in View for the Good of the
Colledge.

11. G. D. Several poor Objects occur, to be releeved.

* 12. G. D. This morning I sett myself to consider,

*With what Eye did my SAVIOUR look upon this World, and all
he little Glories of it?*

And in Conformity to Him, I desired,

That all the Enjoyments of this World might appear contemptib Things unto me.

That no offer of these Things might ever draw me into any Si against the glorious GOD.

That I might be content with a poor; and hard, low, mean Cor dition in this World.

And yett give Thanks for the smallest Vouchsafements of it; Morsel of Bread.

That I may be willing to leave this World, as soon as ever m heavenly Father shall call me out of it.

13. G. D. The Psalmody is but poorly carried on i: my Flock, and in a Variety and Regularity inferior to som others; I would see about it.

14. G. D. A Difficulty, my GOD, Help me witl Prayer and Patience to overcome it.

Oh! may *Cresy Walter's Death*, be sanctified unto *Cres Mather!*

15. G. D. My Brother and Sister at Roxbury, hea: of the Death of their eldest Son abroad. What shall I do to comfort them?

16. G. D. I am not only polishing the *Psalteriun Americanum*, which is now in the Press; but also making Additions to the rich Stores of the Cantional, that so the Various Intentions of Piety may be more fully answered.

17. G. D. The Charge, with the Fellowship of the Churches, lately given in an Ordination, being joined unto the Sermon then preached, which is going to the Press, may serve several good Purposes.

18. G. D. Employments must be sought for some that want them.

* 19. G. D. This Morning I sett myself to consider;

How did my SAVIOUR attend the private and public Worship of God?
And in conformity unto Him, I desired,

That I might converse much with the glorious GOD in the *Religion of the Closett.*

That my part of the religious Exercises in the Assemblies of *Zion*, may be serious, devout, constant.

20. G. D.   My poor Flock! what shall I do for thee? hope, the Sermon preached Yesterday, proves a very Awakening one.   I contrived Yesterday, that the Consid-eration of a *Death approaching*, upon which the Place of every one will *know them no more*, might be sett home, with all possible Pungencies.

I may here take notice of an observable Thing.

What a precious Favour of Heaven it is, to have a Mind moved and acted from above, and under a special Conduct of Heaven!   Towards the latter End of the Week, I found my Mind strongly impelled unto the præparing of a Sermon on Job VII. 10. *Neither shall his Place know him any more: But without any other Intention*, than to have it ly by, for some future and unknown Occasion.   On the Lord's-day-Morning (and it fell out that I must, preach in the Morn-ng,) I had it struck into my Mind, that I may do well to preach the Sermon I had præpared; and make it a funeral Sermon, for a worthy Minister of *Andover*,[1] who died sud-denly the last Week, and add his Character in the close of t.   He was a worthy Man, and very modest and humble; and one who studied much to avoid public Appearances. But I thought, my publishing the Worth of such a Man, and procuring a just Fame unto him, would be but the more proper an Action, and be some Reward of Heaven unto him.   I did accordingly; and enjoyed a very gracious Presence of the holy One with me, in the doing of it.

(VI.)   The Son of this Person, is our Schole-Master, and my Auditor; and he comes to me, for a Copy of my Sermon.   While such a large work, as my *Psalterium*, is in the Press, I have not had so many Opportunities for the publishing of lesser Composures.   But I begg'd of the Lord, that He would continue my Fruitfulness, and make

[1] Thomas Bernard.

and find Opportunities for it. Behold, an Instance! I give my Sermon to my Neighbour, for the Press, under this Title; VANISHING THINGS. *An Essay on the Condition of Man known in his Place no more, when Death has once removed him from it. A Sermon preached on the Death of the shining and yett humble* Mr. Thomas Bernard, *the late Pastor of a Church in* Andover.[1]

On this Occasion, I look'd back to see, how many Persons of Worth, a gracious God has employ'd my poor Pen, publickly to exhibit unto the World, with an Advantageous History, or Character of them. And, I found, no less than One hundred and fourteen men (whereof more than Fourscore stand in the Church-History,) and above twenty Women; besides many more, who have more transiently and occasionally had an honourable Mention made of them.

I now sett myself to glorify the free Grace of GOD unto the Chief of Sinners, in using me thus, to discover unto the World, the Glory of my SAVIOUR, in what He has done for and by His chosen Servants.

I begg'd of Him, the Grace to approve myself so, that what good I have written of others, may not prove my own Condemnation, thro' my own falling short of the like.

I freely consented unto it, that I should myself after all, remain unmentioned after my Death, and ly buried in all possible Obscurity, and never have any Remembrance among the Children of Men. I found such a Love of GOD, working in my Soul, that I would fain disappear and have none but Him to be acknowledged.

21. G. D. My Negro-Servant, *Obadiah;* my Saviour has committed him unto me, that I may bring him up to be a Servant of the Lord. Being deeply affected with such a Consideration, I would use all possible, and exquisite Endeavours for the Instructing and Restraining of him. I have hitherto been too defective in these Endeavours.

22. G. D. The worthy Minister of *Groton* is become

[1] Printed by S. Kneeland for D. Henchman, 1718.

now (and by my means) my Kinsman.[1] I would endeavour in ways of special Kindness and Contrivance, to become useful unto him, and assist him in the fruitful Discharge of his Ministry.

23. G. D. The Author of *the Occasional Paper* having published unto the World, my Letter to *Pillonière*,[2] I now send unto him several Instruments, in hopes, that by his Means, they may serve the good Cause of *Piety* and *Liberty*, for which they are calculated.[3]

GOD knows, what may be the Consequences of publishing the mentioned Letter, which I found called, *A celebrated Letter* and much talk'd of, before this Publication.

24. G. D. Writing to my Brother I renew my Sollicitations unto him, that he would bring my Testimony against *Arianism*, into operation.

And I press Mr. *Bradbury*, to —

25. G. D. Several Miserables, under the Influences of my Charity.

For my Remittances to the *Orphan-house* at *Glaucha*, I gathered eight Pounds of our Money for which Mr. *Belcher* generously furnishes me with a Bill of ten Pounds Sterling : Sent by me now to Mr. *Boehm*, and Mr. *Nauman*.

* 26. G. D. This Morning I sett myself to consider,

The Prayers of my SAVIOUR, what were they, and how managed?
And in Conformity to Him, I desired,
That I may be accustomed unto all Sorts of *Prayers.*
And particularly that my *ejaculatory Prayers* may be innumerable.
That I may be exceeding frequent in my Prayers and make my Visits unto Heaven upon all Occasions.
That I may be exceeding devout, serious, fervent in my *Prayers,*

[1] Caleb Trowbridge (1692–1760), married (1) Sarah Oliver, and (2) Hannah Walter, daughter of Rev. Nathaniel Walter. The second marriage took place September 18, 1718.

[2] François de la Pillonnière.

[3] Simon Browne (1680–1732), now pastor of the important congregation in the Old Jewry, London, issued a *Collection of the Occasional Papers for the Year* 1718, III. where he printed Mather's letter, dated November 5, 1717.

as having the Sight of Him who is invisible, and being duely affected
with the Importance of what is before me.

That I may in my Prayers exercise a strong Faith in God.

And that my Petitions may be well-examined ones, for ever according to the Will of God, and aim'd at His Glory: And with a due Submission to His infinite Wisdom and Justice and Sovereignty; a Resignation to His holy Pleasure.

27. G. D. I will keep continually scattering in my Flock my Essay on, *the Greatest Concern in the world.*

This morning our merciful SAVIOUR gave my Daughter *Abigail*, a safe and a quick Deliverance of a Daughter.[1]

28. G. D. And this obliges me to new Acts, wherein I am to consecrate my Family unto the Lord.

29. G. D. And, Oh! what shall I do, that the excellent Faculties and Attainments, of my Nephew at *Roxbury*, may be made exceeding serviceable to the Kingdome of GOD?

This Day, that young Man is ordained unto the pastoral Charge of the Church there.[2] I am employ'd in some of the public Exercises on this Occasion; particularly, in giving the Fellowship of the Churches; wherein I enjoy the gracious Assistances of the Lord.

30. G. D. I hope I have litt upon a Method of introducing the Gospel into the Town of *Providence.*

31. G. D. The Master of the Grammar-Schole[3] in my Neighbourhood, expresses to me, so much of a Desire to have it a Schole of Piety, that I am animated exceedingly, unto all possible Projections to render it so.

31 *d.* VIII *m. Friday.* This Day, I endeavour, as I use to do; to devote good Part of the Day, unto the Devotions of a Sacrificer.

The Occasions and the Exercises of the Day, were such as of later time they use to be.

---

[1] In the margin is written "about 4h." The child, Abigail Willard, was baptised November 2.

[2] Rev. Thomas Walter. See Sewall, *Diary*, III. 201.

[3] John Bernard.

I particularly cried unto God, That our Colledge might be rescued into a Better Condition.[1]

My Alms this Day were somewhat extraordinary; tho' not worth Mentioning.

November. 1. G. D. Money and Cloathing for some very poor Strangers, lately come among us.

* 2. G. D. This Morning I sett myself to consider;

How did my SAVIOUR use to sabbatize when the Rest of GOD every week return'd unto Him?

And in Conformity to Him, I desired,

That on the *Sabbath*, I may keep a strict Guard, not only on my *Words*, but also on my very *Thoughts*, to have nothing allow'd in them, that shall be unsuitable unto the *Religion* of the Day.

That on the *Sabbath*, I may spend the whole Time, as far as I am able, in the public and private Exercises of Religion.

That when the *Sabbath* arrives, I employ many most affectuous Meditations on the Works of *Creation*, and of *Redemption*, and on the *Rest which remains for the People of GOD.*

That the Arrival of the *Sabbath* shall be alwayes exceeding welcome to me.

This Morning, when walking in my Garden, I had my Spirit raised unto wondrous Flights of Union to my SAVIOUR, of which I may take a Time hereafter to give the Particulars.

3. G. D. Oh! lett me oftner yett renew and repeat my Considerations upon that awful Enquiry; *What Account shall I give unto my Saviour, of my Cares about the Flock, which He has committed unto me?*

4. G. D. Should not *Sammy* be putt upon writing after the Preacher; and begin thus betimes a Stock of Notes, that may imprint upon his Mind the Truths of the Gospel?

5. G. D. What more shall I do, for the Service of my Kinsman at *Brooklyn?*

This Day, I enjoy'd a most gracious and precious

[1] For a letter from Mather to Shute, dated this day, upon the concerns of Harvard College, see Quincy, *History of Harvard University*, I. 523.

Presence of GOD with me, in managing an Ordination at *Brooklyn*.[1]

6. G. D. I have had many Thoughts, whether a Sermon about the awful Nature and Effect of an *Oath*, may not be of great Use unto the People of the Countrey; among whom a rash Præcipitation in the Taking of an *Oath*, is what People are too commonly guilty of. What if I should attempt it, in the Audience of the General Assembly.

7. G. D. Now is the Time, to renew the Motion for *Guardians* to the Christian Indians.

8. G. D. A Scotch Youth, in poverty, and want of Employment, must be provided for.

* 9. G. D. This Morning I sett myself to consider,

The Miseries of a wretched world, how did my SAVIOUR look upon them?

And in Conformity to Him, I desired, that wherever I see any Miseries, my *Compassions* may be moved for them.

That I may with much Concern, and Vigour, and even Raptures, fly to *succour* such as I see in any Miseries.

But above all, that the *Sins* with which I see any offending of GOD, and injuring of themselves, may be *grievous* to me.

10. G. D. I entertain the Flock, with as pungent and useful a Discourse, as I can, on the Occasion given in the tragical Spectacle of a Number in our Neighbourhood, (among which were the Master of the Light-house, and his Wife) who were drowned the last Week, and carried all together to the Grave, with a very solemn Funeral.[2] And at the same Time, I recommend that excellent *Piety*, *an Observation of the Divine Providence in all Occurences.*

Having done this Yesterday, my most Gracious Lord,

---

[1] Rev. James Allen. See p. 483, *supra*.

[2] George Worthylake, his wife Ann, and daughter Ruth. The storm fell on November 3. Shurtleff, *Description of Boston*, 570. Franklin's ballad on the incident (Autobiography, in *Works* (Smyth) I. 239) was translated into French as "La Tragédie du Phare," and re-translated into English as "The Tragedy of Pharaoh."

will still hear my Cries, unto Him, and allow me, and employ me, to bring forth much of that Fruit, by which the heavenly Father may be glorified. My Sermon goes to the Press, and I have an Opportunity, in a more diffusive way to recommend that excellent Piety, which will exceedingly glorify God.

(VII.) It is entituled, PROVIDENCE ASSERTED AND ADORED. *In a Sermon occasioned by the Tragical Death of several, who were unhappily drowned, near the Light-house, at the Entrance of* Boston-Harbour. *With a Relation of the unhappy Accident.*

11. G. D. I must lay certain Charges on my Children, relating to their Conduct, that it be wise, good, patient, silent, and honourable, under some Temptations to Sin, which they may be in danger of.

12. G. D. I have a Nephew entring into the Business of the World, whom I must advise for the best in several Regards.

13. G. D. I must advise with the Governour about several important Services for the Public.

14. G. D. An ungospellized Island, — I hope, I am in a way of getting the Gospel to it.

14 *d.* 9 *m. Friday.* Renew'd Occasions, oblige me to ly in the Dust before the Lord, with the Deepest Humiliations, and the most fervent Supplications. I know not that Man upon Earth, who more wants Pardon, and Pitty, and Succour, from the Glorious Lord!

15. G. D. I don't want for Objects of Charity and Compassion; they ly thick about me.

This Day I gett very far up towards an Union with my dear Saviour; first in Disposition, then in Aim; lastly in Will. And I was dissolved into Floods of Tears, from the Apprehension, which this Union gave unto me.

* 16. G. D. This Morning I sett myself to consider,

What was the Behaviour of my SAVIOUR towards His various Relatives?

I find, that He paid an inviolate Respect unto His Parents; and He took singular Care for the Releef and Comfort of the Person that was more than in the Eye of the Law one of them.

He had Brothers, whose bad Carriage towards him for diverse Years, He bore with Patience; and He never gave over, until they were brought home unto GOD.

He had Kinsmen, whom He took into a most intimate Communion with Him, and qualified them for great Enjoyments in and Services to, the Kingdome of God;

For the Direction of my Behaviour towards my Consort, I often, often, think, How is the Church treated by her Saviour.

I begg'd help of Him, to *go and do likewise.*

17. G. D. Another Master of the *Light-house,* is (with another Person) already drowned.[1] So surprising a Dispensation gives me an Opportunity to lett fall such Passages on the Sea-faring part of my Flock, as may have a mighty Tendency to excite the Motions of Piety in them. God prosper these Endeavours.

18. G. D. My Family is in astonishing Circumstances. Oh! the Patience, the Prudence, the Prayer, that is called for.

If it were not for my calling of a glorious CHRIST into my Mind continually, and the Visits which He graciously makes unto my poor, sinful, sickly Soul, what, what would become of me? I here leave this Testimony to you, my Children, or whatever Hands these papers may fall into: that a Glorious CHRIST conversed withal, will be the Life of the Soul, that has Him dwelling in it.

19. G. D. This Day I find out a remote Relative that I never thought of; one in miserable Poverty. I sett myself to do the best I can for them.

20. G. D. This Day, I attempt the Service, which I have many Thoughts about. I give to the Public and in

[1] Robert Saunders.

the Audience of the General Assembly, a Sermon upon the Nature of an *Oath*, and the Vileness and Peril of a *Perjury*.

Præliminary to this Action, I underwent many deep Humiliations.

But besides all the rest, I had a Hold upon me, and much Fear that I should not have a Voice to go well thro' the Work upon. I considered, that my JESUS is the *Voice of GOD;* and that I am united unto Him. So I believed, that I should speak.

I enjoy'd not only a *Voice*, beyond what was ordinary, but also had a Presence of the Glorious One with me, to an uncommon Degree, in every part of my Service.

21. G. D. A Projection to putt out as many of the Indian Children, as tis possible, unto English and godly Families, is what I would now prosecute, as most likely to answer all good Intentions for the next Generation among them.

22. G. D. A miserable Woman in the Prison, for horribly butchering her child, is a singular Object for my Compassions.

* 23. G. D. This Morning I sett myself to consider:

What was the Conduct of my SAVIOUR in preaching of the Gospel?
I find that He preached with much Frequency; and with oh! what matchless Fervency!

Very plainly; especially in the use of the most enlightening Similitudes.

With great Faithfulness; bearing Testimonies for GOD, and for Truth, without fearing the Displeasure of Men.

And chiefly insisting on the more weighty Matters.

I begg'd Help of Him, to go and preach as like Him, as may be.

24. G. D. It has been my way, when I have had any personal Affliction befalling of myself, then to consider how I may render my Flock the better for them; and what Lessons of Piety should be to my Flock recommended and inculcated. I will do so, at this Time, as wisely as I can.

25. G. D. It will be not only a thing acceptable to GOD, but also a great Convenience and Advantage unto my dear *Sammy;* if I take a religious, ingenious, poor Orphan, who is of the same Standing in the School with him, and give him his Board in my Family.

26. G. D. I have a Son-in-Law, who needs my Advice, in diverse important Articles.

27. G. D. Oh! That I could find the Liesure to form an Enchiridion of the liberal Sciences, which might enable Persons easily to attain them: and at the same time, consecrate the whole Erudition unto the Designs of Piety; that Persons may therein live unto God.

If such a Thing might be accomplished, it might be one of the most useful Things that ever were done in the World.

But I despair, — it seems too late for me: — except, —

28. G. D. I have Thoughts of writing a circular Letter, unto the several Ministers employ'd in the Work of Gospellizing the Indians; upon several important Points relating to that Affair.

29. G. D. Some of my Neighbourhood under Languishments call for my Compassions.

I have been ill all this week; a feavourish Pain in my Head, much afflicting me, every Forenoon.

So that I have not had Strength to sett apart a Day for Supplications, as I use to do.

* 30. G. D. Either I must reserve the further Prosecution of my Design, to consider the Image and Pattern of my Saviour for the Healing of my Soul, for some other Papers, or however I must here make a short Parenthesis, that I may enter one of the Things which I have to delight my Soul, in the Multitude of my Thoughts within me.

I have a Contemplation, which has upon me a most Heart-melting Efficacy.

When the *Cloud of Glory*, which was the *Shechinah*, that had our SAVIOUR, with the *Angels of His Presence* dwelling in it, came down and filled the *Temple* of old, what a grateful Spectacle was it, and what Acclamations did it raise in the Spectators! A godly Man is a *Temple* of God; *a living Temple;* dearer to Him than any *Temple* of *meer Matter*, tho' the most splendid and costly in the World. When our SAVIOUR comes into the Heart of a godly Man, then the *Glory of the Lord* comes to fill a *Temple*, which He has chosen for His Habitation. And our SAVIOUR comes into an *Heart*, which is continually instructing and reforming and solacing itself, by *thinking* on Him. *O Heart* panting after thy SAVIOUR; So kind is thy SAVIOUR, that even at the Call of a *Thought* He will come into thee! A *Temple* so filled with the *Glory of the Lord* is unseen by the Standers-by; *Flesh and Blood* standing by. The *Life* of the godly Man is *Hid with CHRIST in GOD;* It is an *hidden Life*. But GOD sees this *Temple* with Pleasure. The SAVIOUR who *knoweth all things* is pleased with the Sight. His *Angels* make their Acclamations upon it.

A feavourish and a torturous Pain in my Head, has now visited me, and afflicted for the whole former Part of the Day, for now a week together. By means hereof I am this Day chased, not only from the House of God, but also from His Holy Table where His People expected my Administrations. This Thing, attended with other humbling Circumstances, caused me exceedingly to judge and loath myself before the Lord.

But at the same Time, I had my SAVIOUR coming very near unto me. I have not only the infallible Symptoms and Effects of a pardoned Soul, but my SAVIOUR dwells in my Soul; and comforts me with astonishing Emanations and Assurances of His Love.

This Day, I have been in the heavenly World. It is impossible for me to relate what I have mett withal. The Things are unutterable! unutterable! unutterable!

(VIII.) That I may serve the Kingdome of my SAVIOUR in one important Article more; *Glory to GOD in the Highest, and Peace on Earth*, I have convey'd unto the Press, my late Sermon about *Swearing*. It is entituled; THE RELIGION OF AN OATH. *Brief Directions, How the Duty of SWEARING may be safely performed, when it is justly demanded. And strong Persuasives to avoid the perils of Perjuries. Concluding with a solemn Explanation of an*

OATH, which the Laws of Denmark *require to be considered by them, whom an OATH is propos'd unto*.[1]

Two ordination-Sermons are lately published; and with them, there are given to the Public, the SPEECHES which I made, at giving the Fellowship of the Churches on those Occasions. These are the first Speeches of this Kind, that ever were printed in the world.[2]

December. 1. G. D. This is the Morning, in which I sett myself to think, *What may I do for my SAVIOUR in the Service of the Flock, which He has committed unto me?* I can think of nothing, but a renew'd Vigour of *pastoral Visits,* as soon as my Health will allow of them. On this Occasion, I exceedingly bewayled before the Lord, my Slothfulness and Barrenness in my Projections of Service to the Flock for which I must give up an awful Account unto Him. I confess'd before Him, how just it would be for Him to punish me with dreadful Things in my House, while my Behaviour in His House, is to be taxed with so many Negligences and Miscarriages. I begg'd it of Him, that He would instruct me and inspire me, and from time to time, lead me on unto the doing of such Things as may have a Tendency to make my Flock, a wise, an holy and an happy People.

2. G. D. What a singular Engine have I to employ, for the engaging of my Children to become very frequent and fervent in their Prayers to the glorious God. Oh! may I effectually and importunately improve it! And, Oh! may I be in Agony till I see produced in them, the Piety, to which I and they have uncommon Awakenings!

3. G. D. What shall I do? What shall I do, that my Kinsman, who is now settled in the pastoral Care of the

[1] Printed by B. Green for D. Henchman, 1719.

[2] Both sermons were by Increase Mather; the one, at the ordination of Rev. Mr. Walter, in Roxbury, October 29, 1718; and the other, at that of Rev. Nathaniel Appleton, in Cambridge, October 9, 1717. There is no speech appended to the Appleton Sermon.

Church at *Roxbury,* may glorify my SAVIOUR, with his bright Faculties and Attainments?

I will cultivate much Familiarity with him; I will endeavour to bring him into right Sentiments concerning the Kingdome of God, and the Service that is to be done unto it. I will communicate the best of Treasures unto him, on all Opportunities.

4. G. D. My Letter to *Pillonière* having been published and scattered thro' the World, and there being much Notice of it, it may be an Introduction unto my further Appearances in much greater Services for the Kingdome of God. Another Letter, either to him, or to the Author of *The Occasional Paper,* well contrived, may be of uncommon Consequence.

5. G. D. Some aged Societies for Piety, in my Neighbourhood, are languishing; What shall I do, that either they may be reanimated or others may be substituted.

6. G. D. Sundry poor Widows in my Neighbourhood.

*7. G. D. For some weighty Reasons, I must now make an Addition unto my *Daily Prayers.* As my SAVIOUR went up into a Mountain *to Pray,* so would I now every Evening about Sun-sett go up into my Library to pray. The more special Intention of this Prayer shall be, to enlarge in Petitions for Improvements in *Piety;* but yett more peculiarly to obtain Conduct from Heaven for the Management of my Designs to serve the Kingdome of God, and the marvellous Rescue and Increase of my Opportunities to do good, which sometimes the grand Adversary threatens with grievous Mischiefs unto them.

8. G. D. What, what shall I do more, for the Flock whereof I am the Servant?

It has been a Consolation unto me, when my Life has been full of Adversity, that all the Articles of it, have brought forth Revenues unto the People of GOD, and the Flock with which He has betrusted me. My Adversity has yeelded Instructions and Experiments unto them, which they have been the Better for; and I have been rendred the more, fruitful among them. Shall it not still be so?

I meet with some very uncommon Exercises. Now, first; my public Prayers and Sermons, must be more flaming Devotions than ever; there must be more of the Fire of God in them, and what may discover a sensible Improvement of Piety in me under my Calamities. And, secondly; there are certain particular Maxims of Piety which being enabled from the Things which I meet withal, to press more than ever, I must accordingly now recommend with a singular Importunity.

9. G. D. Ah! my poor Family! what Prayers must be obtained and employed for thee! I must use more effectual Methods that the Evenings, both before and after the Lord's-day, be more entirely devoted unto Exercises of Piety.

There are also certain Methods of Frugality, which the growing Difficulties of the Time, oblige us to grow more studious of.

10. G. D. A new Relative appears; a very poor one; and I doubt not a very good one; but one who expects, and must receive many Kindnesses.

11. G. D. I propose a Letter to the Author of *The Occasional Paper*, accompanied with some Communications, which I hope, will prove of a most extensive Service to the Kingdome of God.

11 *d.* 10 *m. Thursday.* This Day was kept as a public Thanksgiving thro' the Province.

My gracious Lord granted me some Assistances of His Grace, for the Work before me.

In the Evening of this Day, I went up into my Library, (as my SAVIOUR did use to go up into a Mountain, to pray,) according to the Custome I have lately taken up. I had my Soul astonished, and full of Consternation, from an Apprehension, that the Vengeance of

God was irresistibly coming out against me; an holy and a religious God, proceeding irresistibly to punish me, yea, to destroy me, for my Sins against Him; Sins in me aggravated above those of any man in the World. Oh! the Agony, in which I lay prostrate and contrite in the Dust before the Lord; crying and begging and weeping for a Pardon: and pleading the Great Sacrifice of my SAVIOUR, that the Wrath of Heaven may be turned away from me!

The next Morning I renew'd my Flight with a Flood of Tears, unto the Fountain sett open for Sin and for Uncleanness; and with such Dispositions towards the Blood of my SAVIOUR, that I could not but beleeve, that a gracious GOD has pardoned me, and that my SAVIOUR will gloriously step in, with His Providence, to stop the Progress of the divine Vengeance against me.

12. G. D. Our Schole-Master is like to leave us. A good Successor is of great Importance. I have one in View; who may prove an Instrument of great Good unto us. I will endeavour his Introduction.[1]

13. G. D. A poor Woman, under long Languishments, with no body to look after her.

* 14. G. D. In my vehement Cries from the Dust unto the Lord for the Pardon of my crying Sins against Him, I consider the Dispositions in the Mind of my dear SAVIOUR, at the Time, when He was enduring the Punishment of my Sins, and making Himself a Sacrifice for them. I find that He was willing to take whatever Cup His Father should give unto Him; that He lamented the Distance of GOD from Him; that He was concerned for to have the whole Will of God finished; that He was concerned for the Welfare of those that were about Him: that He wished the Mercies of GOD unto His Enemies; that He resigned His immortal Spirit unto His Father, for Him to do as He pleased with it. Now I strive till I find the holy One working in my own Soul, something that answers these Dispositions of my SAVIOUR. Thus disposed, I beg with Agony for the Pardon, which my SAVIOUR so disposed, has with His precious Blood purchased for me. And herein I do not aim, at recommending myself by any good Thing in me, unto the Benefit of a Pardon: but my Aim is to gett a comfortable Evidence, that it is a Faith of the right Sort, with which I now fly to the Blood of my SAVIOUR,

[1] Sewall mentions a candidate, Rev. Samuel Angier.

and pursue and receive a Pardon. Yea, these Dispositions assure me, that I am actually alive, and have passed from Death to Life, and so a Sentence of Life is with a Pardon passed upon me. To gain the greater Assurance of this Life, I find, that the Blood of my SAVIOUR is running warm in the Veins of my Soul; quickening of me to mighty Anhelations, after an Imitation of Him, in loving of Righteousness, and Hating of Wickedness, and submitting to God, and perpetually doing of Good; yea, an universal Conformity unto Him. An infallible Token that this precious Blood has been applied unto me.

15. G. D. One of our Deacons, more active than the Rest. I would much consult with him, and oblige him to concur with me, on that Point, *What may be further done for the Good of the Flock*.

16. G. D. A Servant-maid come into my Family. I must speak, yett more explicitly and effectually to her, about her Espousal to her SAVIOUR.

17. G. D. There are in this Town several Families to which I am nearly related. Methinks, I do not visit them often enough, upon the Designs of Piety.

18. G. D. Might I not be furnished with some notable Opportunities to serve the Kingdome of GOD, if I should bring it about, that the Commissioners for propagating the Gospel among our Indians, keep a Day of Prayer together, and I on the Day entertain them with a Sermon suited unto the Occasion, and then publish the Sermon accompanied with some other Things to serve the Cause of Religion in the world?

19. G. D. The Minister at *Rhode-Island* must be followed with new and strong Instigations, to hasten the Gathering of a Church there.

20. G. D. An honest and an aged man of some Consideration in our Neighbourhood, is fallen midst grievous Distraction. Besides other Compassions to him and his Family, I procure a Number of the pious Neighbours to meet and pray together for him.

* 21. G. D. My glorious LORD is leading me into a Practice, wherein He has a wonderful Design, and whereof there will be anon a wonderful Issue.

As my SAVIOUR, when the Evening arrived, would go up into a Mountain to pray, so, when the Dark or the Dusk of the Evening arrives, I go up unto my capatious Library, which is three Stories above my Study, upon the like Intention.

The more peculiar Purpose of these Prayers, (wherein, Oh! what sweet Interviews have I with my lovely SAVIOUR!) is, to beg that the Kingdome of GOD may come on, and that I may be accepted and assisted for the doing of Services to the Kingdome of my SAVIOUR, and that the Devices of Satan to destroy my Serviceableness may be defeated.

But I grow more and more sensible, that I have not enough Acknowledged and glorified my admirable SAVIOUR, as the Lord of ANGELS; and that I have not enough considered the *Angelical Ministry* in my Supplications. I would now more than ever, bewayl that Aggravation of my Impieties and Impurities; The Grief I have given to the Holy *Angels* in them; and with the most repenting Flights of a contrite Heart unto the Blood of the great Sacrifice, obtain the Pardon of them. I would now more than ever entreat the holy SPIRIT of my SAVIOUR, to fill me with Dispositions, that may render me the Delight of His holy *Angels*, and help me to live at such a Rate of Sanctity, Watchfulness and Fruitfulness, as they may with Pleasure look upon. I would now more than ever, ask it of my SAVIOUR, that He would send His *good Angel*, to do me good, in all those Points, wherein the *ministering Spirits*, use to befriend the Heirs of *Salvation*. I have a deep Sense of it upon me, that if I obtain such an Order of my great SAVIOUR, unto His *good Angel* to do me good Offices, as may in the Way I have now begun be waited and hoped for, my Welfare is in a most comprehensive, and indeed incomprehensible Manner provided for. So, I am going on, with my *Evening-Sacrifices*, more explicitly and more copiously than ever, to consider the *angelical Ministry;* and with such Supplications, to ask for the Favours of GOD.

Some strange Things are a coming to me!

22. G. D. The holy Method of Tasting the *Love* of our SAVIOUR to us in every Thing should be sett before the Flock, yett more clearly, fully, effectually.

23. G. D. I am Renewing my Instructions to my dear *Sammy*, for the porismatic Way of Reading the sacred Scriptures. I am wonderfully refreshed, by his telling of me, that he has already used it. I animate and encourage and assist his proceeding in it.

24. G. D. I give a Visit unto my Relatives at *Charlestown;* with Essays to discharge my Duty to each of them.

25. G. D. The Country is brought into dreadful Distresses. And they grow upon us apace towards a great Extremity. Our excellent Governour converses with me upon that Head, and I am with his Assistances, projecting several Things, that may have a Tendency to rescue us from the impending Destruction.

26. G. D. One of those Things, is, an Association of more sensible and Judicious and thoughtful Men, who shall apply their Thoughts, unto the dreadful Case before us.

26 *d.* x *m. Friday.* This Day, I sett apart, for supplications, that I may be supported under my dreadful Distress and carry it well under it, and make very great Improvements in Piety from it.

O my dear SAVIOUR, I was never so near to Thee, never so full of Thee, never so much what I would be, as I am under the dreadful Distress, which thou hast brought upon me.

I had other Petitions also to spread before the Lord.

27. G. D. A poor, froward, wretched Man, a Scholemaster, one suffering extreme Wants, much thro' his own haughty Folly; I must, (altho! yea, *because,* I have suffered great Injuries and Abuses from him,) contrive all I can to gett Releefs and Employments for him.

* 28. G. D. My Entertainments in my Library, when I go up for the Supplications of the Evening, are wonderful! wonderful! Astonishing! Pen and Ink, are too weak Things to utter them!

I must now make as full a Collection as I can, of the

Passages and Instructions, which occur in the sacred
Scripture, concerning the *good Angels*, who belong to the
Armies of my dear SAVIOUR, whereof there is no Number.
And I would successively employ the Hints which these
will give me to amplify upon them, in my Prayers, that the
Ministry of the *good Angels may* be by my glorious LORD
allowe'd and ordered for me.   In my improving and applying these Hints, I find my Heart exceedingly expanding
towards a Conformity to, and a Communion with the
heavenly World.   My Enjoyments are astonishing; It is
impossible for me to write what I meet withal: and it will
not be convenient perhaps, anon, for me to do it, if I could.
Oh! My SAVIOUR, thou makest me a rich Compensation,
for all the Sorrows, which are appointed for me.

29. G. D.   There are some Articles of Supplication,
whereof I may do well to take a more expressive and perpetual Notice, in the public Prayers.   The Flock should be
drawn into the Desires; and hereby also, they will be more
instructed how to pray in their Families.

30. G. D.   My poor *Nancy!* My dear *Nancy!*

31. G. D.   Fresh Occasions I see, to study, that my
aged Parent may be rendred as comfortable as may be.

January. [1718-19.]   1. G. D.   My Lecture occurs on
this *New-Years-Day*.   I take Occasion from the Day, to
inculcate such Maxims and Lessons of Piety, as are proper
for such a Time, and may from thence receive a singular
Efficacy.

That I may be the better prepared for what is before
me, I rise very early, and making a Recollection, I Repent
before the Lord, for all the Miscarriages which the former
years of my Life have been fill'd withal; and give Thanks
for the Favours of Heaven to me in the years; And by a
fresh Flight unto my SAVIOUR, I secure my Happiness,
in case this year should prove the Year of my Death; And
I cry to the Lord, that He would prepare me for all the

Changes and Sorrows, which may be this Year to come upon me.

I enjoy'd very gracious Assistances from Heaven, in my public Action.

2. G. D. Our excellent Governour presses me to form a significant Society of our superiour and principal Gentlemen who may project Methods for the Deliverance of the Countrey from the dreadful Distresses, which it is running into.

3. G. D. There is a Scholar of a very hopeful Character, whose Welfare I would much study for, and bring him into Employments. Ταρδ.[1]

*4. G. D. I have cried unto my SAVIOUR, that He would bestow a more diligent Heart upon me. He does, in a surprising way, hear my Cry. Oh! precious, Oh! welcome, the Scourges, by which my Desire is accomplished! I am now become such an early Riser, that I employ the Light of the Candle, in my morning-Studies. But, oh! the vast Improvement in Piety, as well as in Usefulness which I may, yea, which I do, make from, the Diligence, which I am now rais'd unto. My morning-Visits to Heaven, as well as my evening ones, have new, rich, high Entertainments in them. GOD makes the Outgoings of the Morning and of the Evening, to rejoice with me.

5. G. D. Our Scholemaster being upon a Remove, it is of great Consequence to the Flock, that a good Scholemaster be brought into the Succession.

6. G. D. The Condition of the Schole, will now require me, to take in a Manner the whole Care, of my dear *Sammy's* Erudition. May the Glorious One send His good Angel, to instruct me, how I shall order the child, and how I shall do unto him.

7. G. D. Sometimes among my Relatives, I have reckoned my personal Enemies, with Projections that I

[1] Ward. Robert Ward (died 1732) was a graduate of the College in 1719.

may do good unto them. I am sorry that among my personal Enemies, I must now reckon some of my Relatives; unaccountable Creatures! But I have a little penetrated into their inexplicable Character and Conduct. I must watch over my Spirit, and study to carry it as well unto them, as if they were better affected unto me. And heartily pray for them.

8. G. D. Some Letters unto the Scotch Ministers arrived in our East Countrey, may have a Tendency to hearten them in that Work of GOD, which they have to do, in those new Plantations; and more particularly for the christianizing of the Indians there.

9. G. D. The Ministers of this Town, have their stated Interviews. There is now a good Number of us. May I perpetually contrive, that every time we meet they may hear something from me, which may have a Tendency to render them, wiser and better, and more useful in their Stations.

10. G. D. Another Brother of our Church; a godly Man, is fallen into a crazy Melancholy; I must approve myself a true Shepherd, on this Occasion.

A poor Indian perishing under a Cancer calls for my Compassions.

* 11. G. D. It would be to me many Wayes of mighty Consequence for me not only to obtain a strong Faith of the wonderful GLORY which the Servants of our SAVIOUR shall enjoy in an heavenly Work; but also arrive to clear Ideas, and Sentiments of that Glory. T'wil greatly sanctify me; and it will præpare mee for Triumphs over my Approaching Death: and be of an unknown Advantage; to me and many others.

In order hereunto, I would cry with Importunity unto my SAVIOUR, *I beseech thee, shew me thy Glory.* And I would often make this Glory a Subject of my Meditation, when I go up in the Evening, to converse with Him, in my Library.

12. G. D. Several observable People in our Church, under very disconsolate melancholy, miserable Circumstances. I must on the Occasion draw the Church into Christian and suitable Expressions of Brotherly-kindness, in the Prayers I make on these Occasions.

13. G. D. There is one Child in my Family, whose Condition calls for my more singular Compassion and Concernment, that —

14. G. D. My Kinsman at *Sandwyche*, I may do many Services to him and his. I also see many Services that I may putt him upon doing for the Kingdome of GOD.

15. G. D. I will take my first Opportunity to give unto the Public my Friend *Boehm's* Recapitulation of the Heads, whereon good Men are in this heartless Time of Religion, at work for the Kingdome of GOD; in Hopes of drawing in others to do what they can upon the various Articles.

16. G. D. I am now upon writing Letters for *Europe*. In each of them I will study as exquisitely as I can, what Services to the Kingdome of God, I may putt my Correspondents upon the doing of.

17. G. D. Several People in very poor Circumstances, call for my Assistences.

A worthy Gentleman of my Neighbourhood, having buried a Child last Night, I would this evening Visit his Family, and pray with them, and speak what may suit the Occasion.

* 18. G. D. There is a Book of Piety, which tis observable, all Christians of all Communions, have approved and valued. It is, *Th. a Kempis*, his Book, *De Imitatione CHRISTI*.[1] It may be of some good Consequence for me,

---

[1] This book had an experience in Massachusetts, at an earlier day (1669). "The Court, being informed that there is now in the presse, reprinting, a booke, tit. Imitacons of Christ, or to that purpose, written by Thomas a Kempis, a Popish minister, wherein is conteyned some things that are less safe to be infused among the people of this place, doe commend it to the licensers of the

to read a Chapter in that Book, the last Thing I do, every Night, before my going to my Lodging, till I have gone through it.[1]

The Conclusion of the lvi Year[2]

21 *d.* xi *m.* 1718 [–19.] *Wednesday.* My glorious LORD, has inflicted a new and a sharp Chastisement upon me.

The Consort, in whom I flattered myself with the View and Hopes of an uncommon Enjoyment, has dismally confirmed it unto me, that our *Idols* must prove our *Sorrows*.

Now and then, in some of the former Years, I observed and suffered grievous Outbreakings of her proud Passions; but I quickly overcame them, with my victorious Love, and in the Methods of Meekness and Goodness. *And, O my SAVIOUR, I ascribe unto thee all the Glory of it, and I wondrously praise thee for it;* I do not know, that I have to this Day spoke one impatient or unbecoming Word unto her; tho' my Provocations have been unspeakable; and, it may be, few Men in the World, would have born them as I have done.

But this last Year has been full of her prodigious Paroxysms; which have made it a Year of such Distresses with me, as I have never seen in my Life before.

When the Paroxysms have gone off, she has treated me still with a Fondness, that it may be, few Wives in the World have arriv'd unto. But in the Returns of them (which of late still grow more and more frequent,) she has insulted me with such Outrages, that I am at a Loss, which I should ascribe them to; whether a Distraction, (which may

press, the more full revisall thereof, and that in the meane time there be no further progresse in that worke," *Mass. Col. Rec.,* iv. Pt, ii, 424. The first known colonial edition was made by Christopher Sower, on his Germantown, Penn., press, in 1749; and no edition appeared in New England until after the war of independence.

[1] Nearly seven leaves of the Diary were torn out at this place. The cause is developed in what follows.

[2] These entries are written in a separate note book.

be somewhat Hæreditary,) or to a Possession; (whereof the Symptoms have been too direful to be mentioned.)

In some other papers, I leave a more particular Account of these Things.[1]

But, what I have here to relate, is; that she had expressed such a Venome, against my reserved Memorials, of Experiences in, and Projections for, the Kingdome of GOD, as has obliged me to lay the Memorials of this Year, I thought, where she would not find them.

It has been a Year, wherein I have made more Advances in Piety, than in many former Years. Perhaps, my Journey thro' the Wilderness just expiring, I must rid more way in one year now, than in forty before. My dear SAVIOUR has made the Distresses, which the vile Frames and Ways of my poor Wife have given me, to be the happy Occasions and Instruments, of my Improvements in those Things, which make a rich Amends, for all the Troubles which His holy Wisdome has ordered for me: and they have been welcome to me. As in this Year, I have kept many Dayes of Prayer; (on some of which, I entred some Things relating to the angelical World, which I would not lose upon easy terms:) and I have had such Contrivances for better ordering of my Walk with God, as have been somewhat singular; so for every Day, I have noted, my Purposes of Services for the Kingdome of GOD. For fear of what might happen, I have not one disrespectful Word of this proud Woman, in all the Papers. But this Week, she has in her indecent Romaging found them; and she not only detains them from me, but either she has destroy'd them, or she does protest, that I shall never see them any more.

I have offered unto her, to blott out with her Pen whatever she would not have to be there. But no loving Entreaties of mine can prevail with her to restore them. Only

[1] Fortunately not preserved.

she gives me hope of restoring some time or other, the Papers of the four or five preceding Years, which this un-gentlewomanly Woman has also stolen.

My glorious Lord, will have me dy to every thing: and so I must be Dead, even to those Papers, which are of more value to me, than any temporal Estate I can pretend unto. *But, at thy Command, I resign these things also. I make Sacrifices of them! Sacrifices to the Disposal of thy wise, just good Providence, O my SAVIOUR!*

On the Day when this my LVIth Year commenced, I entred some strong Apprehensions, that before I saw an-other Birth-day, my Life would be finished. There is yett above three weeks time, to have what I apprehended, most literally Accomplished. And it may be, what befalls these Memorials of my Life, may be for an Admonition to me, that my Life itself is terminating. But if it should be ful-filled only in a *Sentence of Death* passed thus on the *Memo-rials of my Life*, how favourably am I dealt withal!

This Loss of the Papers where I entred my Designs, upon the Article of GOOD DEVISED; (the G. D. stood for it 365 times in a year;) calls upon me, to humble myself exceedingly before the Lord, for my exceeding Barrenness in the *Inventions of Wisdome*, to do good, unto all about me.

And, if the *Book of Remembrance* written by me, be lost; yett, a Gracious GOD, may have in His *Book of Remem-brance*, what He may accept, of my poor Essays to do good, when I have thought upon His Name.

They who destroyed *Jeremiah's* Roll, gott nothing by it. This unhappy Woman getts nothing, by what she does unto mine. Her base Carriage to me, makes me only write more than else I should have done: and will but quicken, yea, mightily augment, my Fruitfulness in the little Remainder of my Pilgrimage.

There has been one very gracious and singular Display of the Providence administred by my lovely SAVIOUR.

I have lived for near a Year in a continual Anguish of
Expectation, that my poor Wife, by exposing her Madness,
would bring a Ruine on my Ministry. But now it is exposed, my Reputation is marvellously præserved among
the People of GOD, and there is come such a general and
violent Blast upon her own, as I cannot but be greatly
troubled at.

I will now go on.

21. G. D. This is the Day, on which I still contrive
to be a Blessing unto some or other of my Relatives. Ofter
on this Day, I have thought, how to be so, unto my aged
Parent. But this Day my Thought is a little singular. I
have a Father, who will count every one a Blessing unto
him, who putts him into a Way of being a Blessing unto
others. I am sure, it will rejoice him to be so unto me
whom GOD has made a Son unto him in some uncommon
Circumstances. I cannot enough admire the Mercy of
my glorious LORD, in sparing to me the Life of so excellent
a Friend, even for such a Time of Distress as is now come
upon me. I am too ready to fly unto Creatures. And I
have no Man upon Earth but him to fly to. I will continually repair to him, open my Case to him, open my Heart
ease my Mind in that way.

But, who can tell, what his Prayers may obtain for
me.?

22. G. D. I am aware of certain Points to be inculcated, which the Welfare of this unhappy People mightily
turns upon. And I begin to have in View certain Methods
for the Inculcation of them.

I must look up to my glorious Lord for His Direction

23. G. D. Writing to a Gentleman of notable Capacities in *London*, I animate him, with the best Charms I can
to apply them unto the glorious Intention of serving the
Kingdome of God.

This Day I sett apart, for the Devotions of the Closett

The usual Occasions and Petitions, were what I had in the Day my Eye unto.

But what I more especially considered was the dreadful Distress, which the foolish Woman brings upon me, and upon my unhappy Family.

I never find myself in any danger of sinking in the boisterous Floods, but when I am at some Distance from a lovely SAVIOUR, by my Thoughts of Him, abating. This Day, I was greatly helped from Above, to renew my Flights unto Him, and after sore Conflicts, with dark Apprehensions concerning the Indignation of GOD against me for my Miscarriages, I had my Soul powerfully irradiated with Assurances, that the blessed JESUS, (to whom I am entirely devoted, and for whom I am continually speaking and pleading,) is my Advocate: the Consequences whereof, I took the Comfort of.

As for the Distress now upon me, I declared unto the LORD, that if it were necessary, to finish my Repentance, and quicken my Obedience, and render me more lively in the Service of God, and more useful unto His People, I did heartily consent unto the Continuance of it. Only I cried unto my SAVIOUR, that He would enable me to carry it well under my Distress, and not leave me in any Way to sin against Him. All along as well as now, this has been my main Desire. I have more desired the Grace to behave myself well under my Distress, than to be delivered from it.

But my melted and contrite Heart, was revived with a strange Assurance of a Deliverance near unto me. My SAVIOUR has given a Good Angel, His order to do me good.

24. G. D. Diverse new Objects of Charity, and Compassion.

* 25. G. D. Behold, an Exercise of PIETY, taught me by my SAVIOUR, which has not been commonly thought upon.

When I suffer any Distress, I will make this use of it. I will consider some Distress like unto it, occurring in the Sufferings of my SAVIOUR. Hereupon, I will consider the Love of my SAVIOUR, expressed in such His wonderful Sufferings. I will then consider the Sufferings of my SAVIOUR, as infinitely meritorious; and as particularly purchasing for me, these three Benefits; First, the Pardon of my Sin which has brought my Distress upon me; secondly, the Strength to carry it well under my Distress; thirdly, a Deliverance out of my Distress, when He sees His Time for it. Finally, while I am in the midst of these Considerations, I will reckon my bitter Distress exceedingly sweetened, by the Conformity which there may be found in it, unto any Sufferings of my SAVIOUR; and by the Operation which it has to lead me thus unto Him.

How much was my SAVIOUR grieved, by the ill Treats, which His espoused Jewish Church, gave unto Him!

26. G. D. It has been very much my Study, that whatever Distresses I may suffer at any time, the Flock may have Revenues out of my Sufferings. My Afflictions have been rendred even comfortable to me, by the Prospect which I have had of their proving profitable to the Flock, which my SAVIOUR has committed unto me.

Well, what shall I do, that from the Distresses now upon me, the Flock may reap some sensible Benefits?

One thing that I will now more than ever insist upon, shall be an Experiment, which I have wonderfully made in my Distresses; That a Soul full of a CHRIST will be marvellously prepared and strengthened for all Encounters of Adversity. My Flock shall find me more full of a CHRIST than ever I have been; and more full of Essays that they may be so too.

Moreover, a Man of some Capacity and Ingenuity, who came under the Censure of our church above twenty Years ago, is yett living in the Town. I do this day, write as loving, as charming, as pungent a Letter, as I can for my Life, to recover him out of the Snares in which he is perishing. I do it with earnest Cries unto the glorious Lord for the Success of it.

27. G. D. The Time requires it, and the Condition of my Family calls for it, that we come into the Methods of a reasonable and reputable Frugality for our Expences. My Wife, in her froward Pangs, having happily thrown the Administration into my Hands, I gladly take it. And having paid off my Debts, I now suffer not my Folks to run upon Scores many Articles of our Expences, but still pay as we fetch. I hope, that as an Obedience to my SAVIOUR dictates this prudent and righteous Way of proceeding, so my Family will come into a better Condition to glorify Him.

28. G. D. Certain Points of Conduct, Prudence and Goodness, relating to the Gentlewoman which is my dear Father's wife, that may have a Tendency to his Comfort, are what I have now before me.

29. G. D. There must be something yett more effectually done, that our School may be supplied with a Schole-Master who will serve the Kingdome of GOD.

Provide Bibles, to be scattered in our ungospellized Places.

30. G. D. I am writing Letters, to some Gentlemen beyond-Sea, wherein I animate their Concern to serve the Kingdome of God. And other Letters to our eastern Parts, of the like Tendency.

I am tried unto the uttermost, in my domestic Circumstances. But my dear SAVIOUR so upholds me, so strengthens me, so sanctifies me, and admitts me to such Communion with Himself as makes me a glorious Compensation. If my Distresses are necessary to preserve and maintain the Life of GOD in me, I heartily consent unto the Continuance thereof upon me. But I am sure my SAVIOUR is going to deliver me.

31. G. D. A poor Man, under grievous Distraction, must have my Compassion expressed for him, in all the ways I can think of.

February. * 1. G. D. I will have my Meditations more exquisitely employ'd than ever; upon that Point *What are the Sentiments of the Glorified in the heavenly World?* Oh! Whither may I be caught up in such Meditations? And what holy Impressions may they leave upon me!

My Sermon, this Day, shall touch upon some Instances

At Evening, when I went up to my Library, my gracious LORD, carried me up, into a marvellous Communion with the Glorified; a marvellous Harmony with them.

And I know, that a good Angel of the heavenly World in coming down by an Order of my SAVIOUR to do me good.

2. G. D. I mightily desire, to raise in the Minds of the Flock, a very wonderful Sense of that astonishing Mystery, *GOD becoming a Man in our JESUS*, and instruct them in the Way of improving this Mystery to the most glorious Purposes.

3. G. D. The dreadful Distresses which a furious and froward Stepmother brings upon my Family, as they oblige me to lay upon the Children the most solemn Charges of all possible Dutifulness unto her, so, they furnish me with Opportunities, mightily to press all Piety upon them, and a particular Expression of it in their Prayers and Cries unto the Lord. Oh! may they be brought nearer to GOD, by the sad Things that are come upon them.

4. G. D. The Lord having wonderfully begun to restore my Brother *Walter* unto his public Services, Oh! how affectionately shall I join with him in thankful Contrivances to glorify our SAVIOUR!

5. G. D. I have new and bright Views given me, about a work I have to do, in bearing Testimonies to the Godhead of my SAVIOUR.

6. G. D. I will prevail with Mr. J. *Winthrop*, to furnish me, with some of his Father's and Grandfather's noble

Remedies, and I will make myself the Dispenser of them unto he miserable.[1]

7. G. D.   One of the Ministers in the Town being sick, will in the most brotherly Manner employ Prayers for him.

*8. G. D.   I am endeavouring more than ever to affect myself, with Views of the Aspect which the *Godhead* of my SAVIOUR has upon all the affairs of the great Salvation. This I do, with a particular Intention, to become the better qualified and furnished, for the bearing of a Testimony to the Glory of my SAVIOUR; which I beg Him to assist me in.

My Soul is irradiated, sanctified, fortified, with marvelous Discoveries.

9. G. D.   I am in a Way to form a Society, whose peculiar Intention, it shall be, to consider and prosecute *what may be done for the Good of the Church, which we belong unto?*   I hope for many Services to the Flock, from this Association.

10. G. D.   Oh! my poor, distressed, oppressed Family! Shall not I take the several abused Children, and call them to me in my Study, and there not only with all possible Insinuations and Importunities, press them to consider their present Affliction as a strong and loud Argument for their Turning unto GOD, but also pray with them, and with fervent and weeping Prayers carry them unto the Lord, and also obtain Promises of a pious Behaviour from them.

11. G. D.   A Sermon at the Lecture on the Methods of Piety, wherein one may make ones BIRTHDAY an Opportunity for serious Recollections and Resolutions, may be a Service to the Religion of my SAVIOUR.   To morrow is to be my *Lecture,* as well as my *Birth-day.*   Lett me then endeavour it.

[1] See Vol. I. 3 *n.*

THE COURSE OF MY MINISTRY THIS YEAR.[1]

16 *d*. 12 *m*. [*February*.] 1717 [–18.]   On Luk. IV, 25.   A Sermon, on the Exercises of Piety, wherewith *Widows* are to glorify God.

23 *d*. 12 *m*.   On, Hag. I. 9.   Sins of *Omission;* and particularly Men's Neglecting to *build the House of God*.   (And I administred the Eucharist.)

27 *d*. 12 *m*. *Thursday*.   A general Fast.   On Jam. IV. 3.   How to manage our Prayers, that we may not *ask amiss*.

2 *d*. 1 *m*. [*March*.]   On Col. I. 12.   A glorious Blessedness for the Faithful in a future State, an heavenly world.   Intending several Sermons on it.

9 *d*. 1 *m*.   On, Rev. II. 9.   Good Christians meeting with great Calamities;   But our Saviour *knowing* all.

13 *d*. 1 *m*. *Thursday*.   The Lecture, on Zech. XIV. 9.   The *Kingdome* of our SAVIOUR, to be one day enlarged.

16 *d*. 1 *m*.   On, Col. I. 12.   A Prosecution of an Exhortation, upon what I began a fortnight ago.

23 *d*. 1 *m*.   On Col. I. 12.   The glorious Blessedness of the Faithful, an *Inheritance;* and, for *Saints*.

30 *d*. 1 *m*.   On Col. I. 12.   The glorious *Light*, in the Inheritance of the Saints.

6 *d*. 2 *m*. [April.]   A.M.   At the Old South, on Cant. II. 3.   The *Shade* and the *Fruit*, enjoy'd from our Saviour, (the Eucharist succeeding.)

P. M.   At the Old North, on Col. I. 12.   Finishing what I was upon, the last Lord's-day.

13 *d*. 2 *m*.   On Col. I. 12.   A *Meetness* for the Inheritance of the Saints.

20 *d*. 2 *m*.   On Act. XVI. 14.   An *Heart which the Lord has opened*.   (And I administred the Eucharist.)

24 *d*. 2 *m*. *Thursday*.   The Lecture.   On Psal. XXIX. 3.   The *Voice* of the Lord, on the *Waters*.   Endeavouring an Holy Improvement of the dismal Inundation, which has lately made so much Destruction on the Provinces of *Holland*, and the Sea-Coast of *Germany*.

27 *d*. 2 *m*.   At Roxbury.   A. M. on Isa. LXV. 23.   P. M. on Isa. LV. 8.

4 *d*. 3 *m*. [*May*.]   On Col. I. 12.   My seventh Discourse on *Meetness for the Inheritance of the Saints in Light;* finishing the Sub-

[1] We now revert to the original entries for this year.   See p. 583, *supra*.

ject, with a Sermon of *Expostulations*, for the Life of Piety, which brings to the glorious Blessedness.

11 *d.* 3 *m.* At the Old Church. On Matth. XII. 13.

18 *d.* 3 *m.* On Heb. II. 18. The Way of addressing our SAVIOUR, for Succour under *Temptations*.

21 *d.* 3 *m. Wednesday.* At the Ordination of a Pastor in the Church of the *Baptists.* On, Rom. XV. 7. Our Duty to receive all those, whom CHRIST *receives to the Glory of God.*

25 *d.* 3 *m.* On 2. Tim. IV. 22. The Blessedness of having the Lord JESUS CHRIST *with our Spirit.*

1 *d.* 4 *m.* [*June.*] On Gen. XVIII. 14. Nothing *too hard* for the Lord. The infinite *Power* of God, practically improved, in regard of Distresses.

5 *d.* 4 *m. Thursday.* The Lecture. On 2. Tim. III. 2. *Self-Love*, the Root of Wickedness and Wretchedness in which the World is languishing. The General-Assembly sitting.

8 *d.* 4 *m.* On 3. Joh. 4. The *Prosperity* of a SOUL.

15 *d.* 4 *m.* On Hag. II. 7. The *Desire all Nations* found in our SAVIOUR. (And I administred the Eucharist.)

22 *d.* 4 *m.* On Rom. XIV. 17. The *Righteousness*, which belongs to the *Kingdome* of God.

29 *d.* 4 *m.* On Jam. IV. 13. The vain Presumption of *living* and *thriving* in the World, which People, especially in their Youth, are prone unto. (On the Occasion of an hopeful young Man, who lived with my Son-in-Law, drowned in the Harbour.)

6 *d.* 5 *m.* On Rom. XIV. 17. The *Peace*, to be found in the *Kingdome* of God.

13 *d.* 5 *m.* On Rom. XIV. 17. The *Joy*, in the holy Spirit.

17 *d.* 5 *m. Thursday.* The Lecture. On 2. Tim. IV. 7. How to manage the *Combates* of Christianity, against various Temptations, which Christians commonly meet withal.

20 *d.* 5 *m.* On Neh. I. 11. *Pious Desires*, an Evidence of *Piety.*

23 *d.* 5 *m. Wednesday.* At *Brooklyn*, A Day of Prayer. On Isa. XXX. 18. God *waiting to be gracious.*

27 *d.* 5 *m.* On Act. XIII. 45, 48. The very *different Reception*, which the Word of GOD, finds in the same Auditory.

3 *d.* 6 *m.* [*August.*] On Col. III. 3. Our *Life hid* with CHRIST in GOD.

10 *d.* 6 *m.* On Cant. V. 9. What there is in our beloved SAVIOUR, more than there is in any other Object, most beloved in the World. (And I administred the Eucharist.)

II · 38

12 *d*. 6 *m*. *Tuesday*.   The Lecture at *Roxbury*.   On 3. Joh. 4. The *Prosperity* of a Soul.

14 *d*. 6 *m*. *Thursday*.   The Lecture; in the Room of another who wanted Help.   On 1. Pet. V. 10.   The *eternal Glory* of the Faithful.

17 *d*. 6 *m*.   On Col. III. 4.   CHRIST our *Life*.

24 *d*. 6 *m*.   On Col. III. 4.   CHRIST *Appearing*, and we *with Him*, in *Glory*.

28 *d*. 6 *m*. *Thursday*.   The Lecture.   On 1. Pet. V. 10.   Finishing what I began a Fortnight ago.

31 *d*. 6 *m*.   On Lam. 1. 16.   Our great SAVIOUR, the grand *Comforter* that releeves our Soul.

7 *d*. 7 *m*. [*September*.]   On Eph. III. 8.   The *unsearchable Riches* of CHRIST.

14 *d*. 7 *m*.   On Eph. III. 8.   Finishing what I began the last Lord's-day.

21 *d*. 7 *m*.   Changing with one of the Ministers in the Town, (who wanted such a releef), I preached at the Fourth Church, on Act. XIII. 45, 48.

23 *d*. 7 *m*.   On, Matth. XVII. i.   The Remark our Saviour setts on a *seventh* Day.   And, a View of things in the *heavenly World*, strengthening us to undergo Troubles on Earth.

(Beginning a Course of Sermons, on the Transfiguration of our SAVIOUR.)

5 *d*. 8 *m*. [*October*.]   On Isa. XXV. 6.   The *Feast* in the *Mountain*.   (And I administred the Eucharist.)

12 *d*. 8 *m*.   At the New North.   On Matth. XII. 13.

God ordered for me, a precious Opportunity, to treat very solemnly with the Souls, that are swarmed from me.

19 *d*. 8 *m*.   On Job. VII. 10.   The dead Man's *Place knowing him no more*.   (A Funeral Sermon, on Mr. *Bernard*, of *Andover*.)

26 *d*. 8 *m*.   On Matth. XVII. 1.   *Brothers* united in the Favours of Heaven.   *Relatives* considered in our Essays to do good.   The Gospel *well attested* to.   Great *Enjoyment* follow'd with great *Abasements*.   *Poor-men* raised unto Heavenly Priviledges.

3 *d*. 9 *m*. [*November*.]   On Joh. XXI. 17.   The *Godhead* of our SAVIOUR, and the marks by which a true *Love* to Him is to be discovered.

9 *d*. 9 *m*.   On Matth. X. 29.   The *Providence* of GOD, how to be considered and acknowledged in all Occurences.   (On the Occasion of some Neighbours drowned the last Week; and carried all together unto the Grave, which afforded a very affecting Spectacle.)

20 *d.* 9 *m. Thursday.* The Lecture on Jer. IV. 2. The Religion of an *Oath.*

23 *d.* 9 *m.* On Matth. XVII. i. None going to *Heaven*, but such as our SAVIOUR *carries up.* Seasonable *Retirements* needful to spiritual *Enjoyments. Pains* to be taken that we may enjoy GOD and CHRIST and Heaven; but Pains *well-rewarded.* This lower world, to be left, that we may enjoy a *better World.* The Victorious over strong Temptations finding a wonderful Recompence of their Victories.

7 *d.* 10 *m.* [*December.*] On Luk. IX. 28. 29. The Pattern of our Saviour at *Prayer* to His Father. And the *transfiguring* Efficacy which *Prayer* will have upon the Minds of them that use it.

11 *d.* 10 *m. Thursday.* A Day of general Thanksgiving. I preached on 1. Cor. X. 31. *Glorying* in the LORD.

14 *d.* 10 *m.* On Matth. XVII. 2. The *Glories* of our SAVIOUR demonstrated and insinuated, in the *Shine* of His Face, as the *Sun,* when He was *transfigured.*

21 *d.* 10 *m.* On Matth. XVII. 2. And Mar. IX. 3. Remarks on the *shining Raiment* of our Saviour, in His Transfiguration.

28 *d.* 10 *m.* On Joh. XXI. 17. Managing an Exhortation to the *Love* of a most lovely SAVIOUR. (And I administred the Eucharist.)

1 *d.* 11 *m.* [January, 1718-19.] *Thursday.* The Lecture. On Psal. XC. 9. The Years of our Life spent like the *Telling of a Story.* Entertaining the People with Meditations proper for a *New Years Day.*

4 *d.* 11 *m.* On Zech. XIV. 8. The *Winter* no disagreeable Season for the *living Waters* of the Gospel, to have their *lively Efficacy.* (A very cold, winter-day.)

11 *d.* 11 *m.* A. M. At the New North, on Cant. I. 4.

P.M. At the Old North, On Matth. XVII. 3. and Luk. IX. 31. The *Glory* of the Faithful, after their Departure out of this World.

AS AN APPENDIX TO THE COURSE OF MY MINISTRY,
— IN MY STOLEN PAPERS.

18 *d.* 11 *m.* On Matth. XVII. 3. The *Wonderful Glory* reserved for the Faithful in another World; (Finishing what I had begun before.)

25 *d.* 11 *m.* On Joh. VI. 68. The *Words of eternal Life,* with our SAVIOUR.

1 *d.* 12 *m.* On Matth. XVII. 3. Both *Law* and *Prophets* testify-

ing to our SAVIOUR; and both *Jews* and *Gentiles* having the *same* SAVIOUR, and the *same* Religion. And the *glorified* ones conversing with our SAVIOUR, and with one another.

8 *d.* 12 *m.* On Matth. XVII. 3. The *raised Bodies* of the Faithful, appearing in *Glory*.[1]

To Thomas Prince. M.H.S.

25 *d.* X *m.* [December.] 1719.

MY DEAR FRIEND, — Considering the Agitation in the Minds of people throughout the Countrey on our late *Aurora Borealis*, I knew not, but a Sheet given to the public upon it, might have some considerable Benefits attending of it.

Under the Influence of such a Thought, I wrote yesterday the poor Sheet, which now waits upon you; and which our Patriarch [Increase Mather] on Perusal this morning returns to me, with his *Imprimatur*.

I present the Sheet unto your Acceptance; and submitt it entirely to your Judgment.

If you think it may do any Good, I leave it unto you, to give it unto what Bookseller you please. Only offering my opinion, that the more speedily the Bookseller dispatches it, the more he will find his Account in it. It will probably sell throughout the Countrey, if the Countrey know that it is to be sold. You know the Smiths motto, Dum calet percute.

If you incline to suppress it, I shall in that also be entirely satisfied. Only then, you may do well to give unto one of our Newswriters (to day) the little Paper that has by itself the Account of the *Aurora* in it.[2]

I wholly leave all to you; and thank you for your Servants, which now return to you.

---

[1] On March 12 Mather preached the Lecture, and Sewall makes the following entry in his *Diary* (III. 214): "For my part, the Dr. spake so much of his visions of Convulsion and Mutiny, mentioning our being a dependent Government, and the danger of Parliamentary Resentments: that I was afraid the printing of it might be an Invitation to the Parliament, to take away our Charter. Gov'r would have put it to the vote; but when he saw how hardly it went, caused the Secretary to break off in the midst."

"1 *d.* 1 *m.* [1718–19.] The Repentance of *Sarah Forbes*, whose first born was born four or five Months before the lawful Time, was offered and accepted." *Cotton Mather's MS. Records of the Second Church*, III.

[2] It was printed as *A Voice from Heaven*.

May the Glorious Lord graciously direct and succeed your Studies. I am, Sir, Your Brother and Servt.

Co. MATHER.

To THOMAS PRINCE. M.H.S.

Tuesday Morn. [1719.]

MY GOOD FRIEND, — Our good Friend Mr. *Green*,[1] has undoubtedly something in hand that we know not of.

He has a great and just Regard for the Satisfaction of Mr. *Clap*. The Sermon of Mine, which he has to do for him, is but a single sheet.

He has had it with him, I think, about seven Weeks. About a fortnight ago I had the first half Sheet; not yett, the last.

I don't complain. For I take Mr. *Green*, to be so sincere, and hearty, and pious a Friend, that he will do *all he can* for us. But so it is.

You know, Sir, that in such Things, as that which your Goodness has just now permitted, and even committed unto the Press, much of the Decency and Cogency and all of that will turn upon the Time.

You will therefore, having entred into the Trouble of it, go on to inform yourself, how tis at the Press; and use your Instances, that a proper Dispatch be used.

I should be willing that good Mr *Green* send it me by his Lad, before he compose the latter End of it, because I would correct a Passage.

I know not whether I should have given you the Trouble of these Incitations, if it had not been for the Opportunity it gives me, of presenting a Manuscript unto your Perusal at your Leisure; after which (if I live) I may humbly ask your Judgment upon it. It has long Lain by me. But I am at Length upon sending a Copy of it over to *London*, if you approve of it.

Come; we are now getting into our Operations, of together carrying on Services for the Kingdome of our God, and for the Beloved of our Souls, In whom, I am, Sir, Your Brother and Servt.,

Co. MATHER.[2]

[1] Bartholomew Green.

[2] For a curious letter of Mather to Judge Sewall, written in April, 1720, and James Savage's comments upon it, see 4 *Collections*, II. 122.

"22 d. 1 m. [*March*.] 1719–20. At a Church Meeting, Mr. John Buchanan was chose to the Office of a Deacon.

"The Church also chose Messieurs *John Clark, Thomas Hutchinson, Adam Winthrop, Edward Hutchinson, John Ruck, Samuel Greenwood, John Frizzel,* and *John Charnock,* to act as a Committee, in Concert with the Deacons, on the be-

To Daniel Neal.   A.A.S.

5 d. V m. [July.] 1720.

Sir, — The *History of New England*,[1] whereof you have made a kind present unto me, obliges me to tender you my Thanks for the Favour you have done unto me: and for the Honour that you have done in many points unto my Countrey.

Your performance is the Reverse of what was done by the malicious and Satanic pen of one *Oldnixson* (some such Name,) in his Account of the *English Empire in America*,[2] whose History of N. E. has far more Lies than pages in it, and the more unpardonable, because contradicted in the very Book, which he was at the very same time living on, and railing at.

No doubt some of our people may inform you of certain passages in your well-penned History, which might call for a little further Elucidation; a Thing which is incident unto all Humane composures, and which must not be wondred at. But I hope, they will be all sensible, of the Candour which you generally express towards the Countrey; and of the good wishes which you have to the welfare of it.

We ought certainly to have a grateful sense of it, that any men of worth, should count such a poor, despised, maligned Countrey as ours, worthy of their Cognisance; and much more of such Pains as you have taken to represent us under an advantageous Character unto the world.

But I must confess to you, that my poor Countrey was never famous for Gratitude unto its Benefactors. Nay, we have greatly

---

half of the Church, in all Affairs proper for their Cognizance, (as formerly): but 'the Church now more particularly desired and empowered the said Committee to consider the present Condition of the Church, especially with relation to the Meeting-house, and proceed with what they shall judge expedient for the Welfare of the Church, and in Cases, which the whole Church is likely to be affected withal, to make report unto the Church of what shall be projected and proposed.

"3 d. 3 m. [*May*.] 1720. At a Meeting of the Brethren a Proposal was made by the Committee to mend the Floor of the Meeting-house, and new Model the Seats, with a Provision for a Number of Pews, was accepted and approved, and they were desired to proceed in the executing of it, and also what Repairs of the Meeting-house they shall judge necessary." *Cotton Mather's MS. Records of the Second Church*, III.

[1] Printed in London, in this year. See Sewall, *Diary*, III. 251.

[2] First printed in 1708. John Oldmixon (1673–1762) was a journalist rather than a historian.

dishonoured our Profession, by our Defect in that Vertue. They that serve N. E. expect the Recompence at the Resurrection of the Just. So, that if you hear little from us, that may appear a just consideration of your Merits, you must not be surprised at it. However, some of our best Men, are considering of the most proper Way, to testify their friendly Construction, and Thankful Reception of what you have done for us. And our excellent Governour is not wanting to prompt them unto their Duty in it.[1]

We publish a great many little Things in this Countrey, perhaps I know of one Hand, from which the press has at least Three Hundred times drawn Things, on various Argumts, and in various Languages, into the public. You will excuse us, if we trouble not our European Masters with them: only one, of these because it is the continuation of our History, is now humbly tendred unto your Acceptance.

May you be continued yett many dayes an Instrument of Service to the Kingdome of God. I am, Syr, Your obliged Friend, Brother, and Serv't.

BRIEF ON HOWELL ESTATE.

Reasons, why the Administrator on the Estate of *Nathan Howel* deceased, should be released from His Bonds of Administration, Humbly offered.

I. Tho' his Allowance of his Name, to stand for the Administration, when he was unhappily drawn into it, were no unrighteous Thing, yett it was a very Indiscreet One; It was an Error in him; It was not for the Service and Honour of the Gospel. And tho' he has been well paid for his Indiscretion, in the unaccountable Ingratitude of them who have had the only Benefit of it, yett so great Interests are hurt by his continuance in it, it appears but a Just and Right Thing, that his Bonds be no Longer continued on him.

II. It being in the power of the Judge, to change an Administrator, when there are in his Judgment sufficient Reasons for it, it

---

[1] The College gave him the degree of A.M.

"14 d. 6 m. [August.] 1720. At a Meeting of the Brethren, the Church received from the Committee an Account how far they had proceeded in the new-modelling of the Meeting-house, and voted, that the said Committee should proceed, in seeing and judging what shall be found necessary to be done for the repairing and preserving of the House. As also, that proper Methods be taken for the obtaining in a Way of Subscription, what shall be necessary to defray the Expences of it." *Cotton Mather's MS. Records of the Second Church*, III.

may be Enquired, what Reasons can be sufficient, if those be not so, to Remove the Administrator now Petitioning, which appear in his being a most Improper and Unqualified Person for it. Were he, *Non compos Mentis,* This would be thought Enough to Release him; Now if there has not been Enough either to *Declare* him so, or to *Render* him so; yett there is Enough to represent him as Incompetent.

III. The Administration has been carried on with a most unreproachable Integrity and Fidelity. A most Entangled Business has been transacted, by the managers, with an Uncommon Ingenuity, and Application; Great sums have been saved unto the estate, by the Honesty and Vigilance of their Proceedings, and many Thousands of pounds of Debt have been paid. The Trouble which remains, is very Little in comparison of that which has been already waded through. And so much being done, the Administrator may with a Good Face pray for a Dismission.

IV. Upon the most Exact stating of the Accounts, there appears a very solvent Estate; and when all Debts are paid, there yett remain many hundreds of pounds unto the Heirs. This is a Thing so Evident, that there are doubtless to be found those, who upon a due Reward allow'd unto them for the Trouble, would readily undertake the Remaining Administration.

In the mean time, the sufferings of the present Administrator are so Insupportable, and he is in such peculiar Circumstances, that he cannot but press for a Release from his Bonds, with an Importunity, which he hopes will move the Compassion of them who can deliver him.

COTTON MATHER.

Boston. Nov. 8. 1720.

1721

THE LIXth YEAR OF MY LIFE.

12 *d.* 12 *m.* [*February.*] 1720–21. *Lord's-Day.* This Year, which Oh! the Wonders of the divine Grace and Goodness and Patience, that has brought me to! begins with a Day, which obliges me to enter into the *Rest* of GOD. And very probably, it may be the Year of my Entrance into my *everlasting Rest.*

I take the Opportunity, thankfully to acknowledge the Help of GOD, thro' which I continue to this Day, and the many marvellous Blessings with which my Life has been brightened and sweetened.

And I bewayl my Unfruitfulness under the Means of Good and especially a Variety of Afflictions, which have been in this Time employ'd upon me; and the slow and small Progress I have made in a Return unto GOD.

I also confess with Sorrow, all the Impieties and Impurities, with which my Life has been defiled, and the vile Idolatries in aiming at self, with which my very Services have generally been polluted. And I make my Flight unto the great Sacrifice of my SAVIOUR, for the Pardon of them all.

I ask for the Smile of GOD upon me, in the ensuing Year; and a Soul prepared for all the Changes which it may bring upon me.

But I especially pray, that a singular Growth in an Acquaintance with a Glorious CHRIST, and in the Skill and Care of exhibiting His Glories to all about me, may be the Distinguishing Fœlicity, whereby that year shall be signalized unto me.

* G. D. In Pursuance of this Fœlicity, this Morning in dressing myself, I considered the various Benefits of my several Garments unto me; and from thence I formed agreeable Thoughts of the Benefits to be found in the Enjoyment of my admirable SAVIOUR, and I putt on CHRIST, in doing so.

Having also been lately very ill, and this being the first Lord's-day of my going abroad after my Illness, I suit my Circumstances in that Regard, as well as in my Birth-day, by a Discourse on 1. Chron. XXIX. 15. Our *Days on the Earth are as a Shadow, and there is none Abiding.*

13. G. D. How shall I convey to my Flock, such Sentiments of Piety, that they may fare the better for the Illness which I have lately had upon me, and be Gainers by my Afflictions and Experiences.

14. G. D. Several Points of Cultivation for *Samuel*, to be prosecuted.

Especially, that of determining the End of his pursuing the several Points of Learning which he has in Prosecution.

15. G. D. Think on some noble Subject, which my Kinsman at *Roxbury*, may cultivate for the Service of the Kingdome.

And encourage a Collection that some charitable Gentlemen are Meditating for the Releef of his Necessities.

16. G. D. It may have a notable Tendency to the Revival of the *Boston-Lecture*, and be for the Edification and Satisfaction of the Auditory, if the Lecturers might agree to preach on connected Subjects, and such as the Cause of *Piety* most calls to be insisted on, and such as the Auditory may be aforehand apprised of what may be looked for.

Prosecute this Design.

17. G. D. I would see whether I can't publish and scatter thro' the Countrey, certain Proposals for the reviving and præserving of Piety, by *religious Societies*, well animated and regulated, in every Plantation.

Because of my late Illness, and the Weakness yett remaining on me, I did not sett apart this Day, for Fasting with Prayer, as else I would have done, and as I use to do. Yett it was with me a Day of Sacrifices.

18. G. D. Several of the Flock are distressed with grievous Temptations.

* 19. G. D. A most gracious Providence of my dear,

kind faithful SAVIOUR, has led me to the Perusal of Mr. *Walter Marshal's* Book, on, *The Gospel-Mystery of Sanctification*.[1] In the perusing of it, I find admirable Hints, about the true Methods of arriving to the highest Pitch of *Holiness*, and some Things, whereof I had not so clear and full a Sense as now the glorious Lord has given me. I hope, to improve in Holiness exceedingly by this Communication.

20. G. D. The Committee of the Church, must be stirred up, to renew their Cares and employ their Thoughts, and revive their Meetings, for the Good of the Flock. The Time growes yett more Critical.

21. G. D. My Negro-Servant, seeks Baptism. I must use my best Endeavours to prepare him for it.

22. G. D. What shall I say to the Unhappy R. H. at his taking leave of me, going to the W. Indies.

23. G. D. Something must be done, and I must be at some Expence, for the offer of the Gospel unto our Narraganset Countrey.

24. G. D. Something should be done, that the Interviews of the Ministers every fortnight, may be rendred yett more profitable to ourselves and others.

25. G. D. A Family in the Neighbourhood, where one is distracted.

* 26. G. D. I am collecting into my *Paterna*, several Methods of conversing with my Admirable SAVIOUR, which of late Months I have been instructed in: that so having them together before me, for a frequent Perusal, I may keep in the lively Exercise of them, and may not lose them in my feeble and broken Conversation.

27. G. D. I observe a great Number of People in the Flock, whose Employments are so circumstanced, that while their Hands are employ'd, their Minds are very much at liesure, and others, in whose Business both Hands and Minds

[1] Walter Marshall (1628–1680), a Presbyterian divine, whose chief work, just mentioned, was not published until 1692.

are so I would in a Sermon propose Methods for these Neighbiours to Redeem this Time, especially in such good Thoughts as may be of the best Consequence unto them; and, if I can publish and scatter the Sermon among them.

28. G. D. Warnings to *Sammy!* About this Time, I committ unto the Press, two Treatises, wherein I propose many Services to the Kingdome of God.

First, having obtained a Time of Prayer with the Commissioners for our *Indian*-affairs, they direct the publication of my Sermon to them on that Occasion. And having held some Correspondence with the Missionaries in the *East-Indies*, I take the Occasion to exhibit some very entertaining Things relating thereunto: especially my Letter to them, and theirs to me.

(I) It is entituled, INDIA CHRISTIANA. *A Discourse delivered unto the COMMISSIONERS for the Propagation of the Gospel, among the AMERICAN* INDIANS *which is accompanied with several Instruments relating to the Glorious Design of propagating our Holy Religion, in the Eastern as well as the Western INDIES. An Entertainment, which they that are waiting for the Kingdome of GOD, will receive as Good News from a far Countrey.*[1]

(II) Moreover, observing the grievous Mispence of Time everywhere indulged, and more particularly observing how much there might be a better Husbandry of Time for good Purposes, in them whose Heads are little employed when their Hands are following their Business, and in others whose Heads as well as Hands are very much at Liesure; I preached a Sermon, which I then printed, with a Purpose to lodge it where I come, in the pastoral Visits. Tis entituled, HONESTA PARSIMONIA. *An Essay upon, Time spent as it should be; with PROPOSALS, To prevent that great Mischief, The Loss of Time; and employ the Talent of Time*

[1] Printed by B. Green, 1721.

*so watchfully and Fruitfully that a good Account may at least
be given of it.*[1]

March. 1. G. D. Encourage a Collection for the
Releef of my Kinsman at Roxbury.

2. G. D. I would endeavour that the Governour may
interpose to putt an effectual Stop to those cursed Pamphlets and Libels, wherewith some wicked Men, are endeavouring to Poison the Countrey.[2]

3. G. D. An excellent young Minister, as bright a
Thing as ever this Town produced, who is particularly
insulted and abused by the scurrilous and scandalous Libels,
I would greatly encourage him, and endeavour that he may
not be at all disheartened.[3]

4. G. D. I would endeavour, that a well-qualified
young Gentleman, who is out of Employment, may be made
a Tutor at the Colledge.

* 5. G. D. That sublime Thought, the first Idea and
Archetype of all Creatures, being in the eternal SON of GOD
who is the Wisdome of the FATHER; from whence there
follow Consequences full of Astonishments: I would cultivate it with my Contemplations, and thereby prosecute
my main Intention of His becoming all unto me.

6. G. D. A comfortable Hope, yea, a lively and joyful Perswasion, that our great SAVIOUR has taken us
under the Shadow of His Wings, and will surely do us good,
and make us righteous and holy, and save us to the uttermost, I take to belong so much to a saving Faith, that I
doubt the dropping of this Doctrine by Divines of later
Years, had been a real Disservice unto Piety; and it may

---

[1] Printed by S. Kneeland for J. Edwards, 1721.

[2] A bill entitled, "An act for preventing of libels and scandalous pamphlets,
and punishing the authors and printers," was laid before the House of Representatives, but was negatived on a second reading, March 27, 1721. *Journals.*

[3] Thomas Walter was probably the young minister, and John Checkley's
*Choice Dialogues, between a godly Minister and an honest Countryman, concerning
Election and Predestination,* one of the cursed pamphlets. Walter replied in a
Choice Dialogue between John Faustus, a Conjurer, and Jack Tory his Friend.

quicken Piety in my Flock, and have a Tendency to recover them from that condition of more feeble Christians, in which they are generally languishing, if this Doctrine were in its true Light and with a suitable Inculcation sett before them.

7. G. D. I see, I must again, with the strongest Reinforcements, direct Employments for *Sammy*, that may rescue him from the Idleness, which he is too ready to fall into.

A further Accomplishment for *Creasy*, to render him a more finished Gentleman (Oh! when, when shall I say, Christian) must be paid for.

8. G. D. Writing to my Brother *Samuel*, I propose to him a matter of great Consequence.

9. G. D. I would use Methods, that several of my poor Treatises to serve the Kingdome of GOD, may reach to the *Frederician* University; where tis possible they may be, some of them, translated for further Service.

10. G. D. May I not visit the Watch-house, and there prevail with the Watchmen, to spend their Time in devout Exercises, especially in reading Books of Piety when they are not abroad upon their Duty!

11. G. D. There are several aged People, that I have a strong Disposition to Visit, upon the Intention of bringing their Preparations for Death into its perfect Work.

* 12. G. D. *Temperate in all Things.*

13. G. D. Should not something be done towards the mending of the *Singing* in our Congregation? [1]

14. G. D. *Sammy* now returning to *Cambridge*, I would write Letters, unto some superior Students there to keep a strict Inspection on Him, and oblige him to observe certain Points of good Conduct, which I shall propose unto them.

15. G. D. I have a Kinsman, who needs my Exhortations and Stimulations, to stick well to his Business.

[1] See page 693, *infra.*

16. G. D.   There is a very wicked Party in this Countrey who fill the Land with Strife and Sin, and who are drawing the People into continual Snares, and into such Actions and Follies, as are a Blemish unto us, and threaten to bring horrible Oppresion and Slavery upon us.   And such is our poor Condition, that except the Hand of our glorious Lord, in some wonderful Way deliver the Countrey from two or three Men, who are the very Soul and Staff of the wicked Party, the Countrey must in an ordinary way be ruined, and the Churches of the Lord reduced unto wretched Circumstances, and His Work wherein much of His Glory has appeared, be lost among us.   In this Distress, what can I do, for this poor, ungrateful and unworthy Country, but cry unto GOD ; and unto my SAVIOUR, who has more Pity and Patience for a Congregation full of Murmuring than ever a *Moses* could express for his froward People? Accordingly, bewayling my own manifold impurities, and particularly my own Frowardness under the Provocations of this People, and getting my Soul well-purified from all personal Revenge or Malice against these Men, I carry them unto the Lord, and I earnestly intercede with Him, that the Countrey, which is perishing by their Means, may be delivered from them.   Within these few Hours, GOD has in a marvellous Manner, and at a very critical Moment, smitten with an Apoplexy, one who has been and would still have been the greatest Hinderer of good, and Misleader and Enchanter of the People, that there was in the whole House of Representatives, who are just now come together.[1]   Methinks, I see a wonderful Token for good in this Matter : And I go on with my humble Supplications to the Lord.

[1] "Dr. Oliver Noyes is seized with an Apoplexy, at 10 at night." He died the next day, and prayers were made for him by Rev. Thomas Foxcroft and Rev. Benjamin Colman. On the following Sabbath many ministers "improved the sudden death of Dr. Noyes to awaken all to prepare for the Lord's coming." Sewall, *Diary*, III. 284.

In the Evening I preached unto a large Auditory, where a Society [of] persons learning to Sing, began a quarterly solemnity. On Rev. XIV. 3.[1]

17. G. D. I am this day, in the most solemn way Prosecuting the Design mentioned yesterday.

17 *d. 1 m. Friday.* I sett apart this Day, for Supplications, wherein I carry unto the Lord the affairs about which I am concerned, and cast my Burdens upon Him.

Especially, the Deliverance of the Countrey from the Men and Things that are Snares unto it. An happy Period of my Administration. The conversion of my Son *Increase,* the Preservation of my Son *Samuel,* who returns this day to the Colledge. The Presence of the Lord with me, in the Lecture upon early Piety, which I have the next Week before me.

18. G. D. Several new Objects of Charity and Compassion, more than one or two, present themselves unto me, to be cared for.

* 19. G. D. I grow continually more and more sensible of this: That I cannot apprehend my SAVIOUR except I am first apprehended of Him. I seek my Satisfaction in conversing with Him, and my Consolation in having the precious Thoughts of Him raised in my Mind. But I cannot myself raise these Thoughts; I continue without them, if He dart not His Rayes into my Mind, for the enkindling of them. This therefore must be the Way that I take; when I feel (as, alas, I often do) my Soul at a distance from the glorious CHRIST, who is my Life, I must first lift up a Cry to Him, *O my dear SAVIOUR, shine into my Mind, and send into me the Thoughts wherein I shall enjoy thee!*

20. G. D. I am furnishing myself with my Essay on,

---

[1] He preached on the 16th to the young musicians. "House was full, and the Singing extraordinarily Excellent, such as has hardly been heard before in Boston. Sung four times out of Tate and Brady." Sewall, *Diary,* III. 285.

Time spent as it should be; and I purpose in my pastoral Visits, to bestow it upon those, whose Business affords them Time to have their Minds filled with such Thoughts as may be of the greatest Use unto them.

21. G. D. *Creasy* needs fresh and strong Admonitions to be *diligent in his Business.*

Oh! my God; when, when the *Month* in which thou wilt *find him!*

22. G. D. I will take my religious Neighbour Dr. *Perkins*, into the Number of my Relatives; I will study his Welfare; I will promote his Practice; I will do for him all that I can do for the dearest Brother.[1]

23. G. D. Having invited the Ministers of the City into a Resolution to entertaining the People with eight Lectures on *early Piety;* I do this Day begin the Course, with a Sermon on parental Sollicitudes to see it wrought in their Children, and vehement Expostulations with the Children themselves to look after such a Blessedness.

And tho' I was faint and weak, yett crying to my glorious Lord, that He would send His good Angel to strengthen me, I was after a surprising Manner strengthened in the Service before me. It was a very vast Assembly, that I preached unto; and I stood very long in my Sermon; but my glorious Lord mightily assisted me; and when all was finished, I was less tired and broken, that ever in my ordinary Performances I use to be. Oh! what shall I render to the Lord!

24. G. D. Lord, what shall I do, for a self-destroying People! My foolish, and froward, wretched Countrey, will destroy itself unless two or three wicked Men may feel the Hand of GOD upon them.

25. G. D. A poor Infant of a poor woman perishing under scrophulous ulcers.

* 26. G. D. May I with much Activity of Mind grow

---

[1] John Perkins is mentioned in 1707 as "poor," but paying a rental of £12 for a house. *Boston Record Commissioners,* X. 120. See p. 93, *supra.*

in the Skill and the Use of this Exercise, that whatever I enjoy or observe useful or grateful in any Creatures, I may still form thereupon some Thoughts of the Excellencies in my SAVIOUR, to render Him useful and grateful unto the Children of men.

27. G. D. A Warning unto the young People of the Flock, to beware lest the Essays of the Ministers in the Town, to produce early Piety, prove their impœnitency, but an Introduction to a grievous Mortality among them.

28. G. D. Further Projections for *Sammy's* Welfare at the Colledge.

29. G. D. Animate some charitable Intentions to releeve and support my Kinsman at *Roxbury*.

30. G. D. Several important Things to be mentioned unto the Governour.

But, I am entertaining serious Thoughts upon the Condition of Religion, and of the Dissenters, especially, in *England;* Whether I may not come into such Meditations thereupon, as may carry the Voice of the glorious GOD, and be of great Use, unto them.

31. G. D. My, *Christian Philosopher*,[1] in a vessel blown off our Coast last Winter,) is this Week arrived from *England;* an Hundred of the Books are come. I may glorify God, especially by getting our Colledges filled with them.

April. 1. G. D. Several Neighbours, I see Death approaching on them. Lett me treat them agreeably, profitably.

* 2. G. D. The use of a glorious CHRIST, (or, How the Faith of Him is to operate) in every Part of the Christian Life: this noble Subject, O my Soul, prosecute it with a yett more notable Cultivation of it. And may He assist thee in it.

3. G. D. Two Sermons on the unhappy Condition of those, who walk in the Darkness of a woful Uncertainty

---

[1] Printed in London by Emanuel Matthews, 1721.

about their State in the eternal World, and know not whither they are going; The Flock needs greatly to be rowsed with them.

4. G. D. My miserable, miserable, miserable Son *Increase!* The Wretch has brought himself under public Trouble and Infamy by bearing a Part in a Night-Riot, with some detestable Rakes in the Town.

Oh! what shall I do! How shall I glorify my just, wise dear SAVIOUR, on this deplorable Occasion! And what is my Duty in relation to the incorrigible Prodigal!

Apply to the Secretary who employs him.

5. G. D. My Neighbour, *Perkins*, needs to be advised of something for his Welfare.

6. G. D. Disperse among the Scholars at the Colledge, a Number of my, *Honesta Parsimonia.*

Enter into a Correspondence with *Geneva*, whereto I am invited.

7. G. D. Certain things for the public Welfare, to be projected with the Governour.

8. G. D. A very poor, miserable Family, in my Neighbourhood.

Widows also multiplied.

*9. G. D. I draw up, a Recapitulation of the various Methods to converse with a glorious CHRIST, which His good Spirit has led me to; that so I may by a Review prevent my losing any of them, or my failing in their Exercise; And I propose also to communicate the same unto some special Friends, that they may learn in the like Methods also to glorify GOD.

10. G. D. The very wicked House of Representatives, that satt lately among us, have wickedly encouraged the People to cast Contempt on the Order for the general Fast. And there may be hazard lest some of my Flock be drawn into the Impiety. By what I speak, at the Reading of the Proclamation, I endeavour to save them from it.

11. G. D. My miserable son *Increase*, I must cast him and chase him out of my Sight; forbid him to see me until there appear sensible Marks of Repentance upon him. Nevertheless I will entreat his Grandfather to take Pains for his Recovery.

12. G. D. Some of my Kinsmen, I will endeavour to assist and excite into the Methods of a Society, for a profitable Conversation.

Prevail with my Father to preach the, *Concio ad Clerum,* at the Election.

13. G. D. Encourage the Booksellers, to publish the eight Sermons at the Lecture, for early Piety.

14. G. D. A wicked House at our End of the Town, which proves a Snare and a Ruine to young People; procure the Extirpation of it.

15. G. D. A poor Widow, made so this Week.

* 16. G. D. Now, *Now!* I have a dreadful Opportunity to Try, how far I may find a Glorious CHRIST, a Comforter, that shall releeve my Soul. What can I find in Him to comfort me, under the terrible Distresses, which the Condition of my wicked son *Increase* brings upon me!

17. G. D. Consider seriously and consult with Heaven about it, whether a Course of Sermons on the *Forty-fifth Psalm*, will be a Food which I may do well to treat my Flock withal.

18. G. D. I will write a tremendous Letter to my wicked Son *Increase;* and after I have sett his Crime in order before his Eyes, I will tell him, that I will never own him or do for him, or look on him, till the Characters of a Pœnitent are very conspicuous in him. God prosper it!

Lord, tho' I am a *Dog*, yett cast out the Devil, that has possession of the Child.

19. G. D. My very aged Father-in-Law in *Charlestown*, what may I do further for him?

20. G. D. This Day is a general Fast.

And I this Day bear Testimonies for GOD. And invite my Neighbours to consider His Judgments that are abroad n the Earth, and the spiritual Judgments under which this Town and Land is perishing.

21. G. D. In my Dispatches to *London* this week, I contrive some very extensive Services to the Kingdome of God in the World.

22. G. D. Several of my Neighbours are languishing and they are hastening to the Gates of Death. I would with all possible Discretion and Charity, endeavour to prepare them.

* 23. G. D. O dismal Case! O doleful Case! I am a Man of Sorrows and acquainted with Griefs. But I am now afraid of my Sorrows!

It looks, as if there were certain Sorrows wherein the Sentence of Heaven has putt me into a State of Punishment, tho' I am therein punished less than my Sins deserve. My Crimes have procured an order from GOD, that I must languish under these heavy Sorrows, and Heaven is become inexorable; No Prayers, no Cries, no Tears, must prevail for the Removal of them. There are more than two of these grievous Things; yett I shall in this Place take notice of no more than two. The one is, The Abandonment of my ungodly, distracted, hard-hearted son *Increase*, unto those foolish and vicious Courses, which must bring him to Misery, and throw me into unspeakable Trouble and Anguish and Confusion. The other is, the malignant and venemous Disposition of a great part of the Town and Countrey towards me, with implacable Resolutions to do all they can devise, or their Father can assist them, to ruine my Opportunities to do good in the World.

But if I am indeed in a State of Punishment, and my Iniquity not be purged with Sacrifice nor Offering; in this Condition, how am I to behave myself, and glorify God?

First, I must accept the Punishment of my Iniquity: And I must patiently bear the Indignation of the Lord; because I have sinned against Him; and I will humbly take part with His Holiness and Righteousness against myself; with some Satisfaction of Soul in the View of the glorious One gratified in breaking me to Peeces,

I will entertain every Stroke with that Acclamation, *Just art thou O Lord, and just are all thy Indignations!*

But then, I will most earnestly and with Agony deprecate a share in the Punishment reserved for the Workers of Iniquity in another World; since I am here so judged of the Lord; and plead the Sacrifice of my SAVIOUR for my Deliverance.

Thirdly, My main Concern shall be, what Improvements in Repentance and all Piety I shall make, under my Punishment, and by Means of it. And for this purpose I employ my Thoughts distinctly, on each of the Articles.

Lastly: Yett will I hold on weeping to the Lord, that if it be possible, the Cup may pass from me; and sitt alone, and keep silence, because I have born it upon me, and putt my mouth in the Dust, if so be there may be Hope.

Walking in this Darkness this Day, I had anon a strange Ray of Light shott into my mind, with a Reflection upon this; that I found my Will wonderfully united with my SAVIOURS: and being so one with Him, I must anon see some comfortable Events, which will be greatly to be wondred at.

And in a Prayer at a Baptism in the Afternoon, I could not but with Tears expostulate the Matter after this Manner before the Lord. "O our dear SAVIOUR; Hast thou not commanded us to bring our Children unto thee? Yes, and in obedience to thy Command, we do it, we do it. But, shall Dust and Ashes plead with thee? Lord why didst thou call for our Children? Was it that thou mayst putt them over unto Satan to take Possession of them? Was it, that they might be given up to Blindness and Hardness, and Madness? Was it that they might have the Distempers of their Souls ly uncured, when one gracious Word of thine can cure them? Or, was it, that they might still have their Hearts confirmed in their Sins, when one Touch of thy almighty Arm can give a new Biass to their Hearts? No; No; thou hast called for them, that by thy wondrous Power they may become disposed for the Service of our God. O our God, our God, we will yett beleeve, that we shall see thee doing Wonders for them."

I could not but think on poor *Increase*, when these Expressions were thus educed from me.

24. G. D. A Sermon on *Virtue* proceeding from our SAVIOUR. Contrive an Association of young People, to

idvance Religion among their Brethren, and bring them forwards to the Table [of] the Lord; and bring them into my Company.

25. G. D. Ah, Poor *Increase*, Tho' I spake against him, yett I earnestly remember him, and my Bowels are troubled for him. Is there nothing further to be done? His Grand-father, and his Kinsmen and others, must labour with him.

26. G. D. My aged Parent, I must assist both his Conduct and his Comfort, with relation to our new foolish Builders.

27. G. D. I hope, I have provided a Missionary for the Eastern Indians.

28. G. D. May not I try, whether the Reading of my *Supplies from the Tower of David* may not be introduced among the Students in our Colledges.

29. G. D. Several of my Neighbours have Death, with lingring Circumstances making its Advances upon them. I must assist their Preparations.

* 30. G. D. I am now called unto an uncommon Trial, wherein it will be found, whether I am Dead unto Creatures, or no; and whether having a CHRIST left unto me, I can live upon Him alone. The ungodly Doings in our New-North Church, have caused an Assembly of enraged, violent, boisterous Men, to build a new and very large Brick Meeting house, the finest in the Countrey. To fill their House they prevail with a mighty Number of the Flock which I serve, to join with them; and the Religion of Pues which with a proud, vain, formal People seems to be now the chief Religion of the Town, is too powerful a Temptation for them.

Now on this Occasion, Oh! how sollicitous must I be, to glorify my admirable SAVIOUR! In the first Place, I cry to Him for the Aid of His Grace, without which I can do nothing. *O thou Comforter, who alone canst releeve my Soul, be not thou far from me!*

I then endeavour an entire Satisfaction in the Dissipation and the Diminution of the Flock; especially from these Considerations.

Tis my wise, holy, righteous, and faithful SAVIOUR who has ordered it: and for such Ends as I shall know hereafter, but ought in the meantime to be well-perswaded of.

I shall enjoy a bright Conformity to my SAVIOUR in it, if, just before my Death, I suffer a general Withdraw of my Hearers from me.

I shall still have a CHRIST with me, as the Object of my Studies, and I shall preach Him to as many as He will allow to Hear me.

While I have a CHRIST I have enough, tho' all Creatures desert me.

And who can tell, what my glorious Lord may in all these things be preparing me for!

May. 1. G. D. I must now more than ever look on my Flock with a sacrificing Eye. Tis incredible, what Numbers are swarming off into the New Brick Meeting-house in the Neighbourhood. But it falling unto me, to preach the first Sermon in that Meeting-house, I propose then and there to take my Farewel of them with a most solemn Warning unto them, that they do not perish after all that they have received and heard in my public Ministry.

2. G. D. Accustoming myself alwayes to fall asleep with a Meditation on some Text, that has in it something of my SAVIOUR, I do now, while I am undressing, mention the Text of the Night in the Hearing of my Consort, (and of my Servant, if attending,) with some Thought upon it, that may be worthy to be remembred.

3. G. D. It is necessary for me to Reform something at *Roxbury*.

4. G. D. More must be done, to strengthen the Patience of our Governour.

5. G. D. I send a Number of my, *Honesta Parsimonia*

to be distributed among the Scholars, in the Colledge at
New-Haven.

6. G. D. A poor Man in the Flock, taken distracted;
I must bespeak and procure Prayers for him.

* 7. G. D. This Morning having my Thoughts on the
Sacrifice of my Flock, which I am call'd unto, among other
of my sacrificing Strokes, I considered this: the Men who
are drawing off, are of several Employments. Were they
all of them to be always at work for me in the Way of their
several Employments, what would be my Enjoyments from
them? I have a CHRIST concerned for me, and conversing
with me. While I have so, I am sure of enjoying as much
of what these could help me to, as I have any Occasion for.
But then I find in Him, analogous Blessings that are infinitely superior to all the Comforts, which these Neighbours
could have afforded me.

8. G. D. Must nothing be done to preserve the Flock
from Dissipations! Lett the Deacons be made more sensible
of their Duty.

9. G. D. The sick State of my Consort calls for a
good and a wise Conduct in me towards her.

10. G. D. My aged Father, too much laies to Heart;
the withdraw of a vain, proud, foolish People from Him in
His Age. Lett me comfort him what I can, and inculcate
my Maxims of rejoicing in a Glorious CHRIST upon the
Withdraw of all Creatures from us.

Yea, to obtain and secure this Point with him (and
honour my SAVIOUR) I do in his Name as well as my own,
this day take a solemn Farewel of the People going from
us. I conclude my Sermon; with much Solemnity calling
Heaven and Earth to record, for our Fidelity in the Discharge of our Ministry unto them. And with high Strains
of Sacrificing, I give all the People to see, how easily and
cheerfully we endure their Departure from us; especially
in this Regard that (as the Withdraw of the Disciples from

our SAVIOUR a little before He died,) we saw in it a comfortable Symptom of our drawing very near to the best Hour that ever we saw.

11. G. D. My Opportunities to serve a glorious CHRIST in my weekly Auditory, coming under a very great Abridgment, I must apply my Thoughts, to Projections for the making my Studies more extensively useful in some other ways. And therefore I will Think, whether in my Ministry I may not handle such Subjects, and præpare such Sermons as may by the Way of the Press in *Europe*, serve the Kingdome of God. I think yett more particularly, whether some Discourses on the *Life of Piety* maintained by a *Faith* in the GOD–HEAD of our SAVIOUR, may not be very proper upon that Intention.

12. G. D. I will move a godly Midwife, to procure a new Edition of my little Essay, entituled, *Elizabeth in her Holy Retirement:* that it may be scattered thro Town and Countrey; and occasion be taken from the Circumstances of them who are expecting an Hour of Travail, to quicken their Præparation for Death, and the Exercise of all suitable Piety.[1]

13. G. D. A miserable Negro under Sentence of Death, for the Murder of his Wife, must be visited, instructed, counselled.

* 14. G. D. Finding my Will entirely swallowed up in the Will of my SAVIOUR, and the Enjoyment of a glorious CHRIST that which abundantly satisfies me in the Withdraw of all Creatures from me: and calling to mind, that He sees and knows these Dispositions of my Mind, and has a Delight in beholding what His good SPIRIT has brought me to; inexpressible; inexpressible are the Consolations, which do from hence arise unto me!

---

[1] It was on this day that the freeholders first took notice of the smallpox. The man-of-war, *Sea-horse*, lay in the harbor, with two or three men on her sick with the disease. *Boston Record Commissioners*, VIII. 154.

The Holy Angels will take Pleasure in me. And, GOD will shew Wonders to the Dead!

15. G. D. Notwithstanding the Sacrifice I apprehended myself call'd unto, in the Dissipation of my Auditory looked for, I had yesterday a very considerable Auditory: The People drawn off, were hardly to be missed in the great Congregation. I am surprised at the Spectacle! But I took the Occasion in the public Prayers, to ask, that the Flock which did thus remain, might be more united than ever in Love to one another, and feel such precious Impressions from the Gospel preached here, and have such Visits of Grace here made unto their Souls, as to make them say, *'Tis Good to be here*. There may be a sensible Service to the Flock in this Petition.

16. G. D. My Consort having been for some Weeks languishing, what shall I do, most for her Advantage; especially with a due Improvement in Piety under it?

17. G. D. A Kinsman, serving of CHRIST at *Bristol* must be encouraged.[1]

18. G. D. My *India Christiana* being published, I am sending it into several Parts of *Europe* with Designs to serve the Kingdome of GOD.

Writing to *Europe*, I am sollicitous in a singular Manner to learn the present Condition of the *Vaudois*, on which I have my Eye with great Expectations.

19. G. D. Try, whether my, *Supplies from the Tower of David*, may not be entertained at the Colledge, and become influential.

20. G. D. If I live till to morrow, I purpose to press my usual Practice for this Day, upon my Auditory. To be on the Look-out for objects to show Compassion to.

* 21. G. D. The Time of the Year arrives for the glories of Nature, to appear in my Garden. I will take my

---

[1] Nathaniel Cotton, ordained in 1721, in the place of Rev. James McSparran, who had taken orders in the Church of England.

Walks there, on purpose to read the Glories of my SAVIOUR
in them. I will make it an Emblem of a Paradise, wherein
the *second Adam* shall have Acknowledgments paid unto
Him.

22. G. D.   Is it possible for me to glorify my SAVIOUR
more, or make the House wherein I serve Him to be more
an House of His Glory, than by a Course of Sermons on
His Illustrious MIRACLES? Yea, who can tell what
Wonders He may be going to shew *by* as well as *to* the
Dead?

23. G. D.   I will draw up certain Quæstions, turning
upon the several chief Actions of humane Life, in the right
Stating of the Answers whereto, there lies the Skill of living
unto GOD.   I will putt these Quæstions into the Hands of
my two Sons, that they may form and write proper Answers
to them.   So Try, whether the Life of God may not this
Way come into them.

24. G. D.   Further Services and Kindnesses, to be
done for the *beloved Physician* in my Neighbourhood.

25. G. D.   The Providence of my glorious Lord, still
strangely continuing and multiplying my Opportunities to
glorify Him, it comes to pass, that on my Lecture, there falls
out the Execution of a Negro,[1] who has been instructed and
baptised, and rendred himself a pretty noted Fellow, is
this day to be hanged for murdering his Wife.   A vast
Assembly attends the Lecture; and with a great Assistance
from Heaven, I bring forth many Things which I hope,
will make a good Impression upon the People.   More
particularly, wicked and froward Husbands, (as well as our
Ethiopian Slaves) have this Day, their Portion with a due
Pungency given to them.

26. G. D.   The grievous Calamity of the *Small-Pox*
has now entered the Town.   The Practice of conveying
and suffering the *Small-pox* by *Inoculation*, has never been

[1] Joseph Hanno.

used in *America*, nor indeed in our Nation. But how many
Lives might be saved by it, if it were practised? I will
procure a Consult of our Physicians, and lay the matter
before them.[1]

27. G. D. A poor Man in Prison for Debt; some Care
must be taken of him.

* 28. G. D. The Entrance of the *Small-pox* into the
Town must awaken in me several Tempers and Actions of
Piety relating to myself, besides a Variety of Duty to the
People.

First: The glorious Lord having employ'd me a few
Months ago, under an Afflatus from Heaven, to entertain
the City with a Lecture on *Trouble near*, and foretel the
speedy Approach of the destroying Angel: It becomes me
to humble myself exceedingly, and ly in the Dust. Lest
the least Vanity of mine upon seeing my poor prædiction
accomplished, should provoke the holy One to do some
grievous Thing unto me.

Secondly; I have two Children that are liable to the
Distemper; and I am at a Loss about their flying and
keeping out of the Town. As I must cry to Heaven for
Direction about it, so I am on this Occasion called unto
Sacrifices; that if these dear Children must lose their
Lives, the will of my Father may be duely submitted to.

Thirdly; my own Life is likely to be extremely in danger,
by the horrid Venom of the sick Chambers, which I must
look to be call'd unto; and I would accordingly Redeem
the Time to do what my hand finds to do.

29. G. D. The Diminution of my Flock, and the
wicked Spirit manifested by them, who for the Pride of
Pues, and such vile Motives, are gone out from us, must
quicken my Concern to do good unto them that remain.

---

[1] See Dr. R. H. Fitz's essay on "Zabdiel Boylston, inoculator," in *Johns
Hopkins Hospital Bulletin*, XXII. 314. The *Boston News-Letter*, on May 27,
reported eight cases in the town.

My Labours have heretofore taken singular Notice of two Sorts among us, our young People, and our Mariners. None are now withdrawn from me, more than these. Is it from a Wrath of GOD upon me, for my Miscarriages in the Discharge of my Ministry towards the Objects? I would humble myself, as deserving it. Yett, when I feel my Soul triumphing in my SAVIOUR on this Occasion, I can't but hope, that there may be His Love unto me in it. I wish there be not His Wrath, upon the unfruitful and obstinate Sinners, that are departed.

30. G. D. My two Children, that have their Terrors of the Contagion breaking in upon us; I must lay hold on the Occasion to quicken their effectual Flights unto their SAVIOUR.

31. G. D. A Kinsman, generously doing his part for *Bristol*, under the woful Troubles there, must be encouraged and animated and pray'd for.

My glorious Lord, will still give me to bring forth Fruit unto Him and unto His People.

(III.) Having prevailed with the eight Lecturers of the City, to preach so many Sermons on *Early Piety*, the Booksellers, are upon publishing of them, all in one Volume together. Here mine stands the first, and is entituled; WHAT THE PIOUS PARENT WISHES FOR.[1]

(IV.) It fell unto me, to preach the first Sermon in the New Brick Meeting-house. I made it an Opportunity, to glorify my admirable SAVIOUR ; and I concluded the Sermon with a very solemn Speech, in my Father's Name as well as my own, taking a Farewel of them. The People publish the Sermon. And the Title of it is, A VISION IN THE TEMPLE. *The Lord of Hosts adored; and the King of Glory proclaimed. On a Day of Prayer kept, (May, 10, 1721:) at the Opening of the New Brick Meeting house in the North part of* Boston.[2]

---

[1] Printed by S. Kneeland for N. Buttolph, B. Eliot and D. Henchman, 1721. Each sermon had a separate titlepage.   [2] Printed for Robert Starkey, 1721.

(V.) The Divine Providence having somewhat strangely ordered it, I preached a Sermon, on the day when a wretched Murderer was executed.[1] The Sermon made a great Impression, and served the Cause of Piety. The Booksellers give it unto the Publick; under this Title, TREMENDA. *The dreadful Sound, with which the Wicked are to be Thunderstruck, In a SERMON delivered unto a great Assembly, in which was present a miserable African, just going to be executed for a most Inhumane and uncommon Murder. To which is added, A Conference between a Minister and the Prisoner, on the Day before his Execution.*[2]

June. 1. G. D. In the Convention of the Ministers' Meeting at the Election, I endeavour several Services.

2. G. D. Because of the destroying Angel standing over the Town, and the grievous Consternation on the Minds of the People, I move the Ministers who are the Lecturers of the City, to turn the next Lecture into a Day of Prayer, that we may prepare to meet our God.

3. G. D. A miserable Creature, who has long lain under the Censures of our Church,———

* 4. G. D. It is a Time, wherein we are strongly and hourly expecting our Ships from *England*. I have my important Points of Expectation, which make me unawares long for their Arrival. But I rebuke my Expectation as one dead unto this World, and unto all Things here below. I consider, what are the Things, the coming or knowing whereof now from the other Side of the Water would give me some satisfaction. I find something in a glorious CHRIST analagous unto, and præferrible before those Things; and I take a Satisfaction in Him superior to what any Creatures can afford me. I rejoice in Him, and I am easy tho' I should have nothing else to comfort me.

[1] Joseph Hanno.

[2] Two editions were printed in this year; one by B. Green, for B. Gray and I. Edwards, and the other for Robert Starkey.

5. G. D. I must of Necessity do something, that the Exercise of *Singing* the sacred *Psalms* in the Flock, may be made more beautiful, and especially have the *Beauties of Holiness* more upon it.

6. G. D. My *African* Servant, stands a Candidate for Baptism, and is afraid how the Small-pox, if it spread, may handle him. I must on this Occasion use very much Application to bring him into a thorough Christianity.[1]

[1] On June 6, 1721, Cotton Mather prepared an address to the physicians of Boston in which he called attention to this "new method" of inoculation, and embodied in his address a summary of two letters describing the method, as published by the Royal Society of London. One of these letters was written by Dr. Emanuel Timonius, F.R.S., from Constantinople, in December, 1713, and the other by Jacobus Pylarius, Venetian Consul at Smyrna. The publication by the Royal Society had come to the hands of Dr. William Douglass, then in Boston, and he loaned it to Mather. After Mather's publication Douglass recalled the Society's issue, charged that Mather's summary of the letters was not correct, and refused again to lend the tract for use or comparison. One of the physicians to whom Mather's address had been sent, Dr. Zabdiel Boylston, determined to make experiments upon his own family. The difficulties encountered he told in his *Historical Account of the Small-pox Inoculated in New England* (1726).

He made inquiries among the Africans in Boston, who confirmed the methods employed and the results obtained, telling the story "plainly, brokenly, and blunderingly, and like Ideots," but agreeing in the main features. Having experimented "*with all the Disadvantages* that can be imagined," Boylston became convinced of its efficacy, and in this pamphlet undertook to reply to his critics, to demonstrate the benefit and safety of the practice, and to prove its lawfulness. The chief moral reason brought against inoculation was that it was a heathen practice, and it was unlawful to learn of the heathen. Absurd as the argument seems, Boylston could point out in reply that all the physicians of antiquity were heathen, and that the Colonists had learned from the Indians a corrective to snake bites and the practice of smoking.

Into this controversy Mather, the principal instrument in introducing the method in Boston, threw himself with great zeal, and naturally the moral or religious aspect of the question received his greatest attention. He prepared and printed a tract, giving *An Account of the Method and further Success of Inoculating for the Small pox in London* (1721), but no copy has been preserved. He wrote a *Letter to a Friend in the Country, attempting a Solution of the Scruples and Objections of Conscientious or Religious Nature commonly made against the new Way of receiving the Small pox*, the nature of which may be conjectured from the entries in his Diary. He also caused to be reprinted his *Pastoral Letter to Families visited with Sickness*, which had not been put to the press since 1713, and for which, with good publishing instinct, he now saw a need for a new edition. He induced his father, in November, to put his name to a tract offering *Several Reasons proving that Inoculating or Transplanting the Small pox is a lawful Practise*, etc., which was answered

7. G. D. I have a Kinswoman at this time sick of the Small-pox; but not without hopes of Recovery. As I must now be concerned for her, so when she is able to receive it, I must present unto her my Book of, *A perfect Recovery.*

8. G. D. Having procured the Lecture of this Day, to be turned into a *Day of Prayer*, because of the Calamity impending over the Town, I have an Opportunity of speaking many things in a Sermon this day, for the Good of the Inhabitants, and for the Advancement of that PIETY, to which the Judgments of GOD should awaken them.

By the public Fast which occurred a Month ago, and now again, by that of this Week, I am diverted (the feeble State of my Health not allowing it,) from the Fasting in Secret, with which I use to prepare for the Table of the Lord.

9. G. D. There are some ungospellized Places, which I have diverse Proposals of Compassion to. Especially, *Providence.*

10. G. D. There is a poor Man in my Neighbourhood, roaring under the horrible Torments of a Cancer, in a Seat rarely heard of.

*11. G. D. My glorious Lord, has accepted my Testimonies. My *American Sentiments*, on the present Controversies, about the GOD–HEAD of our SAVIOUR, and the Way of owning it, are published and scattered thro'

by John Williams, "tobacconist," as his critics called him. From this answer is obtained a title of an anonymous defence of the new method, *Sentiments on the Small Pox Inoculated*, of which no copy has been found. Another anonymously printed tract, *The Imposition of Inoculation as a Duty Religiously Considered*, has been attributed to Samuel Grainger; while the author of still another, *A Letter from one in the Country, to his Friend in the City; in relation to the Distresses occasioned by . . . Inoculation*, has thus far escaped identification. A "wicked pamphlet" entitled *Inoculation of the Small Pox as practised in Boston: considered in a Letter to A. S."* etc., excited the ire of Increase Mather, who replied in *Some Further Account from London of the Small-Pox Inoculated*, which reached a second edition. The newspapers of the day contained much on the controversy, and the year 1721 was made as notable by this discussion on inoculation as by the visitation itself.

the Nation. I am indeed hereby exposed unto Sufferings; I feel myself a Loser in some Temporal Interests. But I have my Spirit so rejoicing in GOD my SAVIOUR on this Occasion, that I am sure of His owning me among His Followers and Confessors, and of His Dealing wonderfully with me.

12. G. D. Whether I may not profitably and seasonably entertain my Flock, with some Thoughts on the *Snares of a worldly Mind;* awakened by the marvellous Confusion which the Bubble of the *South-Sea,* has brought upon our foolish Nation![1]

13. G. D. What shall I do? what shall I do, with regard unto *Sammy?* He comes home, when the Small-pox begins to spread in the Neighbourhood; and he is lothe to return unto *Cambridge.* I must earnestly look up to Heaven for Direction.

The State of him, and of *Lizy,* who is in greater Fears than he, I must improve with all the Contrivance I can, to make [it] subservient unto the Interests of Piety in them.

14. G. D. The mischievous Tricks of a rascally Boy, and his foolish and froward Mother, have raised some Discord in my Father's Family. I must with all possible Meekness and Patience, and with as much Prudence as may be, endeavour to prevent evil Consequences.

15. G. D. The Eruption of a new *Volcano,* producing an Island in the Sea, near *Tercera,* is a just Alarum to a secure and sleepy World. It affords Occasion for some Thoughts which may be of use more Ways than one, if the Minds of sensible People may be entertained with them.

(VI.) And behold, at the very time, when I am writing my Thoughts upon the Subject, the Bookseller comes to me, with Desires to have them, that he may give them to

[1] The South Sea Company, incorporated in 1711, ended nine years later in disaster.

the public. So he has them under this Title, *The World alarum'd.*[1]

16. G. D. Move among the Ministers, that our stated Interviews may be rendred more useful unto our selves, and unto the Public.

17. G. D. A miserable Woman, that has long been under the Censures of the Church, presses to be restored.[2]

* 18. G. D. So precious are the *Thoughts* of a glorious CHRIST unto me, and so do I find all my *Riches* and all my *Delights* in Him, that every *new View* of Him, and every *new Way* of conversing with Him, into which He leads me, more satisfies me and ravishes me, than if any worldly Wealth were poured in upon me. And, when upon a Prospect of any Trouble coming upon me, I recollect, *this Trouble will raise fresh Contemplations on my SAVIOUR in me;* I find myself sweetly reconciled unto it, and ready to entertain it.

19. G. D. I must request the Church to meet, that so the Desire of some to be dismiss'd from us, may be laid before them; and I would endeavour that there may be a præparation for Things proper to be spoke on that Occasion.

20. G. D. Oh! what shall I do, that my Family may be prepared, for the Visitation that is now every day to be expected!

21. G. D. Being entirely satisfied in the Skill of my pious Neighbour Dr. *Perkins*, I will take all Occasions to recommend him unto the Use of the Neighbourhood, in the Calamity of the *Small-pox* coming upon us: As well as make my daily Prayers for him.

I will also daily pray, for my Friend Mr. [John] Briggs, whom GOD has made a great Blessing unto me.

22. G. D. I prepare a little Treatise on the *Small-Pox;* first awakening the Sentiments of *Piety*, which it

---

[1] Printed by B. Green for S. Gerrish, 1721.
[2] Abigail Star. See p. 629, *infra.*

calls for; and then exhibiting the best Medicines and Methods, which the world has yett had for the managing of it; and finally, adding the new Discovery, to prevent it in the way of Inoculation. It is possible, that this Essay may save the *Lives*, yea, and the *Souls* of many People. Shall I give it unto the Booksellers? I am waiting for Direction.

23. G. D.   I write a Letter unto the Physicians, entreating them, to take into consideration the important Affair of preventing the *Small-Pox*, in the way of Inoculation.[1]

24. G. D.   Miserables neglected and perishing in Sickness; I must concern myself, to have them look'd after.

* 25. G. D.   Some new Treatises of Dr. *Owens*, about *A Walk with God*, may assist me in my endeavours for it.

26. G. D.   For any of the Flock, that fear the Contagion, (as People generally do, even with Amazement upon them,) to continue with earnest and constant Prayer to the glorious God at such a Time, lett me mightily aggravate unto them the Impiety, the Impenitence.

27. G. D.   Lett me take Advantage from the Fear, which Distresses *Liza*, to quicken her Flights unto her SAVIOUR. And lett me give her, the little Book, which relates the Death of a young French Lady.

28. G. D.   Among the Number of my Relatives, I will take in Mr. *John Briggs*, whom GOD has made a most helpful and useful Friend unto me. I do several good Offices for Him, and pray for him every Day.

29. G. D.   I am writing for *London*, and sending more Things to serve the Kingdome of God.

30. G. D.   The Affair mention'd this day Se'nnight, is begun and has raised an horrid Clamour, which Occasions new Cares upon me.

July. 1. G. D.   A Family of the Neighbourhood, brought into much Darkness, by Mortality.

[1] *Massachusetts Magazine*, I. 778.

One under much Distress of Mind.

* 2. G. D. In my Meditations, on the dying Speeches of our SAVIOUR to His Disciples, I find very astonishing Matters; and very divine Consolations. I hope, to live on those Chapters of *John*, after another Manner than I have ever done heretofore. Oh! that clause, *You in me, and I in you!* How much is comprehended in it! What an incomprehensible Blessedness! [1]

3. G. D. Faithfully speak to the Flock, about the Irregularities frequently committed, in a Contempt cast upon their Covenant, and a Withdraw from the Communion of the Church on very sleight Occasions.

4. G. D. How shall *Sammy* spend his Time, to the best Advantage?

5. G. D. My aged Parent is under Infirmities, what shall I do for his Releef?

Assist him also in a præface to the eight Lectures now coming out of the Press.

And procure the Sermon he preaches to young People, the next Lord's-Day, to be transcribed for the Press, that it may accompany the Eight Lectures of *Early Piety*.[2]

6. G. D. Several Places destitute of the Gospel, begin to appear Fields that may be laboured in. What shall be done for them?

7. G. D. Now and then, I may suggest Passages for our public News-Letter, which may do considerable good among the Readers.

7 *d.* v *m. Friday.* This Day I sett apart for Humiliations and Supplications, that I may obtain from a Reconciled GOD, and a Powerful and merciful SAVIOUR, the

---

[1] "2 *d.* 5 *m. Abigail Star*, who was laid under the Censure of the Church three and twenty Years ago, appearing this Day before the Church with a very expressive Confession of her Crimes, and some Testimony of a reformed Conversation, she was restored unto the favor and fellowship of the People of God." *Cotton Mather's MS. Records of the Second Church*, III.

[2] It was printed the last in the volume.

Blessings of Goodness, and His gracious Presence with me in my Ministry.

One special Errand unto Heaven was, to beg (as good Things for all my Children, so especially) the Lives of my two Children, which are threatened by the contagious Distemper of the Small-Pox; which is now spreading among us; and a Direction of Heaven, what I may do for their Welfare in that, and (for all of them) in all Regards.

Another special Errand was: that my unhappy Administration, which has been the Occasion of so much Trouble to me, is yett unfinished. And my Children-in-Law, have laid a deep Design, assisted with crafty and cruel Adversaries, if they can, to ruine me. I must fly to my strong Redeemer, with Cries for Help against my unjust and wicked Persecutors, and for my Deliverance from them. I am sure, *my God will hear me!*

8. G. D. Some under grievous Consternation, from *Small-Pox* now spreading, must be directed and comforted.

* 9. G. D. The glorious Lord who orders my Condition for me, has order'd me a Condition of considerable *Poverty*. What very little Estate I had, has been sold, and the Money is gone to pay my Debts. I do not own a Foot of Land in all the World. My Salary is not enough to support me comfortably, I meet with many Wants and Straits: in my Diet, much; in my Habit, more. There occur strange Wayes to pull me back, and keep me low, if at any time I have begun to lay by any Thing for the Releef of my Necessities.

NOW tis, that I find a glorious CHRIST becoming All unto me.

I am so far from any Impatience under my Difficulties, that I feel an inexpressible Delight in that Conformity to the Condition of my humbled SAVIOUR, which they help me to. My Poverty makes me, with a very sensible Pleasure to think, *now I am conformed unto the Blessed Jesus, who was poor, and had nothing of this World, that He called His own; and encountred with many Difficulties.*

I think, that while I have a CHRIST concerned for me, and while I can converse with a CHRIST continually, and while my Opportunities to glorify a CHRIST are multiplied unto me, I have the best of Riches; yea, the unsearchable Riches of CHRIST. I really look upon every new Enjoyment of a CHRIST, and every new Advantage

to glorify Him, as a vast Accession to my Riches; and with the same
Eye, that the Men of this World, look upon any new Accession and
Affluence of Wealth unto them.

It is with an unspeakable Pleasure, that I behold my SAVIOUR
having entirely in His Hands, the Supply of all the good Things,
which I have any real Occasion for. I can with a sweet Assurance
rely upon Him, to supply me with all that His Wisdome and Goodness may judge proper for me; and I will not so much as indulge a
Wish for any more.

I look forward and I certainly know, that there is another World,
wherein my SAVIOUR will bring me to inherit all things, and I shall
in that world have enough and enough to make a Compensation for
all that in this World has been denied unto me. *Domine, ubi omnia
mea, Tu Scis!*

10. G. D. The various Distresses come upon the Flock,
in the grievous Disease now beginning to distress the Town,
must be suitably considered by me; my Prayers and Sermons must be adapted unto their Condition.

11. G. D. For *Sammy*, and *Liza*, Oh! what shall I do ?
A continual Dropping of Instructions and Awakenings.

12. G. D. A Kinsman has done bravely and expressed
a noble Compassion, and Self-denial and Courage in accepting an Invitation to miserable *Bristol*. I write as pathetic
a Letter as I can unto him, to encourage him.

13. G. D. The Supplications to be made this Day,
the Testimonies to be born this Day:

Tis a Day of Humiliation thro' the Province, on the
Occasion of the Calamity now upon miserable *Boston*.

14. G. D. Do something further to strengthen the
Governour's Patience.

Write unto our Agent at London, what may be for
our good and his own.

15. G. D. Widows multiply. *Marahs* to be spoken to.

* 16. G. D. At this Time, I enjoy an unspeakable
Consolation. I have instructed our Physicians in the new
Method used by the *Africans* and *Asiaticks*, to prevent and

abate the Dangers of the *Small-Pox,* and infallibly to save
the Lives of those that have it wisely managed upon them.
The Destroyer, being enraged at the Proposal of any Thing,
that may rescue the Lives of our poor People from him, has
taken a strange Possession of the People on this Occasion.
They rave, they rail, they blaspheme; they talk not only
like Ideots but also like *Franticks,* And not only the Physician who began the Experiment, but I also am an Object
of their Fury; their furious Obloquies and Invectives.

My Conformity to my SAVIOUR in this Thing, fills me
with Joy unspeakable and full of Glory.

17. G. D.   What shall I do for that Part of the Flock,
that are fled into other Towns, to escape the Dangers of
the *Small-Pox.*

Accommodate them with Books of Piety.

And unto a Number of them in the Neighbour-Town,
go and preach a Lecture.

18. G. D.   The cursed Clamour of a People strangely
and fiercely possessed of the Devil, will probably prevent
my saving the Lives of my two Children, from the Small-
pox in the Way of Transplantation.   So that I have no way
left, but that of my continual and importunate Cries to
Heaven for their Preservation.   Accompanied with Admonitions unto them to make their own.

19. G. D.   A little Kinsman admitted into the Colledge,
I must procure Subscriptions, towards the supporting of
him there.[1]

20. G. D.   Writing to *London* and *Bristol,* I project
several extensive Services to the Kingdome of GOD.

And I more particularly encourage our Agent, cheerfully to continue his Endeavours to do good for the most
ungrateful and barbarous people in the World.[2]

---

[1] Andrew Oliver, who died in 1774.

[2] Jeremiah Dummer was the agent, and the barbarous people were those of
Massachusetts.

21. G. D. There being several Societies of young People, meeting for the Exercises of Religion on the Lords-day-Evenings, and they generally lying obnoxious to the Danger of the Small-Pox, I would, as far as I can find Strength for it, visit them, and entertain them with Prayers and Sermons that shall be suitable for them.

This Day, I sett apart, for Supplications to the glorious Lord, especially on the behalf of my two Children, that are exposed unto the Dangers of the Small-Pox, and that I may obtain Blessings for all my Children. I also implore the Compassion of Heaven to a Town already under dreadful Judgments, but ripening for more.

And that GOD would requite me Good for all the Cursing of a People that have Satan filling of them; and yett appear to rescue and increase my Opportunities to do good, which the great Adversary is now making an hellish Assault upon.

22. G. D. Some of Neighbours are in very particular Circumstances obliging me to visit them and comfort them.

* 23. G. D. I have my Meditations very strongly employed on that Question:

If I were fastened unto a CROSS, and under all the Circumstances of a Crucifixion, what would be my Dispositions; what my Exercises?

My Answer to it, is written down on a separate Paper.

But I find myself so entirely brought unto such Dispositions, and such Exercises: that I have abundant Evidence that I am *crucified with CHRIST.* And now, Oh, the glorious Consequences!

24. G. D. A young Man in the Flock has made a very hopeful and joyful End, and has gloriously triumphed over Death! To animate Piety, especially among the young People in the Flock, especially now the Fire of GOD is consuming them; I preach a Sermon on this Occasion.

25. G. D. A young Woman (a Kinswoman of my

Wife's,) sojourns in my Family.   Books of Piety, whereof she
appears too negligent must be commended unto her Perusal.

I must also be patient under it, that my own Children
must be turned and kept out of Doors, and their Place be
taken by a Stranger so unacceptable to me.

26. G. D.   I have some Kindred in the Town who
languish under great Fear of the Contagion, that is now
spreading among us.   It furnishes me, with an Opportunity,
to address them in the most effectual Way upon their
greatest Interests.

27. G. D.   The monstrous and crying Wickedness of
this Town, (a Town at this time strangely possessed with
the Devil,) and the vile Abuse which I do myself particularly suffer from it, for nothing but my instructing our base
Physicians, how to save many precious Lives; these things
oblige me, in the Fear of the divine Judgments, to fall
down before the Lord, with most earnest Supplications, for
His Pitty and Pardon to a People so obnoxious to His
Displeasure.[1]

28. G. D.   The Minister of *Wenham* [2] sends to me for
Directions, to regulate and animate the private Societies
of Religion there.   I send him the Directions, with Proposals to make them of a more diffusive Usefulness throughout the Countrey.

I sett apart this Day, as I did this Day Se'nnight, for
Supplications to the glorious Lord.   The Occasions and
the Exercises were the same now, that they were then;
only that I enjoy'd rather more of Heaven, and Assurance,
that my God will hear me!

29. G. D.   Several afflicted People to be visited and
comforted.

[1] The *Boston Gazette*, July 27, 1721, printed a letter on the smallpox, dated
July 25, and signed by Increase and Cotton Mather, Benjamin Colman, Thomas
Prince, John Webb, and William Cooper.   The original MS. is in the Boston
Medical Library.

[2] Robert Ward, ordained January 25, 1720–21, and died in 1732.

A Minister of the Countrey, who meets with grievous Difficulties among a barbarous People, must be releeved and supported.

* 30. G. D. What should be my Conduct under the Outrages and Obloquies of a Town which Satan has taken a most wonderful Possession of?

I must exceedingly rejoice in my Conformity, to my admirable SAVIOUR: who was thus, and worse requited, when He saved their Lives, and came to save their Souls.

I must mightily take heed unto my own Spirit, and watch against all Ebullitions of Wrath, lest being provoked, I speak unadvisedly with my Lips.

I must give myself unto Prayer, and wait with Patience, in a full Perswasion, that my glorious Lord, will restrain and govern the Satanic Fury that is now raging; and that He will anon give me to see my Opportunities to do good strangely multiplied.

31. G. D. I must yett more particularly give to our People, a Sermon that shall most plainly and fully Instruct them, how to gett into such Terms with Heaven, that they may be Ready, for whatever Events the Contagion that spreads in the Town may bring upon them.

August. 1. G. D. Full of Distress about *Sammy;* He begs to have his Life saved, by receiving the *Small-Pox*, in the way of *Inoculation*, whereof our Neighbourhood has had no less than ten remarkable Experiments; and if he should after all dy by receiving it in the common Way, how can I answer it? On the other Side, our People, who have Satan remarkably filling their Hearts and their Tongues, will go on with infinite Prejudices against me and my Ministry, if I suffer this Operation upon the Child: and be sure, if he should happen to miscarry under it, my Condition would be insupportable.

His Grandfather advises that I keep the whole Proceeding private, and that I bring the Lad into this Method of Safety.

My GOD, I know not what to do, but my Eyes are unto Thee!

2. G. D.   I will employ the Witt and Pen of my Kinsman at *Roxbury*, to serve the Cause of Truth and Right on the present Occasion.

3. G. D.   The glorious God has with marvellous Displays of His Free-grace, employ'd me to articulate His Voice unto His People, on many Occasions.   I am inclinable to send over unto *London*, an Essay, of, *Seasonable Reflections and profitable Instructions, produced by the Matchless Distress which the Managements of the* South-Sea Company *have brought upon an unhappy Nation.*   Direct me and Accept me, O my SAVIOUR.

4. G. D.   I will allow the persecuted Physician,[1] to publish my Communications from the *Levant*, about the *Small-Pox*, and supply him with some further Armour, to conquer the Dragon.

I sett apart this Day also, as I have several Præceeding *Friday's*, for secret Supplications; on the same Occasions, and with the same Exercises, that I have the former.

Especially, to cry unto Heaven for the Lives of my Children.

And, to cast indeed all my Burdens on the Lord.

I am sure, that I have obtained the Conduct of a good ANGEL from my GOD and SAVIOUR.

But Oh! how comprehensive a Blessing am I therein made Partaker of!

5. G. D.   The Condition of my pious Barber, and his Family, calls for my particular Consideration.

*6. G. D.   It is the Hour and Power of Darkness on this miserable [2] Town; and I need an uncommon Assistance from Above, that I may not miscarry by any froward or angry Impatience, or fall into any of the common Iniquities,

---

[1] Zabdiel Boylston.   [2] He had first written "detestable."

of Lying, and Railing and Malice: or be weary of well-doing and of overcoming Evil with Good.

7. G. D. My clear Ideas of a *crucified Christian*, I would communicate unto the Flock, and inculcate upon them, with all Faithfulness imaginable.

8. G. D. What further shall I do, for my *Samuel*, (Not mine, but thine, O Lord! For I offer Him up unto thee!) That he may be prepared for what is every day to be looked for!

I will much employ him in preparing of Sermons.

9. G. D. Some Kinsmen in continual Fears of being siezed by the *Small-pox;* I lay hold on the Opportunity to press the Lessons of Piety upon them.

10. G. D. I rejoice in taking Opportunities to preach Lectures at the neighbouring Towns; and carry to them the Glories and Maxims of an admirable SAVIOUR.

11. G. D. Instigate a Neighbour-Minister to take proper Methods, for the Saving of his Life, now in extreme Danger by the Contagion spreading among us.

12. G. D. A poor godly Widow, has lost her only Son, by a sudden and awful Death.[1]

*13. G. D. I propose a particular Advantage unto Piety in me, by reading a Book newly published, on *the Employments and Services of the Blessed Spirits in Heaven.*

And prosecuting that Subject, with yett more penetrating Meditations.

14. G. D. And may I not be serviceable to the Flock by entertaining them, with what of this kind may be proper for them?

15. G. D. My dear *Sammy*, is now under the Operation of receiving the *Small-Pox* in the way of *Transplantation.* The Success of the Experiment among my Neighbours, as well as abroad in the World, and the urgent Calls

[1] Nathaniel Parkman, son of Nathaniel and Hannah Parkman. He was killed by the fulling mill on Neponset River, August 11. Sewall, *Diary*, III. 291.

of his Grandfather for it, have made me think, that I could not answer it unto God, if I neglected it. At this critical Time, how much is all Piety to be press'd upon the Child!

And it may be hoped, with the more of Efficacy, because his dearest Companion (and his Chamber-fellow at the Colledge,) dies this Day, of the Small-pox taken in the common Way.

16. G. D. I know not why I should not press diverse of my distressed Kinsmen, to come under the same Experiment.

17. G. D. The Notable Experience I now have of this New Method, for the Saving of many Lives, yea, and for the Abating and preventing of Miseries undergone by many who do live, and survive an horrible Distemper, enables me to recommend the matter so, that I hope it may be introduced into the English Nation, and a World of good may be done to the miserable Children of Men. I take the Matter into Consideration.

18. G. D. I may propose some agreeable Passages, to be inserted in the *News-Letters*, which may have a Notable Tendency to correct and restrain the Epidemical Follies of the Town.

19. G. D. Some greatly bereaved Parents must be visited and comforted.

* 20. G. D. My Soul makes a glorious Improvement in the prosecution of the Fœlicity, which my SAVIOUR has in those Terms propos'd unto me, *You in me, and I in you.*

And I am now feeding and living upon His most gracious Promise; *If you abide in me, and my Words abide in you, you shall ask what you will, and it shall be done unto you.*

21. G. D. The Committee of the Church, ought to be pressed unto more Expedition in settling of some Affairs, which may have a Tendency to our Tranquillity.

22. G. D. My dear *Sammy*, having received the *Small-pox* in the Way of *Inoculation*, is now under the Fever

necessary to produce the Eruption. But I have Reason to fear, that he had also taken the Infection in the common Way; and he had likewise but one Insition, and one so small as to be hardly worthy the Name of one, made upon him. If he should miscarry, besides the Loss of so hopeful a Son, I should also suffer a prodigious Clamour and Hatred from an infuriated Mob, whom the Devil has inspired with a most hellish Rage, on this Occasion. My continual Prayers and Cries, and Offerings to Heaven, must be accompanied with suitable Instructions to the Child, while our Distresses are upon us.

23. G. D. My little Kinsman, recovering from the Small-Pox, I will direct him, that He draw up and write down, the Returns to the Lord his Healer, which are now to be endeavoured by him.

24. G. D. The Town is become almost an Hell upon Earth, a City full of Lies, and Murders, and Blasphemies, as far as Wishes and Speeches can render it so; Satan seems to take a strange Possession of it, in the epidemic Rage, against that notable and powerful and successful way of saving the Lives of People from the Dangers of the *Small-Pox*. What can I do on this Occasion, to gett the miserable Town dispossessed of the evil Spirit, which has taken such an horrible Possession of it? What besides Prayer with Fasting, for it?

25. G. D. I will assist my Physician, in giving to the Public, some Accounts about releeving the *Small-Pox* in the way of *Transplantation;* which may be of great Consequence!

25 *d.* VI *m. Friday.* It is a very critical Time with me, a Time of unspeakable Trouble and Anguish. My dear *Sammy,* has this Week had a dangerous and threatening Fever come upon him, which is beyond what the *Inoculation* of the *Small-Pox* has hitherto brought upon any Subjects of it. In this Distress, I have cried unto the Lord;

and He has answered with a Measure of Restraint upon the Fever. The Eruption proceeds, and he proves pretty full, and has not the best sort, and some Degree of his Fever holds him. His Condition is very hazardous.

I sett apart this Day, for Supplications to my glorious Lord, on this distressing Occasion. I was enabled by him to make a Sacrifice of my Son, unto Him. I submitted and consented unto it, that if He would please to kill the Lad, even in such aggravating Circumstances of Sorrow, as his Death must now be attended with, I would humbly acquiesce in His most sovereign, just and wise Dispensations. A CHRIST being left unto me, I would entirely take my whole satisfaction in Him alone, and count myself Happy enough, while I have Him to comfort me. But yett, I beg'd for the Life of the Child, that he may live to serve the Kingdome of GOD, and that the Cup which I fear, may pass from me.

I have other Children also at this Time, sick and weak and languishing, and in much Affliction. My SAVIOUR seems to multiply very many and heavy Loads at once upon me. Oh! may He help me to carry it well under them! Oh! may my Carriage yeeld Him a grateful Spectacle!

What can I do, but cast my Burden on the Lord!

26. G. D. Several poor People, sick of the common-Distemper, call for my Releefs, more Ways than one unto them.

* 27. G. D. My blessed SAVIOUR, the Healer of my Soul, has at length brought me to a Blessedness, which nothing in this World, nor all the good Things of a thousand such Worlds, may be compared unto. It was not enough that I should come unto this; I am willing to be stript of all my worldly Enjoyments, and have neither Wealth, nor Health, nor Name, nor Friend left unto me, and find in a glorious CHRIST alone, all the satisfactions which People vainly promise themselves in Creatures.

But I must also come unto this; My dear, dear SAV-
IOUR, thou hast brought me to it! I am content, That I
see no Reward of PIETY in the whole Time of my Pilgrimage upon Earth; and that none of my Prayers have such
Answers here given to them, as I could have wished for. I
am satisfied, in what I am sure, shall after Death be done
for me, by a SAVIOUR, who, I am sure is Himself risen from
the Dead. I can cheerfully take up, with what shall in a
future State be done for me, by a SAVIOUR, whom I can
with a strong Faith rely upon, and give Glory to God.

28. G. D. This miserable Town, is a dismal Picture
and Emblem of *Hell; Fire* with *Darkness* filling of it, and a
lying Spirit reigning there; many members of our Churches,
have had a fearful Share in the false Reports, and blasphe-
mous Speeches, and murderous Wishes in which the Town
is become very guilty before the Lord. Calling upon the
Flock to prepare for the Table of the Lord, I warn them to
repent of whatever may have been in them offensive unto
GOD, and come with suitable Dispositions of Love to GOD
and CHRIST and their Neighbour, lest they provoke Him
to be terrible in His holy Places.

29. G. D. The Condition of my Son *Samuel* is very
singular. The Inoculation was very imperfectly performed,
and scarce any more than attempted upon him; And yett
for ought I know, it might be so much as to prove a Benefit
unto him. He is however, endanger'd, by the ungoverned
Fever that attends him. And in this Distress, I know not
what to do; but, O Lord, my Eyes are unto thee!

30. G. D. That which adds to my Distress, is, that
my Son-in-Law, D. W[illard] is not only languishing under
an unknown Fever, but also grown delirous with it.

My Daughter *Abigail*, within a few Weeks of her Time,
is very hazardously circumstanced with several Infirmities.

My Daughter *Hannah*, has a violent Feavour upon her,
which extremely threatens her Life.

My Sister's Family has the *Small-Pox* broken in upon it. Her Son, Daughter, Grandson.

Tis an abundance of Duty, which on these Occasions I am called unto.

I sett myself to consider, what I could see desirable and comfortable in my *Children*, and what it is, that would render me glad of their Continuance with me: but then I considered, what I could find in a glorious CHRIST, infinitely more desirable and comfortable; and what I can find in Him, that will abundantly satisfy me in the Withdraw of these and all Creatures from me.

These are *my Children*, I am therefore from Nature and from Duty to *love* them.

A CHRIST is the Son of the eternal GOD, GOD must be more to me than *myself*. My highest *Love* must soar away to Him.

I see *my Image* on my *Children*. Does this *endear* them to me?

A CHRIST is the *express Image* of His FATHER. How much more *Dear* should this render Him to me?

My *Children* are *nearly Related* unto me. Not so *nearly* as my SAVIOUR. I am One with Him.

The *Affection* which my *Children* have and show to me, causes me to delight in them.

The *Affection* of my SAVIOUR to me, shines forth in the most incomparable Instances.

My *Children* in their *Conversation* with me entertain me with many Things that are *delectable*.

I find what is beyond all Expression more *delectable* in conversing with my SAVIOUR.

My Children are taken from the *good Things* of this World, which I should gladly have seen them rejoicing in.

My SAVIOUR takes them unto Himself, and unto *better Things* than any that are in *this present evil world*.

My sad Things are welcome to me, because of the Invitations and Opportunities, which they give me, thus to fly unto a glorious CHRIST, and feed and live upon Him.

And in the Skill and Will which He has given me to do so, I enjoy *unsearchable Riches*. I have a sure, a full, a Perpetual Fund of Blessedness.

Being brought unto these Dispositions and Contemplations, I went on, and made a Sacrifice of, my beloved Son and offered him up unto my glorious Lord, with all the Resignation that I could attain unto.

Immediately resuming my Chair, I thought I would visit my Bible, the Store-house of my Consolations; and if the first Place, I found it open at, should not prove the fittest Matter for my Meditations, I would then turn to the Relation of the miraculous Cure which the blessed JESUS wrought on the Son of the Nobleman, and meditate upon it. Unto my Surprize, the Bible tho' under some disadvantage for doing so, by a paper lodged behind the Leaf, it opened at that very place; and the Passage which immediately lay before my Eye, was that *Go thy Way, thy Son liveth*.

Towards the Evening, the Child's Fever arose to an Heighth which distressed us all. But he, under an Impression of such Violence upon him, as if it came from some superiour Original, fell into an unpacifiable Passion, to have a Vein breathed in him. We gratified him, and he had not one uneasy Hour after it; his Recovery went on to admiration.

31. G. D. But tho' the Recovery of my Son is hopefully going on, yett his Danger is not over. And the Distress for his two elder Sisters goes on to an Extremity. Especially, poor *Nancy*, dear *Nancy*, tis the plain Symptoms of approaching Death continually increasing upon her.

Wherefore I sett apart this Day, for Humiliations and Supplications, with Fasting before the Lord. That so I might as a Son of *Jacob*, weep and make Supplications, when I see my Family threatened with Desolations.

September. 1. G. D. What if I should move our Ministers to join with me, in publishing some Directions of Piety, for Families visited with Sickness.

My two dying Daughters!

Especially, dear *Nancy*, in the very Jaws of Death!

My God keeps my Faith in continual Exercise. And

in my Essays to live upon a CHRIST, He does quicken me and assist me wonderfully!

2. G. D. I need not now be at a Loss for particular objects of Compassion. They multiply wonderfully; they become innumerable.

* 3. G. D. A vast Collection of heavy Loads comes at once upon me: Some that I do not mention in these Papers, are added unto them. Full of Resignation to, and Satisfaction in, my SAVIOUR under all I am verily perswaded, that I shall anon find the GOD of Patience, to be the GOD of Consolation.

Dear Nancy dying!

The Physicians give her over, and pronounce it, that she has not many Hours to live. I do myself also resign her; and visit her with many Prayers, in a Day for that purpose.

But I know not what well to make of it; in the midst of all my Darkness, a strange Light breaks in upon my Mind with a Perswasion, that I shall see that Word fulfilled upon the Child, *I was brought low, and He helped me.* The Child herself also returning for a few Minutes to her Sense and her Speech, told me, she had yett some Hope to see that Word fulfill'd unto her.

4. G. D. The Flock must hear me take a very solemn and bitter Notice of it, that tho the Arrows of Death are flying among us, and our young People are afraid of their Lives, yett we are not sensible that any notable Effects of Piety are produced among them. Instead thereof, there is a Rage of Wickedness among us, beyond what was ever known from the Beginning to this Day.

Dear *Nancy*, still adying: and given over, condemned by the Physicians, to dy within a very few Hours.

5. G. D. *Sammy* recovering Strength, I must now earnestly putt him on considering, what he shall render to the Lord! Use exquisite Methods that he may come Gold out of the Fire.

Nibby still dangerously circumstanced.

And *Nancy* still a dying.

6. G. D. The Condition of my Sister *Maria's* Family: (full of affliction;) calls for my great Concern about it.

Nancy still a dying.

7. G. D. In the Circumstances of my dying Children, I am called unto repeated Sacrifices; I must go thro' the Duty of a Sacrificer. But shall I not exhibit unto the People of GOD, the Conduct of a Sacrificer, in such a Manner, that my Trials may be made useful to my Neighbours?

I do it this Day in the Lecture.

8. G. D. I make a Motion among the Ministers to serve the Design of Piety in the sick Families of the City.

To our Surprize, this Day, dear *Nancy* revives, and her Feaver breaks, and gives us Hopes that she may yett return unto us.

9. G. D. Still I don't want Objects for Compassion in my Neighbourhood. They grow exceedingly.

* 10. G. D. That Word of our SAVIOUR, *If the World hate you, yee know that it hated me before it hated you;* my Soul exceedingly feeds and lives upon it. I consider the Maxims and Actions, of my SAVIOUR, which exposed Him to the Hatred of the World: I will entirely conform unto them: and if the World thereupon treat me with all the Aversion imaginable, it shall be welcome to me, I will rejoice in it. The Joy sett before me in my SAVIOUR and in a Better World, gives me all the Satisfaction that can be wished for.

11. G. D. Entertain the Flock, with Meditations on the *lothsome Disease* upon us, in regard of our Sin: whereof we have a lively Emblem in the Distemper that is now raging among us.

12. G. D. What shall I do, that *Sammy* in his new Life may live unto God?

What shall I do, for my two feeble Daughters?

13. G. D. I have two Kinsmen recovering of the *Small-Pox*. What shall I do, to produce in them, the grateful Improvements of serious Piety?

14. G. D. GOD is doing of terrible Things, unto *France;* and the Time comes on, that this *tenth Part of the City* must be over-turned in a mighty Earthquake. It may be a very seasonable Action, if GOD please to direct and prosper it, and very astonishing may be the Consequences of it, if I form an agreeable Instrument, that shall make due Remarks on the Judgments of God, which are distressing and even destroying the French Nation, and call upon the Nation to Repent of the unparallell'd Persecution on the Worshippers of GOD and Followers of CHRIST which brings on them a wrath unto the uttermost, and exhort them *to come out of Babylon*, and instruct them in the *Maxims of the everlasting Gospel*, which they must unite upon. Wherefore, I am now forming of such an Instrument, and putting it into the French Language, and seeking Direction from Heaven, how to procure the Dispersion of it in *France;* and praying and waiting for the Success of it.

15. G. D. A Minister of the New North,[1] having his Consort, by Death taken from him, it gives me an Opportunity, to serve him, and preach for him, and thereby to introduce a more peaceable Condition of Things in our Churches.

16. G. D. Alas, my Afflictions multiply upon me. I cannot number them.

I will propose one comprehensive Service for them. In moving the Selectmen to look for a seasonable Supply of Wood, for the Town; that the Poor may not suffer for want of a convenient Fuel, in the approaching Winter.

* 17. G. D. Instead of any Regrett at the Things which for the present are not joyous but grievous, I will

---

[1] Rev. John Webb, whose wife, Frances, died September 14.

intermix with the darkest and saddest of them, a marvelous Joy upon my Encounter with such Things, as carry on my Crucifixion to This World, and my Conformity to my crucified SAVIOUR, and the Condition of one dying on a *Cross:* because of the Joy sett before me, and the View therein given me, of my Partaking with my SAVIOUR in the heavenly Glories which He has in the future State reserved for His Followers.

18. G. D. How pathetically may my public Prayers represent the various Condition of the Flock in this Time of Trouble before the Lord. Lett me study and contrive to do it in the Manner that shall be most edifying for them.

19. G. D. My unhappy Son *Increase* is again in lamentable Circumstances. A vile Sloth, accompanied with the Power of Satan still reigning over him, ruines him, destroyes him. I must not only repeat my solemn Admonitions unto the impenitent Youth, but (notwithstanding the Provocations he has given me) invite him to come again and live with me, that I may have him under my Eye continually.

My lovely *Nibby*, who was delivered of a Daughter on the Lord's-day, is now in Dying Circumstances. Lord! what a Sacrifice am I called unto!

I am daily with the dear Child, assisting and comforting of her.

20. G. D. My Neece, Mrs. *Eliot*, is also dying.[1]

A Variety of services to be done for her, and for the afflicted Family.

21. G. D. I am using Methods, to gett my *pastoral Letter* to Families visited with Sickness, reprinted, and scattered in our sick Families.

22. G. D. Move the Governour, to assist and promote several important Services.

[1] Maria, daughter of Maria Mather and Bartholomew Green, born in 1693, and died September 21, 1721. She married Captain John Elliott.

23. G. D. The afflicted multiply fast enough. One Day this Week their Condition obliged it, that my Prayers were seventeen, on another Day, twenty-two.

* 24. G. D. The dying Circumstances of my lovely Daughter, in conjunction with a Variety of other Trials, oblige me this morning to preach on, Isa. XXXVIII. 14. *O Lord, I am oppressed, undertake for me.* And I conclude my Sermon with such Terms as these.

"You are sensible, that the Condition whereinto the glorious Lord has brought me, by calling me to the Sacrifices of a *Jephtah*, and the Condition of some nearly Related unto me, has obliged my Flight into these Contemplations, whereupon I have two Things to observe unto you. The one is, that it pleases the Holy One, to make my Sorrows profitable to some few among His People. There are some few among the Children of GOD who fare the better for my Sorrows. And the View of this, renders my Sorrows in a Measure welcome to me. The other is, that a poor Servant of GOD can assure you, from his own happy Experience, that while he knowes he has a CHRIST concerned for him, and feels a CHRIST possessing of Him, and conversing with Him, none of all his Distresses prove too heavy for him. He don't sink under any Pressures, but can rise and soar and sing the Songs which God our Maker has given His children for whatever Night He will have to be passing over them. Oh! prize the CHRIST, for whom you hear our Testimony."

The New-born Grandchild, should have been brought forth to Baptism in the Afternoon, and the Water stood ready for it and the Name of, RESIGNED, should have been put upon it. But its dying in the Time of the public Service prevented it. An Uncommon Occurrence!

25. G. D. Can I edify the Flock more, than by two such Testimonies as I bore Yesterday unto them?

What have I to support me, under the Pressures which the View of my dying Daughter laies upon me? A glorious CHRIST! He is my Life, He is my All. I feel what it is to live by the Faith of the SON of GOD. A glorious CHRIST is carrying my Child unto the Paradise, where she shall be comforted with Enjoyments ten thousand Times more comfortable than any in this World, which my Love to her might have disposed me to have wished for her. All that I can see in her, to endear her to me, I can see much more in a glorious CHRIST, who gave her all that is desirable in her. I could have no Satisfaction in conversing with her, but what I can find, and infinitely more, in conversing with a Glorious CHRIST, whom I have always with me. My SAVIOUR will also take abundant Care of the Orphans, that she leaves behind her.

26. G. D. To strengthen a dear Child in the Agonies of Death, is a sad Work, which I am again call'd unto.

Between ten and eleven in the Evening the dear Child expired. A long and an hard Death was the Thing appointed for her.

Some Account of her, and the Circumstances of her Death, with her Dispositions under them, is given in some other Papers.

27. G. D. The Condition of my widowed Son-in-Law, now calls for my singular Cares, to befriend him, and advise him.

28. G. D. How much may I serve the Cause of Piety, and edify the People of God, if I entertain the Public with such Sentiments as the Faith and Love of CHRIST has given me, on such Occasions as I have now before me!

I do therefore particularly take the Lecture this Day; and entertain the Auditory with Meditations on the *holy Silence*, wherewith we are to glorify GOD, under all the sad Things that come upon us.

29. G. D. There will be *good devised* in my setting apart this Day, as I do, for Prayer with Fasting;

That I may humble myself before the Lord, for all the Sins which the Death of my dear *Nibby* calls me to a Repentance for.

That I may obtain Mercy for the Family that she has
left behind her.

That *Nancy* may have a perfect Recovery; *Creasy* be
made a new Creature; *Liza* have her Life preserved in the
Dangers of the Contagion; and *Sammy* be bless'd in his
Education.

That I may be supported and preserved in my daily
Visits to the sick Chambers, that are so lothsome, and full
of Malignity.

That I may be directed, assisted, prospered in my whole
Ministry.

And have a particular Smile of Heaven on the Essays I
am now sending beyond-sea, to serve the Kingdome of God.

30. G. D. The Afflicted. *Lord, How are they increased*
that affect me:

My glorious Lord, makes me still *fruitful in the Land of
my Affliction.*

(VII.) A particular Direction of the divine Providence
ordered my preaching at the New North Church, the Lord's
day after the Death of the Ministers Consort. There never
were but three Sermons printed, that were preached in that
Church, and all these three have been mine. What I now
preached is one of them. The Relatives have desired it. It
is entituled, GENUINE CHRISTIANITY. *Or, A True Christian
both in Life and in Death glorifying the most glorious Lord
A Sermon on the departure of Mrs.* Frances Web, *the Vertuous
Consort of Mr.* John Web, (*a Pastor to one of the Churches* in
Boston.) *who expired,* Sept. 14. 1721.[1]

(VIII.) I also gave to the Bookseller, my two Sermons
which were occasioned by the Death of my lovely Daughter.
The Book is Entituled, SILENTIARIUS. *A short Essay on
the Holy Silence, which Sad Things are to be Entertained
withal. A Sermon preached at Boston-Lecture, the Day
before the Interment of Mrs.* Abigail Willard.

[1] Printed by S. Kneeland for S. Gerrish, 1721.

Whereto there is added, A Sermon on, The Refuge of the Oppressed; which was preached on the Lord's-day preceeding.[1]

Moreover, My *Pastoral Letter to Families visited with Sickness,* is at this time under a Third Impression;[2] to be dispersed into such Families.

October. * 1. G. D. It is a Time, when people are strangely abandoned unto a froward, raging, lying Spirit; a Time wherein Malice and Falsehood have a mighty Operation among us. Help me, O my SAVIOUR, that I may not be in the least Measure infected with the Vices of the Time. Help me, that with a constant Care of Truth in all I speak, I may maintain the Meekness of Wisdom, and be full of Goodness, in all my Conversation, whatever Provocation to Impatience I may meet withal.

2. G. D. A Sermon on the Death of our promising young People, may be very serviceable.

3. G. D. My Children are with me. I have now three of them (and my wife's Kinswoman) at my Table. Among other Methods of Piety, I would make use of this. Tho' I will have my Table-Talk facetious as well as instructive, and use much Freedom of Conversation in it; yett I will have this Exercise continually intermixed. I will sett before them some Sentence of the Bible, and make some useful Remarks upon it. The Book of the *Proverbs,* is what I begin withal.

4. G. D. My bereaved Son-in-Law, and his Family, must continue a Subject which my Cares and Prayers are to be employ'd upon.

I must consider the special Temptations, which he may be obnoxious to.

5. G. D. Having this Week finished the *Grande Voix du Ciel à La* France *sous La Verge de Dieu;* I am contriving

---

[1] Printed by S. Kneeland.

[2] Printed by B. Green for S. Gerrish, 1721. It was first published in 1703, and again in 1713.

the best Methods I can to obtain the publishing and the
Dispersing of it. Among others, I propose the way of
Holland.

6. G. D. And I will employ the Hand of a Minister
somewhat acquainted there, for that Purpose.

7. G. D. The afflicted still multiply upon me. The
contagious Distemper, seems now at the Heighth in my
Neighbourhood.

The Number of the Sick that had Prayers asked for
them in the Bills at the Old North Church, on the last
Lord's-day, was, two hundred and two.

On the Monday, the Number of my Prayers with the
Sick, added unto those of my domestic Sacrifices, were one
and thirty.

So that I am exceedingly tired, and have little Time
to study.

*8. G. D. My Soul fills with strong Desires, to be
more acquainted with the heavenly World, and more
Initiated here below at the Employments and Enjoyments
of it; Groaning after that Attainment, *Thy will be done on
Earth as it is done in Heaven.*

In order hereunto, I would by way of Præface to the
Prayer which I usually make in my Study in the Beginning
of the Evening, have a Meditation on the *heavenly World;*
the Glories, and the wonderful Circumstances of it.

What a Week must I look for! The Number of Persons
in the Bills for Prayers on behalf of the Sick of the Small-
pox, in the Old North Church this day, amounts to about
315.

9. G. D. The Flock may be profitably entertained
with a Sermon on a *lothsome Desease.*

10. G. D. It is time for me, to renew my Directions
unto *Samuel,* for the Spending of his Time, and carrying
on the Course of his Studies.

11. G. D. What shall I do, that my aged Parent, who

is now wholly laid by from all public Service, may be yett further serviceable and comfortable?

This day, about thirty prayers!

12. G. D. I am consulting with the Governour, how to gett my *Grande Voix du Ciel*, into *France*.[1] And about some other Services.

13. G. D. May I not excite some considerable Persons among us, to project Ways, wherein some great Afflictions which they have suffered in their Families, may be made useful to the People of GOD.

14. G. D. I am furnished with Money, to be dispensed unto miserable Families. My dear *Greenwood*[2] supplies me with a Sum for that Purpose. I'l be as faithful and prudent a Steward as I can: But lett it be declared, that I am not myself the original Bestower of the Charity.

*15. G. D. That Account given of my SAVIOUR, *He pleased not Himself*, I find my Soul penetrate more into the Meaning of it; and grow more deeply affected with it. I will study, that in my Devotions towards GOD, and in my Benignities towards Men I may grow more conform'd unto the glorious Character.

322 in the Notes for the Sick of the small-pox prayed for.[3]

16. G. D. My Prayers with the Sick of the Flock, now take up a very great Part of my Time. I will contrive to make them as pertinent and pathetic as ever as I can. I will also disperse my *Pastoral Letter*, in my Visits.

17. G. D. Dear *Nancy's* Condition.

18. G. D. My Kinsman at *Roxbury* needs to be advised as well as assisted by me, for the Accomplishment of his desire to suffer and escape the *Small-pox*, in the Way of Inoculation.

[1] See p, 665, *infra*.

[2] Perhaps Isaac Greenwood, who married Sarah, daughter of Dr. John Clark.

[3] Written in the margin. The number of bills put up in the church. See p. 683, *infra*.

19. G. D. Consider, with the other Ministers, what further Duty the Distress now upon us may call us to.

20. G. D. A young Minister of the Town, whose Life I have earnestly pray'd for, having suffered but a gentle Visitation from the Small-pox, and being upon Recovery, I propose to make this an Occasion, and him an Instrument, of uncommon Services to the Kingdome of GOD.

21. G. D. Far from wanting Objects of Compassion.

* 22. G. D. Having made a Collection of my Methods to live upon a Glorious CHRIST, I will often peruse them, that I may not suffer any Decay in my Practice of them.

The Sick of the Small Pox in the Notes to be pray'd for, sunk to 180.[1]

23. G. D. The Wounds given to my Flock, in the Deaths which the Small-Pox has multiplied among us, must have a great Improvement made of them for the awakening of Piety in the Survivours.

24. G. D. Poor *Increase!*

25. G. D. My kinsman at *Roxbury*, I will send for him, to lodge at my House, that he may there have the *Small-Pox* in the way of *Inoculation* upon him.

26. G. D. Shall I not endeavour to shew our People, after what manner the Praises of the glorious GOD and His Christ, are to be copiously and affectuously celebrated? I do it this Day; which is a Day of general Thanksgiving throughout the Province.

This Day, towards the Evening, a Fever siezes me; brought on me by Colds taken in my Night-Visits, and by the Poisons of infected Chambers.

Is my Hour come? Tis welcome.

27. I have a View of speedily conquering the Fever with which I am threatened; and not suffering above three or four days Idleness and Confinement by it.

---

[1] Written in the margin.

G. D. I putt a Number of the *Pastoral Letter to Families visited with Sickness*, into the Hands of a pious Physician to be prudently dispersed by him in his Visits.

28. G. D. Still objects of Compassion enough!

*29. G. D. I am still sensible that in my Remarks on the Folly and Baseness continually expressed by our absurd and wicked People, I do not always preserve that Meekness of Wisdome, which would adorn the Doctrine of GOD my SAVIOUR. I use too bitter Terms. I will ask Wisdome of GOD for the Cure of this Distemper.

30. G. D. Entertain the Flock, with a Discourse on the Sovereignty of the glorious GOD, in His Dispensations; going down to the House of the Potter.

31. G. D. I will have our Satureday Evenings in the Family, rescued into more Opportunities, for a Variety of Devotions; about which I will study yett more exquisite Contrivances.

November. 1. G. D. I am giving a Reception in my House to my Kinsman T. W[alter] who is come under the Inoculation of the *Small-Pox*. But I would make it an Opportunity, for my doing and speaking many Things, that may render him yett more serviceable to the Kingdome of God.

2. G. D. In the Lecture this Day, I may edify a few People of this miserable and detestable Town, with a Discourse on a lothsome Disease.

3. G. D. This abominable Town, treats me in a most malicious, and murderous Manner, for my doing as CHRIST would have me to do, in saving the Lives of the People from an horrible Death; but I will go on, in the Imitation of my admirable SAVIOUR, and overcome Evil with Good. I will address a Letter to the Lieut. Governour and other Gentlemen of New *Hampshire*, to obtain from their Charity, a considerable Quantity of Wood, for the poor of this loth-

some Town, under the Necessities of the hard Winter coming on.[1]

4. G. D.   Still, the Objects of Compassion are so many, that I cannot make a particular Mention of them.

Among these, there are several Strangers arriving from *Ireland*, which are to be considered.

* 5. G. D.   By reading an holy Treatise, about a Christian *Crucifixion*, I propose to strengthen my Sentiments of it, and Submissions to it, and my Capacity to entertain the People of GOD with a Treatise on it, which I am endeavouring.

The Number of the Sick in our Bills now sunk to little more than 50.[2]

6. G. D.   It is time to feel the Pulse of the Flock, about an Assistent and Successor in the Ministry.

7. G. D.   There is a Variety of excellent Employments, which I must invent for, and assign to, my Children, each of them: that they may enrich their Minds with valuable Treasures, and furnish themselves to do good in the World.

They may on a Paper proper for it, be more distinctly declared.

8. G. D.   I will consider the young Gentlemen that accompanied my Kinsman for the Inoculation of the *Small-Pox;* as being *pro hac vice* my Kinsmen too.   And I will sett myself to do them all the Good I can, and quicken them to make a right Improvement of the divine Favour to them, in their present easy happy Circumstances.

9. G. D.   The sottish Errors, and cursed Clamours that fill the Town and Countrey, raging against the astonishing Success of the *Small-Pox* Inoculated;   makes it seasonable for me, to state the Case, and exhibit that which may silence the unreasonable People.

[1] The local feeling against Mather was very strong, and on the fourth a meeting of freeholders voted against permitting inoculated persons to come to town. *Boston Record Commissioners*, VIII. 159.

[2] Written in the margin.

10. G. D. May not I animate a noted Minister in the Countrey, to appear on this Occasion?

Letter to *Roxbury*, may enable my Brother there, to do some Service.

11. G. D. A dear Friend, whose Life is in daily Danger of the *Small-pox*, Lett me write unto him, and (if I must lose him, which God prevent!) lett me *Liberare Animam*.

*12. G. D. Reading a nameless Essay, just arrived from *London*, about, *The Temptations of Ministers*, I am inexpressibly suited and pleased; I find my own case admirably exhibited in many Articles. I am awakened unto exceeding Watchfulness, *that none of my Temptations may discourage and enfeeble my usefulness.*

But after these Impressions of the Messages from Heaven so sent unto me, to my Surprise I find, that the Essay was of my own Brother's writing.

13. G. D. Continual Charges unto the young People of the Flock, recovered from the Small-Pox, as they come in my Way, which they do continually, to live unto GOD, and by His Goodness be led unto Repentance; This will be one Article of my Conduct.

14. G. D. What an Occasion, what an Incentive, to have PIETY, more than ever quicken'd and shining in my Family, have I this morning been entertained withal!

My Kinsman, the Minister of *Roxbury*, being Entertained at my House, that he might there undergo the *Small-Pox Inoculated*, and so Return to the Service of his Flock, which have the Contagion begun among them;

Towards three a Clock in the Night, as it grew towards Morning of this Day, some unknown Hands, threw a fired Granado into the Chamber where my Kinsman lay, and which uses to be my Lodging-Room. The Weight of the Iron Ball alone, had it fallen upon his Head, would have been enough to have done Part of the Business designed. But the *Granado* was charged, the upper part with dried

Powder, the lower Part with a Mixture of Oil of Turpentine and Powder and what else I know not, in such a Manner, that upon its going off, it must have splitt, and have probably killed the Persons in the Room, and certainly fired the Chamber, and speedily laid the House in Ashes. But, *this Night there stood by me the Angel of the GOD, whose I am and whom I serve;* and the merciful Providence of GOD my SAVIOUR, so ordered it, that the Granado passing thro' the Window, had by the Iron in the Middle of the Casement, such a Turn given to it, that in falling on the Floor, the fired Wild-fire in the Fuse was violently shaken out upon the Floor, without firing the Granado. When the *Granado* was taken up, there was found a Paper so tied with String about the Fuse, that it might out-Live the breaking of the Shell, which had these words in it; Cotton Mather, *You Dog, Dam you: I'l inoculate you with this, with a Pox to you.*[1]

15. G. D. My Kinsman having received so great a Deliverance, he shall not stir from me till we have contrived and resolved, some very special and signal Service to be done by him for the Kingdome of God.

16. G. D. Ought not the Ministers of the Town, to be called together that we may consider, what may be our Duty and most proper to be done upon the Occasion of Satan so strangely lett loose to possess the Town?

17. G. D. On this Day, I use to think, what good shall I putt others upon doing of? I must now think, how shall I prevent others from doing Evil? Particularly, in spreading false Reports about the Countrey. For this Purpose, I convey unto our News-Writers, a true Account of the *Tuesday-Affair,* which is very much talk'd of, that it may be published.[2]

[1] In his newspaper account of the incident, Mather made the paper read: "Cotton Mather, I was once one of your Meeting, but the cursed Lie you told of —, you know who, made me leave you, you Dog; And," etc.

[2] Printed in the *Boston News-Letter* November, 20, 1721.

18. G. D. Sundry Lives are to be saved, by my pressing the Inoculation of the Small-Pox upon them.

*19. G. D. Certainly it becomes me and concerns me, to do something very considerable, in a way of Gratitude unto GOD my SAVIOUR, for the astonishing Deliverance, which He did the last Week bestow upon me, and upon what belong'd unto me.

Among other Things, I entertain the People of GOD, with a Discourse on the Services done by the good *Angels*, for the Servants of GOD. So will I bespeak more Praises to GOD my SAVIOUR for the Benefits of the angelical Ministry: which alas are not enough tho't upon.

But, behold, what my glorious Lord has brought me to. I have been guilty of such a Crime as this. I have communicated a never-failing and a most allowable Method, of preventing Death and other grievous Miseries by a terrible Distemper among my Neighbours. Every day demonstrates, that if I had been hearken'd to, many precious Lives (many Hundreds) had been saved. The Opposition to it, has been carried on, with senseless Ignorance and raging Wickedness. But the growing Triumphs of Truth over it, throw a possessed People into a Fury, which will probably cost me my Life. I have Proofs, that there are people who approve and applaud the Action of *Tuesday* Morning: and who give out Words, that tho' the first Blow miscarried, there will quickly come another, that shall doe the Business more effectually.

Now, I am so far from any melancholy Fear on this Occasion, that I am filled with unutterable Joy at the Prospect of my approaching Martyrdom. I know not what is the Meaning of it; I find, my Mouth strangely stop'd, my Heart strangely cold, if I go to ask for a Deliverance from it. But, when I think on my suffering Death for saving the Lives of dying People, it even ravishes me with a Joy unspeakable and full of Glory. I cannot help longing for the Hour, when it will be accomplished. I am even afraid almost of doing any thing for my præservation. I have a Crown before me; and I now know by Feeling, what I formerly knew only by Reading, of the divine Consolations with which the Minds of Martyrs have been sometimes irradiated. I had much rather dy by such Hands, as now threaten my Life, than by a Feaver; and much rather dy for my Conformity to the blessed JESUS in Essays to save the Lives of Men from the Destroyer, than for some Truths, tho' precious ones, to which many Martyrs testified formerly in the Flames of *Smithfield*.

20. G. D. I entertained the Flock, yesterday, as I have there proposed.

21. G. D. I must assign unto *Samuel*, such Subjects to form Discourses on, as his late Circumstances may more particularly lead unto.

22. G. D. I have some Kinsmen, (and others as dear to me) whom I will encourage to save their Lives, in the way of the *Small-Pox Inoculated*.

23. G. D. I join with my aged Father, in publishing some, SENTIMENTS ON THE SMALL-POX INOCULATED.[1] CHRIST crowns the Cause for which I have suffered so much, with daily Victories. And Abundance of Lives may be saved by our Testimony. Truth also will be rescued and maintained.

24. G. D. I draw up the Method of Proceeding in the Inoculation of the *Small-Pox*, and communicate Copies of it, that so Physicians about the Countrey may know how to manage it.

24 *d*. IX *m. Friday*. This Day, I sett apart for Supplications: Wherein I enjoyed many sweet Influences of Heaven; assuring me that my Sins are pardoned: and

---

[1] A broadside printed by S. Kneeland for J. Edwards, November 20, 1721, and entitled *Several Reasons proving that Inoculating or Transplanting the Small Pox, is a lawful Practise.* Reprinted in I. *Collections*, IX. 265.

that I shall be rescued out of wretched Encumbrances that ly upon me; and that my domestic Wants and Straits also, shall be releeved.

But this Day, I likewise made an offer of my Life unto the glorious Lord. Being in daily Hazard of Death from a bloody People from no other Cause pretended but this: that I have saved the Lives of dying People, in a way by a gracious GOD reveled unto us; I declared unto my GOD and SAVIOUR, that I am unspeakably willing to dy by their Hands, and that I cannot think of my Martyrdome for Him, without unutterable Joy. I feel my Spirit not only longing for the Accomplishment of it, but even straitned until it be accomplished.

This Day, I also presented unto the Lord, my two præparations; the One, entituled, THE ROARING OF THE SOUTH-SEA; The other, UNE GRANDE VOIX DU CIEL, À LA France, SOUS LA VERGE DE DIEU: entreating Him to accept and prosper them.

25. G. D. My Visits to my Friends under the Inoculation.

* 26. G. D. Will not the *Spirit of Martyrdome*, to which I am arrived, and of which I have such a precious Opportunity to repeat the Discoveries and Expressions, be upon me a Token for good, that I shall be received into the glorious Army?

27. G. D. It is time to putt our Committee upon doing some things for the welfare of the Flock.

28. G. D. *Sammy's* Studies to be directed.

29. G. D. Several Persons at this Time under the *Small-Pox Inoculated*, I must look on as my Patients, and so, my Relatives. I will do the best I can, that they may Resolve on some special Returns of Gratitude, wherein God their SAVIOUR may be glorified.

30. G. D. Writing Letters for *Europe*, I send over many Things, that I hope, will serve the Kingdome of GOD.

And particularly, among the rest, I write a further and a more distinct Account of the *Small-Pox Inoculated*, the Method and Success of it among us, and the Opposition to it; By which Means, I hope, some hundreds of thousands of Lives, may in a little while come to be preserved.

December. 1. G. D. Having drawn up, the Way of Proceeding, in the *Inoculation* of the *Small-pox*, I communicate Copies of it unto the Physicians and others, in several Parts of the Countrey; that so they may be directed in the Practice of it, as there may be Occasion for it.

2. G. D. Some very wicked Persons, must have suitable Admonitions dispensed unto them.

* 3. G. D. In watching against having any Share in the Vices that are now raging at an uncommon Rate among us, I must beware, that I don't harbour or admitt, any Tendency towards the least Wish of Evil, unto such as may have displeased me, in the Contradiction of Sinners, which I so much meet withal. And, if I find at any time the least sudden Inclination that way, I must immediately suppress it and oppose it, with a contrary Wish of all Good unto them.

I must beware, that upon the Provocations, which the prodigious Nonsense, and Folly, and Baseness ever now and then expressed by the People may give me, my Speeches be not intemperate and unadvised, or any Ebullitions of Impatience; any Trespasses upon the Rules of Meekness and Wisdome.

I must beware, that I don't spread any false Reports, and report any thing, but what I [am] well informed and assured of.

4. G. D. Considering the several Classes of People in the Flock, the great Number that have recovered of a terrible Distemper do particularly call for my Consideration. And I would with adapted Prayers and Sermons, awaken them to glorify GOD their SAVIOUR with suitable Returns of Obedience to Him.

5. G. D. My Negro-Servant, must be prepared for Baptism, with some singular Instructions.

6. G. D. Employ particular supplications for the Welfare of the unknown Person, who sought my Death by the fired Granado.

7. G. D. I entertain a Purpose, of writing in the Latin Tongue, a Discourse about the Union of *Lutherans* and *Calvinists*, on the Basis of PIETY; and of sending it unto the University at *Hall* in the *Lower Saxony*. Who can tell, what may be the Consequences? Assist me, and accept me, O my SAVIOUR!

8. G. D. Several Motions are to be made among the Ministers of the Town.

Particularly relating to Days of Prayer, in this evil Time.

9. G. D. Warnings are to be given unto the wicked Printer, and his Accomplices, who every week publish a vile Paper to lessen and blacken the Ministers of the Town, and render their Ministry ineffectual.[1]

A Wickedness never parallel'd any where upon the Face of the Earth!

* 10. G. D. There is a Frame of PIETY, which happy am I, that my dear SAVIOUR has brought me to it!

I have at my own single Expense for many years, maintained a *Charity-Schole* for the Instruction of *Negro's* in Reading and Religion. A Lieutenant of a Man of War, whom I am a Stranger to, designing to putt an Indignity upon me, has called his *Negro-Slave* by the Name of COTTON-MATHER.

On this Occasion, I could recollect a great Variety of Instances, wherein the Point of my singular Endeavours to glorify GOD, instead of having any temporal Recompences,

---

[1] Three newspapers were now printed in Boston, the *Boston News-Letter*, the *Boston Gazette* and the *New England Courant*. The last, published by James, brother of Benjamin Franklin was regarded as the greatest offender.

have been followed with nothing so remarkable as the conspicuous and vexatious Revenges of Satan upon me.

Having done so, my Spirit rejoicing in GOD my SAVIOUR, immediately soared into these two Dispositions.

First; I do and will reckon, that my Interest in a glorious CHRIST, and the Skill and Will to converse with Him, wherewith a gracious God has enriched me, is a sufficient and abundant Reward, of all my Services, all my Devotions.

Next: I am entirely willing to have all my patient Continuance on Well-doing pass unrewarded in this World; and with a strong Faith I can be content, that in a future State, I shall see all my Harvest; reap nothing till I come into another and a better World.

11. G. D. I am astonished, I am astonished at the prodigious Ignorance of our People in Matters of Religion, after all the Instruction bestow'd upon them. Among other Instances, their foolish Talk, about the *Decrees of* GOD, is notorious. I must in this, and in some other Points, endeavour to have the Flock better illuminated.

12. G. D. My Son *Increase*, by a violent and passionate Resentment of an Indignity, which a wicked Fellow offered unto me, has exposed himself to much Danger, and me also to no little Trouble. I must employ this Occasion as much to his Advantage, especially in regard of Piety, as I can.

God graciously gives a good Issue to it.

13. G. D. I am using further Methods to promote the Credit and Practice of the beloved Physician in my Neighbourhood; whom I would embrace as a beloved Relative.

14. G. D. The *Small-Pox* making terrible Destruction in several Parts of *Europe*, I would hasten unto *Holland*, an account of the astonishing Success, which we have here seen of the *Small-Pox inoculated*. Who can tell, but

Hundreds of Thousands of Lives, may be saved by this Comunication.

15. G. D. It may be an Introduction to some good, if I visit the Lecture of the New North Church in my Neighbourhood.

16. G. D. Some lately recovered from the Dangers of the Sm : Pox in the Way of Inoculation must be spoken to.

* 17. G. D. My Brother has a pretty Fancy, in his Discourse of *Temptations;* that Ministers, who meet with Abuses from sorry and scoundrel People, have cause to look on themselves as humbled, on the Account of their having the *Egyptian* Plague of *Lice* upon them. I am very *lowsy*, it seems; and I ought therefore to be very *humble*. Under the Assaults and Insults of contemptible People, I must behave myself, as under the Fulfilment of that Word, *my GOD will Humble me.*

18. G. D. My Auditory strangely reviving and increasing, I may do well, to contrive public Expressions, that may have a Tendency to unite them, and yett further augment them.

19. G. D. Books to be assigned unto *Creasy*, for his Reading.

And oblige him to enrich his *Quotidiana.*

20. G. D. They that have enjoy'd the Benefit of the *Small-pox Inoculated*, being all of them indeed my *Patients*, I would consider them as my *Relatives*, and I would use all possible Methods, that they may improve in Piety under the Favours of God.

21. G. D. I am sending to *Holland* my, *Grande Voix du Ciel à La France*, that it may that way gett into *France*.

I am sending also some other Things into *Holland*, with Hopes thereby to serve the Kingdome of God.

22. G. D. I communicate unto some of our best Ministers, those Papers, which may have a Tendency to

raise them unto the higher Measures of Holiness and Usefulness.

22 *d.* 10 *m. Friday.*   I sett apart this Day, for Supplications.

On such Occasions, and with such Exercises, as employ'd me, when I was last in this way before the Lord.

But especially to obtain my final Deliverance, from the Encumbrance which my unhappy Administration has brought upon me.

And that my Opportunities to do good may be delivered from the Power of the Dog.

23. G. D.   Releefs to be dispens'd unto one, whom I shall employ to pray for me.

* 24. G. D.   I consider, that whatever comes into my Mind, has a Subsistence given unto it there.   The Thing receives a Notionall Subsistence there; which is indeed all that a mind of no higher power than mine, can give unto it.   Hence I infer how watchful I should be over the Thoughts that are formed in my Mind.   My Mind must beware of giving a Subsistence to foolish, and much more to wicked Things; to anything offensive to GOD.   My Obedience and Conformity to the glorious GOD must be expressed, in my giving a Subsistence to nothing, but what shall upon Reflection be found very good.

25. G. D.   The Fearful Withdraw of the holy Spirit of GOD from His Ordinances, is to be so represented unto the Flock, in the public (prayers and) Sermons, as may awaken an awful Consideration of it.

26. G. D.   A new Servant is come into my Family. By lodging Books of Piety in her Hands, and by dropping the Maxims of Religion continually in her Hearing, I will do my best that she may be brought home to GOD, and obtain a CHRIST by being here.

27. G. D.   In my daily Prayers, when I mention my Children to the Lord for His Favours, I must remember

now to make a more particular Mention of my two Grand-
children.

28. G. D.   I thought upon an Action, that might seem
a little fanciful and whimsical, but yett if it be done with
a due Concealment on the Doer of it, it may happen to produce good Impressions on some or other among the chosen
of GOD, who may happen to consider it.

Our Bills of Credit (which are all the Money we have)
Circulate into numberless Hands.   A vile Sett of men,
have contrived, by the wicked Use of their Pens on the
Backs of the Bills, to convey Poison and Mischief thro' the
Countrey.   As the Reverse of this Wickedness, I would
on the Backs of the Bills which come to me at any Time,
write some Text of Scripture, that shall have a Tendency,
to awaken in the Minds of People, right Sentiments of this
World, and of what is passing in it.

I would write —

  See Prov. 23. 5.   See Jer. 17. ii.

or See Matth. 16. 26. or See 1. Tim. 6. 10.

    or See 1. Joh. 2. 15.

29. G. D.   I would move some Gentlemen in *Holland*,
unto several Services.

30. G. D.   A dying Handmaid of the Lord, in Darkness; yea, more than one such.

* 31. G. D.   By a dark and a faint Cloud striking over
my Mind, I begin to feel some Hazards, lest my Troubles,
whereof I have a greater Share than any Minister in the
Countrey, grow too hard for me, and unfit me and unhinge
me for my Services.   I must therefore cry mightily to the
glorious Lord, that I may not faint in the Day of Adversity.
And I must labour exceedingly to multiply the Exercises
of my Conversation with the Comforter who should releeve
my Soul.

January. [1721-22.] 1. G. D.   Some of my Flock,
with whom I discourse occasionally on the Mysteries of

the *Kingdome of God*, wherein His *Will* shall *be done on Earth as it is in Heaven*, seem desirous to be more fully acquainted with those Mysteries, and ask and hear me *privately* upon them.   I am therefore upon forming a Society of Christians agreeable to such an Intention, with Purposes to entertain them at my house once a fortnight, with Discourses on that noble and holy Subject.   And, I hope, that the Society may afford me Opportunities to do for the Flock, some further considerable Services.

2. G. D.   Ah, poor *Creasy!* Poor *Creasy!*
Yett will I not utterly give him over!

3. G. D.   The sick State of a Child, which I am a great Uncle to, calls for my Cares of it, and of my Widow-Sister who is Grandmother to the orphan.

4. G. D.   Shall not I do well to call upon such of my Flock, as have had the Benefit of the *Small-Pox Inoculated*, that they meet at my House for a solemn Thanksgiving to the Glorious Lord?   It may have many good Consequences attending of it.

5. G. D.   There is Danger of some Inconveniencies befalling the Colledge; in which my Advice for a due Temper in Management, privately given, may be of some Service.

5 *d.* 11 *m. Friday.* This Day, I sett apart for secret Supplications.

Especially, that I may be supported under the many and heavy Trials which I encounter with.

And my Opportunities to do Good, be rescued from the Rage of my furious Adversaries; the Floods of Belial.

That my Son *Increase* may yett have a new Heart given to him.

That the Wants and Straits which are come upon me may be releeved.

And yett more particularly, that I may be well delivered out of the heavy Encumbrance which lies upon me, for the remaining Part of the Administration wherein I foolishly suffered myself to be entangled; and that they who intend my hurt may not be able to accomplish it; and that the Lord would raise me up Friends, and lead me in the Way wherein I should go.

In the Evening, I began to see a surprizing Answer to some of the Prayers that had been made in the day.

6. G. D. A poor Widow, perishing of Wounds by a Scald.

* 7. G. D. When the Protomartyr *Stephen* had his Countreymen *crying out with a loud Voice upon him, and stopping their Ears, and running on him, and stoning of him,* he was then so favoured of Heaven, that he could say, *Behold, I see the Heavens opened.* At this Time, I am engaged in the Methods of Supplication and of Meditation, to seek such a Favour, that, I may, *Behold, and see the Heavens opened.* Oh! That with uncommon Flights of Piety and of Purity, and of a Secession from this World, I may soar up to the *Conversation in Heaven,* which I am now preaching on! Lett me in my Devotions particularly exercise, illustrate and accommodate every Article of the *Conversation in Heaven,* which I may be led in my Studies to think upon.

8. G. D. And how can I serve my Flock, better, than by Communicating to them the Effects of my Studies on this noble and holy Subject.

9. G. D. By Supplying of *Creasy,* with Matters to be inserted in his *Quotidiana,* which I will compell him to writing of (and Reading for,) I would hope to spread some Netts of Salvation for him.

10. G. D. My Kindred are to be quickened unto Piety, from the Death of the Child this day to be interr'd, which I am great Uncle to.

11. G. D. Tomorrow is our good Governour's Birthday. I not only present him with my *Genethlia Pia*,[1]

---

[1] Published in 1719. This entry determines the day of Samuel Shute's birth, a fact unknown to the writer in the *Dictionary of National Biography.*

but also putt *Sammy* on addressing an agreeable Poem to him. I hope, in this way to introduce good Services for the Public.

12. G. D. Writing to *South-Carolina*, I send some things, that may be of Service to the Cause of Piety there.

I sett apart this Day, as I did one a Week ago, for Prayer with Fasting before the Lord.

The Occasions, and the Exercises, were the same with what they were this Day se'nnight.

13. G. D. Make an offer to a Minister at *Marble-head*, likely to be murdered by an abominable People, that will not lett him save his Life, from the Small-Pox, in the Way of Inoculation. Offer to receive and cover him.[1]

* 14. G. D. This Thought is very impressive, (*Lord make it more so!*) upon me. When I am going to Prayer, I am *going to Heaven.* With what Love and Hope and Joy ought I to repair thither on all Occasions! But then, that by my Prayer, I may enter into the most holy Place, lett me still preface it, with some Consideration of my Jesus acting as the High-priest of His People there. Lett me also consider, with what Aims and Frames ought my Prayer to be carried on, that it may have some Harmony with the Devotions of the glorified Spirits now worshipping of God in the heavenly World. And when I find my Prayer managed with too cold and vain, and wandring an Heart, lett me consider for the Rebuking of it, how little is this like to what is doing in the heavenly World!

SPOKEN IN A MEETING OF THE MINISTERS.

15 *d.* 11 *m.* 1721 [-22.]

It has been a Maxim with me, *That a Power to do good, not only gives a Right unto it, but also makes the Doing of it a Duty.*

I have been made very sensible, that by pursuing of this Maxim, I have entirely ruined myself as to this World, and rendred it really

[1] John Barnard?

too hott a Place for me to continue in.   But yett, in the Pursuance of it, I have not lett one Day pass me for very many Years, which has not brought with it, shaped and written Projections to Do Good; for which Purpose I have divided the Objects into Classes to be distinctly considered, that so I might be sure to do good unto all. And besides all this, I have scarce at any Time for these five and forty Years and more so come as to stay in any Company without considering whether no good might be done before I left it.   I would not have said this, if I had not lived by Neighbours that compel me to it.   And if they would have me own, that I have been guilty of many Indiscretions, and of præcipitated or preposterous Managements in some of my Essays to do good, I am ready to own it; and shall thank them, to convince me of the Instances.

But, my Opportunities to do good, which have been to me the Apple of my Eye, have been strangely struck at.   Odd Occurences have happened, which have produced unaccountable Combinations in all Ranks of Men, to disable me for doing what I have most inclined unto.

The most false Representations imaginable have been made of me; and of my Conduct.   And tho' I could easily have confuted the Slanders and Clamours, I have rather born them with Silence, and been as the Sheep is before the Shearers, and as a Man in whose Mouth there are no Reproofs.   I hope, I have known what it is to take Pleasure in Humiliations and Annihilations.

I am at length reduced unto this Condition, that my Opportunities to do good, (except among a few of my own little Remnant of a Flock,) appear to me almost entirely extinguished, as to this Countrey.   I must employ my Faculties, in projections to do good in more distant Places.   And I bless God, I have there a Prospect of some Things, whereof I shall know more hereafter.   But at present, *I have done! I have done! I have done* treating you with any more of my Proposals.   If they should be never so good, yett if they be known to be mine, that is enough to bespeak a Blast upon them. Do *you* propose as many good Things as you please, and I will second them, and assist them and fall in with them, to the best of my Capacity.

An ingenous Person in the Company, *Mr. Wm. Cooper,* made the first, and a quick Reply to me, in these Words, *I hope the Devil don't hear you, Syr!*

15. G. D.   I have a strong Impression on my Mind,

that this poor Place will shortly see a tremendous Fulfilment of that word, *they shall go out of one Fire and another* Fire shall devour them. I do to my Flock utter the Warnings of it; thinking it may be serviceable unto them for me to do so.

16. G. D. My *African* Servant must be præpared for the Baptism, which he has been long seeking for.[1]

17. G. D. My personal Enemies, and they that hate me with a cruel Hatred, more and more shew themselves. *Lord*, save me from the evil Disposition of personal Revenges. And if I proceed unto any necessary Chastisements upon any of them, lett me be very careful, that no Trespasses upon the Rules of Charity, be intermixed with them.

18. G. D. There are some Things doing about the Colledge, whereabout my Help is asked, and may be useful.

19. G. D. The villanous Abuses offered and multiplied, unto the Ministers of this Place, require something to be done, for their Vindication. I provide Materials for some agreeable Pens among our People, to prosecute this Design withal.

This Day, I sett apart, for Prayer.

On the same Intentions, and with the same Exercises and Experiences, that I have had, in those of the Weeks preceeding.

20. G. D. A young Bookseller, in danger of exposing himself to the Judgments of GOD, must be faithfully warned of it.

* 21. G. D. What is the Sabbath, but the *Rest of GOD?* I sabbatize aright, if I enter into the Rest of GOD, on the Lord's-Day; and all vital Religion will be kept alive, and flourish and improve in me, by my doing so. Coming to a Rest in GOD, I do this Day enter into the Rest of GOD. But how is this to be accomplished? It is my JESUS, who must carry me into the Rest of GOD; I must look up con-

---

[1] See p. 683, *infra.*

tinually to my JESUS, who has offered and promised, *I will give you Rest.* My Thoughts on Him are to be this Day continual and Numberless.

I must by my Thoughts, and with suitable Affections raised from them, incessantly fly away to GOD; therein saying, *Return to thy Rest, O my Soul; even to the God who will deal bountifully with thee.*

I must have my Thoughts much employ'd upon the *Rest which remains for the People of GOD;* and have many heart-melting Meditations on the Blessedness which GOD, my SAVIOUR has for me in another World.

The Services of the Day, which are an Imitation of what is done in that World, and the Sufferings of my Life, out of which I shall be delivered in that World are to lead me into those Meditations.

If any Thoughts which have any Tendency to discompose my *Rest* in the Views of God my SAVIOUR on this Day dart into my Mind, I am out of Obedience unto Him, to chase them away, and say *Depart from me, ye wicked Things for my communion with my God shall be undisturbed.*

22. G. D. Some of my Flock seem desirous, that I would form a sort of Society, who should at proper times visit me, and receive my Instructions concerning the King-dome of GOD that is to be lookd for, and the Scriptures that relate unto it.

Consider of it.

But I think, I mention'd something of this before. I therefore add, (that there may be *Nulla Dies Sine Linea*) there is a very old Man, whom I would bring into the Church before he dies; and I would make it an Occasion of speaking many pungent Things to the old People in the Assembly.

23. G. D. A Servant come to live in my Family, has not been baptised. I would use all proper Means to bring her into an Espousal to her SAVIOUR, and so to the Con-firmation of it in the Baptism of the Lord.

24. G. D. My Kinsman at *Roxbury*, there are things he must be excited to, and things he must be delivered from.

25. G. D. Something must be done towards the Suppressing and Rebuking of those wicked Pamphletts, that are continually published among us, to lessen and blacken the Ministers, and poison the People.

26. G. D. Several Things of an exquisite Contrivance and Composure, are done for this Purpose. Tho my poor Hand is the Doer of them, they must pass thro other Hands, that I may not pass for the Author of them.

26 *d.* 11 *m.* I sett apart this Day for Supplications, as I have now done one Day in a Week, for several Weeks together.

Especially to obtain, a good Period unto the wretched Encumbrance of my Administration.

The Conversion of my miserable Son *Increase*, and his Rescue from the Power of Satan. And a religious and industrious Mind for my Son *Samuel*.

The Deliverance of my Opportunities to do good, from the Rage of a wicked People; Satanically sett for the Ruining of them.

The Releef of the Wants and Straits which are oppressing of me, and wherein I sometimes am destitute of a Food convenient for me.

I enjoy'd some heart-melting Interviews with Heaven, in the Services of the Day.

27. G. D. Something must be done, for a Stranger, a young Minister, now at *Watertown*, that he may not stumble on dark Mountains.

* 28. G. D. I am gott into a Way, of setting apart one Day every week, for Supplications. And I think, I will try to continue the Practice, until my glorious Lord please to arise and save me.

29. G. D. In my Discourses to the Flock, on a *Con-*

versation in Heaven, I have marvellous Opportunities to feed and serve them; which I study with as exquisite contrivance as I can.

30. G. D. On the Lord's-day Evenings, I have my Domesticks together, and have some agreeable thing read among them. I will single out the most suitable Things I can think of.

31. G. D. My sister mourning under the Death of her only Daughter, is in Danger of offending Heaven, and ruining herself. I must comfort her, advise her, perswade her.

February. 1. G. D. There is great Hazard of Confusions (there are Contentions) in unhappy *Watertown.*[1]

Much of my Counsil and Labour to prevent these Things is called for.

2. G. D. Much good may be done, by making an Extract of Dr. *Harris's* Prælection, *De Inoculatione Varrolanum;* and publishing of it here.[2]

2 d. 12 m. *Friday.* This Day I sett apart for Supplications, on the Matters and in the Methods, and not altogether without the same enjoyments, that have been for such a Day with me, one every Week, for now many Weeks together.

3. G. D. Releefs to be dispensed unto a praying Soul, with a Request that [*unfinished.*]

* 4. G. D. There is a Petition which I am to make in my daily Prayers; and which is to run in such Terms as these: *Lord, Lett the Wrath of my Enemies praise thee, and the Remainder of that Wrath do thou Restrain.*

But, Oh! may I obtain the Grace to imitate my SAVIOUR in my Temper and Carriage towards these unreasonable Enemies.

5. G. D. A Sermon of Things to be expected from a

---

[1] Two new meeting houses were to be erected. *Watertown Records* II. 279.
[2] John Harris (1667?-1719.)

Remnant, may be much for the Welfare of the Flock that continues with me.

6. G. D. My *African* Servant is now propounded, for the Baptism of the Lord. Great Pains am I to take, that he come to it, with suitable Understanding and Affection.[1]

7. G. D. My poor Son-in-Law.

8. G. D. I have a wondrous Prospect of restoring Peace to the Countrey, by accomplishing some unexpected Reconciliations.

9. G. D. Good may be done in our poor eastern Parts, by some Letters thither.

9 *d.* 12 *m. Friday*. This Day I sett apart for Prayer with Fasting on the same Occasions and with the same Exercises, that I have kept such a Day every Week, for diverse Weeks together.

I enjoy'd something of Heaven in the Devotions of the Day.

On each of my important Articles, I repented of the Sins by which I had forfeited the Blessing. I beleeved, confessed, adored the Power of GOD my SAVIOUR to bestow the Blessing. I pleaded, the Glory and Service that would arise to GOD from it, if He should grant the Blessing. And then finally, to express my Faith, and receive the Answer of my GOD, while I was yett on my Knees, I sang a Paragraph of a Psalm suitable to my Purpose; in leading me to which I had a strange Direction of Heaven.

10. G. D. An aged Gentlewoman, eminent for her Bounties to all sorts of Persons (I have been myself a Sharer in them) is fallen into the lowest Poverty; extreme Wants and Straits, have overtaken her. And none of the Ingrates that have partook in her Bounties, will now do any thing for her. I'l send her some Supplies, but ly entirely conceled from her. I stir up some others also to do for her.

* 11. G. D. The Year being so finished, what can I

---

[1] See p. 683, *infra*.

do better, than seriously peruse the Memorials of it, and make the Reflections of Piety that may be proper upon them!

THE COURSE OF MY MINISTRY.

12 *d*. 12 *m*. [*February*.] 1720-21. I preached, On 1. Chron. XXIX. 15. No *Continuance* in, or *Expectation* from, this World. (It being my Birth-day; and also the First-Day of my coming abroad unto the public Services, after I had been for some Weeks confined by Illness.)

19 *d*. 12 *m*. On 1. Pet. II. 9. An *holy Nation*. (And I administred the Eucharist.)

26 *d*. 12 *m*. On Exod. XXI. 19. The Damage in the *Loss of Time*, with Methods and Motives to prevent it.

5 *d*. 1 *m*. [*March*.] On Phil. IV. 4. A glorious CHRIST rejoiced in.

9 *d*. 1 *m*. *Thursday*. The Lecture; On Matth. XII. 20. The *Compassion* of our SAVIOUR, towards the frail and vile Children of Men.

12 *d*. 1 *m*. On Phil. IV. 4. Finishing what I began a Week ago.

19 *d*. 1 *m*. On 1 Pet. II. 9. An *Holy Nation*. (Finishing what I began a Month ago. Before the Eucharist.)

23 *d*. 1 *m*. *Thursday*. The Lecture. On 1. Chron. XXIX. 19 The *pious Mind* which Parents that have any Piety in them, will desire for their Children. (To a very great Assembly with a very great Assistance.)

2 *d*. 2 *m*. [*April*.] On Joh. XII. 35. The sad Condition of them, who leave at Uncertainty, what is to be their Portion for Eternity, and *know not whither they are going*.

9 *d*. 2 *m*. On Joh. XII. 35. Finishing the awful Matter I began the last Lord's-day.

16 *d*. 2 *m*. On 1. Pet. II. 9. A *peculiar People*. (And I administred the Eucharist.)

20 *d*. 2 *m*. *Thursday*. A general Fast. On Isa. XXVI. ii *Learning Righteousness* from the *Judgments* of GOD.

23 *d*. 2 *m*. At the old South. On 3. Joh. 2. The *Prosperity* of the *Soul*.

30 *d*. 2 *m*. On Joh. XV. 25. The Aversion for a glorious CHRIST in the Children of Men, always *causeless*.

7 *d*. 3 *m*. [*May*.] On Luk. VIII. 46. *Virtue* going out from our SAVIOUR, to them that by Faith make their Application to Him.

10 *d*. 3 *m*. *Wednesday*. On Psal. XXIV. 10. Our SAVIOUR,

the *Lord of Hosts:* very particularly in regard of His Authority over the *Assemblies* of His People. (A Day of Prayer at the Opening of the New Brick Meeting-house in our Neighbourhood. This the first Sermon in it.)

14 *d.* 3 *m.* On 1 Pet. II. 9. The End of all that is done for us in our Salvation, to declare the *Praises* of our SAVIOUR.

21 *d.* 3 *m.* On, Joh. II. 10. The *Miracle* of our SAVIOUR turning *Water* into *Wine.* (Designing a Course of Sermons, on our *Miracles* wrought by our SAVIOUR.)

25 *d.* 3 *m. Thursday.* The Lecture. On Job. XV. 21. The *dreadful Sound* in the *Ears* of wicked Men. (Particularly propounding a right Use to be made, of what was to be seen in the Condition of a Fellow that was this Day executed for a Murder, and now appeared in the great Assembly.)

28 *d.* 3 *m.* On Joh. II. 10. Finishing what I began a Week ago.

4 *d.* 4 *m.* [*June*] On Joh. IV. 54. The *Miracle* of our SAVIOUR healing and raising the Son of the Nobleman.

8 *d.* 4 *m. Thursday.* On Amos. IV. 12. *Præparation* to meet our God coming to us, in Ways of *Adversity* and *Mortality.* (The Lecture turned into a *Day of Prayer* because of much Calamity by the Small Pox impending over us.)

11 *d.* 4 *m.* On 1. Pet. II. 9. The Followers of our SAVIOUR, effectually *called,* out of *Darkness* into His *marvellous Light.* Finishing in a Course of eight Sermons my Meditations upon the Text. (And I administred the Eucharist.)

18 *d.* 4 *m.* On Joh. IV. 54 (a second time.) On the Miracle of our SAVIOUR healing the Son of the Nobleman.

22 *d.* 4 *m. Thursday.* The Lecture (for Another:) on Job XXIX. 3. *Walking thro Darkness* by the *Light of God.* (Because of a *dark Time* coming on the City.)

25 *d.* 4 *m.* On Joh. IV. 54 (A Third Time.)

2 *d.* 5 *m.* [*July.*] On 2. Sam. XXIII. 15. The Water of the Well at *Bethlehem.* (At the Old-South-Church.)

9 *d.* 5 *m.* On Cant. II. 14. The *Dove.* (And I administred the Eucharist.)

13 *d.* 5 *m. Thursday.* (A Day of Prayer, thro' the Province.) On Psal. LXXXVI. 4. The *Lifting up of the Soul* unto God under Distresses.

16 *d.* 5 *m.* On Jam. I. 27. Keeping ourselves *unspotted from the World.* (Intending an Improvement of the dreadful Judgment on the Nations in the *South-sea* Infatuation.)

23 *d*. 5 *m*. On Psal. LXXVIII. 63. The *Fire* of Divine Wrath, *consuming* our *young* People. (On the Occasion of the *Small-Pox*, beginning to carry off our *young* People. But one young Man, making a very hopeful and joyful End, under it.)

30 *d*. 5 *m*. On Jam. I. 27. Finishing what I began a Fortnight ago.

6 *d*. 6 *m*. [*August*.] On Cant. II. 14. The Dove in the *Clefts of the Rock*, or, conversing with a suffering SAVIOUR. (And I administered the Eucharist.)

8 *d*. 6 *m*. *Tuesday*. The Same, in the Lecture at *Roxbury*.

13 *d*. 6 *m*. On Joh. V. 5. The Miracle wrought on the *Paralytic*, at the Pool of *Bethesda*.

20 *d*. 6 *m*. On Matth. VIII. 3. The Miracle wrought in the Cure of the *Leprosy*.

27 *d*. 6 *m*. On Mar. II. 5. The Miracle wrought on the *Paralytic* pardoned.

3 *d*. 7 *m*. [*September*.] On Matth. IX. 2. The *Pardon of Sin* declared and assured, unto the repenting Beleever. (And I administred the Eucharist.)

7 *d*. 7 *m*. *Thursday*. The Lecture. On Judg. XIII. 19. The *Wonders* attending our *Sacrifices*. (It being with me a Time of Sacrifices.)

10 *d*. 7 *m*. On Matth. VIII. 5. The Miracle on the Servant of the *Centurion*.

17 *d*. 7 *m*. A.M. At the New North. On Rom. XIV. 7, 8. The Christian both in *Life* and in *Death*, being the *Lord's*, and for the Lord. (A funeral Sermon for Mrs. *Web;* the Consort of the Pastor to the Church there.)

P. M. At the Old North. On Matth. VIII. 5. Finishing what I began a Week ago.

24 *d*. 7 *m*. On Isa. XXXVIII. 14. Our Cry unto the glorious One to *undertake* for us, when we are under *Oppressions*. (It being a time of heavy Pressures.)

28 *d*. 7 *m*. *Thursday*. The Lecture. On Lev. X. 3. The *holy Silence*, that sad Things are to be encountred with. (On the Occasion of my lovely Daughter, with her Infant, now lying Dead.)

1 *d*. 8 *m*. [*October*.] A. M. I administred the Eucharist. P. M. On Job. V. 7. Man *born to Trouble, as the Sparks fly upward*. (On the Death of many lovely, Hopeful young People: especially, one young Gentleman in the Neighbourhood.)

8 *d*. 8 *m*. On Psal. XXXVIII. 7. A Sinful World punished with

a *lothsome Disease*, for Sin a more *lothsome Disease*. (Vast Numbers lying sick of the Small-Pox.)

15 *d*. 8 *m*.   On Heb. XII. 11.   The *peaceable Fruit of Righteousness* produced by our Afflictions. (Many Friends with me, being very much afflicted, with the Death of desireable Relations.)

22 *d*. 8 *m*.   On Job. XVI. 22.   People at their Death, going whence they shall not return. (A very dying time.)

26 *d*. 8 *m*. *Thursday*.   A general Thanksgiving.   On Job. II. 10. How to receive *Good*, and how to receive *Evil* at the Hand of God.

29 *d*. 8 *m*.   On Gal. V. 24.   The *Crucifying* of the Flesh. (And I administered the Eucharist.)

2 *d*. 9 *m*. [*November*.] *Thursday*.   The Lecture.   On Psal. XXXVIII. [7.]   A lothsome Disease.

5 *d*. 9 *m*.   On Psal. CXIX. 96.   An *End* of all *Perfection*. The use to be made of the Sight.

12 *d*. 9 *m*.   On Psal. LXIII. 3.   The Favour of God better than Life. (It being a Dying Time.)

19 *d*. 9 *m*.   On Act. XXVII. 23.   The *angelical Ministry*, employ'd for them that are the Lord's, and that serve Him. (On Occasion of the astonishing Deliverance, the last Week, bestow'd upon me.)

26 *d*. 9 *m*.   On Gal. II. 20.   A *Crucifixion* with CHRIST. (And I administred the Eucharist.)

3 *d*. 10 *m*. [*December*.]   On Psal. XXXVIII. 9.   Our *Desires* and our *Groanings*, yea, the *hidden Desires* which rise no higher than *Groanings*, all known unto the glorious GOD.

10 *d*. 10 *m*.   On Luk. IV. 5.   A *Moment of Time*, enough to survey all the *Glories* of this World. (Accommodating the shortest Day in the Year.)

17 *d*. 10 *m*.   On Phil. III. 20.   A *Conversation in Heaven*. (Intending a Course of Sermons, on that noble Subject.)

24 *d*. 10 *m*.   On Zech. XII. 10.   *Looking on a pierced* JESUS. (And I administred the Eucharist.)

27 *d*. 10 *m*. *Thursday*.   The Lecture.   On Matth. XXIV. 12. The Love of many *waxing Cold*.   Agreeably to the Season.

31 *d*. 10 *m*.   On Phil. III. 20.   A second time.

7 *d*. 11 *m*. [January, 1721–22.]   On Phil. III. 20.   A third time.

14 *d*. 11 *m*.   On Gal. VI. 7.   The *Deceits* which are commonly imposed on People, in the Matters of Religion and Salvation.

21 *d*. 11 *m*.   On Phil. III. 20.   A fourth time. (And I administred the Eucharist.)

28 *d*. 11 *m*.   On Phil. III. 20.   A fifth Time.
4 *d*. 12 *m*.   On Phil. III. 20.   A sixth Time.
11 *d*. 12 *m*.   On Phil. III. 20.   A seventh Time.

TO THOMAS PRINCE.   M.H.S.

12 d. 12 m. [February 1720–21.]   At Night.

MY DEAR FRIEND, — Upon Trial this day, I find my *Locks are cutt.* I performed so pittifully, that my courage for the *Lecture* utterly fails me. Especially considering that the Lords-day (and Table) will follow presently upon it. This last Bout has been the most Shocking, that I have had this twenty years. My Return back to this loathsome World, is unspeakably less pleasant unto me, than the View I had these three weeks ago of taking wing for that glorious World, whereof, oh! could I tell you something of the Glories, which I am now certain are to be there bestowed upon them, who have nothing but a CHRIST left alive unto them!

I durst not ask for the Continuance of my poor Life one day longer, but purely with the Aim and for the Sake of doing Service for the Kingdome of God, while the ordinary Course of Nature supposes a Capacity for them.

For which Cause, I would gladly have served the Lecture (and vexed the Dragon) this Week. But I can't, I can't. Wherefore, if you will be so very kind as to do it, I will entertain some Hope, that by the Thursday after, I may be able to take your Turn, and pay a little of what I shall owe you.

But if you really can't, then, I pray, comply with another Task, which I shall impose upon you. Step in the Morning on my behalf, as far as my dear *Cooper's*.[1] Give my Service to him. Say not one Word, that he owes me any thing. I utterly decline all such Claims, or Terms. But, join your Request with mine, that he would step this week into the Lecture, and allow me to take his Turn, if I live to the Time, and am found able to do it. Lett him know, that it will very much oblige me; and such is his Goodness, I am sure, you need say no more.

And now, I reckon myself safe; that between (you) two, I shall not fall to the Ground.

May our glorious Lord, accept both of you, to do worthily in Israel, and to do more and greater and better services for His Kingdome than have been done, by the poor unfruitful Thing who thus

---

[1] Rev. William Cooper, of the Brattle Street Church.

prays for you; and give you a kinder Entertainment in the World and call you to fewer Encounters with Temptations, than have been seen by, your poor, weary, tired, Brother and Servt.,

Co. MATHER.

To Sir William Ashurst. A.A.S.

SIR, — It was not until just now, that I have, (by a Second and worthy Hand in *London*) understood, the INDIA CHRISTIANA, with my Address unto your Honour, to have reached you. That, and my want of Matter on the Subject which is to be written of, has delay'd my doing the Duty of making a Return, to a Letter which I had the Honour some good while ago, of receiving from you.

And what I have now to write, is perhaps what may procure from your Goodness a Rebuke rather than an Approbation.

I must, in short, confess myself so discouraged by some occurrences, as to apprehend it most proper for me, to propose a Secession from the Board of your Commissioners for the Propagation of the Gospel among the Indians. I am not fond of mentioning what the Things are that have discouraged me. But you may be sure, That if I had enjoy'd the prospect of doing any of the Good, my Soul, has been Travailing for, I should have been afraid of declining my opportunities. Instead thereof, I will enclose a Copy of a Letter, which not long since, I address'd unto Lieut. Governor [William] *Dummer*, as president of that Board; since which, I have received nothing from the Board, that intimates to me, what Notice the Gentlemen please to take of it. I do it, that so, you may see something of what I have wished for, and may give such Directions as in your wisdome you shall Judge most convenient. The Copy of the Memorial that accompanies it, is not in the least offered upon any Design, to obtain from you the grant of the petition in it, or to complain, that it was not granted here. I am entirely satisfied, and yett for some Reasons lett you know another thing that I once wished for.

May our glorious Lord graciously direct and accept and succeed, all your excellent Essays to do Good in the world; and particularly to revive and preserve the Christianity, among our poor Indians, whom Heaven has committed unto your pious patronage. I am, Your Honours, Most affectionate Friend and obedient Serv't.

Apr. 28, 1721.

To Rev. Thomas Prince.   M.H.S.

[8 ber 15, 1721.]

My dear Friend, — If you have no Advice of an opportunity to write unto *Holland*, within three weeks, pray permitt my French M.SS. with the Translation, return to me in the Morning by *Caesar;* Because I would have it come under the View of an other dear Governor at N. *London*, before it goes.

Citra ut valeas.

The Number of the sick in the Bills at the old North to day, amounts to 322.

To Rev. Thomas Prince.   M.H.S.

Sir, — Our Servant, Ezer, after a due Examination of his Knowledge and Beleef, and a due Testimony of his Good Conversation, was Received into the Covenant of GOD, and Baptised Lately with us.[1] For which Cause, his offspring (whereof I hear, part is newly born in your Family) is humbly recommended unto the Christian Baptism with you, by, Sir, Your Brother and Servt.

Co. Mather.

Feb. 24. 1721 [-22.]

To Rev. Thomas Prince.   M.H.S.

[May, 1722.]

O mihi post nullos Memorande.[2]

After I have wished you Joy on what you have heard about the Royal Family, I shall (as I always do) take a singular Freedom with you. Your singular Friendship for me, always emboldens it.[3]

I have long been of the Opinion, that there could scarce be a more

---

[1] See p. 676, *supra.*   [2] Mart. *Epig.* 1. 16.

"27 d. 3 m. [May, 1722.] The Baptism of the Former [William Stirling] was introduced with such Words as these:

[3] "Here is now offered unto the Lord the Child of one who died with good Expressions of a repenting and believing Soul, and giving up her Child unto God her Savior, with Desire that it might in his Baptism come under a solemn Dedication to Him. The pious Grandmother of the Child (Mrs. *Grace Ireland*) who is one of us, does here present it unto us, and you do here before the Lord adopt this Child as your own, and you engage unto the People of God, that you will take all due Care, both living and dying, that it may be brought up in the Knowledge and for the Service of the Lord. The Disciples of the Lord in this Church have hitherto not forbid the Children in such Circumstances to be brought unto their Savior." *Cotton Mather's MS. Records of the Second Church*, III.

comprehensive Service done, than to Lodge in the Hands of the Ministers throughout the Countrey, a Memorial of the Methods which may be taken by them to be very serviceable. No men have such opportunities as they, to be very serviceable.

Now my Two Neighbours, Mr *Thacher* and Mr *Web*, have had such favourable Sentiments for the poor Sermon that was offered you last Thursday,[1] as to press the publication of it, and provide for part of the Charge. Surprized at their Motion, I am come anon myself, into the Opinion, that the poor sermon being Transcribed and somewhat Amended, may answer such Ends, as I ought humbly and gladly and zelously to devote my All unto. And the rather, because my Time for doing, is drawing very near its period. If now I can gett the Assistence of but 50s or 3£ subscribed, I can, I suppose gett thro' the rest of the Expence which the Desired Publication may call for. Wherefore, I will be so rude, as to leave it with you, to Consult with our dear *Cooper* and *Foxcroft*. (*Ambo, et cantare pares, et respondere parati!*)[2] added, unto the two Brethren above mentioned, what, (or, whether anything) may be done about the Matter. I know, you Love to do Good; and you Love the Doers of Good; and you Love, Your Constant Friend, Brother, and Servt.

Co. MATHER.

To Rev. Thomas Prince.   M.H.S.

[June 12, 1722.]

MY INVAULABLE FRIEND, AND BROTHER, — To you I chuse to committ my, MINISTER.[3] I enclose *fifty Shillings* towards the Expence. I have occasionally had some Discourse with Mr. *Fleet* about the work. For that Cause, you must make the first offer to *him*. I Leave the whole to your Wisdome and Goodness. If you, or any of the Brethren, would correct any passage in it, I Entirely resign it unto your Pleasure. I could have Embellished it with many ornaments. But I conscienciously decline the ostentation of Erudition, Lest I disoblige that Holy Spirit, on whom alone I depend for the Success of the Essay. Besides, I have in a considerable Number of other Books, (besides the *Magnalia*,) already pretty well Exhausted a Good Stock of Flowers, which ought not to be presented over again. Yea, this very week, I have an ordination-Sermon published;[4] which

---

[1] May 31, 1722, when he preached to the anniversary Convention of ministers.   [2] Verg. *Ecl.* VII. 5.   [3] The book bore this title.

[4] Delivered at the ordination of Rev. William Waldron, at the new church in the north part of Boston.

I tender to your acceptance we shall reap together the Harvest of this Action, in the First Resurrection.

To Rev. Thomas Prince.   m.h.s.

Tuesday night

Sir, — Your Printer has I suppose, gott ready your, Minister! and it was in some View of the Opportunity which you might have to disperse many of your Books on the Approaching Festival.

Imagining that the Generous Goodness, which has been exerted by you in this publication, does intend a Dispersion of the Books into the Hands of all the Ministers throughout the Countrey, it seems necessary that there should be some Agreement of the Brethren, to prevent your Interfering with one another, in your pious communication. Every One should know, what counties, (or parts of the Countrey,) he will chiefly take for his province in the Dispersion.

And, if you order your Printer to bring me my fifty shillings worth, I will send our, MINISTER, thro' the Colony of *Connecticut*, and some of the more Southern Provinces.

We are thus praeparing for Employments in the Better World. Waiting for which, I am, Sir, Your Brother and Servt.,

Co. Mather.

I am not well! But my poor wife, struck with a Consumption wants and asks your Prayers.

To Thomas Prince.   m.h.s.

Wednesday, 7 *d.* 5*m.* [July.] 1722.

Sir, — The Excellent Spirit of Piety which always Endears our worthy Brother *Sewal*, to all of us as well as to me, and the Intimate Communion and Correspondence of the most Inviolate Friendship, which we always maintain with him, seems to render it suitable, that he should be apprised of our Combination, to begin this Evening a *Conference on the Sacred Prophecies concerning the Coming and King-dome of our Saviour;* And have the offer of a welcome to it. It is possible, that he may have a Less Degree of Relish for those things, than some others; and there is a peculiarity of Constitution in these points, not easy to be accounted for. But then, his objections to our Interpretations, may be of use to us, to prevent our going too Easily into mistakes; and perhaps to establish what cannot be shaken.

It is however fitt, that he should have the Liberty of sharing with us; (as Mr. *Cooper*, I perceive also will.)

I hope, we shall meet in the First Resurrection; In the Faith and Patience of the Kingdome, I am, Sir, Your Brother and Servt.,

Co. MATHER.

When you visit Mr. *Daniel Oliver*, bestow all (or some) of these *Golden Curbs* upon him, to putt upon Head-Strong Fools at the Times when he has occasion to Execut the Law upon them.

To REV. THOMAS PRINCE.   M.H.S.

MY DEAR FRIEND, — Allow me to renew my Petitions and Instances with you, That you would, furnish me, with the best Account you have,

Of the Birds raised at *Newtown*.

Of the *Leviathan* dug up at *Virginia*.

And Enquire into the Story of a *Naevus Maternus* on a Daughter of one *Brown*, a Stiller, which grows, they tell me, very Troublesome to the Marked Damsel.

Our dear Patriarch, is revived this Morning; and wonderfully Comforted. Using the very words, which you used unto him, and Joyfully saying, *I now see, that I was deceived, when I fear'd Lest I might be deceived.* I am, Yours always.

Co. MATHER.

Tuesday, [Feb. 19, 1722–23.] [1]

To REV. THOMAS PRINCE.   M.H.S.

[June 16, 1723.]

MY DEAR FRIEND, — *Vigilare decet hominem qui vult sua Tempore conferre officia.*

In the Circumstances of the Poor Creature, who is this week day to dy by the Sword of Justice, there is a voice of GOD crying to the City.[2]

[1] "10 *d*. 1 *m*. [March.] 1722–23. *John Bushel* made unto the Church an acknowledgment of a Scandal given by him, in being disguised with excessive Drinking, which the Church accepted of." *Cotton Mather's MS. Records of the Second Church*, III.

[2] The idea of a servile insurrection must have appealed strongly to Mather's imagination. Never very numerous in Massachusetts, the negro slaves yet constituted an appreciable part of the population, and with the veneer of civilization upon them, occasionally broke through all bounds. Some of the very striking crimes in colonial and provincial days arose from the enslaved Indians or Africans. In this case the negro had set fire to Powel's house in the dead of night.

Not only the Condition of such Slaves is worthy to be considered, but also the Threatenings which there have been of Laying the Town in Ashes, are speaking Things.

I would humbly propose to you, and entreat of you, to bend your Holy Studies a Little this way, for your approaching Lecture. You may do a work pleasing to God, and useful to men; and you are Excellently Qualified for it; and your performances are to my Knowledge, highly acceptable to my Neighbours, and can be no otherwise to your own.

Pardon the Suggestion, Tis my way to project services for others, as well as myself.   I am, Sir, Your Brother

Co. MATHER.

[ENCLOSURE.]

[June 18th, 1723.]

This Place has Lately been brought into uncommon Distress, by some, of a Foolish Nation.

The Voice of the Lord Cries to the City.

First, the Burning of the Town has been threatened; and there have been many Fires Kindled, in some of which, those of this Foolish Nation, we may suppose, have not been concerned.

While the Decree is not yett Executed (and we have been so marvellously, remarkably, undeservedly præserved) our God calls us.

Not only to Thankfulness for our præservation,

(The Horror of the Calamity if it should proceed, makes the Call to this very powerful.)

But also, to consider what we have to do, that such a Desolation, by those (or some other) Hands, may be prevented.

Repent and Reform, our Sabbath-breaking.   Jer. XVII. 27.   Dishonesty in our Dealing.   See Job. XV. 34.

Contention.   Burning for Burning, was required by the Word of the glorious GOD.   Fulfilled by His Hand.

And Considering by what Hands the Town has been so Endangered, there can be nothing more seasonable and reasonable than for us, to Consider whether our Conduct with relation to our African Slaves, be not one thing for which our God may have a Controversy with us.

Are they always treated according to the Rules of Humanity?

And much more, Christianity which is improved and Ennobled Humanity.

Are they treated as those, that are of one Blood with us, and those that have Immortal Souls in them, and are not meer Beasts of Burden?

Are they instructed, and made to know

Such things, which if they knew, would restrain them from Exorbitancies and Enormities which are Complained [against] them, and render them notable Blessings in the Families they belong unto.

The Common Cavil, that they are the worse servants, for being taught the Knowledge of CHRIST, is a Cursed Falshood; Experience confutes it; It is a Blasphemy; and it is fitter for the Mouth of a Devil, than of a Christian, to utter it.

But then, there is a Voice of Heaven, to the Slaves, on what this poor Creatur is Left unto.

To Beware of the Sins, which may provoke the glorious one to Leave then unto the Last Degrees of Wickedness and Misery.

To study a Dutiful Behaviour unto their Superiours; and that they may b Blessings in the Family they belong unto.

To be Patient in their Low and hard Conditions.

To become the Servants of CHRIST.

Then, what they shall very shortly see, at the End of their Short Servitude. Else a worse thing.[1]

To Rev. Thomas Prince.   M.H.S.

Friday, [July 19, 1723.]

SIR, — Supposing, that it might be some Gratification unto yo to Read, what you could but imperfectly Hear, in the late Comence ment, I now entertain you with it; [2]

[1] "10 d. 5 m. [July.] 1723. At a Church Meeting, *Sarah Wood*, a Widow o our Communion, having been convicted of a Fornication, presented unto the Churcl a poenitent and expressive Acknowledgment: the Church agreed that she shoul continue under Suspension from our Communion for some time, and until she ca return with due Testimony for her good Behavior and Repentance from the Neigh borhood. In the mean Time she was now laid under Admonition. [The censure on Sarah Wood was raised March 29, 1724.]

"The Church now renewed their Choice of the six Persons that are yet sur viving of their late Committee: *John Clark, Thomas Hutchinson, Adam Winthrop Edward Hutchinson, John Ruck,* Esqrs., and Mr. *John Charnock;* and now added Mr. *Thomas Cushing* unto their Number; desiring them to act still in Quality o a Committee for them, as formerly, for a Year ensuing.

"It being proposed, whether the Church would immediately proceed unt the Settlement of an Assistant and Successor in the Work of the evangelical Min istry among us, or delay the Matter: and the Church being a little divided in their Sentiments about it, it was voted, That in Consideration of "the low State wherein our aged Pastor is languishing, the Church propose to set apart a Day o Supplications, to carry his Case unto our gracious God, and to obtain the Direc tion and Blessing of Heaven, with relation to that important Affair, of seeking after a Supply for an Assistence and Succession in the work of the Ministry." *Cotton Mather's MS. Records of the Second Church*, III.

[2] The commemoratory oration delivered by Samuel Mather. It does no appear to have been printed.

"21 d. 6 m. [*August.*] Wednesday. The Brethren of the Church meet, and coming to a Vote, managed by Papers, Whether to *proceed* or *delay*, in the Matter of Chusing an Assistant and Successor in the evangelical Ministry, a considerable Majority of the Votes came forth with *delay* written upon them." *Cotton Mather's MS. Records of the Second Church*, III.

But there is this Encumbrance on your Entertainment.

Our Honourable Friend Judge *Sewal*, was not at the Commencement. He has a kindness for his Little Names-sake, and is glad of any promising performance from him. He has also a Kindness for the Name of *Stoughton*, and is Glad when he sees it celebrated. Communicate unto him, the M.SS. But so that either *he* send it home to me by the middle of the Next week, or Else do *you* take that care upon you:

You will continue your Loves and prayers, for the Lad, as well as for Your Brother and Serv't.

Co. MATHER.

FROM SAMUEL SEWALL.   A.A.S.

In Matherum morientem
Feria Sexta, Augusti 23, 1723.

Quantum per vitam potuit, CRESCENTIUS auxit Doctrinam: dono mortis ADULTUS erit.[1]

SAMUEL SEWALL.

REVEREND SIR, — If my barren vein would have yielded better, I should have more cheerfully have offered it for the Honour of my Excellent Friend. Sir, your obliged humble Servt.

SAMUEL SEWALL.

Boston, pridie calendas Septembres, 1723.

TO GURDON SALTONSTALL.   A.A.S.

October 21, 1723.

SYR, — Of all the Good Works that are done under the Sun, there appears none more worthy of a Christian or more Demonstrative of his being what he professes himself to be, or more pleasing to God, or more useful to men, than that of propagating pure and undefiled Christianity in the world. And your Honours Hearty Zeal to promote this First-born of Good Works, is but agreeable to your Faith, and among the bright Instances in which you adorn the Doctrines of God your Saviour; and the place wherein our God has in mercy to His people Stationed you.

[1] Increase Mather, father of Cotton, died August 23, 1723, "just at Noon, after long and grievous Sickness." He was buried in the north burying place. Sewall, *Diary*, III. 326. The son has fittingly commemorated the father in his *Parentator*, published in 1724.

Tis not unknown unto your Honour and unto many valuable persons under your Government, that in the Town of *Providence* near unto you, there has appeared a Field white for the Harvest. Indeed, some of the first Motions in this Great Affair, were from some Excellent Persons in your Colony.

Our First Essays to Erect an Edifice for the public Worship of GOD, in that place, have mett with such Encumbrances, as appear not at all Marvellous, unto them who consider, that the Great Adversary of the Gospel is not Asleep. These Encumbrances are now in some Degree Surmounted, but the Expences of the Enterprize have been thereby very much augmented. This work of GOD therefore very much needs a further Assistence, from the Bountiful Charity of the Churches in your Colony; who have on many occasions Expressed their Bounty in Collections that have upon Good Intentions [been] called for; But perhaps have rarely done it upon any, of a more noble Importance than this, wherein the Kingdome of GOD, our Saviour, and the Salvation of Souls from Death, are so notably concerned. The Good people in this Providence have done worthily in this matter; and we make no doubt, that yours will not come at all behind them; so that we need add no more, but our humble Request, That for the preventing of Misapplications, it may be proposed, that what money shall be collected, may be Lodged in the Hands of Prudent and Faithful Trustees among yourselves; unto whom, if any Advice from the Ministers in this Town be thought necessary, it will be at all Times readily communicated.

Thus, commending your person and whole Administration, to the divine Conduct and Blessing, we subscribe, Your Honors Most hearty Servants.[1]

To Rev. Jedidiah Andrews.   A.A.S.

Sir, — Tis a great Satisfaction unto me at all times to hear from a Brother, whom I always honour as being a *Vir sui Nominis*. Your unfainting Labour for the Name of your Lord, your service and

---

[1] "22 *d.* 8 *m.* [October.] At a Meeting of the Church, there were forty-nine Brethren present. It was proposed, that the Church might now come to the Choice of an Assistant and Successor in the Work of the Evangelical Ministry. The Choice was made, and the Majority (thirty-four) of the Votes declared it for Mr. *Joshua Gee. John Clark, Thomas Hutchinson, Adam Winthrop*, Esqrs., and Mr. *Samuel Turel*, with the Deacons, were appointed a Committee to report unto him this Act of the Church." *Cotton Mather's MS. Records of the Second Church*, III. Gee (1698–1748) remained with the church until his death.

your patience, I cannot think upon, without glorifying of Him in you. I must beg your pardon, that I forgett sometimes to send you the Little Things that are published among us.

I now address you with Two or Three of our Latest publications; the sight whereof may perhaps also gratify some of your worthy Neighbours.

I am so much a Stranger to Dr. Williams's Charitable but it seems Ambiguous will, (having Long since mislaid and forgott our Paragraph in it) that I know not how to express myself capable of assisting your Desires of coming at the Benefit of it, until I am somewhat more fully instructed; but if you can come at it, you may be sure I shall say, Much good may it do you!

I have Lately written, *Memoirs of Remarkable Things in the Life and the Death* of my deceased Parent; But, it being a Book of it may be Twenty Sheets, it will be diverse Months before our otherwise Employ'd presses can give it unto the public. In the mean time, I transmit unto you, a *Coelestinus* [1] that will bring something of and from the Countrey which he is gone unto.

The Condition of my Foolish Countrey and a Relation of the Follies committed in it, would be a story not worth telling to you.

Lett us Long for the Land of Rectitude. In the way to it, and ye Hope of it, I am, Sir, Your affectionate Brother and Servt.

Boston, N. E. Nov. 5, 1723.

To Thomas Hollis. [2]   A.A.S.

Sir, — By several Conveyances, I have dispatch'd unto you those letters and Packetts, wherein I have after my poor Manner, express'd my grateful Resentments of the Many and Weighty Favours, which I and mine have received from you.

In one of them there are also, the Acknowledgments, which your Son Samuel (your First born) has made of your Goodness to him, and a Copy of his Commemoratory Oration at our Commencement; which, I hope, has reached you.

What I am now to do, is, to render my Brethrens Thanks, with my own, for what you have done about our Memorials; and acquiesce in what has been done by others.

The Truth is, if all the Remonstrances that we make about a Charity so abominably prostituted as that of the *Society*, will only

[1] Printed by S. Kneeland for Nathaniel Belknap.
[2] Nephew of the benefactor of Harvard College.

produce a care of our Diocesan to send over better Missionaries we are best as we are. For the Missionaries they have hitherto sent, have generally been such Ignorant Wretches, and such Debauched and Finished Villians, that Like the Rattle snakes in our Countrey they carry with 'em what warns and arms our people against being poisoned with them.

In the meantime, I am sorry, that a Countrey in which you are daily multiplying your Benefits, affords to you such matter of Trouble, in the Mischiefs which your Charitable and Sympathizing Mind sees us by our Follies bringing on our selves. Our Governour was a person of an Excellent Spirit; and I always thought he studied the welfare of the Countrey more than any one person in it. Had we carried well to him, he would have made us an easy, and had we hearken'd well to him, we had been an Happy, people. His enemies, who began to be so, upon a Rage, which was raised in them from a Disappointment of certain projections to Enrich themselves, which they suffered from his Arrival in the Government instead of another whom they thought they had made their property, never were many; but being very subtil, as well as very spiteful, they gott the knack of perverting and misleading a Majority of poor, and weak (tho' sometimes honest) Countreymen in our House of Representatives; and so they produced *Votes* which any Governor must count Intolerable; and which are Like to overwhelm our whole people, who generally abhor what is done, in Ruines that will be Irretrievable. *The Evil that I feared is come!* How much a Man, who is no Great Seer, did foresee these things, and forewarn our People of them some years ago, I am willing you should see, by casting your Eye on a Sermon;[1] for which Fidelity I have since been an object for the utmost Rage of the Satanic Party, and not only had their printed Libels continually darted at me, but had Attempts made upon my very Life. Nevertheless, after all that I have performed and suffered on the behalf of our Good Governour,[2] I am told, that he dismisses me from the List of his Friends, because of a Misreport that was made unto him, of my being at a Loss how to mention his Voyage in our public prayers, immediately upon his very sudden withdraw from us. But alas, who can tell what is Good for Man? And if our Governour do obtain the Destruction of our Charter, how uneasy will he find himself in his Return unto us? The wretched Men that have provoked him, will still be in our Assemblies, and Continue to do so. At the same time, all his Friends, (and

[1] Probably he refers to *Mirabilia Dei*, delivered November 5, 1719, and printed in the same year. [2] Shute.

none so much as they,) will be rendred miserable: a Good Countrey anon putt into the Hands of Rulers, disaffected unto all the best Interests of it; the Religion of the Countrey insulted, ruined, and by Degrees Extinguished.

But we grow Ripe for Confusions. A fearful Decay of Piety among us, ripens us for them. One Symptom and Effect of which Decay is, a Strange Inclination to Contention discovering itself upon all occasions among us. I'l mention to you an Instance, which you will wonder at!

A mighty Spirit came Lately upon abundance of our people, to Reform their singing which was degenerated in our Assemblies to an Irregularity, which made a Jar in the ears of the more curious and skilful singers. Our Ministers generally Encouraged the people, to accomplish themselves for a Regular singing, and a more beautiful Psalmody. Such Numbers of Good people, (and Especially young people,) became Regular Singers, that they could carry it in the Congregations. But, who would beleeve it? Tho' in the more polite City of *Boston*, this Design mett with a General Acceptance, in the Countrey, where they have more of the *Rustick*, some Numbers of Elder and Angry people, bore zelous Testimonies against these wicked Innovations, and this bringing in of Popery. Their zeal transported some of them so far (on the behalf of *Mumpsimus*) that they would not only use the most opprobrious Terms, and call the Singing of these Christians, a worshipping of the Devil, but also they would run out of the Meeting-house at the Beginning of the Exercise. The Paroxysms have risen to that Heighth, as to necessitate the Convening of several Ecclesiastical Councils, for the Composing of the Differences and Animosities, arisen on this occasion.[1] And if such an Improbable occasion produce them, what is to be expected, when our Great Adversary getts a permission to start more hazardous Controversies? *O! Tell it not in Gath!*

The world is falling into that period whereof one Character is, *The Nations were Angry.* A Spirit of *Anger* is to possess the Nations, and boil up and break out, on all, and even on very small, on the very Least, occasions. In our Countrey people Take all occasions, and seem even to seek occasions for the Ebullition of their Anger against their Brethren. I wish, it were more otherwise in yours.

Having mention'd the period we are fallen into, I will only add, It is doubtless the period, wherein what the Holy Spirit of GOD

---

[1] Mather wrote and printed (1723) *A Pacificatory Letter* on the singing of psalms in church.

has foretold concerning the Consuming of Ten Kingdomes, is to be accomplished.

May all the Blessings of the Man who deviseth Liberal Things, be your portion in such a period. Yea, your Everlasting portion. With such Wishes, I am, Sir, Your most obliged Friend and Serv't.

Boston, N. England, Nov. 5. 1723.[1]

To Isaac Noble.   A.A.S.

Jan. 14, 1723–24.

My Invaluable Friend, — The Correspondence with which you have honoured me, has been so very useful and grateful to me, that I beseech you to continue it.

I take this opportunity, to present you with a few of our Latest Publications; But what I now do, is but a præface to a more Copious and agreeable Entertainment, which, I hope, in Two or Three months (if the Gracious Lord please to spare the Barren Tree so long) may be ready for you.

The Occurrences among us, are too small, to be worthy of transmitting to you.

---

[1] "12 d. 9 m. [November.]. There was exhibited unto the Church, the Answer of Mr. *Joshua Gee*, unto the Choice of him unto the pastoral Charge, whereof they had made Report unto him. His Answer declared his Acceptance of their Invitation.

"The Church voted, that as a Provision at present for his comfortable Subsistence, he should have the weekly Allowance of three Pounds out of the Church's Treasury.

"The Committee that were chosen to report unto him the late Act of the Church, were now chosen to be advised by him (with the present Pastor) about a proper Time for his public Ordination."

"25 d. 9 m. The Brethren of the Church voted:

"That Wednesday, the eighteenth of *December* approaching be the Day for the Ordination of Mr. *Joshua Gee*, to the pastoral Charge of the Flock.

"That the six Churches of our united Brethren in this Town, and the Church of *Roxbury*, be addressed for their Delegates to appear with us on that Occasion.

"That the Pastor do, the next Lord's-day, sollicit the Assembly to advance in their Contribution on the Lord's-day following, what may support the Expense of that Occasion.

"That Mr. *Walter*, Mr. *Wadsworth*, Mr. *Colman* and Mr. *Sewal*, be desired to join with the Pastor (from whom they expect the giving of the Charge) in the Imposition of Hands on the Person to be ordained.

"That Mr. Goodwin, and Goldthwaite and February, join with the Deacons in preparing a proper Entertainment for the Delegates." *Cotton Mather's MS. Records of the Second Church*, III.

A French priest, with Countenance from the Governor of Canada, has instigated our Eastern Indians, to begin a War upon us; animated with an Expectation, that France and the pretender were bringing things to that pass, that would allow all Canada, openly to back them; However, our Merciful GOD has kept more of a Restraint upon them, in their outrages and Incursions, than we could have justly look'd for.

A Faction of unadvised and prejudiced people here, have so disobliged our Governour that he privately withdrew, and has presented a Memorial against our House of Representatives, which has introduced a bad aspect upon our Liberties; But if our charter which is the Hedge about our churches, be on this occasion taken away, the pure and undefiled Religion of this Countrey, will soon feel the bad consequences of it.

A few young Ministers, who have prov'd such Apostates, as to deny and renounce the Ministry of these Churches, and gone home to our Bishop for orders, have made a great Noise at home, as well as here. But they signify very Little, and can draw no Disciples after them, except a few, that are a Scandal and Blemish to the wretched parraselene which they go over to, and serve as a praeservative which antidotes our people against a Church, that have such people for the Only Pillars of it.

Shortly, I may give you a fuller acco't, of these and some other Matters.

In the Meantime, lett the Cry of Peace; peace, among you, be what it will; some of us Live in continual Apprehensions of what the Second Chapter of *Daniel*, (whereof, the Time, the sett Time, is come,) has very quickly, I say, very quickly to do upon you.

In the Faith and Patience of the Kingdoms, I am, Sir, Your Brother and most hearty Servt.[1]

---

[1] " 19 *d.* 11 *m.* [January.] 1723-24. Baptised James Cox. The first Baptism administered by Mr. Gee. And, indeed, the first that has been administered by any Hand, but those of *Mather* (Father and Son) in the Old North-Church, for more than half an hundred Years together." *Cotton Mather's MS. Records of the Second Church,* III.

The last entry made by Mather in these *Church Records* was that of a baptism, performed on February 23, 1723-24. With the first entry in March, the writing changes to that of Rev. Joshua Gee, and only so much as relates particularly to Mather is included in this volume.

1724

THE LXII YEAR

12 *d.* XII *m.* 1723–24. O wonderful! O wonderful! O the Wonders and Praises with which I am to consider the Favours of the gracious GOD, who *hitherto has helped me!*

This Day I sett apart for a DAY OF THANKSGIVING, which I kept in my Study before the Lord. And I enjoy'd a most comfortable, yea, and an astonishing Presence of GOD with me in the Exercises of the Day. No Pen can express my Enjoyments and my Elevations.

In the Morning, under a deep Sense that I am Nothing, deserve Nothing, avail Nothing; I behold my SAVIOUR offering to enter and possess me by His holy SPIRIT, and come to act as a Principle of Life in me, for my Living to GOD; I accepted His offer and resigned my self up unto Him. The Consequence of which was, that I was carried beyond myself in all the Devotions of the Day, and was quickened unto Strains of Piety, which being left unto myself, I should not have arriv'd unto.

Having celebrated the infinite Perfections of God the Father, and the Son and the Holy Spirit; I proceeded then to acknowledge the Blessings of GOD unto me, all, how undeserved, how Distinguishing! in the whole Course of my Life to this Day! And I especially made this a Time of Thanksgiving for my having arrived unto this great Age, free from the grievous Diseases, which carry Horror with them.

Anon, I went on to praise Him, for the Discipline of Afflictions, with which my Conformity to my SAVIOUR has been carried on. And for the Answers of Prayers wherein He has often granted my Petitions unto Him.

I finally, and above all, gave Thanks for the spiritual Blessings in the heavenly Places, which my SAVIOUR has given me the Inchoation and the Expectation of. Adding, my Thanks for the Benefit of that Ministry, in which His good Angels have so often brought His Kindnesses unto me.

[696]

During the whole Day, I intermixed ejaculatory Thanksgivings, on all Occasions and Occurrences.

And I sang agreeable Passages in the *Psalms*, before the Lord.

And I settled the Points in which I must now more than ever be, the Lord's.

But, O the Expansions of a Soul mounting up to Heaven, as with the Wings of Eagles, and united unto GOD in my SAVIOUR, which He brought me to!

And, O the Assurances, of Mercies reserved for me, which my Desires have been much carried forth unto!

My Pen is not able to relate them!

12. G. D. A Family of remote Relatives in *Dorchester;* Lett me do something to serve the Cause of Piety in it.

Unto my Father's Life I add an elegant EPITAPHIUM.

13. G. D. In a neighbouring Town, the Widows have been lately and greatly multiplied. I purpose to purchase a little Number of my Book entituled *A Visit to the Widow*, and send them (undiscovered from whence they come) unto the Minister of the Place, to be by him dispersed among them.

It may be, I shall do so, for some other Places.

14. G. D. The Mischief which the Anabaptists are doing in my Neighbourhood, putts me upon abetting and assisting, the Design of some to reprint my *Baptistes*,[1] and scatter it where there may be Occasion for it.

I sett apart this Day for Supplications, carrying the Concerns of my Soul, and my Ministry, and my Family, and of this poor People unto the Lord.

It was a Day, wherein I found the implored and expected Spirit of my Jesus, enabling me to call upon the Lord, and comforting me with Assurances of Blessings and Mercies reserved for me.

But none of the Devotions in the Day, were more full of the divine Life, than a Prayer made as a Præface to my following Petitions; Wherein I declared unto the Lord, that I did not so much come to ask for good Things, as to express myself willing to go without them; having my Will entirely swallowed up in His. I was more

---

[1] Printed by T. Fleet for J. Phillips, 1724.

sollicitous to be a Sacrificer, and be satisfied in going without whatever my Father and my Saviour will have to be denied unto me, than to come at the good Things, which my Desires would carry me forth unto. I esteemed a Mind so conformed and united to GOD, as better than any of the good Things whereof I was ready to be desirous. All that I would insist upon should be a glorious CHRIST appearing in the most holy Place for me, and Visiting me with Discoveries of Himself, and Influences that should bring me to be continually feeding and living upon Him.

15. G. D. A young Gentleman, to be preserved from Infection by the Daughter of *Babylon*.

* 16. G. D. In all Events, to keep continually acknowledging the Providence of my GOD and SAVIOUR, disposing of all, and acquiesce in His Will in the Disposal. But therewithal take Delight in such an Exercise of Piety, (yea, and in the Occasion for it,) as more desireable, than the Things which I would have desired, but which are denied unto me: This is a way of Living, which I have long, long been used unto. No doubt, my Memorials have here and there Touches upon it; which I remember not. But it being at this Time in a singular Vigour with me, I am willing again to mention it.

17. G. D. More various, exquisite, powerful Projections that the baptismal Prayers may answer a great Variety of good Intentions.

18. G. D. A new Servant is yesterday come to sojourn in my Family. I will do what I can, that she may devote herself to the Service of her Saviour; and learn the Ways of Piety by coming to us.

19. G. D. My dear Sister (as I must call her) Mrs. *Brown*, seems to be in a declining State, and as if she were hastening to the Period of her Pilgrimage. I would accordingly, in as exquisite Ways as I can, assist her præparations.

20. G. D. My large Work, entituled, THE ANGEL OF BETHESDA, is now finished. If my glorious Lord will please to accept of it, it may prove one of the most useful Books,

that have been written in the World. I must now apply myself both to Heaven and Earth, to bring on the Publication of it.[1]

21. G. D. I will encourage my Collegue often to lett me know what he intends to preach upon; that so I may direct him to and supply him with such Books as he may do well to read upon the Subject.

22. G. D. A young Man, an only Son, and a Scholar, is in danger of being bewitched and ruined by our Church of *England*. Something must be done, to rescue him.

On the last *Wednesday* night, my Consort was again taken ill. A Coincidence of several Things, caused me on *Thursday* Morning, to lay aside, the Sermon I intended then to serve the Lecture withal. I was at a Loss what Subject I should preach upon. I could make nothing do. But at length I preached on Jam. v. 8. *Stablish your Hearts; for the Coming of the Lord draweth Nigh*, and pressed Preparation for the Coming of the Lord, as what may be nigh to us, not only in regard of Mortality, but also in regard of remarkable *Events* and *Changes* which might suddenly come upon us.

The Sickness of my Consort grows into a very Dangerous and a very Dubious Appearance.

* 23. G. D. On this distressing Occasion, Oh! how shall I glorify GOD! With what Compassion to my afflicted Consort, should I imitate the Goodness of my SAVIOUR! With what importunate Supplications must I carry her Condition to the Lord! With what sacrificing Resignations must I entirely submit unto the Will of GOD! What a Watch must I keep over my Heart, that not the least unsuitable Frame or Thought be admitted there!

O my dear SAVIOUR, I can do nothing; do thou possess me, and be Thou a Principle of Life in me, disposing

---

[1] A single chapter was printed in New London, Connecticut, by Timothy Green, in 1722, but that is all that has ever reached the press.

and quickening of me to every Thing that is holy and just and good.

24. G. D. I will consult with my Collegue, whether we may not yett accomplish, what I long since proposed; a Society of Persons, who shall consider on that Point, what further Service may be done for the Church? And, what the State of the Flock may call for? Serving as Eyes unto us, to look out for us, and report to us, what may have missed our own Observation.

25. G. D. Oh! the Goodness, the Wisdome, the universal Helpfulness, with which I must endeavour to treat my Consort, under her threatening Languishments!

26. G. D. I have a Nephew, thriving in the World, and strongly engaged in the Pursuits of it.

I must so talk with him, and putt such things into his hands, as may have a Tendency to draw him, unto the Minding of his greatest Interests.

27. G. D. The Practice of setting apart whole Days, for Supplications, which the Ministers began a Quarter of a Year ago; I must call upon them, to continue in it. The Times loudly call for it.

28. G. D. Furnish other Ministers in the Countrey, with my Books of, *A Visit unto the Widows:* and (unknown) Request them to dispense them and apply them.

29. G. D. A Man lately recovered from a dangerous Fitt of Sickness, to be advised.

Some near a Time of Travail, must have my *Elizabeth* putt into their hands.

March. * 1. G. D. I am this Day to instruct my Flock, after the most pathetic Manner, how we must lift up our Eyes unto the Lord, for the Releef of our Distresses, when we are very much distressed, and know not what to do for our own Releef. It being on very many Accounts, my own Condition, I do as well as I can; first privately practise my own Instructions.

I will mention an *Exercise of Piety* which I am further led unto.

I keep an Account of my Benefactors, and their Civilities. It is my Custome, in the last Prayers of every Evening, to mention the Names of those who have done me any Kindness in the fore-going Day, and ask for a Reward from GOD unto them. And now, besides This, upon the Finishing of the year, I would spread my Catalogue of Benefactors before the Lord, and pray for such Blessings to be bestow'd upon each of them, as I may apprehend most suitable to be asked for.

2. G. D. What better Service can I do for the Flock, than what I endeavoured yesterday.

3. G. D. I would instigate my Children to be Blessings unto one another. Particularly and peculiarly I would animate my well-disposed Son *Samuel*, (in whom a gracious GOD wonderfully makes up to me, what I miss of Comfort in his miserable Brother,) to exert his Piety, in espousing *Liza* to her SAVIOUR, and perswading her to the Use of her Pen in writing down the Desires of a Soul returning to GOD.

4. G. D. My gracious and generous Landlord has been so very kind unto me, that I think it my Duty to make him under my Hand, some agreeable Acknowledgments of his Favours. But more than this; I would list him and his among my Relatives in my Projections to do good unto them. And particularly, a Son at the Colledge;[1] To whom I would be frequently dispensing seasonable Admonitions, with Books of Piety suitable for him.

5. G. D. In my Father's Life, there is Mention of a Sermon preached by him, upon, Self-Murder, attended with some remarkable Circumstances! Judge *Sewal*, sends unto me, to recover the Notes of it, that he might now publish it, in hopes of doing some good by it, more than forty years after the Preaching of it. I am somewhat

[1] Governor Thomas Hutchinson (1711–1780).

remarkably directed and assisted from Heaven, for the Recovery of it; and within a few Hours after his Request I send it unto him.[1]

6. G. D. Propose to some of the Ministers, whether it may not be worth the while, and a notable Defence for our invaded Churches; to publish a bare Collection of Passages, Assertions, and Concessions, found in the most eminent Writings of the old Ch: of E. which the Demands of the modern Church run counter to.

7. G. D. I hear of a Family in much Poverty and Affliction. I would be concerned for the releeving of them.

*8. G. D. There is a Passage of *Jo. Nierembergius*, which I lately meet withal.[2]

"I had rather, *Lord*, could it be without Sin, that all should *hate me*, than that they should *love me for myself*. If all the World hate me, I should have but what is mine; If they should *love me for myself*, they would usurp what is *Thine*."

Tis impossible for me to express how much this Passage pleased me: and he that shew'd it me, knew me so well that he thought it would.

O my Soul, thou hast long been disposed this Way. But, press on, press on, till the Disposition come to perfection in thee.

9. G. D. Give the Flock a short sett of as edifying Sermons as may be, on that glorious Epitome of the Bible; Mic. VI. 8.

10. G. D. A Nurse attending on my sick Wife, may be by me look'd on, as one of my Family. I will study what I can, to serve the Interests of Piety with her, and by Discourses to her, in her Hearing, and by Treatises bestow'd on her, endeavour to assist her præparation for a better World.

---

[1] *Call to the Tempted.* See Davis, " Valentine-Vans Currency Pamphlets," in *Proceedings*, XLIII. 440.   [2] Johann Eusebius Nieremberg (*c.* 1590–1658).

11. G. D. My Kinsman at *Roxbury*, intending an Answer, to a vile, horrid, monstrous Book, newly published among us, I assist him with Materials.[1]

12. G. D. I hear of strong Machinations and Expectations among our wicked Ch : of E. Men, to gett our Colledge into their Hands; which will be a most compendious Way to bring a quick Ruine on our Churches. I would apply myself with all proper Awakenings to the Men at Helm, on this Occasion.

13. G. D. Sollicit for Days of Prayer to be kept in the Colledge-Hall, on the Occasion of the Condition, which it is many Ways expos'd unto. Such Things may be attended particularly with many good Consequences to the Students.

This day I sett apart for Supplications to the glorious GOD. Besides the many and usual Occasions for my lying thus in the Dust before the Lord, there is now this come upon me. The Crisis is arrived for the Extremity of my Vexations, from that unhappy Administration, wherein I suffered myself to be entangled seven Years ago. The Vexations which I have suffered from it, all this while, have been beyond all expression miserable. But now I have Arrests laid upon me, for considerable Sums; whereof really I owe not a Farthing. And I have no Prospect of any Out-gate, but by selling all my Goods to pay the Debts, and breaking up my Family. The Friends who might be capable of helping me, keep at a Distance from me, and appear to do little for me. The Relatives on whose Account, I have brought all this Distress upon myself, treat me like Monsters of Ingratitude.

My continual Cries to God, all this while, seem to have no Answer, but a Growth of my Confusions.

And I am afraid of all my Sorrows; it is a wonder, that either Death or Distraction has not in all this while putt a Period unto all my poor Services in the World.

My Supplications this Day, earnestly cry to God, for a good Issue of my marvellous and oppressing Difficulties. But, because I have no prospect left of that, I cry to Him for Grace to carry it well

---

[1] The monstrous book was John Checkley's *Modest Proof of the Order and Government . . . in the Church.* Walter's reply, *An Essay upon that Paradox,* called out a *Defence* from Checkley. See p. 726, *infra.*

under my Calamities, and that I may not be left unto any thing that may dishonour Him.

The Devotions of the Day, were very poorly carried on. I have some way grieved the holy Spirit of my GOD and Saviour. The Comforter that should releeve my Soul is far from me. The Views of a glorious CHRIST that use to support me, are denied unto me. T'is an Hour of Darkness with me. And from the strange Dispensations that I meet withal, sometimes hideous Temptations to Infidelity are shott in upon me.

O Thou strong Redeemer; I sink, I sink; Oh! Reach out thy Hand, and save me!

14. G. D. A young Gentleman in the Neighbourhood needs to have some good Advice given to him.

*15. G. D. My horrible Temptations quickly vanished. On my Cry to my SAVIOUR, He most graciously stept in for my Succour. I felt Him returning to me, with Influences, which marvellously allay'd all the Æstuations in my Soul; There arose Light unto me in my Darkness; and by His Light I could walk thro' Darkness.

I found the Dispositions of Patience under all the sad Things that I meet withal mightily strengthened by the Glorious Power of GOD my SAVIOUR, even to long suffering with Joyfulness.

I look up unto my SAVIOUR, that tho' I am of my self able to suffer nothing well, yett thro' Him strengthening of me, I may be able to suffer all Things.

In all my sad Things, I see an holy, and a righteous, as well as a sovereign GOD, performing the Thing that is appointed for me; and all the Murmurs of Discontent at the Providence that assigns my Portion and inflicts my Trouble, as well as of Envy at my Neighbours, who are not so chastened as I am, and so plagued all the Day, are forever silenced. My submissive Soul saies under all, *Shall not I take the Cup which my heavenly Father gives me!*

In all my sad Things, I beleeve and behold, and admire the Love of my SAVIOUR to me, at work that He may convey to me the Blessings of an healed Soul, and make me a Partaker of His Holiness, and produce in me the peaceable Fruits of Righteousness. I gett my Assurance of His Love to me in all sealed, by my coming into those Exercises of Piety which my Afflictions call me to.

In all my sad Things, I discover a Conformity unto my SAVIOUR, who was a man of Sorrows, and acquainted with Griefs: And it is with an incomparable Satisfaction, that I see myself, suffering with Him; having a strong Perswasion of the blessed Consequences.

None of all my sad Things discourage me; but I retain the firmest Resolutions, and grow stronger and stronger in them, to hold on after the most industrious Manner, serving of GOD, and doing of Good. And I am willing, that my Crucifixion go on, and that I should see no Deliverance, nor enjoy one comfortable Hour in this World, and that all the Harvest of what I am here sowing in Tears, be putt off, unto the other side of Death, and the Grave.

When I see sad Things coming on me, I make them welcome to me, in this View, that now I shall have a notable Opportunity to be made a Spectacle which the glorious GOD will, for the sake of HIS CHRIST, with Delight look down upon: and even the Thing which tries my Faith, is more precious than Gold unto me; better than if there were a present of Gold unto me. I tasted the Meaning of that strange præcept, *Count it all Joy, when you fall into diverse Temptations.*

Upon the Arrival of any sad Things unto me, I sett myself to consider, *What singular Work for GOD, may I take Occasion from this Thing to be led unto?*

And I am now watching over myself, (The Holy SPIRIT of my SAVIOUR, to whom I Resign myself is doing it!) That under my sad Things, I may neither speak unadvisedly with my Lips, nor allow any Disturbance of Mind, and any Discomposing Thoughts, a Lodging in me.

Dark Dispensations, but Light arising in Darkness.

It may be of some use for me, to observe some very *dark Dispensations*, wherein the *Recompences* of my poor *Essays at Well-doing*, in *this Life* seem to look a little Discouraging, and then to express the Triumphs of my *Faith* over such and all Discouragements.

Of Things that *look Darkly* I may touch upon twice seven Instances.

I will not be so vain as to challenge the producing of *any Man upon Earth* who has out-done me, in many of the instanced Articles. But yett I will venture to offer unto Consideration, *what has my gracious Lord helped me to do?*

I. *What has a gracious Lord given me to do,* for the Welfare of the *seafaring Tribe?* In *Prayers* for them; in *Sermons* to them; in *Books* bestow'd on them; and in various Projections and Endeavours, to render the *Sailors*, an happy Generation!

AND YETT, there is not a Man in the world, so Reviled, so slandered, so cursed, among the *Sailors*.

II. *What has a gracious Lord given me to do*, for the Instruction, and Salvation and Comfort, of the poor *Negro's?*

AND YETT, some, on purpose to affront me, call their *Negro's*, by the Name of *Cotton Mather*, that so they may with some Shadow of Truth, assert Crimes as committed by one of that Name, which the Hearers take to be *me*.

III. *What has a gracious Lord given me to do*, for the Profit and Honour of the *female Sex*, especially in publishing the vertuous and laudable Characters of *holy Women?*

AND YETT, where is the Man, whom the *female Sex* have spitt more of their Venom at? I have cause to Quæstion, whether there are twice Ten in the Town, but what have at some time or other spoken basely of me.

IV. *What has a gracious Lord given me to do*, that I may be a Blessing to my *Relatives?* I keep a Catalogue of them, and not a Week passes me, without some *Good devised* for some or other of them, till I have taken All of them under my Cognisance.

AND YETT, where is the Man, who has been tormented with such monstrous *Relatives?* Job said, *I am a Brother to Dragons*.

V. *What has a gracious Lord given me to do*, for the *Comfort* of my *Parents?*

AND YETT, How little *Comfort*, yea, how much contrary to it, have I seen in my *Children?*

VI. *What has a gracious Lord given me to do*, for the Vindication, and Reputation, of the *Scotch Nation?* It may be no *Englishman* ever did more.

AND YETT, no *Englishman* has been so vilified by the Tongues and Pens of *Scotts*, as I have been.

VII. *What has a gracious Lord given me to do* for the Good of the *Countrey*, in Applications without Number for it in all its Interests, besides Publications of Things useful to it, and for it?

AND YETT, there is no Man whom the *Countrey* so loads with Disrespects, and with Calumnies and manifold Expressions of Aversion.

VIII. *What has a gracious Lord given me to do* for the Upholding of the *Government*, and the Strengthening of it, and the bespeaking of Regard unto it?

AND YETT, the Discountenance I have almost perpetually received from the *Government!* yea, the *Indecencies* and *Indignities* which it has multiplied upon me, are such as no other Man has been treated withal.

IX. *What has a Gracious Lord given me to do*, that the *Colledge* may be own'd for the bringing forth such as are somewhat known in the World, and have read and wrote as much as many have done in some other Places?

AND YETT, the *Colledge* forever putts all possible Marks of Disesteem upon me. If I were the greatest *Blockhead* that ever came from it, or the greatest *Blemish* that ever came to it, they could not easily show me more Contempt than they do.

X. *What has a gracious Lord given me to do* in the Study of a *profitable Conversation?* For near fifty Years together, I have hardly ever gone into any *Company*, or had any coming to me, without some *explicit Contrivance*, to speak something or other, that they might be the *wiser* or the *better* for.

AND YETT, my *Company* is as little sought for, and there is as little Resort unto it as any Ministers that I am acquainted with.

XI. *What has a gracious Lord given me to do*, in good *Offices*, wherever I could find Opportunities for the doing of them: I am always on the *Look-out* for them; I forever entertain them with Alacrity; My Life is filled with them. I have offered pecuniary Recompences to such as would advise me of them.

AND YETT, I see no man for whom all are so lothe to do *good Offices*. Indeed, I find *some* cordial Friends. But, how *few!* Often have I said, What would I give, if there were any *one Man* in the World, willing to do for me, what I am willing to do for *every Man*, in the World.

XII. *What has a gracious Lord given me to do*, in the *Writing of many Books*, for the Advancing of Piety, and the Promoting of His Kingdome, *Glory to GOD in the Highest and Good will among men?* There are, I suppose, more than three Hundred and thirty of them.

AND YETT, I have had more *Books* written against me; more Pamphlets to traduce me, and reproach me, and bely me, than any man that I know in the World.

XIII. *What has a gracious Lord given me to do*, in *Alms*, and in Disbursements on *pious Uses?* For whole Years together, *not one Day* has passed me, in which I have not been able to say, that I have done something that Way.

AND YETT, tho' I am strangely provided for, yett I am a very *poor Man*. I have not a Foot of Land upon Earth. Except a *Library* and a little *Househould Stuff*, I have nothing upon earth. And this also I am now offering unto my Creditors, to satisfy for Debts, whereof I never did myself owe a Farthing. My very *Library*, the Darling of my little Enjoyments, is demanded from me. Tis inexpressible, how much this Condition pleases me, gladdens me!

XIV. *What has a gracious Lord given me to do*, in a Variety of *Services?* For many *Lustres* of years, not a Day has passed me, without some *Devices*, even *written Devices*, to be *serviceable.*

AND YETT, my *Sufferings*, they seem to be (as tis Reason they should be,) more than my *Services.* Every Body points at me, and speaks of me, as by far the most afflicted Minister in all *New England.* And many look on me as the *greatest Sinner* because the *greatest Sufferer:* and are pretty Arbitrary in their Conjectures on my punished Miscarriages.

But now, lett me proceed unto my *Dispositions* and my *Consolations*, under these *Dispensations.*

First; I have a clear and strong Perswasion of a *Future State.* I am heartily willing, to wait for the Fulfilment of all the *Promises* in the Covenant of God, until my Arrival at that World, where I shall have all the Spiritual Blessings of the heavenly Places bestowed upon me. I am content, and I can patiently and cheerfully allow of it, that the whole Harvest of my mean Studies to glorify God, should be adjourned unto a *future State.* I do most freely submitt and consent unto the Condition of a *crucified Man*, and am willing to have my Crucifixion go on with a perpetual Succession of Pains and Pangs, without any Prospect of any Outgate, but at and by the dying Hour.

Yea, secondly. I have already received an abundant *Recompence of Reward.* A glorious CHRIST has reveled Himself to me, has conferred Himself on me, has taken Possession of me. The *Views* which I have of a glorious CHRIST, and the *Wayes* which He teaches me, of conversing with Him, and so finding in Him the *Consolations* which it will be in vain for me to seek in Creatures, which are at best but *lying Vanities:* These are a sufficient Compensation for all that I undergo, in being made a Man of Sorrows and acquainted with Griefs. If I never had any other Compensation made for my Troubles, I have here so much, that I need not ask for any more.

16. G. D. All faithful and prudent Methods must be used; that the Flock may be established in the Faith and Order of the Gospel, and the *present Truth;* for the

Prevention of an Apostasy to the vile Superstitions of the Ch. of E. growing upon us: And they must be yett more plainly told, what they go from, if they *go away*.

17. G. D. Among my many other Calamities, under which the Patience of CHRIST in me, must have its perfect Work, I have dwelling with me, a Neece of my wife's, who is a very wicked Creature, and not only utterly deaf to all Proposals of Piety, but also a monstrous Lyar and a very mischievous Person, and a sower of Discord, and a Monster of Ingratitude. The Uneasiness that by her vile Tricks is caused in my Family, is a sore Trial to me. Now may my glorious Lord assist me to be not only patient, but also very prudent under it; and in His Time and Way, deliver me from it.

18. G. D. My poor Nephew, under Languishments, what shall be done for him?

19. G. D. The Churches of this Countrey have been so wickedly misrepresented, in the *Watertown*-Libel, that it appears a seasonable Service unto Them, and unto the Cause of Religion, to præpare and publish an Answer to it; which accordingly I am now adoing.[1]

20. G. D. Tho' I purpose to take my Leave of the Board where I sitt among the Commissioners for the Affairs of the Gospel among the Indians, being dissatisfied and discouraged with their Conduct; yett I would continue my Cares for the Indians. Wherefore I write a Letter unto the Lieut. Governour and the rest of the Commissioners, to sollicit, that they would employ a *Visitor*, to bring them, an exact Report of what State the Indians are in; and what may be further done for them; and so prosecute with better Vigour than formerly, what shall be judged necessary. And several other Matters.

21. G. D. A Family lately arrived from N. *York*, to

---

[1] Probably the "libel" was Rev. William Williams's sermon at the ordination of Rev. Warham Williams at Watertown, June 11, 1723.

dwell in this Place, I would visit on the best Intentions, and unto some Relatives of theirs at N. *York,* as well as unto themselves, dispense Books of Piety.

*22. G. D. My Soul would be particularly affected with a Strain of Piety, to be express'd in certain *Echo's of Devotion* upon the Declarations which the Glorious GOD makes of His gracious Purposes concerning us. For Instance; Our God sais, *I have chosen you.* I would say, Lord, *I chuse thee for my God, and chuse the Things that please thee.* Our God calls His People by the Name of, *His Portion and His Inheritance.* I would say of Him, *The Lord is my Portion, and in Him I have a goodly Inheritance.* Our GOD calls His People, *His Habitation.* I will say to Him, *Lord, Thou art my Dwelling-place and my strong Habitation, whereto I will resort continually.* Our GOD speaks of His People, *I will walk in them.* I will say to Him, *Lord, I would walk [in] thee, and walk before thee in the Land of the Living.* Our God speaks of His people, as *precious* to Him. And in my *beleeving* on Him, CHRIST shall be *precious* unto me. Our God sais, *I have loved thee with an everlasting Love.* My Heart sais, *I love thee, O Lord, my Strength.*

23. G. D. A pathetical Representation of the State of the Flock, before the Lord, in the public Day of Prayer approaching.

24. G. D. The new Servant come to sojourn in my Family, I have great Hope, that her coming into it may prove her Conversion to GOD, and her Espousal to her SAVIOUR. And I shall have great Joy if it may be so. My serious Directions for it, must be repeted.

25. G. D. The threatening Circumstances on the Health of my Kinsman at *Roxbury,* obliged me to study all possible Ways of being serviceable to him, and of assisting his Præparations for what he may be shortly call'd unto.

26. G. D. This Day is a Day of general Supplications thro' the Province.

In the public Sacrifices of the Day, I propose and pursue a Variety of Services.

And I enjoy a marvellous Presence of my God with me in them.

My Prayer was about *two Hours*, and my Sermon *more*.

In the Intercessions on the behalf of the Interest, which our Saviour yett has in this Countrey, I felt a strong, sweet, heart-melting Afflatus, that there should be yett some Effusions of the holy SPIRIT on His People, and a remarkable Blast from Heaven upon the Attempts of evil Men to destroy the Faith and Worship and Order of the Gospel among us.

27. G. D. Having præpared Materials, for the Vindication of our Churches from the *Watertown*-libel, I committ it unto a Minister in my Neighbourhood, entreating him to adopt the Composure, and alter it, and abridge it, as he pleases, and pursue the Work of preserving the Reputation of these poor Churches, in the World.

28. G. D. A young Gentleman that needs my Advice, in several Articles; especially to confirm him in the right Ways, wherein he has been hitherto strangely præserved.

* 29. G. D. It is to me a Thought full of Consolation; that if I have a Glorious CHRIST living in me, and have Him upon my Eye and my Cry unto Him to enter me, and possess me, and quicken me, for every Step of my Living unto GOD, I shall have Him, also suffering in me, and in all my Afflictions He will be afflicted. When I suffer such Things as He underwent of old, when He was a Man of Sorrows and acquainted with Griefs, He will after some sort suffer over again; so that He will support me under what I am call'd unto, and He will carry on my Conformity unto Himself until His Image in me shall be finished and He will by all præpare me for the Glories wherein I shall one day be a partaker with Him.

30. G. D. It being very probable, that thro' the Arrests

712 DIARY OF COTTON MATHER

upon me, for the Debts of other Men, and the Plotts o
them that seek my Ruine, and the unaccountable Aver
sion of my pretended Friends to afford me any effectua
Assistance under my Distresses, my Opportunities o
Service to my Flock are likely within a Month to come unt
a Period, I would exceedingly study (and seek Directio
from above) what most important and pathetic Things
it may be most proper for me to make my ᾿εξόδια ῥήματα
and to take my Farewel of the Flock withal.

31. G. D. My dear, dear *Nancy;* a Child of so man
Afflictions all her Days. The unreasonable and implacabl
Aversion of her Mother-in-Law for her; augmented n
doubt, by the wicked Kinswoman of my Wife, who sojourn
with me, and otherwise adds to her Uneasiness, compell
me to seek some other Place, where I may board her.
must contrive all the ways imaginable, to comfort th
Child, and hearten her, and make her Sorrows profitable t
her. I must also look up to Heaven for Direction abou
the Disposal of her.

(I.) About this time, there is published an Essay
which I wrote long ago; entituled, RELIGIOUS SOCIE
TIES. *Proposals for the Revival of Dying Religion, b*
well-ordered Societies for that Purpose. With a brief Dis
course offered unto a Religious Society, on the First Da
of their Meeting.[1]

In this Essay, there is one thing a little singular. Th
Sermon in it, is one that I entertained my Neighbours witha
before I was a public Preacher, and when I was but sixtee
Years of Age. It may be, this is the first Sermon from on
of that Age, that has been published. Thus my compas
sionate Lord honours me and uses me, and comforts me, i
the Midst of my grievous Humiliations.

April. 1. G. D. The dangerous Condition of m
Nephew M[ather] B[yles] in regard of his Entring into a Con

[1] Printed by S. Kneeland for John Phillips, 1724.

umption, requires me to do all I can for him; especially to prepare him for what he may be coming to.

2. G. D. The memorable *Joseph* was a Type of our admirable JESUS, in this among other Things, that the very Methods which their Enemies took to defeat the Purposes of Heaven concerning them, did but help to fulfill those very Purposes.

I often foretold, that my PARENTATOR[1] would not be gett well abroad into the world, before I should meet with a greater Storm of Humiliations, than most that I have seen, tho' I have seen enough, since I came into the World. It is accordingly come to pass unto Astonishment! A Number of Arrests are laid upon me, to make me pay the Debts of other People, and restore that which I took not away. They that should comfort me, and for my serving of whom, I am exposed unto all my amazing Difficulties, make themselves rather a Terror to me, and encumber the Offer of my Friends to appear for my Rescue. My Friends have also a deep Sleep from the Lord fallen upon them: and tho' they might easily putt a stop to my Confusions, they, like Persons in a Maze and a doze, permitt them to go on, unto such Extremity, that within a Fortnight I must either be lodg'd in the Prison, or forc'd into a private Withdraw, which where and how it will terminate, none can foresee.

The Design of Satan herein, is, utterly to extinguish my Services to the Kingdome of GOD.

Now, that which I would exceedingly study on this Occasion is, that the Kingdome and Interest of my SAVIOUR, may be but the more served, for the sad Things, that I meet withal, and that the Things which happen to me, may be for the Furtherance of the Gospel.

[1] Printed by B. Green for Nathaniel Belknap, 1724. It was the first book on which Timothy Green, the younger, worked, according to the Advertisement at the end of the volume.

This will be accomplished; first, if Patience (with Repentance) have its perfect Work: and my Behaviour under my Troubles, be such, that I may be a Spectacle which Heaven may be gratified with looking down upon.

And then, if the people of GOD may see me so Humble and so silent, and so cheerful, and so full of Resignation to the Will of GOD, and Satisfaction in the Enjoyment of a CHRIST, as to recommend the Ways of Piety unto them.

And, lastly: if I am awakened unto still more exquisite Enquiries, after the Methods wherein my Pen as well as my Tongue, may bring forth more of that Fruit, by which my heavenly Father may be glorified: and if I grow more Industrious in redeeming of my Time, and finishing the work which I have before me.

O My Saviour, do thou grant such Things unto me.

But, behold, the marvellous Appearance of GOD my SAVIOUR! In the Evening of the Day, which had such as these Meditations for the Morning, a most unexpected Thing befel me. Four of the principal Gentlemen in the Church whereof I am the Servant, (men full of Prudence and Goodness,) visited me, and kindly rebuked my Anxieties and Assured me, that they would immediately undertake to extricate me out of my Difficulties, and that without any further Thought of mine, they would see a Period putt unto them.

This fills me with Admiration at the Care which Heaven takes of as vile a Sinner as any upon Earth.

3. G. D. And the Use I would make of it, shall be, to press after greater Measures of Holiness, in all Manner of Conversation: and study how to do more good than ever, without any Dread of the bitter Humiliations which must probably be the Consequences.

But then, in my continual Excitations of others, to be serviceable, I would warn them and arm them for the humbling Things which they must look to meet withal.

4. G. D. I have in view several Persons, who are to
e admonished of their Duty, to join to the Church.

* 5. G. D. Inexpressible Cause have I, to bless my
lorious GOD and SAVIOUR, for leading me to the Papers
f Pious Major *Dorney*.[1] Never have I any where found
tal Piety operating and exhibited more unto the Life,
an in those precious Papers. They have more taught
e to live by the Faith of the Son of GOD, than any thing
at ever I mett withal. I propose to make an Extract
ith my Pen of such Passages from them, as are more
ffectuous and impressive upon me, and gett them thoroughly
igested into my own Experience; and then to do my best,
at the People of God may in my Ministry fare the better
r them.

6. G. D. And, what better Service can I do for the
lock, than to go before them, with Prayers fetch'd and
rm'd from those high Flights of evangelical Piety, which
am thus raised unto! The mighty Pleadings with a
lorious GOD; and Looks to a CHRIST as bringing us
nto Him, which may fill these Prayers, with such raised
otes of the Gospel as are but rarely heard in our Assem-
lies, may leave precious Impressions upon the People.

7. G. D. *Misera mea Conjux in Paroxysmos illos vere*
atanicos, a quibus per Annos quosdam fuerit plerumque
iberata (Vel ego Saltem Liberatus) iam rursus delapsa, mihi,
illam, illiusque filiam, dura ac dira alias perpesso, ingra-
ssime vix tolerabiles creat Molestias, et absurdissimis ac
rdidissimis mutitur Stomachationibus. Haec mulieris In-
niæ per Sanctissimi Iustissimique mei Redemptoris Sapien-
am, in mei probationem ordinata, orationes meas excitat,
igiliasque, ut Patientia mea nunquam deficiat, atque ut
enitentia ad perfectionem et puritatem summam inde per-
ucatur.

[1] Henry Dorney, whose *Divine Contemplations and Spiritual Breathings of*
. D. appeared in 1684.

8. G. D.   To be more thoroughly serviceable unto m
Kinsman at *Roxbury*, especially to assist his Preparatio
for what we have most Cause to be apprehensive of, I ar
thinking particularly to invite him unto the Perusal o
especially two Chapters in my *Angel of Bethesda*, entitule
the one of them, *Desector*, the other, *Euthanasia*.

9. G. D.   There being some vile Books disperse
among our People, to disaffect them unto the Ministry i
our Churches, which call for some further Antidote agains
them.   This is a Point which I am now bestowing som
Study and Labour upon.

10. G. D.   The civil Magistrate being upon the Prose
cution of a wicked Fellow, for a Breach of his Bonds for th
Peace, in publishing and scattering an execrable Book amon
us, there is danger lest they so found the Prosecution on
Bottom that shall have a Controversy of Religion inter
woven into it, as may be anon improved unto our Dis
advantage by a persecuting Adversary, I have had sucl
Remonstrances of the Danger made unto me, as oblig
me to write as proper a Letter as I can, unto the Govern
ment, on this Occasion.[1]

This Day I sett apart for Supplications before the Glorious God
not without the Enjoyment of gracious Assistences from Above.

I entertained the Views and Hopes of a GOD Reconciled unt
me.   I invited and received a CHRIST into me, that by Him livin
in me, I may do Services, and bear the Sufferings, and conque
the Temptations I may be call'd unto.   I turned all my Desireable
into Sacrifices, and I took up with a CHRIST alone, as abundantl
making up the want of all Things.

I carried unto the Lord, the Preparations for the Public whicl
He had assisted me to the Composing of, particularly my, *Boanerges*
and my *Angel of Bethesda*, and my, *Ratio Disciplinae*, that they ma
be brought forth for the Good of Many.

I laid before the Lord, my particular Troubles; especially th

---

[1] John Checkley was the "wicked fellow" and the "execrable book" wa
Charles Leslie's *Short and Easie Method with the Deists*.   See Slafter's introduc
tion in *John Checkley* (Prince Society), I. 39 *et seq.*

)ifficulties which my Administration has brought upon me; and the
orrid, froward, malicious Disposition of my Wife, to hurt me, and
ay dear *Samuel;* that so I may be gloriously delivered from every
'hing that may hurt my Services unto His Kingdome. And I am
are, that *my God has heard me!*

11. G. D. Assistences and Encouragements unto a
oung Gentleman, to be the next Week ordained for the
ervice of the Church at *Charlestown* in *Carolina.*

* 12. G. D. In my Sermon this Day, I am to have a
'assage which the Favour of the glorious Lord that has led
ae to, abundantly compensates to me, what I suffer in the
reat Fight of Afflictions which I am now enduring. And
could not but humbly say so to Him, at the time of my
vriting of it:

(On Joh. XIV. 20.) "We were in *CHRIST JESUS* (1. Cor. I. 30.)
vhen He did those things, wherein He wrought out *Righteousness
nd Sanctification, and Redemption* for us. He transacted still as a
ublic Person, and we were *in Him,* when He did what He did on our
ehalf. Oh, what a most affecting View may we take of our SAV-
OUR, passing thro' the several Stages of the Work, which He did
s a *Redeemer* for us. With what Revived and opened and sharp-
ned Eyes, and how filled with Tears of Joy, may we read the *Gospel*
f our JESUS *obtaining eternal Redemption* for us! To think all
long, *I was in my JESUS, when He did these glorious Things!* This
s a Flight of PIETY, it may be *somewhat new* unto you. *Behold, I
hew unto you an excellent Way,* wherein you may take the *Comfort
f the Scriptures!* To behold your SAVIOUR as having *You in Him,*
vhen He took the Steps of a *Redeemer* from the Time of His being
Manifest in Flesh, to the Time of His being *received up to Glory.*
This *comfortable perswasion* of an *eternal Union* with our SAVIOUR,
aas an infallible, and a never-failing Tendency to make us *holy in
ll Manner of Conversation.* (*After the Thoughts Exemplified.*) It is
mpossible to entertain such Thoughts as these, without soaring up
o a *Conversation in Heaven;* such Thoughts must needs produce a
anctity and *Purity* wherein we shall *mount up as with the Wings of
Eagles!*"

13. G. D. Can I do a greater Service to my Flock,
han by inculcating such Things as these upon them?

14. G. D.   Help me, O my GOD, and Saviour that, —

On this Day, the Glorious Lord accepted me, and assisted me, to manage the Solemnity of an Ordination of a Person going forth to the Work of the evangelical Ministry, in a distant Countrey, from whence we have received the Desire of a Flock, to send a suitable Minister unto them.

The Ordination was performed in one of the Churches of the City, and in the Presence of a considerable Congregation.

It is, I suppose, the *Tenth Ordination*, which has been managed, by the sinful Hand that is now writing.

The Circumstances that have led unto it, will be found in the Speeches made on the Occasion; which I have here inserted.[1]

15. G. D.   My Kinsman of *Roxbury*, under his Languishments is at this time lodging in my Family; which gives me Opportunity to, —

His little Brother doing so too; this also gives me a further Opportunity to, —

16. G. D.   Besides an Opportunity, which I have this Week, to give a Check unto some foolish and wicked Contentions, with which the Devil makes work for us in *Dedham* I have an Opportunity this Day to recommend unto the Inhabitants of this Town, the *Piety*, with which they are to acknowledge the Providence of GOD that supports them and admonish them faithfully of some undoing Indiscretions which they run into.

17. G. D.   I would employ the hand of the Minister at *Weston*, to transcribe and adopt my Materials, for the Vindication of our churches from the *Scotch-Irish* calumnies.

[1] Missing, but from Sewall, *Diary*, III. 332, the name of the person is obtained — Mr. Nathan Basset, who was to go to South Carolina. The ordination service was held in Dr. Colman's church. See *Year Book, City of Charleston*, 1882, 373.

[2] The dispute on Presbyterian ordination raged in this year, and much was printed upon it in Boston and in Philadelphia. Rev. William Williams was the minister.

18. G. D. Good Offices to be done for the young Iinister, that is bound for *Carolina*.

Miserable Scotts to be releeved.

* 19. G. D. Read, *Cole*, of Regeneration.[1] *Rowe*, of emptations.[2]

Tis a Thought full of Consolation to me, and what arries an Animation of Piety with it; that the sad Things hich appear to me, as Punishments of my Offences, and accordingly Accept them, and I don't complain, but say, will bear the Indignation of the Lord, because I have sinned gainst him; they really prove Benefits unto me, and I nd them intended for such; and they have those precious ffects upon me, which proclame the everlasting Love of OD unto me.

20. G. D. I must consult with my Collegue, now the ntermissions of the Winter are over, about the most roper Methods for the reviving and managing of our *atechising*.

21. G. D. *Domi rursus omnia pacata, tranquilla, serena fere Extatico erga me Amore, condita; (tam inexplicabilis st conjugis meae ad Extrema se Vertentis incertissima mu- bilitas!) Me ducunt ad Laudes Dei, ac Majorem in Opere vangelico Industriam, atque mei-ipsius patiens, et sobrium astumque Regimen.*

22. G. D. My Kinsman, M. B[yles] being fallen, I oubt, into a Consumption, I must with all possible Good- ess and Concern, sett myself to do all that I can find roper to be done for a Nephew in such Circumstances.

I am also writing to my Brother at *Witney*.

23. G. D. To exhibit unto the World, a *Collection of e Lives and Characters of eminent Persons, Divines and thers, among the Professors of pure and undefiled Religion*

---

[1] Thomas Cole (1627–1697), *Discourse of Regeneration, Faith, and Repentance,* rinted in London, 1689.

[2] John Rowe (1626–1677), *The Saints' Temptation,* 1675.

(the Dissenters;) may be a Thing follow'd with many an happy Consequences. From the Time that the old Collecto Clark[1] left off about forty Years ago, there may be foun separately appearing sufficient Materials for such a Biog raphy, among the Successors of the Old English Puritans to make a Volumn, which would, no doubt, be quickl bought up, and not want Subscriptions, and might prov inexpressibly useful to the best of Interests. Besides, th Histories that go under the Title of *Lives*, there may b extracted for, and contracted in, such a Work as this, th *Characters* given in funeral Sermons on many excellen Persons, which would make a noble Constellation.

I send over a Proposal of this Importance, unto th Ministers in the City of *London*, entreating them to forwar this Design, and inspect and manage it.

I propose my PARENTATOR, to have a Room in thi Collection.

24. G. D. The Proposal, which I have mentioned, would send Copies of it, unto several Gentlemen, bot Ministers and others; exhorting them to forward it. would also signify unto them, that if I have timely Notic of their Proceeding in it, I would contribute unto the Work by sending them a Collection of Characters given in funera Sermons, published in this Countrey.

25. G. D. Several Neighbours, to be animated unt the Duty, of coming to the Table of the Lord.

*26. G. D. I am still upon Transcribing of selec Passages from dear Major *Dorney:* with Hopes of stron Impressions upon my own Soul from the admirable Strain of Piety shining in them.

How much has my glorious Redeemer taught me t pray, by the Breathings of His good Spirit, which I discer in the Lines of His faithful Servant!

27. G. D. There has been of late among us a Repetitio

[1] See Vol. I. 65 *n.*

of horrible *Self-Destruction*. In such Things the Voice of the Lord cries to the City. I preach to my Flock, as lively a Sermon as I can, upon the *Self-Destruction*, which all that walk in the Ways of Sin are guilty of. I incorporate into the Sermon, all that may appear needful to be spoken upon the Crime of proper *Self-Murder;* that so if any of the Flock are tempted unto it, they may be duely warned against it.

28. G. D. I would have my Servants, (particularly, *Ezer*) learn to write. *Sammy* shall do the Kindness of teaching them.

29. G. D. I am using a Variety of Methods, that my dear Friend Mrs. *Brown*,[1] may not only taste the Consolations of GOD, her Saviour, but even be filled with them.

30. G. D. I am writing to the Corporation at *London*, for propagating the Gospel among our Indians.

May. 1. G. D. Unto the Ministers of this Island, I offer a PROPOSAL, that they would once a Fortnight spend three Hours together; and in every Interview after a Prayer, tender what Answer each one thinks fitt unto a Quæstion proposed the Fortnight before; out of which our Scribe shall draw up such a Conclusion as may be tendered at the next Meeting [and] agreed unto: and the Moderator after this regulating the Expence of Time on each Subject, shall call for what Communications any one has to make on those three Points; an Illustration of any Passage in the sacred Scripture; The State of Religion abroad as well as at home; and any Motion of special Service to be done for the Kingdome of GOD.

My Purpose is, to invite my Brethren the next Week, unto a small Treat, and then make the offer of this Proposal. How it will be entertained, I know not.

2. G. D. The Minister of *Newington*, is at this time in the Town, under Languishments; I must visit him, and

[1] Rebecca Brown, who may be the R. B. of later mention.

study all possible Ways wherein I may be a Comfort unto him.[1]

* 3. G. D.   Tho' I have not always made a Record of such Experiences, yett I will here mention one.

On the last Lords-day, under singular Afflations, in the public Prayers, I was carried forth to pray in an enlarged and expanded Manner, and with much Importunity, that we may see the glorious One do some remarkable Thing for the Destruction of the Pyrates, by which our Coast has been lately infested. The Prayer had so much Notice taken of it, that many People receiv'd and expressed strong Expectation from it, that within a few Days, yea, before the Week was out, we should hear something remarkable. Behold, before the week was out, there comes in a Vessel wherein five or six Captives among the Pyrates that were upon making horrible Ravages among our poor Fishermen, rose, and with much bravery kill'd the Chief of their Masters, and the rest they took Prisoners. The Joy of the City on this Occasion was very notable.[2]

The Notice taken of what there appeared prophetical in my poor Supplications, introductory to it, obliges me in the first Place to treat with inexpressible Caution and Abhorrence, all Elation of Mind, and the very first Motions of any Tendency to Vanity; O the tremendous Consequences, of being any other than a meer nothing, and lying any where but in the Dust before the Lord! But then this Experience encourages me, to hold on praying, and exceedingly watching against every thing that may grieve the Spirit of Prayer (which is a Spirit of Prophecy,) and provoke Him to withdraw from us.

4. G. D.   Here is a Proposal among us, that the three

---

[1] Rev. Elisha Williams, now settled at Newington, Connecticut.

[2] *Boston News-Letter*, May 21, 1724; Sewall, *Diary*, III. 335. The "dreaded" sea-pirate who had commanded the crew, and who was killed in this affair, bore the name of John Phillips, and may have been of the Charlestown family from which Mather took his first wife.

Churches on the Island of *North-Boston*, should unite in a
Lecture præparatory to the monthly Communion; (which
in this Case, must be on one and the same Lord's-Day;)
It appears a Proposal, that may have a Tendency to many
good Consequences. I would as soon as may be advise
upon it.

5. *G. D. Familia mea per furentis uxoris insaniam rursus misere distracta ac turbata; Imo Ministeriumque meum
tremendis periculis Expositum,* —

*Quid agam? Redemptor mi! Quid agam? O mihi
peccata mea condones, meque clementer protegas.*

6. G. D. More to be done for my three Widow-Sisters,
especially, in Prayers together with them.

7. G. D. The sudden Death of that unhappy Man,
who sustained the Place of President in our Colledge,[1]
will open a Door for my doing of singular Services to the
Best of Interests. Indeed his being within a Year of the
same Age with myself, loudly calls upon me, to live in a
daily Expectation of my own Call from hence, but, *my
Times are in thy Hands, O Lord!*

I do not know, that the Care of the Colledge will be now
cast upon me; tho' I am told, it is what is most generally
wished for. If it should, I shall be in Abundance of Distress about it. But if it should not, yett I may do many
Things for the Good of the Colledge, more quietly and more
hopefully than formerly. And more particularly I may do
what will afford an Article for to morrow Morning.

8. G. D. Why may I not write unto the Tutors of
the Colledge, and sollicit for such Things as these.

That under a deep Sense of their great Opportunities to do inexpressible Good unto the Colledge, and unto more than all the Countrey,
and what both GOD and Man expects from them, they would come

[1] John Leverett (1662–1724), who had served as president from January
1707–08. He died May 3, 1724, and a funeral sermon was preached by Benjamin
Wadsworth, who on July 7 was elected to succeed him in office.

into a Combination to invent and pursue the best Projections for the
Well-ordering of the Society.

That they would exert their Powers, to make the Students, become
indeed what they are called, and spend and fill their Time well; and
therefore not content themselves with the daily Recitations (the
matter of which also, ought to be further considered,) but assign them
suitable Books to read, and see that they read them.

That they encourage Sodalities among them; to meet every
Week, for the Communications of their Acquisitions to one another.

That they countenance Industry, with distinguishing Rewards
and Honours to the Meritorious.

That they bring up the Use of the Latin Tongue in Conversation
among the Scholars.

That above all Things, they do what may be done for the Animation and Inflammation of PIETY among the young Men; have personal Conferences with them, on the State of their Souls; cast a kind
aspect on those who associate for Devotions; and add, a special
Care, to have them acquainted with pure and undefiled Religion;
and recommend proper Books of Theology to them; and establish
them in the *Faith and Order of the Gospel* in which the Churches of
New England, have their Beauty and their Safety.

8 *d.* 3 *m. Friday.* This Day I sett apart for Humilia-
tions and Supplications before the glorious Lord. And
indeed, in my domestic Circumstances, I had some singular
Occasions, to be thus prostrate in the Dust before Him:
Entreating that He would interpose with His gracious
Providence and Influence to give a good Issue unto my
Sorrows, and bring Light out of dark Dispensations.

I am comforted with one Token for good upon me;
which is, that my Soul is filled with Praises to my Gracious
and faithful Redeemer, for all the grievous Things befalling
me, by which my Repentance and Holiness is carried on,
and all Sin is made more Lothesome to me. O my dear
SAVIOUR, welcome, welcome, unto me, are the most
bitter Things in the World, if they may but embitter all
Sin unto me!

I left all my Desires before the Lord, relating to my

Ministry, and my Family, and all my Difficulties; comfortably perswaded of my Acceptance with Him.

9. G. D. A Student, who is a Candidate of the Ministry must be assisted, and advised; and Books must be bestow'd upon him.

* 10. G. D. Listening to the Voice of my glorious Redeemer in some Dispensations, I am suspicious, whether He don't call me immediately to attain unto some greater and higher Degrees of Purity (tho' the least impure Thought has long been abominable to me,) than I have yett arriv'd unto.

So, I have resolved, with a CHRIST quickening and strengthening of me, upon several Points of the most consummate, and even uncommon Purity. There is no need of my writing them down in this Place; but that in which they terminate is this; that if the Devil should ever have the Imprudence to try the Throwing of so much as one impure Thought into my Mind, it shall not only be rejected with Abhorrence, but also turn to the Disadvantage of my Adversary, and only Raise me nearer to GOD, with fresh Flights and Looks unto my SAVIOUR.

11. G. D. About the Method of catechising in the Flock and personal and pastoral Visits, concert with my Collegue.

12. G. D. *Res Mira! Domi omnia rursus Tranquilla. Et mea conjux in mei non tantum Amorem flagrantissimum, sed et Admirationem rapta! Postremi illius Furores, a Fidelissimo meo Redemptore in mei Purificationem Consummatissimam sunt Sanctificati! Me Vero oportet maximopere Vigilare, ne hujus puritatis vel minimam in Corde intermissionem aut relaxationem admittam, sed quid faciam, ut conjux mea, non per mei Amorem Solum, sed et per Dei Timorem, servetur ne Spiritus ille malignus, qui nuper illam agitaverit, ad illius Irritationem iterum redeat!*

13. G. D. I assist my Kinsman at *Roxbury*, with many

Communications, for the embellishing and enriching and strengthening, of the Work which he is preparing for the Press in defence of our Churches.[1]

14. G. D. In reading Dr. *Burnett's* History of his Times, I find this passage; "I have upon all the Observation that I have made, often considered the *inward State of the Reformation*, and the *Decay of the Vitals of Christianity* in it, as that which gives more melancholy Impressions, than all the outward Dangers that surround it."

This Passage awakens me, to think on some further Projections, of Things to be done, for the Awakening of the People of GOD abroad in the world, unto a due Consideration of their own Condition; in which they are now generally slumbring and sleeping.

15. G. D. And particularly to write unto my Friends in the *Frederician* University, my Sense of these Things.

16. G. D. The poor condemned Pyrates.

* 17. G. D. Preaching this Day, about the *Hope* and *Gain*, and Fate of the *Hypocrite*, it is of infinite Consequence, that I should make sure of such Dispositions in my Soul, as no *Hypocrite* ever attains unto.

Upon an impartial Search into the State and Frame of my Soul, I find such Things as these produced there.

Such are my Regards to GOD, that I not only make the Serving and Pleasing of Him, the Chief Design of my Life, and the Sense of my being under His View is awful to me, but also, when I am in any Miseries, and I think that He helps me to such a Behaviour under them, as He is gratified in the beholding of, I even take a sensible Pleasure in them.

Such are my Regards to CHRIST, that I not only look up to Him for all the Blessings of Goodness, and particularly

---

[1] Thomas Walter, who published this year *An Essay upon that Paradox, Infallibility may sometimes mistake. Or a Reply to a Discourse concerning Episcopacy.* He did not attach his name to it.

for the Influences that are to quicken me in living to GOD, but also He is become all unto me, and if I may but have Him conversing with me, and possessing of me, I am satisfied in the Withdraw of all Creatures from me.

Such are my Regards to SIN, that I not only hate every false way, but also the most bitter Dispensations that embitter my Sin unto me, and carry on Repentance to a more perfect Work, are welcome to me; I am heartily thankful for them.

Certainly, these are the evident Tokens of Salvation upon me.

Bless the Lord, O my Soul!

18. G. D. There are several Persons in the Flock, who have Sons at the Colledge. These Children I would look upon, as a Part of the Flock, that may be singular Objects of my Cares. I would consult with my Collegue, about the special Methods that may be taken, to form the Minds of these Children, and bring them to good Principles and Practices.

19. G. D. O! Lett my Conversation with my Consort be full of all Goodness, and more than ever exhibit in it a Conformity to the good One, and a Pattern to all Observers!

But then, O! Lett all possible Purity accompany it, and lett me watch against all such inordinate Affection, as may grieve the holy Spirit of GOD!

20. G. D. I would invite my Kinsman T. W[alter] under his Languishments, to sojourn a while in my Family, and make it an Opportunity of all the Good that may be, to himself and others.

21. G. D. I am writing to *Scotland*, and sending my *Parentator* thither, accompanied with some other Instruments, wherein I design more particular Services to the University of *Glasco*.

22. G. D. What shall I think on, to be proposed among the Ministers, at their anniversary Convention the next

Week, to serve the Kingdome of GOD, and the Cause of Piety?

Conversing with some who have Relation to the colledge at *Newhaven*, I would propose what may be for the good of that Society and of the Churches, which have their Expectations from it.

23. G. D.   A young Gentleman of *New-York*, a Person of excellent Piety, and much Expectation, comes in my Way.

* 24. G. D.   It is an unspeakable Advantage, that I find, by having my Eye on the *Hebrew Psalter*, while I am with the People of GOD praising of Him in the Congregations, I am led by the Language of the holy Spirit there, into Sentiments that are very curious and sublime, and Mysteries that perhaps were never discovered there before. These Things notably serve the Cause of Piety with me; and if I could find the time afterwards to write them down, which I hope to do, they may be of some Service to the World.

25. G. D.   Some Sermons on the Character and Confusion of the *Hypocrite*, may be of singular Service to the Flock.

26. G. D.   For my evening Sacrifices in my Family why may I not read Mr. *Henry's* Commentaries on the Psalms, which declare and assist the Frames of Piety, that every Portion is to be sung withal; and make this a Præface to my Singing of it?

This Morning I was taken very ill; feavourish with a violent and wasting *Diarrhœa*, and Cholical Pains accompanying of it.

I was hereby laid aside, from all Opportunities to do Good, in the Convention of the Ministers at the Election.

I endeavoured on this Occasion to glorify GOD, with a Submission unto His Will in every Thing (and of my Life into His Hands) and an Improvement in all the Dispositions of Piety.

After three Days, I revived.

In this Time I wrote some Things, and read more; but I particularly endeavoured, that the Condition of the Pyrates who are to be executed the next Week, may be rendred profitable to the people.

Among the Projections for this, I drew up the Conference I had with them in the Prison, instructing them how to turn unto GOD.

*31. G. D. Having many Thoughts, about the Influence, which the Faith of our SAVIOUR'S infinite and eternal GODHEAD has, upon all real and vital PIETY, I incline to a sett of successive Meditations hereupon. I would particularly every Lord's-Day Morning write a Contemplation on some Article in a Life of Piety, wherein this Faith is of the greatest Consequence for our Living unto GOD.

And in this way, I would propose, not only to animate my own Piety, but also provide Materials for a Book, which I may anon offer to the World.

One of the first Things which the Pyrates, who are now so much the *Terror of them that haunt the Sea,* impose on their poor Captives, is; *To curse Dr M———.* The Pyrates now strangely fallen into the Hands of Justice here, make me *the first Man,* whose Visits and Counsils and Prayers they beg for. Some of them under Sentence of Death, chuse to hear from me, the last Sermon they hear in the World.

(II.) The Sermon is desired for Publication. I give it unto the Bookseller. It is entituled; THE CONVERTED SINNER. *The Nature of a Conversion to Real and Vital PIETY, and the Manner in which it is to be pray'd and striv'n for. In a Sermon preached in Boston, May, 31, 1724. In the hearing and at the Desire of certain Pyrates a little before their Execution. To which is added, a more Private Conference of a Minister with them.*[1]

[1] Printed for Nathaniel Belknap, 1724. John Rose Archer and William White were executed June 2.

June. 1. G. D. Unto a Number of the Flock, who have with extraordinary Benefactions exerted themselves, to extricate me out of my Difficulties, what special Expressions may I make of my Gratitude? There is one I am thinking of, —

2. G. D. Lett *Nancy* go, and offer her best as assistences to her aged, weak, blind Grandfather; whose wife being struck with a Palsey, renders his Condition full of Uneasiness.[1]

3. G. D. I have a Kinsman, a Minister at *Warminster*, in *Wiltshire;* to whom I would send my *Parentator;* and otherwise apply to him.

4. G. D. Having received an Account of Petitions gone home to *Whitehal* against the Countrey, full of cursed Calumnies against the Churches here, from a wretched Crew at *Watertown*, and some others here, I transmitt unto our General Assembly a Copy of it. And I am Considering on further Methods to prevent evil Consequences.

5. G. D. The Colledge is in great Hazards of Dissipation and grievous Destruction and Confusion. My Advice to some that have some Influence on the Public, may be seasonable.

I sett apart this Day, for Supplications, with Fasting in Secret, on such Occasions, and with such Devotions, as I had a Month ago.

My Interviews with Heaven were not this day quite so full of Agony and Impression, as they were on that. Yett they were such that, I hope, the Intentions of the Day are somewhat answered.

6. G. D. A poor young Man in my Neighbourhood, abandoning himself to evil Courses, I do what I can to save him with Fear, plucking him as a Brand out of the Burning.

* 7. G. D. I cannot express how much I find myself affected with that Word, *O Lord, Thou art my Glory.* Besides

---

[1] Sarah Graves, who died in 1731.

the other Intentions of that Word, I find my Soul rising and soaring to this; it shall not only be my greatest *Glory* to know, and serve and enjoy a Glorious CHRIST, but also *His Glory* shall be *mine:* If I may see Him *glorified* in the World, it shall comfort me, as much as if His *Glory* were all my own. It shall be no Part of my Concern, what Esteem have I in the World; but my amiable and admirable Jesus may be esteemed, in this I will find more Satisfaction, than if I myself had all possible Honours heaped upon me.

But then, with what a Zeal shall I now carry on my Purposes, to bear yett more notable Testimonies unto the Glory and the Godhead of my SAVIOUR!

8. G. D. A Sermon to the Flock, on the Method of obtaining that Blessedness, *A CHRIST living in us*, may be a great Service to the Cause of *Piety* in them.

9. G. D. I am not without very great Hopes, that the Designs of Satan to discompose my Family and prejudice my Ministry, are gloriously and eternally defeated; the GOD of Peace brings about those Things, wherein Satan will be marvellously bruised under my Feet. Oh! what shall I render to the Lord! How holily, how prayerfully, with what a Watch against inordinate Affection, yea, and all Tendencies and Beginnings of a Decay in regular Affection, shall I walk before the Lord!

And what shall I do, that poor *Nancy* may be directed, præserved, comforted?

10. G. D. To a new Kinsman, I would convey some Assistence and Encouragements for the Service of God.

11. G. D. I am sending to *Ireland* such Things as may be for the Service of our Churches, and their Defence from the vile Misrepresentation, that some Scotch Incendiaries have made of them.

This Day, I attempted many Services, to the Countrey; preaching the Lecture in the Audience of the General Assembly; showing them the Tokens of our God's Departure from us, and the Methods of preventing it; particularly pressing (in Allusion to what *Isaac* did) that we call Things by the same Names that our Fathers before us called them.[1]

12. G. D. The Indian Commissioners need again to be called upon.

13. G. D. A Family like to be broken to Peeces, I must with Healing Advice endeavour the præservation of it.

*14. G. D. I have a strong Inclination to write, and preach on the Godhead of my SAVIOUR, and the Influence which the Faith of it should have on a christian Life in every Part thereof.

That I may be accepted in this Undertaking, I must endeavour singular Methods of Devotion, and Measures of Purity; lest I be a Cast-away.

I would also, in the evening Prayers of the Closett, cultivate that noble Subject in the most experimental and affectionate Way that may be.

One sweet Way of Conversing with my SAVIOUR, my Mind is at this time running much upon. Whatever afflictive Thing befalls me, it shall quicken me to think on what my SAVIOUR suffered of the like Affliction: and so, magnify His Love; and Hope for some Advantage by my own Calamity.

15. G. D. What further shall I do for the Flock? I will entreat my Collegue to think for me. O! the Barrenness of my poor Invention!

16. G. D. Because I would study all possible Ways of being useful to my Consort, I think on this, among other Things. The Subject of the holy Thoughts which I fall asleep withal, I would still make her apprized of it.

17. G. D. To some of my young Relatives, give the Book that is newly published.

[1] This paragraph was written in the margin.

18. G. D. The glorious LORD having strangely sent me in some Supply for the expensive part of it, I would apply myself, as fast as I can, to prepare my Essay of Directions for Candidates of the Ministry, how to order their Studies, that they may become useful Servants of GOD in the World.

19. G. D. It is proposed, that the Ministers of the City, renew their ancient *Thursday* Inter-views.

20. G. D. A poor drunken Creature, to be warned.

* 21. G. D. The glorious Lord has led me into fuller Views than I have ever yett had, and such as I have exceedingly longed for and asked for, of what shall be the true State of Things in His Kingdome. And I am now satisfied, that there is nothing to hinder the immediate Coming of our Saviour, in these Flames, that shall bring an horrible Destruction on this present and wicked World, and bring on the new Heaven, and the new Earth, wherein shall dwell Righteousness. I purpose quickly to write on these things. In the mean time, I would in all holy Conversation and Godliness, mightily endeavour to maintain such a Disposition of Mind, as the tremendous Descent of my glorious Lord, is to be entertained withal.

22. G. D. Meditating on the evil Spirit chased from *Saul*, by *David* playing on his Harp, I entertained a Thought whether a Sermon that should with an agreeable Artifice employ the Harp of *David*, in Quotations from the Book of *Psalms*, to chase away such evil Spirits, as assault and ensnare the Souls of our People, may not be to the Flock a considerable Service.

23. G. D. In conversing with my Son *Samuel*, what if one Article should be, a Paragraph of some Treatise (as for Instance, my *Coheleth*,) [1] to be translated into Latin; upon the most elegant and refined Latin for which, we would concur in our Sentiments.

[1] Printed in 1720.

24. G. D.   Some of my Sister's Children at *Roxbury*, I address with further Excitations to Piety.

25. G. D.   I am this Week, writing Letters to my dear *Franckius*, and the Professors in the *Hallensian* University. I have in View several great Services for the Kingdome of GOD.   Among other Things I send my, PARENTATOR, to them.

26. G. D.   The Church at *Portsmouth* wanting a Pastor, and being in singular Circumstances and there being a likely Person in View for them, who is in danger of being detained by the Humours of some foolish Relatives, I exert myself on this Occasion.[1]

27. G. D.   Especially, in strong Letters, to the Person, who has it a Day of Temptation with him.

* 28. G. D.   Very strange things have befallen me, to Impoverish me, and leave nothing of this World in my Possession.   I am willing to enter my Sentiments on this Occasion.

I acknowledge the Punishment of my Sins, in the impoverishing Dispensations of an holy and a righteous GOD : and I humble and abhor myself before Him.

I approve the Conduct of Heaven, in keeping such a Balance on the divine Favours to me.   I am richer in the Best of Treasures, and especially in great Opportunities to Do Good, than the most of Men ; and I shall count this Grace to be sufficient for me.

I am to entertain what befalls me, as not meerly a Chastisement for my Miscarriages, but also as an Experiment made upon me, whether I shall count myself sufficiently enriched, in having a glorious CHRIST concerned for me, and visiting of me, and having the Disposal of my whole Condition, so that His gracious Providence will suffer me

---

[1] Rev. Nathaniel Rogers died in October, 1723, and a call was given to John Hancock.   He served only a short time, and in the summer Rev. Jabez Fitch was ordained.

to want nothing that shall be good for me; and by being employ'd in Service for Him.

Finding my Mind full of the sweetest Contentation and Satisfaction in this View of Things, I arrive to a joyful Assurance, that my SAVIOUR is by my Poverty only præparing me for the unsearchable Riches, which He has in the spiritual Blessings of the heavenly Places, to bestow upon me.

I am now, *As having nothing, yett possessing all Things!*

29. G. D. The Spirit of Adoption and of the Gospel, operating after a very conspicuous, impressive, heart-Melting Manner, in the public Supplications, how can the Edification of the Flock, and the Salvation and Sanctity of the People, be consulted more effectually!

30. G. D. *Miserrima mea Conjux, post flagrantissimos mei Amores, rursus in Pristinos dilapsa Furores, ob impetum de Maligno Spiritu per Lyram Davidicam sopito ac fugato, Concionem, summas mihi meisque tentat Injurias, Creatque Molestias.*

Ah, Mi Domine Redemptor; Quid agam, nescio: Sed versus te sunt mei timidi ac tumidi oculi.

Quotidianis precibus, in quibus Filium associatum habeam, gratiam tuam Quærere, est mihi propositum.

July. 1. G. D. They are so near to me on some accounts that if I consider them as Relatives, among the Objects of my Essays to do Good, there will be no Trespass in it.

An honourable Family at *Marshfield*, having lately buried a Daughter, have also had their Son, who was a Captain in the public Service, and should have this day proceeded Master of Arts, murdered by the Indians, with some singular Circumstances of Embitterment.[1] This Day, I write a Letter of Condolence and Consolation to them.

---

[1] The family was that of Isaac and Sarah (Wensley) Winslow; the daughter's name was Anna (1709–1723), and that of the son, Josiah (1701–1724).

This Day, being our insipid, ill-contrived, anniversary Solemnity, which we call, *The Commencement*, I chose to spend it at home, in Supplications; partly on the behalf of the Colledge, that it may not be foolishly thrown away: but that GOD would bestow such a President upon it, as may prove a rich Blessing unto it, and unto all our Churches.

The other usual Matters for my Supplications, were also carried unto the Lord.

And the sad Things which my Ministry and my Family are threatened withal, were particularly considered.

In the Sacrifices which I this day offered unto the Lord I felt astonishing Impressions and Assurances of my being brought nigh to the glorious GOD, and of my Union to my SAVIOUR and His Concern for me.

But, Oh! what Advice from Heaven, is come to me this Day, about my poor Son *Increase!* Yea, how many Times have I been of late overwhelmed with Afflations, which tell me, that —

2. G. D. Expecting many Ministers, to be together this day, from several Parts of the Countrey, I would endeavour, in a Speech unto them, to sett before them such Matters for their Prayers and Cares as it may be of great Service for them to think upon.

This Day I received from *New London*, some copies of a Book, newly printed there. Being willing to be furnished with another Book, to lodge in the hands of my Neighbours and such as I have opportunity to converse withal, I putt myself to some Expense for it; And what now comes out of the Press, is entituled;

(III.) STIMULATOR. *Or The Case of a Soul walking in Darkness awfully and suitably considered. An essay to awaken People out of the Lethargy, which disposes them to continue in a Dark Uncertainty about their Future State, in the World, which is not seen, but is Eternal.*[1]

[1] Printed by Timothy Green, 1724.

What I spoke to the Convention of Ministers, at *Boston* July 2, 1724.

It was a Sentence, which I think I more than once heard fall from the Lips of our Memorable, and venerable ELIOT; *It is no little Notice, which is taken by our Holy Lord, of what passes in the Meetings of His Ministers.* The Ministers of the Countrey, doubtless have their frequent *Meetings;* and in these Interviews, their Discourses and Projections to serve the Kingdome of GOD our SAVIOUR are such as to demonstrate that they remember, He *hearkens to hear* what passes there, and that He has a *Book of Remembrance* in which He enters what passes from them who *think upon His Name.*

That what now passes may somewhat answer such an Expectation, I would humbly ask Leave, to offer unto the Brethren a Word or two, which may *stir up their pure Minds* to the *Remembrance* of some Things, that cannot be well forgotten or neglected.

It is to be supposed, and beleeved, that Ministers being *Men of GOD,* are *Men of Prayer.* And, we not only do ourselves *pray without Ceasing,* but also animate and encourage *Prayer* all we can among the People, whom we instruct how to *pray,* while in that holy Exercise, we go before them.

There are among the many Matters of *Prayer,* which call for our Consideration, very particularly two, or three, which you will allow me to mention, as Points upon which the *Watchmen* on the Walls of *Jerusalem,* should not *keep Silence* before the Lord.

First; the *State of Religion* in the whole World is very deplorable. A fearful Decay and withdraw of *real and vital Piety* is every where greatly confessed and lamented, by those Few that have any thing of it, yett remaining in them. Our *United Brethren,* in Gr. *Britain* and *Ireland* appear to have a dismal Share in this epidemical Wretchedness. It is no small Instance of it, that when there is an horrible Conspiracy in our Nation to dethrone and degrade and ungod the infinite SON of GOD, a very great Part of our Brethren by refusing to *subscribe* those Explanations of the sacred Scripture, which are necessary to distinguish the *Precious from the Vile,* have acted as if they were willing to embrace as their Brethren in CHRIST, the *Vile Conspirators:* they have too much paved the Way for the Countenancing and Introducing of those *Damnable Heresies,* which are inconsistent with the Life of God, and their Alienations from one another on this Occasion, have a tremendous Aspect on them. Certainly, we should *pray* much, that God would avert the Omens; and that we may not be our selves overwhelmed in the *Sleep* of the

Midnight in which the World will be surprized by the Coming of the Lord.

Again, the State of our *Colledge* is not altogether unknown unto us. Our *Colledge* is as great an Interest of this Countrey, as any one that can be spoken of. *Religion* is like to be præserved or betrayed in our Churches, as the Colledge is provided for. A well-furnished, a well-principled Governour of that Society will be of mighty Consequence unto us all. Such a Gift of our SAVIOUR to us, would be more valuable than the golden Wedge of *Opher*. We should count it worth our while to *pray* much for such an inestimable Blessing. And the more so, because there may probably be less Prospect of obtaining it, than is by some imagined.

Finally, Since our Churches are under *shaking Dispensations*, and may look for more; Our *Prayers* for the Establishment of them in the Things that cannot be shaken, are the more necessary. But what *Labours* may do well to accompany our *Prayers!* Private Labours and *public* Labours; And especially in the Dispersing of profitable and seasonable *Books*, into the Hands of our People.

And since the *Ministers* throughout the Land, thro the Folly and Baseness by which our *Bills of Credit* are depreciated in their Circulation, have their *Subsistence* extremely threatened; extreme Wants and Straits are likely to distress us, above any Sort of Persons whatsoever; lett us make this Holy Use of it. That we shall by a more exemplary Diligence and Vigilance in the Discharge of our Ministry, recommend our selves unto the Providence and Protection of our faithful SAVIOUR, who can and will so look after us, that the Quæstion, *lacked ye anything?* shall anon have a strange Answer given to it.

3. G. D. The Thursday Interviews of the Ministers being thus renewed, I would make it my perpetual Study, forever to bring forth something at them, which my Brethren may be the better for.

4. G. D. A young Gentlewoman in dying Circumstances.

*5. G. D. I am astonished at the Visits which the Holy SPIRIT of Grace makes unto the Chief of Sinners. He visits me, instructs me, comforts me, and raises me to such Interviews with Heaven as assure me of my being one that my SAVIOUR intends Mercy for. Oh! may I not

rieve the holy SPIRIT of God, but cherish His Motions,
nd Illapses, and follow His Manuduction.

My domestic Trials, lying so long and so hard upon me,
egin at length to gain so far towards the breaking and
ainting of my Spirit, which has hitherto been so far sup-
orted and wondrously carried through, and I feel the Iron
o entring into my Soul, that I am in great and sad Appre-
ensions, what may be the Issue. I cry to my SAVIOUR,
s *Peter* just ready to sink in the Waves, — *Lord, I am
oppressed, undertake for me!*

6. G. D. A Part of the Flock, have newly signalized
their Kindness to me, and shown me the Kindness of GOD,
n privately collecting and advancing a Summ of considerably more than two hundred Pounds, to pay a Debt of my
wife's former Husband, which I inconsiderately had made
my own, and was now in the Course of Law ready to have
Execution served upon me for. I cannot perceive a Sense of
Gratitude unto me, in those for whom I have been so much
a Sufferer. But my Soul is filled, and even fainting with a
Sense of Gratitude unto the kind People, who thus lay me
under very uncommon Obligations. I must think of some
singular, transcendent, uncommon way to express my
Gratitude unto them. *Teach me, O thou good Spirit of God,
And lead me into the Way of Gratitude, and Land of Rectitude.*

7. G. D. My Daughter *Liza*, is now on the Point of
being disposed of. What Supplication and what Resignation, am I on this Occasion call'd unto! That she may not
be thrown away, and given to such a sorry Wretch, as one
of her Deceased Sisters was! What Advice must I give to
the dear Child, that she may not be unhappy!

8. G. D. Prevail with a Kinsman at *Windsor*, an
excellent Physician; to commit unto writing, the more
notable Things that have occurr'd unto him, in his Practice. His more singular Observations on Diseases and
Remedies; his botanic Discoveries, and whatever else may

be entertaining and serviceable to the World; and communicate them to me, that I may make them so.

9. G. D. There are collected some notable Instances of Piety, among our evangelized Indians. The Publication thereof may serve many good Purposes. I would therefore animate it, and employ my Cares about it, and prevail with several Ministers to join with me in Supervising of it.

10. G. D. Among the Commissioners for the Indian Affairs, there are many things of Consequence to be prosecuted. I would earnestly solicit for Meetings to be called, that these Things may be considered in them.

11. G. D. A poor, godly, gracious Woman, in our Church is in miserable Circumstances, by reason of an unreasonable and a very abusive Husband. Something must be done to direct and comfort her.

* 12. G. D. My God has convinced me, that the second coming of my SAVIOUR, is to be at and for the Perdition of the Man of Sin; and that the tremendous Conflagration which is to precede the new Heavens and the new Earth, is then to carry all before it; and that there is nothing that we know of, remaining to be done, before this astonishing Revolution; so that it may with Reason be daily looked for.

I purpose ere long, with the Leave and Help of Heaven, to write my Sentiments of this important Matter. In the mean time, Oh! what Manner of Person ought I to be in all holy Conversation and Godliness. I desire to live continually under the Power of the Apprehension which I have entertained, and have it govern my whole Conversation.

13. G. D. As far as I may with Edification do it, I would insinuate the like Apprehension unto the Flock, and labour that it may make an holy Impression upon them, to wean them from the inordinate Pursuit of this World, and cause them to be in the Fear of the Lord all the Day long.

14. G. D. I think, I may now permitt *Samachi*, to begin some Essays at preaching the Gospel, in some lesser Assemblies. Begin at the Castle.

But before his first Performance, I would have him, to sett apart some time, extraordinary, with great Solemnity, to dedicate himself unto the Service of the glorious Lord, and Implore the continual Operations and Assistences of the holy Spirit with him.

15. G. D. Resolving to treat *Isaac Greenwood*, as a sort of a Son, I am writing such things unto him, as may be of the last Importance for him.

16. G. D. In Consideration of the distressing Troubles upon the Countrey from a War with the Indians, and the Danger of our Liberties; and a Drought at this time upon us; and that more Influences of the divine Grace may be obtained for us, I move among the Ministers, that more Days of Prayer may be observed; and particularly that on the next Thursday, the Lecture may be turned into a Day of Prayer.

17. G. D. I would move Mr. *Monnis*, the converted Jew, to collect his Remarks in his Reading of the Old Testament; which may mend our Translations, or may lead us to a Sense of the deep Things intended by the holy Spirit of GOD, in His Oracles, which are not commonly observed. A Jew rarely comes over to us, but he brings Treasures with him.[1]

18. G. D. I am writing to a young Gentleman, at this Time in *London*, what may have a Tendency to his future Usefulness in the World!

[1] First on the list of instructors in Harvard College stands the name of Judah Monis, appointed in 1722 to teach Hebrew. He held the position until his death in 1760, when he was succeeded by Stephen Sewall. A MS. Hebrew grammar, prepared by him in 1725 for Jonathan Belcher, is in the collections of this Society. Although he is always spoken of as a "converted Jew," he was not the object of the years of prayers on the part of the Mathers. That Jew is said to have gone to Jamaica and died there "a hardened wretch." *Proceedings*, XLIV. 686.

* 19. G. D.   There is not any one Point, that I have
more cause to be concerned about, or to complain that I
am Defective in, than a wise Redeeming of the Time.   Now,
the glorious GOD will give Wisdome to them that ask Him
for it; And the Redemption of Time was a considerable
Article in the Life of my SAVIOUR, who will imprint His
Image upon me, if I look up unto Him for it.   I will then,
with exceeding Importunity, more than ever seek to the
GOD of all Grace for this Favour; yea, make it a daily
Petition to Him, *Lord, make me a wise Redeemer of the little
Time that remains unto me!*   And I would resign myself
up unto the SPIRIT of my SAVIOUR that He may make
holy Impressions for this Purpose upon me.

20. G. D.   A Discourse on the *two Adams;* how all
the affaires of Religion turn upon them; it may be among
the Things whereby the Flock may be more than a little
edified.

21. G. D.   *Ob revertentes indies, et ingruentes* κονινγις
*vexationes, vereor ne tandem in vexationum Fluctibus pro-
cellosis misere submergar.*

*Extensis tuis manibus, ad Servum tuum alias obruendum,
Redemptor mi, me subleves, oro, ac sustineas.*

*Hi sunt mei ad CHRISTUM Quotidiani, Importunique
Clamores.*

*Necessum habeo dilectissimam meam, et iniquissime
tractatam Filiam et Familia amovere, Et in alijs, indices
mihi, O clementissime JESU, in quibus, ædibus Elevare.*

*Necessum habeo, nequissimam adhuc apud me Commoran-
tem Iuvenculam,* υξορις *perfidam et ingratam Neptim, a meis
ædibus abigere; Quo vero pacto hoc fiet, O clementissime JESU,
dirigas.*

22. G. D.   My old Father-in-Law at *Charlestown,* very
near entring his ninety-third year, and very feeble and sore
broken, what, what shall I do for him? [1]

---

[1] He died March 20, 1725–26, aged ninety-four.

23. G. D. This day, the principal Inhabitants of the City, keep a Day of Supplications, on account of the War and of the Drought. In my Sermon and my Prayer, I have Opportunity, to bear those Testimonies, and pay those Acknowledgments, to the glorious Lord, which may be of some use unto His People.

24. G. D. Rarely does a Jew of any Erudition come over to Christianity, but he brings with him some Treasures of Illustration upon the sacred Scriptures. We have a Christianized Jew at *Cambridge*, who is a great Master of the Hebrew Language. I will putt him upon collecting and præserving the notable Observations, which he makes in reading the Hebrew Bible.

25. G. D. One for whom I have great Reason to be concerned, is made a Widow.

* 26. G. D. I seek and serve a GOD, who waits that *He may be Gracious*. I will sett myself to think, what may be the Errand of the many and heavy Trials, wherewith it pleases Him to exercise me; and the Compliance with it in me He is waiting for, that He may be Gracious to me, and release me from the Exercises. But, yett, at the same time I would be so satisfied in the Improvements of PIETY wherewith He favours me under this Discipline, that I would be entirely reconciled unto the Continuance of them; and be unspeakably more concerned for a right Behaviour under them, than for a full Deliverance from them.

27. G. D. Several of the Flock are under Bereavements; especially one whom I have singular concern for; and more are like to be so. It may be serviceable to the whole Flock, and particularly seasonable to these, if I give them a Sermon, on *GOD supplying all our Wants from Riches in Glory by* CHRIST JESUS.

28. G. D. *Miserrima mea* Κονυυξ *mirum in Modum ab Adversario obsessa ac repleta, in solitos paroxysmos ac Furores tam frequenter ac tam insolita Violentia jam incedit,*

atque in tantam excurrit Rabiem, quod Ministerio meo Fami læque Ruina inde impendere videatur. Imo ad crisim res lam est redacta; Et si Deus Redemptor non Extensa Mann me Ex Aquis eripiat, pereo, obruor, Actum est. In his Do loribus et Angoribus positus quo me Vertam, nisi ad Te, C Deus Misericors, O Christe meum Refugium, ac perpetuun Solatium.

Wherefore I sett apart this Day, for Prayer with Fasting before the Lord.

I humbled myself before Him for the Miscarriages which have provoked Him exceedingly to humble me; and I implored and obtained a Pardon.

I earnestly besought him to assist me unto a right and wise Behaviour, that I may be a grateful Spectacle to Heaven, under my Exercises; and I consented unto the Continuance of them, with a Soul reconciled unto the Holy Discipline. It was with me a Day of Sacrifices; and a glorious CHRIST left unto me, was my sufficient Portion.

But I entreated for such an Interposition of His Providence, as He may see seasonable, and necessary, for the præservation of my Ministry.

I have some Works upon the Anvil (especially one of Directions for Scholars intending the evangelical Ministry,) for which I asked the Influences of Heaven.

My younger Daughter is this week upon a Marriage; and I now ask'd for a Blessing upon her. The Condition of my elder Daughter, was also a Matter of my Supplications.

My Son *Increase!* my Son, my Son!

But my Son *Samuel* intending speedily to begin his public Performances, I now pray'd with him in the Library; and confirmed his Consecration to the Service of the Glorious Lord, and wept unto the Lord for such Favours to him as are to be wished for; entreating that God may be with him.

29. G. D. In the Day of my Catechising I will consider my Catechumens as my Children.

This Day, I propose to insist on several of the more important Quæstions, in the Way of a Catechism for Concience among them.

And to preach them a Sermon on, *See, thy Son liveth.*

30. G. D. Cases wherein the Welfare of Churches is oncerned, are laid before me.

This Evening I married *Liza*, to Mr. *Edward Cooper.*[1]

31. G. D. I hope, we have provided a Chaplain for an xposed Garrison; whom therefore I would instruct, and dvise, and animate.

Inexplicabilis, inexplicabiliter mutabilis, mea conjux deositis Furoribus, ad Mentem novam ac Sanam Est reversa, neque summis cum Amoris Ardoribus amplexata.

Being by the unhappy Entanglements of my Wife's nd her Daughter's Estate, brought into a Necessity of aying a Debt of more than two hundred Pounds, for an state which I was never one penny the better for, and eing so exhausted, that I have nothing to pay it, except he Creditor please to take my Library, which tho' so ery dear to me above all temporal Possessions, I offer to Deprædation:

A little Number of my Flock, generously joined for my Deliverance; and privately and presently advanced the um that was necessary for my Deliverance out of my Entanglements.

(IV.) I was thinking, how to Express my Gratitude unto a People, who have so obliged me, and expressed such tender Care of me. Among other Projections for this urpose, I take a Discourse on the *Unsearchable Riches of CHRIST*, and with an agreeable Dedication of it unto the Flock, declaring what I should be to them, and what they have been to me, I am at the Expense to publish it; proosing to present it particularly to my benefactors, with heir Names written by my Pen, in the Front of the Dedica-

[1] She died August 7, 1726.

tion. I would hope also, that my Confessions of my Duty
may be some Directions and Incentives unto other Pastor
for their Duty, when it arrives, as I intend it shall, to man
of them. It is entituled, THE TRUE RICHES. *A Tender o
Glorious and Immense Riches, to all that are willing to accep
thereof. In an Essay on, The unsearchable Riches of CHRIST.*

August. 1. G. D. The pious young Minister of *Mal
den,* last night had his House, and all the Estate that wa
in it, laid in Ashes.[2] What shall be done for his Comfort

* 2. G. D. That I may be more fruitful in my well
advised Inventions to do good, and that I may be under :
more effectual and sensible Conduct of Heaven in them, :
would when I come to consider the Quæstion, *What Good i
to be done!* feel and own myself to be Nothing, and unabl
and unworthy to do any thing, and so resign my Mind up
unto the Influences of my SAVIOUR, with such an Ac
knowledgment and Supplication as this; *O my SAVIOUR
lead a poor, dark, dead Creature, to such Thoughts and Works
as may be pleasing to thee!* That it may be no longer I
who project Essays to do good, but a *CHRIST living in me*

3. G. D. My Manner of treating the Flock, in my
Sermons is, with abundance of Artifice, to spread the Netts
of Salvation for them, and so propose the Truths of the
Gospel, that if at the Moment of the Delivery, they receive
them with Acts of Compliance, and come unto the Language which I gett ready for them, they are unawares taken
in the Netts, and they shall be found among the saved of
the Lord.

Accordingly, Communion with our SAVIOUR being the
Top of our Blessedness, that so the Flock may be drawn
into it, and be blessed of the Lord, I preach a Sermon
upon it, so contrived, as even to surprise them into the
Enjoyment of it.

---

[1] Printed by B. Green for Nathaniel Belknap, 1724.
[2] Rev. Joseph Emerson. See Corey, *History of Malden,* 481–484.

4. G. D. My Daughter *Liza*, being married, I would ith all possible Solemnity, bestow the best Instructions pon her, for the ascertaining of her Espousal to her SAV-)UR, and her good Conduct in her Family.

But, Oh! what shall I do for her elder Sister?

5. G. D. And what shall I do, that my new Son-in- ,aw may prove a wise and a good Man, and a Blessing to ll concerned in him?

6. G. D. A woful Indifferency and Formality in the rand Business of Religion, being become the epidemical Ialady of the Time, and a Token to be trembled at, I hought it not amiss to entertain the Public at the Lecture ʻith a Discourse on, RELIGION IN EARNEST.

7. G. D. What shall be done for the poor People at *hattam*, whose Minister deals foolishly with them?

The Church at *Stratford* sends for Advice in a Case, on ʻhich I advise them as well as I can.[1]

8. G. D. A poor indigent, unhappy old Man to be ɔokʻd after.

One whom I have cause to love and prize, made a Widow.

* 9. G. D. O my SAVIOUR, help me to make an Holy Jse of what I see in a Minister, become an unaccountable ;lave to the Drink which intoxicates him; and impeni- ent and incorrigible after many Admonitions, whereof I nyself have dispensed some, unto him, to bring him unto Repentance.

I would exceedingly adore the Free-Grace of Heaven, into the Influences whereof alone, it is to be ascribed, that am not given up to the Bondage of that, or some other Lust, which might have bewitched me, and befooled me, ind confounded the whole Work of God, wherein I am :oncerned.

I would exceedingly implore the Aids of Grace, that I nay, with the Pardon of my Offences, be in so much Favour

[1] Hezekiah Gold was settled here from 1720-1752.

with my Redeemer, that He would lett no Iniquity of an
sort have Dominion over me.

My SAVIOUR, wo to me, if thou depart from me
Wherefore, O Forsake me not!

10. G. D. That I may not neglect my own Vineyar
in the awakening Sentiments which I propose to offer unt
the World, concerning the second Coming of the Lord, an
the tremendous Conflagration that must accompany it,
have thoughts of Preaching to my own Flock a Sermo
upon that awful Subject; and make Demands of that hol
Conversation and Godliness which is called for.

11. G. D. *Samachi*, did on the Lord's-day, two Day
ago, begin the public Services of the evangelical Ministr
(at the Castle) tho' he be not yett quite eighteen Years o
age. I am distressed for him, that he may be very humble
and modest and self-diffident; and that he may not mak
more Haste than good Speed in his public Appearances an
Performances, and that he may with a mighty Industry la
in a good Stock of Treasures wherewith he may come t
the Service of the Sanctuary. My continual Admonition
and Remonstrances to him, shall not be wanting.

12. G. D. My languishing Kinsman of *Roxbury*, is a
this time in my Family; may I be directed from above t
treat him in a Manner suitable to his feeble and threatning
Circumstances.

I am now informed, that yesterday the six Men, who cal
themselves the Corporation of the College mett, and Contrary to the epedemical Expectation of the Countrey, chose
a modest young Man, of whose Piety (and little else) every
one gives a laudable Character.[1]

I always foretold these two Things of the Corporation
First, that if it were possible for them to steer clear of me,

[1] The choice fell upon Rev. Joseph Sewall, who declined the office. See
Quincy, *History of Harvard University*, I. 329. The six members of the Corpora-
tion were, Henry Flynt, Benjamin Wadsworth, Benjamin Colman, Nathanie
Appleton, Edward Wigglesworth, and Edward Hutchinson.

ey will do so. Secondly, that if it be possible for them) act foolishly, they will do so. The perpetual Envy, ith which my Essays to serve the Kingdome of God are eated among them, and the Terror that Satan has of my eating up his Quarters at the Colledge, led me into the rmer Sentiment. The marvellous Indiscretion, with which ie affairs of the Colledge are carried on, led me into the tter.

It proves accordingly. Now, tho' the senseless Manage- ient of these Men threatens little short of a Dissipation to ie Colledge, yett I have personally unspeakable cause to dmire the Compassion of Heaven to me on this Occasion. ho' I have been a Man of Sorrows and acquainted with riefs, yett none of the least Exercises that I have mett ithal, was the Dread of what the Generality of sober eople expected and desired; the Care of the Colledge,) be committed unto me. I had a dismal Apprehension f the Distresses, which a call to *Cambridge* would bring pon me, and I was afraid of all my Sorrows. But, the leight and the Spite of my six Friends, has produced for ie an eternal Deliverance. I doubt, I have expressed iyself, with a little too much Alacrity, on this Occasion!

Lord, Help me to a wise Behaviour!

13. G. D. Hasten, hasten, O slothful *Mather;* in dis- atching thy Treatise of Advice to the Candidates of the Ministry, thou mayst thereby do more Good, than twenty Presidents of Colledges!

This Night my unaccountable Consort, had a prodig- ous Return of her Pangs upon her; that seemed little short f a proper Satanical Possession. After a thousand un- epeatable Invectives, compelling me to rise at Midnight, nd retire to my Study that I might there pour out my soul unto the Lord; she also gott up in an horrid Rage, protesting that she would never live or stay with me; and alling up her wicked Niece and Maid, she went over to a Neighbour's House for a Lodging; Doubtless with num-

berless Lies, which a Tongue sett on Fire of Hell, woul
make no Conscience of.   In the mean time, I with my So
Samuel and my Daughter *Hannah*, retired up to my Librar
where we together kept a Vigil, and sang Passages in th
LVI. Psalm, and poured out our Supplications.

Towards the Morning, I went unto my Bed, and enjoy'
some Repose.

I verily beleeve, there is not in all these Regions a
Husband, who treats a Wife, with more continual and ex
quisite Endeavours, to please her and serve her, and mak
her comfortable at home, and reputable abroad.   And i
is astonishing, how she can invent Occasions for the Out
rages that she will fall into, after the lucid Intervals whicl
are filled with Expressions of the most enamoured Fondnes
for me.   What was pretended as the Introduction to th
present, was, that forsooth, for a Day or two, my Look
and Words were not so very kind as they had been.   A mer
Fancy and Whimsey!   But the bare telling her so, threv
her into these Violences, wherein she charged me witl
Crimes, which obliged me to rebuke her lying Tongue
with Terms I have not been used unto.

14. G. D.   Something should be done, by the Minister
of this Place, to rebuke the wicked Spirit of the Ministe
at *Harwyche*, who incessantly labours to disturb the Peac
of the churches.[1]

15. G. D.   A young Student in my Neighbourhood, ir
peculiar Circumstances.   J. M.

* 16. G. D.   The eternal Release, which I have latel
received from all Expectation of Employment in the Servic
of the Colledge, is a Dispensation of so much Mixture, tha
I am sollicitious for a right Understanding of it, and a righ
Behaviour under it: Sollicitous to find out, what senti
ments and what Actions my GOD and SAVIOUR now
calls me to.

[1] Rev. Nathaniel Stone.

First: Had the Care of the Colledge been devolved upon me,
esides my finding it a Station infinitely troublesome, the Labours
ad Fatigues of it, would have undoubtedly hurried on my Dissolu-
on. I could never have lived a Year to an End!

And yett, perhaps I am to dy immediately at home, and GOD
ay have mercifully diverted the Colledge from a Choice which would
ave immediately terminated in fresh Troubles to them.

Again: Had the Care of the Colledge been committed unto me,
had enjoy'd precious Opportunities to have done good unto all
ae Churches in the Countrey, and this, in a Way of living unspeak-
oly Agreeable to me. The strange Abridgments and Obstructions,
hich I have seen on my Opportunities to do good, when my Zeal
·r it, and my Thirst after exquisite Projections to accomplish it, are
· insatiable, has a dark Aspect upon me.

And yett, Light may arise in this Darkness. Who can tell what
·pportunities to do good may be yett reserved for me? Besides, the
·race which I have already received in that kind, especially con-
·dering my prodigious Unworthiness may well be sufficient for me.

Finally: The præferring of a Child before me,[1] as my Superiour
· Erudition, or in a Capacity and Vivacity to manage the Govern-
1ent of an Academy, or in Piety and Gravity, this is what, for several
.easons, it would be a Crime in me to be disturbed at. I hope, that
1y SAVIOUR who has taught me, will help me, to take all possible
atisfaction in it.

17. G. D. My Flock does generally consist of People
hat are in a *middle Condition* of Life; not very *rich*, not
·ery *poor:* such as live Tolerably, yea comfortably, and
·re able to do good unto others. I preach them a Sermon
n *Agur's* Prayer;[2] to render them content with their
:ondition yea, thankful for it.

18. G. D. The dreadful Condition of my Family, Tis
·xpress'd in some other Papers.

O the humbling Dispensations of my GOD unto me!
·he, whom I have perpetually studied in the most exquisite
Vays, to serve, and please, and gratify, and have even
·ndone myself to oblige her, not only does by her unac-

---

[1] Sewall was in his thirty-sixth year.
[2] Proverbs, xxx.

countable Humours, ever now and then breaking forth i
prodigious Paroxysms, wherein she expresses the greates
Hatred and Contempt for me, prove the most heavy Scourg
to me, that ever I mett withal, but also takes, variou
Methods, all she can to ruine my Esteem in the World, an
the Success of my Ministry, and strike out the Apple of m
Eye, my Opportunities to do good in the World. GOI
knows, that she has no manner of Reason to treat me i
the Manner that she does.

I still keep in my Eye, the Conduct of my SAVIOUI
towards His Church.

But, I have nothing left in View, but a total Extinctio
of my Opportunities to do good.

However, I will still *give myself unto Prayer.*

I have hitherto had (besides the numberless Ejacula
tions of an *Eye ever towards the Lord,*) but SIX more set
Prayers in a Day, and more solemn Visits unto Heaven
I will now carry 'em on to Number, SEVEN: And there
fore, it shall be my Custome, immediately upon my rising
from the Table to retire, and pour out my Supplication
unto GOD. And the principal Subject and Intent of then
shall be, To bewayl all my sinful Impurities, and obtai
the Rescue of my Opportunities to do good, from the Mis
chiefs which do threaten them, and comfortable Circum
stances relating to the Death, which is approaching to me
and, it may be, some other Matters hereafter to be though
upon.

My dying Father's Desire, *to Do Good while I Live, an*
glorify CHRIST in my Death.[1]

Moreover, my Consort's leaving of my Bed, when I an
a Person of whom there cannot be the least Pretence o
my being a Person universally acceptable, affords me Occa
sions of particular Supplications, that the Holiness anc
Purity whereto I am so singularly called of GOD, may have

[1] Written in the margin.

its perfect Work, and that I may no longer so foolishly dote as I have done, upon a Person who treats me with such a matchless Ingratitude, and Malignity.

I have allow'd *Sammy's* beginning his Performances in the Work of the evangelical Ministry. But I will not countenance, his proceeding too soon or too far, in public Appearances.

19. G. D. My dear, dear Friend, and Sister, Mrs. R. B. having marvellous Afflictions come upon her in the Condition of her only and foolish Son, I must sett myself exceedingly to support and comfort her, and because at this time she is out of Town, write unto her.

20. G. D. While I am this Morning, about projecting of Services for the Kingdome of God and what I may do to build up His House, I have sad Advice of His going on to pull down mine, with dreadful Dispensations. Nevertheless I will not at all abate, but greatly improve, in my Activities to do all the good that He will allow me to do, and particularly study, what special Thing I may do for His People, under the fresh Awakenings and Contusions which His Providence gives unto me.

For, I am now advised, that my Son *Increase*, is lost, is dead, is gone. The Ship wherein he was bound from *Barbados* to St. Peters had been out five Months, and was not arrived; and some singular Circumstances of the Vessel also concur to confirm the Apprehension that it is perished in the Sea. Ah! My Son *Increase!* My Son! My Son!

My Head is Waters, and my Eyes are a Fountain of Tears! I am overwhelmed! And this at a Time when the domestic Inhumanities, and Diabolisms which I am treated withal, are so insupportable! O my God, I am oppressed; undertake for me.

But, the Soul of the Child! If the Papers which he left in my Hands, were sincere and His Heart wrote with his pen, all is well! Would not my GOD have me to hope so?

II · 48

My SAVIOUR yett affords me this Light in my Darkness, that He enables me, to offer up all the Sacrifices He calls me to!

And as for the continual Dropping which I suffer in my Family, I freely submitt and consent unto it, that the Glorious Lord should continue the Sorrows of it upon me all the few remaining Days of my Pilgrimage, and never give me any release until I dy; only lett me obtain this one Thing of Him; a Soul full of a CHRIST! A mind, not only assured of His being my SAVIOUR, but also sensible of His gracious and quickening Influences, and continually irradiated with the precious Thoughts of Him.

21. G. D. Yett once more, Lett the Proposal for the Trial of Candidates for the Ministry, be revived among the Ministers.

22. G. D. A young Student, whose conduct has been irregular, but who now pretends to desire and purpose better.

* 23. G. D. My Opportunities to do good (the Apple of my Eye,) I find again violently struck at, and all possible Pains are taken, by such as have the least Cause of any under Heaven to do so, to fix a vile Character on me among the People of God, and invite them to look upon me as a Person from whose Hands the Bread of Life is by no means to be received. This is at a Time, when I have a Variety of heavy Calamities upon me; and especially, that heavy, heavy, heavy and amazing Heap of Distresses, which I have in the Death of my Son *Increase*, my Son, my Son! under which, they that should comfort me, add unto my Troubles.

In the Midst of these my Troubles, when I am almost overwhelmed, yett I declare unto my glorious GOD and SAVIOUR that I freely submitt and consent unto it, that my Sorrows may continue, yea, multiply upon me, unto the last Moment of my Pilgrimage, which cannot but now be just upon me. Yea, that my Opportunities to Do Good, the very last and cheef of my Sacrifices, be extinguished; if I may but be assisted from Above unto such a Conduct, that I may prove a grateful Spectacle unto Heaven under my Trials; and if

I may have a Soul full of a Christ, fill'd with the precious and Impressive Thoughts of Him, and feel His gracious Influences and be assured of my having Him concerned for me.

But in the multitude of my Thoughts within me, when I was giving up all my Opportunities to do Good, as lost and gone, and utterly destroy'd by such as ought to have been the greatest Comforts unto me, I have that Word strangely born in upon me. *I am thy Shield, and thy exceeding great Reward.* My GOD has brought me to this; that a glorious CHRIST is my *exceeding great Reward.* I have taken up with it, as the very Top of my Ambition, and the very Sum of my Blessedness, to enjoy HIM for mine. If I may but have HIM, I judge that I have an *exceeding great reward,* and a sufficient, an abundant Compensation for all the sad Things that I meet withal; Yea, what will make Amends for it, tho' I am stript not only of all my other Enjoyments, but even of my Opportunities to do good, which are the dearest Things in the World unto me. Upon this, I received a joyful Assurance from the Lord, that He would be a *Shield* unto me, and that they who go to hurt me should not be able to do it; but then, my Soul was grieved for the Hurt, which they will do, yea, have done, unto themselves and for the terrible Things which are to come upon them.

In the Evening of this Day, my poor Wife, returning to a right Mind, came to me in my Study, entreating that there might be an eternal Oblivion of every thing that has been out of Joint, and an eternal Harmony in our future Conversation; and that for the expressing and further obtaining of this Fœlicity, I would now join with her, in pouring out Supplications to the Lord: and resolve to pray oftener with her, than ever heretofore. I did accordingly. And the Tokens of the greatest Inamoration on her part ensued upon it.

24. G. D. The Death of my son *Increase.* Ah, my Son! my Son! Is there no Fruit that I should bring forth upon it, for the Awakening of our young People, betimes to turn and live unto God?

The little Damsels of the Flock, have so deserted the Catechising, that I have now for many months intermitted the Exercise. Yett I will make one Experiment more;

and accordingly this Week I have directed their Attendence
on me, declaring my purpose to take my Measures according to what Appearance they now make at the Time and
Place appointed.

25. G. D.　In my Family, Things are again strangely
returned unto the former Tranquillity.

But, that they may continue so, my Purpose is, (tho'
I now make seven sett Prayers in the Day) to pray oftner
with my Consort, than formerly.

26. G. D.　Tis the Day when I expect the little Damsels
to attend upon my Catechising.　I propose to treat them,
with some very moving Thoughts on, Psal. CXIX. 147.
(*There appeared near 100.*)

27. G. D.　The Death of my Son *Increase*, among the
peaceable Fruits of Righteousness, which, — Oh, that it
may yield unto me, — I have many Thoughts whether I
should not be putt upon making one Essay more for the
Awakening and Animating of *early Piety*.　Consulting of
Heaven, whether I should *proceed* or *desist*, the Direction
is, *proceed*.

28. G. D.　Some Churches need Advice in Difficulties,
among them.

This Day, I sett apart for Supplications before the Lord; humbling myself unto the uttermost, in the Sense of the sad Things,
wherein my GOD has humbled me: and especially, the Sense of the
Sins and Crimes wherewith I have provoked Him to dispense terrible
Things unto me.

The Exercises as well as the Occasions of this Day, were many
of them such as I have had heretofore;

But then I had this Day before me, the new Grief, which the
Death of my poor Son INCREASE has brought upon me.

I exceedingly loathed and judged myself before the Lord, for the
Sins of that Child, as being on some accounts my own; and for all
my other Sins, which have procured such astonishing Rebukes of
Heaven upon me, as in the Case of that unhappy Child, I have mett
withal.　And from the Depths I cried unto the Lord, with whom there
is Forgiveness, that He may be feared.

I begg'd it, of the Glorious Lord, that I might have the Grace to carry it well under this, and all my Trials; and that I might be fruitful in the Land of my Affliction.

I sett myself more particularly to beg, that the Death of my Son, may produce very special and very notable Fruits of Righteousness: and that the Sermon which I may preach (and perhaps print) on that Occasion, may be blessed for the good of many. Yea, I humbly declared unto the Lord, that if the Death of my Son, might bring in any Children to GOD, it would be a marvellous Compensation for my Sorrows on this Occasion, and mightily quicken me and comfort me, in the Resignation, wherewith I sacrificed my Son unto Him. This Disposition I could not but look upon, as a Token for good upon me; and it revived me, when walking in the Midst of Trouble.

Yea, the Good which I find that I gett, and am awakened into Endeavours to gett, by the sad Things that befall me, I consider, as a Token, that tho' my Sins have brought such sad Things upon me, yett my Sins are pardoned.

29. G. D. A miserable Man of the Church fallen into Scandal.

* 30. G. D. It being my Course, to call upon my Glorious God and Father seven Times a Day with more solemn Addresses, besides what I do in Prayers of the ejaculatory Sort without Number, I am willing here to give some Account concerning the Matter and Purpose of them.

I. At my first Arrival to my Study, I make the Prayer which presents my daily Petitions to the Lord, for myself and others.

I begin it, with an Improvement of those Meditations on a glorious CHRIST, which it is my constant Care to have my Soul in the Night-Watches fed withal.

II. At a fitt Hour, I have my Family-Sacrifices; in which I particularly consider what the Portion of the Sacred Scriptures then read, leads me to take Notice of.

III. At or near the Hour of Twelve, I do again in secret, prostrate myself before the Lord; and particularly spread before the Lord, the Condition of my Family, and the several Branches of it; and with a good Issue to whatever Difficulties may be lying upon me.

I also carry my Countrey unto the Lord, and in a more particular Manner pray for what Mercies the Condition of it may call for.

I likewise beg, that I may have right Sentiments concerning the Kingdome of God, that is to be look'd for, the Characters and Approaches of it.

IV. Rising from the Table, which is usually between two and three o'clock, I renew my Supplications; wherein I more particularly employ the Portion of the sacred Scriptures, which [I] had singled out, as the Subject for part of my Table-Talk; And then, I cry unto GOD for the Success of my Ministry; and for the Rescue and Increase of my Opportunities to do good, which thro' the Devices of Satan are continually struck at. But above all, that I may be prepared for my dying Hour, and that an *easy Death* as well as a happy Death, may be allowed unto me. *O My SAVIOUR, For an easy Death! For an easy Death! For an easy Death! I earnestly look up unto thee!*

V. About the shutting in of the Evening I make a new Visit unto Heaven, wherein I acknowledge and celebrate some Glories of my SAVIOUR, whereof I have had a previous Contemplation; or some Operations of the holy SPIRIT, wherein the Life of PIETY with me, may be concerned.

I also look up to my GOD, and SAVIOUR, that I may have His good ANGEL employ'd in the doing of good Offices for me.

VI. Towards the Time of going to Rest, I sing something of a *Psalm* with my Domesticks, after I have entertained them with some Thoughts upon it. And then make a Prayer, on such Points, as I apprehend proper for the *Evening-Sacrifices*.

VII. Before my going to Rest, I retire, and give Thanks to the glorious God, for such Favours as are never to be forgotten with me; and particularly for such as in the Day now past, may fall under my more particular Observation. And if any had shown me any special Kindnesses in the Day, I do more especially ask for the divine Recompences to them. I then bewayl the more observable Miscarriages of the Day, and ask for the Pardon of them, and of all my Miscarriages. Finally I committ myself, and my all, into the Hands of Him, whereof I may say, I know, whom I have beleeved.

31. G. D. What can I do better for my Flock, than entertain them, with such a Sermon of *Early Piety*, as the Death of my Son leads me to!

September. 1. G. D. That *Samachi* may make some further Improvements and be encouraged in his Industry,

I give my Countenance and Assistance, unto a Journey, which he desires to take unto *New London,* and so unto *New-Haven,* that he may be present at the Commencement there.

2. G. D. What shall I do, for my new Son-in-law? Endeavour to establish him in the Exercises of Religion, particularly aboard the Ship he is Master of.

3. G. D. Advice to be sent unto *Bristol,* upon some Difficulties about Apostates there. The *Thursday* Interview of the Ministers disbands again. Differences arising at *Bridgwater;* GOD helps me to compose them.[1]

4. G. D. Some of the Ministers in the Town should be putt upon writing unto the wilful, furious, wretched Minister of *Harwich,* to cease his always grievous Ways of embroiling the Peace of the Churches, in those Parts of the Countrey.

5. G. D. A poor old Man at *Concord,* wanting to be helped into the Church there, I write a Letter thither for him, having first removed his Difficulties.

O the astonishing Dispensations of Heaven! must it always be so, that I must see a Sentence of Death upon good Things; and then will the GOD of Patience and of Consolation, give me to see some Comfort in them! We are surprized with very probable Advice, that my poor Son *Increase* is yett living: that the Vessel wherein he sailed, after a long, long, sad Passage, wherein it had spent all its Masts, was arrived into a Port of *New-found Land.*

If it be so, Oh! may the Distresses of the poor Prodigal bring him home to GOD. Oh! may I yett see strange Answers and Effects of the Prayers that have been employ'd for him!

* 6. G. D. What fresh Matters of Contemplation, and Supplication, have I now before me!

---

[1] A new parish — the East parish — was set off in 1723, and October 28, 1724, Rev. John Angier was ordained. Mather may refer to that, or to the difficulties of Rev. Benjamin Allen, pastor in the South parish. Mitchell, *History of Bridgewater,* 46, 47.

This hopeful Advice concerning my Son that was dead and is alive, need not hinder my entertaining the Flock this Day with such a Sermon as the Advice of his Death, has putt me upon præparing as one Essay more for the Awakening and Animating of early Piety.

But I do it this day, and have a mighty Presence of the glorious Lord with me, in the doing of it.

7. G. D. I think to print the Sermon of Yesterday, and scatter it especially among the young People of the Flock, whereof I am the Servant.

Lord, Thou hast lifted me up, and cast me down, Oh! Lett there not be thy *Indignation* and *Wrath,* in what is done unto me! To day, the good News of poor *Creasy's* being rescued and revived from Death, is all come to nothing. T'was another Vessel. *O my Father, Thy will be done!*

8. G. D. *Samachi* may be made an Instrument of some Good among the Ministers and others at *New-haven,* by Means of the Things, which this Week I write unto him.

This Day, the Lieut. Governour and Council, desired the Ministers of the City, to meet with them in the Council-Chamber, and spend some time extraordinary, in Humiliations before the glorious Lord under the Distresses which the Indian-War brings upon us, and Supplications for Success to the Forces now going forth against the Enemy.

I enjoy'd gracious and precious Assistence from Heaven, in my Part of the Services.

9. G. D. I supply my Kinsman at *Roxbury,* with certain Materials, which he publishes, to enlighten the Minds of Men in several Points of great Importance at this day to the Countrey.

10. G. D. The divine Providence throwing into my Hands this Day an Opportunity to serve the Lecture, in the Room of a Brother that is indisposed, I make it an Opportunity to entertain the People of GOD, with such Things as, I hope, will prove seasonable and serviceable unto

many. Especially, with regard unto Fears that exercise them.

11. G. D. I propose, the next Week, to invite the Ministers of this Island unto my Table, and then actually concert with them, the Projection for the Establishment of a profitable Conversation.

12. G. D. More Widows produced in the Neighbour-hood.

*13. G. D. My glorious Lord calls me to a singular Exercise of Piety, Patience and Humility under the Trial of being one *despised and rejected of Men.* The Sleight and the Spite, with which the Corporation of the Colledge have treated me, when I had such a Testimony in their Conscience as well as with the whole Countrey, to the Erudition, and Capacity and Activity for doing of good, and Fidelity to the Religion of the Churches of which it may be hoped that the Lord has bestowed something upon me; this occasions Town and Countrey to be inquisitive into the Bottom of the Contempt, which they have cast upon me; and many wild Guesses are made on this Occasion to my Disadvantage. It becomes me to be very silent, and with meekness of Wisdome to concoct it, and ly in the Dust before the Lord who makes me so much a Castaway, and not complain of it, if I am also a Stone, which the Builders have refused.

This Day I read over the Book which contains the Life of Mr. *Gearing,* and his Experiences; and the Marks of an Interest in CHRIST, that my Soul may further improve in experimental Piety.[1]

14. G. D. I am treating the Flock, with two Sermons on our SAVIOUR, gathering the Children of Men as the affectionate Bird the Chickens, under his Wings. I repeat

---

[1] William Gearing, author of a *History of the Church of Great Britain* (1674). He also published *The Sacred Diary, or Select Meditations for every Part of the Day* (1679).

the clocquing Voice of our SAVIOUR as affectionately as ever I can; and apply it in a singular Manner unto our young Ones.

15. G. D. Lett *Nancy* read the Experiences of a young Gentlewoman, published with the Life of Mr. *Gearing.*

And Visit —

16. G. D. What shall I do for my new Son-in-Law, who is now upon a Voyage?

17. G. D. Proposing as soon as I can, to publish my Sermon on the Death of my Son *Increase,* for the Animation of *early Piety,* I am thinking, whether I had not best add, my Sermon on the *Sparks flying upward.*

18. G. D. A Minister of some Note among us, being entangled in the Wretchedness of excessive Drinking, and a great Flock being in hazard of being ruin'd by it, I would move the Ministers of this Island, with whom I am associated in a *profitable Conversation,* to join with me, in a solemn Letter of Rebuke and Advice unto him.

19. G. D. A very poor old man in my Flock, must be instructed and comforted with singular Assistences.

* 20. G. D. By reading the *Christognosia,* of *Steygman,*[1] I propose to furnish myself, with Stores for Thoughts on the *Glory* of my SAVIOUR, which are the very Life of my Life, and must be the Salt of my Ministry. And by reading what he writes, *De vero Christianismo,* I propose to brighten and strengthen my Sentiments on a Subject which I have already done something to cultivate.

21. G. D. With my Collegue, lett me concert a List, of such as we may apprehend qualified for our Communion, and then with private and proper Applications unto them, call upon them to do their Duty in the Matter.

22. G. D. I am informed, that my Son, *Samuel,* in the Journey to *New-haven* from which he is not yett returned, has had the uncommon Respects of the Degree of M. A.

[1] Joshua Stegmannus, *Studii Pietatis Icon, sive Christognosia,* 1630.

conferred on him, at the Commencement there. If it be true, he is distinguished, by being a graduated Mr. of Arts, while he is yett short of eighteen years of Age. He also meets with much Esteem as a Preacher at these early Years. On these Accounts, I must mightily inculcate on him, the Maxims of Piety, of Industry, of the profoundest Humility, that he may express a due Gratitude unto the glorious Lord who so remarkably smiles upon him; and a Conduct so full of Wisdome, that he may not make them ashamed who have promoted him, and that he may not fail the just Expectation of the World concerning him.

23. G. D. The Children, which are this day to attend the Catechising, are unto me as my Relatives. Besides my other Contrivances to come at their young Souls, I would this day preach as pungent things as I can to them, on the Children of *Bethel*.

24. G. D. Being well-assured, that the M. CC. LX years for the Man of Sin, are up, I am sure, our High-Church must go down; and I will take the Occasion from hence to animate as many Testimonies as I can, against its vile Idolatries and Superstitions.[1]

25. G. D. The Interview of the Ministers on this Island, for a *profitable Conversation*, being established, there shall a proper Number of Ministers from the Neighbourhood be invited into it.

This Day, I sett apart for Supplications on the same Occasions and with the same Exercises, that I had a Month ago.

But with a special Regard unto the sad Case of my Son *Increase;* that I may have Light arise in Darkness to me under it; and that I may after a suitable Manner make the Sacrifice which I am call'd unto; and that the Discourses which it has awakened me to præpare for the Public may be published and prospered.

A Blessing on my Son *Samuel* in his Journey homewards, was also a Petition of Importance with me.

The Publication of several Composures, which have long been

[1] See p. 805, *infra*.

waiting for it, was a Matter which I now also importunately carried unto the Lord.

26. G. D. A poor Woman perishing under a Cancer, I must make a singular Object of my Compassions.

* 27. G. D. The sudden Death of my intimate and honoured Friend, the excellent Governour *Saltonstal*, on this Day Se'nnight, who was a few years younger than myself, — how much must it awaken me to be *always ready*, and as fast as I can, *do with my Might what my Hand finds to do*, and what I would wish to have done before I dy!

O my God, and SAVIOUR, quicken me, assist me, and lett an *easy Death*, (Oh! for an *easy* as well as an *happy Death!*) conclude my Labours and my Sorrows!

28. G. D. To entertain the Flock, with a Sermon on the *Golden Candlestick!*

This Day, the Church meets, partly to employ the *Golden Snuffers* of the Sanctuary in the Discipline due to an Offender; charged with lewd Attempt of Adulteries on several Persons. The Lord help me, to make this an Occasion of speaking such Things, as may cause all the People to fear GOD and receive Instruction.[1]

29. G. D. On the Death of my Son *Increase*, my first Care is, to make my dreadful Sacrifice after a suitable Manner.

But then, I would contrive as exquisite Ways as I can,

---

[1] "A copy of two Votes drawn up by the Reverend Dr. Mather, at a Church Meeting 28 *d.* 7 *m.*

"The Church, from what they have heard, apprehend it their Duty unto Mr. N. *Wheeler*, who stands accused of lewd and very scandalous Behaviors toward several Women; and a Duty owing to the Honor of our holy Profession and Communion, that he should stand suspended from our Fellowship at the Table of the Lord, until he arrive to us with such Testimonies of an humbler watchful, and exemplary Carriage, and such Expressions of a true Poenitent as may be for our more general Satisfaction.

"Voted, that the Church's Treasury pay the rent of the House in which our Pastor the Rev. Mr. Joshua Gee resides; and also advance the Sum of twenty Pounds for the Fuel of his Family for the Year current and annually, till 'tis otherwise ordered." *MS. Records of the Second Church*, III.

that at and by his Death, a poor Child, who did no good in his Life, may do good in the World : that the Child may be an Instrument of good after he is dead. I think, I have contrived a Way for it, which may anon be mentioned.

30. G. D. My excellent Sister, Mrs. R. B. is fallen into such an Extremity of Affliction by a foolish Son, who has wasted her, that she is in extreme Danger of being hurried into the Grave. I am under the greatest Obligations of doing all that I can, to assist and comfort her.

(V.) A godly Woman having been carried thro' many Afflictions, thought herself bound in Duty, to invite her Friends unto a Consort with her in the Praises of GOD her SAVIOUR: and having had a more particular Experience of the Truth in that Word, Psal. CXIX. 92, *Unless thy Law had been my Delights, then had I perished in my Affliction,* she desired me to furnish her with a Discourse upon it. I did so, and she published it. It is entituled, THE NIGHTINGALE. *An Essay of Songs among Thorns, or The Supports and Comforts of the Afflicted Beleever.*[1]

October. 1. G. D. It may be a Service unto the Public, for me to bestow a funeral Sermon on my honourable Friend, Governour *Saltonstal*; and give him his deserved Character.

I do it this Day in the Lecture.

2. G. D. And I send it unto *New-London*.

3. G. D. A young Gentleman, bound for *Europe;* Fortify him against his Temptations.

* 4. G. D. Ever now and then, when I am conversing with Heaven in Supplications, I have a Thought struck in my Mind, which I never had before, and which I know not that any other Man has had before;

A Thought full of Light and Warmth, and of an heart-melting Efficacy. Tis my Infelicity, that I have not had the Time or Strength to write so many of them, as I should have done.

[1] Printed by B. Green, 1724.

But because it is now the *Lord's-day* with me, I will enter a Thought of Piety, by which the Sanctification of the Day, may be more than a little animated. This is the Day, which the Lord has made considerable by His Resurrection from the Dead upon it. His Resurrection from the Dead, was his Acquittance from the Debt of Punishment which we ow'd, (for on His own Account He ow'd none) unto the Justice of GOD. Accordingly, when we sanctify this Day, and celebrate it, as we ought to do, we not only putt in our Claim to a share in that Acquittance, but also have an Assurance of it. When we conscienciously and religiously Sabbatize, we may be assured of it, that we have a Share in that Justification which our SAVIOUR and Surety rising from the Dead, received on the behalf of His chosen People. God says to the careful Sabbatizer; *Be of good Comfort, thy Sins are forgiven thee.*

Oh! That this *Joy of the Lord* may be my *Strength*, in sabbatizing to Him!

5. G. D. Some things, to be done with relation to the Seats, in the Meeting-house.

6. G. D. My Son *Samuel*, having found so much Acceptance of his Performances in the Neighbourhood, it will be expected, that he should be exhibited unto his Grandfather's and Father's Church in the Neighbourhood. I advise him therefore to prepare a Sermon, on Exod. xv. 2. *My Father's God, I will exalt him.*

7. G. D. I have two Nephews both which are now so struck with a Consumption, that their Lives are to be despaired of. I am to treat them accordingly, and assist their preparations.

8. G. D. I am now making Remittances to the *Royal Society*, which, I hope, will be not an unuseful Entertainment.

9. G. D. I am also making fresh Instances to forward the Design of collecting and compacting the Lives and Characters of pious Puritans.

10. G. D. A godly Woman of my Neighbourhood, under the Torments of a wicked and froward Husband, and bereaved of a Daughter that was a great Comfort unto her, what shall I do for her Support in her Affliction?

A Man and his wife in my Neighbourhood, living in much sinful Discord, I heal their Contentions.

*11. G. D. Another of the many Things darted into my Mind, when I am addressing Heaven with my Supplications, is this: the meritorious Obedience of my SAVIOUR to the Law of the glorious GOD, had a Voice in it. The Sufferings of my SAVIOUR were Petitions to Him for such Favours of Heaven to be bestow'd upon us, as they purchased. The Wounds of my dying SAVIOUR, did as opened Mouths, petition for such Blessings to us, as the Blood which issued from them, was the Payment of a Price for. When therefore I pour out my Prayers to the Glorious God, they are in Conjunction with the Supplications, which there were in the Sacrifice of my SAVIOUR: they do but utter the Language of the Sacrifice. With what Faith, what Hope, what Joy may my Prayers be animated from this Consideration!

12. G. D. The last Week there died in this Neighbourhood a Damsel, about sixteen years old,[1] who in the last Days of her pious Life, expired with marvellous Triumphs over Death, and such uncommon and heavenly Expressions, that I thought it might be a Part of my pastoral Watchfulness, to entertain the Flock, and particularly the young ones of it, with a Relation of them.

13. G. D. Some further Projections, for dear *Nancy's* Welfare.

14. G. D. And my dying Kinsman at *Roxbury*.

15. G. D. I purpose, if I can, to draw a number of our Ministers, into a Combination, to erect and revive a *Society for the Suppression of Disorders;* which may go on upon such a Plan, as in this Town such a Society formerly went upon; and a World of Good was accomplished.

16. G. D. A Council to meet in this Place, and at my House, upon the distressed Case of *Portsmouth*.

[1] Mrs. Rebecca Burnel.

17. G. D.   A gracious Widow in this Neighbourhood, fallen into great Affliction by the Death of her only Son.

* 18. G. D.   Much edified in Reading of *Gerhard's Meditationes Sacrae,* one of them, the last thing, before I go to Rest.

19. G. D.   Some in the Flock, under grievous Exercises, To be accommodated with a Discourse on being *chosen in the Furnace of Affliction.*

20. G. D.   What shall I do, that my Carriage towards my Consort, may have in it yett more Conformity to my Lovely SAVIOUR?   I think of many Instances, wherein I will endeavour it unto the uttermost.   Especially, in Compassion to her with regard unto the Things which threaten her Comfort.

But that I may improve to the highest in this matter, I would pray much oftener with her, than I have done heretofore.   Oftener than in our monthly Action of that Importance.

21. G. D.   The little Damosels of the Flock, are to be treated with me, as my Children.   This is the Day for the Catechising of them.   I would this Day treat them with a Discourse on Ps. LXIII. I. *Thou art my GOD, Early will I seek thee.*

22. G. D.   The Revival of the horrible Persecution in *France,* revives in me, an Enquiry, whether I may not resume the Essay, which I made three years ago, to send into *France,* an Instrument in the French Tongue, that is calculated for the awakening of the People there, to reform their Impieties, or to expect the tremendous Judgments of GOD.[1]   I sent it into *Holland,* and have had no Account concerning it.   I am inclinable to be at the Expence of printing it here, and so sending it into *France,* as many ways as I can.   *Direct me, O my SAVIOUR!*

23. G. D.   The unhappy State of Religion at *Rhode-*

[1] *Une Grande Voix du Ciel.*

Island, calls for some Consideration, and the Minister there is to be putt upon the doing of his Duty.

Something to be done relating to *Canterbury*.[1]

This Day I sett apart for Supplications, with the same Exercises and on the same Occasions, which employ'd me a Month ago.

Unto which there were now some others added.

Especially, that the glorious Lord would pour out His Holy SPIRIT on my Son *Samuel*, and assist him and accept him, to serve His Kingdome, and be particularly with him on the Lord's-Day approaching, when he is to stand in his Grandfather's Pulpitt, and Minister before the Lord.

And that I may enjoy a glorious Presence of the Holy One with me, in a great Council of Churches, which is to meet at my House the next Week, that they may consider the Condition of *Ipswyche* and *Portsmouth;* and see a good Issue of the important affair.

24. G. D. Good Offices to be done for oppressed and afflicted Slaves. These have often occurr'd, without my making in these Records any Mention of them.

*25. G. D. Oh! If I had an holy Heart, how much might I live in Heaven, while I am on Earth. Yesterday, to the seven stated Prayers of the Day, there were added, a Prayer with my Widow-sisters in the Evening; a Prayer with a gracious widow under Darkness; a Prayer with my Consort præparatory to the Communion; which raises them to the Number *ten.* How many ejaculatory Prayers passed in the Day, cannot be numbred.

Now, that I may be more Heavenly in and by these Exercises of PIETY, I propose often to præface them with such Thoughts as these; *I am now making a Visit unto the Heavenly World! I am going, where my SAVIOUR is making a continual Intercession for me. I am going, where I hope ere long to be received into everlasting Habitations.*

This Day, my Son *Samuel*, (while yett short of eighteen) appeared in the Pulpit where his Father and Grandfather

---

[1] Samuel Estabrook was the minister at Canterbury, Connecticut, where he remained until dismissed in June, 1727.

before him, have served our Glorious Lord; and preached
on Exod. xv. 2. *He is my Father's God and I will exalt
Him.*

26. G. D. On the special Presence of our Glorious
Lord, in the Midst of His Churches, I entertain the Flock
with such things as, I hope, He will make awful and useful
to them.

27. G. D. Oh! when, when, will my two Daughters
exalt the GOD of their Father, by laying hold on His Covenant, and confirming it in the Communion of His People,
at the Table of the Lord!

I must not leave my Instigations, till it be accomplished.

This Day, the Delagates of ten Churches, mett in a
Council, at the Place of my present Habitation. My
spacious Hall, was handsomely filled with a venerable
Appearance. The Occasion was, the Desire of the Church
at *Portsmouth*, to obtain a Translation of one of the Pastors
in the Church at *Ipswyche*, to them.[1] They placed me in
the Moderator's Chair. And my Glorious Lord, unto
whom I had look'd up with much of Agony for His Assistence, enabled me, to manage the affair in my hands, after
such a Manner, that they who were present, apprehended,
that we had an uncommon and very special Presence of
our Lord with us. The Result of the Council is in other
Papers. They adjourned for three Weeks.

28. G. D. Lord, what shall I do, for my two Nephews,
whose Life drawes near to the Grave, — that [*unfinished*].

(VI.) 29. G. D. It may be for the Service of Piety
among very many People, especially our young ones; to
allow the Publication of a Discourse, which is now in the
Press; entituled,

LIGHT IN DARKNESS: *An Essay on the PIETY, which*

---

[1] See p. 734, *supra*. The council considered Fitch's acceptance of the call
to Portsmouth.

by Remembring the Many Days of Darkness, will change them into a Marvellous Light. With a notable Exemple of it, in a young Person, in the Seventeenth year of her Age meeting her Death with uncommon Triumphs over it.[1]

30. G. D. My best Instructions and Assistences, to a young Minister, bound for the Service of the Gospel, at *Cohanzy.*[2]

31. G. D. A godly Woman in my Neighbourhood, mourning under the Death of what was most of all desireable to her, in her Children; and vexed with a very wicked, and froward Husband.

(VII.) Preaching lately a Sermon on, Job. III. 25. one of the Hearers came to me, for a Copy of it. It was a Sermon which the Death of my Son INCREASE led me to. Tis published under this Title. TELA PRÆVISA. *A short Essay on Troubles to be look'd for. A Wise Expectation of and Preparation for Troublesome Changes, recommended unto the Strangers and Pilgrims in this present Evil World.*[3]

(VIII.) Moreover, That I might serve several good Purposes, I sent my Funeral-Sermon on Governour *Saltonstal,* to his Widow at *New-London,* who immediately published it. This is the Title. DECUS AC TUTAMEN. *A brief Essay on the Blessings enjoy'd by a People that have Men of a Right Character shining among them. Offered in Commemoration of that Good and Great Man, the Honourable* GURDON SALTONSTAL *Esqr, Late Governour of Connecticot-Colony,* New England.[4]

November. * 1. G. D. I find my Dispositions to find all my Delights and all my Riches, and all my Honours, in a glorious CHRIST, grow exceedingly.

It is a marvellous Consolation and Encouragement unto

---

[1] Printed by S. Kneeland for Nathaniel Belknap, 1724. It was preached on Mrs. Rebecca Burnel.

[2] Salem county, New Jersey.

[3] Printed by B. Green for Thomas Hancock, 1724.

[4] Printed by T. Green, 1724.

me, in my Supplications, to think, that there was a Voice in all those Acts of Obedience, which my SAVIOUR paid unto the divine Law, and more particularly a Voice went from the Wounds of my suffering SAVIOUR, as with open Mouth demanding the Blessings of Goodness for His People; and all my prayers to the glorious GOD, are nothing but the Repetition of that Voice; and so they reach to Heaven with a marvellous Concomitance and Efficacy.

2. G. D.   I take in hand the Word of GOD as a mighty *Hammer which breaks the Rock to Peeces*, (preaching on the Text that calls it so) and then, I particularly single out the several Sorts of Transgressors which the *Hammer* is more especially to be employ'd upon; and I give adapted Strokes of the *Hammer* upon them. Oh! may they be effectual!

3. G. D.   I putt my Son *Samuel* upon two Things. The one is, a more exact Method and Order for his daily Studies.

The other is, A more particular Concern in him to do all possible Good unto his two Sisters.

And yett more particularly for *Nancy*, to supply her with such Things as it may be most proper and useful for her to read; and also what her Pen may be employed upon.

4. G. D.   A Kinsman come to sojourn and study in *Boston*, is to have my best Assistences given to him.

5. G. D.   This Day being a public Thanksgiving, thro the Province, I thought it might be a Service to entertain the People of GOD, with a Discourse on the devout Methods to be used, in keeping a Day of Thanksgiving, which all the Churches in the World, but ours, (and ours now too much) are Strangers to.

The Lord graciously assisted me in the public and private Services of the Day, and help'd to the Attainments and Enjoyments, of a Sabbath filled with His Praises.

6. G. D.   I must furnish the Deputies which our Coun-

cil sends unto *Ipswyche*, with Matters to manage the Cause, which we send them upon.

7. G. D. A young Man, whom his Uncle, a worthy Minister in *London*, recommends to me.

8. G. D. I find the reading of Mr *Cole's* Discourses, to be serviceable to me; in several Hints I take from them, to nourish and quicken, the Spirit of the Gospel in me; and PIETY upon evangelical Principles.

9. G. D. I propose to entertain the Flock, with, first, the free Offer, which our SAVIOUR makes of the Water of Life to us; and show [how] our Faith is to receive the Offer. And then, (if I may be spared so long,) to entertain them with the apostolical Catalogue of Graces, to be added unto Faith.

10. G. D. *Liza*, is in circumstances, which I may lay hold on, as an Occasion for me to press upon her the Attainments of the most serious Piety.[1]

18. G. D. I visit my dying Kinsman at *Roxbury*, and assist him all I can, to præpare for what is before him; And I also carry to him some temporal Releefs, under his domestic Difficulties.

19. G. D. I entertain the Public this Day, (the General Assembly sitting) with some faithful Instructions, how we may come to have the Face of GOD in His CHRIST so shining upon us, as to save us.

20. G. D. My Letters to *Ipswyche* and *Portsmouth*.

This Day I sett apart for Supplications, as I use to do.

Little that is new, occurred for, and, in the Day. I earnestly declared unto the Lord, that I ask'd no Blessings from Him, which it was lawful for me, to be willing to have denied unto me, but I præferred an Heart willing to sacrifice those Blessings, before them all. Such a sacrificing Heart was what I now chiefly insisted on; and I declared with the greatest Alacrity, that a Soul full of a CHRIST, and sensible of a CHRIST concerned for me, and quickening of me, should satisfy all my Desires: I would ask for no more.

---

[1] A leaf has been torn from the record.

I also besought of the Lord, that if I asked for anything, which He saw would not be for His Glory and Service, He would not grant the Petition I asked of Him.

I then particularly pray'd for a Smile of GOD, upon my Attempts to publish and scatter my Essay to convey His great Voice unto *France*. And upon my Essay to instruct the Candidates of the Ministry, which I design speedily to return unto.

And that He would smile on what I have to do the next Week, in an Ordination at *Medford*.

By a marvellous Operation of the divine Providence, all things are come to Rights in my unhappy Family.

*21. G. D. An abominable Fellow in my Neighbourhood abuses his godly, humble, patient Wife, intolerably. Every body dreads the Consequences. This Day I write as well-contrived a Letter as I can unto him.

22. G. D. The Corporation of our miserable Colledge do again (upon a fresh Opportunity) treat me with their accustomed Indignity and Malignity.[1] But, Oh! may I take Pleasure in the Opportunity, which I have to glorify my GOD and SAVIOUR, with a Disposition which He may with Delight look down upon!

First; I am entirely Satisfied in the Allowance which my sovereign, wise, just and good LORD grants me, of Opportunities to do good in the World. I am content, that they should be all at His Disposal; and thankful that I have what He has indulged unto me.

Secondly; I look unto Him, for His Help, to govern my Resentments of Affronts, that may be offered unto me; and bear them with a Prudence, and Patience, and Silence, that may adorn the Doctrine of GOD my SAVIOUR.

Thirdly: I rejoice, I rejoice, I feel a secret Joy in it, that I am thus conformed unto Him who was despised and rejected of Men, and the Stone which the Builders refused. That I may demonstrate this Joy, I would utterly forbear

[1] Rev. Benjamin Colman was chosen to be President of the College, November 18, 1724, but declined the office, and Benjamin Wadsworth entered upon the duties of President July 7, 1725.

aking any Step (as I easily could many) to throw Confusion upon the Men, who would make me low in the Eyes
of all the Countrey. A Man in black, may deride these
Things, under the Name of, my *Extasies*, but, I bless GOD,
I know the Meaning of them.

On this Lord's-day, I found myself much indisposed.
And returning home from the public Services of the Forenoon (to which I was graciously assisted,) I had so much
of a Fever siezing on me, as confined me from going abroad
any more. I had three Maladies now to conflict withal.
A *Cough* which proved a grievous Breast-beater; an *Asthma*
which often almost suffocated me; and a *Fever*, which held
me every Afternoon. In the Time of this Confinement, the
glorious Lord enabled me, to study how I might approve
myself a Spectacle which Heaven might with Delight look
down upon; especially, with a patient and submissive
Resignation to His Will, in my uneasy Circumstances; and
with a continual Struggle to have such Thoughts formed
in my Mind, as might be fitt for a Temple of GOD: Particularly, I imposed it as a Rule for me, that whenever any
Fitt of my tedious and irksome Coughing should come upon
me, I would strive to have some new Thoughts of the
blessed JESUS raised in me. And I was gloriously supported
by the Comforter who releeved my Soul, and caused me
to triumph over the Fear of Death, and enabled me to sing
the Songs of the Lord in a strange Land, and entertain my
Visitors with such Flights to the Heavenly World, and Views
of it, and News from it, as, I hope, honoured Him, and had
a great Impression upon them.

After five Weeks, of Confinement, the God of my Life
returns me to my Study, and to a Prospect of serving Him
again in the Public Sacrifices.

It was a comfortable Circumstance, that my own Son
was one of those, who supplied the Pulpitt for me.

The Month of *December* passed along as a *Month of Vanity*.

And yett in this Month, I read over several considerable Books, yea, went thro' much of some *Folio's*, which made some Addition to the little Stock of Erudition, with which I would be somewhat qualified for the doing of some good Work about the House of my GOD.

In this Time also, I gott into the Press, (and corrected the Press-work of it) an Essay in the French Tongue, which I had præpared before my falling Sick.

(IX.) I have a strong Apprehension, that *France* is very near a mighty and a wondrous Revolution; and that it is not easy to do a greater Service for the Kingdome of God, than to sett before the French Nation, the horrible Wickedness of that cruel and matchless Persecution, with which they have exposed themselves to the tremendous Vengeance of GOD; and therewithal to instruct them in the *only Terms*, which the Friends of a *Reformation* must unite upon, and exhibit unto them an incontestible System of *pure and undefiled Religion*, and a scriptural Fulmination upon the Corruptions of Religion with which the Man of Sin intoxicates them. The glorious Lord has helped me to do this, in an Essay which I putt myself unto the Expence of Publishing; under the Title of, UNE GRANDE VOIX DU CIEL À LA FRANCE. And I apply myself immediately to Methods of getting it convey'd into *France;* which I have already a various Prospect of.

(X.) Moreover, being sollicitious that the grievous Calamity befalling me in the Death of my poor Son *Increase*, may yeeld some Revenues of Service to the Kingdome of GOD; and that the Child, who did so little Good, but much ill, in all the Days of his Life, may do some good at his Death; I took the Sermon I preached on that Occasion, adding to it another that is agreeable; and with a considerable Expence enabled the Bookseller to publish them. While it was, in the Press (which also was in this Month) a strange Hand of Providence made such an Accession from others, to my own Disbursements, that I could add a third Sermon, to the Book, wherein I may yett more notably serve the Designs of Piety. All these are concluded, with an Instrument of a Soul repenting and returning to GOD; which is a Copy of a pœnetent and pertinent Writing left by the poor Child on the Table in my Study, before his going off. So it makes a bound Book; whereof the Title is; THE WORDS OF UNDERSTANDING. *Three Essays.* I. *The PHILO-MELA, with, the Notes of Morning-Piety.* II. *The EPHEM-ERON, or, Tears dropt on Dust and Ashes.* III. *JONAH, or, The Dove in Safety. Occasion'd by some Early Deaths which require such Notice to be taken of them.*[1]

About this Time, a new Matter of Distress comes upon me. *Lord, what Sacrifices dost thou call me to!*

My Son, my only Son, *Samuel,* whom I have at home with me, in a Conversation and a Cultivation, that affords me the greatest Consolations among the *Creaturulæ Conso-latiumculæ,* which I am releeved withal, is earnestly sett upon a Voyage to *England,* and there is a Coincidence of many Circumstances, to accelerate the Execution of his Purposes, which I was in hopes to have delay'd another Year. The Expences of his Voyage, he thinks, are wondrously provided for. His Uncle (his Mother's Brother,) accommodates him with a good and great and strong Ship, and what Money he has Occasion for; and he has also an Interest of his own to support him. He proposes to improve in his Accomplishments for Service; but much more, to do considerable Service for the Church of GOD, by bringing forth such Things as with the Help of Heaven I have prepared for it. If I cross his Inclinations, I know not what grievous Temptations I may throw him into. He has a strange Perswasion, that he shall be prospered: and his Friends generally agree to encourage him. Full of Distress, I cast my Burden on the Lord. If this Child,

[1] Printed by S. Kneeland for J. Edwards, 1724.

must after his two Brothers, be buried in the *Atlantic* Ocean
I sacrifice him, O my GOD and SAVIOUR, I sacrifice him t
thy Holy Pleasure! If I have a CHRIST left unto me,
shall rejoice in Him, and reckon that I am still happy enough
tho' every Comfort in this World be taken from me.

But I am satisfied.[1] The Matter will Issue well.

January. [1724–25.] 1. This is the first Day of m
Return to my Study; and I begin the Year, with suc
Recollections and Supplications as a new Year should b
entred withal. My published Essay on, *A Year well-begun*
has described them.

G. D. A fruitful year, beyond any that ever I saw!

2. G. D. In the Time of my Sickness, I dispense
Alms to the Poor; and especially some that were languishin
under Sickness.

* 3. Returning to this evil World, I seem to be upo
a new Song. The very little Time that remains of m
Pilgrimage thro' this evil World, must be carried on wit
new Measures. No Time is to be lost. I must be a
Work for my Glorious Lord continually and assiduously
and more than ever.

I think to leave off the Custome of entring so largel
the Memorials of, GOOD DEVISED, in these Papers; but fa
from abating the Number of the *Devices;* and indeed a grea
Part of the daily Number was never entred.

But, I would record my Improvements in the Senti
ments and Practices of Piety. And for my *Purposes to D*
Good, I would every Satureday in the Evening, record ver
brief Minutes, of what I have thought in the week, on th
seven Heads, which I use to employ them on.

Such more considerable Things also as befall me in m
Life, may come into the Records.

These Things may be sufficient. For me to be mor
laborious in these entries, may be a disservice to tha

---

[1] Two lines of text obliterated.

Redemption of Time, of which I must now be more than ever Studious.

G. D. I know not what better Service to do for the Flock I am returning to, than to entertain them with two Discourses on Phil. 1. 21. How CHRIST is the true Christian's *Life*, and what *Gain* such a Christian shall have by his Death.

A gracious GOD, has marvellously interposed in the Affair of my Son *Samuels* Voyage. He seasonably disposed me to prevent his going by the Way of the W. *Indies*. Then he ship'd himself on a Vessel bound more directly for *London*. Here also the divine Providence ordered something to fall out, which putt a Delay and a Defeat upon his Inventions. This is the Effect of my Cries unto the glorious Lord, that if the Child's Voyage might not be for the Service of His Kingdome, and the Welfare of the Child himself, He would graciously putt a Stop unto it. The calm Resignation and Satisfaction, with which the Child entertains the Disappointment of a Matter which his Heart was exceedingly and passionately sett upon, is a Token for Good. I have also had an Opportunity to make a Sacrifice of my only Son; and yett without the actual Accomplishment thereof, to receive him again as from the Dead. G. D. I hope to improve these Occurrences, as great Obligations upon both of us, to apply our selves unto such Things, as may effectually demonstrate, that GOD has meant them unto Good.

At the Hour of Twelve, I use to have a short Interview with Heaven, wherein among other Things, I particularly carry the Condition of my Family unto the Lord. G. D. I find it an excellent Introduction and Ingredient of this Communion with Heaven, to take a Sentence of the sacred Scriptures, and find out what is in it, and feed for a while upon it, and conform to the Sentiments of Piety, which it leads me to. The Like, for my Evening-Prayer.

I find my Soul, with strange Raptures into Heaven, in this
Exercise, præpared for the Supplications, which I pour out
unto the Lord.

9. My Kinsman at *Roxbury*,[1] lies a dying; full of Distress and of Darkness about his future State. With much
Importunity and Impatience, he calls for me to be fetch'd
over to him. I have the Satisfaction to strengthen him in
his Agonies, and advise him, and comfort him; and leave
him with a sensible Satisfaction, and a good Hope thro'
Grace arrived unto him. The Prayer-hearing Lord, enabled
him to dy the next Day, with joyful Triumphs over the last
Enemy.

G. D.   Some remote Relatives in *Dorchester*, I this Day
consider, with transmitting Books of Piety to them.

* 10. My Glorious Lord often enlightens me and enlivens me, with such Sentiments of His Gospel and His
Kingdome, and such Insights into the Mystery of CHRIST,
as have a most heart-melting Efficacy in them. I am sorry
that I have entred no more of the PRECIOUS THOUGHTS, in
my Memorials. But for the little Time that remains, I
hope, to make more frequent Entries of them.

Where pr. Th. appears in the Margin, those PRECIOUS
THOUGHTS, have some Notice taken of them.

Pr. Th. We have a SAVIOUR, who is our Advocate in the
Heavens, and by His potent Intercession saves us to the uttermost.
He receives those of our Petitions, which find an Approbation with
Him; and presents them to the FATHER, and undertakes to prose-
cute them and accomplish them; and Him the FATHER heareth
always.

O my dear SAVIOUR, the Petition which I bring unto thee, is,
that thou mayest be glorified in making me Partaker of thy great
Salvation; in making me a Servant of thy Kingdome, a Member of
thy Body, an object of those precious Works, wherein thou dost
fulfil the good Pleasure of thy Goodness upon thy chosen, and that
I may come to live unto GOD, and bring forth much of that Fruit, by

---

[1] Thomas Walter.

which the FATHER will be glorified. My Heart is not sett upon any Petition comparable unto This! And now, may I not be assured of it, that such a Petition as this, will be approved and allowed and accepted with thee; and that thou will prosecute it and accomplish it; and that it will be grateful unto the eternal FATHER, whose Glory will be Thine, in thy obtaining of it? It cannot be otherwise! And this Assurance now fills me with a Joy unspeakable and full of Glory!

Points of Consideration.

G. D.   My Bereaved Relatives at *Roxbury*.
My Decaying Nephew in Boston.
The Redemption of a Captive.
One of my Flock, fallen by excessive Drinking.
Several poor Widows.

G. D.   The Case of the *Fear of Death*, to be with a well-studied Answer spoken to. How much good may be done in the Flock, by a proper Discourse upon it?

15. The Feebleness, which continues upon me, since my late Sickness, excuses me from setting apart this Day, as I use to do every Friday, approaching to the Table of the Lord. I serve a gracious Lord who desires Mercy and not Sacrifice, and who delights not in the Miseries of His Creatures. My Eyes also are continually unto the Lord.

And I sett apart the Afternoon of the Day following, for such exercises of Piety, as might have a Tendency to præpare me for the Interviews with Heaven at the Holy Table.

16. Pr. Th. Whatever holy Frames and holy Thoughts, I have raised in me, were first of all produced in my Holy JESUS. My SAVIOUR is the first Recipient of the Holy SPIRIT, in those gracious Influences, with which His whole mystical Body is to be animated: and whatever Holiness is produced in His People, is first in Him, as the Archetype of it, and the Fountain of Life whence flow down the gracious Influences by which we are quickened for Living unto God. If I am enriched with any holy Frames and holy Thoughts they are such as have been, for the Kind of them, in the Mind of my lovely SAVIOUR.

Here I see a Reason, why the holy Frames and holy Thoughts which are at any time formed in me, find Acceptance with the infinitely holy God, and He looks down with Delight upon them. No only has my SAVIOUR made Expiation for the Iniquity which thro my Corruption, does attend my holy Things, but also they are such a He has beheld already produced and existing in the Son of His Love.

Here again I see the Meaning of having the *Face of GOD* shin upon me. It is the CHRIST of GOD that is the *Face* of GOD. H shines upon me, when He forms holy Frames and holy Thoughts i me. I have Him in me, when I have these from Him in me. H withdraws, He hides Himself, He keeps at a Distance from me, i the Withdraw and Ceasing of these. The continual Presence o these, may cause me to sing with Joy, *Now I have CHRIST in me, th Hope of Glory!*

Here, finally, I see the Method of obtaining holy Frames and hol Thoughts, when I am destitute and desirous of them. The Metho is, to look up unto my JESUS for them; It is to have a Wish of thi Importance, *O Holy SPIRIT, Form thou in me such Holy Frames an Holy Thoughts, as Thou has fill'd my SAVIOUR, withal! O my Saviour send thou down the Impressions of thy Holy SPIRIT upon me!*

Reccomend unto *Samachi*, to be attentively read many things, — but especially, *Dietericus, his Antiquitate Biblicae.*[1]

To *Nancy, Baxter's, Poor mans Family-Book.*

Some agreeable Books, to a Nephew, coming to live, a Prentice, in my Neighbourhood.

21. G. D. I thought it might many Ways be a Servic to the Cause of Religion, if with a Discourse on the Honour which GOD will putt on the Servants of our SAVIOUR, I should endeavour a proper Commemoration of my Kinsman, lately deceased; and particularly, give some Account of his last Hours, and the remarkable Repentance an Assurance, to which he arrived in them. The Lord graciousl assisted me and accepted me to do this, in the Lecture thi Day.

(XI.) And on the same Day, I gave the Discourse unto

---

[1] Conradus Dietericus (Dietrich), author of *Analysis Evangelicorum* (1631).

he Bookseller; entituled, CHRISTODULUS. *A Good Reward* *f a Good Servant. Or The Service of a Glorious CHRIST,* *ustly demanded and commended from a View of the Glory with* *hich it shall be Recompensed. With some Commemoration of* *1r* Thomas Walter.[1]

Poor Objects of Charity releeved this Week.

Books of Piety, dispensed into several Parts of the ountrey.

* 24. Pr. Th. Certainly, there is a Disposition to give, 1 one who desires and who directs to have a Gift asked of im. It may especially be supposed of a Father, that if e bids his Children to ask a good Thing of him, he is dis-osed, yea, resolved for the Bestowing of it.

My most Gracious God has advised me, invited me, yea, com-anded me, to come and ask for His Blessings. His Word is, *Ask,* *nd it shall be given you.* And the Blessings which He bids me to sk of Him, are the best of Blessings; the greatest Things that can e thought of; and such Things as will make me beyond all Imagi-ation happy; bring me to perfect and endless Happiness. I may hen conclude, If I ask such Blessings, they shall be conferred upon ne. The Lord only waits that He may be Gracious, and stays for othing but that by asking of them I may be prepared for His 'avours. O my GOD, with what a joyful Assurance may I come nto thee now, for such inestimable Blessings as these; that I may e united unto my SAVIOUR, and by His Blood be reconciled unto hee; and have His Image imprinted on me, and feel Him dwelling n me, and quickening of me, to live unto thee; and that I may be illed with the Love of GOD, and employ'd in Service for Him, and e made an Instrument of His Praises! I am assured that thou wilt rant such Blessings unto me. And then I am assured, that thou vilt bless me indeed; and I shall have Goodness and Mercy forever ollowing of me.

G. D. The scandalous Profaneness of those who even o old Age, neglect præparing for and approaching to the Table of the Lord, is to have yett more pungent Rebukes estow'd upon it.

[1] Printed by T. Fleet for S. Gerrish, 1725.

G. D. A Thing to be done for the Satisfaction of my Consort.

G. D. Some foolish Steps taken, to draw the civil Government into interposing and inhibiting ecclesiastical Censures upon Offendors. I am giving seasonable and effectual Stops unto them.

G. D. By Conversing with some Physicians, I hope to gain some Augmentation of the Stores, with which I would propose to do good in the world.

G. D. A very wicked and vicious Gentlewoman, my Admonitions unto her, and my Essays to bring her unto Repentance, tho' they have been frequent, they have been too oblique. I shall be more easy in my Mind, if by a nameless Letter she be more directly, cogently, faithfully dealt withal.

* 31. Pr. Th. and G. D. In a Sermon which with the Help of Heaven, I have just now composed, I give this Description of a SOUL wherein PIETY is *Flourishing*.

"Tis a Soul, whose *Prayers* are *without ceasing;* very *frequent* very *fervent;* poured out from a Soul swallowed up in *Aims* at the Glory of GOD ; full of *Resignation* to His Will, and Reliance on the *Intercession* of the *Advocate in the Heavens*.

"A Soul that prizes and propounds *Communion* with GOD in all religious Performances, and cannot be satisfied without it.

"A Soul that remembers, *GOD is acquainted with all my Ways,* and therefore, not only steers clear of *secret Sins*, but also will not allow those *Frames* or *Thoughts* in the *Heart*, that may be offensive to Him.

"A SOUL that is a mighty Enemy to *Mispence of Time*, and is troubled if many Hours have been so spent, that a good Account can't be given of them.

"A SOUL that is ever *Devising of Good*, and studies to be a Blessing in all *Relations*, to all *Societies*.

"A Soul that looks upon all that it has, or could wish to have with a *sacrificing Eye*, and can readily forego, and give up, and part with every thing that GOD will have to be denied unto it.

"A Soul able and willing to dy, and that when Death approaches can *sing* in the *Valley of the Shadow of Death*, and find it but a *Shadow of Death;* and can say *I have nothing to do, but to dy; Nay, I have not this to do neither; For I am already dead unto all things here below:* So, triumphing over the *Fear of Death*, and beginning to *sing the Songs of the Lord*, even in a *strange Land*; the *Songs*, which none but those *chief Musicians*, the *Redeemed from the Earth*, are skilful at. This is the Soul, which *flourishes in the Courts of our GOD.* Oh! For such a SOUL! Oh! For such a Soul!

"A CHRIST, a CHRIST conversed withal; This is what will produce a Soul so *flourishing* in PIETY. Without this, O SOUL, Thou wilt be no other than a *barren Figtree.* If we would *flourish in the Courts of our GOD*, it must be in *living by the Faith of the SON* of God, and by continual Flights unto our SAVIOUR. Tis a SOUL full of a CHRIST, that is the *flourishing SOUL:* A SOUL which makes *daily Visits* to Him with affectuous *Contemplations* and *Supplications:* A Soul which often beholds the *Pattern of all Goodness* in our SAVIOUR, and labours to *resemble* Him, to *imitate* Him: A SOUL, that can't bear to be long without the *precious Thoughts* of Him; *A Dove in the Clefts of the Rock!* Oh! for such a SOUL!"

Now, This is what I am striving for. Yea, O my SAVIOUR, I hope tis what thou hast in a comfortable Measure brought me to.

But I was taken so ill the last Night, with a Relapse into my Cough, and Fevers, that I was not only diverted from the public Services of the Lord's-day but also confined all the following Week.

I used all the Methods of Piety I could think on, to glorify my faithful GOD and SAVIOUR, under this new Visitation.

February. Several Services public and private, were attempted under the confinement by Sickness, which the first Week of this Month finds me under.

Especially this. I apprehend it may be a most comprehensive and unspeakable Service, unto the Cause of Piety, yea, and the Establishment of our Churches in their Aversion for the episcopal Ways whereto some are apostatising, if I should publish an History of "glorious Effects of

II · 50

Grace, remark'd in the Church of *Scotland*, suffering for its Opposition unto an abjured Prelacy, and a Collection of memorable Speeches uttered by some of her dying Martyrs."

My Gracious Lord has helped me this Week, under my Languishments, to make a notable Progress in this Collection.

* 7. G. D. When I sitt alone in my Languishments, unable to write, or to read, I often compose little Hyms, agreeable unto my present Circumstances, and sing them unto the Lord.

Vast Numbers have I had of these; which are immediately all forgotten. But tho' none of them have been hitherto recorded, I will here insert one of them; inasmuch as I design to use it again, and often upon Occasion.

Having found my Mind for some time without such precious and impressive Thoughts of GOD my SAVIOUR, as are the Life of my Spirit, I thus mourn'd and sang unto the Lord.

> O Glorious CHRIST of GOD; I live
> In Views of Thee alone.
> Life to my gasping Soul, oh! give!
> Shine Thou, or I'm undone.

> I cannot live, my GOD, if thou
> Enlivnest not my Faith.
> I'm dead; I'm lost; oh! Save me now
> from a lamented Death!

For the Return of my Health, I added.

> My glorious Healer, thou restore
> My Health, and make me whole.
> But this is what I most implore;
> Oh, for an Healed Soul! [1]

---

[1] A leaf has been torn from the record.

The Course of my Ministry.

16 *d.* 12 *m.* [*February.*] 1723-24. I preached, on 1. Cor. III. 23. Our Acknowledgments of the *Right* which our Saviour has unto us: after four Sermons, on *all Things* made ours through Him. (And I administred the Eucharist.)

20 *d.* 12 *m. Thursday.* The Lecture. On Jam. V. 8. Being præpared for the *Coming of the Lord*, in unknown *Events* and *Changes*, as well as in the Approach of Death.

23 *d.* 12 *m.* On Prov. XI. 23. The *good Desires* of the Righteous.

1 *d.* 1 *m.* [*March.*] 1724. On 2. Chron. XX. 12. Our *Eyes unto the Lord*, for the Releef of the Distresses, wherein we *know not what to do.*

8 *d.* 1 *m.* On Mic. VI. 8. A glorious CHRIST, the *good One.* (Intending a Course of Sermons, on that Epitome of the Bible.)

15 *d.* 1 *m.* On Mic. VI. 8. *Piety*, in all the Exercises of it, *good* for us.

22 *d.* 1 *m.* On Prov. XV. 8. The *Sacrifice of the Wicked.* (Præparatory unto a general Day of Prayer, to be this Week attended.)

26 *d.* 1 *m. Thursday.* A general Fast. On Exod. XVII. 11. A Continuance in *Prayer* and *Faith* (uplifted Hands,) on the Behalf of the Church in the Distresses of it.

29 *d.* 1 *m.* On Mic. VI. 8. The Doing of *Justice.*

5 *d.* 2 *m.* On Mic. VI. 8. The Loving of *Mercy.*

12 *d.* 2 *m.* [*April.*] On Joh. XIV. 20. The *Union* between our Saviour and His People. (And I administred the Eucharist.)

16 *d.* 2 *m. Thursday.* The Lecture. On Deut. XXXIII. 7. The *Blessing* which a People enjoy when their *Hands* are made *sufficient* for their Support in the Service of GOD: adding a Warning to our People against the needless and foolish Expences, which plunge us into Insufficiencies.

19 *d.* 2 *m.* At Roxbury. On Rom. VIII. 16. The *Testimony* of the holy SPIRIT, unto our Adoption. (Both Parts of the Day.)

26 *d.* 2 *m.* On Hos. XIII. 9. The *self-Destruction*, which they that walk in the Ways of Sin, may be charged with. (On the Occasion of several noted Persons lately laying violent Hands on themselves.)

3 *d.* 3 *m.* [*May.*] On Mic. VI. 8. *Walking humbly* with our GOD. (My fifth and last Sermon, on the *whole Duty of Man*, according to the Gospel of *Micah.*)

10 *d.* 3 *m.* On Psal. CXIX. 104. *Hating every false Way.* (On

the Spectacle, which we have, in what the *false Ways* of our Pyrates have brought them to.)

17 *d*. 3 *m*.   On Job. XXVII. 8.   *Hypocrites*, who are they, and what the Hopes and the Gains they may arrive unto, and what comes of them at the Last.

24 *d*. 3 *m*.   On Job. XXVII. 8. (A second time.)

31 *d*. 3 *m*.   On Jer. XXXI. 18.   A *Pœnitent* *bemoaning* himself, and praying for his own Conversion. (At the Desire, and in the Hearing, of two Pyrates that are to dy two Days hence.   To a great Assembly, and with a great Assistence.)

7 *d*. 4 *m*. [*June*.]   On Gal. II. 20.   How to obtain and enjoy the Blessedness, of living to GOD, thro' a CHRIST living in us. (And I administred the Eucharist.)

11 *d*. 4 *m*. *Thursday*.   The Lecture.   On Num. XII. 9.   The Tokens of GODS departing from a sinful People, and the Methods of preventing it.   The General Assembly sitting.

14 *d*. 4 *m*.   On Job. XXVII. 8.   (The third and last time.)

21 *d*. 4 *m*.   On Act. IX. 6.   A Soul returning to GOD, with a changed Heart, willing to *know*, and willing to *do*, the whole Will of GOD.

28 *d*. 4 *m*.   On 1. Sam. XVI. 23.   How the *Harp of David* is to be employ'd, for the driving away the *evil Spirit!*

5 *d*. 5 *m*. [*July*.]   On Isa. LXIII. 10.   The Evil of *provoking* the holy SPIRIT of GOD.

12 *d*. 5 *m*.   On Luk. XIX. 9.   *Salvation* come to the *House* and *Soul*, and with the Tenders of the Gospel.

19 *d*. 5 *m*.   On Rom. XVI. 7.   What it is to be in CHRIST, and what are the Marks of them that are so.

23 *d*. 5 *m*. *Thursday*.   A Fast kept by the Inhabitants of *Boston*, on account of the War and the Drought.   On Job. V. 6.   Our Concern with the glorious GOD in all our afflictive Troubles.

26 *d*. V *m*.   On Phil. IV. 19.   A glorious CHRIST having a rich Supply for all our Wants, in His glorious Riches.

2 *d*. VI *m*. [*August*.]   On 1. Cor. I. 9.   *Communion* with the Son of GOD.   (And I administred the Eucharist.)

6 *d*. VI *m*. *Thursday*.   The Lecture.   On Isa. LXIV. 7.   *Religion in earnest*.   The sad Proofs, that there is little of it.

9 *d*. VI *m*.   On Eph. V. 14.   The Call to *arise from the Dead*, and the *Light* which a glorious CHRIST will give to them who do so.

15 *d*. VI *m*.   On Prov. XXX. 8.   *Temporal Blessings* to be asked of GOD.   And Contentment with a *convenient Allowance* of them.

23 *d*. VI *m*. On 1. Sam. XXV. 29. On a *Soul*, bound up in *the Bundle of Life*.

30 *d*. VI *m*. On Psal. CXIX. 147. *Early Piety*. One lively Essay more, for the Animating of it. (Awakened by the Death of my Son *Increase*. And now, in the first Place, addressed unto the Assembly of the *New North* [Church], unto which there is a great Resort of young People, from several Parts of the Town, and particularly from that which has formerly satt under my Ministry.)

6 *d*. VII *m*. [*September*.] On Psal. CXIX. 147. Giving to my own Flock the same (with some other) Things, that I gave the last Lord's-day unto another.

10 *d*. VII *m*. *Thursday*. The Lecture. On Psal. LVI. 3. *Fear* cured by *Faith* at the Time when we apprehend ourselves in the most fearful Circumstances.

13 *d*. VII *m*. On Matth. XXIII. 37. Our SAVIOUR *willing* to gather our Souls under His Wings; and People perishing because they are not *willing* that He should save them.

20 *d*. VII *m*. On Matth. XXIII. 37. Finishing what I began the last Lords-day.

27 *d*. VII *m*. On Rev. I. 12. A Church answering the Character of a *golden Candlestick*. (And I administred the Eucharist.)

1 *d*. VIII *m*. [*October*.] *Thursday*. (The Lecture.) On Prov. XI. 11. Good Men great Blessings to the People, whom God bestows them on. (A funeral-Sermon for Governour *Saltonstal*.)

4 *d*. VIII *m*. On Job. III. 25. A wise Expectation of and Præparation for, troublesome *Changes*, to befall us. (Occasioned by the Death of my Son *Increase*.)

11 *d*. VIII *m*. On Eccl. XI. 8. *Remembering the many Days of Darkness*. (With a Relation of the marvellous Triumphs over Death, in a Child of this Neighbourhood.)

18 *d*. VIII *m*. On Isa. XLVIII. 10. *Chosen in the Furnace of Affliction*. (Occasion'd by the grievous Trials, wherewith some are exercised.)

25 *d*. VIII *m*. On Rev. I. 13. The *special Presence* of the glorious Lord, in midst of *golden Churches*.

1 *d*. IX *m*. [*November*.] On Jer. XXIII. 29. The *Word* of God an *Hammer* that *breaks the Rock to Peeces*. Employing some singular Strokes of the *Hammer*, on certain particular Occasions.

5 *d*. IX *m*. A Day of public Thanksgiving. On Col. I. 3. The Methods of *Thanksgiving*. Particularly of keeping a *Day of Thanksgiving*.

8 *d.* IX *m.* On Rev. XXII. 17. The *Water of Life* offered *freely;* and, how the Offer is to be received.

15 *d.* IX *m.* On Rev. XXII. 17. A second time.

22 *d.* IX *m.* On Rev. XXII. 17. A third Time. (And I administred the Eucharist.)

3 *d.* XI *m.* [*January*, 1724–25.] After the longest Confinement by Illness, that I ever had in my Life, I this Day returned unto the Flock of God; whom I treat with a Sermon, on Phil. I. 21. CHRIST, the *Life* of the true Christian.

10 *d.* XI *m.* On Phil. I, 21. (A second time.)

17 *d.* XI *m.* On Phil. I. 21. (A third Time.) And I administred the Eucharist.

21 *d.* XI *m.* The Lecture. On Joh. XII. 26. The Honours which God bestows on the Servants of our SAVIOUR. (A funeral-Sermon for my Nephew.[1])

24 *d.* XI *m.* On Phil. I. 21. (A fourth time.) Finishing my Sermons upon it.[2]

ADVERTISEMENT. A.A.S.

To Confute a Vile Calumny, which I am told, is cast upon me, That I directed or advised, or some Way Encouraged the unhappy *Daniel Willards* Creditors to arrest or trouble him, it might be Enough to say, that such will appear the Nonsense and Folly of the Calumny, to every one, who considers my circumstances relating to him that it must confute itself; None but an Idiot (or such as take me for one) can believe it. But I further declare That there is not the Least Syllable or Shadow of Truth in it. Nor has he any one Creditor in the world, that ever would offer or whisper, the Least Intimation of such a Thing. I have done that poor Man Good and not Hurt, all the Days of his Life; and as he knows I never yett spoke one Angry Word, so I have never done one Hurtful Thing to him since he was born. And until just now I remember not that I ever knew who so much as any two of his Creditors were; besides myself, who am, I suppose, by far the greatest Creditor he has, but have never to this Hour made any Demands on him, or done any thing for my own Security. I know not how well to express myself in stronger Terms. But such Abuses as these, are no more than what I am daily treated with. May Patience have its perfect work on all such occasions.

C. M.

Feb. 28, 1723/4.

[1] Rev. Thomas Walter.
[2] Here ends the Diary of Cotton Mather, so far as it has been preserved.

To John Dean. A.A.S.

Sir, — Your pious Desire, to have a Sermon preached on the Eleventh of December (Last) was what I had the fullest Resolution and Expectation to have answered, according to my first understanding of it; and accordingly I præpared a Sermon, for a Commemoration of your never-to-be-forgotten Affliction and Salvation.

My purpose was to have assembled a good number of pious Gentlemen, at either Dr. *Boylstons*, or my own Capacious Hall, and there to have spent an agreeable portion of Time, in proper Devotions, especially giving Thanks and making Prayers, on your behalf, accompanied with the sermon; which I proposed then to have printed with the story of your affair, as I did the like Ten years ago.

As for the price of a Sermon, I know none Established in this Countrey. Much less would I have Look'd for any pecuniary Acknowledgment of Mine; who have preached so many hundreds of sermons, without any Temporal Requitals. Only if something has been advanced for the Charge of the Impression I might have allow'd of That.

But when our worthy and Hearty Friend, Mr. *Borland*, arrived unto us, he told us, he thought my proposal, did not in all points quite answer yours. He thought, that you suppos'd the Bells might be rung, and a promiscuous congregation come together on this Occasion, in one of our public Churches; as it might be done in *England*. Upon this View, it was considered, That such a practice being altogether unusual in our City, it might meet with some Inconvenient Misconstructions. And the Religion of this Countrey also not Encouraging the Anniversary celebration of any Stated and Certain Days, any thing that Look'd that way openly done might be misinterpreted. So we agreed, the dropping of the matter at this time, and not proceeding until we receive your further Directions after the True State of the Case, as it is now represented, has been considered with you.

In the mean time, I bless the Glorious Lord-Redeemer, that He continues in you a grateful sense of His Favours; which doubtless you also Endeavour to Express with perseverance in all the Steps of a Godly, and sober, and Righteous Life; And may the final Issue of all be, a Rescue from the worst of Ship-wrecks, and a share in the plentious and Eternal Redemption, which will bring the People of GOD unto the full Enjoyment of Him. With such wishes, I am, Sir, Your hearty Friend and servt.

Mar. 31. 1724.

To Thomas Prince.   M.H.S.

SIR, — Tis, I confess, a weakness in me, to communicate unto you, the enclosed Papers; For, to be free with you, the Ministers of this Town appear to me, the *most unbrotherly and unsocial Tribe* of their Profession, that I beleeve, is in the whole World.

But I do it, because, I have some Apprehension, that I must within a few Days, or Weeks, take a Step, which much more than all *New England* will ring of, and I am willing to distinguish *you* from the rest, with giving you some Satisfaction aforehand about the Circumstances leading to it.

I have nothing under Heaven to ask of you, but your Prayers: and your prayers for nothing but this, *that I may be strengthened with all might, according to the glorious Power of CHRIST, unto all Patience and Long-suffering with Joyfulness.* And, if you think fitt, some Advice to my Son, if he find occasion to ask it.

I will send *Ezer*, and in the Evening, for the Return of these papers, and of *Gog* and *Magog*.

(Only that about, THE STATE OF RELIGION, which you may keep a few Days; and which you *may* (tho' I beleeve, you *will not*,) Shew to Judge *Sewal*, and Col. *Fitch*, but if you do, yett leave it not in their Hands.)

I wish you and yours, all the Blessings of Goodness; and a Condition very much the Reverse of what is ordered for, Sir, Your Brother and Servant

Co. MATHER.

Apr. 1. 1724.

To Lieut. Governor William Dummer.   A.A.S.

SYR, — My Disobedience to the Command which your Goodness laid upon me, the last Thursday requires a Just Apology; and yett it will require the mention of such unmentionable Things, that even that may render another Apology necessary.

An Indisposition then upon me unfitted me for the payment of my Duty. But Concomitant with it, I laboured under several Discouragements.

I need not say, that I apprehended my well-known Circumstances of prosecution to restore what I took not away, rendred it a Disgrace unto such a Table, as well as unto any Pulpitt, for me to make my Appearance there. These perhaps are since a little altered.

But I must confess also, that I have thought myself directed by the Government, (for the serving whereof I have exposed myself to sufferings much beyond any man in the Countrey,) to look upon it as a peece of proper Modesty, to be as little as possible in their presence, ever since they did above a year ago, with sufficient Expressions of Displeasure, silence my pen, and forbid the printing of any more about, the State of Religion. I was accordingly to the best of my Capacity, with a Better, Endeavouring to do comprehensive service for the Countrey and Religion, and surely if I had not been reckoned a person worthy of the greatest Contempt, I had been by some one or other of the Council spoken with, before the Countrey (who much Expected the Continuation of their Satisfaction) had been made sensible that the Government was offended at me, as publisher of dangerous Libels. Being thus treated as an offendor, I have I hope with all decent Patience commanded a Silence to my speech aequal to that which my Superiours commanded for my pen: but I have with a modest Recess, for now a twelve month, retired from the old Familiarities of the Table, as well as other Freedoms, which I had been once used unto: It appearing to me always rude for an Offendor to do otherwise.

The Suspicion of an Aversion in the Government more for me than for other Men, was very much strengthened, and confirmed; When the offence taken at me was for a Quotation of a passage, which was but a Complaint of a vile party in the Ch. of E. which complaint is made continually by an Army of the most famous Divines in the Established Church. And yett, in the same News-Letter, under the Title of, [*published by Authority*,] there is an Allowance for whole pages of the bitterest Invectives against that *Potent and Swaying party* of the Ch. of E. as Monsters of Impiety, and representing the Four *Stuarts* on the Throne, as prodigies of Weakness and Baseness and Perfidy; and the Late Queen, as the Favourite of High-Church but Leaving the World, under the blackest Infamy. And all this from a paper well-known to be highly offensive unto the King and present Ministry.[1]

To be disheartened into a peaceable Withdraw as far as may be, from all public Exhibitions when I see myself under such (I would not presume to say undeserved) Marks of Dislike from those to whom I ought always to pay all due Deference, may be smiled at as Vapour; yett this Vapour will appear to be Reason unto one under the power

[1] Probably refers to the letter signed "Cato," which, copied from an English source, occupied more than three pages of the *Boston News-Letter*, March 12, 1723-24.

of it; having at the same time a thousand other more heavy Loads upon him.

There is yett another Thing, wherein I should reconcile myself unto your Honour, before I can have the courage to do as I have used heretofore to do.

A man for whom Honour is not seemly, has been so Gentlemanly as to show here and there a Letter with which your Invaluable Brother had obliged me. Now, tho' I would much sooner have died, than have been guilty of so vile an Action, as to betray a Friend, and to his Enemies what 'he writes unto me; yett this Disaster befalling me, has entirely and eternally shutt me out of his Friendship; and your Honour may well judge, you have cause to shutt me out of your Favour also. Now, I can give no Account of the Disaster but this. The Villains, I mean, especially THREE, have certainly Employ'd one of their Brethren, to do an abominable Thing. One of their Tools, riffled Mr *Penhallows* closett, and convey'd unto them from thence, a Letter of Mine to him, which gave to four, their true Character, But so meanly was I then deserted, by those who ow'd me more Protection that I was drawn into the Iniquity of asking their Pardon. And I must now say, my Study has been knavishly, and c-kishly riffled. But about the same time, that this Letter of him that was once my Friend, was in this rascally manner siezed upon, I had six pounds of Money also stolen; which was enough to bear the Expence of several Tankards. If they would please to tell, how they gott the Letter into their hands, tis possible I might guess how my Bills of Credit were disposed of. This is my Case. And tho' the person more immediately injured accepts not my Vindication, yett, it may be, his Honourable Brother, may upon a calm view, think me rather unhappy than culpable, and use a Lenity in the Censures to which I am obnoxious.

I have now declared some of my Discouragements, under which yett I hope, neither your Honour nor the Board, will ever find me any other than an easy, honest, well-meaning Man; one who will not, cannot strike? one who will forever study to be quiet, and lead a peaceable Life under your aequal Government; and one who at the worst, will study to make no other than an Humble, and a Decent use of all the Frowns he meets withal; And now, if after this, your Honour have any further Commands to lay upon me, you shall never find me fail of due obedience.

The publication of my PARENTATOR, having mett with no Interruption, I take leave to present it unto your Honour, especially for the sake of the Charter-Story in it; and I do it with earnest Prayer that you may long enjoy your Opportunities to do good with the Divine Assistance and Acceptance, in the singular Enjoyment whereof you make us an happy people; subscribing, Your Honours, Most obedient serv't.

Apr. 4, 1724.

To Lieut. Governor John Wentworth. A.A.S.

Sir, — It is with more than a little Concern of Mind, that we behold so considerable a Flock as yours at *Portsmouth*, so much in the uncomfortable Condition of Sheep without a Shepard; and your prudent and Faithful Agents meeting with no better Success of their Indefatigable Endeavours to obtain a Supply for you. We are Sensible, that so Conspicuous and Important a Station as that in *Portsmouth* ought to be filled with a Person of Rich and Bright and uncommon Abilities. If one in whom you can generally unite as being such an One do not immediately appear, the Holy and Humbling Providence of the Great God therein is to be adored. But it is a Blessing worth some waiting for; and we are not without Hopes, that a God who waits that He may be Gracious, may bestow it upon you, when you shall be more prepared for it. It may be, the Glorious Head of the Church Expects to be, with yett a more particular Solemnity and Importunity sought unto; that He may be duely Acknowledged in such a Gift of His unto you. There are several very Hopeful Candidates of the Ministry, which we are told may be in a very Little Time *shown unto Israel* and when the methods of prayer and Patience have been a Little further persisted in, He that once opened the Eyes of one in a wilderness to see an unexpected provision made for her, may show you where the Waters of Life may be ready for you. While the present Necessity obliges you to the Trial of a Little waiting, we cannot but earnestly recommend it unto you, as what will be a Token for Good; That you do not fall out by the way, for you are Brethren. Divisions and Contentions among your Good people, and Especially if they proceed so far as to threaten any Interruption of the pure and undefiled Religion, in which you have hitherto flourished, will not at all Mend your Circumstances, but give an opportunity for the Devices of Our Great Adversary to do unknown and Endless Mischiefs among you. Your Beauty and Safety will be in your adherence to Those Golden Maxims of the Gospel, Be kindly affected one to another, with Brotherly Love, in Honour preferring one another; And, Lett us follow the things which make for peace, and things wherewith one may Edify another. And we are well assured, that your Honour, will Employ the wisdome and the Temper and the power, with which our Good GOD has furnished you, to preserve as much as may be, an unity of spirit in the Bond of Peace, among a people, who are made happy by your Influences.

With hearty supplications That our glorious Lord would confer a Man of understanding and a Pastor after His own Heart upon His Destitute people with you; and therewithal Assist and Accept you in the whole Administration of your Government, we subscribe, Your Honours, Most sincere and faithful servts.
Apr. 11. [1724?]

To Thomas Bradbury.[1]   A.A.S.

Sir, — It is my Duty to glorify GOD in you; and I do it, giving Thanks to Him for the services which He Enables you to do for His Kingdome and Interest in the World.

The Last Essay of that Intention, wherewith you favored me, requires very particular Expressions of my Gratitude.

I wish my Parentator, which I now present unto your Acceptance, may among them find, with you, at Least, what the Law Calls, an Acceptilation.

I have no Expectation that any thing performed by my Mean Hand, should find any great Reception on your side of the Water.

Especially since the prodigious Depravation of Gust among you, which renders every thing unpalatable, but what shall have Qualities, which I will never be Reconcil'd unto.

I wish a passage in the two hundred and first page may have a due operation among our Brethren; But this is more than what I can Look for.

It is an Insupportable Grief unto us, that so many of our Brethren should so openly declare, that they Look not on the Faith of our SAVIOUR and Eternal Godhead, as Essential to Christianity and salvation; and that they can receive to the Regards of Brethren in Christ, those Idolaters who acknowledge no CHRIST but one that is infinitely Inferiour and Posterior to the Eternal Father. We behold it, and are grieved, That your pretended Irenicums do purposely and perpetually Leave out the Faith of our Lords Eternal Deity, when they pretend unto an Enumeration of our Fundamental Articles. Tho' they themselves are not gone over to the *Arian* Infidelity, yett by these perfidious pretensions and overtures for Peace,

---

[1] See *Dictionary of National Biography*, VI. 150.

they take a fearful step towards the Sacrificing of the most Glorious Truth, and the Delivery up of the Holy City into the hands of Infidels. We are afraid, we are afraid, lest our Brethren hereby procure to themselves a sad share in the Consuming Blows, which I cannot but again and again tell you, are hastening on a sinful Nation, a people Laden with Iniquity.

In some few parts of this Countrey, especially where piety is very much decay'd, there have appear'd Little Parcels of Ignorant, Vicious Contemptible people declaring for the Ch. of E. Which yett, as Litigious and Scandalous a Crue as they commonly are, they would never do, if they had not the Hopes of being Excused from all the Charge of Maintaining any Ministry, by having parsons maintained for them, from the stock of your Society *pro propaganda Fide,* Than which there never was more shamefully misapplied and prostituted Charity in the world.

It would amaze you to hear of the Occasions on which the Ch. of E. is here declared for. But I will mention One, which a Little belongs to a Point, about which you once enquired of me.

[A mighty Spirit, as in the Letter to Hollis.] [1]

Very Lately, a Little Crue at a Town Ten miles from the City of Boston, were so sett upon their old Howling in the public Psalmody, that being rebuked for the Disturbance they made, by the more Numerous Regular Singers, they declared They would be for the Ch. of E. and would form a Little Assembly for that purpose, and subscribed for the Building of a Chapel; and expect a Missionary to be sent and supported from your Society (aforesaid) for the Encouragement of half a score such Ridiculous Proselytes. But we suppose, it will come to nothing.

Our Late Apostates, make no hand on't. And Cutler [2] for whom they have built a New Church in Boston, has by high Flights rendred himself so odious unto the Body of our People, and rendred the more temperate and moderate part of his own Congregation so disaffected unto him, that he has no very Encouraging Auditory; and his Arrival here, is as much a Disservice to the Ch: of E. as almost anything that could have happened. The vile High-flying Leslaean [3] pamphletts they disperse among us, meet with such victorious Answers as tend greatly to the Establishment of our Churches.

---

[1] There is no such passage in the draft of the letter to Thomas Hollis.

[2] Timothy Cutler, who served the North Episcopal "Christ Church" from its foundation in 1723 to his death, in 1765.

[3] Charles Leslie.

My Invaluable Friend, Mr Reinolds, in a short letter some while ago, seem'd upon dismissing me from all Expectation of his taking any further Notice of me (as for some years before indeed, he took very Little,) because of his having his time so much taken up in his controversy with Mr. *Brown*.[1] I wonder a person of so bright Abilities can think such a Controversy a thing, in which the spending of much Time should be necessary. I pray, when you see him, give my service to him, and inform him, That his Adversaries pamphlett has here done him no manner of Damage; but been Entertain'd with greater Expressions of Dislike and Contempt than one would care to mention; and the Author censured and condemned as one of a very unchristian spirit, and uncivil Conduct. I would not that my Brother *Reinolds* should have one uneasy Thought about him. I have now done for him this time.

Apr. 22, 1724.

To Colonel Winslow and His Consort.[2]   A.A.S.

My honoured Friends, — In the General Condolence wth you, upon the Sorrow which you have Lately mett withal, I take a very particular Share; and think it my Duty to give you some few Expressions of it.

But, how can I better Express it than in my Earnest Supplications which I therefore make to the Glorious Lord, that He would Enable you to Glorify Him in the Sacrifice which He now calls you to?

If not a Bird of the Air falls to the Earth without the Will of our Heavenly Father, you may be sure, that the Child hatch'd under your tender Wing, is not fallen, without the Will of Heaven ordering it. And you cannot have a better proof that you are the Children of God, than by your patient submission to His Will on such an Occasion; and your submissive saying, *The Cup which my Father has given me, shall not I drink it?* The Cup which is now given you indeed is Bitter Enough. But if the Sense of the Hand which it comes from and of the End which His Wisdome and Goodness has in giving it, quiets you, His Comfortable Voice unto you is; *I will be a Father to you.* And being thus His Children, you have a Better Name, than what the Son and the Daughter He has obliged you to part withal, could have help'd you to.

It is a Great Sacrifice that you are now putt upon. But you will

---

[1] Simon Browne.   [2] See p. 735*n*, *supra*.

approve yourselves the Genuine Children of *Abraham*: and so prove your claim to the Blessings of His Covenant. [Illegible] the Reluctancies of nature to it. Withold not the child whom you have Loved, when God calls you to offer it up. So it shall be said, *Now I know, that thou fearest God*. And verily, There is more solid comfort in this Assurance, than there can be in the Enjoyment of any Child, whereof you might say, This same shall comfort us. Your Blessedness in the world to come, will be in an Holy Priesthood. And that you may be in this world Initiated for it, Your SAVIOUR will now have you to be Holy Sacrificers. You will be notably such, when upon the Death of Lovely and Hopeful Children, you *hold your peace*, and only say, *The will of the Lord be done*, and beg of Him that the Influences of His Grace may Effectually subdue, all the Rebellion of yours against it.

A Trial, yea, an Exquisite one is now made; Whether there be any thing Which at the plain call of God, you cannot Resign unto Him? Or, whether you will not now seek, and hope to find, that satisfaction in having a Glorious CHRIST Concerned for you, and conversing with you, which we Expect in Vain from the Creatures, which forever are found no better than Lying Vanities. If being thus tried, you come forth as Gold, and approve yourselves noble Sacrificers, it will [be] an Infallible Token for Good, that you have a part in the Grand Sacrifice which your SAVIOUR has offered for His people; and shall have a part, among those, whom the Blood of the Lamb will bring to walk in white Robes, and serve Him in His Temple.

Most certainly, If the Repeted Strokes of Mortality upon your Family, be of use unto you; To bring sin unto Remembrance, and carry on Repentance to its Perfect work; To animate your prayers, and your cares that you may be perfect and Entire in your Essay to conform unto the whole will of GOD:

To wean you from a World, wherein you see an End of all Perfection: and make you seek the Things that are Above;

To Quicken your Thorough praeparation for your own Death, which the Death of such Relatives, does Loudly admonish you to be daily Looking for; These Blessings will be a Rich and a Full Compensation for the Loss of what have been taken from you. True PIETY will dispose you to count them so. Death in such a way brings the truest Life with it; yea, what is better than Life. And Light will arise unto you in the Darkness, which Death has brought upon your Tabernacle.

But, there is the less Need of my Expatiating unto you upon these

Consolations of God, since you have an Excellent Pastor, who has you under his Continual Cultivations, and Loves you Exceedingly, and has the Tongue of the Learned, able to speak a word in season to you; And from him you will continually hear those Good Words, which, I hope, will make your Hearts Glad, when they are stouping with Heaviness.

I here Enclose a small Addition to them, as a sign of the Affection, with which I am, Your cordial, constant, sympathizing Friend. July 1. 1724.

To Thomas Bradbury.   A.A.S.

SIR, — So Lately have I written to you; (with a present of my PARENTATOR,) that I thought I had Little more to write, but an Acknowledgment of the Satisfaction I have this Day received in the Letters of last *April*, with which I have been favoured.

My more particular Sentiments, about the Two Gentlemen-Brothers (I wish I could say, on all accounts, Gentlemen,) whose odd usages of me, have made me to·be (as all their Friends here seem now to be) Ashamed of my Hope, concerning them; As also my Sentiments of that violent Man, their Antagonist, now with you.[1] I make my Neighbour *Dennis* Master of them; and he shall Entertain you with them.

When I thought, I had nothing else to write about, I was immediately by a Letter from another, Led into an affair with you, of as great Importance with me, as most that can be mentioned.

A Composure, which not I, but the Grace of God with me, prepared for the public some years ago, Entituled, BOANERGES, or, *The work of the Day*, I am told, is Lodged with you. My Heart rejoiced, when I understood This; and I was ready to use the word, which an Army of Good Men Engaged in a Good Cause once began a Battel with, *Now for the Fruit of Prayer!* Many a prayer (not without an agreeable Resignation) has been made unto the Glorious Lord, That He would Employ His Good Angel, to make to be heard the Voice of His word, in that *Boanerges*. And now think I, My Bradbury, who has already Laid me under vast obligations, by bringing my *Christian Philosopher*, to serve the Great End of my Life, is to do the part of the Good Angel again on this occasion.

I am sure, that he is of my Catholic Principles; and that he will be particularly pleased, with the Care which I perpetually take, under them, to shutt out all *Arians*, and their Brethren, from any Share in

[1] May refer to the Dummers.

the Union of Good Men upon the Basis of Goodness, and the Maxims of the Everlasting Gospel.

Syr, If this Treatise may by your Means be brought into the world, you will soon find, thousands of Good Men, who will tell you, that a greater service to the Church of. God could not easily be thought of. I pray you, I beg you, I do with the greatest Importunity, besech you to favour it.

I Entirely Committ the Work into your Hands. I give you full power, to omitt; or Alter, any passage in it, as you shall in your wisdome, (to which I always pay all possible Deference) Judge Convenient. You will also see, (as you did in your former Kindness) that the press-work be well corrected.

For a further Animation of the Work, you may, if you think it necessary; assure your Bookseller, That if he will risque as many of the Books as may be allow'd for Ten Pounds in our Money, I shall (if Living) upon the Receit thereof pay that sum unto his order. But the Book will certainly sell.

I now add no more, but pray your Acceptance of Two Little Things, for the offer whereof (such Little Things!) I can make no Apology, but This; That they are just now published.

May the Glorious Lord, be with you in all your unfainting Labours for His Name, and for His Sons Name. *Stand*, O Bradbury, as αἴσιμος τύπτομαι

I am, In the Faith and Patience of the Kingdome, Your Brother and hearty Servt.

July 13, 1724.

To Isaac Greenwood.   A.A.S.

My dear Child, — It is as Cool Waters unto a Thirsty Soul, that I hear what I do, of you and from you. But it is above all, a singular satisfaction unto me, to understand, that in the Midst of the Pleasant Studies, which do at an uncommon rate accomplish you, you still retain your Disposition to serve your Glorious End, in the work of the Evangelical Ministry. It is most certain, that notwithstanding the many Discouragements and Humiliations, which that work may be attended withal, tis the best that a short life can be devoted to; and the Consequences if it be very well allowed will be of all the most comfortable in the Day that is daily to be Looked for. I hope, you will be a grateful Spectacle to Heaven in it; and that the Field of your Actions, will be your own Countrey; which tho' it be not in all points what you would have it, yett all things con-

sidered, the only Better Countrey to be desired, is the Heavenly
The Sooner you Return to us, the Better; for that which is mor
Precious than Money, spends apace; and we Long to be reaping th
Fruits of your Excellent and Exemplary Industry.

Whatever Lies within my Reach, to promote your Acceptanc
and usefulness among us, you may depend upon. And if somethin
should happen that some foretel, and many desire, but I don't car
to mention, you may be sure, I shall consider you as my son, an
appear with more zeal to gett your proposals answered, than if yo
were by Nature so. But, Child, you know, tis Early Days in ou
Little Countrey; and meritt is very Little regarded here; and th
most useful Erudition is not what we are fondest of. Tho' the Col
ledge has a Revenue, to Encourage the Profession of the Mathe
matical Sciences; yett I durst not promise, that a Sufficient Numbe
of Scholars will shew themselves whose payment of a proper premiun
joined unto That, will be a Suitable Subsistence for a Professor o
That, and of Experimental Philosophy; or not be content with wha
their ordinary Tutors may do for them. So that, if you cannot return
to us, with a Mind Aequilibrious on that point, I am so much unde
the Power of the *Hypo*, as to say, Then Lett the Scale turn for a
Dismission of that Expectation and of the great Expence that must
accompany it. But, Return, Return, O Novanglian, Return, Return.

And yett, oh! That before That, you may be the Happy Instrument, of bringing our *Boanerges* into Operation. If I could think
it possible, to do a more serviceable or a more seasonable thing for
the Church of God, I would not ask it with so much Importunity.
But I do ask it with the greatest Importunity. And for a Little Animation of the Design, which I have my Heart more than a Little
sett upon, I now add, that if you or the Bookseller do risque so many
of the Books hither, as at a just price will fetch Ten pounds of our
Money, your Order for it, at the Receit thereof, shall be answered.

At this time I add no more; But my Earnest Supplications,
that the glorious Lord would furnish you for and employ you in, good
work about the House of your GOD: and safely and quickly return
you to, Your cordial and constant Friend.
July, 16, 1724.

To Gurdon Saltonstal. A.A.S.

Syr, — The Reason of your Suffering so seldome the Trouble of
my Letters has been my Apprehension of your Honours being supplied from other hands with better and fuller Intelligence of every

thing worthy of your Enquiry; and my sense of the many ponderous Affaires, which take up your precious Time, *quum tot sustineas*, wherein to Divert you, may be to Injure many others. To which I may add, That it were a crime to break in upon your Honour, while you are perusing your *Burnettian* History, which be sure, you can not Leave off, when you have begun to read it.[1] My own Little Experience tells me, That Correspondences with Persons of Consideration, make an Article of so much Figure in the Business of Life, that if Discretion do not, yett Necessity will, bring it under Limitations. And lett this also be admitted as an Apology, for one [of] my Dull Capacity, when your Honour may otherwise interpret my Silence, as a peace of Disrespect or Negligence.

But, it is a great Satisfaction unto me to have a fair pretence for the writing of more Letters unto a person for whom I have so high an Esteem, in the occasion which I have in those wherewith you have Lately honour'd me. I gladly take the opportunity to Render Thanks from all the United Ministers of the City, with my own, to your Honour, for the Goodness and Candour with which you have Encouraged a Collection for the Meeting-house at *Providence*. May it be recompensed in the Blessings of that glorious One, who cast a Benign Aspect on him, who had from the people of GOD, that Recommendation; He *hath Loved our Nation and built us a Synagogue.*

As for the Money Collected, we pray That Mr *Adams*[2] may transmitt it unto Mr *Cotton*[3] of *Bristol*, who is the Chief Manager, and a very Generous One, of what is now doing for the House of God at *Providence;* and who will so apply the Money as will doubtless be to the content of the proper persons to whom he will anon give an Account of the Stewardship.

Having so briefly dispatched that Point I pass into the Dispositions of a further and more than a Little Satisfaction, in the place assigned unto your Honour at the Board of the Commissioners for the Gospellizing of our Indians; and the Hope it gives me, that it will not only procure something more Effectual than what has yett been done for your *Monhegins*, but also inspire a New Vigour into all our Motions.

I must confess, every thing has appeared under such a Languid Aspect with us, and I have seen so much, and so Little, that I did half a year ago, address for a Release from any further obligations to the Business. But if your Honour will please to be one of the

---

[1] The first volume of Burnet's *History of his own Times* appeared in 1723.

[2] Eliphalet Adams.   [3] Nathaniel Cotton.

Number, it will so fetch me out of my Despondencies, that I shall be willing to return unto the Colours from whence I began a Desertion. For, tho' your Distance will not permitt us to Enjoy much of your presence at the Board, the Desires that your pen may convey to us, will generally have the Force of Commands, and I shall myself always think it my Duty, unto the best of my power, to prosecute them.

It is a Time of many Distresses and confusions with us; and God knowes what may be the Issue of them. Redeuntem Vix usquam videbimus. It is particularly Remarkable, That among the many Frowns of Providence upon us, we do not see it smiling on our Ch. of E. Adversaries. The Standard-bearer of it here, sinks under Epidemical Contempt and Hatred, and his Flock is become a Little sorry, Scandalous Drove, which have Little but Baseness and Impiety and Jacobism to distinguish them.[1]

As for the world in general; it is most certain that the second coming of our God and Saviour will be at, and for the Perdition of the Man of Sin; whose period of 1260 years is now finished. And it is as Little to be doubted, that the Flames wherein the Lord comes, will bring on the tremendous Conflagration, which is to precede the New Heavens and the New Earth wherein shall dwell Righteousness. Nor do we any where see any thing but the world fearfully Ripening for such a Revolution: And the Sleep of Midnight growing into the deepest Lethargy, among the professors of our Holy Religion; which has now in a manner every where almost given up the Ghost. Your Sagacious Wisdome, needs no Intimations of Mine, what is to be Look'd for.

May we be Ready for all Events.

I wish to your Honour, and your Lady the best of Blessings, and subscribe Your Honors, Most hearty serv't.
Aug. 3. 1724.

To Gurdon Saltonstal.   A.A.S.

Sir, — Much more than Thirty years ago, Leading an Infant by the hand, thro' a Room in a Grandfathers house at *Charlestown*, I was guilty of so much Impertinency, as to say unto a poor Mad Woman then in the Room, *Is not this a pretty Damsel?* The mad woman made me this wise, and sober and pungent Answer, *The Crow thinks so, Syr!* The Rebuke and Satyr so pleased me, that I gave her (what I could not now do) a *Splendid Shilling*, to reward her for

[1] Timothy Cutler.

so useful an Admonition; and I hope, it has been much more than a shillings worth, of use to me, unto this very Moment.

A Young Man,[1] who counts it well worth his Travel and Expence, to visit *New London*, only to come under Notice with your Honour, is also ambitious of Riding in your Guards to the Commencement at *New-haven*. His having spent so much Time not altogether unprofitably in the studies which he has follow'd so close, as to deserve a play-day, causes me to Countenance his proposal; But much more, the Benefit of Waiting on your Honour, which it will be impossible for him to do, without some Improvement. It is proper for me to give your Honour some Account of him; tho' how to do it, without incurring the Censure of, *The Crow thinks so*, is not very Easy. He has been unawares drawn two or three times, into public Performances: But tho' he has mett with Uncommon Acceptance, yett he resolves to stop, and not by any means appear frequently in public, till more months of Qualifying Study have passed over him. All I shall add, is, That I am told he is Esteemed for a Early Piety, for a manly Discretion, for some Erudition, and none of the worst Tempers; or, at Least, *The Crow thinks so*. He wishes, that he had been of a year or two Longer Standing; and then he would have humbly Supplicated, for Leave to have stood as a Candidate and Competent for a Degree, in a Colledge which his Father has been sometimes a Small Actor for; and where the Memory of his Ancestors would bespeak some Easy Terms for his Admission to so much Honour, tho' his Learning should not be aequal to that of many others. But it must be enough unto him, to be Admitted as a Spectator, among them who wish well to *Yale Colledge* and would lay hold on all opportunities to putt all possible Respects upon it. So I Leave *Ascanius* under your Honors favourable Patronage.

What remains, is, To rejoice with your Honour, in Governor Burnetts victorious Demonstrations, that the Man of Sins M.CC. LX. years are up.[2] Then, I am sure, High Church must go down apace;

---

[1] His son Samuel. See p. 759, *supra*.

[2] To this same subject another fragment of a letter to Governor Saltonstall relates:

"I look upon Colonel *Burnetts* Late *Essay on the Scripture Prophecies*, as the most penetrating, Judicious, Decisive Essay, that has ever yett-been made upon that noble Subject. He does not Expatiate into Copious and verbose Amplifications; but in a Concise way, wherein every word has its weight, he gives those Explications which carry Demonstrations with them. He has instructed us and obliged us with some Illustrations, which we never Enjoy'd before; but such as have in them an Evidence, which compels us to give a good Reception to them.

and our Apostates have taken a very wrong Time to run into a Fall ing House, and have shown Less Instinct than some other Animal famous for the Reverse of doing so.

May a Continual Smile of Heaven be upon your Person, and you Honourable Family, and your whole prudent, patient, self-Denying Administration. So prayes, Your Honours Most obedient Servt. Aug. 31, 1724.

To Mrs. Gurdon Saltonstal.[1]   A.A.S.

Madam, — All these Regions unite their Tears with yours. The Brightest Man that shone in those Regions has Left us. We mourn with you; and we mourn for you. Our Sorrows have a Tincture o Sympathy with yours; upon whom (as well as upon us,) the Breach is Like one of the Sea, which cannot be heal'd. Nothing but a Glori ous CHRIST, can make up your Loss; Tis your Happiness that you have Long been Acquainted with Him; Long been Espoused unto that glorious Lord.

What that Excellent person, who Led him to these Happy Studies (our Late Presi dent sir *Isaac Newton*,) has been to the world, in *Philosophy*, this must his Hon ourable Scholar now be in Prophecy; and be acknowledged as a Dictator; above all Contradiction. There is indeed no Little Proof of our being arrived unto the *Time of the End*, (and that he has calculated right) in our having *Daniel* so admi rably opened unto us.

"I know, you will study (in modest humble, prudent ways) to do Good, wher ever you come. Lett one of your Essays in your Journey be to command this late Performance, unto the serious Perusal of the Gentlemen where you come, and lett my Character of it be known, and how much it may be wished, that by Studies of the Prophecies wisely managed (which have been so Foolishly neglected, and so profanely derided,) we may be rescued from a share in the Epidemical Sleep, wherein the world is to be surprized by the Terrible Day of the Lord. The 1260 years being Certainly up, there are most certainly those Terrible Things to be every Day Expected, which I doubt, we are but poorly prepared for.

"I am sure, if the M.CC.LX. years be up, High-Church must go down. Accord ingly, I have two things to inform you of, and you may particularly Exhibit unto my Honoured Brethren, the Trustees of *Yale Colledge*, the Information which I now give you. That miserable Apostate Cutler, Experimentally finds the Frowns of our glorious Lord, upon his Apostasy. First, A Lady of High-Church whom you know, the Last week declared unto me, That she had been at *Cutlers Church*, and it was amazing to see, how few there, and what a sort of shabby people they were; and what a shame it was that such a man should be under such contempt among us. Others of the Auditory did this day Se'nnight, speak to the same Effect unto my worthy Collegue. Secondly; This Day Se'nnight, I read in Letters from *London*, that our *Cutlers* High Principles, were strangely going down the wind in the Ch: of E. and growing out of fashion."

[1] See p. 765, *supra*.

There are Two Duties which I now feel incumbent on me.

The one is, To address you, with what I take to be the most supporting Sentiments on the present Occasion. This I do, as well as I
can, in a small Treatise, in which the Title will presently inform you,
that it is, Your Now Names-sake spoken to.

The other is, To pay some Just Regards unto the Memory of my
Honourable Friend.

This I have done, in a Late Sermon; the Notes whereof I now
humbly offer you. They being my First Notes, which I could have
no Time to gett fairly transcribed, I doubt the Discourse is hardly
Legible. But you may yett Read in it, Something of my Apprehensions concerning the Excellent Character of the Departed. The
Hearers all said, There was not a Word too much; you and I shall
both of us think, Tis' all much too Little. But the Time would allow
no more; and I Endeavoured much in a Little. I am not so vain
as to think that it is worthy of the press; or that one so mean as I
am, can add any Lustre to so good and so great a Man. It will be
Honour Enough to it, that it be Lodg'd in your Scrutoir. But, if it
be your pleasure, that it should go abroad, instead of what may come
to you from a Better and a Nearer hand, your Neighbour *Green*,[1] is
used unto my Copies. But I should Earnestly desire my very valuable Brother Mr *Adams*,[2] to preface it with an agreeable *Dedication*
to the Lady, whose Merits ought to be acknowledged in Conjunction
with those of the Deceased.

May we yett for years Enjoy your presence with us; and may
the Comforter that will releeve your Soul never be far from you,
So prays, Madam, Your Disconsolate and almost Inconsolable Kinsman and Servt.

The very great Civilities which my Son has received from you,
madam, as well as from the dear Governor, will never be forgotten
with us.

To Lieut. Governor Dummer.   A.A.S.

Syr, — Inasmuch as the Good Providence of God has placed your
Honour, at the head of the Commission for the Affairs of the gospel
among our Indians, as well as the whole Government of this extended
province, I thought it my Duty to venture upon One Request more,
on the behalf of dying Religion among those miserable objects. And
in so doing I hope to have so done my Duty, that I may without

---

[1] Timothy Green, printer.   [2] Eliphalet Adams.

offence ask Leave to Retire in this point also, as I have thought I
have not wanted sufficient Intimations that it may be judged proper
for me to do, from all Interest whatsoever in any other matters o.
public Importance.

The work of Gospellizing the Aboriginal Natives of this Countrey
is one of *New Englands* peculiar Glories. That it Labours under
grievous Difficulties and Discouragements, is not at all to be wondred
at, considering what lies at the Bottom of all. But the Greater they
are, the stronger must be the Application of the Instruments to sur
mount them. The conduct of the Commissioners has many eyes
upon it; yea, Greater Eyes, than those of the Governour and company on the other side of the water.

To Retrieve what is wanting, and produce numberless Good
Effects, I could make an Humble Proposal to your Honour and the
Board; That the Commissioners find out a Man of Discretion, and
Probity, and Activity, and constitute him, *A Visitor of all the Indian
Villages.*

This *Visitor* may with an Exact Scrutiny, find out, what may be
found among the Indians that wants to be Redirected and Reformed
or better provided for. And He may by Enquiry of the most pru
dent and best affected among the *English*, Learn, what would be most
Advisable to be done for the *Indians*.

And He may Return from his Visitation, furnished with Proposals, which the Commissioners may without needless Retardation
under the Notion of writing and Waiting for further Informa
tions, (which may confound the best proposals, and has often
it may be, done so,) Immediately find ways and means to put
in Execution.

The Visitor may carry Instructions from the Commissioners, and
a copy of all the Articles, which his Enquiries are to proceed upon
The Visitation also may be renewed and repeated, as often as the
commissioners may judge Convenient. And if their Servant be well-
paid, the Money may be well-spent.

The Commissioners Once Employed such a Visitor and it was
one of the most useful Things that ever they did, and if his Report
had been acted upon, as it should have been, and not thrown by, it
had been followed with many very happy consequences.

I shall add no more. But only Entreat, That your Honour, would
please as soon as may be to procure needful meetings of the commissioners, and Lett the Languishing State of many things be Enquired into.

At Martha's Vineyard, for how many years has the settlement of the Lands been Left unaccomplished, where a Revenue of an 100 £ a year, might be as Easily brought in as 50 £ and things would be better, if such a person as Mr. *John Chipman*, may be added unto one of the Mayhews, powers to do what is hitherto neglected.

At *Punkapoag*, (where an honest Labourer in the work of Christianity among the Indians has had but Eight pounds, for the Labours of near twice Eight years,) Things are in a Condition, which calls for a more thorough Inspection.

I could mention many more, Occasions for somewhat more Vigour to be Exerted in the Proceedings of the Commissioners.

I would be Thankful for what opportunities I have sometimes had of being patiently and favourably heard speaking at the Honourable Board of the Commissioners; and would humbly move, That since by Mortality, or some Enfeebling Circumstance in the Approaches of it, there is now Left not so much as one Minister among the Commissioners, they would please to think on some Nomination for a Substitution to be commended to, and confirmed by the Governor and Company at home; And if a Minister or two should come into the Nomination, perhaps there might be some Advantage in it, as well as Decency for the Commissioners do not Look upon the Business of the Board, as if it were meerly or mainly to save money or manage a Discrete and Frugal Merchandise; but principally and perpetually to Invent and pursue the best Methods of serving the Interest of pure and undefiled Religion among the Indians.

May our glorious Lord, graciously direct and succeed the pious Essays of His Faithful Servants, to do the work of His Kingdome, which you are all most cordial and constant Friends unto.

And may a singular share of Blessings rest upon your Honors Person, and whole Administration, with such wishes, I take Leave; and subscribe, Your Honours, Most affectionate and most obedient Serv't.

Mar. 20, 1724.

To Benjamin Colman.[1]   A.A.S.

SIR, — Nothing that I have mett withal, (and continue to meet withal) causes me to lay aside my zelous concern for the welfare of the Colledge, which you have under your Government.

I think it my Duty therefore, to inform you, that within these

[1] An earlier letter to Colman, dated November 6, 1724, is in *Proceedings*. XLIV. 260.

few Hours, I am (from one whose Time and Heart is more with son
Folks than I wish it were) inform'd of great Machinations and Expe
tations, to see the Colledge demanded into the hands, of a Daught
of Babylon; and notable over-haulings.

On this occasion, Lett me not be thought an Overbusy I
termeddler in affairs which I have been sufficiently forbidde
from any meddling with, if I humbly offer two Things to yo
Consideration.

The Colledge is in a most precarious uncertain, unsafe Conditio
for want of an Incontestible Charter, you know whose Maxim it wa
(and whose it will be) That when the Cow was Dead, the Calf die
in the Belly of it; And how often and how Long our General Assem
blies acted, as Confessing of it. Whether this be True and Just o
no, the men whom you know too well, will as soon as they can procee
upon it. Several Opportunities, and even Invitations, to gett
Royal Charter for the Colledge, were in a wretched Manner, and o
wretched Intentions thrown away. We have now a King on th
Throne, who is not so much in the Interests of High-Church, and wil
not be so fond of doing what K. *James* himself (as my PARENTATO
will tell you) confess'd a Most unreasonable Thing, but that, if th
Dissenters at home will so far Lay aside their *Unbrotherliness*, as t
join their Intercessions, we may hope to obtain a Charter. What
wish for, is, That Mr. *Colman* may be prevail'd withal, to step ove
the Atlantic and Employ the Talents wherewith GOD has furnishe
him, to sollicit and prosecute this matter; and that the Colledg
Treasury may (with other Assistences) be at the Expence of an Hoo
to Catch a Salmon. I Entreat you think of it. And if there be any
Service that I can do, in forwarding the Design (tho' it be very Little
that I can do in this or any other matter) I shall upon your Directior
do all that I am able.

In the Mean time; I remember the Time, when Days ol
Supplication, have been kept in and by the Colledge. If there
were such kept at this Critical Time, who can tell, how many good
Consequences may follow upon them. There is doubtless a Number, even of the under-graduates, whose prayers may help, *caelum
tendere etc.*

And others not so well-disposed may on such Days be in the way
of the greatest Edification. While such Things are by you carrying
on there, I will associate myself with some of my Fellow-Christians
here, in Harmonizing Exercises.

Tis possible, the same Indescretion, which attends all my other

ssays to do Good, may be discerned in this also.   But it is address'd
nto one, who knows how to forgive, and Candidly accept, His Brother
nd Servt.

Iar. 6. 1724–25 [1]

To Thomas Prince.   M.H.S.

[January 31, 1725–26.]

My dear Friend, — and one of my dearest!

If you ask, *How I do?*   I can scarce allow myself Air Enough, to
ive you an Account, in the Terms of the Letter the poor Souldier
t *Casco*, wrote unto my Brother *Walter*, at *Roxbury*.   Yett for part
f it, I may.

If you ask, *What I do?*   Alas, Methinks, my Name is *Do Little;*
ho' in *Deed* and in Worth, much Inferiour to him that wore that
Name.

I am hastening unto the Work of my *Triparadisus*.   But perhaps
naking more Haste unto the *Paradise* of GOD.

The Less I *do* myself, I think, I must Contrive the more for
thers to do.

And as there are several small services to Good Interests, which
. may take an opportunity to mention unto you, if I Live to see
ou: [By the way, Ask Mr. *Cooper* and Mr. *Foxcroft*, if I this
Day wrote nothing to them?]   So there is One Very Important,
Extensive Peece of work, which you must give me Leave to assign
ver to you.

Our, Agricola; Good Master *Henchman* has it; and it has been
nany weeks in his Hands.   Now, if he saw Cause to go on with it,
pon a sufficient Encouragement, I cast the whole care (under the
glorious Lord, who always does All!) upon *you*.   I Leave it, with
ou to direct him, and advise him; very particularly about the method
of sending the *Proposals for Subscriptions* (which he has in his hands)
nto the Countrey Towns.   Mr. T. *Green*, will I suppose, be so kind,
is to help us all over *Connecticut*.   Perhaps, I may add, *Excite* him
too, against Loss of Time; and against Living at the *Sign of the Snail*.
You see, how I sett you to *ploughing;* even under the *Cold;* yea,
Because of the *Cold*.   The *Harvest!* The *Harvest!*   It is near, Lord
come Quickly.   The rest (I want strength; my side akes with This!)

---

[1] On June 29 the Church, "having taken into Consideration the Difficulties
our reverend Pastors labor under by the high and excessive prices of all necessaries
of Life," voted a weekly allowance of four pounds to Dr. Mather, and of three
pounds ten shillings to Dr. Gee.

I reserve to another Time. I am, Your Brother, *As merry as on*
bound for Heaven.

Co. MATHER.

(Mrs. *Askews* subscription)

Let no *vulture's eye* see the enclosed but let it, at your own time
return safely to me. The fair copy met with a strange deliverance
which at another Time I may tell you of.

To THOMAS PRINCE.   M.H.S.

SIR, — That you are as Cordial and Constant a Friend unto me
as any I have in the world, Endears you not unto me, so much a
your being such a Friend of our glorious CHRIST, and of His Truth
and Cause and Kingdome in the World.

Some Expression of it, I have seen in your Favour to the, *Ratio*
Disciplinae; wherein I have seen the *Kindness of God.*

That work will certainly prove one of the Usefullest Things, tha
ever were offered unto the churches. Their perpetual Confirmation
and Establishment in the *Faith and Order of the Gospel*, and their
Vindication to the (Court and) world, will be but some of the conse
quences, that will be found upon its publication.

Our great Adversary thinks so. Hence, he obtained a permission
t'other day, to scatter two thirds of the Copy, unto the four Winds
of Heaven, in Loose Leaves, whereof, some were taken up by strangers
others were found in a Garden, others in a wood-pile; when, if it
had been to save my Life, or one worth ten thousand of mine, I could
not have recovered it. But, the Angel of the Lord Look'd after it.
Not a Leaf, nor a Line of it, is missing!

The work proceeds. Nine-sheets are now printed off.

But, So, Now, our Good Bookseller does declare, the work shall
stop; not a sheet more shall be done.

He'l tell you *his* Reason, if you ask him. And I have told you
Mine!

I don't wonder that such a work must be brought forward with
a *Struggle.* Tis a sign, tis for the Kingdome of God!

I had not writt a Word of all This; but only to introduce my
Request, that you would Visit Madam *Saltonstal*, from whom I
Learnt yesterday, that you may hope to find her a Noble Subscriber.

See Isa. XXXVII. 3. with LXVI. 9.

I add no more, but that I am, Sir, Your Brother (and Servt) in
the Labour, and service and Patience of the Kingdome.

Apr. 5, [1726.]

C. MATHER.

To THOMAS PRINCE. M.H.S.

[May 23, 1726.]

SIR, — It appears to me, that *Just Sentiments on the present Con-*
dition of the PROTESTANT RELIGION, are what our Churches as well as
those of *Europe*, need greatly to be instructed and Excited with.
our prayers as well as *Theirs*, are called for; and may have their
operation, on the sad Occasion.

I have not forgotten, the Folly and Baseness, with which our,
present *State of Religion*, was treated. Yett I am not thereby discouraged, from allowing, that if you think it advisable, you may give
this to Mr *Gerrish*, for Publication; and if he have it out, by the *Elec-*
tion-day Morning, he will be no great Loser by it. You will please
to Correct Every thing in it, (as well as the press-work,) and lett
Every thing about it, be just as you would have it. I Leave all to
your Discretion and Activity.

But, Continue of the Opinion, it may be a very useful paper;
and may have prayerful Consequences.

If it be cavill'd at, I can show a much more obnoxious one of Dr.
Owens, published in a worse Time than ours pretends to be. I am,
Sir, Your Brother and Servt. CO MATHER.

Munday Morn.

For your marvellous, and Victorious Pryn, I mightily thank you.

To ROWLAND COTTON. A.A.S.

26 *d*. VIII *m*. [October.] 1726.

SIR, — When will the Angry Man, who wrote the Enclosed, have
done persecuting of me?

A Long While ago,[1] hearing you and the worthy Ministers of your
Neighbourhood basely reflected on, for ordaining a Minister, who had
confessed unto Mr. *Stone*,[2] that he had never studied Divinity for one
month (or some such small space,) by way of preparation for the
Ministry, before his Entrance upon public preaching; (or to this
Effect, which, I think, I have seen asserted under Mr. *Stones* hand:)
I replied, I was well-assured *This could not be true*. For, besides what
I myself knew of the studies follow'd by him, I was informed by Mr.
Cotton,[3] how long he had studied Theology in *Ireland*, under as famous
and worthy a Tutor; as Mr. *Stone* could have wished for him.

[1] In 1718.   [2] Nathaniel Stone, of Harwich.
[3] Rowland Cotton, of Sandwich.

For my saying This, I was assaulted and insulted by Mr *Stone*
with a very strange Letter and Language. which for some Reason
in a very ancient Book, I did not care to give any Answer to. I sent
the letter to you; desiring you to rectify his mistakes; and Excuse
me from having any thing to do with a man, so full of evil-dispo-
sitions towards me; lest I should unawares trespass on the Rule of
that meekness and Patience, which ought always to govern me. After
this, I don't remember that ever I spoke any thing about it; but once
to my Brother *Colman;* who ever treats me with Candour in Expectation, that he would also do the same Good office; which, if he did
not forgett it, I beleeve, he did. You were pleased after this, (and a
great while ago) to tell me, That Mr. *Stone*[1] promised to have done
with his Clamours about Mr. *Osborn:* And I don't know, that I have
ever had occasion since then to say any thing about the Matter.

I have done all that was needful for me to do, that sin might not
Ly upon him; And that *you,* and other very Good Men, might not
have a vile Representation given of you. I have said nothing but
what is Exactly True on this occasion; and nothing, but what I had
a Loud call to speak when you were abused as ordaining a most
Ignorant Creature.

But the enclosed will give you to see how much he has done with
his clamours.

I hope, you have not Lost his former Letter; (tho' I Forgett all
but the general Strain of it; nor do I desire Ever to see it again.
The second, wherein I am sorry to see him so much Like the Troubled
Sea, I now send you, with my Request, that you would either shew
this touchy brother his Errors; or tell me plainly, whether Mr. *Stone*
did say True, when he said, That Mr. *Osborn* confessed, That he had
never studied *Theology,* any time before his Entring on the preaching
of it. If he did say True; I will humbly own, I have wronged him,
and ask his pardon. And you shall as humbly own to me, that you
have imposed on me, and ask mine. If what he said, were entirely
False, then, I pray, perswade him, to forbear his charging me with
Lying, and with being an *Eminently Immoral Man,* and the rest, that
you have in the Letter. Perswade him, that he would cease multiplying to me occasions for that *overcoming of Evil with good,* which he
derides me for. I pray, take this Task upon you. For I will not
beleeve so wise and good a Man as Mr. *Cotton,* to do such Ill Things
as Mr. *Stone* insinuates, in the Instrument he hath sent about the

[1] Samuel Osborn. See Freeman, *History of Cape Cod,* II. 89. A letter of
Stone on this case, dated June 19, 1718, is in Prince MSS. 101.

ountrey. And I will by no Temptation (if I can help it) be drawn to Loseing time in having any thing to do, with a man who hath far cast off all the Rules of Decency.

May our glorious Lord, Enable both of us to be Followers of the ood one; and give a better Frame of Mind unto some of our dis-mpered Brethren. I am, Sir, Your kinsman and serv't.

To Thomas Prince.   M.H.S.

Sir, — With many Thanks for the Liberty you have indulged e, I return your Laborious *Many-Reader*.

About the *Illustration*, Extracted from him, which I now send ou, some time or other (if we Live) we may change a word or two.

I am this morning in a Querulous Humour.

Very many Months ago, a Number of Ministers who once were athers to Mr *Clap*,[1] address'd him, with their tenderest and most oliging Admonitions, and Exhortations, and perswasions to Reform great and public Scandal, that he had Long persisted in. He took o notice of them. And yett, the Ministers of this Town, appear fraid of so much as telling him, That they dislike his Conduct.

At the same time, the State, and at Last the Pen, of the Scatter-g Flock makes a Loud Cry unto us, and gives us the fairest oppor-inity and Introduction for our Advice to them that can be. All elay carries Destruction in it; and yett all we do, is to Lett them now, that we shall delay giving them the Advice their Difficulties ll for, till we have some Direction from Mr. *Clap* to do it.

The Two Letters you ordered yesterday (tho' I, who would ever ubmitt unto your better Judgments have signed them,) I verily ear, are only to harden a Melancholy Man in a Gross Iniquity. And nly to Lengthen out the Time for the great Adversary to accomplish he Scattering of the Holy People; and ruining a valuable Interest.

I would not abound in my own Sense; and I am very sensible of y being more liable to mistakes, than my Brethren. However, I ust confess, I don't understand our Conduct.

But, I *very well understand* the meaning of the Indecency and ndignity I am treated withal; To order me to draw up Letters, and nake me Lose my Time which grows more and more precious to me, nd own that I have exactly follow'd my orders, and then turn 'em pon me again, and substitute instead of them, that which can be f ńo *other use*, but only to render *Them useless*. I say, *I very well*

---

[1] Nathaniel Clap, pastor of the Congregational church in Newport, R. I.

understand it. However, you'l find me, very patient and Easy, an under no other Impression from it, but only a Resolution to Look myself as Excused for the time to come from the Labours of yo Clerkship.

I am willing you should Lett Mr. *Foxcroft* see my simple Sent ments.

May our Glorious Lord help us wisely and meekly to bear on anothers Burdens, (what we sometimes Lay on one another,) an keep us always united in Services to the *Kingdome of the Stone*, tha we may have our share together in the *Kingdome of the Mountain* And Love one another, when I am, Sir, Your affectionate Broth and Servt

Co. MATHER.

Friday Morn. Jan. 13. [1726–27.]

To THOMAS PRINCE. M.H.S.

[Boston January 24, 1726–27.]

SIR, — Having first Expressed my Satisfaction on what you hav written to Mr *Watts*, I will freely, and in the most open-hearte Manner, offer you a Little of my Opinion, about the *Disquisition* which that Man has Lately published.[1]

I take him, to be a very Disqualified person, for the Managing the Vast Subject he has undertaken ;

He is not only too shallow for it ; but also Led away with a Spur ous and Criminal Charity, for those Abominable IDOLATERS, th *Arians*, and ready to Embrace as Brethren in CHRIST, those ancien and perpetual Enemies of CHRIST, whom to treat, as a great par of the Dissenters are WICKEDLY come to do, is an High-Treason of greater and blacker consequence, than ever an *Atterbury* was charge withal.

His complements to that execrable crew of Traitors (I mean, th Arians) are unChristian, and scandalous, and have a Tendency t destroy the Religion of God. His Attempts, to compound wit them, on these Two Anathematizable Terms ;

First, That there is no Eternal Son of God ; [welfare, poor *Assem blies* Catechism !] and that there is no Filiation in the Godhead, bu this, That God (*sabellianically!*) created a super angelical Spirit good while ago, and intimately possessed him : —

Secondly, That an Holy Spirit in the Godhead, may be called *Person*, as the Grace of *Love*, and some other things, are *Personalize* in the Scriptures ; —

[1] Isaac Watts. See *Dictionary of National Biography*, LX. 69.

These Attempts will be Detestable, to all that think, *The Faith once delivered unto the Saints*, worth Contending for.

Could his predecessor once again take his pen into his hand, he would Charge him with nothing Less, than grievous *Haeresies*.[1] His Answer to *Biddle*, for That!

For my own part, I Look on the part which our Brethren, (I will not now say, *United Brethren*,) have taken in Countenancing the Conspiracy to dethrone and degrade and ungod the Eternal SON of GOD, as having a deep share in preparing the world for that *Catastrophe*, which my, *Diluvium Ignes* warns you of. [You have not yett Readd, the Two Last Leaves of it.]

As for you, *My Son*, [If not my *Age*, yett allow my *Love* to call you so!] I will say one Thing to *you*. *Take heed unto your Spirit*. The Candour, or Humour, in the Spirit of Our Friend on the other side the water, has betray'd him into a most mischievous Treachery to the Faith of the Gospel and unhappy Disservice to the Best Cause in the world. I highly approve and admire the Goodness of your Spirit, and the Equanimity wth which you Look upon Displeasing Things. But yett, watch over it, Lest you admitt of an *Indolence*, where an Holy Zeal shall be called for; and where a *John* himself would be a *Boanerges*, with zealous Testimonies; and Lest you unawares at some time or other Hurt a Glorious Cause, by an Air that may carry too much Complaisance, where warm Expressions of the greatest Abhorrence, are what our glorious LORD would be most pleased withal.

Haec raptim et ἀυτοκελευστί from Sir, Your most affectionate Brother. Co. MATHER.

Mr. *Henchman*, has the AGRICOLA;[2] you will give the Enclosed unto him, when tis fill'd as far as you think fitt. And ask him to carry it, with the AGRICOLA, to Mr *Checkley*, if he purposes to do an thing about it.[3]

[1] Watts had succeeded Isaac Chauncy in the pulpit.

[2] A tract of Mather, *Agricola, or the Religious Husbandman*, appeared in 1727, printed by F. Fleet for D. Henchman.

[3] "28 d. 11 m. [*January*.] 1727-28. A.M. At a Meeting of the Brethren of the Church, the following Proposal was offered and approved; and it was agreed that notice hereof should be given to the whole Assembly in the Afternoon.

"Whereas in the holy Providence of our Lord his aged Servant, our Rev'd and dear Pastor (Dr. Cotton Mather) is visited and bro't low by Sickness, which takes him off from those Exercises of the pastoral Care, whereby God has greatly

endeared him to us, and threatens his Removal from us by Death, which we woul
deprecate as a most awful Frown of Heaven:

"We do therefore desire and appoint next Wednesday afternoon, to be se
apart and employed in humble, poenitent and earnest Supplications to God ou
Savior, that it may please him to restore and confirm the Health of his Servan
and prolong his Life and Usefulness, as a rich Blessing to his People.

"And we humbly desire the Rev'd Mr. Colman, Mr. Thacher, and Mr. Sewa
to assist in the Services which are called for on this Occasion."

Cotton Mather died February 13, 1727–28, one day beyond his sixty-fift
birthday. On the day of his death the church over which he had so long preside
passed the following vote: "Whereas under the awful and humbling Bereavemen
wherewith the great and good Shepherd has visited this Flock, the united Pastor
of the Town are in a course of preaching with us; according to the usual Metho
of expressing their pious Regards to a deceased Pastor, and his bereaved Floc
and Family: it is therefore ordered and appointed, that as a token of the lik
Christian Regards, the usual Salary be continued to the bereaved Family, and tha
the Deacons accordingly give the same to Mrs. Mather for the support of th
Family, from the Death of our late Venerable Pastor, till the said Course of preach
ing be finished." On April 2, 1728, the Church voted to Mrs. Lydia Mather th
sum of one hundred pounds, to be paid in monthly instalments of five pounds
On January 28, 1730–31, Samuel Mather was chosen to be assistant to Rev. Joshua
Gee. *MS. Records of the Second Church*, III.

TEXTS USED BY MATHER

TEXTS USED BY MATHER[1]

ACTS

CHAP.	V.	VOL.	P.
2	37	I.	116
4	12	—	116
5	31	—	38
6	8	—	18
8	23	—	118
9	5	II.	190
—	6	I.	116
—	—	II.	788
—	31	I.	119
10	4	I.	190
—	44	II.	32, 287
11	15	I.	219
—	25	—	251
—	26	—	246
13	2	—	99
—	45, 48	II.	593, 594
16	2	I.	202
—	14	—	117
16	30	I.	116[2]
—	31	—	116
21	7	II.	400
—	14	—	504
24	25	I.	152
26	28	—	120
27	23	I.	355
—	—	II.	680
—	25	I.	355

AMOS

4	12	II.	678
6	6	I.	116
8	2	II.	219, 286
—	11	—	509

CANTICLES

1	4	II.	510, 595
2	3	—	508, 592
—	14	—	401,[2] 678, 679
—	16	—	33
5	1	—	509
—	2	I.	120
—	6	—	117
—	9	II.	593
—	10	—	400

CHAP.	V.	VOL.	P.
5	17	I.	116
8	6	II.	401, 506, 508
—	7	—	402

- I CHRONICLES

4	10	II.	285, 286
15	31	—	289
19	3	—	167
—	15	—	677
29	3	—	289
—	11	I.	590
—	15	II.	289, 602
—	19	—	286, 677

II CHRONICLES

1	7	I.	119
12	12	—	149
20	12	II.	787
25	9	I.	180
32	2–8	—	220

COLOSSIANS

1	3	I.	416
—	—	II.	789
—	12	—	530, 592[7]
2	7	I.	392
3	2	II.	507
—	3	—	593
—	4	—	548
—	5	I.	288

I CORINTHIANS

1	9	II.	788
—	30	I.	503,[2] 504, 505, 506, 507
3	16	I.	541[2]
—	23	II.	787
6	9	I.	287
7	29	—	416
—	35	—	590
9	26	II.	362, 400[2]
10	14	—	399
—	31	—	595
11	28	I.	120
—	30	—	168
—	31	—	39

II CORINTHIANS

CHAP.	V.	VOL.	P.
1	3–11	I.	434
2	11	—	389[2]
—	—	II.	388[2]
3	18	II.	399
5	5	I.	103
—	14	II.	219
—	17	I.	118
—	20	—	120
7	11	—	592
11	27	II.	168
12	4	—	163
13	5	I.	118
—	—	II.	29
—	14	—	542[3]

- DANIEL

4	8, 10	I.	249
18			
—	34	II.	163
5	27	I.	541

DEUTERONOMY

4	10	I.	119
26	17	I.	391
32	3	—	591
—	5	—	414
33	4	II.	234
38	7	II.	787

ECCLESIASTES

1	4	II.	163
—	15	—	165, 167
2	14	—	165, 287
4	9	—	27
7	2	—	163
—	9	—	507
9	5	—	509
—	10	I.	117
—	—	II.	437, 506
—	12	—	507
11	8	II.	789
12	5	I.	365, 391
—	10	II.	399
—	14	—	234

[1] Superior figures represent the number of sermons preached upon the text.

INDEX

INDEX

831

Morse, John, **1**, 525*n*.

Mortality, early, **2**, 217, 222; in church, 490, 493, 501.

Mortification in a minister, **1**, 107.

'Mortification of Sin,' **1**, 108.

Morton, Charles, **1**, 269*n*.

Moses, Lord's anger against, **1**, 2; speech, 51.

'Mother's Catechism,' **2**, 25.

Mother-in-Law, Medford, **2**, 361.

Mottos, **2**, 28.

Moulton, Bridget, **2**, 291*n*.

Moulton, Jane, **2**, 291*n*.

Mount, Richard, **1**, 550.

Mouth, thoughts on, **1**, 2, 50.

Moxtershed, Ralph, **2**, 459*n*.

Musculus, **1**, 159.

Mystery of the Trinity, **2**, 14, 40, 66; of Godliness, 14; of Jesus, 590, 591.

Nævus maternus, **2**, 686.

Name of God, things to be done for, **1**, 73.

Nantes, Edict of, **1**, 41*n*, 134*n*.

Nantucket, Mass., **2**, 248, 370.

Naples, **2**, 171.

Narraganset country, **2**, 603.

'Narrative of the Miseries of New England,' **1**, 141*n*.

Natick, Mass., **2**, 125; Indians at, 182, 252.

Naumann, ——, **2**, 563.

Neal, Daniel, letter to, **2**, 598.

Neau, Elias, **2**, 238*n*, 300, 550; apostasy, **2**, 89.

'Necessary Admonitions,' **1**, 436.

Necessity of Nature, thoughts on, **1**, 357.

Needham, Ezekiel, **2**, 198*n*.

Needham, Mass., **2**, 197.

'Negro Christianized,' **1**, 177*n*, 564, 598.

Negroes, rules for company of, **1**, 176; baptism of, 278; **2**, 43; christianizing, 570, 598; thief, 351; soceity of, 364, 532; charity school, 379, 478; servant, 383, 384; named Mather, 663, 706; insurrection, 686; return, 706.

Neighbor, troublesome, **2**, 135; conduct to, 348, 457, 464, 494.

Neighborhood, tempers of, **2**, 149.

Neighbors, contentions, **2**, 212.

'Nepenthes Evangelicum,' **2**, 244.

Nephew of Mrs. George, **2**, 556; his own, 567, 700, 782.

Nesbit, ——, **2**, 410.

'New and remarkable Discoveries of the Spirit of Quakerism,' **1**, 572.

Newbury, Mass., church of England at, **2**, 147; service for, 194; case of, 218, 223, 231, 327.

New England, ingratitude, **1**, 140; church history, 166; representation on,

168; sins of, 214; Satan shakes, 329; charters, 403; distribution of books, 523; account of, 295; churches of, 302, 327, 412; Sabbath, 337; Neal on, 598.

'New England's Faction discovered,' **1**, 134*n*.

Newfoundland, **2**, 171.

New Hampshire, **2**, 380; Shute visits, 392; politics, 422; wood, 655.

New Haven, Conn., invites Mather, **1**, 42, 53; Warham Mather, **2**, 87, 134, 147, 759; church, 319, 321.

Newington, Conn., **2**, 721.

New London, Conn., **2**, 231, 759.

New-modellers of churches, **1**, 364.

'New Offer to the Lovers of Religion,' **2**, 283, 309, 310, 330.

Newport, R. I., **2**, 815*n*.

News, thoughts on, **2**, 83.

News-Letters, **1**, 71*n*; **2**, 638.

Newton, Sir Isaac, **2**, 806*n*.

Newton, Mass., **1**, 353; **2**, 226, 227, 371, 397, 470, 473, 474, 475, 529, 534, 686.

New Year's day, **2**, 579, 595.

New York, reform, **1**, 268; Pelagian doctrine, **2**, 60; Church of England, 151; dissenters, 353, 473; family from, 709; young man, 728.

Nicholson, Francis, **2**, 35, 173; arrives, **2**, 290.

Niece, to be admonished, **2**, 80; wife's, 709, 712, 742.

Nieremberg, Johann Eusebius, **2**, 702.

'Nightingale,' **2**, 765.

Noble, Isaac, **2**, 541, 694.

Non-attendance on church, **2**, 10.

Non-conformists, prayer, **1**, 42; condition in England, **1**, 312; **2**, 143, 145, 148; Long Island, 132.

Nonesuch, frigate, **1**, 148*n*.

Northampton, Mass., **2**, 234.

Norton, David, **2**, 36.

Norton, John, **1**, xv.

Nottingham, Earl of, **1**, 500; **2**, 172.

Nottingham Galley, **2**, 71*n*, 791.

Nova Scotia, **1**, 398*n*.

Nowell, Samuel, **1**, 208*n*.

Noyes, James, **1**, 190*n*; **2**, 303*n*, 321*n*.

Noyes, Joseph, **2**, 321*n*.

Noyes, Nicholas, **1**, 151, 190*n*, 437, 551.

Noyes, Nicholas, Jr., **1**, 190*n*.

Noyes, Oliver, **2**, 382*n*, 403; letter to, 417; stricken, 607*n*.

Nudigate, Sarah, **1**, 551.

'Nuncia Bona,' **2**, 329.

Nurse, considered, **2**, 702.

Oakes, Thomas, **1**, 138, 139*n*.

Oakes, Urian, **1**, 207*n*.

Oath, nature of, **2**, 110, 566; sermon, 569, 571.